PATHWAYS
TO
MADNESS

PATHWAYS
TO
MADNESS

BY

JULES HENRY

VINTAGE BOOKS

A Division of Random House, New York

Library of Congress Cataloging in Publication Data

Henry, Jules, 1904–1969.
    Pathways to madness.
    Includes bibliographical references.
    1. Family—United States—Case studies.
2. Interpersonal relations. 3. Psychology, Pathological.
I. Title.
[HQ728.H395 1973]   616.8'9'071   72–7499
ISBN 0–394–71882–8

To my wife Zunia,

who has been the liberating force

in my life

Life lures us with small favors

to commit great crimes

Preface

This book is written for children. I hope it will help reduce the misery in their lives; and I hope some parents, because they have read it, will be able to save themselves some suffering by avoiding some mistakes with their children. Some may be made aware that usually we do not know what we are doing to them.

In 1948, in a paper entitled "Common Problems of Research in Anthropology and Psychiatry,"* I said that since lack of scientific knowledge of family life was an obstacle to understanding emotional illness, researchers should live for a short time with families of the emotionally ill. The idea was, as might have been expected, ignored by "the profession." Years later, however, Bruno Bettelheim made it possible for me to do the work with the aid of Ford Foundation funds he had at his disposal. I am grateful for his help, his insight and his confidence in me. I am grateful also for the opportunity to learn from him and his associates.

The first product of my studies of the families of psychotic children was a monograph entitled "L'Observation naturaliste des familles d'enfants psychotiques," published in Paris in 1961.† In 1963 I published "The Portman Family" and "The Ross Family" in my *Culture Against Man.*‡

This book is not only a study of pathways to madness but also, indirectly, an account of some changes in myself, as the years passed between "L'Observation naturaliste . . ." and completion of "The Keen Family," which is the final study in this volume. Meanwhile the world changed too—the sense of doom, of helplessness, was not quite as strong in the world when I published my first study as it is now—and as the world crisis deepened my work was affected: I think my own understanding was improved.

About half this book was written during my tenure as a fellow of the Center for Advanced Study in the Behavioral Sciences, and I am most grateful to its director, Ralph Tylor, a sensitive man who knows how to say "Yes," and to its staff. I also want to thank Washington University for the year off. I wish I could thank by name the organizations that introduced me to the families discussed here, but to do so would violate privacy.

I have discussed every page of this book with my wife, and it is likely that some of its weaknesses might have been eliminated had I accepted more of her suggestions. I am also grateful to Berenice Hoffman for superb editorial work. I want to thank Barbara Willson for her patient and scrupulous copyediting.

* *American Journal of Orthopsychiatry*, Vol. XVIII, pp. 698–703.
† In the journal *La Psychiatrie de l'Enfant.*
‡ Vintage Books; New York, Random House.

If this book communicates its message, others besides myself will be grateful to these families for their co-operation in the research. I am afraid that I have sometimes written about them in language that may seem strong; yet none of us is free of the kinds of problems they have, nor entirely free of their defects, and I have tried to make this clear.

J.H.

Contents

PATHWAYS
TO
MADNESS

Introduction

The Naturalistic Study of Families

In this book I describe five families, four of which had an institutionalized child, only one of whom made a home visit during the study. The fifth family was one in which the mother had had two alleged psychotic episodes before the study began and one a couple of months later. In that family, the oldest child had been diagnosed as mentally retarded, with behavior problems.

When studying the Rosenberg family, I had my own room in the house,* where I lived for a week. I did not actually live with the Jones, Wilson or Metz families, but arrived each day around breakfast time and left when the family retired for the night. The observations of the Keen family were done by a young woman to whom I have given only the name Susan, to protect the anonymity of the family. She arrived at the Keen home at seven in the morning and left when the family went to bed. I spent eight and a half days with the Joneses, five with the Wilsons and a week with the Metzes, and Susan spent a week with the Keen family.† Each family was observed for about one hundred hours, and the notes of the observations are the basis for this book. The identity of all the families has been disguised, as have certain details, but the description of their behavior has not.

I have done this study because I believe that direct observation of families in their native habitat, going about their usual business, will furnish new insights into psychotic breakdown and other forms of emotional illness, and suggest new ideas for prevention and treatment. Other motivations were my wish to understand family life better and to study man in his day-to-day surroundings. The last is the compelling goal of my scientific life.

I am repelled by the artificiality of experimental studies of human behavior because they strip the context from life. They take away from it the environment, without which it has no meaning, without which it has no envelope. I require the actuality of what is nowadays called the "existential human being" as he lives his real life. I have to see *that person* before me; and what I cannot see as *that actuality*, what I cannot hear as the sound of *that voice*, has little interest for me. Human life fills me with a wild, intoxicated curiosity. A result is that in my studies I try to combine disciplined observation with a comprehensive interpretation of life in its complex interrelations.

In this book I offer no "typologies," because human phenomena do not

---

* This is true also of the Portman and Ross families, discussed in my *Culture Against Man.*

† More details about the conduct of these studies are given in the Appendix, where I also attempt to answer questions that might arise about possible distortions caused by the presence of the observer, how the cases were obtained, how notes were made, etc.

arrange themselves obligingly in types but, rather, afford us the spectacle of endless overlapping. Hence I have no family "types" and no statistics, only intensive analyses of the variety of family experience. The less we know about family life the easier it is to set up categories, just as the less data we have the easier it is to write history.

I am not a stranger to statistics or to "interviewing methods." I was trained in "nondirective" interviewing at Carl Rogers' laboratory when he was at the University of Ohio. I have also been an interviewer and study director on many surveys, and there was a time when I could even run my own sorts on old-fashioned IBM sorting equipment. The equipment has been revolutionized since then, but the social-science material fed into it is still largely the same old jazz. I have designed and carried out fixed response as well as "open-ended" surveys and published my own statistical studies. It is my familiarity with "hard" research that has made me skeptical.

It is a commonplace of scientific history that the first valuable hypotheses are developed out of good observations of natural-occurring phenomena. In my research I assume that the study of *human* psychology—as distinguished from that of pigeons, rats, mice and sundry other lower animals— is merely beginning and can profit from naturalistic observation: observation of human beings in their native habitat. There is a great dearth of such material but an enormous amount of premature theorizing, based on studies of highly artificial laboratory setups or, even worse, extrapolation from experimentally controlled behavior of lower animals. That Americans have been willing to take the rat and the pigeon as paradigms of man confirms the fact that we have learned to consider ourselves as little more than pigeons or rats. Our humility is to be admired, perhaps, but the resulting contribution to a science of man is questionable.

In psychiatry, on the other hand, while the research subject is the human being, he has not been studied in his natural surroundings of home, school and place of work, going about his business, but in the psychiatrist's office or, to a lesser extent, in institutions.* In this book I try to show how understanding human beings is furthered and the opportunities for new theoretical insights are provided by a return from the laboratory and the consulting room to man in his natural surroundings, and by observing him through the successive transformations of his activity as he moves through his daily activities and cycles of feeling—out of calm into rage, out of rage into love or sorrow, and so on. Life has an inner calculus, which is the passage of existence through time, through one state into another, by leaps and by infinitesimals, from one mood to another, from one person to another, from one embrace or one struggle to another, to its final summation and dissolution.

The Study of Sanity

This book is an attempt to show how much more data is needed in order to understand pathogenesis and how that data can be obtained and used.

* Nowadays a few psychiatrists are attempting to do psychiatry with families in the home. These are periodic, brief family meetings.

It is, furthermore, the beginning of what I hope will, in the next few years, become a description of the fundamental intellectual structures underlying evaluations of normal and abnormal. I ask such questions as: What is our concept of an infant? How do we *think* about an infant, and what is there about our notions of infancy that causes us to say, "She is a wonderful mother," or "She is a terrible mother"? What is our conception of house-keeping that leads us to say, "She really does/does not know how to keep house." We constantly make instantaneous, intuitive judgments about the mental status of other people, about the "correct" and the "bizarre," but what is the intellectual structure of these intuitions, and how valid are they for judging sanity?

What is the intellectual structure of sanity itself? We know that it has something to do with our understanding the relationships of time and space to objects and people, and with a person's relationships with other people and with objects, etc. We know that it has something to do with understanding crucial differences, like that between infant and adult, for example; with perceiving the contradiction or the consistency in behavior and language, and so on. In this book I attempt a close analysis of what the *something* is. I begin with an analysis of the integration of the assumptions, shared with all other "sane" people in our culture, about how reality is constituted; and I study how these assumptions become part of everyone's thinking, become "mind" itself, become the fabric of "sanity."

I am also concerned with illusion and "as-ifness" as constituting part of the structure of sanity, perhaps one of its most substantial parts. How can Professor Hilquist go on teaching year after year, when he knows that very few students are able to learn what he has to teach, and that practically none of the others will ever use what they have learned? Is it not the illusion of effectiveness that enables him to continue? He acts *as if* he were effective when he is not, because he has to feel effective to earn a living and to "keep going." Consider another type of illusion: here are Aurora and Cynthia smiling and chatting, or Professors Ghoul and Lauter conversing. In these encounters there may be much disinterest and even dislike, yet each person harbors the necessary illusion that he is pulling the wool over the other person's eyes. The illusion must be maintained in order for people to carry on. The illusions of concealment, of safety, of deceiving the other are part of the absolutely necessary structure of consciousness. The illusion keeps us sane.

As-ifness, as a stable reaction, is the expression, *in action*, of illusion. The illusions, installed in our heads by culture, are part of the structure of consciousness of every sane person. When we meet a member of another culture, therefore, the question is not, "How different is he from me?" but, "What is the difference between his illusions and mine?" This would mean that two cultures may seem very different on the outside—different dwellings, different ways of getting a living, even different religions—but they would be very much the same if the members had similar illusions. This idea brings Japan, Dobu,* Kwakiutl† and the United States all very close together.

The difference between the as-ifness of average people and that of the

---

* A small island in the South Seas.
† An Indian tribe of British Columbia.

families discussed in this book is, perhaps, that the latters' illusions are in some ways different from ours—that some of their illusions are not culturally acceptable and are more dangerous, or, rather, dangerous in ways that are different from the average illusion.

Invariants

The book begins an exploration of the invariant forms of activity underlying social adaptation. I call them "invariant" because these activities and conditions are found in all human societies, though they take different forms in each. For example, in introducing the Wilson case, I examine the concept of availability, and arguing that availability of human beings to one another—of parent to child, of husband to wife, of clan to clan—is a necessity of social existence, I study how unavailability can create pathology. Of course, this does not mean that the only problem in the Wilson household is unavailability or that no other family in the book has such a problem. It simply means that the Wilson family particularly invites a discussion of it. The Rosenberg family is introduced by an essay on sham because this is one of the main problems here; but shamming is universal. Also, the fact that an essay on sham introduces the Rosenbergs does not mean I believe the only thing troubling the family is sham, or that no other family in the book suffers from it. Many things trouble the Rosenbergs, and I discuss these things throughout the analysis of the case.

Sham and availability are but two of the invariants I discuss; there are many others.

Alternatives to Some Psychoanalytic Interpretations

I am much concerned with suggesting alternatives to the psychoanalytic hypothesis of the death wish of the unconscious, for I feel that in many cases there are reasonable alternatives to it. If we assume that the underlying structure of consciousness, the culturally determined framework of judgment and perception, is acquired through learning, it follows that some may learn it well, others poorly and some may not learn it at all. The ordinary person considers the latter strange and intolerable. But something more serious is at issue, for under the influence of a theory of unconscious destructive motivations, we have come to think that people who do the "wrong thing" are motivated by unconscious hostility or death wishes. When they come late to appointments, forget to give medicine, feed the baby food that seems too hot, and so on, we are inclined to blame it on unconscious hostility. In the essay on "Time, Space, Motion, Objects and People," which introduces the Jones case, I discuss the difficulty in distinguishing between perceptual defect—failure to learn the frameworks of judgment and perception—and unconscious hostility. Since Dr. and Mrs. Jones have many difficulties involving this very issue, the Jones case is the best one in which to examine it. The problem is acute in the Keen family too. I do not, of course, insist that all the stress in these families arises from perceptual defect, or that there is no such thing as unconscious hostility.

The Complexity of Family Life

In disturbed families, as in others, difficulties arise from many causes, and for this reason I have gone to great lengths to illuminate the complexity of family life. Nearly every matter I discuss warrants a separate essay, perhaps, and in this book I have often had to compress issues into a few pages and sometimes even into a paragraph. Studies have too often reduced psychopathology to a few explanatory "mechanisms" derived from current orthodoxies. A purpose of this book is to get away from reductionism. Orthodoxy impoverishes life—life itself, and the description of it. I want to show how rich existence is, even though it often appears that it is rich merely in misery.

No single bit of behavior can be considered alone; the significance of any event can be evaluated only as part of a configuration of events. Possibly the main problem with which I have struggled in this book is to put things together so that the reader and I can relate events to one another in context and in time: what I see today must surely be related to what I perceive tomorrow—a fight today has a carry-over which affects how tomorrow shall be experienced and lived.

I do not believe in the "commonplace." If a women peels an onion; if a man reads a newspaper or watches television; if there is dust or no dust on the furniture; if a parent kisses or does not kiss his child when he comes home; if the family has eggs or cereal for breakfast, orange juice or no orange juice, and so on through all the "trivia" of everyday life—this is significant to me, if for no other reason than that commonplaceness proves the family sane. So my observations are full of "commonplaces," and the reader may sometimes be a little bored with my insistence on presenting and analyzing them. I proceed on the basis that science advances by relentless examination of the commonplace; that some of its greatest discoveries have been made through fascination with what other men have regarded as not worthy of note.

Who's to Blame?

Not long ago, when a child had emotional problems, orthodoxy "blamed" the parent, and the blame was a kind of incrimination, because it implied that the parent hated the child. A new orthodoxy now blames the child for the parents' disturbance, and the reasoning is that the child was born so strange that it drove the parent crazy. As one distinguished psychiatrist said, "When the social worker said to me, 'How can the child stand such a mother?' I replied, 'How can the mother stand such a child?'" Thus the new orthodoxy regresses a hundred years. This book is, in general, a basis on which to examine both new and old orthodoxy. The method is best illustrated in the Keen case, for Mrs. Keen, who had had two psychotic episodes before the observer arrived, treated her eleven-month-old baby and her three-year-old and ten-and-a-half-year-old children in very much the same way. The controversy between the two orthodoxies is akin to the nature versus nurture controversy, and, like it, will be settled perhaps when we have many cases in which the same mother is observed taking care of different children.

Similarities between Disturbed Families and "Us"

I try to show in this book that families which have a psychotic child are very much like all of us—that the main difference between "them" and "us" is that they seem to go to extremes and do too many things that are upsetting. They are often very much like everybody else in most of the things they do: they follow most of the routines of life just like other people. So much of their activity seems within "normal limits" that in much of what I have written I do not use the word "pathology"! Thus much of this book is simply a description of family life, with judgment regarding health or pathology reserved.

This book is, in considerable part, a request for compassion toward those who irritate us most. The clinical records of Mrs. Metz show the anger she aroused in all who worked with her in connection with her disturbed son, but that anger interfered with a correct interpretation of her. She was a very unhappy woman who also had made her son very miserable, but before one could help the son, one would have to develop compassion for the mother, in order to help her to help her son. This brings me to the humanistic aspects of the book.

The Book as Humanistic

I perceive these families as Greek tragedies without gods. They seem destined to misery and even to catastrophe because they were locked in by their past and by the configurations of love, hate, anxiety and sham which became established in the home, rigid as the walls. The faceless equation $I = 2^n - n - 1$ (see the Appendix), which is merely an instrument for counting the number of constellations of personal relations in the family—mother and father; mother and child-one; father and child-one, etc.—states also the almost unshakable character of the relationship between each member of the family and every other. Orestes had one relationship to his sister, another to his mother, and another to his father's soul, and these relationships, controlled by Destiny, drove him. So it is in families, but, of course, without the gods. When we think about an average family we say, "This is the way the Billingses are," but when we feel a family is disturbed, we tend to say, "This is the way the Joneses are driven." If we put together the past history of the mother and father and the constellations of personal relations established in the family—largely by virtue of the relationship between the parents—we have my conception of a family destiny; in other words, the force is not the supernatural any longer, but the family's history.

Thus I have written about these families around central themes and around themes integrated into configurations. But just as the configuration of the *Oresteia* is spun from the totality of Greek culture, so the threads that have been taken up and woven into their own destiny by my families come from *their* culture. The quality of life in these families is their particular creation of what they have taken from the culture without being aware of it. I view them, however, as just as helpless to change their destiny without outside help as Agamemnon was helpless to change his destiny without a god. This book will get no sympathy from those robust, bumptious ones who believe that man—and they in particular—can seize life and compel it to do their bidding. The people in this book will look to them like congenital weaklings, lacking guts, intelligence or both.

I have tried to keep technical language out of this book, not only because it is ugly and incomprehensible to most people, but also because it is ugly and incomprehensible to me. Much is ambiguous in the human disciplines because everything is so poorly defined and because different writers use the same words with different meanings. Therefore, everyday language is usually clearer than the technical vocabulary. Renouncing it and searching for clarity in ordinary language was good discipline, for it compelled me to rack my brains for what I really wanted to say.

Yet this book is not entirely free of jargon. A convenient term I use repeatedly is *configuration*. A configuration is a complex interweaving of values, institutions, emotions and actions. In the Wilson family, for example, the inability of each parent to commit himself to the other, their drive, their incapacity after marriage to give up their old families to form the new one, their preoccupation with material rewards, and the sham resulting from all this, had terrible consequences for their first child and is making of their second a calculating, though attractive little girl. The configuration is all of this put together in the writer's head and demonstrated through marshaling and presenting the facts.

The idea of configuration comes principally from the German philosopher-historian Wilhelm Dilthey. Almost any quote from Dilthey would illustrate why he is important to this work, and I give a few lines below:

> The task of all history is to grasp the system of interactions. The historiographer penetrates more deeply into the structure of the historical world by sorting out and studying individual contexts . . . The most fundamental of these contexts is the course of an individual life in the environment by which it is affected and which it affects . . .
>
> Every life can be described, the insignificant as well as the powerful, the everyday as well as the exceptional.*

Family contexts are historic, in the sense that they express our time and culture and are themselves micro-movements in history. The tragedies of the Joneses, the Rosenbergs, the Metzes, the Wilsons and the Keens are minute, quintessential expressions of the total tragedy of our age. So the

* *From Wilhelm Dilthey: Pattern and Meaning in History*, ed. and with an introduction by H. P. Rickman (Harper Torchbooks; New York, Harper & Row, 1962).

reader will not find anything so bizarre in this work that it will be beyond his comprehension. On the contrary, he will often be struck by how average is the life of these families that have created and endured deviance of the most serious kind. This is the key to understanding the families and why I think the reader will understand them: he has either lived through it himself, known people like these people, or, since the same psychic currents flow in him as in these families—because he and they are of the same historic epoch—he understands intuitively.

What This Book Is Not

This book is not an effort to prove that psychosis is created by family life only, that the families described are psychologically deviant altogether, or that families like them always produce psychosis. The data with which to argue these issues rigorously do not exist, and I acknowledge that until we have a large number of studies of families with and without psychosis, inferences about what is pathogenic will be subject to considerable error.

On the other hand, to insist that these families are *no* different from any other would put a therapist in an impossible position, for he would have no reason for attempting to modify behavior which, before his eyes, seems to be having psychologically destructive consequences. Of course, everything depends on what one considers destructive, and we thus confront the perduring problem of choice, between folded hands ("Wait until all the facts are in"), and action based on knowledge conditioned by probable error.

Pathways to Madness is not an attempt to disprove biochemical or genetic theories of causation. Though, except in a very few instances, genetic factors are strongly influenced by environmental ones—including the family—so that the former can never be thought of as *alone* determining psychosis—this book is not to be construed as coming to grips with that issue. My position on the nature-nurture issue is outlined in my paper "Culture, Personality and Evolution." *

The controversy will be closer to resolution when we have many studies, along lines suggested in this book, on families that have no psychosis as well as on families that do. Meanwhile, intransigence on either side is bad for science. There is no doubt that biochemical research will turn up some important discoveries, especially if research is started on random samples of children studied from birth, so that we can have biochemical data on people *before* they become ill, and not just on people after they have become ill. Longitudinal biochemical and naturalistic studies on the *same* families would be ideal.

* In *American Anthropologist*, Vol. LXI (1959), pp. 221–26.

PART I

The Jones Family

INTRODUCTION

On Anger and Quarreling

Quarreling is a fundamental feature of human society; and society could not have developed without it, for it is one of the most important ways of controlling people. Yet, because it does not have a formal structure, like a lineage, a ceremonial or a government, quarreling is relatively unstudied by anthropologists. Because it does not have a visible paraphernalia and obvious ritualistic movements; because it does not have totem poles, ceremonial houses or masked dances, it has been ignored as an area of formal study. Books and movies abound on religion, kinship, economics, hunting, praying, baby tending, housebuilding, etc., in exotic cultures, but there are none on quarreling, even though it is everywhere.

In psychoanalytic theory, hostility is considered an instinct or a drive, and like the sexual drive it is assumed to exist in a kind of pure state. Love between man and woman is a cultural expression of sexuality, and just as we do not know of a sex drive in man unmodified by culture, so we do not know of an expression of hostility unmodified by culture. Anger and quarreling are the social expressions of hostility, as love between man and woman is the social expression and experience of sex. Wherever there are people there is anger, though it varies in frequency and intensity, and above all in the quality of the feeling and accompanying attitudes. So also, the aftermath of anger, the individual and social conditions following an angry outburst, is different everywhere.

Since most people experience anger, nearly everyone knows something about it. Almost everybody knows what it is to be angry, but most of us have defended ourselves against full knowledge of its complexities. Every student is aware, for example, that sometimes a professor makes him angry; on the other hand, he is likely to be less conscious of the fact that when he becomes angry at some professors he experiences a frightful mixture of anger and fear, at others a feeling of anger and suffocation, at others a feeling of anger and humiliation or futility, and so on. A thorough study of anger would explore all of its intensities and mixtures, its *modalities*.

Modalities of the feeling. Anger is felt and expressed in different ways, depending on cultural and individual factors. For example, among the Kaingáng Indians of southern Brazil,* the term for anger translates as "to be dangerous toward," but also implies fear of the target. In stories and in conversation it becomes clear that the Kaingáng, like many among us who become frightened when angry or angry when frightened, actually feel an

* See my *Jungle People* (Vintage Books; New York, Random House, 1964).

amalgam—anger-fear. On the other hand, many of us also feel anger-hate; and although these feelings are frequently considered the same, a person can be angry without hating. Anger can also be associated with depression or with alienation from the target or attacker.

If anger is taboo, one may feel ashamed or guilty if he gets angry, in which case the emotion actually felt would be anger-shame or anger-guilt. On the other hand, if for some reason a person is shamed, he may feel angry because of it, and his complex feeling will be shame-anger. Where anger is taboo, the experience of it is tinged with shame; but if one gets angry when one has been shamed, the shame is overcome by the anger.*

If I feel righteous anger, if my anger has been somehow legitimized by a personal excuse or by the culture, my feeling is quite different from the anger I feel if it is unrighteous. In the first case I feel anger combined with a feeling of expansiveness; in the latter my anger is accompanied by inner doubt. Since self-righteous anger tends to become addictive, there are people who bloom, so to speak, in the hot sun of their own anger. They are a bane. People prone to self-righteous anger feel unfulfilled when they are not angry, and may even suffer from sensations of lassitude and incompetence. It is necessary for them to eat somebody for breakfast every day. This is the Jeremiah syndrome. On the other hand, people who tend to feel anger as unrighteous avoid it as too painful; they tend to withdraw from the Jeremiahs, not so much because they are afraid of them as because they cannot stand their own anger.

It is common among American parents, especially those with teen-age daughters, perhaps, to experience an intolerable mixture of anger, fear, futility, desperation, doubt and self-righteousness when arguing with their children. Since the parent is often not sure he has the right to be angry, because he is not sure of his own point, he feels, in his anger, that he will never be able to convince his daughter; and since he no longer has the prerogative, whether he is right or wrong, of beating her, he feels he can neither convince nor cow her. Hence his growing feeling of futility. Meanwhile, since he still believes that his daughter is in danger if he cannot protect her by dissuading her, and his own authority is in danger if he loses the argument, fear and desperation come to join his so-called anger. From the outside and to an untrained eye, the parent may merely seem angry: the emotions, however, are so mixed, or, as I have called them here, amalgamated, that it is really a question of whether the term anger should be used at all. What strikes us, then, is that to describe the feeling, the word *anger* is employed rather than the words "doubt," "futility," "fear," "desperation," "self-righteousness," etc.

If Mr. Quigley is angry with his daughter Jane—with all the complexities of feeling this involves—often all that Jane, a creature of our culture, can perceive is that she is the target of anger, and she is usually unable to perceive the other emotions that are part of the angry display. As a creature of her culture, Jane is trained in blindness to the emotional accompaniments of anger; and she therefore reacts to her father's anger as if it were merely that. Thus angry interchanges are often ambiguous interchanges, not only because of lack of clarity in the arguments but because of the lack

---

* Ruth Benedict has described this for the Kwakiutl Indians of Vancouver Island. See her *Patterns of Culture* (Boston, Houghton Mifflin, 1961).

of training in emotional perception. A sensitive person can perceive the other emotions that are present along with the one that is salient to everyday perception.

Thus anger is not a pure emotion but a physiologic possibility that becomes associated with cultural or idiosyncratic factors in such a way that other emotions are felt simultaneously. As a matter of fact, it is merely linguistic poverty that makes us say "anger" when we are really talking about amalgams of feeling in which the angry feeling is only one factor. Failure to examine emotions analytically leads to the acceptance of very complex feelings as simple ones.

Modalities of expression. Anger may be felt but unexpressed or it may be expressed in a variety of ways, ranging from mere change of facial expression to an orgastic, self-consummating outpouring, accompanied by shouting, obscenity, blows or torture, depending on the culture and other circumstances.

In all cultures, anger is related to status. In our own, "nice respectable people" are "refined" in their expression of anger, and "only animals scream and shout." One expects women in our culture to be more restrained than men in expressing anger, while among the Pilagá Indians of Argentina and East European Jews, it is precisely the opposite. Among the Pilagá, angry women may engage in screaming insult bouts, whereas it does not occur among the men. Thus, in all cultures there are rules for the expression of anger, and the degree to which a person allows himself to be governed by them is a measure of his social acceptability.

Attacker and target. It is one thing to attack, quite another to be the target of anger. Depending on the culture and on idiosyncratic factors, the target of anger may experience some modality of anger; or he may experience pleasure, panic, alienation, numbness, a loss of respect for the angry person and for himself, and so on. After the angry outburst, attacker and target have the problem of recovering from anger—as from a sickness; or there is a period during which the anger "subsides"—as if it had been a flood of blood rushing to the head; or there is a period during which "things calm down"—as if the anger had been a storm and one now had to pick up the broken pieces of life's structure and put them together. Expressions like "recover," "subside," "calm down" are labels for dispositions to experience emergence from anger in a culturally or idiosyncratically determined modality. The attacker may have a post-anger experience that is not the same as his target's. Maybe after he has "blown off" he "forgets it," while his target remains alienated, withdrawn, frightened or depressed. Maybe while he is "simmering down," his target is preparing to retaliate.

Perception of people alters when we are angry. The attacker may view himself as having "enough moral courage" or as being "enough of a man" to express anger; and he may view his target as being "enough of a man" or as "too scared" to fight back. Similar considerations apply to the target's perception of the encounter. These perceptions are distinct from the perception of the underlying fault that caused the quarrel in the first place. For example, a husband may attack his wife because he thinks she is imposing on him, but his perception of her as an antagonist in the fight—how he views her in terms of whether she fights back or bursts into tears, for example—affects the quarrel also. Related to this is the type of target from which an attacker derives the greatest satisfaction. If, for example, he finds rage a consummating experience, he may require a target that can drive him to pinnacles of rage, and may be deeply disturbed by a person who does not fight back—for example, a wife who dissolves in tears and "has hysterics." Failing to get the gratification he needs, he may come to perceive his target as contemptible, as withholding gratification, and so on.

The aftermath. Usually the antagonists in a quarrel come out of it feeling different. It is probably in their tendency to make the assumption that after a quarrel things are the way they have always been, that some people in our culture show most clearly the notion that time is reversible. Typically, the anger-prone attacker is a time reverser who can never admit that his antagonist has not forgotten the encounter, as he has. His anger "passes off," and since *he* feels as if "nothing has happened," it is incomprehensible that the other person should not feel that way too. If he is a little more mature he may attempt to reverse time with the magic of the apology or comfort. Thus the problem of emotional repair is complementary to the problem of emotional damage; and underlying all efforts at repair are the assumptions that repair is possible, that a means can be found that is adequate to the task, and that repair is desired.

Quarrels are usually triggered by disagreements over actions or ideas. A quarrel has a temporal reference: it "flares up" at a particular time and after a while it "is over." On the other hand, there can be a "long-standing" quarrel, or the "flare-up" may "quiet down" but continue to "reverberate" through other activities. Quarrels derive either from the fact that people strive for disparate goals, or they may have the same goal but perceive the pathway to its attainment differently. On the other hand, no quarrel can arise in either case unless the parties are involved in their goals, for without involvement there can be no striving. This will be true even when the manifest *goal* is spurious and the underlying involvement is in *the quarrel itself.*

Assertiveness and anger tolerance. There can be no quarrel if there is no resistance, for even in the presence of the deepest involvements there will be no quarrel if the people involved give in or withdraw. But resistiveness must be two-sided, for if one person resists and the other withdraws, there is no quarrel, merely unilateral shouting, etc. In the presence of resistiveness a quarrel can still fail to materialize if neither party persists but decides to "drop the issue." "Dropping the issue" is the opposite of "forcing the issue"; and it is the latter that converts a mere difference of opinion into a quarrel. Thus resistiveness alone is not enough to make a quarrel. The probability of a quarrel occurring is greater the more A forces against the resistiveness of B. On the other hand, if B's resistiveness is indirect or covert, a quarrel may be avoided as long as A does not perceive the resistance.

Since withdrawal is a consequence of anxiety, it is related to how much anger one can bear. On the other hand, withdrawal from an impending quarrel can also be a "respectability phenomenon," for some believe that nice, respectable people simply do not quarrel. When quarreling is perceived as degrading, anxious withdrawal derives not so much from the hostility of the attacker as from expectation of shame deriving from the degradation implicit in merely quarreling.

Quarreling and the self. When quarrels become entangled with feelings about the self, the quarrel becomes a contest, and people fight back and force the issue. Then the anger that started the quarrel is blended with fear of losing the quarrel and anticipatory shame lies beneath the surface, sustaining fear and egging anger on. At the very bottom is sorrow, waiting to burst into tears, to go into mourning and even to push for suicide (as in the Trobriand Islands) if the self is destroyed in the battle. This capacity to anticipate what one will feel often makes anger disproportionate.

The self may become involved in a quarrel, however, not only because the quarrel becomes a contest but also because the original interference may seem to block the possibilities of the self—for example, when a parent refuses to let his child go to college or a child objects to the remarriage of his parent. Within limits a quarrel is man's salute to life, especially in our culture. It becomes the negation of life when it kills—either the body or the soul.

Since quarrels are so closely related to the self and its thrust toward its possibilities, a quarrel can become a situation in which one's self seems to be maximizing its possibilities; in which the self really comes into its own. The raging combat in which a person feels his self attacked and counterattacks with slashing insult or physical violence then seems, in its intoxicating effects, to present the self with the blinding vision of its consummation. In such, usually pathological, cases, the quarrel as consummatory experience is an important end in itself. When the quarrel is a consummatory experience for her husband, the best thing a wife may be able to do for him is create occasions for intoxicating rage, and later his contrite tenderness may be her reward. On the other hand, her failure to provide him with adequate stimulus to rage may be resented as a deprivation: her greatest contribution to his well-being may be her capacity to enrage him. What happens to her in this pathological process is another question.

While the capacity to anticipate what we will feel often makes anger greater than the occasion warrants, so does the capacity to see the adversary as other or as more than he is. When, for example, Black is having a run-in with Burke, and "something about Burke" reminds him of something else—maybe his own father—Black's rage may expand without limit. Since the same thing may be happening to Burke, the run-in becomes a savage encounter in which not only our self but everything we have ever dreamed or feared become the enemy, embodied now in the antagonist before us. The ability to fight a thousand demons hidden inside the visible adversary often gives an angry encounter a nightmare quality. To perceive the adversary as he really is, stripped of the costumes and the masks with which imagination and the unconscious have endowed him, marks an important difference between mature and immature anger.

In passing, it may be remarked that rats, pigeons, cats, dogs and even chimpanzees are incapable of these transformations or, in the language of psychoanalysis, transferences. Psychologists would do well never to compare human anger to rat "frustration."

Quarrels often have the function of driving one of the antagonists into a role he does not want. They may be triggered by a disagreement over some small matter—who will open the window or the door or cut the meat—when the real issue is that the role of husband or wife or one of the children is being questioned. This kind of quarrel may have a peculiar fierceness, because when a person's role is threatened, so is his self. Since behind the role lurks the self with bared teeth, driving a person into a role can be like trying to drive a tiger into the skin of a sheep—or, of course, vice versa.

Blame. Many quarrels get started or pushed along because somebody blames somebody else. Blaming somebody, of course, is a way of attacking him or defending oneself against him, but quarrels become especially bitter when antagonists rake up the past or anticipate the future. The argument, for example, that "Willie's accident last year was your fault, and if he gets hurt again it will be your fault" contains the possibility of almost unlimited quarreling because blaming has lost its temporal boundary. While there will probably be no quarrel if one of the people blames himself or accepts the blame imputed to him by the other, a person who cannot accept blame but always blames others makes life intolerable. Whoever blames others while habitually raking up the past and anticipating the future is, however, an acute threat to sanity. Thus, in a violent argument the combination of anger and anxiety provide a person with certain kinds of information and ideas that might otherwise not interest him: he can use them as ammunition.

When some people quarrel they "blow things up out of all proportion" and try to "make nothing" of the facts used by the opponent. The importance of facts is distorted because the will to win—the will to status—has become connected to memory, the usual control system of perception. This underscores the familiar observation that often things are remembered not as they were but as we wish them to be, and that the world interprets facts not as they were but as is convenient. It is obvious that lower animals are incapable of this.

Another characteristic of quarreling is that opponents may "drag in" matters that "have nothing to do with the case." Our perceptual sphere is expanded in anger by the need to win, so that it comes to include the most distant associations. Just as the angry perception blows things up, it also spreads out to include matters having no (or only the remotest) relation to the immediate issue. All of these "defects of anger" can be included in what might be called "irrational memory."

The environments of quarreling. Family quarrels are affected by the underlying life situation, by strivings for impulse release or control and by the presence of spectators.

1. The most important feature of the *underlying family situation* is the quality of the relationships in the family. Quarrels are less likely to start if the members of the family trust one another and treat one another as equals, than if everybody in the family tries to dominate the others. If the family members are generous, quarrels are less likely to start than if they are stingy; and probably one of the greatest spurs to quarreling is the feeling among family members that they are being exploited by one another. Certainly the assumption of infidelity guarantees quarreling even when husband and wife are faithful. They then watch one another to see who makes a move that seems to confirm the suspicion of domination, infidelity, and so on. When people are ready to fight over trivia, when they are always alert for cues that will release their pent-up feelings, they are hypervigilant

for triggering cues. To an outside observer, family quarrels may appear so air-drawn that he is unable to believe that he saw what happened under his nose. He may, for example, be unwilling to believe that a stream of invective could really have been triggered by the trivial event he just witnessed. In a sense he is right, for unless he has observed the family for a long time, he cannot have observed the real cause—the underlying family situation. Hypervigilance is an outstanding characteristic of disturbed relationships, and it is so closely related to family tension that one can say that the worse the tension the greater the vigilance.

When people are unassertive, however, they may be quite tense and vigilant but rarely let their anger out. Then inner rage produces secret blame; they store up resentment on the basis of their distorted perceptions, while the secret enemy—husband, wife, child—is aware only of a growing coldness, sullenness, tendencies to sudden outbursts triggered by petty, almost invisible incidents.

When somebody is looking for trouble, people may learn to be very careful not to do anything that may start a fight. This wariness is the complement of readiness for triggering. Under such circumstances people give the impression of "walking on eggs" and "looking for a fight" at the same time: one is mobilized against oneself, to prevent a triggering cue from "slipping out," and against the other person, in order to keep him quiet. This is cold war.

2. Quarrels are determined by the extent to which they are accepted as vehicles for release of hostile or masochistic impulses, for the expression of heretosexual or homosexual impulses, etc.

The peculiarity of cultures in which quarrels are common is that although often nobody seems to want them, they keep occurring; that although one or the other parties to the quarrel seems to wish it would not occur, the quarrels occur so frequently that they give the appearance of being "wanted." Sometimes what is wanted is not the quarrel but its affective release: it is a release to insult somebody—if only one could "do without" the ensuing quarrel!

3. In some families husband and wife will never express serious disagreement "in front of the children" or "in front of strangers." On the other hand, some people quarrel particularly in front of others in order to humiliate each other publicly, in order to degrade each other in front of the children or in order to win the children over to their side. In direct observation, such parading does not occur as often as concealment, but it must be considered in connection with the argument that people try to conceal their disagreements from an observer.

Frustration tolerance. Consideration of these factors alone makes the concept of "frustration tolerance" irrelevant in the present context. If in any situation a person is uninvolved and unassertive, has such a great tolerance for the anger and resistiveness of others that he can put up with it without resorting to counterassertion, and if he has a general low-tension level, is wary of other people while being nonvigilant for triggering cues himself, he will not quarrel. If in addition the culture—family or general—disallows quarreling in the family while nourishing narcotizing attitudes within it, the chances of a person's ever getting into a quarrel are nil. When the components of quarrel structure are analyzed in this way it becomes clear that at least after early childhood, the "frustration tolerance" as a biological concept is too reductionistic.

The course of quarrels. If a feud be considered a quarrel, then it is obvious that some quarrels end only when the parties and their descendants are dead. Considering the fact that some married couples quarrel constantly and that each quarrel tends to become merely the aftermath expression of the preceding one, some marriages give more the appearance of feuds than of unions—or rather, the union is accomplished through feuding. In the present discussion, however, I have taken a quarrel to be essentially a transitory outburst of anger in which people feel themselves attacked, and retaliate or defend themselves. Under this definition quarrels follow a course, from outbreak to aftermath. While the course of a quarrel is set largely by the factors mentioned, the quality of the concomitant anger is determined also by how the issue is perceived, and the modality of this anger has in turn an affect on the course of the quarrel. If Professor James says to Professor Smith, "That's a meaningless question," a quarrel may start, depending on how Smith perceives James's remark: for example, he may perceive the remark as James's "manner of speaking" and therefore "not to be taken too seriously," or as an affront to his mind or status. In the first case Smith may simply elaborate his original statement in order to show James its true meaning; in the other case Smith may become very angry, and a quarrel may start. The course the quarrel takes will be subject to the modality of Smith's anger and on whether his anger makes James angry. If Smith feels a mixture of anger and contempt, his outburst may anger James and spur him on to say things that further enrage Smith. On the other hand, if Smith is ashamed of being angry—because it is not befitting a professor and especially a professor of Smith's status—he may contain his anger. If Smith feels absolutely self-righteous, because "one does not talk to a scholar that way," he may feel so expansive, so wrapped in the shining purity of his position that he perceives no limits to the rage his righteousness permits him to pour on James's head.

Just as the character of the mutual onslaught is affected by the modality of the anger, so also is the aftermath. The course of a quarrel is determined also by the goals: does a person wish to crush his opponent, win the battle or merely "blow off" and demonstrate his selfhood?

All quarrels pass through a cycle. (The cycles through which a person passes during a quarrel affect the mood of the aftermath.) For example, there is the original provocation, then anger; then, perhaps, mounting anger and possibly the addition of a new emotion, perhaps hatred or contempt, which did not seem to be present before; then, perhaps, a gradual diminution of rage; or, perhaps, no dimunition but mounting rage, until somebody leaves the field. Obviously the phases through which the cycle passes vary with the culture and the responses of the antagonists.

Other aspects of anger and quarreling will be brought out in the study of the relationship between Dr. and Mrs. Jones.

Time, Space, Motion, Objects and People

Time

Time determines relationships among all animals. Winter and summer, indifference and rut, maturity and immaturity, night and day, "early" and "late" form the framework of existence. Wherever we find man, however, the pattern of his life-in-time is modified by culture, and the less he is under the brute domination of natural forces the more his actions become subject to culturally determined laws of time. In our culture, where the temporal frame is set by the requirements of a competitive world industrial system, fathers have jobs that are varied enough, the needs of the children are different enough and the temperaments of the people are diverse enough to give every family its own time variations: its own pace, its own times to get things done, and so on. These, nevertheless, are mere variants of the overall configuration of time set by the culture.

In the following pages I discuss aspects of culturally regulated time and its distortions.

The concatenation of events. The average man knows the time relations of his actions to his family's. He is aware, for example, that if he is not home "on time," dinner will be "kept waiting," "the kids will be hungry and screaming" and his wife "worried and mad" because she "couldn't imagine what had happened" to him, and because, since she has to go out, his getting home late has "spoiled everything." The expressions in quotes demonstrate the close connection between time and mood in our culture, and show that everyone must learn that his movements in time are connected with other people's feelings. It is by no means usual in the world that a person's actions *in time* have this tight connection to other people's moods. Time binds us in action to our wives and children in this culture, but it does more—it binds us to their emotional life. There is no culture outside the industrialized ones where anxiety, rage and contentment are so minutely affected by time. Thus, while it is true that the *idea of time* emerges first in a baby's relations to his parents, time is saturated with love, rage and anxiety from the beginning. Hence time as a feeling; hence time as flowing invisibly in our blood and our lymph. "Prick me and I bleed time!" is a motto for man-in-the-West.

Let us imagine Mr. Tutwell eager to get home for a special event on Tuesday night. He is delighted that he has "gotten my desk cleared off" and is "able to get away" and "beat it home" on time, but he happens to have the bad luck to run into Evans, who "can't stop talking." "Tied down" by Evans, Tutwell "gets very nervous" because he is thinking of "Ella and the kids waiting" for him, with the result that he "cuts Evans short"; Evans is hurt and Tutwell feels terrible. The quotes again refer to time-saturated actions and feelings and show that our language has many forms created by our unique time configuration. Thus, in our culture, time helps to shape language.

The cultural configuration of time demands our submission; it requires that we renounce impulses that interfere with it. This is the *austerity of time*. When impulses are too powerful, culturally determined modalities of time are disregarded and when other people are not involved we can deal with this kind of time as we please.

But in our culture, time is regulated also by hope, for what makes the middle-class person stick to the groove of time is the organization of his life, and his life is organized by his hopes for himself and his children. Where there is no hope—as, for example, in a Negro slum—time loses significance. To paraphrase an old proverb: When hope flies out the door, time flies out the window. In disorganization of the time sense, much more is involved than can be revealed by the day-of-the-week, month-of-the-year time test for schizophrenia, for what is at issue in disorganization of the cultural time sense is a failure to perceive or an inability to submit to the cultural configuration of time, or both. In Negro slum culture it is the same —only that without hope, learning about time is impossible. It is not that the poor Negro has a "delicious indifference to time," but that he never learned it. Give him some hope and he will be happy to renounce his "delicious indifference."

Sensitivity to temporal cues. If Mr. Lane wants to visit his friends on a Sunday afternoon, he must remember to stop watching TV at a particular time because he knows it will take him half an hour to shave, shower, dress and drive over to the Williamses' (by the main highway, because the short-cut is blocked). Thus everything Mr. Lane has to do in connection with his visit is touched off (or cued) by what preceded it and by what follows and since such cues exist in every series of actions directed toward an end, I call them *immanent temporal cues.* A sense of how events must be adjusted to one another in this way is sensitivity to immanent temporal cues.

A friend of mine climbed a famous mountain with one of his children and promised a younger one that when she was old enough he would do it with her. Meanwhile he grew older and short-winded, but six months before his daughter's twelfth birthday he went into training for the climb, so that by the time her birthday rolled around he was in trim. This is sensitivity to immanent temporal cues!

Since sensitivity to immanent temporal cues depends on knowing how our own submission to time affects others, an important ingredient in it is empathy. Between friends and lovers, between parents and children, empathy transforms astronomical time into social time; between employer and employee, between sergeant and private, between teacher and pupil, fear transforms it. Thus a question for all in our culture is, What winds the spring of our clock—the key of empathy or the key of fear? Dreams have given us the answer, "It is fear," for dreaming of time is dreaming of being too late.

It is often imagined that people without a sense of time really have "an unusually large amount of unavowed disregard for others which exploits [this] constitutional factor for its purpose." * On the other hand, since the perception of time is learned and since so much may occur in a family that upsets a child's ability to perceive the world clearly, it is difficult to be sure when a person's failure in relations with his fellows is due to unconscious

* Sigmund Freud, *The Psychopathology of Everyday Life* (Mentor Books; New York, New American Library, 1960), p. 81.

disregard of them and when to disorganizing learning experiences as a child. The difficulty grows when the experiences not only disorganize his capacity to perceive correctly but lead him to disregard others also. If a child's mother keeps him waiting for meals until he is wild with hunger, feeds him at six on Monday, at seven on Tuesday and at five-thirty on Wednesday, or promises to do something on a certain day and does not, he may not only develop a very poor sense of time but he may also become indifferent to the wishes of others. Encountering him as a husband, a wife would find it impossible to tell whether he pays little attention to her meal-time schedules because he is insensitive to time or because he is insensitive to people.

In *The Psychopathology of Everyday Life*, Freud says:

> If I *resolve* in the morning to carry out a certain intention in the evening, I may be *reminded* of it several times in the course of the day, but it is not at all necessary that it should become conscious during the day. As the time for its execution approaches it suddenly occurs to me and induces me to make the necessary preparations for the intended action.*

Being "reminded" is the dynamic factor in sensitivity to immanent temporal cues. Freud does not point out, however, that having resolved "in the morning to carry out a certain intention in the evening," a person has to schedule his activities in order to finish *in time* to carry out his evening "intention." *Submission* (to the temporal interlock) combines with *memory* (of what has to be done) to form the central complex of sensitivity to immanent temporal cues. Any failure along the line is attributed by Freud to a "counter-will." †

Disregard of others is a gift to us from the high cultures, for in tribal societies, far-flung compulsory *regard* for others is provided for within the kinship system and is guaranteed by inevitable rewards and punishments. At the same time, ability to respond to temporal cues depends on the imposition in early childhood of strict impulse controls. Although most people in our culture restrain the desire to wander from the compelling path of time, they are naturally unaware of the enormous amount of training they needed as children to prevent them from doing so. We even have the verb "to dawdle," which means "to wander from the compelling path of time." From the standpoint of the Arunta aborigine on his Australian wastes, our culture has so many distractions that it is a wonder that we ever manage to get home at all. Yet we do; and most people keep their appointments and during the day accomplish what they are supposed to.

In view of the exacting training necessary to make us do this we have to know, in dealing with different kinds of people, whether an instance of failure in time is caused by unconscious factors specific to the instance, whether it is a general expression of "an unusually large amount of un-avowed disregard of others," whether it is caused by an impairment of the culturally determined time sense, or whether it is related to all three. In no case can we find the answer unless we have a view of the person's behavior over the entire range of his activities.

Fixed and flexible time. Success dominates time in our culture; and

* *Ibid.*, p. 78.
† *Ibid.*, p. 83.

wherever it becomes the issue, time loses its flexibility: in games, in business, in taking examinations, it is all the same. The time of an appointment with a successful and powerful man is less flexible than that with a weak one. In lovers' meeting time, there is more flexibility, but keeping a sweetheart waiting too long may lead her to think she is not valued, and the courtship becomes a failure.

Aesthetic time is the most inflexible of all, for if a conductor's beat is off or the musicians do not co-ordinate, the music falls apart; and if a dance group cannot time well, they bump into one another and lose the dynamics, and the performance becomes ludicrous. It is probably in relation to aesthetic time that *Homo sapiens* can experience temporal failure most acutely and even symptomatically; violent anger, sweating palms, irritation of the skin and at the roots of the hair, a tendency to laugh wildly, and so on, are a few of the symptoms in a sophisticated audience present at a performance in which the timing is off. All relations in our culture have a fixed or flexible time schedule, and after twenty or thirty years we usually come to know how this works. Some people do not learn.

Bound and unbound time. Everyday affairs bind the time of all of us. A man's time is bound from the moment he opens his eyes in the morning until he quits for the day, by the necessity to wash, shave and dress, and to have something to eat and get to the station on time in order to get to work on time and to stay there until it is time to check out. None of that time— from getting up in the morning till quitting time—is his own, because he has sold it to the job. Sold time is bound and is governed by fear. Time not so bound, time that is not sold, is unbound and is therefore free for empathy and love. Unbound time has become so important in our culture that we have given it a special name, "leisure," whose very origin in an ancient French verb meaning "to be permitted" underscores the argument that bound time is fear time. To "dawdle" and to be "at leisure" are two expressions invented to convey the idea of escape from bound time.

Since, in our culture, consistent failure to fulfill the demands of bound time is accompanied by savage punishments (like losing one's job for being late), time becomes associated with so much anxiety that unbound time tends to become bound. In this way, fear time encroaches on empathic time. The dialectical opposition between bound and unbound time is, on the one hand, liable to make people rebel against bound time, and on the other, treat unbound time as if it were bound. This helps us understand both those who do nothing on time and those who have to fill their unbound time (leisure) with time-binding activities: club memberships, card games, do-it-yourself activities, and so on. A consequence of the fact that for most men in our culture the time between seven in the morning and six at night is bound and governed by punitive economic sanctions is that unbound time creates serious psychological hazards. People who are unable to cope with unbound time and who always have to keep busy are categorized by sociologists as being under the sway of the "Protestant ethic"—a cliché used to explain the malaise related to leisure time. In this way sociologists get rid of the problem of explaining why millions of people who neither protest nor are ethical try to fill up their unbound time by making it appear bound. The simple issue is that if not binding one's time in productive labor has the consequence of loss of livelihood and sinking to the bottom of the social scale, then not to use time in productive labor—to disengage time from work—is simply to set anxiety free. When work binds anxiety, not to work frees it.

> Work binds time.
> Work guarantees livelihood.
> Livelihood binds fear.
> No work, no livelihood.
> Time and fear are set free.

Appropriate and inappropriate time. In Camus' *The Stranger*, Meursalt is sentenced to death because he had no sense of what is appropriate. The fact that he went to a movie—and a comedy at that—on the day of his mother's funeral turned the court against him during his trial for murder. I am not concerned with this kind of right and wrong time, for Meursalt's defection from respectable custom really has to do with *occasion*. A semantic peculiarity of our language brings clock time together with occasion and etiquette, and uses the same adjective, "appropriate," for both.

In this section, however, I shall talk only about moments in clock time when it is appropriate or inappropriate to do something. In middle-class culture you don't phone your friends at nine o'clock on Sunday morning and usually not after ten o'clock at night, nor do you ask them to dinner at five o'clock in the afternoon, because, since you know they function on a physiological schedule that is culturally determined, you don't expect them to be hungry at five; and you know they like to sleep late on Sunday because that is a way of emphasizing the difference between bound and unbound time, and of "catching up on sleep." In our culture sleep runs eternally away from us; we never get enough of it and we try hard to hoard it, so that if we "don't get enough sleep the rest of the week" we can store it up again on the weekend and put it back in the sleep bank. An early phone call on Sunday morning is a bank robbery—"he robbed me of three hours' sleep," we say poisonously of a person who calls too early. Thus, in clock time the hands point to vulnerabilities that are half folk myth, half reality, but a reality always bent by culture. I think that the inappropriate *moment* is distinguished from the inappropriate *occasion* by the fact that the former is always linked up with a culturally determined physiology while the latter is connected with business, etiquette, or taboo.

Before, after, now, during, later, and until express the matrix of temporal thought (regardless of culture and regardless of whether the language has these words). In our culture, even babies have to learn to do things *now*; that something will be done for them *later*; that they have to do one thing *before* they do another; and so on. The conceptions of anticipation, postponement, filling in time between two points, the now and the later, etc., have to be grasped before one can be oriented in time. A decision to do something is often followed by a period during which other things may occur—like the decision in the morning to go to the theater in the evening—but since nothing must be done to interfere with going to the theater, the period between the decision and the going is really like bound time. Disturbed people overlook these obvious circumstances.

Two Illustrations

On Thursday Mr. Williams got up *before* his usual hour because he knew that the heavy snow that fell all night would delay him. The roads were slippery and traffic crawled, so although his gas was low, he decided not to stop at the service station *now* but to wait until *later*—on the way home. During the unusually long wait at the railroad crossing he tried not to waste time, by going over some of the customers' lists *before* he reached the office, but the raising of the barrier caught him and he didn't wake up until the angry tooting of horns shocked him out of his absorption. In his anxiety he stalled the car and kept sliding down the embankment until the tire treads caught. He got to the office somewhat upset by the experience and started to rush through the papers in order to get them finished before Mrs. Leeds, his secretary, wound up the reports. "I'm ready now, Mr. Williams," she said. "But I'm *not*," he replied.

You can see that Mr. Williams calculates his minutes carefully, moving therefore from one anxiety of time to another: getting so deeply absorbed in using up the minutes that it irritates others; trying to get ahead of time, falling behind time, trying to anticipate his secretary, rushing and, at last, failing—his secretary was ready before he was. Mr. Williams' very capacity to foresee the stream of events affects his movements, his heartbeat and, above all perhaps, the mood of other people.

The next story is a fantasy about a two-year-old's problems with "before," "after," "now" and "later":

"Mommy, make my boat go." "Not *now*, darling, Mommy's busy. *Later*." "But Mommy, it won't go." "*Later. After* you've had your lunch." "But I'm not hungry *now*, Mommy." "I mean *later*. You know, *after* Mommy has vacuumed the rugs and the milkman comes. Then lunch. *Later*." "*After* Daddy comes home?" "Oh no, a long time *before* Daddy comes home." "Not *after*?" "No. Because Daddy always comes home a long time *after* you've had lunch." "And *after* Pussy has had lunch?" "No. Pussy always has his lunch *later*; *after* Daddy comes home." "Mommy, what's 'before' and what's 'after'?" "You have breakfast and then you have lunch. That's 'after.' You have lunch before you have supper. That's 'before.' " "Mommy!" "Yes, darling?" "Please make my boat go."

Since disturbed people often fill in-between periods with activities that ultimately interfere with what they had decided to do, it becomes a problem for the observer to decide whether ambivalence or misperception is at issue. But misperception must be considered a possibility whenever we are dealing with learned perceptions, and certainly in *Homo sapiens* social time and social timing are in this category.

Circumspection. Heidegger coined this term* for the process of perceiving things in their relationship to other things, and I shall use the term in the same way. A person who is able to perceive what he does in relation to how it affects others, who sees his time schedule in relation to the time schedules of others, is capable of circumspection; and a person lacks it who does things as if other people didn't exist or who always gets mixed up in

---

* Martin Heidegger, *Being and Time,* trans. by John Macquarrie and Edward Robinson (New York, Harper & Row, 1962).

time. Later I extend the term "circumspection" to cover the capacity to see any relationships at all.

LIGHT AND DARKNESS

Everywhere and at all times, the experience of light and darkness is intensely subjective, determined by the culture, and varying with age, sex and other social circumstances. "Under cover of darkness" incidents occur that are impossible or at least unlikely in "broad daylight"; and the empathic adult treats fear of darkness as a situation for more intense communication with his child. A striking feature uniting almost all of mankind is that night is the time for sex and crime, both intensely subjective experiences. The Pilagá Indians of Argentina, imagining that sorcerers are abroad at night, stay in their villages; in our culture a man perhaps conducts himself differently toward the same woman at night and during the day.

Side by side with the folkloristic and aesthetic aspects of light and darkness, realistic factors enter the relationship between parents and children. In our culture a parent is supposed to make sure that his child can see at night. A dim light should be left in the bathroom; at night on a rough pathway the parent should have a flashlight; he must not let a very young child go out alone because the child might get lost. It is this capacity to increase his protective activity at night that sets the usual parent off from the disturbed one. A disturbed parent may never be able to anticipate that although it is light when he starts on a trip with his child, it may be dark on the way back, so he goes unprepared, or he may grandiosely imagine himself equal to all things—a creature of night as well as day, he can find his way through darkness like a bat. Of course, matters might very well be turned around so that a parent fills his child with exaggerated fears of the dark. In our culture, darkness provides a test of rationality; in more primitive conditions the phantasms of darkness become frozen into supernatural systems.

Space

In our culture* the conception of space includes the following: *extension:* distance, direction, size, height, depth, and *position:* on the table, on the stove, on the floor, etc. In middle-class culture and above, everyday functions are separated from one another in different rooms. Cooking is done in the kitchen and not in the bathroom or bedroom; one keeps all of one type of clothing in one drawer of the dresser; pots are in cabinets, on tables or hung on the wall and not kept on the floor, and so on. Position is central to order, and when everything is in its "right" position a place looks orderly. The expression "he knows his place" shows that the same notion

* Conceptions of space are culturally determined in many ways and therefore receive a great variety of linguistic expression. My more or less Cartesian analysis would be different were I analyzing the spatial conceptions of a tribal people. I do not give an exhaustive analysis of our cultural conceptions of space, but rather touch on the more usual ways of looking at it.

applies to people, and the fact that it is used for the socially disfranchised more than for others shows that the lower we sink in the social scale, the more we get lumped with objects.

EXTENSION

Unless we have an intuitive grasp of the culturally significant aspects of extension, we can't get along. We must adjust *distance* to time so that we will not live too far away from work or go so far away for lunch that we will not get back to the job in time. Often a primitive man has to be sure not to go so far away from the village that he will not get back before dark. On the other hand, distance is not always related to time; for example, houses everywhere are spaced according to culturally determined feelings about how far apart they should be; and Hall* has pointed out that in different cultures people stand at different distances from one another while talking.

An Illustration

The house on Vandermeer Street looked great to Mortimer. It had nice trees and the street was quiet, so he paid a month's room rent in advance on Sunday and moved in his belongings. But on his way to work on Monday he realized that he should have asked the landlady how long it would take him to get downtown to his job in the morning, because the traffic was so heavy that instead of the fifteen minutes Mortimer had figured, it took nearly forty-five. That meant half an hour's less sleep. He was finicky about his food and guessed he could eat in that nice-looking place a few blocks from his job. But again he had miscalculated; the streets were crowded at noon and the place was jammed, so he had to settle for a greasy spoon nearer the office; and instead of the leisurely lunches he had looked forward to, he found himself rushing like everybody else. Another thing about the house he lived in was that it was much closer to other houses than he was used to, so he would laugh to himself and say, "Whose bathroom am I in now?" He was afraid to play his hi-fi loud, too, and that was a loss because he loved the booming sound of the basses.

Mortimer knew a girl—Dorothy Pennington—whom he had met when she was on a visit to his hometown. He called her up and they went dancing. Since Dorothy was a bit young, her parents insisted that she be home not later than twelve-thirty, even on date nights, so Mortimer couldn't take her to a really good place but had to stick to something closer to her house. Dorothy was pretty, with a demure, childish manner, thus Mortimer was stunned and delighted when she wouldn't sit on the opposite side of the booth at the Cock and Hen but made him sit beside her, and when they got on the dance floor she snuggled up close right away. It was too bad she had to be home so early—and it was too bad he had fouled up on the distance between his rooming house and the job, because not only did he have to bring her home on time, but if he took her out on week nights he'd have to get home to his own place in time to get his sleep—he had to have his eight hours a night—or else he wouldn't be worth much the next day.

* Edward T. Hall, "A System of Notation for Proxemic Behavior," *American Anthropologist*, Vol. LXV (1963), pp. 1003–26.

It is clear that in social life there is no such thing as the pure extension of mathematics, because in social life extension involves other people and a great range of other circumstances that affect our perception of it. In the little story about Mortimer, Vandermeer Street—a spatial idea—is subjectively experienced by Mortimer as pretty and quiet. The range of subjective experiences of the house and street is enormous, for the space on which the house stands is related to Mortimer's job, to his sleep, to his going to the bathroom, to his desire to play his hi-fi set, and even to his sexual life. Dorothy lives so far from his rooming house that he has to think twice before taking her out on a weekday night. His subjective experience of space is also affected by notions of good and bad girls and of age, for he never expected that a demure and rather young-looking girl like Dorothy would be so eager to leap class-determined space barriers. The question for him then became, Is she a "good" girl? And related to this is the sexual-spatial phrase, How far will she go?

Direction, perhaps the most important social mode of extension, is linguistically the most highly elaborated. Toward me, away from me, northward, southward,* toward the inside of the house, toward the house, toward the outside of the house, upstream, downstream, toward the river, toward the forest, up, down, are some of the modes of direction that must be expressed formally in some languages. In English we can talk about motion without indicating direction, but not in Pilagá. For example, I can say "Cybele has gone," without mentioning in what direction she left, but in Pilagá I would usually have to say at least "Cybele went home." Although it is a truism that *Homo sapiens* has to know not only that he is moving but also in what direction, the truism turns out to be useful when we learn that disturbed people often couldn't care less in what direction they are going; and as Margaret Mead and Gregory Bateson have pointed out, if a Balinese is removed from his usual directional landmarks he becomes very anxious.† In a group of forest nomads like the Kaingáng Indians of Brazil,‡ direction is determined largely by the location of food animals: a flock of feeding birds or a tapir's track determines the direction in which a band of Indians will move, and there is no orientation to points of the compass or landmarks. Many New Yorkers cannot tell north from south, but they do know uptown and downtown. On the other hand, a shut-in may forget. Thus orientation to direction is determined by participation in the culture.

Direction is often perceived in terms of what we imagine to be the conditions of the pathway: safe or dangerous, long or short, well or poorly lighted, in good or bad repair, etc. Obviously, however, such categories have

* Poets understand the significance of *-ward,* our lone directional suffix. Thus Keats's

> My heart aches and a drowsy numbness
>   Pains my sense
> As if of hemlock I had drunk
>   One moment hence,
> And lethewards had sunk . . .

and Dylan Thomas' famous lines

> The gentleman lay graveward
>   with his furies.

† In *Balinese Character* (New York, New York Academy of Sciences, 1942).
‡ See my *Jungle People* (*op. cit.*).

no objective existence, for they are themselves culturally determined perceptions, tied into a network of material and intangible determinants. The following illustrates the point: one day I was returning from fishing with Sidingkie, a chief of the village in which my wife and I were living among the Pilagá Indians, when I noticed that instead of taking a direct path to the village he was taking a circuitous one, keeping rather far away from other villages. When I said, "Your pathway is a long way around," he answered that if he went directly to his village he would be seen by people of other villages, who would bewitch him for not sharing his catch. This incident supports the view that pathways are culturally determined, that usually human life is not governed only by the objective characteristics of pathways, and that perception of the pathway is always subject to radical modification by emotions and by one's relations to other people. Extension unmodified by culture exists nowhere, not even in Euclidean geometry.

Size seems always to involve accommodation, suitability and an ideal. In classic Japanese art the ideal feminine mouth is tiny, in our contemporary culture the feminine mouth should be large and "warm." The pelvis of the figures used to display women's clothing in American store windows are always much smaller than that of the average woman, whereas Renaissance paintings give women broad hips. The difference possibly represents the decline in woman's importance as mother and her rise as a consumer. These are differences in ideals. A short man is not suitable for a tall woman in our culture because tall woman/short man does not accord with our ideal. A man cannot wear a felt hat that slides down over his ears, but he can wear a woolen hat that way. In the first case the stylish accommodation of head to hat should expose the ears even in freezing weather; in the second case the point is to keep the ears warm. At a more concrete level— buildings have to be of a certain size in our culture to accommodate an anticipated number of people, to bring in enough income, and so on. But the size must also express the aspirations of people and institutions.

At first glance, the *height* of objects seems not to have much connection with people; yet many judgments of height are based on our feelings about them. A person is very careful about height when he is with someone he loves, because of the danger of falling, so "too high" may mean "too high for Willie," although it may not be too high for his father. A tall person does not put things "too high up out of everybody's reach," and he hangs pictures at other people's eye level, not his own. If I am living with somebody I don't put things "so low down that a person has to break his back to get them."

While it may be possible to talk about the modes of extension without reference to culture and to other people's convenience, safety or peril, it is not possible to live that way. This being the case, understanding of extension comes not from disengaging it from "the world," but from perceiving how it becomes involved in human life.

POSITION

In our culture, position is more important than extension, because in a culture as loaded with material objects as ours we have to have everything in its place. What makes position even more important is that all of extension has been applied to status, so that we speak of the pathway to success, social distance, big men and little men, high and low social position, and so on. I am not concerned with these social analogies here, but rather with the original meaning of position as it refers to the place occupied by material objects.

In our culture, position has become a subcategory of perception, in the sense that we can tell instantly whether things are in order or in chaos; we feel disorder like prickly heat. Although we have few words to express it, position affects thought so much that we become upset when objects are out of place or when people "do not know their place."

Having the instruments in the right place is the result of perceptual consonance between surgeon and nurse: they both understand order in the same way—at least as it applies to the operating room—and they know that order is indispensable to the task. They know also that it is to the benefit of both of them if order is maintained, and that it is essential to the life of the patient. Perceptual consonance is absolutely necessary to the functioning of any culture and is related to tradition, task, survival and mutual self-interest. We can follow the general rule; when people perceive things in different ways they belong to different cultures—or they might as well.

Motion

Chimpanzees, gorillas and gibbons all walk differently because their gaits are genetically determined, but the way people walk is modified by culture. Patterns of motility—of walking, running, creeping, swimming, and so on—vary from culture to culture, and even with age, sex and social position within cultures. A professor usually does not run across the campus like a student, and in our culture, boys and girls throw a ball differently. The way a Chiriguano Indian woman walks is different from the way a Pilagá Indian woman does and while the forest-roving Kaingáng Indian walks with a bounce—as if he were constantly stepping over fallen logs —the Pilagá Indian of the Chaco flatland has a swinging, low-footed rhythm, partly because he rarely has to lift his feet to step over anything.

In all activities there is a certain pace and a certain configuration of movement. This is clear in team games where, as in football or basketball, for example, the players move in accordance with an intuitive feeling of how everybody else has to move. The same is true of the dance. On the other hand, when I stroll along with a three-year-old, I adapt my pace to his and when a man with some empathy in his bones walks with his wife, he adjusts his long steps to her shorter ones. When a person drives his car through midtown, he observes one speed limit, but when he is out on the highway, he follows a different one—and usually figures that the highway patrol will not pick him up for going ten miles over the posted limit. When there are youngsters in the back of his station wagon, a father who thinks about his children does not speed around curves, because unless the children are strapped down they will be knocked about. Some disturbed people cannot follow the configuration of movement prescribed by their culture; they lack circumspection here as they do in time.

Thus the motion of mathematics and physics is an idealized essence of pure units, but wherever man has a hand in it, motion is patterned by culture.

Objects

In the kitchen of any good housekeeper, pots are more or less classified and kept together: she has one kind of pot in one place and another elsewhere; the pots she doesn't use very often are usually stuck away on a lower shelf, so that you have to have a very good back to get at them. Thus, in a very broad sense, she keeps all the pots that serve one purpose or related purposes together and separate from others. Pots are made to fit her hand and the stove—and the design of pots has changed enormously over the years as manufacturers studied the shape of women's hands, the design of stoves, learned and cared more about how women's hands get burned on hot pot handles, and so on. Manufacturers have also thought out types of pots, pans and grills for making poached eggs, frying hamburgers, steaming rice, etc. They have become more and more sophisticated about the job a pot has to do (its function), where it is going to be (its position—hanging on the wall or shoved away in a drawer), the woman who is going to use it (the person) and the object on which it is going to be used (the stove). They have learned what everybody has to learn about all objects, viz., that objects are in a culturally determined relation to a complex of other objects, people, functions and positions. Manufacturers and their designers have gained in circumspective capacities.

Objects must be kept in condition. You have to have all the buttons on your clothes, even if the buttons are useless—as on the cuffs of men's suits or the purely decorative buttons on women's dresses. Things have to be clean too, but there is a standard of cleanliness for every object: you don't have to keep pots and dishes as clean as you keep surgical instruments, but there is a point beyond which a pot becomes "filthy." Knives ought to be sharp, but a table knife doesn't have to be as sharp as a steak knife and even a steak knife doesn't have to be like a scalpel. The refrigerator must not be "jammed with all kinds of junk so you can't find anything," furniture must be dusted and clothes that are white cannot be merely washed and clean—they have to be gleaming. That is why "Dazzle, the new detergent that will make your clothes 40 percent whiter" has come to be a commercial expression of a culturally determined criterion of condition ("You should see the condition of her linens, they're *gray*. I bet she never uses a bleach").

Outlined above are the fundamental points of view that determine the everyday metaphysic of objects. Unless a person has mastered this system he will be in difficulties with other people in addition to having problems purely his own.

People

Protectiveness is the center of viable human relationships. Relationships cannot last if people are not sensitive to one another's feelings and to the physical dangers they face. A parent who constantly humiliates a child destroys the child emotionally, and if he is careless about material conditions, the child will die or be killed. The same thing applies to the relations between husband and wife, and between friends. Space, time, motion and objects become involved in protectiveness, because unless a person's circumspective capacities are well developed, he will not be able to perceive dangers and will do disturbing things. A mother who sets up a feeding schedule for her infant, for example, but cannot stick to it because she lacks sensitivity to temporal cues makes her baby wait too long between feedings, so the baby suffers severe hunger pains and then eats too fast. If the mother alternates between feeding the baby too soon and feeding it too late, this is bad for the baby, too. But such behavior can come also from the fact that the mother has no empathy for a young organism and sees no reason why a baby can't wait half an hour for its meal if *she* can.

In order to protect a person, you must have some feeling for him and be able to perceive the interconnections between time, space, motion, light and darkness, objects and people, but even if you understand that precautions have to be taken to avoid the dangers of darkness, deep water, high rocks, driving around sharp turns, etc., and even if you have feeling, it still is no good unless you are able to perceive the actual dangers and make the effort to protect somebody. Many caring people who seem able to understand the nature of danger in the abstract don't seem to see it when it is before them. Even when they do, they cannot protect anybody, including themselves, for a variety of reasons: because they are afraid, because they dissociate their fear, because they want to hurt themselves, and so on.

All cultures and all families institutionalize norms of protectiveness, and the tendency of our culture to lose them is expressed in the fact that while psychiatry is preoccupied with overprotection, it has shown relatively little interest in underprotection. There are many works on the overprotective mother, and a whole folk ideology has developed around "momism," but there are no works on underprotectiveness and no folklore. Underprotective —called "neglectful"—mothers are handled by social agencies and by the police. Psychoanalytic concern with overprotection is a reflection of the middle-class background of analysts and their patients. Carelessness— neglect—has seemed to belong so much to poverty that psychoanalysts would naturally ignore it. Protectiveness is central to ethical systems and occupational codes in our culture because solicitude for the other person is the idea on which they all stand.

To sum up, time, space, motion, light and darkness, and objects cannot be disengaged from social life, for they are affected by culture and formed into different configurations in different cultures. Having learned the configuration, most people allow themselves to be guided by it, but disturbed ones may be unable to. The result is that they create trouble for themselves and for others, and often one cannot tell whether the trouble they cause is due to lack of circumspection or to disregard for other people.

Since, in the study of the Jones family, such problems of interpretation are important, I have been at pains to outline the issue in advance. The first problems I discuss arise in connection with an arrowhead hunt I went on with Dr. Jones and his two young sons on the first day of my visit. On that "expedition" Dr. Jones violates so many "ordinary precautions" that the average person would say he is mixed-up or careless, and the psychoanalytically trained might decide he is "hostile" or "sadistic." Let us turn to the observations.

THE JONES FAMILY

Dr. Edward Jones and his wife, Ida, are in their thirties. He is a dentist. His wife, who had some college, stays home, keeps house and takes care of the children: Bobby, age seven, Jackie, age three; and Harriet, about seventeen months old. At the time of my visit Tommy, about nine years old, diagnosed autistic when he was about three years of age, was in an institution. Mrs. Jones is pregnant.

An "Archaeological Expedition"

Dr. Jones decided that we should go out into the country to see a mound which he said contained arrowheads.

(First day.) Dr. Jones, Bobby, Jackie and I drove out into the country to find an Indian mound and search it for arrowheads. We came to a little stream, and taking off our shoes and socks, we began to wade along it because Dr. Jones said that this was *the* way to the mound. There was broken glass in the stream and Dr. Jones said there might be danger from snakes as well.

Jackie, the younger boy, got frightened and complained of the cold. He was also afraid that the water was too deep for him. Dr. Jones paid little attention. Occasionally he stooped and picked some broken glass out of the stream. We wandered alongside the stream, up on the bank, down into the stream, up on the bank again, and the stream became difficult here and there. Several times I carried Jackie, but finally Dr. Jones carried him for a long distance as Jackie continued to complain of the cold; it really was quite chilly for that time of the year. At last we reached a point where it was no longer possible to go on because the stream was too deep. We climbed up the bank through poison ivy and encountered a barbed-wire fence over which we climbed while Jackie whimpered. No one was scratched on the wire. We found ourselves at the far edge of a wide field covered with weeds, brambles and berry bushes, and we had to walk across it, barefoot, of course, in order to reach the road that bordered on the far side. I carried Bobby across the field and Dr. Jones carried Jackie. Dr. Jones was surprised when I offered to carry Bobby and tried to dissuade me, saying that Bobby was too huge and heavy. I found him neither huge nor heavy; as a matter of fact, I scarcely felt his weight even though the going was difficult. In the Jones case history, both Dr. and Mrs. Jones, but especially the former, had referred to Bobby, the seven-year-old, as "huge," "strong," etc. Because of this I was prepared for a giant, but I found him an ordinary, rather good-looking kid.

Throughout the entire "expedition" Bobby took matters without any whining; only Jackie complained. At last we reached the road and walked back to the car. We drove about a quarter of a mile, to an old house where Dr. Jones spoke to a woman about our desire to explore the mound just behind her house. We could have reached it in the first place simply by driving there instead of trying to wade to it along the stream. We climbed the little mound and found no arrowheads or anything that looked as if it had belonged to an Indian. Moderate scratching around showed that this little mound was not an archaelogical mound at all but a natural geological formation of rotten shale.

Dr. Jones was never able to free himself of the idea that I was a formal academic anthropologist. Throughout my stay he kept bringing up paleo-anthropology, evolution, genetics and archaeology, in spite of the fact that he knew that my fundamental interest was in the emotional problems of children, in spite of the fact that he had met me at the Agency,* where I had spent many hours recording the family's history as told by him and his wife, and in spite of the fact that I never evinced interest in paleoanthro-pology. The "archaeological expedition" is the first example of his stereotyp-ing me in a role I did not fit. Dr. Jones does this not only because of his perception of me but also because his perception of himself as a man of broad range requires him to encounter me in "scientific" dialogue and ac-tion. As we see here, and as we shall see again later, a rather grandiose perception of himself often pushed him to absurdity.

I turn now to an analysis of Dr. Jones's relation to space, and I will emphasize his subjective experience of space as it relates to his personality.

There are times when even an average person will take chances. For example, if a man rushed into such a stream to save his child, there would be some correspondence between the risks and the goal. But what kind of goal is a hypothetical mound with hypothetical arrowheads? In a culture like ours, whose economic system is based on "risk" and "venture" capital, and where most believe that the essence of existence is taking chances, the inability to balance the risk against the end is a common failing—and so is the fear of taking any chances at all. Automobiles are often wrecked and the people in them killed by drivers who do not consider the risk because they are driven by this culturally determined inner compulsion to take risks. In pathologic risk taking, however, the risks seem bizarre and the danger more obvious than in the average long chance. Broken glass, open cans and potholes in the bed of a stream are clear and present dangers.

Having stood up to extremely threatening parents throughout his child-hood and youth, Dr. Jones became frozen in permanent readiness for com-bat, and his behavior in the stream expressed the image of himself as brave, defiant and surviving. The light from the stream having passed through this image, Dr. Jones could no longer see the stream in its material relations to himself and the rest of us. In this we are all very much the same, for space, time, motion, objects and people do not exist in an objec-tive state for anybody, but are perceived through a self the culture has formed, and this self has its own eyes with which it perceives its own real-ity. It was as necessary that I be perceived as Dr. Jones's self-image deter-mined, as it was that the stream be perceived as his self-image required.

Thus the expedition became an illusion. I was not interested in arrow-heads (my role wasn't there), the stream was impassable (the pathway wasn't there) and the arrowheads, literally, were not there. Reality was

* In all cases mentioned in this book, the organization caring for a disturbed per-son is called "the Agency," "the Institution," etc.

ignored and the excursion became an "as if" phenomenon;* it was a dream in Dr. Jones's head.

But why didn't Bobby or Jackie refuse to go on? Why didn't they turn around and go back to the car, or just get out and refuse to budge? Their *inappropriate acquiescence* was the complement of their father's persistence. *This acquiescent participation in what is dangerous* is based on the fact that dangerous situations are also rewarding—as we shall see.

An Outing

Around five-thirty in the afternoon we all left for a picnic at the lake in Latham Park. Preparations had been very hectic because Dr. and Mrs. Jones dawdled and delayed a great deal and did not plan. The result was that Dr. Jones became very anxious that we might not get to the lake in time for a swim, and began to abuse his wife. She seemed to take it in rather good spirit, hitting back at him—not very violently and not raising her voice. It is characteristic of Dr. Jones that when he is under tension he abuses his wife. He also tried to force her out of the kitchen to take care of Harriet (the baby), but she would not leave, saying that he exaggerates the amount of time it takes her to get the baby ready. On the other hand, she delayed things herself by insisting that all the children be bathed before we went on the picnic. Dr. Jones went into the bathroom a couple of times to urge the boys to hurry, and to threaten Bobby that he would not go on the picnic if he did not hurry. In the kitchen Dr. Jones also brusquely urged his wife on.

During the preparations Dr. Jones kept insisting that many things did not have to be done but Mrs. Jones insisted they did, and her way prevailed.

Dr. Jones did not help with the lunch dishes, so Mrs. Jones did them herself. Meanwhile Dr. Jones talked to me about the academic world: writing papers, social climbing, and so on. This went on for a long time. Every once in a while Mrs. Jones would say something, but since she was at the sink, she actually said little. At last, when the dishes were done and put away, she came and sat down and joined the conversation, saying, "Oh, I'd much rather sit and talk than go shopping." It is obvious that if Dr. Jones had helped with the dishes, things would not have been so long drawn out, and if they both had not been so leisurely about their preparations for the picnic, the arguments would not have occurred, nor would the pressure have been applied to the kids by Dr. Jones to hurry with their baths.

Mrs. Jones asked her husband to weed the garden and pick some corn while she was shopping, and he kept busy doing that. Bobby and Jackie took me for a long walk. When we returned, Harriet, who was in Dr. Jones's care, got lost, and although he sent Pookie, the dog, to look for her, it was I who found her, at last, under the porch, safe and sound. When Mrs. Jones returned from her shopping, at last we got off.

When we started to build a fire at the picnic grounds we discovered that Mrs. Jones had left the grate at home, so there was nothing on which to broil the hamburgers. Dr. Jones became abusive and called her an idiot. When he was out of earshot she admitted to me that she had been stupid to forget it. He called out to her that she really never wanted to go on picnics, anyway, and that the reason she forgot the grate was probably because she didn't want to go. Meanwhile she

* The "as if" phenomenon is discussed in some detail in Part II, "The Rosenberg Family."

dished out orange drinks and potato chips to the famished children, who were gathered around her.

Dr. Jones's suggestion about cooking the hamburgers was that they be held between split branches, but I said that this would divide the meat down the middle so that it would fall apart and into the fire. I at last suggested that we fry the hamburgers on aluminum foil. Dr. Jones felt it absolutely necessary to add hickory and sassafras to the fire because, he said, this would give the hamburgers a wonderful taste. He plunged into the woods and was gone about ten minutes, returning with an armful of leaves and branches which he stuffed into the fire, but they contributed nothing to the taste of the meat. By the time he returned, Mrs. Jones had made the patties, which were placed on the foil and the foil on the fire, and Dr. Jones fried them. They were quite good.

After we had eaten, Dr. Jones insisted that the children go to the toilet, so I accompanied the kids there, about the distance of a city block. Not long afterward Dr. Jones started to go there with Bobby, who apparently had to go again. They were about to leave when, because it was quite dark, I suggested that they take a flashlight, and Dr. Jones decided that it was a good idea. He came back for one, and I was struck by the fact that he hadn't thought of it himself.

Before Dr. Jones and Bobby went to the toilet they walked down to the nearby stream, and Dr. Jones went leaping from rock to rock in the water, making a noise, calling, "This is a challenge!" Bobby followed along, not leaping from boulder to boulder but carefully feeling his way with his feet from stone to stone. They went upstream about a hundred feet and came back without mishap. It was interesting to me to see Dr. Jones running these rather serious risks, because on a previous occasion I had had a discussion with him about the self-destructiveness of people in our culture. He had acknowledged the fact but equated self-destructiveness with "rising to meet a challenge."

During the picnic the only person to whom Dr. Jones really devoted time was Bobby. He first helped Bobby swim in the lake, and then went leaping from rock to rock in the stream while Bobby tried to stick close to him, clinging from rock to rock.

Notice that Dr. Jones is the principal actor in all the consequences of the long-drawn-out delay: the family gets into difficulties because husband and wife cannot plan, and the husband acts out. He is the explosive charge; he is "consequent-prone"; he is the one who goes around making things even more difficult. Under stress he is less able to restrain his impulses than the little boys.

Instead of looking at the delay as a consequence of general inability to organize ("lack of circumspection"), it might be interpreted as a result of the fact that Dr. and Mrs. Jones did not want to go on the picnic in the first place. Yet, since Dr. Jones likes to swim, speaks of outings as "going for a swim," and likes to leap about in rocky streams, he might have wanted to go, but not his wife. She was the major cause of the delay and her husband says she doesn't like picnics, but when one person in a troubled relationship interprets the other we have to be skeptical, because it is partly through mutual misinterpretation that family troubles are maintained. Dr. Jones made his own contribution to the delay by sitting around talking instead of helping with the dishes. Neither ambivalence about going nor insensitivity to temporal cues, however, caused Dr. Jones's attacks on his wife, for they were the expression of underlying hostility.

Homo sapiens is extremely sensitive to disturbances in his arrangements of time, space, objects and people. Upset the order of events in our culture and a kind of madness afflicts us. People have varying immunity to this sickness, but there are few who do not become restless with the fever of cultural time. Since this sensitivity can make deliberate distortion a weapon of choice in domestic strife, it creates difficulty for an outside observer who is trying to decide whether a distortion in arrangements arises from hostility or from disturbed perception. The only conclusion I can come to in the present instance is that the picnic difficulties were due both to ambivalence about going and to lack of circumspection.

Dr. Jones's image of himself also disturbed his relationship to the waning light and to Bobby, for as he leaped from boulder to boulder in the semidarkness, calling out, "This is a challenge," he led Bobby into danger, as he had on the way to the arrowhead "mound." A few months later the boy fell over a twenty-foot spillway while wandering in a stream with his father. Though Bobby escaped permanent injury, he was badly hurt. "*C'est la vie,*" wrote Dr. Jones in his letter to me. When I knew Bobby, he had no visible capacity to stay out of danger; some, I suppose, might call him brave. As we observe Bobby, at seven years of age, acquiesce time after time in his father's confusions, we realize that Bobby is learning a distorted view of time, space, objects and people. Or, to put it another way, he is learning not to see the world as most people do. Bobby, by going along with his father, collaborated in his own jeopardy. On the other hand, if his mother had been sensitive to the danger (and willing to act), or if she had thought that she would be heeded, she might have insisted that at least Bobby come out of the stream. I wonder, nevertheless, whether, in view of the hostility between her and her husband and between her and Bobby, she was silent because she was unaware of the danger, because she was afraid of being ignored or insulted, or because she didn't care whether they got hurt or not. The last is the gravest of all possibilities and will be examined at length in the study of the relationship between her and Bobby.

Primitive people do not, as a rule, go on picnics* and do not depart from ordinary routines except on ceremonial occasions. The Kaingáng Indians,† nomadic hunters of southern Brazil, break camp at dawn on the basis of the previous day's hunting reconnaissance. The men having decided where to camp next, the group moves: their few effects are packed into baskets in fifteen minutes or less; from the night's fire each woman takes a brand for the next camp; babies are hoisted onto their mothers' backs, and with the men in the lead, they leave. Everything happens so fast that time ("duration") is reduced almost to a point, because the demands of their kind of life are inexorable. The decision is communal, and nobody stays behind; no man or woman decides not to go; no one fusses and delays. But the Jones picnic was not inevitable; they were not controlled by a group, the picnic was outside of routine, and since it was not an inevitable requirement of existence itself, they could dawdle and delay, and flounder in the temporal and structural peculiarities of the culture without perishing. There is a limit to confusion in all cultures, which is set by the ultimate need to survive. People like the Joneses, who are sane but confused, seem to go to the

---

* In his *Sexual Life of Savages in North-Western Melanesia* (Harvest Books; New York, Harcourt, Brace, 1962), Bronislaw Malinowski talks about the picnics of the Trobriand youth.

† See my *Jungle People* (*op. cit.*).

brink of existence: a few more steps and they would require special care to be saved from destruction, but as we have seen with Bobby, and as we shall see further, they are terrifyingly close to it. In psychotic confusion, however, a person may so endanger himself or others that society has to step in to protect them.

When Dr. Jones blamed his wife for forgetting the grate she blamed herself, avoiding a fight by acting as if there was a household rule that made the grate her exclusive responsibility—perhaps because pots and pans are her responsibility. A picnic, however, creates a small domestic revolution, when the conventions that bind people to objects are forgotten, and everybody except perhaps the young children takes care of everything. Husband and wife check to see if they have everything they need. To turn around then and blame a wife for not sticking to her usual functions is absurd. Normally it would be unreasonable for the cook—Dr. Jones, in this case—to blame somebody else for forgetting the cooking utensils, and furthermore, insulting his wife could not make the grate materialize. Such pointless, unjust and humiliating blaming is common enough, but if the accused is not somewhat mad he does not blame himself unless he has been intimidated or is just as mixed up as his accuser. We would call that a *concordant misperception,* an expression of the inability of both of them to adapt to a new situation.

But perhaps everything happened simply because Mrs. Jones hates picnics, as her husband implied, but couldn't refuse to go on this one. What I saw, then, would be a more or less unconscious protest and way of punishing her husband for making her do what she did not want to do. Accepting blame for the grate would be an oblique way of acknowledging the "crime" of not liking picnics altogether. This would be typical displacement: instead of admitting a big truth (that she never wanted to go at all) she would "confess" to an untruth (that forgetting the grate was all her fault). She would be like a man advised by his lawyer to confess to a lesser crime he did not commit rather than risk trial for a big one he did commit. In this case the lawyer would be Mrs. Jones's unconscious, which, like everybody's, is always ready with legal tricks to help us escape inner punishment for evil impulses.

I cannot decide which interpretation is right—the one based on confusion or the one based on unconscious motivations—for the Joneses are so lacking in circumspection, so unable to organize their lives that if I were to decide that everything here was motivated by unconscious factors and thus "convict" Mrs. Jones of not wanting the picnic in the first place, I would end up by accusing her of wanting Bobby to be injured, her children to go hungry and the observer to think her a fool. Furthermore, as we shall see later, I would have to accuse Mrs. Jones of desiring the destruction of her baby, whom she obviously loves, although she is exceedingly careless with her.

If we had followed Dr. Jones's suggestion of how to roast the hamburgers, they would have fallen into the fire. This idea was not merely impractical but involved Dr. Jones's misperception of himself as well. Imagining himself primordial man, Dr. Jones saw the picnic as a savage bivouac where primitive materials are used to meet primeval challenges, and in such a setting bent twigs are more fitting than aluminum foil. Dr. Jones could not keep silent, because that would have acknowledged ignorance and failure; yet his idea was no good and he tried to compensate by doing something dramatic, "primitive" but futile—putting boughs of sassafras and hickory on the fire. A useless idea was followed by a compensatory hollow gesture based on the same fantasy of himself—that he was a forest creature, strong and resourceful, among the shadows and the leaves.

A similar situation had developed on the arrowhead hunt. Though unforeseen dangers began to appear when we had been in the stream a short time, Dr. Jones could not turn back. Yet continuing on resulted in a defeat, which really could have been a kind of victory if he had simply said quickly, "It's too dangerous here; let's get out." This compulsion to keep going lies behind the hamburger incident also. While such determination is a valuable characteristic in our culture, the difference between disturbed and undisturbed expressions of it lies in the extremes to which a person goes, in the ends he seeks, in whether he perceives all obstacles as threats to his self-image, and whether, in attempting to compensate for a setback, he becomes absurd. A disturbed person will force the issue in the pursuit of all goals, will go to extremes in the face of all obstacles, perceive the obstacles as threats and attempt to compensate for setbacks by self-defeating behavior.

Disregard versus Perceptual Disorder

There is an underlying hostility between Dr. and Mrs. Jones, and Dr. Jones does not hesitate to humiliate his wife. Often when he forces the issue and is underprotective, his wife acquiesces by remaining silent. Much of Dr. Jones's behavior seems to derive from insensitivity; yet, on the other hand, it is difficult not to believe that misperception and lack of circumspection contribute: Dr. Jones is disorderly about his appearance and his car. For a man of his status he is sloppily dressed; his pants are baggy, his sport shirt flops around, he never wears a jacket except to church and his hair is mussed.

The following are some observations on the problem of time and space: Dr. Jones was thinking of starting a second "feeder" practice in Kington, and it seemed to me not only that he had no time for it, but that such an arrangement would also undercut his home practice in Latham, because he wouldn't be around enough to take care of it. The following is a record of our conversation:

> Dr. Jones thinks that if he starts a practice in Kington it will be all right if he is there between seven and eight-thirty in the morning. He thinks this is all that will be necessary. I suggested that if the practice is worth anything it would occupy much more time than that, and he brushed it off with a laugh, saying, "That's probably so."

While in this example indifference to others is less clear than the gross miscalculation, in the next one indifference seems an issue.

> (Second day.) It was about twelve-thirty now and Dr. Jones was quite late for lunch. Bobby was very hungry and asked me whether he could have a sandwich.

I said, "Don't ask me, ask your mother," and she said, "If you're hungry, take a sandwich," so he did. Mrs. Jones wondered, rather mildly, what had happened to Dr. Jones. Bobby, who had gone out, came back, saying that Dr. Jones was looking at a vacant old hotel. At last, after one o'clock, Dr. Jones came home. He told his wife that they could have the old building for $14,000. He thought it would be a good idea if they lived in part of it and rented out the rest as apartments.

Although Mrs. Jones did not say a word about the building while Dr. Jones was holding forth, she had said to me in private, before he came home, that it was an enormous place, from which I inferred that she thought it too big to be manageable. It seems to me characteristic of him to think of buying that place, for it is obviously an overambitious undertaking. The Joneses could live in only a very small portion of it, and the reconstruction of the rest into apartments would require an enormous internal conversion job and run into a great deal of money. In this connection I am reminded of the idea he had yesterday of going fishing at six o'clock this morning: he and the boys would leave the house at that hour and they could go fishing before he went to the office. They did not go.

We could say that Dr. Jones dawdled in the old building at lunchtime because he was unaware that his wife and children might be hungry. Some might even suggest that he delayed in order to make his family suffer because in his childhood he had, perhaps, hungered in the same way. But then, why did he get involved in that huge building? Surely this was a misperception of space, objects and even of himself. But if *it* was misperception, why wasn't his apparent indifference to his family's hunger a function of a disturbed time sense rather than of some unconscious hostile need to repeat through his family what he had experienced as an infant and child? It could be argued that the grandiose involvement in the building and failure to perceive at once the overwhelming problems involved in remodeling, etc., were also related to childhood experience: expressions of insatiable needs deriving from childhood deprivation. *Yet the disturbed perception remains.* Whatever the underlying "cause," the failure to relate his delay to his family's mealtime is clear.

I included my notes on the proposed fishing expedition in order to indicate the direction in which my thinking was already moving on the second day of my visit.

Delayed Eating

Late meals in the Jones family were due to confusions on outings or to Dr. Jones's coming home late. Since delayed eating is a common feature of disturbed households, I discuss all the material on the Jones family. Some examples have been presented; I give others below.

On our return at three o'clock from a trip to Great Mountain Drive, Dr. Jones was called away and did not have time to eat his lunch.

Mrs. Jones was very hungry but would not eat while her husband was away. At last she could stand it no longer and we both ate two slices each of bread and butter, but she wouldn't serve anything beyond that. (She had given the children lunch when we got home.)

When Dr. Jones had been called away, he said he would be gone only a few minutes. He did not say, "Don't wait for me; you just have your lunch." While we were waiting Mrs. Jones said that in the early stages of pregnancy she used to try to wait for him, but she couldn't stand it because waiting so long made her dizzy; therefore she would have her meal before he returned. I wonder why she found it necessary to wait until she was dizzy?* While we were waiting this afternoon she said she didn't know what to do, whether to sit down and eat or wait until he returned. I said nothing. There is so much indecision about this matter that there must have been a blowup between them at one time in connection with her eating when he was not home.

At last Dr. Jones returned, at about four o'clock, and we three sat down to eat.

• • •

Dr. Jones usually stops off at the grocery store to pick up incidental things the family needs, although his wife does the major shopping. He is most often asked to bring a loaf of bread, and sometimes lunch is delayed because the family has to wait until he comes home with the bread so they can have sandwiches.

Over and over again I have been impressed with the enormous feeding delay in this family, particularly with respect to the boys. It seems to me they always have to wait a very long time between the development of hunger and its satisfaction. This is part of Mrs. Jones's general configuration of disorderliness. Today the kids were fed at one o'clock.

Time was dragging on past one o'clock, and as usual, Mrs. Jones said she didn't know whether to feed herself and me or not. Dr. Jones was supposed to bring home a loaf of bread. On the other hand, she did have hamburger rolls in the refrigerator. Mrs. Jones knew I had ordered a taxi for two o'clock to take me to the railroad station (for I was about to depart), yet she did not offer me lunch. At last, at one-thirty, I asked for something to eat.

Meals are held up because Dr. Jones is often late, and because Mrs. Jones is slow to feed anybody without him. She says that in the past she delayed her own meals until she was dizzy; and she will not even feed the boys until they have waited a long time. I have used the term *pathological even-handedness*† for behavior in which parents inappropriately treat their children the way they treat themselves and each other.

Some enormous force must be at the source of Mrs. Jones's indecisiveness; it is surely the tense relationship between her and her husband. At this point, then, the circumspection theory does not help, for it is not that Mrs. Jones does not perceive the relationship between time and feeding but rather that her combining the perception (of the late hour and of hunger) with the appropriate action (feeding people) is prevented because it is somehow incompatible with family relations. It looks as if Mrs. Jones had agreed not to eat and to delay feeding the boys until her husband was fed too; and this "agreement," which was for the most part not violated during my stay, is probably backed up by Dr. Jones's anger if he finds that his family has finished eating when he comes home.

Let us turn now to Mrs. Jones to see whether, in her case, actions hurtful to others are deliberate, unconscious or caused by lack of circumspection.

---

* It was a serious oversight on my part not to have questioned Mrs. Jones about this.
† In my discussion of the Ross family, in *Culture Against Man* (Vintage Books; New York, Random House, 1963), Chapter 9.

Mrs. Jones

Her Behavior with Harriet: Hostility or Confusion?

Harriet seemed a happy baby, and her many spontaneous approaches to her mother showed that she was accustomed to a warm reception. Since observation (see pages 57–60) convinced me that Mrs. Jones loved Harriet, I interpret the following as due to lack of circumspection.

On the second day Mrs. Jones and I were talking on the front-porch steps and Harriet was playing nearby.

Harriet would run all the way down to the edge of the walk heading toward the road, and Mrs. Jones would go running after her in a jolly way and catch her just before she got out into the road, and the baby would laugh joyously. Harriet took this as a game, and Mrs. Jones went running after her two or three times to prevent the baby from running into the road.

Other observations indicate:

When our backs were turned for a moment Harriet got out almost to the middle of the road, and a huge oil truck came tearing around the corner and missed the baby by about ten feet. We then went back to the porch, and the chasing game between Harriet and her mother developed again. After Mrs. Jones had chased the baby twice I asked her, "Do you like this?" and she said no but changed it to "I do." When the baby ran off a third time I asked, "Would you like me to chase her?" and she said, with a great feeling of relief, "Oh, please do!" So I chased the baby but that was the end of her running because the real fun was to be picked up by her mother.

. . .

Dr. and Mrs. Jones and I were talking to some neighbors. Suddenly we looked around, and there was Harriet right out in the middle of the road. They have a peculiar faith that Pookie, their dog, can bring Harriet back, for they send him after Harriet. However, the dog obviously does not understand his mission, for although he goes barking in the direction of Harriet, he runs prancing past her and does nothing to head her off. This happened twice this afternoon while we were outside and her parents had to go and get her.

Perhaps it would be too much to expect an average mother to realize that when she makes running toward the road a game, she is teaching her baby to run toward danger; but we can expect an ordinary mother to prevent her seventeen-month-old baby from repeatedly running toward the road. And it seems reasonable to expect that even a stupid mother would stop playing after her child has just escaped being hit by a truck. I therefore infer that Mrs. Jones is unable to put together running toward the road, getting into the road, and death. Perhaps husband and wife have an exaggerated *fleeing from death**—a reaction formation against fear of death, which makes

---

* This powerful figure comes from Heidegger, *op. cit.* Analyzing the average, everyday attitude toward death, Heidegger says that it "is a constant fleeing in the face of death. . . . [it is] *evasion in the face of it* . . . and concealing it." The average individual, he says, does not face the certainty of his own death, thinks of it as happening only to "others," etc. See Section H 254.

them act as if it were not "there"—as if there were no danger. Since, in that case, the Joneses would not smell death even if it were under their noses, flight from death would account for their *pathological composure*, which is the opposite of overanxiety.

I had the impression that Mrs. Jones believed it would be easier to get Harriet to eat if she did not fill her up at mealtimes, but she kept giving the baby scraps of food between meals because Harriet seemed to be hungry a lot. It is necessary to know this in order to understand what follows.

(Fifth day.) Mrs. Jones had to give some medicine to Harriet, who has had diarrhea for several days. Mrs. Jones says her husband thinks Harriet has a bug. I wouldn't be a bit surprised if it was picked up right in the Jones household: Mrs. Jones never puts the butter away because, she says, it gets so hard in the refrigerator that it becomes too difficult for her to use, so she spreads Harriet's toast with butter that is almost fluid. She is almost equally careless with the milk, which she lets stand around uncovered in the summer heat. At the same time Mrs. Jones crams everything imaginable into the refrigerator, so that it really is a problem to get things in and out of it.

Mrs. Jones mixed Harriet's medicine with the milk that had been standing around.

Harriet was supposed to be given the medicine six times a day, but although I was in the house until eight o'clock, I saw Harriet receive her medicine only once, at two o'clock. This, more than anything else, seems to me evidence of Mrs. Jones's sloppiness, for she is mad about the kid. She constantly smiles at her, puts her forehead to the baby's, and so on, and the baby responds warmly.

The next day, in response to something I had said, Mrs. Jones told me she had given the baby the medicine the prescribed number of times the day before. On the seventh day of my visit:

Harriet still has diarrhea. Mrs. Jones fed her at lunchtime and then suddenly remembered she had completely forgotten to give her baby the "cocktail," meaning the milk mixed with medicine. Dr. Jones asked at lunch whether she was giving the baby skimmed milk, and she said yes, but the milk she was using was homogenized.

On the eighth day Harriet still had diarrhea. In all this time Dr. Jones did not ask his wife whether she had given Harriet the medicine and did not comment on the fact that the milk and butter were always standing around on the cupboard.

Mrs. Jones's way of feeding the baby increased the chances of reinfection because she kept giving her bits of buttered toast and small quantities of milk. Thus even as she made disorganized attempts to treat Harriet's diarrhea she might have been promoting it by giving her butter and milk with high bacteria content, and by giving her the medicine in homogenized instead of skimmed milk. It does seem confused also to feed the baby butter all day long, when homogenized milk is removed from the diet because the fat in it facilitates diarrhea.

One day the baby sat down in poison ivy not far from the house, but Mrs. Jones did not take her home and wash her off. Harriet did not get a rash.

ANALYTICAL SUMMARY

1. *Time*. Mrs. Jones's insensitivity to immanent temporal cues appears in her repeatedly forgetting to give Harriet the medicine.

2. *Space*. Mrs. Jones lets the child run toward the road and get into dangerous situations repeatedly. These perceptual failures are sustained by pathological composure. Her difficulties with space are further illustrated by her cramming the refrigerator unnecessarily.

3. *People*. It could not be said that Mrs. Jones's attitude toward Harriet was unprotective, but rather that her lack of circumspection resulted in her being unprotective and that lack of circumspection reinforced her pathological composure. It was not that she didn't love Harriet, but rather that she couldn't be anxious because she did not perceive danger. She did not see danger, perhaps, because she was "in flight from death." These factors made her act as if Harriet's world was safe when it was unsafe.

4. *Objects*. It was not only that Mrs. Jones did not perceive the importance of keeping milk and butter in the refrigerator in hot weather, but that she did not see its importance *in relation to Harriet*, either. Since Mrs. Jones is very bright in other matters and has the advice of a physician, her carelessness cannot be ascribed to "routine stupidity."

Finally we may consider Pookie as an object, although the Joneses consider him a person. Whoever has lived with dogs knows that they are so intelligent and emotionally so sensitive that one comes to half imagine that the dog is a kind of person. This is especially true when dogs are around young children, for then they often appear to consider themselves children, too. There seems little doubt that the Joneses have united this common human feeling to a Lassie-like stereotype gotten from children's books and the movies, and created an imaginary beast who can somehow be depended on to rescue Harriet. Thus, just as Dr. Jones metamorphosed me into a "stones and bones" anthropologist because it suited him at the moment, so Dr. and Mrs. Jones transform Pookie into a canine human who will conveniently take responsibility for the baby. They acted as if Pookie *were* human.

5. *Biological inappropriateness*. Because Mrs. Jones is insensitive to immanent temporal cues and cannot put things together (lacks circumspection), her behavior often turns out to be biologically inappropriate. Even though she obviously loves Harriet, as we shall see later, her behavior is inappropriate to the brink of death. I think this applies even to her failure to take the baby home to wash off the poison ivy. Poor perceptual faculties can thus make a loving mother look as if she didn't care, but it makes no difference to a child whether it is killed by hostility or by disorder.

On Learning to Love Danger

Since, when Harriet toddled toward the road, her mother went gaily after her; and since, when the baby was out in the middle of the road, Dr. or Mrs. Jones sometimes sent the dog to get her and then ran after her themselves, without ever punishing the baby; and since, therefore, it was all great fun for her, Harriet was learning to court danger because danger was fun. The same thing has been happening to Bobby, through closeness to his father in dangerous fun. What, then, of some unconscious "death impulse"? If in later life Bobby and Harriet seem to love peril, would it be because they are "self-destructive"? If Bobby, who has love fights with his father, should have to be violent with his sweethearts, would it be because he had sadistic impulses toward women? A person never learns to feel in a simple way: there is no love pure and simple, because one always learns to love in association with a parent who has his own peculiar way of expressing it and wanting it, and when a child grows up he will understand, feel and want love as he learned it. What seems, therefore, often to go along with love (violence, for example) is not necessarily some intruding, unconscious impurity that must be removed. Nor does it necessarily have to be the expression of a repressed impulse that forces itself demoniacally into love; in fact, it need not be what-goes-along-with-love at all, but instead its very essence—for the particular individual or for the particular culture.

Death might have come to Harriet as a consequence of her mother's carelessness, but since Mrs. Jones does other things carelessly too, like housekeeping, for example, it would be wrong to ascribe her carelessness with Harriet to unconscious death wishes toward the baby. The point at issue is that since violating the component systems may endanger life and therefore make it appear as if a parent had such wishes, it is necessary for this very reason to look at such violations first as disturbances in perception. The accusation of the death wish is so serious that all alternative interpretations must be explored first. The tendency has too often been to leap to the most accusatory interpretation first, and this has continued because, in the absence of direct observation, it has been impossible to observe parents over a broad range of their activity.

Mrs. Jones as Housekeeper

In his life story* Dr. Jones said that he insists on considerable routine in his life but that his wife is chaotic. The following observations document the story.

Mrs. Jones had a lot of dry clothes to fold up, so while we were talking I helped her fold and put them away. In this way I was able to see that the drawers of the children's dressers were in a state of total confusion. Mrs. Jones and I were discussing the conflict between her and her husband over her disorderly housekeeping, so I said, "What would it mean to you if you were to keep the house in order?" and she said, with tremendous emphasis, "It would mean giving up living." When I asked her what she meant by "giving up living," she said, "Well, I would have to give up everything in order to keep the house surgically clean and to keep the floors polished." The expression "surgically clean" occurred over and over again—she says her husband wants the house surgically clean—but really the idea of surgical cleanliness is totally irrelevant in considering her housekeeping. It is not only that dirt is visible, but also that everything is out of place. I asked, "What would you have to be in order to keep the house clean?" and she said she would have to show administrative ability and would have to

* I.e., in his case history. Prior to my home visit, I had spent the better part of a day with each parent, interviewing them.

know how to manipulate people. The idea seemed to be that she would have to assign everybody his particular task and keep the kids from disrupting things.

. . .

As I was holding Harriet in my arms, the baby opened a cupboard and took out a box that had contained crackers. There were only a few crumbs. Mrs. Jones had told me there were a few crackers in it.

It seems to me that there is no point at which Mrs. Jones makes a concession to order. It is true that things get done, but nothing on time. It is true also that there are furniture, clothes and bedclothes in the house, but much is out of place.

These data show that in attempting to understand Mrs. Jones's "carelessness" about Harriet one has to go far beyond this, to study her over the entire range of her activity, and then we see much that is loving and much that, though harmful, seems to be part of a general tendency to disorder. The component systems are not systems for Mrs. Jones. Not only are objects out of place—time itself is out of place; the temporal underpinning of life-in-our-culture is simply "not there" for her. Giving Harriet her medicine at the proper time is therefore no more possible for Mrs. Jones than having the household objects in their proper place.

Since in saying that to give up disorder would be to give up living, Mrs. Jones equates order with death and disorder with life, *disorder is fleeing from death*. We shall return to this issue later.

Mrs. Jones fights with disorder just as some women fight with order, nagging their husbands for not picking up their things. In many everyday matters Mrs. Jones does not perceive interrelationships that are present, but at a deeper level she feels interrelationships that seem objectively not present, or even bizarre. For example, to bring some order into that house would not mean giving up living. It would not be necessary to keep the floors polished and the house surgically clean. On the other hand, since becoming orderly would mean succumbing to her husband, her tendency to disorder becomes transformed into a drive, and order looms like annihilation; everything she says about giving up living seems objectively true.

. In his life story Dr. Jones said his wife was "moving toward chaos." In one sense the interrelationships between the factors she sees necessary to order *are* present, for the simple reason that for her to keep things in order, she would have to keep after her family to put things away, and since her husband and Bobby are very stubborn and get angry easily, she would have her hands full with them.

No day passed in the Jones household without anger, quarreling and violence. Husband and wife got angry at each other, and Bobby persecuted Jackie. Since anger and quarreling are universal in human society and since they loom large in the Jones family, I introduced this case with an essay on anger and quarreling. The following sections give further substance to it.

A Brief Summary of the Life Stories

In telling their life stories, the Joneses are eloquent, incisive, truthful and intense. Unlike many, who try to cover up, the Joneses were searching and explicit, and I had the feeling they were not yet done with searching, that they were trying to understand what had happened and was still happening to them.

Dr. Jones's mother, he says, was hard, brilliant, well organized, violent, driving and vengeful. She had no illusions about people. She disciplined her children rigorously, and if they deviated from her tough moral criteria, she cut them down with ridicule. Dr. Jones believes he has much of his mother's violence, but he has also her dread of receiving anything from anybody and her distrust of and isolation from people. His mother tried to be a good mother to Ed. She tried to nurse him but he got sick on her milk, and before the right nourishment was ultimately found, almost died. As Ed grew up his mother pushed him ambitiously and waited on him.

His father was a self-made man, a stable, hard-driving, authoritarian fighter who finally came to terms with Ed only when, as a youth, Ed threatened to fight it out with him toe-to-toe. Then his father began to show some respect for him. The motto in this family seems to have been: "Batter your way through and always fight back." The elder Jones was a man of many talents, and since Ed felt he could never meet that intellectual challenge, he chose a vocation in which he would not have to compete with his father at any point. Mr. Jones was always testing Ed, apparently for his toughness, for his willingness to meet a challenge. "I survived," Ed says, but he became hard and difficult. He shares his father's tendency to be deliberately ambiguous.

Ida Jones scarcely knew her father. Because he traveled a great deal and because of his relationship to her mother, he was a kind of amiable but aloof visitor. In spite of this, however, no hostility between Mrs. Jones's mother and father appeared on the surface, for anger in front of the children was absolutely taboo; the expression of any intense feeling was not permitted in that house. So Ida grew up without the faintest idea of what a family was really like, of what it meant to live with and take care of a husband, of what it was to be a real wife in a real home.

Though hardly a careful housekeeper, her mother was a consistent but not harsh disciplinarian. Ida thinks now that her mother protected her too much against the other children in the family. Overshadowed by them, feeling she was nothing at all, Ida was never close to anyone. She still rates herself very low and considers her autistic son Tommy her failure. However, the fact that ambition was not a fetish in her home, as it was in Ed's, seems to have saved her from utterly abject feelings of self-deprecation. The only model of achievement Ida had was her transient, mysterious father. Ambition and drive play a very small part in her life.

Ida and Ed deprecate their reasons for getting married and never mention love as a motive; yet it is clear, from what Ed says, that during the first months of marriage, before Tommy was born, he really gave himself up to this beautiful, gentle-appearing, low-keyed woman. He trusted; he was able to take; he was even able, he says, to become dependent. All of this was obscured from her, however, and still is, by the shattering impact of his rages once Tommy was born. When Ed talks about Tommy's infancy he discusses his wife's inability to cope with the entire situation, her withdrawal, her failure to perform her wifely duties or to have anything done on time, and of the drying up of this "oasis," of the turning away of this woman to whom he had resigned himself in trust, dependence and hope. He felt betrayed. Tommy, he says, was a threat to everything he had expected, and had begun to hope for, in his marriage. He fought back, trying to compel Ida to give him what he needed, trying to drive her away from the baby. Her will collapsed and Tommy was lost.

When Ida talks about Tommy's infancy, all she can think of is her husband's rages, her own terror, confusion and collapse, her shutting out her baby's crying. She ended up by leaving Tommy alone, isolated in his room. Alienated from her husband, she became indifferent to her baby—eventually she felt nothing for him, she says. Each of Ed's outbursts left her feeling more distant. Her failure to fight back made Ed contemptuous and frustrated and enraged by the fact that for a long time after a fight she remained distant. He could not comprehend why when a fight was all over for him—when he was, in a sense, relaxed—she could not forget too. Since he usually apologized for his excesses, he could not understand her long, shut-in aftermaths. But his uninhibited violence made him an enemy to her, put him outside her social system. She felt no security. For Ed, rage was transient thunder during which he achieved self-realization; for her, it was destruction of a relationship—she thought that only gutter people acted like him. Why she remained with him never became clear to me, though I pressed her to explain. Perhaps the fact that Ed was faithful and seemed honest played a part. Over the years, she says, she has learned to handle him, to fight back, even to enjoy stabbing at him where it hurts most. She can still spur him to red rages, but she tries not to go too far. In spite of her care, however, he is still capable, even now, of outbursts that terrify her.

Nowadays they feel that their relationship is incomparably better than it was. Tommy's illness was a shock to them and they have had some psychiatric help with their own problems. They have become much more interested in religion than ever before and speak of "feeling close to God." Meanwhile, each remains wary of the other.

ANALYSIS OF ANGER AND BLAME

In the light of his urgent needs, and considering the doubts and ambiguities in the marriage, Dr. Jones's angry impatience seemed legitimate to him, and his wife's panic merely an effort to escape responsibility and, perhaps, to hide an underlying lack of love. Because urgency can be aware only of itself and therefore makes everybody else's reality fit the world created by it, no countervailing facts can be imagined, much less tolerated. In these circumstances urgency is truth: it is the metaphysics of anguish. Yet Dr. Jones's misinterpretation of his wife's collapse was one of the many that would spoil their lives, even until the day of my arrival. It is striking that Dr. Jones never indicated to me that he was aware of his wife's terror, nor did she say she ever told him. How many husbands and wives ever dream of letting the other know how anger affects them?

"We were both frightened," says Dr. Jones when he describes Tommy's complete dependence on his mother, and Dr. Jones's response, as he says, was to "fight back." Put another way, his reaction was fear-anger, which expressed itself in fighting. The Kaingáng Indians felt fear this way, yet the feeling is not strange to our culture: we all know people who express their anxiety in petulance and quarrelsomeness. But Dr. Jones was extreme, and his swift capacity to transform anxiety into rage collided with his wife's inability to cope with anxiety. In the dialectic of the confrontation he reached consummatory rage, she collapsed and Tommy was abandoned. Though he did not leave the house, Tommy was a deserted child.*

A human being can feel anger, hate, fear, pain and joy all at the same time in a quarrel—the joy deriving from witnessing the adversary's misery as one drives a weapon home. As the quarrel wears on, there comes a point when an intimate is metamorphosed into an enemy—a stranger. The worse the fight, the more it transforms the antagonists, and hence the ancient truth that those who quarrel become enemies. The critical point at which this occurs is precisely where the assertion of anger of a friend becomes transmuted into joy in hurting what is now an enemy. When the basic relationship is negated, the intensity of the fight can increase without limit, for the restraint imposed by the relationship-feeling is now destroyed, permitting the fight to develop as between strangers. But the horror is that the antagonists are not strangers, for the very condition of fighting requires that they have common interests.

Apology, prayer, "comfort" and "remorse" may help the attacker after the quarrel, while doing nothing for the target: though wounds may heal, the scar is left. What stands out in Dr. Jones's story is justification of his rages and description of his wife's collapse—how she behaved *during* the quarrels. What she emphasizes is how she felt for a long time *afterward*. Perhaps an attacker remembers best his effect on the target and the reasons he gave himself for starting the fight, while the target remembers best his feelings in the aftermath. If the target remembers the aftermath best, he must remember the quarrel longer. This points to the fact that no matter how angry and self-righteous the attacker may feel, his opponent will remember the fight the more vividly if he is hurt the most.

During a serious fight, antagonists metamorphose each other to fit the circumstances. Dr. Jones saw his wife as a weak, disorganized, cowardly, untrustworthy woman who deserved what she got; she saw him as a foul-mouthed, mad-dog hoodlum-out-of-the-gutter. He could not perceive this and she did not tell him. Dr. Jones was blinded by rage arising from unmet needs and from feeling betrayed; yet if he could have seen what his rages were doing to his wife, it would have interfered with his "legitimate" anger,

---

* Domestic desertion—leaving a child to cry unattended—is often impossible in tribal societies because tribal peoples do not tolerate a mother's leaving her child alone this way, and because there are usually plenty of people around to take care of a baby if his mother has to be away. Thus private enterprise regarding babies, and the shutting up of families away from one another in apartments and houses so that the cries of their children cannot be heard by outsiders, is a gift to us from civilization—and so, of course, therefore, is autism.

while on the other hand his blindness prevented him from getting what he was fighting for because his rages alienated his wife. Mrs. Jones has never perceived the source of her husband's rages, in his feelings of deprivation and in his feeling that he had been sold down the river.

If, when a fight is over, the two people do not tell each other how they feel, they will drift apart. Since the victim shuts the enemy out, the enemy cannot tell what has happened to his target and what is going on. On the other hand, since the aftermath is the longest dimension of the quarrel, that is just the time when communication ought to be best. The trouble is that although communication is most active and most destructive during a quarrel, it usually drops off afterward—precisely when it is most needed. This is the paradox on which quarreling relationships are impaled, and explains why they degenerate.

Since the reward in fighting usually derives from self-affirmation and from making the adversary miserable, each is vigilant for signs indicating that the other is getting too much out of the fight, that he is not suffering enough, or in some cases that he is suffering too much. Mrs. Jones tries not to let her husband see how scared she is because this would be a score for him. As a quarrel becomes more intense, vigilance heightens; the initial care in concealing one's feelings breaks down; wariness (of the antago-nist's response) is drowned out; and in the dialectic interplay, violence mounts to the point of mutual destruction, collapse or flight of one or both adversaries.

Over the years Mrs. Jones became wary, and now backs down enough to keep her husband's rage from boiling over. Quarreling may support her self-esteem, but it is hard to keep it within bounds because she so enjoys goad-ing her husband. Once started, the quarrels drag on because both want to win; neither wants to back down, for to keep quiet or to accept blame is degrading in our culture. Mrs. Jones says that nowadays she avoids striking back selfishly and can be a little more reasonable and controllable in strik-ing back, and this is close to what I usually saw in their house—although in some fights she gave as much as she took. Another change seems to be that her husband is no longer easily provoked.

When Mrs. Jones hits back, Dr. Jones gets more than he bargained for, because although he wishes for somebody who, by striking back, would make his outbursts appear legitimate in his own eyes, he does not want thrusts at his "weak spots."

Some people go into a quarrel bristling with weapons: sarcastic mutter-ings; bitter references to the adversary's past, present, future or imagined delinquencies; shouted imprecations, or unjust, air-drawn accusations; im-plications or direct statements of rejection or determination to leave; tears, silence, slamming doors, stalking out of the room, even threats of violence, or its reality, and so on. Others fight with few and feeble weapons. They are almost speechless and easily dumfounded and overwhelmed by the irra-tional or monstrous accusations and behavior of the opponent. They can think of little to say (or don't want to say what they think); they spurn display or do not know how to; they know they are right but do not know how to say it; they sputter, they cannot even cry or retreat. Most people are a mixture. Some can carry out a plan in a quarrel; some do it intuitively, irrationally and well. It is likely that the strategy, tactics and logistics of domestic quarrels are related to ethnic background and education.

Mrs. Jones talks about alienation as if only she felt it; yet she says her husband was often unwilling to come to an understanding before going to sleep. He doesn't share her views on the rules of behavior. The question is then, Who is alienated? Since Dr. Jones did not want to come to an understanding, he must have been just as alienated as she. This is the quintessence of mutual alienation—of drifting apart in the aftermath, of *post-conflict drift*. It is aggravated by new accusations in which each blames the other for misbehaving after the quarrel; it is fire still glowing in the old ashes, and such unresolved blame is the source of future fights. The ghosts of unresolved blame lie uneasy beneath the headstones of the family failures, wandering restlessly in some quarrelsome, tormented night to admonish, harass, astonish and afright.

Unresolved blame is an *admonition* to desist from blaming; the blame that *harasses* is the blame used while raking up the past; the blame that *astonishes* is the blame about which we say, "I'm stunned that you drag *that* in!" And the blame that *afrights* is the blame that is unreasonable and heinous.

Out of the paradoxes and contradictions in the relationship between Dr. and Mrs. Jones emerge the following: Dr. Jones would get angry, never really able, however, to confront the underlying cause—his disappointment in his wife as a woman. Not comprehending the deep sources of her husband's rage, Mrs. Jones goaded him on, until sometimes his rage would become obscene. She told me he has even attacked her physically. As bedtime approached she felt that according to the rules (her rules!), they should come to an understanding, so in spite of the fact that her feeling of alienation was still strong, she tried in some way to bring this about. Her husband was often still alienated himself. As she sees it, however, he seemed to recover more quickly and then started blaming her for her slow convalescence. So, borne on mutually inflicted pain, they drifted.

Direct Observation of Quarreling

The behavior of both Dr. and Mrs. Jones is so disorderly that it is usually difficult to decide whether or not its mutually harmful effects are intentional. Disorder dominates almost the entire range of their lives. From the reasons for their marriage to the details of housekeeping and other conduct, Dr. and Mrs. Jones seem unable to get most things straight and keep them connected like average people. Following Heidegger, I have called this weakness *lack of circumspection*.*

Their life story shows that Dr. and Mrs. Jones have quarreled seriously

* Though, as explained earlier, I owe the term "circumspection" to Heidegger (*op. cit.*), he does not examine the problem of *lack* of circumspection.

and often ever since Tommy was born. Because I saw a great deal of it during my visit, I examine in this section quarrels not discussed before.

The Battle of the Spectacles

(As Dr. Jones was coming up the stairs Jackie playfully threw a pillow at him and broke the bridge of his glasses.)

Dr. Jones asked his wife to help him mend the glasses with adhesive tape. She wanted to hold them one way and he wanted her to hold them another, and he forced her physically to hold them his way.

The glasses became a battleground because Dr. and Mrs. Jones turned a disagreement into a fight for survival. Since everywhere minor disagreements become transformed into battles, I conclude that *Homo sapiens* has a strong tendency to do battle over trivia. Such contests, however, are struggles for the survival of a vital part of him—his self; the fight for survival of the self—no matter how trivial the immediate cause—is a form of *flight from death*. Thus every "fight over nothing" is a fight *against nothingness*, a fight against becoming nothing, which may sometimes be a fight *because* one is nothing.

Long-standing mutual hostility and contempt must underlie this fight, for it could not occur, particularly in front of a stranger, if husband and wife respected each other. However, since such parading tells an observer how they feel about each other, this may have been the purpose of it, for each seemed to be saying to me, "You see what I have to contend with?"

Suppose the quarrel started as a simple difference in point of view—in the fact that Mrs. Jones thought her way of holding the glasses best and her husband thought his way best—for after all, many common efforts have failed because of differences in points of view. Imagine the old-fashioned way of making a hole in stone, in which one man holds a long spike while another pounds the head with a sledge hammer. The men could not collaborate if they did not see the hammer-spike-man-stone relationship in the same way. This seemed to be involved in mending the glasses, but Mrs. Jones made an issue of it and Dr. Jones would not listen to her but forced her to do what he wanted. Thus what happened was not caused by a simple difference in point of view, but was, rather, an expression of underlying feeling.

Only if a person can at least imagine the possibility of an idea alternative to his can he listen to a contrary opinion, but this can happen only if he is not too involved in his own notion, and furthermore, he must respect his co-worker and not feel threatened. But since this was not the case between Dr. and Mrs. Jones, they froze in their own positions and fought it out.

Many joint undertakings have disintegrated because of this. Often the members of a team start to work together because they respect one another; they seem able to perceive many implications in the undertaking and to be able to entertain the possibility of alternative solutions to problems; yet because they begin to feel threatened and because they become deeply ego-involved, they end up by losing respect for one another and becoming rigid.

The result is disintegration of the project or negligible success. The incident of the glasses, therefore, is the model of joint neurotic stupidity. It might be called the "team" syndrome. In one combination or another its components form the booby trap of academic research and even of everyday social learning.

There is still another way of looking at the quarrel over the glasses. Why do Dr. and Mrs. Jones adopt different points of view in the first place? Maybe they have to simply because their hostility is so great that any situation can become a battleground of viewpoints. We all know of relationships —even among our friends—of which we say, "They hate each other so much that if he says it's black, she's bound to say it's white." Many a parent of an American adolescent is aware of the fact that if his child knows that an idea comes from him, there is a good probability that the child will call the idea no good. Under such circumstances the problem for an observer is to understand how agreement can occur at all. Thus what looks like a difference in perception can explode into a major quarrel if the relationship between people is bad to begin with, or a bad relationship can create what looks like irreconcilable differences in points of view; it is usually impossible to tell which is which. Whatever the situation, the self is always the ultimate arbiter.

An observer living with a contentious family for a week witnesses many of the aftermaths of quarrels, and the next selections from the field notes are observations of the aftermath of the argument over the glasses a little later in the day.

In a discussion about golf Dr. Jones said that golf was a ridiculous game because there was no violence in it. He said he likes games like tennis, in which the shock of the opposing players can be felt. He likes violent games, he said.

Looking back at the incident of the glasses, I now see clearly why, when Dr. Jones started to ridicule people who play golf, Mrs. Jones taunted him in a barbed way, but the barbs did not seem to penetrate. She kept at him in the same manner as we talked on a variety of subjects. She also got after him for saying that Bobby and Jackie like to hear only stories of violence without happy endings.

We cannot assume that an aftermath ever ends, and as quarrels become numerous, life itself becomes an aftermath. Thus the adversaries carry their anger to the grave: on the brink of death they are vigilant for hostile cues,* and at a funeral, perhaps full of regrets that the corpse had the last word. In the light of this probability the funeral ceremonies of tribal peoples, with their ritual wailing and self-mutilation, are in part ceremonial denials or affirmations of hostility to the corpse rather than expressions of grief; they are ritualistic resolutions of the perduring aftermaths of numberless tribal conflicts. When life becomes an aftermath, time is saturated with anger, fear, suspicion, alienation and depression. The probability is small that a person living a continuous aftermath will feel time in an average, everyday way. He finds that time drags—is stretched out—or he attempts to fill in time, anxiously trying to make it pass. Of course, living the aftermath, with all the preoccupations this implies, makes it difficult to concentrate on the everyday details of life.

* See my *Culture Against Man* (*op. cit.*), Chapter 10.

The Bible as Battleground

The following is my account of a Lutheran Bible study meeting I attended with Dr. and Mrs. Jones.

The Bible study group was made up of earnest and intelligent men and women who were searching for answers to questions like: What is faith? Can you trust people? Can you trust God if you don't trust people? What is the origin of faith? What makes a good religious leader? Can a religion be strong if leadership is weak?

One of Dr. Jones's first acts was to attack St. Paul for what he considered Paul's pretentiousness—his pretense of humility while at the same time holding himself above everybody else. Nobody agreed with Dr. Jones. This reminds me of the violent attack he had made on a couple who left early. Dr. Jones attacked them for being rigid and unwilling to look at themselves. Meanwhile Mrs. Jones kept saying gently, "Oh, oh," as if she did not agree with her husband. But that was all she said.

During the course of the discussion Dr. Jones argued that faith in man is impossible, and that faith in man is entirely different from faith in God. In this he opposed almost the entire group. Then Dr. Jones developed the following ideas: (1) It is completely impossible for man to become one with God because man can never achieve perfection. (2) It is totally impossible for man to be united with man, because all men are basically individuals. (3) All men are weak and full of error and evil.

The limelight was focused on Dr. Jones, since he was in complete opposition to everybody and was very threatening to them because he said he didn't trust anybody; and one woman, passionately religious, apparently, said that if his position was correct it would destroy her reason for living.

When Dr. Jones said that he had no faith in anybody, his wife asked, "You mean to say you wouldn't even trust me not to be unfaithful?" and right out in front of everybody he said, "No."

When Dr. Jones said he had no faith that his wife would not betray him, and when he later said people are weak and may change completely from one day to the next, Mrs. Jones said this was a signal for her to go out and have a good time.

As we left the meeting, one of the women asked him to repeat his position. He then mentioned a number of persons who had tried to trick him. It is interesting that he did not mention anybody who had ever been loyal. There is no doubt that his wife took all this declaration of no faith and distrust in a personal way.

During the meeting Mrs. Jones had taken an active part in the discussion. It was a very different kind of Mrs. Jones from the one I encountered in trying to get her to talk about personal matters. It is interesting that she challenged her husband in public to tell her whether he believed she would ever betray him.

As we emerged from the meeting Dr. Jones at once lit into his wife for not having told the baby-sitter where they were, and the two wrangled about this all the way home. The argument was about whose responsibility it is to tell the baby-sitter where they can be reached. Dr. Jones said Mrs. Jones should do it because she is the one who deals directly with the baby-sitter, not he; and she said they should both take the responsibility. However, he kept insisting that she should do it; if two people took responsibility, nobody took responsibility. She responded that she's all concerned with telling the baby-sitter what to do with the children and is liable to forget. She didn't give an inch in the argument. He was characteristically crude and she was characteristically resistant but not crude. His attack is very destructive, even when he doesn't use destructive words. His attitude is very brusque, as if he were talking to an inferior.

Eager to hear something about the aftermath of last night, I asked Mrs. Jones whether she and her husband had talked about it, and she said, "We only talked about it a little bit." I said, "It was quite a business," and in her usual way she made some comment that was off the main issue. I brought the subject around directly to her husband's lack of faith in people, and she remarked that she believes this goes back to the fact that when he was an infant he got no real mothering. She said she believes this made it impossible for him to develop a relationship with people or any trust in them. When I raised the subject of his having said he couldn't trust her, she said she *doesn't know* what it means.

As Dr. Jones and I were driving along, I brought up the subject of his lack of faith in people, and he said he had raised the issue at the Bible study meeting yesterday primarily in order to test the people there, because he wanted to know whether they would have faith in him should he make any mistakes in his work. He said also that he was worried that if he gets too close to people he will become vulnerable, and this is somehow related to people's faith in him. When I reminded him of how concerned Ida was last night when he made statements about not trusting her, he laughed and affirmed that of course you can't absolutely trust anybody. After he had gone on for some time about all the people he can't trust and why, I asked, "Well, aren't there any people in your life who have been loyal?" and he said, "Yes, and one of them is Ida"; and then he mentioned one or two others. He said, however, that the cost of finding people you can trust is enormous—meaning that you use up a great many people trying to find a few you can trust. He said the people at the meeting were all confused—they talked about having faith in people but he doesn't believe that any of them really do.

I

The protest of the woman who told Dr. Jones that if his lack of faith in man was justified "it would destroy her reason for living" is reminiscent of Mrs. Jones's exclamation that "it would mean giving up living" if she had to keep her house in order. Dr. Jones's rages make clear that *for him living is making others fear for their lives.*

The group had come together to study faith in the light of the life and epistles of St. Paul. They were hoping that in these they might find some basis for believing that faith, of itself, gives hope. The first thing they heard from Dr. Jones, however, was a violent—a killing—personal attack on a sacred symbol. This was followed by his attempt to demolish by logic what hope remained: while the group expected to come away with renewed hope, Dr. Jones tried to show there was none. Christianity rests on God, Jesus, Mary and the apostles. If the apostles are degraded, much of Christianity becomes null, for their utterances become the mutterings of degraded men. What was threatening in what Dr. Jones had to say was not so much that St. Paul was "only a man," but that he was a pretentious one; and though pretense may lead, it can only betray. Dr. Jones denied the possibility of positive relations among human beings, and whoever did not agree with him was exposed to personal affront, like the couple that left before the meeting was over. Attacking the group, first by assaulting the foundations of religion and then by challenging the premise of the meeting—that faith in man is possible—Dr. Jones undermined the very reason for the meeting.

Dr. Jones turned the group, including his wife, against him, thus confirming his belief that he could have faith in no one and that he was therefore indeed a lonely man. If Dr. Jones's intention had been to use the group to prove to himself once again that he stood alone, if it had been his intention to use it to legitimize his basic distrust, he could not have planned his strategy better.

A couple of days later, however, Mrs. Jones agreed with her husband that the members of the group were "unrealistic about their own ability to have faith in others." Thus husband and wife united in legitimizing Dr. Jones's attack. Mrs. Jones no longer counted herself among the unrealistic ones, but had joined "the enemy"—her husband—in the interest of maintaining domestic tranquillity. Thus the aftermath of the quarrel with the group has been resolved. This introduces the problem of analyzing the Bible study meeting as a quarrel.

2

Dr. Jones seems to have felt a certain expansiveness and pleasure as he warmed to his destructive attack, and as the group centered attention on him. As a direct aftermath of their quarrel during the meeting, Dr. and Mrs. Jones had an angry encounter over the baby-sitter, but as an aftermath of Dr. Jones's quarrel with the group, husband and wife reached an understanding; through the doctrine of "realism," his position at the meeting was legitimized, his status raised, and the group's lowered. Family respect was stabilized by viewing the group with contempt. Thus Dr. and Mrs. Jones worked on his tensions with the group as a substitute for working through their tensions with each other. The fundamental issue was displaced in favor of permitting the *domestic ambiguity* to continue. Dr. Jones's quarrel with the group, which had become their quarrel, was used as a *family resistance* against further exploration of their domestic difficulty. Note that the respect-contempt polarity, which plays its part in their discussion of the group, is precisely what interferes with a good relationship between Dr. and Mrs. Jones.

In his attack Dr. Jones was playing the role of a sharp and outspoken man with the courage to tear away shams. It is an open question who won the argument, but there seems little question that he ended up on the periphery of the group—which is precisely where he had to be. As he says, as a matter of personal choice he has always been a lonely person.

Feeling that the people distrusted *him*, he then accused *them* of not having faith in—or trusting—anybody. This created the opportunity for expressing self-righteous anger against those of false pretentions to faith. His strategy was to undermine their faith in themselves by questioning their judgment of themselves, thereby forcing the group to have faith in *him*—a strange, distorted and miserable hope. As he said to me, he had raised the issue primarily in order to test the people there, because he wanted to know whether they would have faith in him. This is better interpreted, perhaps, "in order to force the people to be faithful to him." There is no self-criticism here, and not even an apology for having embarrassed his wife in public.

Since a man who has little faith in himself cannot expect others to have faith in him, there must always lurk close to the surface of his consciousness a dread that people do not trust him. He must therefore constantly try to smoke people out, to find some way of forcing from them the dreaded confession that they indeed do *not* trust him. And coupled bizarrely with this is the contrary hope that even as he compels them to confess that they do not trust him, they will really say that they *do* trust him.

Most striking in the argument between Dr. and Mrs. Jones about his lack of faith in her is the parading—the inappropriate dragging in—of their domestic conflict into the Bible study. Mrs. Jones felt so threatened that then and there she tried to force her husband to say that although he had no faith in other people, he at least had faith in her. It would, however, have destroyed his argument and undermined his purpose, and besides, it would not have been true for a man so fundamentally distrustful. When he refused to declare his faith she could have remained silent; or she could have said, "How silly can you get?"; or called him "rat" or worse; or challenged him to give evidence to his assertions; burst into tears; or left the meeting. But instead she strengthened his position by saying that he was giving her a signal to go out and have a good time. Though this was logically inappropriate (i.e., there was a lack of congruence between the issues and the means of dealing with them), it was not parlor-logically inappropriate, for she transformed the tragedy into a middle-class joke; and by making the attitude publicly acceptable, robbed the confrontation of its tragic potential. It was dissociation in public—detachment of the feeling from the event. The domestic ambiguity was covered up and the underlying conflict concealed from her own and from public eyes; in this way the domestic ambiguity became a *public ambiguity*.

The fundamental lack of trust displayed at the meeting was treated as a joke, but the relatively minor issue of trusting Mrs. Jones to instruct the baby-sitter was fought out as if it were a matter of basic distrust. Such analogic displacement of feeling occurs when it is too threatening to bring the real issues into the open and put the feelings where they belong. This is a relatively common human failing; even around the campfires of tribal peoples, the anthropologist who talks their language can hear them arguing about one thing when the real issue is something very different, and much more threatening.

The net result of the encounter was that the family pathology was covered up. Thus the function of the processes I have discussed is to act as resistances. They are homologous, in the family, with the mechanisms of defense in the individual. The mechanisms of defense conceal the individual's motivations from himself; the processes I have mentioned conceal the problems of the relationship from the participants. While the mechanisms of defense prevent the individual from facing his self, the processes of domestic ambiguity prevent the members of the family from confronting one another. Thus, *in pathological relationships minor disagreements become struggles for survival of the self, and major ones are deprived of significance.*

Was there anything in the relationship between Dr. and Mrs. Jones that would make him distrust her, in spite of the fact that she had never been unfaithful? It is not necessary for a person who makes love with a faraway look in the eye—a person who can never completely give himself up to love, or who is alienated in some way from life or from his spouse—to commit an act of unfaithfulness, especially if the spouse has insatiable needs. And so it was with Mrs. Jones. A woman of great reserve who had never recovered from her husband's outbursts, she could not give him the impression that she was completely his. It was a vicious circle: since she could not really give him what he needed, he flew into rages in which he flailed about wildly, and she became alienated and still less able to give. This confirmed his feeling that she could not give him what he needed and resulted in distrust. The seed of distrust will sprout in a bed of unmet needs.

The day after the meeting, Dr. and Mrs. Jones were tender to each other. As a matter of fact, I had not seen such tenderness between them before: when Dr. Jones came home at noon he kissed his wife on the lips and she responded, and lunch was lively. This evidence of affection reminded me that in discussing her husband, Mrs. Jones rarely said anything good about him. In the evening they brought out gin and tonic and we listened to Burl Ives records. As we drank, Mrs. Jones became rather gay and several times tweaked and gently poked her husband on the knee and arm, but he made no visible response.

Malice or Carelessness

Since Dr. Jones's apparent lack of circumspection so often penalizes others, one wonders whether it is not really an expression of underlying hostility. In the next example, his wife says it is.

Dr. Jones had returned from the office and we were finally eating our dinner, when Harriet appeared in the hallway, crying out. Only I noticed because my position at the table enabled me to see her in the hallway. I saw that feces were running down Harriet's left leg, and I indicated to the Joneses that something had happened. Dr. Jones got up at once, went down the hallway, picked up the baby, took her into the bathroom, washed her off and set her on the pot. He wiped the feces off the hall floor. His wife continued to eat. When Dr. Jones came back to the table she got up, went into the bathroom and discovered that he had thrown the feces-filled panties into the toilet, and she called out from the bathroom, "You're a mean man." He said, "Why?" and she answered, "Oh, you know," and he became very angry. She said, "Well, the panties might have been flushed down the toilet," and he said, "Oh, you idiot! If you could see them you wouldn't flush them down the toilet." She did not retort. She remained in the bathroom a little while longer and then came back to the table and finished her dinner.

Though he was probably tired and hungry, Dr. Jones did not hesitate to interrupt his meal to take care of the baby, but instead of thanking him for it his wife found something to scold him for. When he flares up she shifts from accusing him of being mean to blaming him for being careless. If she had persisted in name-calling, however, he might have gotten much angrier than he did. I presume that what she expected him to do was to rinse the diaper out in the toilet bowl and put it in the hamper.

Here is another example of a flare-up over an unfinished task:

Dr. Jones started to wash the dishes and his wife asked him why he was doing it. He said jokingly that he did it so he could goof off later. Though he washed and wiped the dishes, he did not put them away, and when his wife remonstrated with him he talked to her roughly and called her "idiot."

When some men do women's work they feel they have put themselves out enough, so they don't have to be particular about finishing up the details. But this is galling to a woman not committed to such "role segregation," as the sociologists call it. She may feel that by leaving the rest for her, the man is reminding her that he has really been doing her job—that he is doing her a favor; and this makes her angry because she finds it humiliating. "He knows his servant will clean up" may be the unspoken bitterness.

On the other hand, Mrs. Jones may have read meanness into what her husband did because she probably has had so much experience with such behavior of his, seeming innocently careless but actually hurting her, that she has come to believe all such "oversights," "omissions" and "mistakes" deliberate. Dr. Jones himself spoke to me with pleasure about this sort of thing in describing how his father could irritate people with hurtful ambiguities. Perhaps it is general that in disturbed relationships a person is blamed for what he does wrong and not rewarded for what he does right. Here the minor incident became the entire incident, and was used by Mrs. Jones to destroy its positive side; her husband ended up being punished for doing good.

When the good a person does is negated by the one for whom he does it, the beneficiary doesn't have to be grateful and can maintain whatever antagonism he has for his benefactor by harping on the supposed evil. Under these circumstances "you do nothing for me" becomes an entrenched attitude, and it is unnecessary for the beneficiary to do anything for the person who helped him. The attitude is summed up in the unspoken refrain "I don't have to be grateful or to be dependent on you." In this way Mrs. Jones's attitude comes to parallel her husband's, and the absolutely necessary reciprocity between members of a relationship is sapped and the way opened to distrust and hostility. Meanwhile, punishing her husband for his help will certainly interfere with his usefulness.

The following occurred later in the day:

While the three of us were in the kitchen Harriet was crying in her room. She cried and cried but neither Dr. nor Mrs. Jones made a move nor said a word to her. At last Mrs. Jones said to her husband, "If you happen to be passing by the bedroom, would you glide in there and do something about your daughter?" He asked, laughing, "Why didn't you simply say, 'Go in and take care of Harriet'?" She said, "You know what you would have said if I had done that," and he replied, "What would I have said?" and she answered, "You would have said, 'Go to hell.'" He laughed and replied that he would have said "Okay," but she repeated, "You would have said, 'Go to hell.'"

Since Dr. Jones readily looks after Harriet, I think his wife's way of putting her request is really related to the panty incident. Perhaps she is afraid of another blowup, but I believe other things are involved too. She may be testing her husband to see whether he is still angry enough to be irritated if she asks him to take care of Harriet, and by saying "You would have said, 'Go to hell,'" she makes it difficult for him to be nasty again. She may also be trying to make him feel guilty over his last outburst, and by implying that he is mean enough to tell her to go to hell just because she asks him to see how his daughter is getting along, she indirectly wins the panty fight—he is, she seems to be saying, a mean man *anyway*, who will even raise hell about looking after his own baby. Meanwhile, her bantering attitude makes it difficult for her husband to get angry. These speculations suggest that in the aftermath of a domestic quarrel there will be (1) testing for residual anger and for attitudes toward similar future issues. (2) Veiled accusations and efforts by the adversaries to make each other feel guilty. (3) Efforts by the loser to get revenge on the basis of some other issue, thus enabling him to feel that he won the previous quarrel. This is time reversal and search for residual victory. (4) One or both adversaries will try to bring about a resolution of the quarrel. This is particularly important, and is probably a vital difference between serious family disturbances and other kinds.

The Core of the Issue

Just before I left, the Joneses had a serious quarrel, which I did not witness. Mrs. Jones told me about it.

She said she had felt very strongly that the lawn had to be mowed because, since it looked very bad, it did not help Dr. Jones's practice any. When she asked him to mow the lawn he went upstairs to change his clothes, but time passed and he did not return. When she went upstairs, there he was, lying down in the baby's room. She asked him to go downstairs and mow the lawn, which he did, but later that evening he blew up at her. When I asked Mrs. Jones what he said she replied, "Oh, mostly he was critical of my puny mind." She said the outburst was violent, and she cried a little as she told me about it. He said she was trying to push him around and that whenever he tried to relax and rest she always found chores for him. "That isn't true," she said. "Many women load their husbands with chores as soon as they come home, but I don't do that." He knows his wife's a Milquetoast and won't fight back. She says she won't do it because she doesn't want to make a scene in front of the children. She thinks that the reason for the lack of relation between the importance of the incident and the dimensions of his rage is that he feels that once he gives up this kind of violence, she will become a nag or demand that he comfort her, or both. His outbursts, she says, are consciously aimed at forestalling both. In this connection she said also that he doesn't want to have to be sympathetic with her. He doesn't want to have to comfort her.

Somewhere along the line I asked her if he was angry with her because she didn't work on his problems, and she thought it used to be that way but it isn't as bad now; that she does try to work on his problems. In this connection she mentioned his hatred of golf, and her having pointed out to him that by not participating in golf with the people around there, he is cutting himself off from social relations and harming himself. He feels, she thinks, that if he has to play golf with these men, he will have to get too close to them. She agreed, when I suggested it, that his playing golf would be an acceptance of conformity.

She mentioned again that her husband was annoyed with her for keeping the house disorderly, and that he had brought this up during the argument. He also brought up her mother, and she feels that dragging in her mother is "hitting below the belt." She feels that arguments should be played according to rules and that dragging in extraneous things like her mother is a violation of the rules and of what she calls "sportsmanship in argument." She says that in an argument she always has to fight according to the rules. He told her during the argument that her keeping the inside of the house in disorder was no different from his leaving the outside of the house in disorder. I asked what the disorderliness in the house meant to her, and she said, "You know we are competitive." I asked, "In what way?" and she explained, "We both struggle to maintain ourselves," to which I replied by asking, "In what way?" and she said, "We both try to keep up our ends of the argument."

In connection with mowing the lawn, she said a number of times that her husband ridiculed her interest in it because it was based on the opinions of others, and that she was more interested in the opinions of others than she was in his getting a rest. She said that situations such as developed yesterday are deliberately provoked by him. She said that he has only mowed the lawn once since they've been there, and she knows that if she does not keep hammering away at it, the lawn will never get mowed.

(Later that day.) Dr. Jones was in very good spirits because he has a number of new patients. His wife hovered around him smiling and made me feel that his outbursts serve the function of making her more submissive and solicitous.

I interpret Dr. Jones's outburst as an effort to compel his wife to have care for his need for solicitude and trust, but his wife still cannot see this problem, and to my questions about meeting his needs she responded by saying that she watches out for his practice and tries to get him to respect golfers. Since the basic issue is beyond her, Ed is in a constant state of latent fury, intensified by his strong inherent tendencies to violence. The more violent he is, however, the more defensive and hostile she becomes, and the less able to perceive the underlying problem. Her feeling that he wants to block any effort to get him to be solicitous appears to be a projection of her difficulty in being solicitous of him. Thus, as usual, behind the trivial cause of a quarrel lie the basic sources of the poor relationship, and Dr. Jones's feeling that his wife is unaware of his disappointment at her failure to perceive his needs is verbalized as her refusing to let him rest. In this way the underlying conflict is again covered up, while a trifle establishes a battleground. Perhaps her refusal to eat without him is an effort to prove to him that she cares.

After the fight Mrs. Jones, feeling crushed, blamed her husband, legitimizing the blame through the idea that he had provoked the fight in order to erect barriers and prevent her from becoming a nag. Thus, in such families, "explanation" is a resistance that prevents insight into the underlying conflict.

Further interpretations are probably possible, but the central issue is that *Ida's action made it possible for her husband to perceive in her again a woman who could never be trusted to put him above all other considerations*. Whatever her motivations, she ended up reinforcing the family pathology.

I turn now to the rules of argument. Phrased in terms of rules, of not "hitting below the belt," of "sportsmanship" or of "keeping one's end up" in an argument, a quarrel is a contest. But although for Mrs. Jones, time and objects have no rules and although she cannot follow rules for protecting a baby from illness and death, she has a clear conception of rules of quarreling. Such troubled people are often intensely aware of rules that to most people are relatively immaterial, but they fail to apply them where they seem essential to others. Since her husband does not perceive the contest as she does, they fight differently. Earlier I related the use of "dirty" tactics to anxiety and to the determination to win. In the present instance Mrs. Jones is anxious and determined, yet she cannot "fight dirty" like her husband because these rules mean too much to her. How is it that she has to abide by rules when her husband does not? Perhaps because, for her, it is better to be dead and unblemished than to be alive and "dirty." Or it may be that no matter what the outcome of the fight, she always "wins" because she "fights fair" and emerges "morally clean," i.e., superior to her husband *anyway*, because he fights "dirty."

Anywayness is important in fights in our culture. "I was right anyway" means that even though it looks as if my opponent won, I was really right. "Anyway" implies that the manifest outcome of a conflict is not its real one—that the loser knows better. Since anywayness reserves to the defeated the belief that matters really ended up in his favor, a loser can view the outcome in a different light from the way others do. In our culture, fighting according to the rules while the adversary does not is a back door to secret victory. Anywayness complicates the aftermath, for the winner of an argument may not know that his defeated adversary feels he won anyway. Anywayness softens defeat and creates ambiguities and delusional victories.

It looks as if Dr. Jones's attacks make husband and wife more attractive to each other; yet I do not think that we should infer from this that the fighting is merely the expression of a sadomasochistic relationship. Rather, their attempts to wound each other—to humiliate and frustrate—seem to express long-standing bewilderment and mutual disappointment. Neither one is capable of coming close to the other, and as they drift they seem to reach a point where the anxiety and hostility erupt into a big quarrel which, in the aftermath, brings them closer for a while. There is a drift toward an affectionate meeting, until the positive consequences of the fight are gone and a new one starts on the noxious residues of the last.

The fights originate in Dr. Jones's feeling that his wife cannot be trusted to care for him, and are aimed at compelling her to prove that she can be. Though in both cases she seems to have missed the point at the conscious level, her increased demonstrativeness suggests that unconsciously she understands in some way. The fact that she appears unable to hold on to it shows once again that although the unconscious can prompt one to do necessary things, it is difficult to learn definitely what the unconscious has to teach.

Since quarreling is an assertiveness which brings Ed and Ida closer together for a while, their quarreling is a flight from death of the self and of the relationship. They are not the only ones who feel most alive when they are fighting, and in warm—in human—contact only during reconciliation. They are part of that vast multitude whose flight from death of the self is given expression in fights with others and in the reconstitution of the aftermath. Thus the inner self seems to counsel, "You will die unless you fight," but, like a Greek oracle, it does not say with whom.

In this family Dr. Jones expresses and endures anger more easily than his wife; he is much more likely to force the issue and frighten his wife, and he holds the economic power. Thus, from the standpoint of "domestic politics" in the United States, he is the stronger. As we say, "he can take it and dish it out" more readily than his wife. I would guess that the growing disorder in the house (as Dr. Jones said to me, "Now things are more toward chaos than ever") has been a consequence of her suffering the most: her expanding disorderliness is a measure of the increasing quantity of unresolved residues of fights. But on the other hand, her own defenses and forms of retaliation enable her to get back at him and even intensify his anger. When things calm down she tests to see whether he is still angry; she makes accusations, attempts to avenge herself and imagines that somehow she has won, anyway. Freud discovered the mechanisms of defense; we need to know more about the *mechanisms of recovery*.

The Relationship between Mrs. Jones and Harriet

The Phenomenology of No Anger

Mrs. Jones's attitude toward the baby is the opposite of the relationship with her husband, but it is not one merely of patience, indulgence and forbearance, for that would imply that if Harriet does something annoying Mrs. Jones covers up her irritation with an indulgent attitude. In this section I explain how I perceive Mrs. Jones's feeling for Harriet—her first girl after three boys—and why it has the qualities I see.

A person's reaction to somebody who breaks a rule or interferes with him can never be explained by simple-minded frustration-aggression theories. In the first place there is the question of what rule is broken and what is interfered with. Then there is the question of who broke the rule or interfered, and how, in general, the frustrated person feels about rules and his own goals. We have to consider also how one feels about the particular person who breaks the rules and interferes, and how the blocked person feels about himself. If Smith thinks little of himself he will react differently to interference or rule breaking than if he believes that everything in his life counts because he himself is significant, that it matters whether he lives or dies, that what he wants and does is somehow important to his self. Furthermore, a person whose every impulse is urgent will tend to fly into a rage at any interference, provided, of course, that anger is permissible to him and the culture.

A man may insist that his wife adhere strictly to rules he may permit his children to break, or he may allow one of his children to break a rule while holding another strictly to it. A person may feel his self-image involved no matter what is going on between him and a certain individual but never feel so involved with another; in the first case he is hypervigilant for any action that seems to interfere with him, while in the second he may not even perceive it. He may accept any kind of interference from one person but not brook the slightest from another. Some people feel humiliated even if their dog disobeys, and will punish the animal for that reason. Their motto is, "I wouldn't let a dog do that to *me*"—and they mean *dog*. If a person is tormented by a nameless guilt, he may be exceedingly tolerant of all rule breakers, or he may, on the other hand, become a Torquemada.

It may be important for a person to balance his attitude toward one individual against his relationship with another, and if so, his response to similar events may be different in each case, because of the balance he needs in his life. If, for example, a woman like Mrs. Jones is in constant turmoil with her husband over broken rules and frustrated wishes, she may look to her child as the one who will provide her with a relationship in which all rules and wishes are subordinated to a single wish, the wish for oneness. Then she will be vigilant for whatever threatens oneness, and rule breaking and disobedience will not be permitted to cause hard feelings. It is very simple and obvious—we do not let little things upset us with somebody we are determined to love; therefore most things that loom large in the eyes of others appear small through the glass of love.

Finally, we must consider a person's attitude toward "the world": if he is in flight from it, if its rules are largely an annoyance to him and he observes only those which keep him out of trouble, thus admitting him to peripheral association with society, then he will often not even perceive that people break rules. Further, if he is also a person of mild desires, interference with them will not disturb him much. I think this is very much true of Mrs. Jones.

Thus, when one studies the attitude of a mother toward her child's naughtiness, one must consider the total context.

Tranquillity is the outstanding quality in Mrs. Jones's relationship with her baby. Classically, tranquillity is achieved through withdrawal from the world; by a suspension of the world, wherein the world is present "out there" but is not permitted to enter consciousness enough to stir up worldly feelings. Thus tranquillity is dependent largely on exclusion.

Mrs. Jones's relationship with her baby is a retreat. In it she is alone with her baby's absolute loyalty and love, and hence the baby can do no wrong. Only when Mrs. Jones's life with her husband and with Bobby (see infra) is understood can the full significance of this withdrawal be grasped. I shall examine some moods and qualities of this *flight from anger*. It is placid; movements are slow except for Mrs. Jones's occasional jolly chasing of Harriet, and she rarely gives even a sign of irritation. The relationship seems to have only the modalities of gentleness and tranquillity. Yet this very striving for tranquillity makes Mrs. Jones rather underprotective: there is no forcing on her part, but rather coaxing. Faces are composed or smiling, and sounds are low; the self-image is not exposed, so there is neither defensiveness nor a desire to crush. Hence, mother and child are not blind to each other's goodness, and they want to touch and handle each other. Scarcely any words are spoken by the mother, and for much of her behavior the ideal of motherhood in our culture seems adequate legitimation. Since most of the communication is nonverbal, it is understandable that although Harriet is a little more than seventeen months old, she does not talk. Mrs. Jones feels no need to explain her mood; and if it has an aftermath, it can be only a quiet reminiscing and a continuing enjoyment of gratifications, rather than an effort to reconstitute a damaged self-image.

This mood can best be communicated to the reader by examination of the field notes.

A Loving Relationship

Since I have described situations in which Mrs. Jones endangered the baby, some may think Mrs. Jones does not love Harriet. I have said that this is not so, and now I try to prove it.

Harriet, the seventeen-month-old baby, was nearby, being picked up every once in a while by her mother and cuddled. Showing some interest in me and in the cordial we were drinking, she was given some to drink. Dr. Jones and the neighbor lady carried on a lively conversation. Mrs. Jones showed mild interest in them but was really almost totally absorbed in Harriet. While Dr. Jones was outside picking corn, Mrs. Jones and I watched TV for a while, although I must say she watched it very little because she was again much absorbed by Harriet, whom she kept on her lap and seemed to enjoy a great deal. Harriet was up and down and up and down, on her mother's lap, then back in her highchair.

After a while Mrs. Jones got up, went to the highchair, and smiling warmly, lifted Harriet out and put her on the floor.*

Later we were walking slowly along the road when Harriet saw part of a top, a rather large, dirty piece of red, white and blue tin, lying at the edge of the road, and headed for it. Her mother said, "No, don't pick it up," but Harriet picked it up anyway and carried it all the way home.

Absorbed in her baby, Mrs. Jones pays little attention to the conversation between her husband and the neighbor or to the TV; and when Harriet clings to the tin Mrs. Jones lets it pass. Just the opposite could have happened: Mrs. Jones could have shooed Harriet away in order to participate in the conversation, or she could have watched TV and ignored the baby; and she could have raised a big fuss about the piece of tin and snatched it out the baby's hand. But she enjoys the baby too much to get interested in the conversation or in watching TV; and she is too underprotective and too determined to keep her relationship with the baby tranquil to make a point of the piece of tin.

Harriet kept climbing up and down the porch stairs, and Mrs. Jones watched carefully to see that she came down backward. A couple of times the baby successfully walked down some steps frontward, but Mrs. Jones always indicated anxiety. Harriet not only climbed up and down the stairs but also leaned over the banister, and her mother was worried lest the baby do more than lean. Harriet was placing herself in situations that provoked her mother's anxiety and made her get up in order to save her. Mrs. Jones frequently held Harriet on her lap. The baby smiled a great deal and cooed. She is rather quiet and placid. She is that way in the highchair also and feeds herself.

Harriet "escaped" and ran around the side of the house under the porch, and her mother went after her, got her out and with a piece of rope tied the door that leads to the underside of the porch. Through all this Mrs. Jones was unhurried, gentle and in close touch with the baby.

* For examples of what can happen when a seriously disturbed mother lifts a baby out of a highchair, see the Keen case, Part V.

When Harriet had finished lunch Mrs. Jones asked her to come into the bathroom so she could wipe her face, but the baby ran away. Mrs. Jones followed her, and Harriet, laughing uproariously, bent over a chair and then ran over to where I was sitting and bent over me. Mrs. Jones got hold of her and wiped her face with a damp cloth. Then Harriet climbed up on me, leaned against my chest and sucked her thumb, and her mother came and picked her up and carried her off for her afternoon nap.

Mrs. Jones and the baby can hug each other almost whenever they please. Harriet is a happy child; she is placid, but she is daring, competent and confident, too: confident of her mother and confident about climbing up and down stairs. In our culture this is a happy baby. Mrs. Jones's main problem is that she is not protective enough. Perhaps Harriet is a little too confident—insensitive to danger—because it is hard for her mother to be harsh or even to interfere.

Among the Pilagá Indians of Argentina a baby of Harriet's age would already be playing outside the house on the village compound with children several times its age; and its mother, far from keeping the child close by, as Mrs. Jones does with Harriet, would try to get it to go outside so she could do her work. Pilagá mothers do not feel they have to prove themselves good mothers by constantly being near their children. Furthermore, a Pilagá village is safe for an infant, while in our culture the house itself, with all its glass and gadgets, is dangerous. Where space is dangerous, where good mothers keep an eye on the baby, where there is nobody else to take care of him and when the mother has time, it is possible to have a pattern of maternal care like Mrs. Jones's. Because of the configuration of our component systems, Mrs. Jones cannot permit her child the separateness—sometimes called autonomy—which a Pilagá woman must allow hers. Thus the Pilagá baby, far from being dependent, actually has more autonomy than one of our own. But the Pilagá child's independence does not last, nor does it expand into the sphere of ideas, because, just as in our culture, the pressures to conform are strong.

Mrs. Jones went into the lake with Harriet but wore a blouse and shorts instead of a bathing suit. The baby was delighted to be in the water and cooed, yelled and laughed. For the entire hour that we were in the water Mrs. Jones handled Harriet, lifting her up and down and swishing her around in the water. Mrs. Jones seemed to be enjoying it very much, though she told me later that it had been a great strain on her back. Dr. Jones did not help with the baby. He spent about two minutes trying to show Bobby how to swim. The boys were left to themselves in the water but no difficulties developed. Dr. Jones and I swam out to the float and back.

The leisurely hour-long swishing in the warm and sunny water conditions the baby to quietness. It takes a very quiet baby to be content to hold on to her mother's hand and be swished around—and nothing else: Harriet is learning to be like her mother. The water play is a paradigm of Harriet's early education in time, space and motion; and one wonders whether, later on, our middle-class American notion of time as a torrent of many whirlpools will not be intolerable to her, as it now is to her mother. If, when she grows up, Harriet cannot keep to any schedule or is often late, an observer, not knowing her past, might interpret this as an expression of "a great deal of unavowed disregard for others." Were the long-drawn-out experience in the water repeated often enough, water might come to have a special place in Harriet's feelings—as something safe and to be loved. Then it would be difficult for her to perceive water as threatening, and even a clear and present danger in it might not overcome the benign perception learned in childhood.

Had Mrs. Jones interrupted the play from time to time to go and sit on the grass to rest, Harriet might have made a fuss trying to get back to the water. Then the only way Mrs. Jones could have had a rest would have been through her husband's helping her. But he was swimming, and we know that there was real danger of a quarrel if she tried to take him away from it. So, by swimming *away*, Dr. Jones brought mother and baby *close*, but because Harriet had learned to love the water, her mother's back began to hurt. On the other hand, if Mrs. Jones had been a different kind of woman —ready to interfere in her child's pleasure—she would have come out of the water and forced Harriet to stay out no matter how much the baby struggled and cried.

Thus the dialectic that brings mother and baby close together for an hour of tranquil, water-borne play derives not only from the fact that Mrs. Jones needs to turn away from the turmoil of her life but also from the fact that she does not interfere—she lets her husband swim away and leave her to take care of the baby alone, and she won't interfere with the baby's delight. Obviously, the more Dr. Jones leaves mother and baby together, the more the baby's perception of the world—the baby's consciousness—will come to resemble her mother's. Thus, in a very narrow way the *social structure of relationships compels the structure of consciousness.*

When a parent's intervention in his child's play is discussed, the stress is usually placed on how it affects the child, but intervention obviously affects the parent also—it often gives him something he needs. We really know next to nothing about the way the average *parent's* needs shape the child as he intervenes in the child's play. True, we all know of some father who became a businessman, when he actually wanted to be a professional ballplayer, and then kept drilling his son to be an outstanding player, so that the son became a third-rate lawyer. We have heard about the mother who wanted to be an Olympic skater but married and had a daughter whom she tried to turn into an Olympic skating champion. But we need systematic studies of run-of-the-mill cases, those that don't call special attention to themselves—like Harriet, Bobby and Jackie. As for Harriet, the Water Baby, we see that play is an assuagement for the mother; a surcease from tension; a proof that she can make *something* love her; a proof, perhaps, that she is not entirely "an idiot."

The day after the first picnic I went with Mrs. Jones when she took Harriet for a walk, and we talked as we rambled along.

While we were carrying on a conversation, Harriet kept running away and coming back and climbing up on her mother. She would run away and her mother would chase her, laughing, and Harriet laughed uproariously. The baby did not run far. At last Mrs. Jones clasped her; the baby leaned against her mother's bosom and sucked her thumb while Mrs. Jones nuzzled her and smiled. A couple of times Mrs. Jones tried to get the baby to go away, but she didn't try very hard and the baby stayed. Meanwhile I felt guilty for having intruded into the baby's life by questioning her mother.

My intrusion was not permitted to disturb seriously the involvement of mother and baby. Mrs. Jones did not irritatedly shoo the baby away, and the baby did not become whiny and clamorous.

I have suggested here that in the process of making the baby her own, a mother teaches it certain conceptions of the universe—of time, space, objects, and so on. For such empathic absorption of the universe by the baby it is probably better to use "imbue" rather than "teach," for the idea of contact with the universe through another person is not quite captured by the terms "learn" and "teach." When one is imbued in this way—as if sun, water and time were filtered to one through the body of another person—it becomes difficult to change one's perceptions, for change would be a kind of death—a detachment from the person through whom the universe was absorbed. Thus consciousness itself is learned and acquired through another person. From the time we are born we are taught *how to be conscious*. Consciousness is a sociocultural phenomenon, and the consciousness of a Pilagá Indian baby is therefore very different from that of an American one.

Babies and Breakage Anxiety

Harriet came into the kitchen, a pair of binoculars draped around her neck and a few things in her hands. She played for a few minutes and then went to the drier and kept slamming the door. She did it about ten or fifteen times but Mrs. Jones made no effort to stop her, although I was made anxious that she would break it. Harriet kept right on until she opened the door of the drier and saw a piece of clothing blocking the door. So she pushed it out of the way and was then able to close the door. Mrs. Jones remarked that Harriet likes to close doors.

What slamming the drier door means to a middle-class American is illustrated by my anxiety. But it did not seem to bother Mrs. Jones, nor did she worry about the binoculars. Even the fact that it is hard to get household appliances fixed in Latham does not upset Mrs. Jones. Once again, what creates difficulties with her husband—carelessness about property—eliminates them between Mrs. Jones and the baby. Mrs. Jones does not care much about objects such as gadgets, furniture, and so on, so they don't loom up to ruffle the relationship between her and the baby. The more you are involved in objects, the more difficult it is to become wrapped up in a baby. Only after we have transmitted to it our own anxieties about objects can we live with a baby. But how could it be otherwise?

Feeding

Quiet self-reliance, reflected in almost everything Harriet does, characterizes her feeding also. At seventeen months she is eating all by herself.

Harriet was seated in her highchair, drinking milk and eating a snack. She was left to feed herself and seemed to be quite comfortable, while her mother busied herself around the kitchen getting supper.

Harriet's quietness and placidness are also evidenced by her quietness in the highchair and the tranquillity with which she feeds herself. On the other hand, she is not rigidly anchored to the highchair, for she frequently climbs out. Sometimes she does not have to do it because her mother lifts her out.

Harriet somehow got into the kitchen and Mrs. Jones picked her up and put her in the highchair. She set her lunch before her—a mixture of soup and meat—and gave her a little spoon with some kind of ring on the end. Harriet fed herself expertly and then whined intensely for milk, which Mrs. Jones gave her. The cup of milk left a mark on her chin, and Mrs. Jones laughed a little when I said that Harriet had a beard.

When Harriet had finished her meal, a difference developed between the baby and her mother because Harriet didn't want to give up her spoon. She was perfectly willing to give up the empty cup, but not the spoon, and she yelled. Mrs. Jones solved the problem by bringing her a cracker and a little milk in a cup, and the baby gave up the spoon. After she had finished eating, Harriet climbed over the edge of the highchair. Mrs. Jones said to me, "Harriet's capable of descending all the way alone," but she started to help her down. Harriet fell part of the way but did not cry. Harriet does not cry when she falls or bangs her head.

Harriet's mother is not pathogenic, making the highchair a prison. The baby seems a tranquil transient there, though she is far from apathetic. Clamoring for milk, climbing out of the chair, yelling over the spoon—she is quite a self-assertive little girl. Her relative quietness has not been used against her.

Mrs. Jones set Harriet in the highchair and kept feeding her morsels of food—a piece of ham, a piece of toast, a glass of milk; and she kept feeding her this way as the baby asked for more.

. . .

I got to the house at about one o'clock in the afternoon. Dr. Jones had not yet come home and the boys were hungry, but they were kept waiting. Harriet, however, was seated in the highchair feeding herself and getting quite messy. Dr. Jones came home after I had been there for about fifteen minutes; he walked into the kitchen without looking at the baby, but after he had been there awhile he did notice her and saw that she was covered from head to foot with food. This annoyed him and he complained loudly to Mrs. Jones and to the baby. He picked her up and gently scraped the food off her body with a spoon, and fed the scrapings to her, and she accepted this. He showed considerable anxiety that she might urinate in the chair. After he had scraped her off, he held her like a sack of flour while her mother removed her panties and shoes. Mrs. Jones objected to the way he held her and called it an "indignity." He then set her on the potty, where she remained for quite some time.

. . .

Harriet was in her highchair now, eating toast and drinking milk. Then her mother gave her some jello mixed with milk, which Harriet splashed all over the highchair and onto the floor. Mrs. Jones and I wiped it up; she was mildly concerned that Harriet hadn't eaten any of the jello. Harriet can hardly be called a fat baby, but she's not thin either. I suppose she's just an average baby. What constantly impresses me is her quietness, but, of course, Mrs. Jones is very quiet too.

. . .

Harriet was in a chair feeding herself. She was given a portion of jello mixed with milk, which she spilled all over herself as usual. I have been very much struck by the fact that Harriet is given so little to eat, and again I was struck by the small amount she was given this evening. While we were seated at dinner eating fish sticks, Harriet demanded some again and again, and she got three of them, more bread and a cup of milk. It is obvious that the supper she got was not adequate. She eats often, and as soon as she is placed in the highchair she begins to eat whatever is given her—I think she is hungry a considerable part of the time. It may very well be that her mother gives her only a little bit of food in order to make her so hungry that she will present no feeding problem. Certainly the child is no problem whatsoever in this regard: she will eat practically anything in sight.

The fact that indirectly Dr. Jones abets his wife's unwillingness to give anybody anything to eat when her husband is not at home, delays the meals, and that Mrs. Jones feeds Harriet as described above, gives further support to the argument that parents' disorientation has consequences that are biologically inappropriate. The contrast between Dr. Jones's demand for order and his wife's lack of interest in it is dramatized by the fact that when Harriet is sloppy her mother is worried because the child has not eaten the food, but her father is upset by the messiness—and this is what first attracted his attention when he came home. Paradoxically, then, the man who is so concerned with orderliness is the same man who scrapes food off Harriet's body and feeds it to her. Here "food must not be wasted" takes precedence over "food must be uncontaminated" and "baby must be kept healthy." After cleaning the baby and feeding her her own dirt, so to speak, Dr. Jones continues to show greater concern for order than for the baby, by worrying about her urinating in the chair and by putting her on the potty. He does nothing to affirm the baby's dignity, nor his affection for her. Now, his wife, who is unable to keep to a medication schedule and who endangers the baby's life in other ways—she may even be underfeeding the baby—suddenly objects to the way her husband holds the baby because it is an "indignity." Holding the baby "right" must have significance for this mother, who is treated with contempt by her husband and who wants a oneness-relationship with her baby. When the *baby* is held like a sack of flour, it is perhaps as if Mrs. Jones were held like one.

Elimination

Harriet's diarrhea has been discussed. Considering the relationship between mother and child and Mrs. Jones's general indifference to rules, we would expect that Harriet's elimination would not cause trouble between her and her mother. I give below the rest of the data I have on the subject.

[When Mrs. Jones and I were on the steps outside and Harriet was playing around] Mrs. Jones said, "Oh, she wanted to go to the bathroom and I didn't have sense enough to know it." The baby's pants were wet and Mrs. Jones let her wear them.

While Bobby, Jackie and I were playing on the floor Harriet wet her pants again and Bobby said, "Oh, she's wet," but Mrs. Jones did not change the baby.

. . .

When Harriet went up on the porch she urinated in her jumper. Her mother noticed this but did nothing about it.

. . .

Harriet was now finished eating and Mrs. Jones wanted to take her to the bathroom. Rejoicing that the baby had not moved her bowels or urinated, she picked her up and carried her toward the bathroom, but Bobby was there and she told him to hurry. He took his time, however, so she came back into the kitchen and sat down to eat her lunch, holding Harriet on her lap and playing delightedly with her, and the baby was equally delighted.

Not even elimination, so often a cause of conflict, so often a strain-bearing function in parent-child relations, causes tension in the bond between Mrs. Jones and her baby. On the contrary, it is Dr. and Mrs. Jones who get into arguments over it. This sort of thing is common enough in our society: mother and baby may be getting along fine—no trouble over baby's eating, sleeping, elimination—but somebody else, mother-in-law or husband, for example, does not like the way things are going and makes a fuss. Where there are no completely agreed-on criteria for raising a baby, anybody's impulses may compel him to inject himself where he is not needed. When, in addition, there is some underlying tension between the intruder and the mother, the impulse to interfere is released even more readily: then hostility toward the mother may masquerade as interest in the baby.

Bathing

Harriet was not bathed much; I have only two notations in my record.

When I came in, Mrs. Jones was in the bathroom finishing Harriet's bath. She was spraying the baby with cool water from a small hose, and she and the baby seemed to be having a good time. Then Mrs. Jones picked Harriet up in a towel, wrapped her in it, carried her into her room, sat down with the baby on her lap and finished drying her. Then she dressed her, brought her into the kitchen and set her in the highchair.

. . .

Mrs. Jones was giving Harriet a bath and the baby was crying bitterly while her mother sprayed her with the hose. When I asked Mrs. Jones why the baby was crying she said it was because she was afraid to get the water on her face.

I think the real reason was that the water was cold: when Mrs. Jones wanted to take a bath she raised quite a fuss because there was no hot water. At any rate, Harriet tried again and again to get away from the hose, even though the water came nowhere near her face. At last the bath was finished and Mrs. Jones wrapped the baby in a towel close to herself. She took her to her room, finished drying her, set her in the crib and left her there. (Harriet howled when she was left alone but her mother paid no attention.)

This is a very different Mrs. Jones. Here she is callous to Harriet and even appears to offend the baby's dignity. The oneness has broken down, and mother and baby are made separate through conflict. In the following sections we will see other instances of this process.

Crying

Harriet would bump her head from time to time but never cried, and this is probably because of many past experiences like the following:

(Going under the table, Harriet bumped her head.) She went over to her mother and put her head on her mother's lap and her mother patted her and said, "Oh, you didn't hurt yourself."

What examples I have of Harriet's crying occurred when she was isolated or cooped up. Why her mother objected to her crying when hurt but not when she was isolated is an interesting question. Perhaps it is because the Old American value system was willing to deny physical pain but not prepared to deny the stress of isolation—it would have been too dangerous—for babies that do not cry out of loneliness, that do not protest their isolation, will become defective organisms.

Mrs. Jones called six o'clock "hell time": she would be getting supper ready, the baby had to be fed, the boys were home and taking baths, playing around, and fighting and yelling. Like many mothers who want to get the baby out of the way for a while, she sometimes put Harriet in the playpen in the baby's room and kept her there in spite of her screaming.

After Harriet finished eating Mrs. Jones put her in the playpen, but the baby didn't like it there and kept screaming. Mrs. Jones paid no attention. Harriet jumped up and down, then sat down and thrust her legs between the bars of the pen, but Mrs. Jones, having put in a few toys, left her there. At last Jackie came along and removed a box from under the pen and Harriet began to worm her way out, but she could not make it without Jackie's help and kept yelling and howling while Jackie helped her, and at last she got out. At this point Mrs. Jones came along and I asked, "How does she get the box out from under the playpen?" She said she thought Harriet got some help from Jackie; and Bobby said, "Yes, Jackie took the box out from under the playpen."

Mrs. Jones did not angrily dump Harriet back in the pen nor bawl Jackie out for conspiring in the escape. Dr. and Mrs. Jones often get angry with each other because one of them breaks a rule or ignores a desire of the other, but in her relationship with the baby, it is precisely because Mrs. Jones does not bother with rules or insist on her own wishes that she is able to reduce conflict. Of course, this is due in the first place to the fact that Mrs. Jones has no reservations about her love for Harriet. But it is due also to the fact that in some circumstances carelessness about order and rules is a useful attitude with a baby. Thus we see that in the same family a characteristic that sustains a hostile relationship can foster a tranquil one. The fact that carelessness about rules and order helps the relationship between mother and baby but impairs that between husband and wife suggests that carelessness is a general characteristic of Mrs. Jones—not something she somehow uses against her husband, but rather a constitutional factor which may come out in any situation. The situation itself is inert, so to speak; it is our perception of it that determines whether it should be labeled hostile or not.

In our culture, sanctioned by the distinction that it is legitimate to confine a baby alone in a different part of the house, the infant becomes separate from the rest of the family. In Mrs. Jones's disregard of Harriet's objection to cold water, and in her telling the baby that her head did not hurt when she bumped it, we have already seen two examples of the learning of separateness; in the playpen-isolation complex we have another. The configuration of separateness—what is generally called "individuality"—is culturally determined, so that it must take different forms in different cultures, and "becoming an individual" is associated with a system of values, notions of what is legitimate, and with culturally determined orientations toward the component systems—time, space, motion, objects and people.

The oneness of mother and baby is being broken largely through stress. Harriet is often cooped up away from her mother, and not infrequently her pain and discomfort are ignored or pooh-poohed. Thus her individuation is being brought about in a typical middle-class American way. It would be far-fetched to argue that Mrs. Jones does these things deliberately in order to break the oneness with her baby; yet in every culture mothers, without thinking about it, use certain measures for separating themselves from the baby. The commonest is weaning from the breast. Anthropologists have on the whole been so uninterested in children that all we can expect from most of them is some laconic statement about the age of weaning. We are rarely told what else a mother does to separate herself from the baby. Perhaps she delays for longer and longer periods her response to the child's crying like a Pilagá mother; perhaps she stimulates the child and then looks away—acting as if the child were not there—as in Bali.* Whatever we see Mrs. Jones doing with Harriet that implies separation is psychological weaning, whether Mrs. Jones does it with that in mind or not.

In the next examples Harriet is again isolated and protesting.

While we were sitting at the kitchen table Harriet, who was in her room, started to cry again, and she cried and cried but nobody paid any attention to her. This gave me goose flesh. At last Mrs. Jones said to her husband, "Maybe you ought to go in there," and he answered, "Oh, I went in there before, and all she wanted was to get out of bed." Nevertheless, after another minute or so he did go in and she quieted down.

Normal human beings everywhere respond attentively to a baby's cry, but the form of the response, the time between first cry and adult response, and how violent the crying has to be before the adult responds vary among individuals and cultures. And so does the willingness of adults to respond. Adults reserve the right to decide the legitimacy of the child's cry and the conditions under which they will respond. The form of response can vary all the way from taking the child on the lap at once and nursing it, to first scratching on the outside of its mosquito basket, as among the Mundugumor,† and then reluctantly nursing it if the crying does not stop. The time range can obviously vary also: some in our culture respond to crying at once, others let the child cry a short time, still others a long time before responding. Since crying ranges from whimpering to paroxysmal crying and screaming, adult response varies along this dimension also—some may wait for the paroxysmal cry before responding. Though "legalizing" the

* See Mead and Bateson, *op. cit.*
† Margaret Mead, *Sex and Temperament in Three Primitive Societies* (Mentor Books; New York, New American Library, 1951).

grounds for crying according to some canon of value is not unique to our culture, in many families it seems as if every time the baby cries, he has to prove he has a right to do it before he gets a response. It is true that in all cultures, the older a child gets, the more the grounds on which adults will respond to crying become specific and restricted, yet it is rare indeed for a tribal society to define the crying of even a seventeen-month baby as illegitimate and therefore to be ignored. In our culture the illegality of crying focuses on two ideas: that the child will be spoiled and that the parent will be exploited. These can be disregarded, however, if the parent decides that the reason the child is crying is "serious." The right to decide what is serious is reserved to the parent.

In our culture, solicitude is far from being an absolute, even with an infant, but is related to competitiveness, achievement and toughness. On the other hand, there is a lesser ideology which, since it is related to tenderness and warmth, affects parental response differently. The former dictates relative disregard of crying, the latter favors quick and frequent response.

It is apparent that Harriet's merely wanting to get out of bed was not, in Dr. Jones's view, a legitimate excuse for crying, and since he could not think of one, he was unwilling to act on the baby's reason. In our culture, going in to the baby has to be "justified" by the baby, so every one of its cries implies a legalistic argument between baby and parent; a kind of debate over an infantile bill of rights, in a constitution that nobody really understands, but of which the parents are drafters, supreme court and executors—or executioners. Since much emotional illness, including, I believe, primary infantile autism, is caused by isolation*—the situation where a mother goes in to the infant only to feed and change it—it is clear that our values make a big contribution to disturbances in early childhood. On the other hand, one can imagine the parent who constantly looks for an excuse to "justify" going to and hovering over the baby, and so welcomes every peep out of it. In our culture this produces the "overprotective" mother.

If there were a different spatial configuration in the usual home, with only one room instead of several, the issue of "going in" would never arise at all. Thus the cultural configuration of space also plays a part in the drama of Harriet's crying. All a baby has to do is cry—this is the primordial biological fact. But the cry is uttered in such an intricate cultural context that it cannot get answered until all the absurdities that *Homo sapiens* has built around himself and around babies have been somehow answered and overcome—often by other absurdities.

At last, under his wife's reluctant urging, Dr. Jones did go in and the baby stopped crying. I do not know why Mrs. Jones did not do it herself, but she frequently asks her husband. Thus in the Jones family no rigid decision has been made about which parent is to take care of Harriet—this much at least has been eliminated in this family from the tangle of cultural factors that complicate response to the infantile cry.

After Dr. Jones left, Mrs. Jones suggested that we go into the living room where she could finish her coffee, so we did. The blower that ventilates the apartment is in the baby's room, and it began to squeak and finally woke her and she started to cry. Mrs. Jones went in there and the baby became quiet, but as soon as her mother walked out Harriet started to cry again. Mrs. Jones, however, got

* See the Wilson case also, Part IV.

a batch of color slides and began to look at them and show them to me. This must have taken about ten minutes, and all that time Harriet was crying. Having finished looking at the pictures, Mrs. Jones went in to the baby again and talked to her and she quieted. But when Mrs. Jones left her the baby started to cry, so she went back.

The second or third time this occurred I went to the baby's room and saw Mrs. Jones lying down on the daybed holding the baby. I went back to the living room, and from there I could hear Mrs. Jones singing an aria from an opera, and as she sang the baby stopped crying. Finally Mrs. Jones left the baby's room, singing as she went out, and Harriet did not cry again.

At one point Mrs. Jones brought Harriet into the living room in order to quiet her, but Harriet got down from her mother's lap and headed for the kitchen, and Mrs. Jones said,

"Oh, so you want a drink of water," and she went and gave the baby some water; and I heard her say, "Why didn't you say so?" (Harriet does not talk.)

The following are the remaining examples of family response to Harriet's crying:

Harriet was put to bed by her mother. The baby cried there for a couple of minutes; nobody went to her and she stopped crying.

. . .

Mrs. Jones set Harriet on the potty in the bedroom, where the baby remained until she raised a clamor and her mother went in and took her off and put her to bed.

Mrs. Jones asked me whether I wanted a cup of coffee, and since she was going to have one, I said okay. So we went into the kitchen and sat down and had coffee and talked. Meanwhile Harriet set up a howl from the crib, but Mrs. Jones paid no attention all the time we were having coffee.

. . .

When Jackie came home Harriet went upstairs with him; her cries had been audible for some time on the porch, but Mrs. Jones had done nothing about it.

One wonders about a family where, although their seventeen-month-old child has had an intestinal upset all week, nobody says, "I wonder whether her tummy is hurting her?" when she cries, and where nobody looks worried or runs in to see whether the baby is in pain even when the crying lasts a long time. Thus the common American practice of "letting the baby cry" persists here under inappropriate circumstances.

For Mrs. Jones, union with Harriet is a flight from the world; the two appear to form an encapsulated mother-baby universe into which Mrs. Jones retreats from the tension and ambiguities of life with her husband and the two boys. Things are clear-cut between Harriet and her mother; it is clear that they love each other. Thus love, clarity, submergence of and diminished concern about herself, an easygoing attitude toward rules, flight from the world and a yearning for oneness have given to this relationship a tranquillity unmatched by any other in the house. It is also the most isolated.

Since the relationship of Mrs. Jones with her baby is the opposite of that with her husband, the gentle affect of one allays some of the baneful consequences of the other. Mrs. Jones submerges herself in Harriet, and along with this goes diminished concern about her own wishes. In contact with

Harriet she sheds what causes rancor with her husband. In addition, the characteristic that troubles her husband—her relative carelessness about order and rules—does the opposite with the baby. Mrs. Jones doesn't think much of herself, and were the relationship with her husband not so threatening, she would probably not be pushed to the fighting we have seen. Mrs. Jones's impulses to assert herself and to fight are not strong, and she might let much slide were she not strongly provoked. In her involvement with Harriet, rules and her own desires are subordinated to the wish for oneness. When she isolates Harriet, it is so she can finish her housework or in order to put the baby to sleep.

The Relationship between Dr. Jones and Harriet

When Dr. and Mrs. Jones are together with Harriet, she is sometimes a source of conflict between them. But even though Dr. and Mrs. Jones get into quarrels over something connected with the baby, Harriet is not adversely affected, as Tommy was. Parental tensions are not discharged on Harriet, although she may be the *occasion* for the expression of underlying hostility.

Dr. Jones is not secure with the baby. His uncertainty is illustrated by the following.

Harriet and I were on the porch. We hadn't been there for more than ten minutes when Dr. Jones drove up. When I saw him I said to the baby, "Look who's coming," and when Harriet recognized him she smiled. When he saw us on the porch, Dr. Jones said something about Harriet's smiling because I was holding her, but it was obvious that she was smiling because her father had come along, so I said, "She started to smile when she saw you."

Although Dr. Jones ignored the baby when he came home from the office, when he picked her off the potty in the bathroom he held her up above his head and put forehead to forehead in a very pleased way. Upon this the baby smiled, and he said, "What have I done to deserve the smile?"

Perhaps it is because a new life is still difficult for Dr. Jones to accept that he feels the baby does not accept him. As in all cases of projection, Dr. Jones flies in the face of the facts, as we see above and in the following:

Shortly after the boys and Harriet were in bed, Dr. Jones came home, and this was a signal for the boys to jump out of bed and for Harriet to start crying for her daddy. So he told the boys a story, a very short one, and they went back to bed; then he went in and held Harriet and sang to her and put her back to bed.

At the Bible study meeting, Dr. Jones said he did not trust his wife; now we perceive that he cannot quite trust his baby. Well, if one cannot trust anybody, why trust a baby? He says that the smile she gives him is really for me, a stranger; when he holds her above his head as he takes her off the potty, the smile cannot really be for him because he does not deserve it. He says these things not only because he feels unlovable but also because he has a dread of trust and does not want to be involved in a relationship of trust. Since he does not trust people, he does not really want them to trust him, because if they trust him they will put burdens on him, and having burdens, he cannot be free. Dr. Jones would like people to trust him when it is convenient for him, and as much as is convenient for him.

In *The Neurotic Personality of Our Time*,* Karen Horney points out that although most people in our culture are distrustful to some extent—probably because they are aware of the fact that this is a culture in which people do not present themselves as they are—a disturbed person doesn't trust anybody or demands excessive proof of trustworthiness.

Here is the last of the scanty material I have of Dr. Jones alone with Harriet. Of course, he can't be alone with her much because there are others in the family; because he isn't home much; and because the baby goes to bed early.

Harriet had been set on the potty, and somewhere in here Dr. Jones got up and removed her. He sang Harriet to sleep. One of the songs he sang was "Dolin Corie." I didn't recognize the other song, though he often sings it to her when singing her to sleep.

"Dolin Corie" is a sad and ghostly song about a dead moonshiner. It tells of the attack on Corie's still by revenue agents, of his death and burial, and of his ghost. Since violence and ideas of violence, danger and death permeate even Dr. Jones's best relations—as with his boys—and because it is so difficult for him to have empathy for anything, I reserve judgment on the specific significance of his lulling his baby to sleep with such a song. Yet it is evident that Harriet is fond of her father; she crows when he comes home, smiles at him, and falls asleep in his arms.

THE AUTHOR'S OPINION SOME YEARS LATER

I finished this analysis a few years ago when, aware of the great difficulty of understanding this complex man, and perceiving that he was drawn toward his family in an intricate and contradictory way; when, aware of Dr. Jones's wish to be a real husband and father, I could yet see the problems he had in attaining this end, I was perhaps moved to overlook certain troubles while stressing others. For this reason I may have gone astray in attributing his wariness with Harriet to general fear of trust rather than to his continuing difficulties with his wife, because his not paying attention to the baby when he comes home—or rather, his delay in paying attention—his talking first about her messiness, his scraping food off her and even feeding it to her, though he knows she has diarrhea, may be related to his persisting inability to trust his wife and therefore to feel comfortable with the baby.

Meanwhile, I want to stress that he does pay attention to Harriet; he does clean her, he doesn't like to see her messy; he does wipe her feces off the floor and take her to the toilet; he does sing her to sleep, and so on. He is trying to be a good father—and the baby obviously likes him.

* New York, Norton, 1966.

The Relationship between Dr. Jones and His Sons

INTRODUCTION TO BOBBY

Although the relationship between Dr. and Mrs. Jones was bad when Bobby was conceived, they went to great lengths to prevent miscarriage. At that time it was already suspected that Tommy was psychotic. When the new baby came along, Tommy was so hostile to him that Mrs. Jones often had to intervene to prevent his hurting Bobby. Tommy was not removed from the home, however, until Bobby was in his second year. Both parents described Bobby to me as a cheerful little fellow but when I saw him, he had a depressed expression and rings under his eyes. His conversation was sprinkled with destructive fantasies, though he could be imaginative in other ways too. I am aware that nowadays violence and even horror are common on TV and in comics and even penetrate the play of nursery school children,* but it seemed to me that destructive fantasies were unusually common in Bobby's communication with me. That he expected me to be interested was due in part, I think, to the fact that horror-and-death-oriented communication was rewarded by his father.

Bobby seemed bright to me, but his mother and father said that though perceptive, he was not intelligent "in the usual sense." On the other hand, though to me Bobby looked physically average, his parents considered him extraordinarily big and powerful; his father called him "almost freakishly big and strong." As far as that opinion is concerned, I would say that if, like Dr. Jones, you let even a seven-year-old slug you with all his force (see infra), the pain will impress you enough to make you exaggerate his strength. Admittedly, Bobby's agility was astonishing.

Bobby is physically courageous: for example, he climbs over perpendicular surfaces even a cat would not attempt, and on the arrowhead hunt, although Jackie complained, Bobby did not. He likes to be thought of as a fighter and boasts to his father of clobbering other children, but to his father's disgust, he sometimes whines like an infant as he climbs on his lap. Bobby sucks his thumb a lot, sometimes with signs of embarrassment. He trusts his father but is openly at war with his mother. In the life-story interviews, her relationship to Bobby was the part of her life about which Mrs. Jones was least accurate, and my observations show that it is the part about which she deludes herself most.

INTRODUCTION TO JACKIE

At three years of age Jackie is still very, very much a baby: he is constantly clamoring for his mother, he whines, screams, sucks his thumb, likes to crawl up on people, is always crawling on his mother and still would like her to take him to the toilet and clean him. His speech and fantasy are garbled.

* See my "Death, Fear and Climax in Nursery School Play" in *Concepts of Development in Early Childhood Education*, ed. by Peter Neubauer (Springfield, Ill., Charles C. Thomas, 1965), pp. 112–43.

Outstanding among my impressions of today is Jackie's constant whining, and about six o'clock, when he was taking a bath, his eruption into an almost uninterrupted series of piercing screams which almost gave me an earache. At last his screaming became so disintegrating that his mother threatened to slap him on the mouth if he did not stop, and since he did not, she slapped him lightly on the mouth, but he kept right on screaming and she did not slap him again.* (The record does not make clear here whether the screaming is due to Bobby's teasing.)

Mrs. Jones and I sat in the living room watching a movie on television. Jackie crawled close to me and leaned against me, not looking at the screen. He was going through some sort of fantasy with a suction cup he was mouthing and trying to stick on his knee and on his hands. The cup was covered with saliva, and Jackie was saying a lot of things, none of which I could understand. Later on he got on his mother's lap and talked in a garbled way about a taxi-boo. This is a song on a record which his mother then asked him to sing, but he made a few tuneless sounds and stopped. Jackie does a great deal of exceedingly garbled talking to himself and to people. It is difficult for both his parents and me to figure out what he is trying to say.

On TV there developed a typical movie fistfight which Bobby watched deadpan, but over which Jackie crowed with delight, simply howling with delicious laughter. I have never seen him laugh with such pleasure.

. . .

Jackie often crawls up on me, always seeking to be picked up and held. There is no doubt that he goes hammer and tongs after cuddling, caressing and kissing, and he manages to get a lot of it. Bobby does this much less. Bobby is a whirlwind of hostile aggression, while Jackie is a whirlwind of affectionate aggression.

. . .

Jackie tried to tell a story about three glasses but was constantly interrupted by Bobby, who was silenced a couple of times by the mother's saying, "Give Jackie a chance to tell his story." The three glasses had all kinds of vegetables in them. Jackie got off on the subject of what was in the glasses and became so fascinated with it that he never got beyond that point—especially since Bobby constantly interrupted him.

. . .

(Jackie fantasied while drinking orange juice.) The fantasy had the following elements in it: a rubber band tied up with sticks that whirled around in the air; then a helicopter came along and it all went up in milk; and there was bomb. When Mrs. Jones asked Jackie where his friend Mary was, he said she was in a trap. His mother answered, "Well, maybe you can get her out of the trap." Jackie said, "But that trap is surrounded by a whole lot of other traps." Later I asked Jackie what the trap was like and he said, "It had a hook in it," and I asked, "What kind of hook?" and he said it was red and brown.

Relationship of Dr. Jones to Bobby and Jackie

The fact that many of the most intimate moments of Bobby and his father occur when they are confronting danger together suggests the strong association in Dr. Jones's personality of intimacy, danger and even violence. The following is further evidence:

Tonight as the boys were about to go to bed, Dr. Jones and Bobby began a "roughhouse." Bobby, without giving his father a moment's rest, kept attacking

* The reader will note that on the following day she again slaps him for screaming.

him violently with both fists and open hands, poking at his eyes and pulling his nose and cheeks.

I think a little more ought to be said about the motor behavior in the roughhouse. Bobby clenches his fists and holds them before him somewhat below his chin. His father assumes the attitude of a boxer, his left shoulder raised to protect his chin, his left arm extended in the position to deliver a left jab. They spar a bit this way, the boy lashing out as violently as he possibly can, first with one fist, then with the other. Dr. Jones corrects the boy's technique, asking him, for example, why he doesn't use his left for a jab. The child doesn't dance around like a boxer, however, but simply lashes out with both fists, sometimes with hands open. There is an alternation between lashing out and leaping from the bed onto his father's neck, seizing him and clinging to him. Dr. Jones would reach out and tap Bobby here and there. Bobby, however, got in many hard blows, particularly on his father's arms. Every once in a while Dr. Jones would pick Bobby up and dump him on the bed (this all took place in the kids' room). Bobby would stand up on the bed, wiggle his face in a sort of mock attacking way, and then leap on his father, throwing his arms around his neck, and his father would grab him. It seemed to me a rather tender embrace but at the same time violent. Bobby quickly changed the apparent tenderness to slamming, pulling and yanking. It should be emphasized that in all this the father and son were playing. Dr. Jones was careful to avoid hurting the child, and Bobby didn't seem to be vicious. He appeared to lash out, however, with all his strength. This kept on and on until Dr. Jones told Bobby to stop.

Jackie participated too, beating his father's buttocks with his fists with all his strength. He threw a cardboard carton and a wooden block at him. When Dr. Jones stopped the roughhousing, he was rather pale and obviously fatigued. They also threw pillows at one another, and Jackie threw his stuffed giraffe at his father. Mrs. Jones looked in from time to time but did nothing to stop what was going on. Using persuasion and strength, Dr. Jones at last quieted the kids. All three got into one of the beds and Dr. Jones told the story of Bloody Valley, a valley nearby which was bought from the Indians by the settlers. As the whites settled in the valley they gradually pushed the Indians back until the latter became enraged, attacked the settlement and wiped it out. Bobby asked, "Children too?" and Dr. Jones said, "Well, I don't know anything about children, but they were all massacred."

Commenting on the roughhouse later, Dr. Jones told me that

in order for Bobby to like him, Bobby has to beat him up, and that if Bobby doesn't have a chance to do this he falls into a depression. Dr. Jones apologized for not having these sessions every day, saying, "Sometimes when I get home from the office, I'm just too tired and I shouldn't do that sort of thing when I don't enjoy it." I said, "And of course the kids would know right away that you didn't enjoy it."

In the intake interview Dr. Jones had told me that in these roughhouses he has to make believe he is hitting back at Bobby so that Bobby will feel he has a right to hit his father—to really resent him and beat him up. When Bobby sees he can do that, says Dr. Jones, Bobby feels everything is well between them. Since Bobby is "almost freakishly strong," he really hurts, but, says Dr. Jones, since fighting his father physically is a way of coping with his authority, it is very important that Bobby feel he can do it with impunity. But Dr. Jones did threaten to spank Bobby, he said, when the boy came crying to him after some trouble he had had with some children. So Bobby turned around and "licked" one of them, and this has been "a source of wonderment and power" to Bobby. I was able to witness something of the consequences of this training in violence:

As soon as Dr. Jones came home, Bobby gave an account of having beaten someone up. Dr. Jones said, "Well, you didn't do it to Billy, did you, because Billy is so small?" And Bobby said no, he did it to somebody else who is bigger, and his father said, "Well, that's good." In other words, the child is rewarded for having beaten somebody up, even though he may well have done it in fantasy only. The boy he mentioned is nine years old, whereas Bobby is only seven.

Since in contemporary American culture fathers are not semisacred figures any more, and since the amalgam of violence-affection belongs to our masculine culture, we are used to the idea that father and sons will "rough it up a bit" and therefore the roughhouse pattern does not seem bizarre. In this way, and (in the Jones family) with the added endorsement of psychiatric theory used by Dr. Jones to suit himself, the roughhouses become ceremonial expressions of mutual affection and hostility. When Dr. Jones says that Bobby has to attack him to see if things are well between them, he means that Bobby has to do it to find out whether Dr. Jones can be trusted, and Dr. Jones lets his children attack him so he can show that he trusts them. In proof of his acceptance of their blows, Dr. Jones lies down with the boys and continues the pursuit of violence through a fantasy tale of death. Love and death have come together in this nursery!

(In the roughhouse, violence—one factor that separates Dr. and Mrs. Jones—is detached from anger and unites Dr. Jones and his sons. Thus once more we see that what creates conflict in one relationship in a family may create its opposite in another.)

What is the difference between putting the boys to bed with a tale of death and putting the baby to sleep with a song of death? People who enjoy violence will entertain their young with songs and stories of it. We know this from the ethnographies of primitive people, and the *Iliad*, one of the bloodiest stories on record in our cultural tradition, was used to teach Greek children. Dr. Jones said the kids like stories with a lot of violence best and don't like stories with happy endings—they scoff at them. His wife disagreed and mentioned one they liked very much, about a little boy whose mother was a witch, but who, transformed by magic, became a very nice person. Dr. Jones says Bobby likes spooky stories. He will ask, "Daddy, frighten me!" and from under the covers, will say, "Oh, I'm so scared I have goose pimples!" On the second day, when the boys were ready for bed, they asked me to tell them a story, so I turned out the light in their room and sat down on the floor by Bobby's bed, one kid pressed close on either side of me, both sucking their thumb, and I told a story about a farm boy who was able to help his parents develop better crops. The kids listened attentively and quietly, and when it was all over, said several times that they enjoyed the story very much. On another occasion I made up a story about a boy who visited the kingdom of the fishes, and later, one about an Eskimo boy who was taken to a strange village by a reindeer. All of these were nonviolent and relatively anxiety-free stories. The kids seemed to enjoy them, and they even asked for a repeat of the story about the little boy in the kingdom of the fishes. After the story about the Eskimo, Bobby told "Goldilocks and the Three Bears" very clearly.

Since the kids can enjoy nonviolent stories, I assume that interest in violent ones comes to them not only from the atmosphere of violence in the culture as a whole but also from their father's preoccupation with violence and danger. Dr. Jones teaches his boys to love violence and danger; his wife teaches Harriet to love quietness. Each child, in the shadow of his parents, learns a particular way of perceiving the world and human relations.

Institutionalized Violence

Culture ritualizes arrivals and departures. The boys marked their father's arrivals with mock warfare, and his departures with attempted imprisonment. I have half a dozen records of this; here are some samples:

When Daddy returned, the boys became very animated and flocked around him, and Harriet stood up in her crib and crowed. Violence ensued between Dr. Jones and Bobby as soon as Daddy appeared, for they threw pillows at each other, but Dr. Jones told Bobby to calm down. Bobby did not calm down before he had taken several hefty smacks at his father.

. . .

When Dr. Jones came breezing in from the office he was, of course, attacked by the boys. The loaf of bread he was carrying was snatched out of his hands by Jackie, and he yelled to him not to crush it. He came into the kitchen and kissed his wife tenderly and she responded. At the lunch table he gruffly called Bobby and Jackie to order. Mrs. Jones fixed Dr. Jones's lunch but she did not eat while we were there. After rushing through lunch, he and I left precipitately, with the boys trailing after him and Dr. Jones telling them to let go of him. This was done in a rather brusque but cheerful way.

. . .

When Dr. Jones came home he nuzzled all the children briefly. He was the typical busy father: he comes home breathing heavily, hoping to eat fast and get back to the office.

He was in a great hurry to get away, so when the children dashed after him to follow him as he left the house, their mother called after them, "Don't torture Daddy; you can watch him from the window."

Once in a while, the encouragement of violence boomerangs:

Dr. Jones had started up the stairs when I heard him suddenly yell sharply at one of the boys, "I told you not to do that!" I went upstairs to find out what had happened, and discovered that Dr. Jones's glasses had been knocked off and broken by a pillow thrown by Jackie. Jackie was lying on the sofa, eyes closed, sucking his thumb, but actually he had retreated into that curled-up position from his father's anger. Then Dr. Jones picked him up, carried him to bed and told him to stay there. Jackie burst into tears and cried inconsolably until his mother went in and bent over him. She told him he had done wrong, that he had been told repeatedly not to do what he had done. She knelt beside him on the floor speaking gently. Dr. Jones was quite annoyed but did not rant or storm about the house, nor was Jackie slapped.

Since attacking father is an expression of love, it must be difficult for the children to make a distinction between when to attack and when not. Hitting their father with a pillow as he comes up the stairs is usually rewarded, because he shows that he is pleased. Since his parents' explanation of his fault could not make sense to Jackie, there is a contradiction here between past experience (i.e., having love and fun with pillow heaving) and the scolding. All that Jackie might remember from his parents' explanations is that although he may batter his father, he must be careful not to break his glasses. As a matter of fact, Dr. Jones removes them for roughhouse.

Extension of Destructive Impulses

The boys' violence extends to children outside the family, but the association between violence and affection may be expressed in relationships with a friendly adult male outsider also. I give examples from the extensive record:

The first thing Bobby mentioned to me when he came home from playing with the neighbors was how he had beaten up one of the boys over there, showing me with his fists what he had done and saying *"Pow–wow–wow"* in time to the movement of his fists. Jackie imitated him, saying he had done the same thing.

. . .

When the boys came home from playing with their friend I was upstairs, and Jackie immediately wanted to wrestle with me. He tried, in a playful, smiling way, to drag me down on the floor, and I got down. I wasn't clear about what he wanted to do until Bobby came along and said, "He wants to wrestle with you." I said, "I'd rather not wrestle," or something like that. Then Bobby wanted to "fight" with me and began to swing his fists at my hands and arms, but I said, "I'm not the fighting kind of guy." So the kids quieted down without any manifest discomfort.

Bobby asked me whether I would play a game, and I said I would. When I asked what game he would like to play he said, "I'll be a prisoner and you try to catch me." So he was a prisoner a couple of times and I caught him; then I was a prisoner and he shot me. After we played escaped convict for a while and I shot Bobby and he shot me, I suggested we play hide-and-go-seek. The kids did not know it, but quickly understood when I explained.

Since little boys often act out destructive fantasies in play and see much violence on TV, it would be absurd to say that Bobby and Jackie get this kind of thing from playing with their father. Rather, encounters with him reinforce the play pattern they find in the outer world.

Escaping from prison is a common game among children in our culture, and is played spontaneously even in nursery school.* Since a prisoner is a person captured, manacled, tried, found guilty and deprived of liberty, and since escape flouts persecutors and retrieves freedom, jailbreak is a game of choice for children, the perfect abreaction of their daily experience with adults. In this context, freedom is perceived as precarious, and guilt and punishment as constant probabilities. The immanence of freedom, the ex-

* See my "Death, Fear and Climax in Nursery School Play" (*loc. cit.*).

perience of freedom as the inevitable environment of life, is thus already problematic to childhood in our culture; it is acted out in the play escapes of children, and in the dreams of adults.

Because an important quality in the relationship between Dr. Jones and his sons is tender violence, I infer that the relationship expresses Dr. Jones's *dread of tenderness.* Also, since Dr. Jones is afraid of closeness and since unadulterated tenderness is impossible for him, he must inhibit it in the boys. Yet we see that Dr. Jones yearns for his children. Sometimes he seems able to meet tenderness directly, as when he holds Harriet's forehead to his own or sings her to sleep, but even this is encumbered by ambiguities, like his distrust of her smile, or by his singing her to sleep with "Dolin Corie."

When Dr. Jones enters, space erupts: objects hurtle through space, children fling themselves at him, objects crash and sometimes break. Time, which hung empty, suddenly becomes crowded with events that burst like rockets on Dr. Jones and all around him, as the boys run from their room and "mow him down" on the stairs and the baby stands up in her crib and crows. Time, space, motion, objects and children are activated, and violence is almost always there as tenderness presents itself, armored for collision—as violence presents itself for affectionate embrace. The following captures the tension:

When we had pushed our chairs back from the supper table, the boys came zooming into the room, and Bobby threw himself on his father's lap and Jackie on his father's lap behind Bobby. They did not go near their mother. There was certainly a great deal of climbing on Dr. Jones today—much more than on his wife, although there was a period after dinner when she had Jackie on her lap while Bobby was on his father's. It may very well be that one of the reasons why the boys are so hot after their father on a Sunday is because this is really the only day they can have him; the rest of the week he is busy. But this climbing on their daddy and his holding them on his lap is one of the numerous instances throughout this day when he fondled the kids. Mrs. Jones had Harriet on her lap much more than she had the boys.

Only a father who is loved and trusted can get such receptions.

Father as Authority

Western culture debates the issue of authority nowadays because authority is losing its basis, as the authority of God, parents and the state are called in question by man's corroding disappointment—and his ensuing sense of nothingness—in which he comes to understand more and more that control is exercised not for his but for somebody else's benefit. Loss of the ideological and emotional foundations of authority produces the often hypocritical "I am doing this for your own good," and this loss is caused by the destruction of the foundation of social life—mutuality of goals and work. Perhaps one should not say "authority," but rather "traditional authority," for what is losing its basis is not so much authority as old authority. Everywhere in the contemporary world the issue is the same, the use of control against the subject in the interest of the authority.

As "imp of fun," Dr. Jones is the center of a whirwind of fun, and his discipline is relatively mild. Just the reverse could be the case: a father's pleasures with his children could be minor but his discipline a major experience—harsh and shattering. Dr. Jones's disciplinary voice is harsh, but not his discipline. As a partner in play he is relatively passive, while the boys hurl themselves affectionately upon him. In imposing impulse restraints, however, he is the active one. So, in loving action Dr. Jones permits himself to be an object, while in discipline the children are his object. Obviously he could actively have made them the object of his affection as well as the object of his discipline. In love, he belongs to that large class of people, often referred to as narcissistic, who let others come to them.

The boys readily accepted their father's control; they were not spanked while I was there, and I believe that their acquiescence was the complement of mutual affection and respect. I now review the observations on discipline:

When Bobby and Jackie came upstairs and saw Dr. Jones seated at the table in his shorts with no shirt on, they said, "Daddy, you're naked as a pig; drink wee-wee and eat poo." Dr. Jones called Bobby in and told him this was no way to talk and that if his friends' parents heard him talk this way, they might not allow him to play with their children. Bobby started to walk away, but Dr. Jones said, "Did you hear that?" and Bobby said, "Yeah," and continued to walk away.

Bobby's teasing Jackie eventually brought Bobby into a clash with Dr. Jones. When his father came home, Jackie came weeping into the kitchen, where Dr. and Mrs. Jones and I were seated, and complained that Bobby had either teased or hit him. In a loud, gruff voice Dr. Jones called to Bobby to come in, and demanded to know what he had done. Bobby said he had hit Jackie because he had asked Jackie for something and Jackie did not know where it was. As Dr. Jones was bawling Bobby out, Bobby started to walk away but his father called him back and asked what he meant by going away like that.

I was reading an interesting letter to Dr. and Mrs. Jones which I had received from a student of mine who had gone abroad. Bobby and Jackie tried to inject themselves into the situations, but were silenced by Dr. Jones. Jackie became more insistent than Bobby and was yelled at by his father and told that if he didn't stop he could go to his room. This stopped him, but about half a minute later he walked off in a huff and did not appear again until the rest of the family was halfway through lunch. He made his appearance moving very slowly and cautiously along the corridor toward the kitchen and hiding in the corner of the wall between the hallway and the kitchen. Everybody saw him but pretended not to, except Bobby, who kept calling everybody's attention to him until his father growled and told him to stop teasing his brother, adding, "If Jackie doesn't want to be seen, we won't see him." Jackie was very giggly. At last, after staying out there in the corridor for quite some time with nobody paying any attention to him, Jackie came into the kitchen, sat down in his chair and had lunch. Meanwhile the baby was sitting in her highchair quietly eating.

The kids asked for ice and Bobby got into his chair and received a piece, and Dr. Jones put a piece in a glass for Jackie and set it at Jackie's place. Jackie wanted his father to hand it to him, but he refused. Finally Dr. Jones said, "If you don't take it I'll throw it away," but Jackie would still not come and get it, so Dr. Jones turned around and picked Jackie up and brought him over to the table and handed him the glass. This was done in a jocular way.

As we left the house to go up on the mountain, Bobby and Jackie said they wanted Cokes. But Dr. Jones said we couldn't stop for Cokes because we were in too much of a hurry. I had the definite impression that hurry had nothing to do with it. This reminds me that Jackie asked for a drink of orange juice when we were in the house, and that Dr. Jones at first said no but that his wife said it was all right to give him some, so Dr. Jones did. Dr. Jones's objection to giving Jackie orange juice at that time was that orange juice is for breakfast.

Dr. Jones's discipline is mild and his tenderness is sometimes violent. In loving his children, he has a dread of tenderness, and disciplining them, he shuns violence. Thus, while his form of tenderness may hold his children at arm's length at times, his discipline does not impede his boys' approach to him. There seemed no aftermath of these mild expressions of paternal authority, and even Dr. Jones's outburst when Jackie broke his glasses was not serious, considering what might have happened with a different kind of father.

In disciplining the boys, Dr. Jones often appears more concerned with their social behavior than with his own status. Even when the boys say, "Daddy, you're naked as a pig; drink wee-wee and eat poo," Dr. Jones appears to care more about preventing trouble with other people than with defending his own image. The only time he seems a little worried about this is when Bobby starts to walk away as he tells him not to use bad language. As a matter of fact, in most of the examples just reviewed Dr. Jones is protecting as well as controlling. No incident becomes a battle—*only love can be a battle*, as in a roughhouse. When disciplined, the children never make a fuss, shriek or run away, and though speaking as a determined father who is sure of himself, Dr. Jones never treats his boys with contempt. It is probably this attitude, united to mutual affection, and the violent but affectionate play that inhibit the development of tantrums and shouting, and make the boys—particularly Bobby—so remarkably acquiescent to their father.

The following is another illustration of Dr. Jones's brand of authority:

Bobby was particularly noisy. He got his parents rather annoyed by pouring milk on his ear of corn to cool it off. This somewhat upset his mother. Bobby was so boisterous that his father threatened to ask him to leave the table unless he quieted down, and as usual Bobby obeyed. He made faces at his father, wrinkling his nose and his forehead, and Dr. Jones said, "Oh, you're a chipmunk."

Several times Bobby stood up on his chair and several times he curled up on it while eating. He ate mainly with his hands. At the other end of the table was Jackie, who is quieter but eats in more or less the same way.

It is a comfortable table, everybody being at ease. There is no effort to sit on the kids. When they seem to get out of hand, their father takes a strong stand and Bobby quiets down. At last, when everything had been eaten except dessert, the apple pie was brought out of the refrigerator and the kids immediately went into a frantic tizzy about the size of the pieces of pie they wanted. They screamed and screamed for large pieces until I was deafened. Bobby was particularly raucous and at last had to be quieted by his father in a severe voice. Dr. Jones then gave Bobby a very large piece—larger than anybody else's. When Jackie was asked how large a piece he wanted he indicated with his hands and arms that he wanted a piece twice the size of the pie. He did get a good slice. When Dr. Jones handed Bobby his piece he said, "You might have a bad dream," but this did not faze Bobby, who downed the piece very quickly.

When Bobby finished he clamored for brownies, but one of his parents said, "The apple pie is your dessert, and that's all there is to it."

As we watch the Jones children at table, we are struck by what the parents let pass and what upsets them. The only time Mrs. Jones becomes visibly annoyed is when Bobby pours milk on his corn, and Dr. Jones objects to extreme boisterousness and to Bobby's pouring milk on his corn, but not to his curling up or standing in his chair, or to his screaming for pie. As a matter of fact, this is rewarded by giving Bobby the biggest piece. Dr. Jones exerts authority here only when the noise gets too much for him; in this incident he cares less about teaching the boys what would protect them from social criticism than about his own peace and quiet. Since Dr. Jones can stand a great deal of noise and wild jumping around, however, the boys push the limits.

The parents can tolerate a great deal of disorder because they have no particular commitment to order, and it causes Mrs. Jones less anxiety to let things slide than to try to interfere. Dr. Jones's anger is mild and he never seems to feel personally challenged by misbehavior, nor does he sulk or bear a grudge. Through all his relations with his children, however, one gets the impression that because he has a dread of trust, Dr. Jones can never let down his guard.

The Relationship between Dr. Jones and Bobby

METAMORPHOSIS

I have presented a great deal of material that bears on the relationship between Dr. Jones and Bobby, but since Jackie was always present and since Dr. Jones seemed occupied with both boys at once, observations in which Bobby and his father are concentrating on each other help to delineate the relationship between the two of them more sharply.

(First day.) While Bobby was playing with the toy (that I had brought him) Dr. Jones repeatedly asked him to tell him what he was making. Bobby was repeatedly unable to answer or repeatedly did not answer because, so it seemed to me, he really didn't know what he was making; he was just putting things together. Bobby had made a sort of cart, and Dr. Jones said, "That looks just like a tumbril," which went completely over Bobby's head and he asked, "What's a tumbril?" Dr. Jones didn't answer. By asking Bobby what the thing was, and then saying what Bobby's toy looked like, Dr. Jones seemed to keep pushing the kid. At one point Dr. Jones said, "Oh, I can't figure out what you've done," and Bobby said, rather testily, "Don't you think that I can figure it out?" This indicates also the kind of give-and-take between Bobby and his father. Bobby often talks rather abruptly to his father in what seems to me a typical middle-class way. Jackie, who is only three, seems to me to be still too vague and foggy to be able to take the kind of stand Bobby does.

My impression of what was going on here is that Dr. Jones feels challenged to be able to guess what Bobby is doing, and defeated when he cannot. He seems to want Bobby to tell him he has guessed right, but Bobby takes it to mean that his father thinks he doesn't know what he is doing. Thus the situation has become a competitive one for both of them.

What does Dr. Jones think he is doing when he says, "That looks just like a tumbril," but doesn't answer when the boy asks him, "What's a tumbril?" Well, he has at the least said something bizarrely incomprehensible and out of reach of a seven-year-old child and then fails to answer when asked to explain. I have a similar instance from the sixth day:

Last night at supper, when Bobby and his father got into some sort of an argument, his father said, "That's *a posteriori*, Bobby."

Such language puts the father out of reach; perhaps it makes him appear possessed of a mysterious lingo, quite beyond the child's powers of comprehension. For Bobby to understand him he would have to be well on in college, but he is only a seven-year-old. Since Dr. Jones is communicating with a somebody who isn't there, a somebody who cannot decode the signals he is sending, let us call this *phantom communication*. At the same time, Dr. Jones has metamorphosed Bobby—made him into a college boy. There is a kind of transient illusion about Bobby, and perhaps about himself. Even if Dr. Jones was doing it all just in order to impress me, the way he tries to impress me is significant.

There is nothing bizarre in the process itself: the appearance of an outsider on the scene always transforms the relationship between parent and child. Suddenly the child's qualities—good or bad—become magnified and exquisitely visible. Latent antagonisms, idealizations, yearnings and hopes may thrust to the surface, feelings parent and child have barely acknowledged emerge, and a certain artificiality may even appear and subside when the outsider has gone. This sudden eruption of latent feeling is something all parents experience: the "audience effect," transient though it may be, reveals the parent to himself, reveals parent and child to each other and reveals both of them to an observer.

When Dr. Jones creates the "archaeological expedition," when in the presence of Bobby he leaps from rock to rock in the thickening dusk, and now, with these linguistic mystifications, Dr. Jones is saying something about Bobby, about himself and about his relationship to Bobby. He is pushing Bobby beyond his Bobbyself, he is trying to go beyond himself and he is presenting himself to Bobby as a father making unrealistic demands—on his child and on himself.

In the next incident Bobby is trying to be just a little boy:

When Bobby finished eating he came around and crawled on his father, but before he crawled he began to whine, and his father said, "What's that?" and Bobby stopped whining. Dr. Jones objects very much to Bobby's frequent whining.

I think Bobby is whining like a little kid who is being pushed too hard to grow up, to be masculine and to be tough, and who has cut himself off from his mother too soon.

The relationship between Dr. Jones and Bobby is tender, within the limits permitted by the mixture of tenderness and violence, a kind of norm established for the Jones family culture by Dr. Jones. It is tender within the limits established by the powerful survival drive of Bobby and his father. It seems to me that pushing Bobby intellectually is related to the roughhouse: in the latter, father and son compete physically; in the former, Dr. Jones is beginning to push his son to compete intellectually. Bobby is fond of his father: he likes to fight him and crawl on him, and he usually responds quickly to his father's growling, nonviolent discipline. Bobby is old enough and strong enough and sufficiently detached from his mother to develop a strong attachment for his father, and Dr. Jones has found a way of loving and trusting his son. But Jackie is too young yet; too timid, too close to being a baby, to really have come within his father's orbit. That is why, although my notebooks contain seventeen notations of Bobby alone with his father, I have only six of Jackie with him; and that is why, although I have eighteen notations of Jackie with his mother, I have only ten of Bobby with her.

I think that Dr. Jones has to have a certain type of interaction with a child before he can really trust him. Their meetings have to be collisions violent enough to make Dr. Jones feel the interaction, whether at the physical or emotional level—as in an argument. Dr. Jones has to be able to feel his son fighting back. At seven years of age, after assiduous training, Bobby is able to *give* this to his father. By this time he thinks he wants it himself; yet in contact with me, he was quite ready to settle for a gentler type of relationship with a man.

The Relationship between Mrs. Jones and Bobby

It is impossible to examine this relationship without including Jackie, because he is often present when Bobby and his mother are, and because much of what happens between his mother and Bobby is a result of what Bobby does to Jackie. This will be used to analyze the relationship between Bobby and his mother, and the study of the relationship between Jackie and Mrs. Jones will appear in the next section.

Insult and Provocation

Bobby shouted "bosom" at his mother and threatened to "sock" her in the bosom for not getting him ice when he wanted it. She said nothing when he threatened to hit her. Once when she, Bobby and Jackie were all together in the bathroom, Bobby was talking a lot about bosoms and she remonstrated gently.

Bobby said to her, "You are drinking wee-wee and eating poo," but she paid no attention.

I mentioned an article to Mrs. Jones which I had read in the paper about parents' being afraid their children don't love them, and she said she thinks that sometimes she is afraid too, especially in the case of Bobby, because Bobby has said, "I don't like you," or "I hate you." I then said, "Yes, he has threatened to hit you too," and she said yes and that is all she said.

After his father had gone Bobby made a curious and ingenious arrangement out of four strings of the Venetian blind. Suddenly he let go and the blind fell with a clatter but did not become dislodged. Mrs. Jones scolded Bobby briefly.

While we were in the kitchen Bobby again made what he called a "patrol house" by tying the strings of three Venetian blinds to the arm of a chair. Mrs. Jones remonstrated, pointing out that he was tearing the cords. He did not give up easily, and she had to insist.

⋅ ⋅ ⋅

When we got back from church Mrs. Jones went into the bedroom to change her clothes. Bobby was in the room with her and kept calling out to me, "Look, my mother is naked as a pig," and all she did was remonstrate.

⋅ ⋅ ⋅

I am beginning to see now what the relationship between Bobby and his mother must be. Bobby is the incarnation of his father's earlier extreme violence and she is afraid to come to grips with Bobby because she dreads him as the embodiment of his father's evil genius. When she is trying to get Bobby to do something, her approach is supplication, which becomes threat if he does not consent. When Bobby sat down to lunch he knocked over his milk and it spilled on the floor. His mother started to wipe it up and I said, "Maybe you could get Bobby to wipe it up." She said, "That's a good idea," and asked Bobby, but he refused. At last he said, "Go ahead and spank me." She asked, "Do you want me to spank you?" He said again, "Yes, go ahead and spank me." She said, "Well, I will if you don't wipe it up," so he slowly got off the chair and did something in the direction of wiping. Actually he didn't do very much of it; his mother did it.

During lunch Bobby provoked his mother by again referring to bosoms. He kept saying "bosoms, bosoms, bosoms," and at one time said, "I'll hit you in the bosom." Mrs. Jones glared at him. Jackie took up the cry of "bosoms" too.

After a while Bobby came home. He had a rubber dagger in his hand. As soon as he came near his mother he poked it in her face and almost in her eye. She remonstrated crossly.

When his mother tried to stop him from making his patrol house today he called her "stinky," ordered her out of the room and delivered himself of other insulting remarks, to which she responded with looks only. She said to me, "I suppose it will get much worse before it gets better."

In the course of the struggle over the patrol house Mrs. Jones made a number of insulting remarks to Bobby. Of these I remember only "dirty face" and "pig." I would characterize the interaction between Bobby and his mother as one of rather intense struggle accompanied by insulting remarks and other kinds of hostile communication. On top of all this, out of the window will come Mrs. Jones's voice asking Bobby to do something, and of course he won't. For example, she wanted him to bring the cartons of milk upstairs but he did not do it, though she asked him in a very sweet voice.

If I hadn't been there, things might have been much worse, perhaps; Bobby might have been taking advantage of his mother's unwillingness to make a scene before a stranger in order to be nasty. However that may be, one could not say that mother and son are exactly fond of each other, or that the relationship is tranquil. In a typically guarded way, Mrs. Jones brought out her real feelings about Bobby when she told me she was afraid that maybe he didn't love her. From his mother, Bobby wants only material things and angry responses to his provocations, and he has learned what provokes her most: yelling "bosom," fooling with the Venetian blinds and tormenting Jackie. Mrs. Jones dreads Bobby; although she responds with insults to his contempt, she tends, on the whole, to tread softly when dealing with him; for the most part she is inclined to let him go his way. Thus her general tendency to be careless and underprotective is supported by estrangement.

Enforcing the Law

What can happen when Mrs. Jones takes a strong stand is illustrated by the following:

Mrs. Jones wanted to listen to the Secretary of State discuss foreign affairs on TV. The kids had been watching TV all afternoon, but when she entered the living room to turn to the program she wanted, she met with the wild and determined resistance of Bobby, who finally rolled over on the floor screaming. She became angry and made him go into the boys' room with her. She sat on the bed and threatened to spank him if he didn't stop. He lay down and said, "You stink, you stink," but she merely remonstrated mildly with him. She also said something like, "After all, you see TV all the time; I'm asking for it only for a short time," all in a reasonable but rather tense tone. Several times he tried to walk out of the room, saying harsh things as he went, but she called him back and he returned under threat of being closed in the room. After she had leveled off, she took up the same problem with Jackie, who proceeded to dissolve into baby howls. She told him that if he didn't stop she'd close him in the room, and he stopped after a while. I then said to her, "That was some time" (meaning that was some time she had with the kids), and she said, "Oh, what did the Secretary say?" as if I were referring to the program. It seemed to me that what she had been through was serious enough to have carried over for a short time at least, but she certainly acted as if she had put the whole thing out of her mind by the time she returned to the kitchen.

In studying the collisions between the boys and their parents, one is impressed by the boys' capacity to stop their "misbehavior" and to yield eventually. Bobby could have rushed from his room to the TV set and fought to defend it, and he didn't have to go into his room at all, but could have run into another room or down the stairs and out of the house. Mrs. Jones's reasonableness is impressive too, and she does not pile up punishments: although she makes Bobby go into his room, she does not hit him or yell at him for saying he stinks. The two have inner controls that prevent conflicts from becoming disorganizing.

We know Mrs. Jones believes it is not respectable to show anger, especially in front of an audience, whether strangers or her own children. Yet Bobby, by "cutting at the soft spots"—to use her phrase to describe her backlash at her husband—provokes her to anger, which she tries to conceal but which shows in her eyes. Ultimately she retaliates by insulting him. Whatever she may wish to do in front of an observer; however she may wish to appear to me, the *onslaught of the impulses of her child compel her to reveal her true feelings.*

"Bosom," Bobby's most telling weapon, must have been employed many times before and its use rewarded by his mother's anger, otherwise he would not have tried it again. Furthermore, it must never have been radically interdicted, and hence must have achieved a kind of legitimacy. In many families there are forms of childish insult that always anger adults, but continue to be used because the child is not punished severely enough to make him stop; the insult is half condoned in order that nothing worse will happen. *In all societies the breaking of some rules is ignored or condoned in order to avoid more serious disturbance, or to let the agent of enforcement save face.* This is the basis for hidden legitimacy. In the Trobriand Islands a chief usually ignores his wives' adultery because it would be impossible to enforce abstinence, especially since by having many wives, he deprives younger men. In general, adultery flourishes there because it would cause uproar and suicide to try to prevent it.

The fight of this mother with this little boy opens up the whole problem of law enforcement, for the Battle of the TV set, fought in countless homes, involves some conception of law. Whether it is a mother quarreling with her child over a monster trivium, or whether it is a street fight, a teen-ager struggling for his rights aganst his parents, or even a tribal chief faced with the adultery of a wife, there is a generalization about law enforcement that applies in all cases. The probability that any agency (parent, teacher, police, tribal chief, etc.) will attempt to enforce a rule or law is tied up with the dimensions and legitimacy of its power, its expectation that things will be better or worse if it acts, and with the risk of losing face if it fails. In the case of parents, there is the special problem of losing love.

Anybody who thinks of enforcing a law may become inactive or dilatory, or he may act impulsively as he balances one factor against the other and tries to decide what to do. Any parent who ever tried to make his child do something has run some or all of the following questions through his head: "Do I really have the strength to make him do it?" "Do I have the right to make him do it?" "Will things be better if I make him do it, or is it better to leave him alone?" "If I make him do this, won't he get even worse later on?" "Is he going to make me look ridiculous?" "Will he hate me?" There is no place in the world where such questions are not central to the issue of law enforcement—from making Willie go to bed to stopping a political demonstration.*

In the light of all this, there is little likelihood that Mrs. Jones will impose her wishes on Bobby. She may question whether she really has a right to object to his insulting her; she has little physical power, may even question her right to use it; and she probably does not expect matters to be better after a run-in. Although she feels he does not love her now, there is still a chance she may recover his love, and she fears running the risk of its irrevocable loss. Furthermore, there is always the danger of losing face.

When Mrs. Jones wants to hear what the Secretary has to say—a matter of little importance in her life—she exerts all her power, but when Bobby

---

* I am aware that this is a very inadequate discussion of what determines how laws are proposed and passed. Sometimes laws come into existence in the face of the absurd and merely create new problems; they cannot be enforced but efforts are constantly made to do so. Laws against intoxicants, drugs and certain political parties are good examples. Given a weak political structure, all laws become absurd; only sporadic efforts are made to enforce them, only people who are politically weak are punished for disobeying, etc. The formulation I have given above is intended to show that the disciplinary activities of Mrs. Jones do not express merely the relationship between a mother and child in a corner of the world but are part of a general human problem.

insults her, the most he gets is a glare. She behaves as if it were unimportant, and/or she had no power, and as if, were she to act, extreme disruptive behavior would result, and she would lose face and love. I am inclined to think she is right; and I believe that is why she was more ready to fight over the TV set than over the insults. Since Bobby's struggle over television is not a clear and unmistakable symptom of a bad relationship, Mrs. Jones is willing to fight too, for the underlying misery of their conflict is less likely to be revealed in a quarrel over television than in one over insult. Thus by choosing to do battle over an issue that is remote from the real one, Mrs. Jones is doing the same thing with Bobby as she and her husband do with each other.

Hostility, distrust and contempt play an overshadowing role in the relationship. Since, however, Mrs. Jones cannot accept quarreling as a way of expressing her hostility, and since she is afraid of his outbursts, she has further reason to avoid getting into a scrape with him. Quarreling is often a way of driving a person into a role, but since Mrs. Jones avoids it by letting Bobby do very much as he pleases, he drifts. Let us call this phenomenon *role drift*. Bobby, however, may not be entirely comfortable this way, for he asked his mother to spank him if he did not wipe up the spilled milk.

Because of their mutual hostility and contempt, the possibility that the two of them could have arrived at an amicable solution of the TV problem is remote; and since, after the encounter—as a matter of fact, after all collisions between Bobby and his mother—there was no attempt at reconciliation, they just drifted apart. Mrs. Jones tries to avoid or lessen the pain of these confrontations by appearing not to be seriously involved, but I suspect that her sugariness, her half-hearted protests, then angry looks and insults, and finally her determination in the tempest-in-a-tea-pot war over the TV set, express anxiety and a sense of failure. What an observer perceives is mutual estrangement of mother and son, and her feeling that the boy does not love her.

On some occasions an unwillingness to "make a scene" in front of me may have affected the way Mrs. Jones behaved with Bobby, but on the other hand his frequent resistance, his insults, his ordering her around and her forms of retaliation indicate weak maternal authority and a mutual indifference and even contempt.

Bobby's hostility to his mother also comes out in his attacks on his brother. This continuous torment drives Jackie and his mother closer together, and Bobby ends up being a kind of half orphan. This, in turn, pushes him closer to his father, consolidating the identification. Through this dialectic the personalities of the boys become polarized; Bobby's more and more in the direction of violence, independence and struggle for survival; Jackie's toward clinging and a stretched-out babyishness. Such is the dialectic of "individuation."

(After Jackie broke his father's glasses.) The period between giving the boys their dinner and Dr. Jones's return was chaotic. In the first place Jackie wouldn't eat. He gave all his ham to the dog and then demanded that his mother feed him, crying rather wildly. At last she did come and fed him a couple of mouthfuls and then went away. This occurred several times. Jackie and Harriet spilled their milk and I helped Mrs. Jones wipe it up. Harriet urinated in her high chair and I helped her wipe that up. Meanwhile, Bobby teased Jackie unmercifully, threaten-

ing to burn his Davy Crockett cap if he did not stop crying. This only made Jackie
cry more desperately, until Mrs. Jones came in and told Bobby to stop.

It was now about seven o'clock. Bobby and Jackie got into the tub with about
five inches of water and a lot of bubble bath. Jackie immediately began to scream
again. He had been screaming pretty continuously from the moment supper began and I attributed this partly to his upset over having broken his father's
glasses. However, according to Mrs. Jones, in the bathtub his screaming was
caused by Bobby's teasing. When I went into the bathroom Bobby was threatening to throw suds into Jackie's face, and he did. I wiped a bit of suds off one of
Jackie's eyes. Fortunately no suds got into them. Jackie rubbed his eyes against
my hand. Mrs. Jones came in and took Jackie out of the tub, first washing the
soap off with a small hose attached to the faucet. She dried him and put on his
pajamas. She was quite irritated with both boys. (I then washed off Bobby and
partially dried him, and he finished the job himself.)

When the TV viewing was finished, Jackie lay down on one of the easy chairs
and Bobby went and leaned over him. Very quickly Bobby was viciously pinching
Jackie's face and made him cry. So Jackie went in to his mother and she cuddled
him on her lap. She said nothing to Bobby. Jackie gets quite a bit of cuddling
and other solicitude on the basis of small injuries. For example, when we went
to look for arrowheads, Jackie scratched his knee superficially and sought comfort from the adults.

While Mrs. Jones and I were having supper we began to talk about teasing,
and she said that Bobby teases Jackie unmercifully and can always find a weak
spot. She told me that her sisters tried to tease her but that her mother overprotected her in not letting them do it.

In the next extract I give much more than Bobby's attack on Jackie because the record presents, within a very short time span, a broad sample of
one of Bobby's potentialities.

Bobby and Jackie were outside in front of the house with Mrs. Jones and me.
Bobby made a bow and shot an arrow directly into Jackie's face, just missing
the eye. When I gasped, Mrs. Jones noticed what had happened and sent Bobby
upstairs. As he started to go, he turned and said to his mother, "You come upstairs, too," but she replied, "You just go ahead." Bobby seemed completely un-
repentant. Just prior to shooting the arrow at Jackie, Bobby was also entranced
with a slingshot made of a piece of leather. He slung a couple of stones at us but
hit nobody. He had a small stick on the end of a string which he whirled around
and almost took my nose off. I told him to stop. He also threw stones, using just
a piece of string as a sling. Nobody got hurt. Bobby also lay on his back on the
lawn wrestling with the dog as he pulled on a rope which the dog held in its
teeth. Meanwhile Jackie was merely in evidence. At one point Bobby insisted that
I tie his hands behind his back. At first I refused, but when he insisted, I tied
his hands in such a way that although it would seem tight, it would be very easy
for him to free himself. Sure enough—Bobby held up the rope triumphantly,
showing me that he had escaped.

When we came in from out of doors Mrs. Jones wanted Bobby and Jackie to
take a bath. The bathtub stopper could not be found, but the boys had to get into
the tub together regardless. Bobby monopolized the rubber hose they generally
use for rinsing off and became completely absorbed in playing with the water instead of washing himself. Jackie, who was in the rear of the tub, tapped Bobby
and received a blow on the back that made him scream. Jackie rubbed soap on
Bobby's hair and called it a hairdo. Bobby then rubbed the soap on Jackie's head

hard enough to make him scream again.* The pattern of interaction between the boys consisted in Bobby's teasing and Jackie's crying out. (I have yet to see the friendly interchange between these children that was described to me by Dr. and Mrs. Jones.) At last Mrs. Jones came in rather irritated and washed Bobby and rinsed him off with the hose—all in a good mood. (This is another interesting thing about her—she can switch from anger to non-anger very rapidly; nothing seems to last.) When she got Bobby out of the tub he dried himself, and at her insistence put on his pajamas. But then he came back into the bathroom and teased Jackie, and his mother drove him out. Then she tried to wash Jackie. His unremitting, ear-piercing screams at last drove her to the point of threatening to slap him on the mouth, and she did.

When Mrs. Jones is together with the boys, one has a strong impression of anger and pain, and the predominant feeling seems negative—Bobby is hostile to Jackie and vice versa, and Bobby and Mrs. Jones are hostile to each other—but there is also something positive between Jackie and his mother as he runs to her from Bobby's beating and teasing. On the other hand, when the father is alone with the boys, matters are very different, for the relationship between the boys is suspended as they hurl themselves affectionately on their father. Here the feeling is positive, not only because Dr. Jones is open to both boys, but also because they have suspended their antagonism for the moment as they lose themselves in their father. And this is the fundamental issue between Bobby and Jackie—they either ignore each other or fight. Or, more accurately, Bobby teases or beats up his brother or ignores him. Mother is the catalyst that precipitates Jackie's torment; father holds it in suspension. When Bobby is told to, he stops abusing Jackie and bides his time. He has settled for brief, savage encounters, in which he can strike hard and withdraw before meeting with serious punishment from his parents. Bobby's skill in being able to perceive when he may lose, and his ability to sense that his mother is also afraid of defeat and therefore often unwilling to fight, protect him from seriously disturbing encounters with her. It is this sharp *vigilance for danger cues* that usually saves him from injuring himself when taking physical risks with his father. Courting danger, Bobby has become alert to its signs. He should make a good gambler or racing driver. One imagines that all his life he will enjoy the thrill of escape.

Jackie's narrow escape from the arrow in the eye illustrates the consequences of Mrs. Jones's inappropriate composure, for the arrow was the climax of a dangerous activity that had begun with the stick zooming through the air on the end of a string, then going on to slingshots and stones. Mrs. Jones's silent acquiescence in these tricks could only have encouraged her son to continue, and in view of the fact that she had not objected to Bobby's other dangerous play, one wonders whether Bobby really understood why he was being sent upstairs.

The chances of Mrs. Jones's intervening to protect Jackie against Bobby are small, considering that in her view, her mother overprotected her by defending her against her older sibling. Several days later Mrs. Jones again talked of how she felt about Bobby's tormenting Jackie:

* I do not imply that these actions of Bobby's were so painful as to make his brother cry out. Jackie was in such a state of continuous upset that he was constantly mobilized for screaming.

On the porch steps we talked about the differences between Jackie and Bobby, and Mrs. Jones said that the difference has always existed. She thinks it's principally because Bobby did not really have an older sibling to knock him around the way Bobby knocks Jackie around. Referring to Bobby's tormenting Jackie, she said she thinks it does Jackie a lot of good. She said also that Jackie gets upset when Bobby is not around.

And again on the following day:

Today Mrs. Jones asked me, "Are my children normal?" and I said that they certainly are, and asked her, "What do you think?" and she said, "I think they're too normal." When I asked her what she meant she said she thought they were too noisy and rough. She expects Harriet to be just as rough, nasty and noisy as the boys.

Confronted with this half-tamed Bobby, Mrs. Jones has tried to come to terms with him by assuming ferocity to be the norm in little boys; and in this view, preventing his tormenting her or Jackie would be illegitimate and even harmful. Meanwhile, since she still seems to harbor the hope that she has not lost Bobby's love, and since fear of the final loss of it may be impossible to face, she is willing to sacrifice Jackie to this hope. Thus Jackie's torment may be ransom for his mother's hope, and the magnitude of the pain she lets him endure is the precise measure of that hope.

Everywhere and at all times, people have sold out others in ransom for their hopes. A mother may let one child mistreat another in order to gain the love of the first, or she may allow her husband to mistreat a child in order to hold her husband's love. A child may be nasty to his mother to please his father, or a husband miserable to his wife to court a child. A politician sells the Negro down the river to hold the votes of his white constituents. The tendency to barter with people's misery as with goods, to bargain away the well-being of others in order to gain prestige, money, love or merely safety is an inherent potentiality of *Homo sapiens*.

Because Mrs. Jones's belief in "toughness" and her fear of losing Bobby's love interfere with her protective functions, Jackie must develop the feeling that his mother is not to be trusted. This is made even more likely by the fact that when Bobby torments his brother, sometimes Mrs. Jones, no longer able to tolerate Jackie's screaming, slaps Jackie on the mouth. Thus, in the dialectic interplay between Bobby's ferocity and his mother's wavering, *Jackie is punished for suffering too much*. It is like beating a wounded man because one cannot stand the sight of his blood. More realistically it is like punishing the Negro by denying him civil rights for being "an animal," when the reason for his social defects is precisely the fact that he has suffered for two centuries from being treated worse than an animal. Thus again there is reflected in this little family *a historic tendency of man-in-our-culture—to punish our fellows for the very faults that have been wrought in them by our own injustice, short-sightedness, confusion, hostility and fear.* The vicissitudes and sufferings of any family are but the reflex of biohistoric processes that shape—and punish—us all.

We defend ourselves against another's wretchedness by becoming annoyed with him. Yet Mrs. Jones did not slap Jackie until she was at her wits' end; this was the day Bobby shot an arrow at Jackie's eye, brought down the Venetian blind with a clatter and fought the Battle of the TV.

Such were the anxiety and hostility generated by Bobby that his mother ended up *reversing the actor*—blaming his brother instead of him. But the reversal was a double one, for she behaved not only as if Jackie were to blame for the screaming, but also as if she were the target of *Jackie's* abuse (his screaming) instead of Jackie's being the target of *Bobby's* abuse.

Thus, while Bobby may drive his brother to his mother, her exasperation and wavering prevent Jackie from becoming too close to her.

The Doctrines of Eating

I now take up another kind of situation in which the two boys are alone with their mother.

Dr. Jones had not yet come home for dinner. Mrs. Jones served Bobby fish sticks, green peas and corn on the cob. He took his milk and poured it all over the plate. First, however, he put the fish sticks on the corn. Everything was a mess. He then had his cup filled with milk again and squeezed a lemon wedge into it and drank it. He also poured milk on the table. He ate with his hands. His mother remonstrated against all this in the mildest way. As a matter of fact, she let most of it pass. Jackie imitated Bobby by putting a piece of lemon in his own glass of milk. Bobby squashed some peas on his corn, as if to give it green eyes, and he ate the corn that way. Jackie was not as bad as Bobby. After Bobby had drunk the milk with lemon, he asked his mother for another piece, got some water and squeezed the lemon into it. He got some sugar and salt, both of which he put on the lemon slice but not into the water until he had shoved the lemon into the water. He drank that. Jackie shoved his own hand into his glass of milk; his mother gently insisted that he take it out and at last he did.

While some may wish to see in this behavior an expression of Bobby's hostility to his mother and surmise that she tolerates it because she does not want to precipitate a showdown, there are other ways of looking at it. A good hypothesis to follow is that any human potentiality will come out if a person wants to express it and if the culture does not forbid it. While in many instances the "wants to" requires some explanation, in the case of table manners it seems obvious enough that reasonably imaginative children will do anything with their food if nobody interferes and if the food does not become inedible. This being the case, the behavior of a psychotic child who has not been able to learn how to eat can look just like the behavior of a nonpsychotic child who is imaginatively experimenting with eating while the adult does not insist on table manners (rules).

Considered in this light, Bobby's table manners need not be a way of annoying his mother, even though she does let him see she does not like what he is doing. It is not necessary to suppose that everything a child does that irritates his parent is done for that reason. Meanwhile, we must consider the possibility that Mrs. Jones is using Bobby's distortions against him. For example, after he has made a complete mess (from our point of view!) of his milk, giving him more lemon could only encourage him to continue his bizarre behavior, and thus help consolidate his mother's image of him as "pig," etc.

While in all cultures there is a certain amount of arbitrariness about eating rules, even in our culture they are, to some degree, founded on a logic inherent in the nature of utensils and food. I dub this "the logic of containers." For example, liquids have to be put in receptacles that have a form related mechanically to them so that they will be contained, and solids, since they will not escape so readily, often may be placed in receptacles of different forms. This is about as far as mechanics will carry us, perhaps. Beyond this lie the doctrines of table manners, which I have sketched in below.

1. *The doctrine of solids.* Certain classes of solids may be mixed together (like meatballs and spaghetti, for example), but others must be kept separate (like corn on the cob and peas).

2. *The doctrine of fluids and solids.* Certain fluids and solids may be put together (like noodles in soup), but other mixtures are taboo (like a piece of lemon in milk). On the other hand, even when certain contacts are permitted, they must occur according to rule. It is permitted, for example, to warm corn kernels in milk but not to pour milk over warm corn on the cob.

3. *The doctrine of fluids.* Some fluids may be mixed together, but mixing others is taboo. One may put milk, cream or liquor in coffee or tea, but not water or lemon juice in milk.

4. *The doctrine of the table.* It is taboo, whether serving or eating, in middle-class culture, to put food directly on the table rather than in a receptacle. One should not do this even with bread, and the taboo is never broken in polite society, although it is in impolite society. One might say that the measure of social status—or of the importance of the occasion—is the frequency with which food is placed directly on the table; the more often it is, the lower the status or the more casual the occasion. It is likely, for example, that even in polite society a bread platter may be forgone at a barbecue or picnic, and fruit placed right on the table. The more one puts food right down on the table at ordinary or formal mealtimes, the more one is flouting cultural regulations—and our deepest sentiments—about table behavior. To put one's bread on the table is, perhaps, pardonable, to do it with corn on the cob is outrageous, but to deliberately pour milk on it is unthinkable.

5. *The doctrine of bodily position.* Ordinarily in our culture, one "sits up straight at the table" ("Don't sit there slumped down, Billy!"). To stand up in one's chair while at table or to curl up in it is unthinkable for adults, however intimate they may be, and in middle-class homes, is impermissible even in children.

6. *The doctrine of communication.* This doctrine embraces the following: (a) What may be talked about. "Disagreeable" topics are taboo. (b) How loudly one may talk. In polite society voices should be muted. Only low people "scream at each other" at the table. (c) Who may talk. (d) What kind of sounds may be made. Usually only conversation is permitted. Whistling, belching, singing, etc., are taboo.

7. *The doctrine of quantity.* At all levels of society except the poorest, it is hoped that people will eat to their heart's content. Limits are set, however, on the amount of food that may be put on the plate at any one time. The rule is to ask for several helpings of food, not "pile it on" one's plate, for to do so suggests greediness.

The assemblage of doctrines constitutes a configuration of eating in our culture. The incident above shows how far Bobby has distorted table manners—and how far his parents let him go. Bobby is obviously "guilty of all the crimes in the book"—crimes against eating regulations. His "delinquencies" in this regard again raise the question of how far the perceptual system of the Jones children is distorted through being brought up by parents who have perceptual problems. There are two issues: (1) Do the parents perceive "wild" food behavior as inherently immoral—the attitude of many middle-class parents? (2) Do the parents see the connection between such behavior and social acceptance? The present data suggest negative answers to both questions. I conclude that Bobby's and Jackie's eating is one more evidence of their parents' lack of circumspection.

However, middle-class squeamishness should not blind us to the fact that *distortions are creations:* the ability to see everyday phenomena in new relationships is the essence of creativity. On the other hand, since it is also the essence of schizophrenia, there is a point where creativity and pathology resemble each other. This should not lead us astray.

Bobby, the Child Outside of Time

Bobby and his mother have almost reached a dead end. She is tormented by a combination of hostility to Bobby, hope of regaining his love, fear of his attacks, and contempt for him as a little pig. Bobby goes his unsmiling way; joyless, aloof from his mother, provoking her primarily through tormenting his brother, whom he has helped reduce to a screaming, dependent, beseeching, three-year-old infant. Bobby finds it easy to hurt others, and his emergence into his mother's awareness is often a demoniac cataclysm—as if Mephistopheles had leaped through the window and alighted on the floor, poised and menacing.*

Just as his mother searches out for attack the "weak spots" in his father's personality, Bobby has found weak spots in his mother's. We may count this also among the "gifts" of civilization—that having given us a self, it has taught us also how to find the vulnerable spots in others. Right now there is no visible way out for either Bobby or his mother; too miserable to tell the truth when she originally gave me the case history, she had to describe their relationship as good. Thus direct observation contradicts twelve hours of interview. Although Bobby appears to want nothing from his mother, except, perhaps, routine care, she wants him to love her, and this may be why she is not firmer in her discipline. Since, however, she lets Bobby go his way and makes little effort to shape his role, the task falls to the father. Bobby may want to get back to his mother's arms but he cannot find the route, and he is unable to express his yearning in a way his mother understands.

The relationship between these two is like Mrs. Jones's relationship with her husband, only much worse, for with Bobby there is not one moment of mutual enjoyment. Bobby is the incarnation of his father's worst characteristics during the first years of marriage, when the bond between husband

* My indebtedness for this image will be obvious to students of Søren Kierkegaard's *Concept of Dread*, trans. by Walter Lowrie (Princeton, N.J., Princeton U. Press, 1944).

and wife had reached the breaking point without breaking. Bobby's present personality is a caricature of his father's antagonism to his mother, but although the relationship between his father and mother has improved, Bobby's personality seems to have remained frozen. Thus in one sense it has outlived itself, for although the relationship between his parents is not a happy one, Bobby's fury does not have quite the function it once did, as an expression of his father's rage and disappointment. Yet Bobby still wages war against his mother. He is like those desperate Japanese soldiers who still held out in the jungles and mountains of the Pacific islands long after the end of World War II. The evolution of the family has rolled over Bobby. Like a Devonian fish swimming in the ocean deeps, he is marooned in the family's past.* Many a child is like this. He comes into his personality when it expresses the underlying tensions in the family; but though husband and wife may move on to a better relationship, the child remains frozen in the personality acquired in an earlier period. *He is a child outside of time.*

The Relationship between Mrs. Jones and Jackie

Jackie was sitting on the floor in the doorway to the kitchen polishing his father's shoes. He had the two shoes, a box of polish and a rag. He came to me to have me open the box of polish. He didn't know what to do after he had put the polish on, and when I pointed out that he had to have a clean rag to rub them with, his mother got up and got him a brush and rag and showed him how to do it. Then he went to his mother to show her the polished shoes. She complimented him several times, telling him what a good job he had done.

A struggle developed between Jackie and Harriet over the cover of the shoe polish, and there was squealing on both sides. Mrs. Jones paid relatively little attention. At one point Jackie took a toy away from Harriet and shoved it out of her reach. Mrs. Jones gave some mild attention to this. Such struggles are rare and exceedingly mild.

I never saw Bobby do any favor for anybody, but Jackie is helpful now and then. He helped Harriet escape from the playpen, he shines his father's shoes, and in the next incident he brings up the milk from the porch.

Mrs. Jones wanted Bobby to bring up the milk from downstairs but he would not do it, though she asked him to in a sugary voice. So Jackie went, making a special trip, and came up with the two cartons of milk under his arm. He was roundly praised for this by his mother. This was a signal for some insulting remarks to Jackie from Bobby.

Every time he helps his mother while Bobby refuses, Jackie moves closer to her by a factor of two, and Bobby drifts away that much, because while

---

* "The consequences of our actions grab us by the back of the neck, blithely disregarding the fact that we have meanwhile 'reformed.' " From Friedrich Nietzsche's *Beyond Good and Evil,* trans. by Marianne Cowan (Gateway Edition; Chicago, Regnery, 1955), p. 89.

Jackie gets closer by helping, Bobby loses ground by refusing. Since Bobby remains inflexibly hostile and Jackie acquiesces, Bobby has no destiny in this triangle but isolation. Furthermore, Jackie's helpfulness can only intensify Bobby's hostility to him; the more Jackie leans on his mother, the more his brother hates him. Pushing the geometric analogy to its logical conclusion, ultimately the triangle must become a straight line as Jackie and his mother blend. This polarizes the boys between masculinity (Bobby) and femininity (Jackie). This too is "individuation" and "identity choice."

Bobby hates Jackie so much that he tried to put out his eye. Thus, when unchecked, the dialectic of the relationship between these three drives Bobby to ever more serious attacks, and Jackie to dependency and babyishness. This is the point to which their mother's inappropriate composure, her underprotectiveness, her failure to reconstitute her quarrels with Bobby and her fear of him and hope for the return of his affection has caused the relationship between Bobby and Jackie to drift.

By shouting "bosom" at his mother, by distorting his table manners like Bobby and by joining him in the tantrum at the TV set, Jackie seems to be trying to come to terms with Bobby. But the risk of losing the tie with his mother is too great for Jackie to go very far in this direction. He is like a diplomat who calculates the chances of collision with one coalition if he flirts too openly with the other.

Bobby's enemies are his mother and Jackie. Jackie, however, seems at times inclined to attack his mother in order to get on Bobby's good side, and, perhaps, Mrs. Jones ignores Jackie's screams in order to court Bobby or at least in order not to antagonize him further. We may state this law of unstable coalition by saying that when an aggressor (Bobby) attacks two friends (Jackie and his mother), they may either intensify their bond or court the aggressor by attacking each other. The final outcome is determined by how much they trust the aggressor and each other, and how much they expect to gain from courting him. The dialectic of the relationship between Jackie and his mother does not give either of them such choice, however, for Jackie dare not really reject her and she dare not turn him against her: each has too much to lose.

In real life the dialectic of coalitions does not work itself out as in a small-groups laboratory because real life is affected by too many emotional factors specific to a situation, and this in turn is determined by past events or its history. In real life every coalition has a history, and history exists in family coalitions just as it does among nations. What small-groups studies do is relieve one of the embarrassment of history.

Continuing with the incident of the cartons of milk:

This reminds me of Jackie's fantasy about rubber bands, milk and helicopters. I asked Jackie where the milk came from, and he said, "Out of a carton." I laughed and said to Mrs. Jones, "You see, this is the modern child." * Mrs. Jones was made rather anxious by Jackie's answer, however, so she kept asking one question after another to get him to say that milk comes from a cow. When Jackie said milk comes from a carton, his mother asked, "Where does the carton come from?" and he said, "The milkman." His mother asked, "Where does the

* All I can say about my laughter here is that it makes me blush now.

milk come from before it gets to the milkman?" and Jackie said, "It comes from something else." Finally, the only way she could get him to say it was by asking, "Does milk come from an animal?" and he said, "Yes, it comes from a cow."

In spite of garbled speech and fantasy, Jackie can think logically, but this is the only time during my stay that Mrs. Jones deliberately pushed him to think. She was, perhaps, provoked to do it because she was afraid I might get the wrong impression. Over the years she has written me spontaneously from time to time to say that her children are developing well. When I was there, however, it seemed to me that Mrs. Jones herself was mainly interested in having warm relations with them.

Jackie likes to stay close to her. Though she tries to get him to go out, he likes to hang around. She does not try very hard. She is fond of him and he likes to climb on her. A selection from the many observations of Jackie alone with his mother or with his mother and Harriet illustrate the point:

Jackie came into the kitchen, and since I was sitting in his chair, he objected, so I got up and he sat down next to me. I played "This Little Piggy Went to Market" a number of times with him, as he kept asking me to do it over and over again. Mrs. Jones repeatedly beamed on both of us, and said at one point, "He's a love-bunny." I must say that Jackie is a charming child. The only thing about which he really gets riled up is food, for he has a way of flying into a passion if he doesn't get precisely what he wants at the moment. For example, at lunch he became furious because he didn't like the peanut butter and olive sandwiches, and we couldn't figure out what he wanted. He kept making a tremendous noise until his mother brought him a peanut butter and jelly sandwich. At lunchtime Mrs. Jones spontaneously turned away from the conversation that Dr. Jones and I were having, to gently stroke Jackie's face and chest. While Mrs. Jones and I were talking, the conversation was stopped by Jackie's crawling up on her lap.

* * *

Mrs. Jones sat down, preparing to eat her lunch. She held Harriet on her lap, playing delightedly with her, and Harriet was delighted too. Meanwhile Jackie crawled up the back of the chair behind her and wanted to sit on her lap. Since this was impossible, he crawled around on her back, nuzzled her and bit her. She seemed to enjoy the nuzzling and called him to attention when he bit her. She seemed to be having a wonderful time, enjoying the two kids. Considering the fact that Jackie and the baby act as if they *expect* her to be responsive, I would say that this was not a demonstration put on for my benefit.

* * *

Mrs. Jones made several efforts to get Jackie out of the house. He would not pick up any of her suggestions and just hung around. When he saw us drinking coffee he asked her for some, but she said, "How about having some orange juice?" She gave him some, which he gulped down thirstily. Mrs. Jones told me that Bobby and Jackie like to play together, but I said I really hadn't seen them playing together since I was there. She showed some anxiety, and said they do play together, particularly in the morning before the parents get up. She said Jackie misses Bobby very much when he is not around. She said also that the kids like to play together in the bathtub.

Jackie courts his mother and likes to stick close to her. Her authority is mild, tempered with praise and never contemptuous. Were it not for Bobby, it is likely that the relationship between Mrs. Jones and Jackie would be more tranquil.

Conclusions

The destiny of this family was set by the parents. When they married, Dr. Jones was violent, distrusting and desperately needful; his wife dissociated strong feeling and was unaccustomed to violence and to frank expression. Mrs. Jones had never really known what a family was. Dr. Jones had, but his mother and father were constantly fighting cutting, intellectual battles. Dr. and Mrs. Jones fought desperately, even coming to blows, and Tommy was a casualty. Since he became autistic and since they have had some psychotherapy, it has been possible for Dr. and Mrs. Jones to live together. Now they have had three more children, two somewhat upset, and the third, the first girl, calm, active, poised and intelligent.

The data of the Jones case have been given; but the meaning of the Jones family to one another, and what they might mean to us, has not been given; nor is it possible for me to say what the Joneses really mean to one another.

It seems to me that theirs is one of many families molded by tragedy—even by a tragic destiny. Given their own backgrounds, the married life of Ida and Ed was almost certain to be shadowed by misery. Tommy became a sacrifice; but through the damage to him, the parents acquired some wisdom. It is a kind of legend of Abraham and Isaac worked out in an obscure family in an obscure corner of the United States, for as Abraham, the obscure shepherd, penetrated to the essence of divinity through his willingness to sacrifice his son, so the Joneses gained more wisdom about themselves and about their family through the real sacrifice of a child. They even became very religious.

I am not suggesting, of course, that the understanding gained when Ed and Ida lost Tommy gave them the insight of the Hebrew shepherd; they merely learned that if any life at all was going to be possible for them, they would have to change.

The story of the Jones family, with its structure of tragic destiny, has often been repeated in my experience with psychopathology: the predetermination of lives by early family experience; the meeting of two depressed, self-deprecating and isolated people, each of whom perceives, quite incorrectly, the possibility of his own self-renewal in the other; the first child, who bears the total misery of his parents, and whose soul is destroyed—or nearly destroyed—and the beginning of wisdom in the parents when it is already too late for the child—all this is fairly common in the annals of psychopathology.

The Biblical story is of a motivated God, concerned to try the faith of the most humble; but today we view the situation of the Joneses differently. We are born into a culture which, on the one hand, trains us to be hard-driving, ambitious and cruel; to grow a thick, resistant skin around our feelings and to wall ourselves off from others. Just the right amount of toughness, resistance (in Freud's sense) and dissimulation will enable us to exist without unbearable misery, and with some happiness. But if something occurs, as it did in the Jones case, to make one too tough, too hard-driving, too resistive, too unaware, too concealing of his feelings and thoughts, he will bring so much suffering on himself and others that he will sacrifice a child. For some, this becomes a way of fulfilling a tragic destiny and it may alter the course of their marriage. This happened to Ed and Ida Jones.

The difference between the ancient and the modern "tragic motif," as Søren Kierkegaard pointed out,* is in the nature of the determination of action: in the ancient tragedy, destiny was determined by the gods or by fate, while in modern tragedy it is determined by what Kierkegaard calls our "inheritance"—what our parents did to us because the culture had done it to them. The understanding that in both cases the individual is bound, so that he has little choice, is the beginning of compassion; and our ability to suffer with these people because we know they cannot escape is the essence of sorrow.

In the rest of the book I follow these themes.

* In *Either/Or*, Vol. I, trans. by David A. and Lillian M. Swenson (Anchor Books; New York, Doubleday, 1959).

PART II
The Rosenberg Family

INTRODUCTION

The Anatomy of Sham

Sham is a combination of concealment and pretense: concealment of how we really feel and pretense of feeling something different. The capacity for sham is universally human, for everywhere the anthropology of tribal peoples gives evidence that even as we do, they conceal their true feelings. Social life compels deception, for even the most truly innocent among us are constantly compelled by fear to act as if they wished to do what they would rather not do, to conceal their feelings while abstaining from doing what they would rather do, to put on a good face while associating with people they would rather avoid, to hide their emotions while avoiding people they would rather not avoid, to smile when they would rather not, to be sober when they would rather laugh, and so on. Engineered by fear, sham is a bridge between the undesirable and the necessary, making the undesirable useful and the necessary bearable. The real problem is not whether to be a sham, but to understand when to drop the mask and when to put it on.

The Circle of Sham

Imagine social life as a set of concentric circles: the innermost is the ideal circle of truth—where there can be no concealment; and the outermost is the circle of sham, where concealment and pretense are the best policy and where truth would be gross stupidity. Ideally, the inner circle is reserved for those we love and who love us, but we know we cannot or dare not tell the whole truth even to them. Only God can stand the truth, for, in the first place, He knows it anyway, and in the second, He can forgive the truth in us because His love is infinite. In this formula—absolute knowledge combined with absolute love—are contained our feelings about truth: that there is always something we conceal and that what we conceal is often so terrible that only absolute love can accept it. Hence the relationship between sham and fear, between truth and love. But, of course, we often fear even those we love—a fact to which some common phrases bear witness: "Don't tell my wife, or she'll murder me"; "Don't let Johnny see it, or he'll never forgive me"; "If you tell my mother, I've had it," etc. Though even the innermost circle of relationships is not free of deception and fear —not free of sham—there is an enormous difference between these white deceptions and the massive black sham practiced in the outer world.

After the inner circle, the next area into which sham expands is our close circle of friends, then our second class of friends, then, perhaps, relatives by marriage, then "the organization"—office, university, etc. With each move outward from the innermost circle, relationships become more and more fraudulent. But when I say "fraudulent," I do not mean necessarily that there is a deliberate effort to deceive; I mean simply that the obligation to be open about our feelings diminishes and that the obligation to conceal increases. Concealment is a social obligation, expanding in proportion as we move outward from our closest, our subjectively most significant, relationships. Hence we always think it a bit peculiar when a stranger confides in us, but at the same time we understand that he does it because he "has nobody to talk to," i.e., nobody he really loves and trusts enough. We know that he unbosoms himself because, since he will "never see me again," his incommunicable truth is as if it had never existed.

Black Sham and White

One has to make a distinction—always fuzzy but always necessary—between black sham and white. Black sham is used to exploit and even to destroy people; white sham is merely socially necessary concealment and pretense. One uses black sham to sell a person down the river or to beat him out for a job, and white sham simply to get along with others—even one's own mother. Black sham is killing sham—like black magic; white sham preserves social relations. When men sit around a table at a committee luncheon, the air may be electric with mutual hostility and scorn, yet they all put on pleasant faces, crack jokes and bellow committee laughter. This is white sham; the committee could not meet at all and the necessary business could not be transacted if they were all to show how they feel. If one or more of these men has it in his head to dislodge the chairman of the division, secretly awaiting the moment to introduce a subtle motion of censure, he is practicing black sham against the chairman, even while using white sham with his co-conspirators.

There is an ever-widening series of circles where sham is more and more expected, tolerated and even required, but when this model is reversed we have pathology, i.e., if sham is present in the *family* and truth in the *outer* world, or if sham runs riot so that there is just as much of it in the family as in the outer world. In such cases a person fears his family more than or as much as the outside world, or he may even fear the outer world less than his own family. To get along in life without too much misery one must at every moment be able to manage sham; this is the essence of being middle-class. But when sham breaks loose, runs wild and contaminates relationships instead of protecting them, one is sick and makes others sick. This happens when a person is afraid; when he is fear-ridden, even his children become threatening.

Sham and the Inimical

Sham is related to distrust, which is, paradoxically, a form of belief—a belief in unreliability, a belief in the inimical. Sham is an expression of the metaphysic of the inimical and therefore embodies our feelings of vulnerability. The more vulnerable we feel, the more likely we are to conceal our feelings and erect a façade. Hence women are greater and more skillful practitioners of sham than men—but not because women are born with more social savoir-faire but because they are more vulnerable than men. Men have the reputation—less and less deserved nowadays as men become weaker and more like women—for being more open than women, and to the degree that this is true, it is because their social position has been more secure and more self-determined. Even today the pathways to status are straighter and more self-determined for men. The more open the road to status, the more self-determined it is, and the more open the face; hence the boss is freer to speak his mind than the peon, the professor freer than his student, the white man freer than the Negro with whom he deals. Sham belongs more to weakness, to vulnerability, and openness belongs more to strength, so openness and sham—two universally human capabilities—are related to status and inimical power as the hand is to the glove.

There is no culture without a metaphysic of the inimical, and the fact that life becomes organized as an escape from it, and that ceremonies and charms are developed to ward it off, proves that the metaphysic exists in people's minds even though never elucidated systematically. Often the inimical is projected outside the society, becoming a supernatural that we pretend to adore while concealing our terror of it. When the inimical is a foreign power, we prepare for war while speaking of peace, shake hands with its envoy and drink the health of his country, while plotting behind his back. But in all cases, much of life becomes organized so as to bind this inimical force, and sham is one device for doing it. Since such thought systems are found everywhere, we can say that *Homo sapiens* has a strong inherent tendency to develop a metaphysic of the inimical; in other words, *Homo sapiens cannot live without it.* As long as the inimical is kept *outside,* the group's fear of the inimical helps integrate life within the group; *it is when fear is so great that the inimical can no longer be imagined as outside the group that madness is upon us.* It is characteristic of pathological social systems, whether countries, tribes or families, that the inimical is imagined to be right *inside* the walls, and it is characteristic of many mad men that the inimical is felt to be inside their souls. Hence, individually and socially, there are two "ideal" kinds of madness: that in which the inimical is felt to be outside and that in which it is felt to be inside. Corresponding to these are two forms of sham—one to mislead the outside enemy and another to deceive the inner.

Deceiving the Inner Self

The expression "self-deception" reveals awareness of a self conceived as an enemy to be misled, and to whom, therefore, we should apply forms of sham most likely to keep him away—outside consciousness. When the self is an enemy, we hate and want to kill it. Hence the use of black sham against the self, and hence the sadness and madness of those who use it—or rather, try to. Black sham is directed against a self that protests too much against one's present conduct. Ordinarily when someone says, "I hate myself," he is not talking about what I deal with here. When someone says, "I hate myself," he usually means that the inner self—the "I"—is free and alive and kicking hard enough to bring him into line. The self-hatred of which I speak here, however, is the opposite; it is a hatred of the "I" for the very reason that the "myself" is determined to pursue its course and will crush the "I" by misleading it—by developing pretenses and by concealing from the "I" "myself's" real motivations. Of course, this is impossible to do because, since the "I" has its spies everywhere, it can ferret out the most elaborately concealed motives.

Let us imagine that a man has a good-looking, intelligent, creative wife who loves him, looks after him, and so on. In other words, she is a paragon. But he is not, and so becomes obsessed with "another woman." Now he begins to imagine flaws in his wife, delusional annoyances—and he presents himself to his "I" as disgusted with his wife. He also imagines the new woman to have phenomenal qualities his wife lacks; he might even imagine an entirely new philosophy of life in order to legitimize his obsession with the second woman. All this material he presents day in, day out, moment by moment, night and day to his "I." The man knows it is all pretense; he knows that all this "evidence" is mere perjury, amassed and presented, as before a jury, in order to mislead his "I" and conceal from it the real fact: that he is obsessed with the second woman, that he is weak and that basically he doesn't have a leg to stand on. At last, imagining that he has really swamped the "I" with evidence, he is able to leave his wife and live with the other woman. But this action leaves the initial condition the same, for the "I" is like a rebelling people crushed by superior force: though they have been subdued, the idea is still alive among them, to make the enemy uneasy in the night.

Such problems gave rise to psychoanalysis, the art of healing by revealing the concealed within us. While Freud was not the first to explain that conscious motives are but shams—proclamations by the conscious self of the inaudible promptings of the unconscious—he was the first to elucidate the machinery of sham, i.e., the famous mechanisms of defense.

Some Ramifications of Sham in the Family

We would expect children to conceal and pretend more than their parents and other adults because they are weaker, and even a loving parent is often inimical to childish wishes. Yet unless the children fear the parents much more than they love them, we don't expect them to pretend or conceal very much. Of course, even the most loved and loving child will have moments of fear when he will hide his feelings from his parents. In addition, every parent and every culture has its particular fears, which, embodied in the child, lead him to conceal. Some cultures tolerate a child's anger at his parents and consider childish outpourings of rage an indication that the child will be a great warrior. But since in our culture it is sinful or merely insulting for a child to get furious with his parents, children often cover up their rage. On the other hand, when parents do not love a child and conceal this fact while trying to act as if they did love him, a condition is given for madness. This takes us into the deep underground of sham.

Let us imagine a woman who believes she has married beneath herself: she feels her husband is not much intellectually, and economically she knows he is not a success, but she gets married because a woman should be married, and because she has tried and failed to attract other kinds of men. He marries *her* because he wants a home and because, knowing his defects, he is aware that he could never do any better. She is not good-looking, not very smart, and he knows she has a terrible temper. The horror of sham is now on its way, for he suspects she married him because he was the best she could do, and he feels she looks down on him. She has a similar view of him: she believes that he married her because, being the kind of man he is, he thinks he couldn't do any better. Thus marriage begins with people who have low opinions of themselves, and before it is fairly under way they have low opinions of each other. There is no love in the union, but much necessity and a great deal of sham. At the wedding, which celebrates expediency rather than love, bride and groom ache with the feeling that everybody knows the circumstances. From now on, life for this couple must be a precise patterning of sham: neither must ever reveal that he suspects why the other married him, and he must never let his attitude toward the spouse's defects come out. Hence silence is the rule, conversation can occur only about the most formal matters, and life is anxious. A consequence of sham is that these people cannot really talk to each other: since any topic that might conceivably lead in the direction of truth must be avoided, evasion becomes an obsession. The children become high-tension wires bearing the electricity of parental deception. Can the mother trust Johnny not to tell his father that . . . ? How does the mother know the father isn't telling Johnny that . . . ? The child is the creation of the parental sham. Who knows how such a child might be subtly punished because he seemed to prefer one parent? Who knows how often the parents, distrusting each other, might try to "pump" the child until, unable to bear this fear of entrapment, the child first resists and then gives up communicating with his parents altogether? Then it is the *parents'* turn to distrust *him*. What is he thinking? What does he have against them that he doesn't talk? That he shrinks away when they approach? That he suspects their slightest inquiry or command? His "negativism" is interpreted as contempt and he is punished for "not respecting your parents."

Or we can imagine another possibility—any one of a thousand. The mother, distrusting her husband's attitude toward her—suspecting that he is using the child against her, perhaps telling the child lies, perhaps pumping him to find out what she said about the father—decides to simplify her life by keeping the child away from the father. If the child goes near the father, the child is suspected by the mother, and if he stays away from the father, he is suspected by the father. In this way space itself becomes a demon. The father can try the same tactic as the mother. Or the child may seem to the mother a means of overcoming her disappointment in the father and of getting back at him for marrying her without love. So she pushes the child to intellectual feats, driving home to the father his mental weakness and at the same time binding the child to her. All of this can only turn the father against the child. In this way, intellect also becomes a demon and study a nightmare.

Meanwhile, because the parental antagonism is worked out through the child, the fundamental sham remains hidden. Since whatever happens between the parents and the child is—must be—considered as caused by the child, the underlying pathology of the parental relationship remains concealed. Let us put it more strongly: the child must be blamed for everything in order to prevent the parental sham from coming into the open. So the parents get along well together and allow each other freedom to do more or less what they want with the child, while believing they really love it. In this way the child's destruction becomes the "salvation" of the marriage: the marriage has seemed to "turn out well"; the only trouble is that such nice parents have had such bad luck with their children.

But the plot against the child goes further, and can even have the effect of bringing the parents closer together than they ever were before—not in love but in conspiracy. In the first place they have to conceal from each other the fact that they harbor a mutual distrust. This can be done simply by shifting the burden of suspicion: it is not that the father is pumping Johnny to get evidence against the mother, but that Johnny is bearing tales. It is not that the wife tells Johnny one thing and the husband another, but that the child is confused or "negativistic." It is not that Johnny can no longer bear the burden of being pushed in order to gratify the mother and show up the father, but that he has lost interest in school. Husband and wife therefore are united in sharing the burden of a "difficult child." But since the child of such a marriage may radiate difficulty—resisting, shrieking, yelling in his misery—the parents are drawn together in plotting how to outwit him. At this point the child distrusts everything, so that he may turn even a well-intentioned act against the parent or view the good intentions unresponsively and with suspicion. The child has become the embodiment of the basic distrust that doomed the marriage in the first place.

What I have described occurs only if the child is active and curious. If he is apathetic—indeed, if he quickly discovers that curiosity and a desire for mastery will earn him nothing but bumps on the head—things will turn out differently. If he is inactive, plays little, gets fat, stays by himself, avoids all problems, gets up when he is told to, sits down when he is told to, eats what is set before him, sits quietly on anybody's lap, he is considered a "good" child and both parents like him. He does nothing to tear off the family mask. His only problem may be that he goes to the toilet in his pants, but this form of resistance can be tolerated if he is a nice child otherwise. Indeed, if he is not subject to severe toilet training—as a reward for being nice—it may help calm him down and make him even nicer. Meanwhile he "cases the joint"; everything he sees and hears in the house tells him to lie low, not to think, not to resist, to cover up, not to be a self if he wants to escape torment. In this way he conserves his strength, but in this way, paradoxically, he can also die spiritually; his self is always racing against death, for the soul that lies too long inactive forever dies. Hence the acute relationship between the self and time: the self must perceive *when* to emerge and *how* to do it, for if it comes forth too soon and too vigorously, the lethal properties of the environment—of any environment—will kill it. Out of all of this issues the sham of acquiescence, for the pathologically acquiescent child, who really lives in terror of his parents, conceals his inner consternation behind a façade of compliant indifference.

Sham and Some Popular Clichés

Alienation. Since the term comes to us from Hegel and Marx—in other words, from the German—I can get a better grip on it by looking at the original. The German words are *Entfremdung,* the process of making strange or foreign, and *Entäusserung,* to be put outside. Thus alienation is *withdrawal* from something—becoming strange or foreign to it, being *put out* or *taking one's self out* and thereby becoming a stranger—separated. Since humans feel vulnerable when they are strangers, the emotional essence of alienation is fear and hostility, and *sham is the expression in action of alienated vulnerability between people who cannot get away from each other.* Sham is thus a phase of condemnation; it is a passport to that social hell where there is no escape from other people.* The same applies to the soul. When, between the "I" and "myself" there is a difference that cannot be resolved, so that the "myself" tries to gull the "I" with sham, the two are alienated; and we say, "He is a stranger to himself," or better still, "He is his own worst enemy," a simple and beautiful way of stating the enmity that exists between the "myself" and the "I." When husband and wife are estranged—though married and living together—because the marriage was a sham in the first place, they inexorably create alienated children. The resistive and the acquiescent child are both alienated in their own way.

Alienation, in its most painful form, occurs in a social system such as the family, for example, when satisfaction is demanded but cannot be obtained; when, as in the family, unity is necessary but division is the reality, and when frankness is impossible. Alienation is a product of dependent inseparability—a phenomenon of chained flight. Alienation is a complex emotion, made up of feelings of estrangement, powerlessness and vulnerability: a person feels cheated and that he is cheating; he feels contemptuous and belittled, and covers up his vast hostility with—sham. Sham is the outer face of alienation.

When parents and children, though living under the same roof, become strangers to one another, sham develops grotesquely. Alienation as part of daily practice can be expressed by avoidance, fighting or sham, but usually by all three together. Cooped up within the four walls of a modern dwelling, unable to escape one another, the members of the family find that complete

---

* As in Sartre's *No Exit* (Vintage Books; New York, Knopf, 1955).

avoidance is impossible, and the ambiguities and traps laid by shamming repeatedly provoke arguments and rage. In an organization, alienation can and must be borne without avoidance and fighting, but in the family, since the parents cannot fire the young children, the explosive potential of alienation cannot be and need not be contained; and *where love is not, sham is not enough.* Hence alienation in a family is always expressed in extremes: massive lying, plotting, avoidance, fighting and distrust. When parents and children are alienated, benevolence is suspected as a sham, as a means of entrapment, and even the apparently innocent question or intention is felt as a concealed weapon.

Identity loss. "I'm forever trying to fool myself" expresses the inner sham of a person suffering "identity loss." To say that anyone has a sense of identity is only a short way of stating that one part of him is not always trying to gull the other part. Alienation and identity loss are both products of dependent, dissatisfied inseparability, and they label different ways of looking at the division in the soul.

Identity loss, or better, identity absence, must be distinguished from a crisis of identity* in one who is hesitating among available choices and has made no decision yet. The second type of identity problem has a future; the first is rooted in the past. When an adolescent says, "I don't know who I am," we have to discover whether he means he can't make up his mind what he will do with his life, or whether he does not know what has been *done* to his life.

A culture like ours, which heavily rewards the capacity for sham, must also produce a pathology of sham, whose symptoms range from the smiling masks of the perfectly normal people next door ("You never know *what* Mrs. Figbert is thinking") to schizophrenia. In between are the uncountable miserable ones who "don't know who or what they are."

Dealing with Sham

Since Erving Goffman has written a magnificent book on this subject called *The Presentation of Self in Everyday Life,*† there is little left to say. Every culture standardizes its own form of sham, and it must provide ways of dealing with it too. If I know that Professor Adams is a sham I must do two things. In the first place, since I am a well-socialized individual, I must not let him know that I know he is a sham. (Goffman, with exquisite insight, has called this "tact.") Children must do the same thing with deceiving parents, and the aged must do it with the patronizing young—they must not let them see that they see through them. If I let Adams know I see through him, it will be impossible for us to get along. Tact, therefore, is white sham. Society rewards me for shamming by making Adams my "friend," but as I smile at him and listen to his fraudulence, I begin to hate myself for shamming. Society has played me a dirty trick; it has promised

---

* Cf. Erik Erikson, "The Problem of Ego Identity," in *Identity and Anxiety: Survival of the Person in Mass Society,* ed. by Maurice R. Stein, Arthur J. Vidich and David Manning White (Glencoe, The Free Press, 1960).

† Anchor Books; Garden City, N.Y., Doubleday, 1959.

me rewards in terms of "comfortable living" for being a fake, and here I am
suffering. What shall I do? Actually, society, in promising me rewards for
sham, is itself a sham, or better, a lie. But now I am blaming society instead
of blaming myself. I then blame myself, saying, "You are a sham yourself.
Tell Adams what you think of him and become an honest man." But this is
impossible. As a matter of fact, Adams is not the only sham I have to deal
with face to face, day in, day out. Can I, like Cyrano, surround myself with
a Spanish ruff of enemies? Obviously not; I have neither his nose—nor his
rapier. I therefore have a choice, either to *do* something about Adams or
hate myself.

Thus the second thing I have to do about Adams' being a sham is to
develop arguments with which to plead my case before my "I." In other
words, I "may be as pure as snow and as chaste as ice" but the mere presence of Adams can make a sham of me.

A child makes shamming a natural part of his life by seeing his parents
practice it, and turning the tables on them, gives at least one good rewarding deception in return for each of theirs. There is, however, a sicklier way
of learning sham, which occurs when the parents feign for the child a love
they do not feel; then the child who comes through this sham alive learns to
pretend to his parents that he is taken in by this, while enduring with sorrow and concealed hatred the fact that he is not loved. He then receives a
graduate certificate in black sham, for he will use his skill at deception
against the world and be most dangerous with those he says he loves.

On the Conditions for the Emergence of Truth

This discussion has nothing to do with truth as information, with questions like "What is the capital of California?" or "How many atoms of oxy-
gen are there in a molecule of water?" or "What are the fundamental
building blocks of the universe?" For most of us the really serious problem
of truth is ethical truth—the truth that involves our relationship to other
people and to the human condition in general: to war and peace, to poverty
and comfort, to openness or concealment, to care for others versus selling
them down the river, and so on. The real problem has to do with the revelation or protection of ourselves and others, leading them astray or enabling
them to walk in a clear direction. The fundamental question is, "Under
what conditions do we abandon sham and allow the truth to come out?"
This question makes the assumption that we know the truth and can reveal
or withhold it by an act of will.

Proposition 1: Truth comes out when there is nothing to be afraid of

This is the primordial condition for the emergence of truth, and all
other conditions take second place in relation to it. It is the opposite condition for the practice of sham, because sham is motivated by fear. To say
that truth comes out when it is socially innocuous or that truth comes out
when it is profitable is simply to state special cases of the general proposition. Even the statement "truth comes out when one has the courage to tell
it" is, in a sense, a special case of the general proposition, for courage

cancels fear. The point is that many people who have the courage to tell the truth when it seems socially dangerous to do so are individuals who know their strength; who, as a matter of fact, have a nicer perception of the probabilities of social punishment than those who habitually avoid it. (For example, in the United States the danger of official persecution for unpopular political opinions is radically overestimated by most people; the continuing strength of the United States is still its ability to tolerate many—though by no means all—shades of deviant opinion.) At any rate, it is clear that absence of fear is a prerequisite for the emergence of ethical truth.

The truth that appears when there is nothing to fear has a very different relation to the self from the truth that emerges as a function of courage, for in the first case it is merely routine, while in the second it is self-maximizing. Every time a person takes his timidity in hand and tells the truth while his heart flutters just a trifle, he is so much the better for it—he feels. Thus the paradox: truth without fear is scarcely worth the telling. And thus the neurotic paradox that a truly frightened person will feel uplifted by an ego-enhancing wave of courage even if all he tells you is that there is soot on the tip of your nose!

Proposition 2: Truth comes out when one person wants to hurt another

In ordinary everyday existence, under pressure of rage or hate, shams are broken down and "the truth comes out." Revelations made under such strong emotions transcend fear and make us ignore the consequences. Rage and hate, breaking repeatedly through the wall of domestic sham, constitute the environment of truth in disturbed family relationships.

However, we must be on our guard against truth that emerges under such circumstances: it is often a pseudo truth—a stored-up rumination developing out of the innumerable difficulties of domestic life, but not really believed. Pseudo truths are notions created by the capricious mind to justify our anger when matters don't go the way we want them to.

In sum, there are three kinds of ethical truth, according to the conditions under which they emerge. The first is routine truth, the innocuous truth whose telling could not possibly hurt or offend anyone. This may be a purely hypothetical class of truth, with no adherents at all; at one time or another, we are probably all put out by even the most obvious ethical truth. The second is the truth of courage, and the third is the truth of rage and hate. It is clear that they serve very different functions in the soul, and make very different contributions to happiness. The first leaves sham untouched, because it never was involved to begin with; the second breaks through social shams; and the last tears away domestic shams, unveiling the family disaster. It is against this truth's coming out that the family must guard most alertly; it is against this truth that the family erects domestic defenses just as the soul erects inner defenses against the truth about iself. I have called the former *domestic ambiguity*.

The Dialectic of Nothingness

> So she passed the nullity of her
> days, the blank stretch between
> hour and hour. She could not
> know oblivion, for there was al-
> ways the hollow sound of Time
> recalling her, not to herself, for
> she had no self, only a bundle
> of small griefs and fears, and
> mountainous furies—but to the
> fact that the days were passing,
> in a darkened and mournful
> procession towards the grave.
> —EDITH SITWELL,
> *Taken Care Of*

The possibility of becoming nothing appears in dreams as failure, as being lost, crushed or put in prison. In dreams each single fear is a concentrate of a multitude; hence the power of dreams to urge us on—out of one fear into another. It is the destiny of all fearful things to escape from one fear, merely to have it rise as a new one from behind the next rock. But the fear of nothingness is the basic one—the pattern, the mold, the matrix—from which all others issue. Why argue about "man's fear of death"? Whether or not we fear death, what we encounter in our dreams is a polymorphous fear, which presents itself now as death, now as failure, now as being lost, caught in the act, or as imprisonment for nameless crimes. There are there-fore many fears that are not of death, but only one fear of death. The fears of non-death, the historically generated fears, are the basic question.

Life in our culture is a flight from nothingness. This fact has been evaded by recent psychology through the invention of the notion of "effec-tiveness" ("mastery," *mutatis mutandis*). Psychology tells us that what we really want is to feel effective—perhaps like a bulldozer or the man run-ning it, or maybe like a cook baking a pie, or like a professor receiving requests for reprints of his papers, or even like a soldier cutting down the enemy with a machine gun. This is a robust idea, fit to print on the flag of a muscular nation—like SPQR on the standards of the Roman legions. The silent anguish of many of us, however, warns that many who are frightfully effective feel like nothing nevertheless.

At any rate, acting on something, being effective, is somethingness, and ineffectiveness is an abyss out of which we try to climb by acting on some-thing. The trouble with being merely effective is that not only does it often fail to destroy the feeling of nothingness, but it also wrecks the peace of others. We are all familiar with this panic of ineffectiveness—it is more effective in smashing the life of other people than in saving anybody from the abyss. Hence the truth of the matter is that action stemming from the feeling of nothingness, from despair, only makes the object of the action despairing.

Effectiveness that is merely flight from nothingness gives rise to a darting destructiveness in which he who feels he is nothing hurls himself upon others in order to escape his illness. He might pick a "particular object" for his darting destructiveness and might vent on him all his emptiness, hatred, envy and fear. In other words, this "particular object" becomes the inimical one, the imagined agent of his suffering. It is very likely that this "particular inimical one" is the very opposite of himself—that it represents fullness, or a striving to be something. Imagine, then, a parent who feels like nothing, with a child who is striving to become something. What irony to have such a traitor in his own house! His own flesh and blood—a living contradiction of himself! Isn't this disrespect? Shouldn't this fullness be rooted out, destroyed, perhaps packed off to a madhouse?

Whence comes this immense sense of nothingness? Obviously out of having had something destroyed. A child was born, and cherished, perhaps, for a brief while. There was a peeping out of the soul to see if the coast was clear, if the weather was good, some sunlight around and a little moisture —the soul having put down some tentative roots. And then the thing was crushed. But it was not obliterated; there was a distant memory of something that had been or almost had been. And this memory, so dangerous to look upon because it reminds one of what he *had* been and had never *become*, because it fills the soul with bursting rage that should not erupt on others (and on the recollections of those who crushed it)—this memory is the headstone of the *something* that makes the disease of nothingness possible, or rather, inevitable. Thus our compassion for that thing which was crushed and for that being who now stands before us, the cemetery of himself, yet visiting on those around him the persecuting phantom of his mutilated soul.

But actually he can create nothing but death. Though it is better that he be immobile, he butts around between paralysis and harmful movement. Startled, he blames it on the *object* when the object he touches withers. He cannot imagine that he is the cause of death, for in the first place, it is beyond his imagining, and in the second, he feels powerless. Hence the *innocence* of nothingness, and hence the paradox that whoever is destructive by his nothingness walks in innocence. His motto is, "How could I, who am powerless, hurt anything?" or "In weakness there is innocence."

And hence the sham. For when a man is nothing, he lives only by impacts from the outer world; he is a creature external to himself, a surface of fear moved by the winds of circumstance: one circumstance colliding with another—that is the ebb and flow of thought. Or he is a cyclone of fear in which impulses from the outer world collide at random. The problem then is to deal with each particle—or rather, to frustrate its portentous probabilities. Hence sham. Reality is not to be considered; *it is to be defeated.* Hence sham.

I insist on the difference between being driven out of life and withdrawing from it. For example, a man sees around him crowds of people whom he disdains ("Worms! Scum! Who wants them?! To hell with them!"). Wrapping his splendid mantle of self-regard about him, he withdraws. *This is an active choice.* The child who has been teased and misled, who has sucked the breast and found it dry, withdraws from human beings. Sizing up the human race, he decides it is not for him. Perhaps he goes mad, but he has *acted:* an act of considered madness, perhaps, wherein the distinction between being driven out of life and deserting it is hard to make. On the other hand, there are those who have been whipped out of life without a chance to withdraw with some self-respect. Beaten and beaten again, sent to sleep with the pigs, they have been *driven out of life*. The madman who has deserted life surveys it: sitting on the edge of his asylum cot, mopping a snake pit floor, swallowing his "medication," eating cafeteria unspeakables, making innumerable plaster casts of Santa Claus in "occupational therapy," his eye is cocked at the world, which daily confirms to him the perils and ambiguity of return. He who has been driven out of life looks at the world with longing; he who has withdrawn from life regards it with fear.

But the man who is nothing is also condemned to watch life, as if he were at the movies or in front of a TV set. He may fall asleep from time to time as the spectacle bores him. But this also narcotizes the pain of nothingness. His own family may become a spectacle, alternately putting him to sleep with its routines and moving him to action by its excitement.

Yes, he may even get married, for there is a certain charm in people with nothingness—just as in those phthisic females in the paintings of certain Flemish masters, whose closeness to death gives them a frail and melancholic appeal. The depression of nothingness tones a man down, and his essentially spectator feeling about life makes him quiet—a very attractive quality to those repelled by strong action, especially by sexual action. So passivity is mistaken for gentleness and reticence, and uncertainty for honesty. The absence of spark is appealing to a companion who has none himself and may feel threatened by it.

In a state of nothingness there is a panic of time—a frantic effort to escape from it. Like a defeated soldier, he who is nothing flees from time, the enemy, for time is a bullet in the back. In flight from time he is prone to drop off to sleep, to stare emptily into space or at TV—purely autohypnotic activities. But hence, also, his living *through* others, for the activity of others, since it is positive, is life for someone who is nothing, filling up time, giving him a sense of being alive. The life of others penetrates him like a mystic shaft; he floats and feeds in the bloodstream of those who are something, and is unable to distinguish between his own form and the bodies of those who transfuse life into him. *This is identification through nothingness.* But since this parasitic life is also one of envy, hate and fear, the man who is nothing is fickle, and suddenly he is capable of treason, without knowing it—for nothingness, remember, is also innocence. Hence the treason of the innocent; hence, also, the clear difference between love and identification through nothingness. Love says, "I am more than myself because of you," while nothingness says, "I am less than the dust beneath your chariot wheels." Identification through nothingness is auto-annihilation, but an auto-annihilation by one who cannot stand himself.

The Dialectic of Pain

When somebody tries to compel a child to obey by hurting him physically, the child has these choices: (1) to yield and endure; (2) to endure and resist; (3) to yield while appearing to endure and resist; (4) to endure, resist and fight back while appearing to yield.

Yielding and enduring. The worse the pain, the greater the enemy's haste and determination; and the less the child's tolerance for pain, the more likely the child will be to yield. Yet most of life's pain is not torture (although average children can be exquisitely cruel to one another); the enemy's timetable is often vague and he is inclined to give up when a victory seems costly. What principally decides whether a child withstands or yields is his ability to tolerate pain and how badly he wants what he is suffering for. A parent who is going to rely on pain must *teach his child to yield to pain.* This he can do, however, only if the child has not learned to endure pain, and a child learns to endure pain if he has been exposed to much of it—or *if withstanding has been rewarding*—if withstanding has rendered him a valuable inner service. It is this possibility that opens the way to an understanding of the dialectic of pain.

Enduring and resisting. If a parent becomes enraged when a child laughs or takes his blows impassively, this may give the child so much pleasure that the parent loses the power to compel him to do anything, no matter how hard the parent hits. While an average child may start to cry even as he stands shaking before his parent waiting for the first blow, a child for whom the parent's baffled rage is a reward stands expressionless or even smiling because anticipation of his parent's defeat narcotizes fear: even as the blows fall he takes pleasure in consciousness of his parent's *panic of ineffectiveness*, and redoubled violence simply communicates to the child awareness of the parent's mounting sense of impotence—and of the child's own strength. What in the average case is an encounter between a disobedient child and a parent angry at what the child has done, here becomes a war between a child disciplined to pain and a parent not disciplined against himself, who, perceiving the child as a threat, hardens in a determination to break him. The comparison with war is exact; the parent's aim now is to destroy the child, and the child, since he is weak, can only fantasy the death of the parent. Like enemies, they absolutely distrust each other, may even conspire against each other, and this warfare has the ultimate effect of destroying both of them; the parent plows deeper and deeper into his own sickness, and as he does so, makes the child's worse, too.

But if the child is not driven mad by hate, resistance gives him a sense of self and purpose, and hatred becomes an opium for his pain. His hate is also a defense against intrusion, against the substitution of an alien self for his own self—however sick it must become with hate. In this way the ability to bear pain—or technically, the learned capacity to endure pain—becomes a vindication, a victory of the self. This outcome gives us an alternative view of "masochism"—and makes us wonder what it really is.

Now, this child's brother or sister is very different, more average; he is in terror of the parent's rage, cries before he is struck, wriggles in pain as he is beaten, bawls that he will be good—in other words, gives the parent complete satisfaction. Hence the blows are lighter, stop sooner and may even be followed by a certain erotic parental tenderness. This is a favored child, much more likely to get some profit out of life, surely more likely to stay sane than the other.

Since the orientations of which I speak are learned and are determined by culture, it would follow that in some cultures relatively minor physical pain has a tremendous effect on a child, while in others—like that of the Plains Indians, for example—even severe physical stress will be borne without flinching. In that case, weapons must be found to afflict the soul and thus make it vulnerable to ridicule, humiliation, loss of love, guilt, and so on. Vulnerability to the weapon used to force him into line must be cultivated in a child; thus, in a satanic way, we are moved without being aware of it, to make our children vulnerable even as we protect them, and thus it is the mark of successful child nurture that we make our children neither invulnerable nor excessively vulnerable.

Mephistopheles is at the elbow of the best of us when we are trying "to whip our child into shape." (The expression itself is very interesting!) What can we do to prevent Johnny from, let us say, "crossing the street by himself"? Well, we'll "keep him in the house all afternoon" if he does. But that may not work, because he has a grand time playing in his room. Well, we can make him go to bed early, while other children are still playing outside. But that may not work, either—he keeps right on crossing the street. The point is that he likes lying in bed because he has such wonderful fantasies there while sucking his thumb. He may even masturbate. It is clear that Johnny is invulnerable to punishment by separation. As a matter of fact, we are merely helping him learn how to get along alone. At last, driven by the fear of having our child hit by a car, we smack him—real hard—shouting, "Don't you ever cross the street without a grownup or you'll catch it worse!" And he stops. Against our will, and without knowing it, we have been experimenting with the child's vulnerability pattern. We have been making him vulnerable to physical pain by not using it, and inuring him to separation by using it when it merely draws upon the child's inner resources for living a lonely existence.

Yielding while appearing to endure and resist. This occurs when the attacker would feel nothing but contempt, and would even redouble his blows, were the victim to yield too quickly. Here the victim is really terrified and suffering, but covers up because he has learned that he will suffer even more if he gives in too soon—if he doesn't give his persecutor the gratification of breaking down a resistance or, at least, of a good workout. Thus the contempt for the victim who yields too quickly, often expressed as contempt for a coward, is really hatred of one who withholds gratification by yielding too soon. Obviously this behavior is possible only when the attacker—like white hoodlums in the South, storm troopers, etc.—does not enjoy beating unresisting flesh.

I have been writing about the dialectic of collisions between children and parents, but there is a kind of dialectic that may occur only between children: *enduring, resisting and fighting back while appearing to yield* is such a case. Here one child puts up with pain but hits back while appearing to submit, because he must gratify the enemy but cannot fight him openly, either because the blows would become too heavy or because he needs his persecutor, and would lose him were he to deny him sadistic gratification. But when the pain is intolerable and the victim is getting sick and tired of submission, he must find a way to resist and fight back without appearing to. Obviously this must be a somewhat friendly—sometimes called "hostile-dependent"—relationship because, since attacker and attacked need each other, both are willing to overlook the ambiguity in what is going on. For example, the attacker, while never hitting with full force (if he did, the victim might be driven to retaliate or go away), might also be willing to ignore the fact that the victim is "surreptitiously," without appearing to do so, battering him in one way or another. For his part the victim may be willing to endure the blows because this is his hold on his persecutor.

Hostility and Dependence

A characteristic relationship among big-city boys—so beautifully described by Henry Roth in *Call It Sleep*—is a hostile-dependent one. The better fighters, usually the bigger and stronger boys, lord it over the weaker ones, beating them up from time to time—but not too badly, because they need them. In exchange for being close to the big guy, the smaller boy offers his body (usually only for beating) and his services—running errands, picking up cigarette butts, stealing a little bit for him from his own home or from stores, and so on. On city streets, even among "nice boys from good families," a vicious boy but an excellent fighter can have a whole train of other children happy to be near him. There is nothing seriously degrading in such a relationship, and the pain of what soul shrinkage may occur in the weaker ones is put to sleep by the warmth of the gang and the proximity to power.

All of this is very well known; however, it is not emphasized that the hostile-dependent relationship, usually considered a pathological form, is so common among city boys that any boy who cannot endure it is out. But the paradox of maleness in our culture is that in maturing, a male raised on city streets has to divest himself of these feelings and reverse them; he must—in technical language—unlearn in manhood what he has learned about male relationships as a child.

The development of a hostile-dependent relationship among children in the small space of the American home may destroy the chances for normal relationships outside. Locked behind the four walls of the home, often sleeping in the same room, the children may develop the hostile-dependent relationship that acquires the obsessive and intoxicating quality of a true hostile-dependent love affair. The main difference between this kind of hostile dependency and one outside the family is the absence of obsessiveness in the latter. The leader of a neighborhood crowd of boys extends his dominion over all of them, but all beneath him are—*mutatis mutandis*—hostilely dependent on one another. Besides, they are not always together, and coalitions in the average neighborhood crowd are forever changing; since space outside the home does not close in on the children to suffocate them in limited opportunities, pathology, stemming from the parents, will not be constantly reinforced—nourished—in the same relationship, but diffused among several.

The danger implicit in dependency between siblings is symbolized in the image of the older child chasing the younger one home ("Get th' hell outa here—g'wan home!"). When the older child threatens the younger with "a kick in the shins if you don't beat it," he is unwittingly encouraging the younger to be independent, while defending himself against becoming just as dependent on the little one as the little one might become on him. We are so accustomed to thinking of the problem the other way around that we are not aware of the possibility of the big one's being dependent on the little one.

The Dialectic of Weakness and Strength

There is a time in life when weakness is strength: because adults are compelled to take care of an infant, his feebleness exercises a compulsive force over them. It was this power in weakness that led psychoanalysis to the notion of "infantile omnipotence"—the idea that since adults presumably leap to do an infant's bidding when he cries, the infant therefore must surely develop the belief that he is omnipotent. If, went the reasoning, this infant had great big adults at its beck and call, causing the mother's breast and other good things to materialize just by crying, this infant should—that is, if the adult were in the baby's place—get the idea that he had the power to make anything materialize. Since no psychoanalyst has been able to put himself precisely in the place of an infant, the notion of "infantile omnipotence" must compete forever with the equally probable notion of infantile feelings of impotence—the infant's feeling that he can do nothing without the help of the o'ershadowing adult, and that he is absolutely and pathetically dependent on adults for everything outside his own body. At any rate, since in our culture the child's weakness does exert a compulsive power over normal adults, one way of looking at this fact is to say that the infant's weakness is his strength.

This strength in weakness is not permitted the child indefinitely, for in all cultures—although different cultures follow a different pace—the child is expected gradually to take care of himself. Depending on the culture, strength through weakness is gradually stripped away from the child—and the child's attempts to hold on to it are punished by ridicule, scolding, blows, and so on.

As the child's weakness ceases to be strength, strength itself takes on a more positive definition: at each age the idea of strength undergoes a subtle reformulation in line with the culture's goals. A good man; a man of standing; a good gardener, trader, fisherman; a man who knows how to keep his mouth shut; an intelligent, creative, daring man; a good warrior, a fierce man—all are cultural definitions of strength. But most cultures hold this strength in line, and "excessive" capability—or rather, the *exercise* of it—is discountenanced. Margaret Mead's *Coming of Age in Samoa** contains the best description we have in anthropology of the control of excellence. Every culture must have a way of cutting talent down to size—or channeling it so that it does not blow the culture to bits by interfering with the possibilities of other people or by upsetting traditional patterns of thought. In warping good brains into the physical sciences, particularly into war and space research, our own culture provides a good example of the channeling of intelligence so that it will not interfere with traditional thought on socially sensitive problems. Here the explosive power of mind is directed to areas where it cannot possibly overthrow accepted social structures, and the high cash rewards in the "hard" sciences often make thinking about the social system seem irrelevant, trivial and even ungrateful. This principle—that the brains of the most alert and original must be channeled into personally rewarding and socially conventional endeavor—has widespread applicability. In discussing the "morphology" of economic backwardness, Paul Baran points out that in underdeveloped countries, economic manipulation absorbs "some of their societies most capable and dynamic individuals," but "at the same time wastes, corrupts, and destroys a vast quantity of what is perhaps the scarcest productive resource of all: creative human talent." † Whether under- or over-developed, every culture provides forms of rewarding intellectual waste and generates sabotage that dissipates the gifts of its most talented members in activities which leave the basic social structure undisturbed.

Since in pressing beyond the perimeters of traditional mental habits, strength becomes weakness because it is vulnerable to attack, the inquiring mind draws about itself an appearance of stupidity in order to be permitted to think at all, and it is the major function of formal schooling to teach us how to be stupid in culturally acceptable and profitable ways—in other words, how to be strong—for in teaching us to be stupid, the society has our own good at heart.

There is no absolute punishment for stupidity, no matter how exuberant and suffocating it may be, but intellect, exercised without limit, provokes a ferocious attack from society. We must not, therefore, turn against the school for its idiocy, since, by reinforcing that protective stupidity first imported to us in the family, it renders most of us an invaluable service. To paraphrase an old proverb, "Where stupidity is strength, 'tis folly to be smart," and as every civilized person knows, this is well documented by the lives of Socrates, Bruno, Galileo, and most recently, by William H. Whyte, Jr.'s *The Organization Man*.‡ In our culture the earliest expression of the danger of excessive ability is found in Aristotle's conception of the golden mean.

Within limits—the limits of congenital idiocy or economic incompetence§—stupidity is strength and intellect is weakness in all cultures. This may lead to pathology when intellect is too heavily penalized and stupidity

---

* Mentor Books; New York, New American Library, 1956.
† *The Political Economy of Growth* (New York, Monthly Review Press, 1960).
‡ Anchor Books; Garden City, N.Y., Doubleday, 1957.
§ In the overwhelming majority of cases in Western culture, really serious economic incompetence is caused by social disenfranchisement.

too highly rewarded. The strong anti-intellectual strain in our national character* was at one time a national strength because it stimulated attacks on the kind of egghead thinking that might have interfered with the emergence of the United States as a muscular, capitalist, expansionist nation. This strength, however, became at last a weakness—for a while at least—in the mid-twentieth century, when the achievements of intellect in physics, chemistry, mathematics, biology and medicine began to multiply contributions to health, warfare and profits. Meanwhile, since intellect is still a threat to social structure, stupidity is entrenched in government and the social sciences. From these well-known and rather hackneyed considerations we can derive the generalization that to every historic epoch belongs its own brand of stupidity because that is the strength it needs, and that what is strength through stupidity in one era becomes weakness in another, but the extirpation of brains at the wrong time is pathological because it creates weakness. In order to exist, every culture must know when to reward weakness and when to punish strength.

This rule is as applicable in a family as in a nation, for every family must be careful to draw an equitable line so that it does not persecute its truly strong members. It must love the child who grasps the world too quickly just as much as the one who grasps nothing—or acts as if he grasps nothing—at all. The pathogenic case is the one in which the latter is loved too much and the former is resented and even feared—the embodiment of the inimical. A parent must feel strong in order not to hate the former or favor the latter: while it is comfortable never to feel scrutinized, to feel exposed before one's own child, naked before that level gaze, is miserable. It is here that the temptation lies to convert a child's strength, his mind, into a vulnerability. The consequences of rewarding stupidity by favor are not serious, for this is the way of the world. Though the peril of hating a perceptive child is that the child may be destroyed, most children, after a few frightening successes at seeing through their parents, learn that it is better not to look too far below the surface. In subtly punishing his child for perceiving too much, however, a parent makes it possible for the child to take the first steps in accomplishing for himself his own intellectual sabotage. Making oneself blind to parental weakness is the very first act of achieving the proper level of culturally essential stupidity, i.e., strength. My feeling is that the process starts in infancy. This should be studied—maybe by a grant from the National Institute for Mental Health.

The Transfiguration of Innocence

Only those who have walked in the shadow of guilt can know the transfiguring experience of being innocent. To the average person, oppressed from the age of two by the fact that he is less and less rewarded for doing what he is supposed to do—because it is taken for granted—and instead pun-

* Described in Richard Hofstadter's *Anti-Intellectualism in American Life* (Vintage Books; New York, Random House, 1965).

ished for not doing it, the experience of being innocent may become an almost palpable thing. If we consider also the accusations heaped on him—for not eating what is on his plate, for leaving his clothes lying around, for not respecting his parents, for being ungrateful or for not telling the truth, and add to this the harm he does to his own soul by lying to it and suppressing it—it is easy to understand why, in our culture, even the average person must feel guilty all the time, and why, therefore, a situation in which he can feel "it's him, not me" may be exhilarating, and in extreme cases, even transfiguring. When a person is sick with guilt, the need for innocence is a kind of addiction, and every day he looks for something to happen that will make him feel innocent. He might even develop a need to trap people or to snoop around in their lives. For one who needs to be innocent, who day in and day out must feel this drug chemically in his blood, the world, quite naturally, seems full of evil people, and he therefore is able to look upon himself as a lamb, a Mr. He-wouldn't-hurt-a-fly.

The thrill of innocence must be most intense in an executioner.

Space and Time Again

As a child is growing up, his relationship to space changes. At first he is restricted to a crib and to the confinement of his mother's arms. Then he is in a bed or creeping around on the floor from room to room. Later he is outside, alone, but only on "our side of the street," or perhaps in a neighbor's yard or apartment. In a few years he goes to school, perhaps many blocks away from home, going there and back with other children or alone. Concomitant with each of his changing relationships to space there develops a different unfolding of the emotional life: the absolute, perhaps tranquil, dependence of the infant; the lesser dependence but more turbulent life of the creeper; the greater independence of the schoolchild, floundering now in the sea of emotion created in him by the encounters with teachers and the flood of other school children. The relationship between changing emotional life and changing orientation to space seems circular, until we ask the questions, "Suppose a twelve-year-old boy always stayed in the house after school—wouldn't it be bad for him? Wouldn't there be something wrong with him?" We recognize that a boy of that age has to run around, go skating, go over to the park, and so on. But this is not only because "that is the life of a boy in America" but because everything that is happening to him at that time—the things he learns in class, the stimulation of the other children and the possibility of using his muscles in new ways—impels him to move around on a big scale. But something is taking place in the emotional life of a boy of twelve in our culture: more and more, he wants to get away from his parents, especially from his mother. Staying away from the house—exploiting the freedom-giving potentialities of space—is an expression of the growing resistance to the old ties. Shutting him up would be like drying him up; and if he shut himself up it would be a sure sign that he was drying up—becoming "odd." It would indicate that he could not solve his dependency problems with his parents.

Thus space and time are amalgamated with the emotional life of the growing child. Time—cultural time, in the form of changing experiences and changing expectations—presses the personality inexorably on, and together with the press of time the culture offers and imposes changing modes of space. To the inner change there is a corresponding outer change, and while time is experienced as a change in the self and in one's relationships to people, space is experienced as an outer configuration that corresponds to the changes which, as a function of cultural time, are taking place within and toward other people. Our cultural metaphysic must become part of our flesh and bone, part of self, part of our breathing and heartbeat if we want to survive, if we want to stay out of the hospital and the lunatic asylum.

All writings on children—from Freud to Spock—discuss the child-in-time, but the fact that there are no geographies of children's movement proves the obvious: when we think about children, our thinking is overshadowed by time as phantasm. Thinking about the child-in-time is anxious thinking; thinking about the child-in-space is more likely to be accompanied by real fears—of the child getting lost, of being hurt, of becoming a nuisance to Mrs. Figbert, and so on, and although we lose these fears as the child grows up, we never lose our fears about the child-in-time until our son is "established" and our daughter married to a "nice boy with good prospects." Fears about the child-in-time last a long, long time, and are symbolized by such expressions as "He's twenty-five and hasn't made anything of himself yet"; "It's about time he settled down"; "She's a nice-looking girl but here she is twenty-five and she hasn't got a husband yet." We fear time more than space in our culture, and so, in line with the universal law, we have spun a complex folk metaphysic of time—even dividing it into folk stages—hypostasized in the theory of psychosexual development—but we have only the mere beginnings of a metaphysic of space for our children. The metaphysic of time—expressed in the psychoanalytic theory of the oral, anal, phallic, latency and genital phases, in the IQ tests, school-achievement tests, etc.—is an anxiety-binding metaphysic, as they all are. Erikson's chart of psychosexual development* is the most perfect expression in print of the metaphysic of time from the psychoanalytic point of view. Depending on how old your child is, you can stick him in one of Erikson's boxes—and your child is defined! Erikson's own awareness that his system doesn't really define anything, however, is proved by the fact that having put it on paper in the beginning of the book, *he never uses it again.* Like all metaphysics, the child-metaphysic-of-time reassures us that we understand time; all we have to do to know where our child is or should be in time is to refer to the little numbers, slots, boxes, etc., provided by the metaphysic.

I have written these introductory essays in order to help the reader understand the Rosenberg family, or, more candidly, to convince him that

* In *Childhood and Society*, rev. ed. (New York, Norton, 1964).

he ought to see the family as I do. Sham, the fear of nothingness, pain, hostile dependency, weakness, strength, the yearning to be innocent, space and time—conditions which affect the lives of many in our culture, are, in the Rosenberg family, formed into a unique configuration which is their culture, the special environment of their misery.

THE ROSENBERG FAMILY

Mr. and Mrs. Rosenberg, now in their forties, are immigrants from the ghettos of Eastern Europe. When I visited them their eldest son, Abraham, sixteen years old, was in an institution, but Irving, who was between thirteen and fourteen years old, and Benjamin, his twelve-year-old brother, were living at home. Mrs. Rosenberg seems to have had enough education to enable her to hold a full-time job as a file clerk in a printing company, but her husband has had very little. He works as a craftsman, repairing furniture.

Mrs. Rosenberg

In a conventional case record Mrs. Rosenberg would appear as "dominating" or "overadequate"; yet she really is not far different from the traditional mother of the Old World *shtetl*.* Her husband is out of bed at five o'clock and gets his own breakfast, and she is up at six. She wakes Ben and Irving at seven-fifteen, makes their omelet, prepares lunch for them and puts it in the refrigerator, and gets things ready for dinner, leaving instructions for Ben: what to give Irving for lunch, when to turn on the oven for the meat loaf, what to give me to eat, and so on. She says of her day, "I'm tired before I start." She talks incessantly. During the day, when she is at the office, she calls up and checks with Ben to see what happened with the repairman, whether Irving got his breakfast, whether I have been fed, etc.

Even though Mr. Rosenberg was at home, it was she who introduced me to the boys when I arrived, and the next day it was she who made the knots in their ties when they dressed for graduation from Hebrew school. At the office she takes the first step toward being friendly. "You have to be a friend to have a friend," she says, and she hoards supplies so that when the girls run out of something, they will depend on her to have it. Since she keeps track of where everything is, the girls come to her for information and are amazed at what she knows.

When she gets home from work she walks right into the kitchen, cleans up and gets dinner. Then she washes the dinner dishes, prods the boys to do their homework and falls into bed. At home she is restlessly busy, like a

---

* The *shtetl* was the East European Jewish community so well described by Marc Zborowski and Elizabeth Herzog in *Life Is With People* (New York, International Universities Press, 1962). On pp. 131–32 the authors point out that most *shtetl* women were gainfully employed, often away from home; they were usually more worldly than their husbands and spoke the national language better (Polish, Russian, Hungarian, etc.).

good Jewish mother, even jumping up from the table in the middle of a meal to water the plants. Yet she is so weakened by a debilitating chronic illness that she needs to see a doctor regularly. The trip to the doctor is a tortuous, hour-long journey by bus. It is only a few minutes by car—but the Rosenbergs don't have one. Sometimes her cousin drives her there; if he happens to be going in that direction, he'll call her suddenly, and she'll drop whatever she is doing, gulp down her food and be ready when he comes by.

Mrs. Rosenberg is one of five survivors out of eleven children. Though she resented her father, who preferred her sisters, Mrs. Rosenberg, always considered the "mean one" in the family, took care of him in his old age; after her self-sacrificing mother died, Mrs. Rosenberg shared an apartment with her father, her husband, her sister Tillie and a married sister and her son. (Tillie continued to live with the Rosenbergs until she herself got married. I was given her old room while I stayed there.) Mrs. Rosenberg had kept house, but her father had done the cooking (her cooking is unspeakable). She complained that her father would not let her sleep in the same bed with her husband "because it wasn't orthodox"; in a really orthodox family in the *shtetl*, husband and wife do not sleep in the same bed. "And there I was, married," she said, "and had nobody to sleep with." Now the Rosenbergs have a double bed.

For a long time Mr. Rosenberg had been too sick to work, so to "protect" him his wife kept everything about the children from him. What could have been so terrible about the children that "everything" had to be kept from him?

"I was a poor student," Mrs. Rosenberg says, so she did not go to college, like her girl friends. They married rabbis but "I had no luck," she says of her own husband. But he is a good, honest man, and if she had it to do over again she would marry him. To prove it she told me of a dream in which she saw many people with masks. One took his off—and it was her husband (an honest man in a mask!).

On the third day of my stay I said to Mrs. Rosenberg, "You say that your husband is such a good man, but the children seem to be closer to you." She quickly replied, "Well, he hands all responsibility and decisions over to me. He even gives me the money." * She is the "tough one," she says, and I noticed that while her husband might wish to shilly-shally or put things off, she would box him in, so he could not escape doing what they had decided was necessary. She was able to find work even during the Depression— sometimes she even had two jobs. "When I want something, I don't give up," she said.

Though her husband has been a disappointment, Mrs. Rosenberg tried to varnish her reservations with the account of the dream of the honest man unmasked. She cannot consciously know that her dream really told her that she feels her husband is a man in a mask. She talks in riddles, revealing and concealing at the same time. Challenged directly, she may lie to defend her husband.

It was hard to carry on a conversation with Mrs. Rosenberg because she

* The woman of the house is the mother of the whole family, including the father." *Ibid.*, p. 291.

seemed always to be thinking of something else or to be defending herself, as she ambled among contradictions and vagueness. She was anxious to tell me, however, how poor the family was now, and how dependent on relatives; how people tried to take advantage of her and her husband, and how those you believe are your friends try to use you. In one form or another these ideas came up spontaneously over and over again as she talked to me: because the Rosenbergs were poor, they were given money by relatives. They never had anything to call their own before they got this house; they wear hand-me-downs; her husband is exploited by relatives and friends who ask him to do jobs for them and then complain that the price is too high; the man who sold them shrubbery tried to cheat; the store where they bought the radio tried to avoid honoring the guarantee; some relatives never do a thing for the Rosenbergs; a man for whom Mr. Rosenberg did a favor never reciprocated, etc., etc., etc. Mr. Rosenberg, however, never talked this way. Mrs. Rosenberg may have been afraid that I would spy for the Agency caring for Abe and then report on their financial status. If so, she was never able to lose this fear, and repeatedly created opportunities for emphasizing misfortune.

This Old World Jewish woman who felt the lack of a higher education, who saw her friends marry learned men, whose husband was "no luck" and chronically ill (as she herself was)—this woman, who in her own eyes was nothing, had a brilliant first-born son, Abraham.

Mrs. Rosenberg compares Abe with Irving, for often when I pressed her about Abe, she would speak belittlingly of his brother. At the same time, she wonders how Irving knows she and his father prefer Ben to him, since they treat Irving and Ben equally. Bennie was an "accident" ("I didn't want him in the worst way"), but he turned out to be a good boy and there is no doubt that he is prized far above the others. Ben is "Mama's boy," she says to him affectionately.

Even before the family façade finally crumbled, Ben and Irving were alternately withdrawn, openly hostile or slightly responsive to their mother in my presence, and her atrocious cooking made matters worse (Abe had even complained about it to his social worker).

Nobody made as determined an effort as Mrs. Rosenberg to appear "right" to me. Into this pathetic "plot" she attempted to draw her husband and the two boys, but Mr. Rosenberg never accepted her plan, though he did not tell her; and though the boys seem to have tried, they could not keep up the front—their counter-impulses were too powerful. My first day's notes contain the following:

Mrs. Rosenberg is a pleasant, plain, dark-haired woman. When I arrived she was in the kitchen getting dinner; she came to the door, greeted me with a smile and let me in. There was some stiffness, but it seems she controls the standard social techniques. I sat down in the living room and she came out of the kitchen a few times to talk to me. She said she has worked in an office a long time and enjoys office work.

The next morning:

When Irving came into the kitchen (for breakfast) there was an exchange of kisses, and when Ben came down, she turned her head and called out musically, "Good morning, Bennie!"

At the week's end, my notes read:

> Mrs. Rosenberg has been looking very haggard, bewildered and frightened. There is no doubt that these kids have their parents over a barrel, and terrified. Mrs. Rosenberg looks beat.

This is a woman about whom one says, "Things just seem to get dumped on her head," or "Poor Mrs. Rosenberg, if it isn't one thing it's another; she got a raw deal, and it just keeps on getting more and more raw. She just can't seem to get any pleasure out of life." Even when recognizing how blind and destructive she has been, one remembers also her background, the agitation of her daily life, how hard she takes everything, how conscientious she is and how consistently, yet how unsuccessfully, she works at being a good mother. The following from my notes on the third morning illustrate some of the points of which I speak:

> It took her a long time to fall asleep, she said, and then she woke up in the middle of the night. She was terribly upset by what had taken place between her cousin and the authorities at the synagogue the evening before, and it spoiled the pleasure of her sons' graduation from Hebrew school.
> After the graduation ceremony there were refreshments downstairs in the basement of the synagogue. The festivities were held in two rooms, one for the parents and guests of the graduating students, another for children not graduating. Mrs. Rosenberg's cousin tried to bring his two children into the room reserved for the graduating students, their relatives and guests, but was blocked at the door and got into a tremendous argument, which was terribly embarrassing to his wife and to Mr. and Mrs. Rosenberg. The result was that during the festivities Mr. and Mrs. Rosenberg were very agitated, particularly the latter, who was so upset she couldn't talk.
> She was also disturbed by the fact that the brother of a girl friend is in very bad shape. He has been in and out of a mental hospital repeatedly. Sometimes he gets well and comes home, and then he takes a turn for the worse. He had just had to return again, and this upset Mrs. Rosenberg very much because it reminds her of Abe. She had a terrible dream, which she did not tell me. She was feeling very bad this morning and very tired, and I'm pretty sure she must have been happy when I suggested driving her to work.
> On the way she talked about all the things she has to do in addition to her job. She has to call the vegetable man, the butcher and the grocer to get things delivered. She is in a constant state of agitation over all the things she has to do, and she said, with striking insight, "You always put other things in the way of things you are worrying about." Then she told a joke: one man was telling another about how to cure a cold. He said, "You have a cold and you take a very hot bath and then stand in front of an open window." The other man said, "But that will give you pneumonia!" And the first man said, "Yes, but you will be rid of the cold." Mrs. Rosenberg sees herself in that position. Behind this constant driving activity of hers there is a great push of anxiety.

So one would say of her, "It isn't enough that she has her own problems to worry about, she has to get upset about her cousin and even about her girl friend's brother!" But we know that when a person is bursting with anxiety, when he is like a river levee holding back a flood, any added little thing can make the anxiety spill over and flood him in the night, destroying sleep. This is Mrs. Rosenberg today.

To sum up: in the sense of getting things done and even getting her husband to do what she wants him to, Mrs. Rosenberg is the most adequate person in the house. Incessantly talking, ordering, driving, nevertheless she barely restrains within her an explosive mixture of anxiety, rage, suspicion, dependency, confusion and feelings of vulnerability, worthlessness and helplessness. She married a man for whom she has little respect, who can take no responsibility and who has been sickly all his life, and although he has given her three children, one has become very severely emotionally disturbed and Irving is badly disturbed. Only Ben seems a possibility; he has so much of what she really wants in a child—acquiescence. Yet even from Ben she gets little, and there are days when the two boys together drive her to desperation. Though in a "clinical" or "case history" sense she is "dominating," she is unable to dominate her life. And even when she dominates or tries to dominate her family, her aggressiveness returns to her in visible or hidden waves of resentment and withdrawal. Actually she is imprisoned by the enemies she has created in her own household.

Mr. Rosenberg

In a conventional case record Mr. Rosenberg would appear as "inadequate." Here is my impression from the field notes of the first day:

Mr. Rosenberg, because of his air of passivity, gives the impression of being shorter than his dominating wife. His worn clothing hung baggily on him. Simply and without ceremony he came and talked to me. Superficially he is completely unaggressive. In the evening, when Irving and Ben came home from Hebrew school Mr. Rosenberg did not get up but I did, and it was Mrs. Rosenberg who introduced me to the boys. They said nothing and went into the kitchen to have supper.

While Mrs. Rosenberg was giving the boys their supper, Mr. Rosenberg and I sat in the living room. So the bustle in the kitchen revolved around Mrs. Rosenberg.

Mr. Rosenberg's father would never let the family know how much money he was making. He was a "religious fanatic," and that is why, says Mr. Rosenberg, he himself has no interest in religion. However, the Rosenbergs keep the Hebrew dietary laws. In contradictory fashion Mr. Rosenberg wants the boys to continue in Hebrew school, even though he rejects religion and, in many ways, Judaism. One day in *cheder*,* he says, some rich kids tore some pages out of the Torah and blamed him, and since he is of a poor family, the *melamed*, or teacher, who also happened to be his mother's brother, beat him bloody, and his mother beat him too, even though he denied having had anything to do with the mutilated Torah. After his beatings he never went back to *cheder*. "In the old country," Mrs. Rosenberg added, "nothing the children said ever mattered." By *shtetl* standards, there is nothing surprising in these beatings, nor in Mr. Rosenberg's mother's refusal to listen to him, yet these experiences permanently undermined his feelings for things Jewish.

* The first school in the Jewish education of a child.

When he was a child in Europe, Mr. Rosenberg was hit in the head with a rock thrown by a Russian boy, but, says Mr. Rosenberg, since the Jews owned all the businesses in town, anti-Semitism was justified. Mr. Rosenberg ridicules the Jews' proclivity for multiplying synagogues in this country. He thinks the reason they do so is that somebody in the congregation makes money out of it. The money spent on synagogues, he says, might better be spent on hospitals. The Rosenbergs live in a predominantly Jewish neighborhood and associate almost exclusively with relatives.

As a child, Mr. Rosenberg suffered extreme hardships, and when he came to America he worked for years in a factory. He tried to go to night school, but "you know, you can't learn very much at night school after working all day." Today his accent is still very heavy, and this, combined with a general tendency to garbled thought, sometimes makes him difficult to understand. His wife's English is far better.

Mr. Rosenberg has worked for many years at a modest wage for an uncle who took care of him when he came to the United States, and although he cannot remember when he last received a raise, he has nothing but good to say about his uncle. Mrs. Rosenberg, however, resents the low pay, and when he points out that his uncle pays him when he is sick, she says, "He pays his sweeper too." Up at five o'clock in the morning, Mr. Rosenberg gets to work by seven, sits down, relaxes and reads the paper. Because of his chronic illness, he finds that it still makes him sick to hurry, so if he gets to work early he can be more leisurely on the job. Getting to work early also has something to do with his uncle's having been so good to him. Except for the bit about reading the paper—and it is true that *nobody* can relax in the Rosenberg home—everything else about the explanation of the early rising is unclear to me. If, for example, the idea of getting to work early is to start early so that he won't have to hurry—and no craftsman wants to be rushed —why does he read the paper? And how does getting to work at seven o'clock repay his uncle's kindness, when all Mr. Rosenberg does is sit around and read the paper?

After he married, his wife's family became a haven for Mr. Rosenberg. When he was sick and unable to work, her sisters supported him, his wife and the children; and these sisters have not ceased to contribute, along with other relatives on the wife's side, to the Rosenberg income. Yet Mr. Rosenberg resents his dependence and often told me how "queer" his wife's relatives are. He talks against his relatives by marriage on his own side too.

On the fourth day of my stay with the Rosenbergs I took a long walk with him. Here is my diary:

Mr. Rosenberg said he wanted to tell me everything, to be absolutely truthful. He said his wife is very violent. She beats the boys with her fist or with a strap when she gets very angry, and she used to beat Abe, who hates her. She would take Abe around to show him off. Because of her constant badgering, Abe once threatened to commit suicide and locked himself in the bathroom with a razor, which he did not use, however. He said his mother was driving him to desperation. This precipitated their seeking help with Agency X, and then, after waiting around for two years and nothing was accomplished, with Agency Y.

According to Mr. Rosenberg, he and his wife have always gotten along well; they're always happy together and always help each other, even though she has an ungovernable temper—like the rest of her family. A sister of hers drank a whole bottle of iodine in a rage. He said he wouldn't let his wife know he had told me all this because "Mrs. Rosenberg wouldn't want me to go too far in telling you about the family."

Mr. Rosenberg says that he never really gets angry, and that his wife never really gets angry at him because he is not the kind that fights back. He can handle her. He protects the children against her rages.

He hates to take charity. Abe is being taken care of by the Agency and this upsets Mr. Rosenberg a great deal, for he contributes only $10 a week. Someday he would like to return all the money.

His wife's family has a lot of eccentrics in it. Her brother, the engineer, behaves queerly. Her sister Tillie is a really dominating woman, just like Mrs. Rosenberg, he says.

No matter how much an East European mother loved her child, she might hit him if she got angry enough and words did not do any good, but from Mr. Rosenberg's story it sounds as if his wife's ungovernable temper —a disgrace to a Jewish house—drives her to extremes. By his description of himself, however, Mr. Rosenberg is, in *shtetl* tradition, a really good Jew, who never gets angry at his wife. On the other hand, while she is very Jewish in trying to hide the family "shame" from the world, her husband tells me, an outsider, that he holds her responsible for what happened to the children and that Irving had at one time written some insulting things about her on their wall, for which he does not blame him. Thus Mr. Rosenberg, while usually hostile to Irving, is—without knowing it—in cahoots with him against the mother. This is one of the several deceptions in the family.

Mr. Rosenberg hates to "take charity." "I don't want to take anything from anyone";* people give you things only in order to get their clutches on you, he says. So, like his wife, he is torn between the actuality of vulnerability and the necessity of being dependent on the one hand, and the yearning to be independent on the other. What people might do if they get their clutches on him was never made clear. Thus, for Mr. Rosenberg, as for most of us in one way or another, unbearable actualities created undesirable necessities which bring into being unrealizable yearnings. This is perhaps the first law of man-in-civilization. As for the equation "vulnerability = dependence = yearning-to-be-independent," it holds as true for the "organization man" and for any child in our culture as for the Rosenbergs. For millions, it projects the will-o'-the-wisp of freedom.

Although Mr. Rosenberg made breakfast the Saturday I was there, he does not ordinarily help his wife with the housework, for no East European Jewish husband would. At home Mr. Rosenberg works a little in the garden, sits around staring into space or watching TV. Aside from mealtimes, parents and children have little contact. Mr. Rosenberg departs from this rule when he interferes in the fights between the boys, and when he snuggles up to Ben, of whom he is really fond. Then, in a radical departure from the *shtetl* pattern for fathers, he will fondle him, and might even thrust a hand under the boy's buttocks.

---

* Zborowski and Herzog repeatedly point to the ready acceptance by *shtetl* Jews of help from others. "For the majority of breadwinners in the *shtetl* the prospects of self-sufficiency are low, and the need to 'go to people' for help is an ever-present threat." *Ibid.,* p. 257.

On the other hand, Mr. Rosenberg ridicules Irving behind his back, thinks him a weakling and a blow-hard, and considers his respiratory difficulty "a weapon." Yet he admires him ("How does he manage to get all A's when he does no work?"). Since Irving does study, his father's failure to see it is a misperception—one of many Mr. Rosenberg has of his son. But Mr. Rosenberg is worried about Irving with reason—he's afraid he'll go the way of Abe.

"I'll have a problem," he remarked to me on the day before I left.

"You've got one already," I said.

Mr. and Mrs. Rosenberg never touched each other in my presence; never even sat next to each other in the living room during the week I was there, though they do sleep in a double bed. Mrs. Rosenberg says of her husband, she "had no luck," and to him she became a force with which he coped by effacing himself. Getting along together, then, is an accommodation by avoidance, and Mr. Rosenberg gives his wife a free hand with the boys, to beat and scream at, for although he avers that he protects the children from her, his "protection" cannot amount to much if she is able to hit them with fist and strap. So the children's misery is ransom for their father's peace and quiet.

Mrs. Rosenberg can live with her poor, uneducated and weak husband only by refusing to admit to herself how ungratifying he is. But after all, what other kind of husband could she have gotten, plain-looking orthodox Jewish girl without money? For his part, feeling her low evaluation of him, Mr. Rosenberg cannot help resenting it. They have lived together for nearly twenty years, neither telling the other of his disappointment; each, nevertheless, letting the other see how he felt; neither trying to escape. What could they have done? Where could they have gone? Their marriage became what has been called an "emotional divorce." *

Learning to live with a person you do not love and respect, learning to live with a person you know neither loves nor respects you is merely learning how to die, how to walk around as a shell, how to deny what you feel, how to hate without showing it, how to weep without tears, how to declare that the sham you live is the true reality and that it is good.

Mr. and Mrs. Rosenberg try to make the best of a sham, but although they "learned to live with each other" (whatever that means), the children are too much for them because there is no foundation for a loving relationship with the children, and intellectually neither parent has the capacity to cope with them.

In the outer world, both mother and father failed to develop the capacity to make themselves very effective; at home, they could attempt to feel effective with their children; yet effectiveness meant largely using the children and imposing discipline, and the dialectic of this is merely withdrawal or resistance or both.

Observing the parents' daily lives at home, I found that nearly all of their time was devoted to getting things done—to servicing, to ordering, to giving commands and yielding to requests, to staring at TV or into space. No word of warmth, no smile, no expression of appreciation or consideration

* See S. Fleck, "The Families of Schizophrenics," in *The Etiology of Schizophrenia*, ed. by Don Jackson (New York, Basic Books, 1960).

passed between husband and wife. An act of solicitude was rare. On the other hand, husband and wife never fought and there was no sign of disagreement—nor of agreement, either. Between Mr. and Mrs. Rosenberg there was rarely any conversation.

The tragedy is that Abraham and Irving were born to this household, for it is an iron law of our culture that a mother and father living a sham can only damage their children. Furthermore, what could such parents do with such children? Deprived by circumstances and upbringing of the intellectual and emotional resources essential to dealing with superiority, they could parade it, push it—attempt to subdue it, but when it turned on them they felt vulnerable and reacted with violence. Fundamentally, neither parent was prepared for anything but acquiescence in children, and when they did not get it they became anxious and resentful. Benjamin therefore came to represent good—acquiescence and calm—and Irving evil—restiveness and anger.

Benjamin and Irving

Angel and Devil

The contrast between the boys is enormous: Irving is leaner and markedly more handsome than his brother. In school Irving gets the highest grades and is a captain in the student patrol; Ben's grades have lately gone down and he is not in the patrol at all. Though bright, he does not have his brother's unsettling, incisive brilliance—or if he does, he has learned to conceal it; he does not talk much. Irving and Ben lack the synchronized, fluid mobility of the usual lean and limber American boy: on the school ball field, when playing with products of American athletic culture, Irving is sent to pick daisies in the outfield. When boys and girls play baseball together, the girls use the occasion to provoke the boys sexually, but they never come near Irving. I did not watch Ben on the ball field, but when he played with Irving I could see that he was at least as awkward.

Except for the necessary trips to school, close to home, and for private games with a small rubber ball on the pavement outside their house, Irving and Ben did not go out. While I was there, only one friend phoned, and the brothers called no one. In anger and at peace, in play or just watching TV, once away from school they had practically no one but each other, their parents, and a (despised) teen-age male relative who came occasionally to play and get a meal. In this isolation the brothers are like their parents.

Ben is acquiescent—"Mama's boy" and papa's joy—but to Irving acquiescence is submission, and if he can possibly escape he will do nothing to help anybody in the house. Ben is Irving's "slave," performing many little chores for him—even, I was told, to the extent of looking up words in the dictionary for him. If Ben refuses, Irving beats him. Ben, however, says he enjoys these scrimmages and that he likes being his brother's slave. Irving calls using people "efficiency" and is proud of it, but he needs Ben, and even gets into his bed at night to sleep with his arm around his brother, pressed against his back, as I saw. With contempt in her voice, the mother told me that Irving has to take Ben along if he goes to the downstairs lavatory in the middle of the night.

Ben is much more than his brother's slave; he is maternal, even somewhat wifely, waiting on Irving, hovering over him, accepting him in sleep. And Irving lords it over his brother and beats him up, though constantly demonstrating his own dependence.

Master and Slave or Child and Mother?

At noon on the second day of my visit I got my first view of the relationship between the boys.

When Ben came home after school for lunch, he asked whether I would have tuna fish or meat. When I said I'd have fish, Ben set out the tuna their mother had left us. Then, after wandering around and turning on the TV, which he did not look at, he made a tuna sandwich for Irv.

Meanwhile Irv was outside on patrol; his post is practically outside the door. Ben called him in, and Irv came in and sat down and ate his sandwich while Ben heated up a very big chunk of meat. There was more than enough meat for a family, and it took quite a long time to heat, but he only took a small piece of it. Irv said with a smile, "Ben is my slave," and he spoke of his own "efficiency," saying he is more efficient than Ben. He calls his exploitation of people "efficiency." He says he directs Ben, telling him what to do. Ben says he does what he's told because if he doesn't, their mother "would get mad and kill both of us," so when Irv goofs off, Ben does the work of both. Ben hustled around the kitchen just like Mrs. Rosenberg. It was Ben who asked me whether I wanted this thing or that with my lunch—never Irv.

All of a sudden Ben asked me whether I knew how to play a certain ball game. When I said no, he started to tell me but Irv took over the description, and Ben asked plaintively, "Can I tell him?" So Irv kept quiet and Ben told me.

During lunch Irv talked a blue streak about having been made captain in the patrol, how kids look up to him now, how he can order them around. Ben performed his mother's function in the kitchen, while Irv performed his mother's function of talking.

The school authorities rely on Irving: perceiving virtue in his tendencies to tyranny, they made him a captain. Yet his parents have no confidence in him; they resent his efforts to enslave Ben and accuse him of selfishness, timidity, showing off and talking big. Thus life at home is made more difficult because the parents dislike in Irving what the school rewards, and because Ben accepts what the parents abhor. Since Irving is unreliable at home, his mother asks Ben when she wants something done. On patrol Irving watches over other children; at home Ben watches over *him*. On the other hand, although Irving shows no interest in his brother's welfare, Irving's welfare is his brother's concern; more so, even, than it is their mother's, for Ben has the capacity to minister, in a pathological way to be sure, to Irving's inner needs. Ben perceives and ministers to the unmet needs of the whole family; in his strange way he is the only one who makes living in this family tolerable.

Ben asked Irv if he had had his milk; so Irv asked him, challengingly, if he had had *his* milk. Ben tries to be a mother to Irv, even to the point of provoking him by anxious hovering; even to the extent of somewhat taking on the maternal anxiety and dominance. What could be a more perfect expression of this than the question, "Have you had your milk?"

(Third day.) As Irv left the house to go to school after lunch, he gave Ben directions for cleaning up.

While we were eating lunch the air-conditioning man, who had come to look at the broken unit in the boys' room, rang the bell. Ben jumped up from the table to let him in and went upstairs with him. Nothing came of it because they were not expecting him and the mother had left no money.

When Mrs. Rosenberg called up around twelve-thirty, Ben answered and told her about the repairman. She wanted to know if Irv had had breakfast, and Ben, on my instruction, told her I had made breakfast for him. (On the day after the graduation ceremony at the synagogue Irv had refused to get up, so at Mrs. Rosenberg's request I fried the omelet she had prepared and gave it to him when he got up.)

Later I offered to take Ben someplace—any place he wanted to go—but he said, "Not just now; I have to wait for Irv because I don't know if he has a key." When Irving came home I asked him whether he carried a key and he said, "About ninety-nine percent of the time," and showed me his on a long chain.

I asked Ben how it was that he did all the chores and he answered, "Because Irving doesn't cook so good and because Irving gets dressed fast in the morning and comes downstairs," so Ben is left upstairs to make the beds.

On the fourth day I took Ben to a delicatessen in the shopping center:

I asked him whether he would like some pickles. He thought for a moment and then said, "I don't think Irving needs any." I asked him if *he* wanted something, and he said, "I don't need anything."

Ben, the embodiment of the maternal presence, exerting its *benevolent* force when the mother is not corporeally there, accounts for his own activity through his brother: *Irving is the metaphysic of his brother's existence. Irving's tyranny and dependence give his brother a reason for existing. Irving is Ben's flight from death.* Even when Ben's reasons for not going out have nothing to do with Irving's not having a key, Ben explains his own behavior as if it did. It is common in psychiatric theory to speak of the symbiotic relation of a child to his mother; here we have it between brothers, expressed *as if it were a relation between mother and child.*

(Fifth day.) Irving was in the kitchen and Ben was in the living room when Irving asked Ben if he wanted some orange juice. Ben turned to me and said, "Irving wants me to drink up what is left of the orange juice so he can make lemonade in the container." When Ben refused the juice, Irving poured it into a glass, and when it overflowed he got another glass, which he set down in the puddle, and then poured the rest into the second glass. The puddle remained on the table the whole afternoon, until about five o'clock, when Ben wiped it up. By that time most of it had evaporated.

Using the container that had held the orange juice, Irving used a concentrate to make lemonade, punching only one hole in the can. He did not offer any of it to anybody.

There is a limit to Ben's obedience: he won't drink orange juice he does not want; he often waits a long time before performing a task and sometimes refuses altogether. Knowing how selfish his brother is, when Ben is suddenly offered something he surmises it is not out of solicitude, and a few minutes later Irving reinforces skepticism when, having made lemonade, he does not offer any to his brother.

Ben asked me whether I wanted hot dogs for lunch. I asked him if he was going to have them and he said yes, so I said I'd have some too. Ben put on the water, and when it boiled, Irving put the franks in one at a time, gingerly, from a considerable distance, acting as if there was danger of a hot geyser erupting from the pot. He looked scared.

Though Ben is the one who asks me about my lunch, he turns cooking the frankfurters over to Irving because he has a great deal of anxiety about the stove. Once, when he put a meat loaf in the oven, he asked Irving to light it.

Irving's relations to physical things puzzle me, and I am reluctant to interpret his reactions. He doesn't seem to perceive objects the way most of us do: for example, his trying to pour all the orange juice into one small glass and punching only one hole in the lemonade can, whereas most people would punch two to facilitate the flow. So I am not ready to say that he is "disappropriately fearful" of the hot water in which the frankfurters were cooked. After all, he does so little in the kitchen, maybe it never entered his head that he could lower a string of frankfurters slowly into the water. Perhaps the same reasoning applies to the orange juice and the lemonade can: Irving is waited on so much, he may simply be inept at doing anything around the house—like his father, for example.

At any rate, what the frankfurter and meat-loaf incidents prove is that Irving will help Ben out when Ben is scared—even at some possible risk to himself. It is something like taking care of the weaker sex.

The record of the day continues:

I told Irving I would like to see some of his drawings, since his mother had told me he draws well, so he looked for his stuff in the drawer of a chest in the living room but could not find it. He asked Ben where it was and Ben said he thought it was downstairs; Irving sent him down to the basement and Ben found it. It was some drawings of astronauts.

When an observer stays in with the boys he perceives a constant interplay between them in which Irving tries to assert himself over Ben. Irving does not always get precisely what he wants, but he gets enough to maintain the *appearance of dominance*. In this way—by *relative* submission— Ben does his brother a good turn; he manages to make him feel big.

Since Ben had no school after twelve o'clock, afternoons were long drawn out, excruciatingly empty and boring, and he started to exist only when Irving came home.

After Irving came home from school, the boys went outside to play ball. They asked me if I would like to come out and watch. They played with a small, soft rubber ball. They set a very small box on the pavement and Ben stood behind it, while Irving stood about fifteen feet away and threw him the ball. Irving was pretending to be a pitcher. Although he pitched very weakly, I could see from the way he fingered the ball that he fantasied throwing fast curves. Both boys pretended they were professional ballplayers and took their names. The game consisted of Irving's trying to throw the ball over the plate (i.e., the box). If it went over it was a strike, otherwise it was a ball. Irving was the main person in the game. Ben frequently missed the ball. You could see he wasn't very good at it. When he threw the ball back to Irving, it was not quite in a feminine way, but it was not masculine. Irving didn't throw the ball in a masculine way either. They played alone all the rest of the afternoon. Their mother says they enjoy so much being with each other that they don't need other children, but now I believe that their failure to mix with other boys is related not only to the general fearfulness cultivated in this household, but also to the fact that neither boy is really masculine. I asked Irving about their playing alone and he said they usually do.

Without a masculine figure in the house, and dominated by the mother, the boys, anxiously dramatizing, acting out with each other the overshadowing meaning she has for them, have not been able to develop like average American boys. The anxiety generated by their mother and the need to master it, the opportunity to master it through working it out on each other, and the domestic absence of the father—present in body but absent in capacity—have brought it about that the boys reinforce each other's feminine tendencies. The lack of masculinity intensifies their isolation, because boys and girls avoid them.

Since the foundations for their roles as American boys were never given to Irving and Ben in the family and since they remained isolated from other children, the culture could not perform its essential task, which is to help build roles. Once a child has received in the family the basic qualities from which his role in society can be formed, other children gather around and pound him into shape. But if this foundation is missing, the other children shy away as if he were diseased, which permits the unusual child to continue along his unusual path. The school authorities are happy to undertake Irving's further development because they see—or think they see—in Irving's conscientious control of other children a trait they can use. But most other children of Irving and Ben's age perceive nothing in the boys they can use, so they avoid them, making it easy for Irving and Ben to withdraw from the culture. When I got there they were already pretty far out—which means, far out from their peer culture.

As they play their pathetic, physically undemanding ball games, requiring no glove because they use a soft rubber ball, standing only about fifteen feet apart (instead of the usual thirty to forty feet, for boys their age), they imagine themselves big-league stars, and Ben plays his role of foil for Irving; before Ben, Irving can indeed imagine himself a star pitcher, as he does fairly frequently.

After school Irving and Ben began to play the same ball game as yesterday. Before they went outdoors, Irving complained that his arm had been thrown out by the eighty pitches he had made last Saturday. He said that now he understands why big-league pitchers have to rest between games. He beat Ben, as usual.

Since in our culture boys dream of being big-league players and since they learn to throw a ball like professionals, only without their virtuosity and power, there is nothing strange in Irving's fantasies. What makes them pathetic, however, and gives them the quality of parody, is that his throw is so feminine—the wrong accompaniment to the right fantasy.

The boys were playing chess and I watched. Irving constantly accused Ben of taking too long to move; he kept up an unremitting barrage. Irv said, "It takes me fifteen seconds to move—I plan ahead." The game ended when Irving check-mated Ben. In response to Irving's hurrying him, Ben said, "You have to have patience. You have to concentrate." Irving scarcely hesitated before making his moves; and he was no doubt able to do that because he got Ben so rattled by his drumfire that Ben made many mistakes.

Irving was very proud of the move he made in checkmating Ben. When Ben lost, he said to Irving, "I got more points than you."

A little later he called Irving a "waster" for not having eaten his custard ear-lier.

Irving left to go on patrol, and I went along to watch him. I saw him stop two little girls on suspicion of having stolen flowers from a neighbor's bushes as they walked along on their way to school. He told me he would report it to Miss X— someone in the "office" who apparently supervises the patrol. Irving seemed rather conscientious and somewhat officious in his job as roving officer. As a patrol captain, he is supposed to roam from post to post and see how others are doing.

Irving had left his dishes for Ben to do. Later, just before his mother came home, Ben washed and wiped all the dishes.

Irving is grossly unfair in the chess game because he cannot wait. Here are two more examples of Irving's need to have everything happen right away:

Just before dinner, Ben had gone to buy a ball. Irving jumped up from the table, took the ball, went into the living room and began to play with it. He bounced it, he went out to the porch with it, and then began to badger Ben to come out and play with him, without giving Ben a chance to eat in peace. Mrs. Rosenberg remonstrated with Irving, saying he should give Ben a chance to eat, and Irving stopped.

.   .   .

Ben and Irving were getting ready for a game of baseball—the kind of box game you buy in a toy store and which you play indoors on the floor or table. To play it you have to prepare with little cards, etc. Irving kept hurrying Ben and threatened not to play if Ben didn't get organized quickly.

Were it not for these additional instances I would have thought that hur-rying Ben in the chess game was just a way Irving had of confusing him in order to win. But when one studies Irving across a range of his activities, one perceives that he simply cannot wait. As a matter of fact, he has diffi-culty suffering any interference at all and he will quit a game or start beat-ing up Ben if Ben misses the ball or makes wild pitches. Irving can let out on his acquiescent brother what he had to bottle up in dealing with his parents or the world.

Through Ben and through others he can dominate, like the little girls bringing stolen flowers to school, Irving reaches for a semblance of *pride*. His brother, however, having renounced domination, has to bolster his self-esteem with the residue of defeat—with anywayness ("I got more points than you") and with accusations ("You're a waster"). Ben has the *patholog-ical pridelessness* of the parents, but Irving will not renounce pride. This is his most serious "defect": *he is hungry for pride in a household that has given up hope of it.*

One evening their cousin Sol came over and, paired with Ben, beat Irving and Sam, a neighbor, in a ball game. When the others had left, Irving, who usually defeats Ben, asked him to play ball, but Ben complained that he was too tired.

Irv then proceeded to beat up Ben, striking him viciously, throwing water at him, but Ben merely laughed as if he were enjoying it. Angrily Mr. Rosenberg tried repeatedly to interfere, but without result.

It is interesting that in all this pommeling—and sprinkling with water—Ben never protested but their father got very angry.

After a while Irving went upstairs and his father yelled after him. One of the things he said was, "Who are you?" In the context it was belittling, and Irving answered back. Then Mr. Rosenberg said, "You don't respect your parents," and Irving answered, "You don't respect me!" which, of course, is the crux of the matter. This was followed by dead silence.

Meanwhile, Mrs. Rosenberg was in the kitchen checking her groceries, washing the huge collection of fruit and preparing for tomorrow's meal. She took no part in the altercation.

Although Ben renders Irving an invaluable service by letting his brother pour out his chronic peevishness on him, Ben's apparent enjoyment may infuriate Irving even further. Fights have an attraction for the father, too, because they provide an occasion when his chronic anger with Irving can be *legitimately** expressed, while at the same time he can imagine that in defending Ben he is coming closer to him, demonstrating his love, his fatherhood and his manhood. Mr. Rosenberg and Irving are acting on the assumption that Ben is being hurt; if they were to admit to themselves that Ben really enjoys the fights—as I shall demonstrate—neither Irving nor Mr. Rosenberg would have anything to gain, Irving would lose the pleasure of believing he is punishing his brother, and his father would lose the pleasure of believing he is protecting one son while combating the other.

In the midst of these ambiguities Irving and his father get into a serious quarrel in which they express mutual disrespect, and Irving silences his parent by confronting him with the truth—that he does not respect his son. Why didn't Mr. Rosenberg say, "I do respect you, but I don't like what you do"? Or was it that he found the idea that a father should respect his son shockingly novel?† Thus, in the act of trying to be a good father to one son, Mr. Rosenberg becomes a bad one to the other.

The anger between Irving and Ben is very different from the anger between Irving and his father, for in the first place, the anger between Irving and Ben is mostly in one direction—Irving is angry with Ben but there is little sign of it in the latter; and theirs is an anger without hate, without enemies. Between Irving and his father the anger is mutual—father and son are enemies and despise each other. Mr. Rosenberg's interfering relieves some of his anger against Irving, just as Irving's attack on Ben relieves some of Irving's pent-up despair. In the dialectic of the conflict, however, Ben derives the maximum benefit, thriving on his brother's exasperation with life and on his father's and brother's hostility toward each other.

Beginning with Irving's defeat in the game, the itinerary of anger is as

---

* In *shtetl* families this kind of fighting could not be tolerated in a *sheyn* (fine) family, but was expected to occur in a *prost* (low) family. See Zborowski and Herzog, *loc. cit.*

† In *shtetl* culture, all the emphasis was on the family's respect for the father. *Ibid.*

follows: Irving, always full of pent-up rage and needing to vent some of the exasperation of his latest defeat by defeating his brother, becomes infuriated when Ben refuses to play, and attacks him. But Ben only laughs, probably increasing his brother's anger. Then Mr. Rosenberg, always full of pent-up hostility toward Irving, gets angry at Irving's hitting Ben, the father's favorite, and interferes, further intensifying Irving's rage, which is now transferred to the father. The two end in mutual recrimination: *truth comes out*, and the father is silenced and probably further angered against Irving. If Irving were not so articulate and so incisive it might have been better for him. This is one of many instances where being too perceptive and too articulate damages Irving with his parents. He is thus not only vulnerable through his weaknesses, but he is vulnerable because of his strengths, too. In pathological environments, a person is rendered vulnerable by his strength; every family must guard against transforming its members' powers into liabilities.

The analysis continues with records of a couple of big fights:

After Irving came home a fight developed between him and Ben and went on intermittently for about forty-five minutes, with Irving pounding Ben, and Ben alternately laughing and complaining that Irv should not try to make him do the work and clean up the house when Irving wasn't doing anything himself. Irving pounded Ben on the arms and back, and Ben pushed his buttocks against him. Irving pushed Ben into a closet on the ground floor and beat him with a shoe and with his knuckles. Part of the time Ben really seemed to be enjoying it. Irving would chase Ben into a corner and beat him on the back with closed fist and with his elbows and sometimes squeeze a knuckle between Ben's ribs, like a screw. He threw Ben down several times. Ben would remonstrate that Irving was doing nothing himself. He never hit Irving back but sometimes tried to overpower him. Neither hit the other in the face nor in the forepart of the body. At last, Irving, tired and quite pale, gave up and sat down in the living room on the settee.

At six o'clock Mrs. Rosenberg came home. I said hello but neither of the boys did. Ben, however, immediately complained to her that he had tried all afternoon to get Irving to go outside but that he wouldn't.

Though ingenious and vicious, Irving is restrained; sparing his brother's face, he *limits* his beating to the less vulnerable parts of the body. And Ben does not fight back—rather, he fights backward, shoving his buttocks against his brother's genitals and belly, so that what is a comfort in sleep becomes a weapon in war—a typical enough feminine maneuver—thus presenting Irving with an insoluble paradox,[*] and reducing his fighting élan. The brothers have entered into a silent entente: Ben will not fight back hard if Irving does not hurt too much. When Ben does complain, it is not so much because of the pain, for he enjoys the fights, but because Irving wants to get him to do all the work. Since Ben protests his role as slave in which the master does not share the task, he is a slave without being a slave; he has accepted the obligation to work and now objects that he is being forced to do what he professes to like doing. And Ben is able to protest because Irving won't hurt him too much, because he has learned how to resist and wear his brother down, because Irving is weakened by years of

* It fits the category of actions described as the "double bind" in "Toward a Theory of Schizophrenia," by Gregory Bateson, Don D. Jackson, Jay Haley and John Weakland, in *Behavioral Science*, Vol. I (1956), pp. 251–64.

respiratory difficulties, because Ben is bigger and stronger now than when he first assumed his role, and because of his ingenious way of fighting back by fighting backward. So Irving's effectiveness is cut, and he quits with only a negotiated peace: Ben does some of the work, and when the mother comes home Ben tries for recognition by playing the goody-goody boy—his brother's keeper, the keeper of his mother's son. What I find striking in the announcement that he tried to make Irving go outside is the assumption that his mother cares—and he is correct, for she herself tries to get the boys out of the house.

In our culture, decisions have to be made about who will command and who will petition and, indeed, about whether in some circumstances there will be any commands at all, and those decisions determine who will be on top and who on bottom. But usually a division into commanders and petitioners, into those who give orders and those who obey them, is also a division into those who frighten and those who fear, and into those who have the privilege of anger and those who must choke on it or find subterranean outlets. The enormous difficulty *Homo sapiens* has had in making such decisions has lead some cultures to renounce command and obedience altogether and has made man in our culture long for their abolition. So on the one hand we have created tyrannies, and on the other, pseudo democracy— the illusion of no command so well described by William H. Whyte, Jr., in *The Organization Man*.

When Irving wants Ben to do something, he gives orders and tries to compel Ben if he resists, but when Ben wants something of Irving he has to plead. Anger is Irving's privilege; subterfuge is Ben's necessity. Thus we can say that to each member of a family and at different times of his life his privileges and compulsions pertain, his openness and subterfuge, his anger and fear. And each complements the others, as do Irving and Ben, whether in pathology or in health. However, as time passes, people change; whoever was effective may begin to feel ineffectual and even defeated, and this is Irving's condition. Also, the peculiar spatial configuration of the Rosenberg life—boxed in and isolated—and the boys' inability to develop broad ties outside the house make Irving's situation difficult indeed. In the family he is dependent on his brother for any experience of effectiveness, and as Ben grows stronger and cannier, and therefore more effective himself, Irving's possibilities are reduced; *the environment is becoming more and more impervious to him.*

Since the boys leave the house only for an occasional errand, to go to school or to play on the pavement just outside the door, it is easy for the parents to become immediately involved in their doings, and hence it is impossible to give an account of the behavior of Irving and Ben without including the parents.

On the very evening after the fight I have just discussed, the boys had a bigger fight. Although Ben was obviously winning it and enjoying himself, the father intervened to protect him, blamed Irving, and Irving blew up. Since the fights give Mr. Rosenberg an occasion for expressing his hostility to Irving and his attachment to Ben, it is next to impossible for him to stay out of them.

The Big Fight

ACT I, SCENE I. *The sidewalk in front of the Rosenberg house.*

When I went outside I found Irving beating up Ben again. They wrestled; Ben, as usual, seemed to enjoy it. Mr. Rosenberg soon came out, got angry and tried to separate them, blaming Irving. Soon the father went indoors and Irving attacked Ben. Ben began to give Irving a hard time by falling on top of him. When Irving left, as if to stop fighting, Ben called him "chicken," so Irving came back and continued to fight. Once Ben got a headlock on Irving and pinned him to the ground. It was obvious that Ben was practically inexhaustible and was causing Irving more and more difficulty. I believe that when Irving wanted to quit, it was because he was tired. It was striking to see Ben constantly provoke Irving to continue to fight, even though Irving pommeled him so and dug his knuckles into him. At one point Ben came over and asked me to hold his glasses.

At last, when Irving seemed really exhausted, he went inside. I followed him into the kitchen, where he was sulking, apparently very angry. He did not respond to something I said. Then he began to scold his father for blaming him for attacking Ben. He was in his usual state of mounting rage. His mother and father continued to blame him and he kept getting angrier and angrier.

I went outside to play with Ben, but I could see what was going on in the kitchen and I heard Irving screaming. Then he seemed to attack one of his parents physically—it seemed to me it was his father. Later his father said it was the mother, but she said it was the father. Then I heard Irving go into the bathroom, slamming the door behind him, and I went inside. Irving was in the bathroom, sobbing and coughing, and his parents were very tense.

As Irving becomes less effective, his brother won't give him a chance to withdraw gracefully but rubs defeat in. Yet, when Irving finally quits, Ben does not crow—he is restrained in victory as his brother is in violence.

The ceremonial combat, through which Irving's past superiority has been affirmed, is losing its meaning. As Ben grows older and stronger it is no longer easy for him to remain a little boy, merely passively effective, a parody of his mother. As the roles of the boys evolve, their positions change relative to each other, and their pathology evolves, too, adapting itself to the boys' changing roles. *Thus role and time constitute the interpersonal environment of evolving pathology.* Meanwhile, the father, unable to perceive the reality of the fight because of his own needs, intervenes where he is not needed, and where, as a matter of fact, he is doing Ben more harm than good—because Ben is trying to become a real boy by crushing his brother; doing Irving more good than harm—because he is saving him from defeat. The following night, when the relatives were over, and Mrs. Rosenberg's brother, the engineer, asked Irving why he had attacked Ben, Ben said he himself enjoyed the fight, whereupon the engineer turned to Mr. Rosenberg and said, "So obviously your interference was entirely unnecessary and uncalled-for."

Mr. Rosenberg said Irving was in the wrong—since he was on top, he must be in the wrong. But actually, when he came out to interfere, the boys were lying side by side on the ground. Mr. Rosenberg said he was afraid Irving would injure Ben—that he might throw a knife.

ACT I, SCENE 2. *Kitchen and hallway of the ground floor of the Rosenberg house.*

There is a small lavatory, and just beyond it is the kitchen. Irving, in the lavatory, is heard sobbing and coughing. The parents alternate between talking to him through the door and conferring with each other in the kitchen. His mother does most of the talking to Irving.

Mr. and Mrs. Rosenberg mixed efforts at appeasement with hostile comments on Irving's behavior. We had originally decided to go to the park this evening, and Mrs. Rosenberg said, "We're going now, and you'll be left behind." Irving shouted tearfully, "Go ahead!" His mother kept telling him to come out. I cannot remember much of what was said, as the parents stood outside the lavatory door, but it was mostly inadequate to the situation and only enraged Irving, even after his sobbing had quieted down. His tearful voice could be heard through the door. One of the things he kept saying was, "You cause me so much heartache in this house. I have nothing but heartache in this house. You blame everything on me. You are doing to me what you did to Abe."

Part of the time I sat in the kitchen with Mrs. Rosenberg, who pretended to be reading a magazine. I asked her, "Do you know what you're reading?" and she answered no. She told me that Irving used to have bad respiratory trouble but that the condition had been quiet for about three years. "He's having the beginning of an attack now," I told her, and she looked at me incredulously.

Mr. Rosenberg approached the lavatory door angrily and threatened to unscrew the lock. Then, in spite of the fact that I had told the parents I would not go to the park if Irving didn't come along, Mr. Rosenberg said, "Dr. Henry says he wants to go." He then added, in a voice that was, for him, gentle, "Don't come out for my sake, come out for Dr. Henry's sake."

Somewhere in here one of the parents asked Irving, "Why do you stay in the bathroom?" And he replied, "Because this is the only place where there is solitude."

After sitting for some time in the living room, Mr. Rosenberg joined his wife and me in the kitchen. He said, "We must get them a bicycle," and the parents talked about that for a while. Their idea was that there should be one bike for the two boys, and Mrs. Rosenberg remarked that the boys had a bicycle once but had never used it.

Both parents were very anxious as they talked about the boys' being bored and not associating with other children. They said the trouble is that Ben seems too young for Irving, that Irving hangs around the house with nothing to do. Mrs. Rosenberg feels that everything that happened tonight was due to boredom.

Mrs. Rosenberg promised Irving he could stay up as long as he wanted and watch his favorite TV show. She said, "Come on out, Irving, you'll miss your favorite TV show," but Irving clamored back, "You never do anything for me." She protested how much she had done, resentfully denying his accusations. The father's statements were mostly hostile rebuttals of what Irving had said. Every time his mother reminded him of what she had done for him, Irving became sarcastic and told her how great she was. Mr. and Mrs. Rosenberg spoke of their love for him, and Irving ridiculed them. Mr. Rosenberg accused Irving of wanting to cause the family pain and Irving told them they caused *him* a great deal of pain.

An effort to appease Irving was to offer him chocolate cake, but he said that the cake in the refrigerator was only fit for pigs, and that at that time of night no bakery was open.

In talking to me in the kitchen Mrs. Rosenberg said that what made Irving mad was being confronted with the fact that he must have been the aggressor, since he was on top of Ben. (Note the misperception.) Ben said the whole thing started because he got very tired and didn't want to play ball any more and because he had made two wild pitches, which annoyed Irving very much.

Through the door comes the sound of Irving's weakness and the words of his sorrow, his rage, his feelings of exclusion and lovelessness, his fear of becoming like his brother Abe, and his accusations that his parents are making him that way. All this frightens and angers the parents, who remember that just before Abe was taken from the home, he too had locked himself in the bathroom, taking along a razor with which he threatened to kill himself. Since Irving's collapse has the effect of frightening his parents and of extorting some appeasing gestures and protestations of love, especially from the mother, it looks as if that were Irving's purpose; as if the whole thing were a hysterical seizure aimed at cowing the parents; as if the illness, as his father had told me in confidence, were merely a "weapon." Actually, however, the incident makes Irving's unbearable position stand forth with great clarity, for his parents are mostly frightened and resentful. Since there are no endearing, beseeching words for Irving, no words of comfort, no tears, we have to ask: When a severe respiratory illness is a "weapon," what is won and who is threatened? When a mixed-up parent starts interpreting his child's behavior, let us be on our guard! If Mr. Rosenberg believes Irving's illness is a weapon, surely he must think himself the target, and we conclude that the father's reaction to his son's illness is anger-anxiety. Thus, what anxiety he may have experienced while Irving was in the lavatory was due not only to the stirring up of memories of Abraham's suicide threat but also to a feeling that the illness was being used against *him*.

Irving is not merely a difficult child. He is inimical. He is a physical sensation, an atmosphere, an environment to these parents; a threatening cloud, impending malice—especially to the father—concretely expressed in Mr. Rosenberg's assertion that he interfered in the fight because he was afraid Irving might throw a knife. Although the parents never told me that Irving had ever thrown anything at anybody, there is some trifling evidence that he might have thrown something at his father, for he did attack, or made as if to attack, him during the height of his rage. Now, who in his right mind would want a knife thrower in the house? Is Mr. Rosenberg preparing the way for his son's exit? Can one live in peace in the conviction that a son would throw a knife at another member of the family? And believing this, how can a parent restrain his fear and hatred? So Mr. Rosenberg's remark that he was afraid Irving might throw a knife cannot be passed over as a mere manner of speaking; it is, rather, the familiar phenomenon of pathogenic metamorphosis (provided, always, that Mr. Rosenberg was telling the truth!). Since pathogenic metamorphosis is a pathological distortion of perception, it is in a class with other forms of pathological distortion of perception—like seeing Irving on top of Ben when he was not, and perceiving Ben as in need of protection when he was not. Or to put it another way: when, in his view of the fight, it looks to Mr. Rosenberg *as if* Irving were on top when he is not and *as if* Ben were in distress when he is not—this is pathological distortion of perception. It really makes little difference to the development of the tragedy whether Mr. Rosenberg is avoiding the truth or suffering from perceptual distortion; the result is the same: a phantasmic world in which one cannot discern what is substance and what is shadow. The point is that *nothing he said to the engineer about the fight reflected the actual existing reality of Irving and Ben.* If Mr. Rosenberg believed what he said, it was *his* reality; if he did not, it was merely a defense of his own behavior stimulated by the embarrassment of the moment.

One could say that "it is only natural" for the parents to be myopic, for when a bigger brother fights a smaller brother, the former must be to blame; after all, the younger one would never provoke the older one deliberately. What average parent would imagine that the little one would get pleasure out of being beaten? However, since the fights are common, occur a couple of times a day and have been going on for a long time, strong forces must be at work compelling the parents to see Irving in the wrong. At the same time, Mrs. Rosenberg avers that though the boys fight, they love each other and will defend each other against any attack from the outside.

Turning now to the problem of Irving's "guilt." From Irving's point of view Ben is, in a sense, to blame for the fights: since Ben is his brother's acknowledged slave, he naturally deserves a beating when he does not obey. This would account for Irving's intense sense of injured innocence, and even offended dignity, when his father blames him. Obviously, Mr. Rosenberg doesn't perceive the master-slave relation as Irving does. Yet Irving lives by it and feels persecuted when his father disagrees. Once, as we shall see in Act 4, he actually got his father to blame Ben, but it did not carry over to other occasions.

Injured innocence, a sham plucked conveniently by the unconscious out of its rag bag of excuses, is not the only issue in Irving's hysterical protest, nor is it the foundation. Or, let us put it this way: although Irving is innocently injured, the fight with Ben is not the crime for which he feels punished. The real crime is for having been born Irving—the second male who would not knuckle under; who, affirming his self, became selfish and resistive and able to penetrate sham with fatal intelligence and humiliating insight.

We turn now to the argument through the lavatory door. Through that door pass the recriminations, the sorrow, the protestations of love, the ridicule, the feeble parental lies and promises of reward not uttered face to face. There is a screen between Irving and his parents as he cries, "You cause me so much heartache in this house. I have nothing but heartache in this house. You blame everything on me. You are doing to me what you did to Abe . . . You never do anything for me!" Having reached a pitch of wretchedness, Irving withdraws and clamors *through the door* what he otherwise keeps largely to himself. His suffering provides the occasion and the door a protection and a threat—the threat of suicide—as the parents are held at bay, fearful and helpless. Locked in the lavatory, he acquires a power over them he did not have before, and he pins them there outside the door as he tries to achieve through terror what he cannot do otherwise; as he attempts to wring from them what they cannot give spontaneously. But the more he is driven to do this, the less likely it is that he will receive the love and respect he wants. Hence the paradox that in order to obtain love, a disturbed person will use the very devices most likely to alienate those from whom he wants it, and this must occur because the withholding of love has made him so hostile that he ends up attempting to use hostility itself to achieve its opposite—love. But it occurs also because parents usually couple coldness with hostile behavior.

An alternative interpretation of Irving's outburst would be that he is not seeking love at all any more, but just wants to punish his parents and make them let him do what he pleases. Thus, in their extremity, some children will accept permissiveness instead of love, and some parents become permissive in order to get the unloved child off their backs.

But what could *these* parents have done? Could they have stopped the accusations and left out the threats? What can parents who do not respect their child do when he goes to extremes because he cannot stand their disrespect? There is really very little left for them but to make promises and tell lies. And if they are perhaps afraid that their child will commit suicide when he is locked in a room, all they can do is try to induce him to come out. But how does one do this with a child for whom one has no respect or love? It is interesting that the very untruths the parents told— about going to the park, for example—were the kind one would use to deceive a two-year-old. Thus, in the process of trying somehow to diminish the gap between themselves and their son, the parents canceled themselves by treating him like an infant. In the very process of persuading Irving to come out they convinced him that there was no good reason why he should. So an argument among disturbed people cannot move to a fruitful resolution because the dialectic of their communication drives them apart. And they drive apart because their feelings for one another are of the kind that separate people. In this, Irving and his father are more extreme than Irving and his mother.

Now I see that I may have gone too far; after all, Mr. and Mrs. Rosenberg could have left Irving in the lavatory and told him to go to hell, or laughed at him, or ignored him. However, they did none of these, and their very anxiety and the maneuvers they went through suggest that there was still something positive between Irving and his parents—even between Irving and his father. This is what family therapy might yet have to seize upon; it is the remaining health that might be expanded by treatment. And now we detect a further paradox—that although the incident remained unresolved, there may have been enough positive in it to convince Irving that even though he did not have a whole loaf of bread, he had at least a little.

Gestures of love keep the hunger for it alive, causing suffering because they give hope. Thus there is another diagnosis of Irving's illness—it is unfulfilled hope—and he has all the symptoms characteristic of tantalizing hope: excessive demands, noisiness, aggressiveness, inappropriate expectations and insatiability.*

ACT 2. *The living room of the Rosenberg home.*

The room is furnished in standard Grand Rapids style. On the floor is a rug that is the same pastel color as the walls. There are no paintings. A TV set faces the sofa.

* In this connection, see my *Culture Against Man* (Vintage Books; New York, Random House, 1963), pp. 396–400.

Irving, looking very tired, his eyes red from crying, has come out of the lavatory and joined the family in the living room.

With his back to everybody, Irving began to play with the Venetian-blind cord. This so angered his father that he got up, went over to Irving and told him to stop it, but when Irving did not obey, the father seemed to think better of it and went back and sat down on the sofa. He said nothing to Irving for the rest of the evening. Mrs. Rosenberg told Irving he might break the blind, and if he did, there would be no money for a bicycle. Irving scoffed at the idea of his getting a bicycle, saying she would never give it to him, and she replied, "Well, you'll see. Did I ever go back on anything I said to you?" Irving said nothing.

After Irving stopped playing with the cord he slumped down on the floor between a chair and the window, with his back to the TV set, and remained there until his parents went to bed. Through all this Ben sat watching TV next to his father.

When Mr. Rosenberg was getting sleepy, he put his arm around Ben and nuzzled him. He rubbed his head against Ben's and put a hand under Ben's buttocks. Ben did not counter-snuggle, and after a while, with both his hands, withdrew his father's hand from under his buttocks. (At dinner this evening, when Irving was out of the room, Mr. Rosenberg patted Ben on the thigh and said, with a warm expression, "Bennie.")

Talking roughly to his parents in the living room, Irving said that his mother can't stop talking, even in her sleep, to which she replied, "How can you tell, you're asleep!" Irving said that neither his mother nor his father loves him. Her listing all the things she has done for him, like taking him to the doctor when he was sick, drew his scorn and contempt. She said, "Doesn't my taking you to the doctor when you are sick prove I love you?"

At one point Irving went into the kitchen and his mother set a dish of ice cream before him twice, but he pushed it away both times, with a disgusted expression.

Protesting mildly, Ben was shoved off to bed by his father and urged up the steps by his mother. She later told me that Ben had said he'd get Irving a new *Mad* magazine tomorrow. She related this with satisfaction, indicating to me what a nice boy Ben is. (I have no record of Ben's having actually done this.)

At last Mr. and Mrs. Rosenberg went up to bed and Irving went into the kitchen, picked up the little radio and turned to the ball game. He got himself half an apple too. He and I were alone now, Irving in the dining room and I in the living room. He said nothing. I don't remember whether I spoke to him, but if I did there was no reply. After a while I got up to go upstairs. I said good night, but there was no response.

The next day Mrs. Rosenberg told me that she had gone down to him—he doesn't like to be alone—and asked him if he wanted to go to bed. He said, "Just a minute, until I'm finished," listened to the radio a little while longer and stopped. She went up to bed with him and kissed him good night and he kissed her good night.

That night, for the first time, I saw Irving asleep in Ben's bed. They were lying in dorsoventral position, Ben's back against Irving, and Irving's arm around Ben.

The quarrel has passed into the aftermath. The argument continues, but Irving and his parents are more relaxed. The father no longer protests love but instead threatens Irving and then withdraws into cuddling with Ben, a hand under the boy's buttocks. Irving's back is to his parents, emphasizing separateness, loneliness and scorn. Dialogue continues with the mother, and as she offers appeasement and proof of love, Irving is contemptuous. Resistive to the end, he makes no gestures of reconciliation, demanding that such gestures come from his parents, and when everyone else goes to bed he remains downstairs, alone. Unreconciled, he may still be hoping he can extort one more positive gesture from his parents, and if we can believe his mother, he did, for she said she came downstairs and urged him to bed.

We must not overlook the fact that Ben does nothing to defend or comfort Irving; what he did demonstrates to his mother what a nice boy he is, by telling her he will buy Irving a new copy of *Mad*. Considering the fact that the magazine would be available to Ben, too, that the boys' copies of *Mad* are very ancient, and that the mother would have to give Ben the money, Ben's offer sounds deceptive.

Ben could have done many things to help his brother. He could have told his parents that Irving had wanted to stop fighting but that he had thrown himself on top of Irving, pinning him with a headlock. He could have joined the parents in urging Irving to come out of the lavatory; he could have sat next to him on the floor in the living room, or told his parents to leave his brother alone, or burst into tears of sympathy, etc. By inaction, Ben divorces himself temporarily from his brother and goes over to his enemies. The perfect illustration of such quiet treason is Ben's usual acquiescence to his father's cuddling, his accepting affection from the one most responsible for his brother's misery—from the man who keeps blaming Irving for doing to Ben what Ben himself says he enjoys. Can Ben be blind to his own duplicity?

ACT 3. *The next day (Sunday). The living room.* The aftermath continues.

When I came down this morning Irving was prone on the floor looking at the newspaper. When he did not respond to my "Good morning," his father prompted him, but he still did not respond. Mr. Rosenberg was making breakfast, but when he offered something to Irving, the boy rejected it angrily. Instead he took a fresh roll from the bag and began to eat it.

Mr. Rosenberg beckoned to me surreptitiously and showed me where Irving had ripped some of the tiles from the wall in the lavatory. He told me that Irving is very destructive and that ordinarily his mother would have given him a licking for this, but that because I was there she didn't. He told me Irving said he removed the tile because it was loose.

While I was in the kitchen eating breakfast Mr. Rosenberg told me how worried he was about Irving but didn't know what to do about it. I said again, "take him to the Agency," but Mr. Rosenberg said that they took too long to effect a cure. He felt that although Abe had been there for several years, they had accomplished little with him.

After a while Irving and Ben came into the kitchen and had a lively discussion about the Yankees and about baseball in general.

Mrs. Rosenberg was the last one up this morning and called downstairs, "Ben, bring me a fly swatter!" I had to go upstairs anyway, so Irving, who had apparently gone to get it, handed it to me and I took it up. She said, "Sorry to have bothered you."

When I came down, Irving and Ben were wrestling laughingly in the living room and Mr. Rosenberg recognized that this was a harmless activity. They were wrestling in their usual position.

Irving's anger at his father is undiminished and Mr. Rosenberg maintains his ambiguous role, offering Irving food, the symbol of reconciliation, while secretly beckoning to the observer in order to show him the damaged lavatory wall. Irving's open rejection of his father's food is the counterpart of his father's covert disdain of him. Irving shows some willingness to come to terms with his mother, however, when he gets the fly swatter for her, even though she had asked Ben for it. Her real feeling about Irving is contained in this request, for by asking Ben rather than him, she betrays the distance that separates her from the older boy. She could not have said more clearly, "I don't want Irving to get it, I want Ben."

The parents do not think that their ambiguous attitude toward Irving—their efforts to give the appearance of love while withholding it—constitutes a "problem," for the obvious reason that their own life together has been this kind of sham. As they see it, their present problem with Irving is the same as they had with Abe—a disturbing child whose condition was not influenced by anything they may have done.

After the fight with his parents Irving slept in the position in which he feels secure—pressed against his brother's back, his arm around his brother's neck; the next morning Irving and Ben are having a hilarious time wrestling in the same position. Nothing is changed between them, and this is demonstrated further in Act 4.

ACT 4. *The same day. First outside the house, then in the living room.*

Today another fight developed between Irving and Ben. I did not see it, but apparently this is what happened: when Ben pitched the ball so that Irving missed it, he got sore and quit, and Ben began to play with a boy next door. Then Irving took away their ball; that's how their fight started. Mr. Rosenberg remonstrated angrily with them and blamed Ben. This I saw. The mother at once offered to get Irving a ball all to himself but he refused. The fighting continued in the living room and the mother said that when Irving was in this mood it was better to leave him alone.

This time, when the boys fight, the father, who can't stay out of things, blames Ben. He has been influenced temporarily by events of the night before, but only to the degree that he blames the wrong person. Every fight is his fight. He likes to fight as a missionary of peace. It gratifies him to be a hawk in the name of a dove, and he becomes one even while blaming his favorite, so great are the attractions of belligerence in the name of peace, in the name of righteousness, in the name of his own innocence. In the language of the *shtetl*, he fights to maintain *sholem bayis*, domestic peace. It gives him a sense of effectiveness to do this and allays his pervading sense of powerlessness; it permits self-righteous anger to this man who says, "I never get angry," but we know that self-righteous anger is addictive because it is self-affirming.

Meanwhile, it is Mrs. Rosenberg again who, by offering Irving a ball all to himself, tries to placate, to do something different from scolding and blaming. She seems to be wrong about what Irving needs at the moment, but deep down, as we shall see, he appreciates her efforts.

The fight has not altered the relationship between the boys or between Irving and his parents. Mrs. Rosenberg remains harassed, anxious, floundering, conciliatory and relatively isolated; Irving is hostile, withdrawn and uncompromising; Ben continues as the object of constant attack by his brother; and the father, persisting in interfering and blaming, is relatively isolated.

About ten o'clock the next morning I was upstairs in my room when all of a sudden I heard a loud noise. I went downstairs and saw that there was a fight between Irving and his mother about his not eating the sandwich she had made. First she had made him a sandwich of lox and bagel, but Irving said the bagel was too hard, so she warmed up a roll. He took just one bite of it. She was pressing him to eat it, but he refused and went to the refrigerator to get a soda pop. This made his mother very angry and she yelled that she had made him a sandwich and that pop was no fit breakfast.

Since soda pop has a special significance in the relationship between Irving and his mother, I interpolate here an observation made a few days previous to this encounter:

Irving got on the subject of his addiction to pop—Pepsi-Cola, Seven-Up, etc. He said he simply must have it, and accused his mother of having made him an addict by inducing him to drink it one hot day. He didn't want it but she had insisted. First he drank one glass and then another, and ever since, he has been addicted to pop. He said he had become saturated with it, that his blood had turned to pop and had bubbles in it.

Later, after the sandwich incident, Irving and his mother got into a discussion about some charges made to her for photographs, which she did not understand and which she was trying to get Irving to explain. He tried, without success, and they ended up in an angry argument. Subsequently:

Now Irving and Ben were fighting. The parents let them alone at first, Mr. Rosenberg saying they should fight it out. But they kept on and on until one of the parents broke it up, saying, "Enough is enough." Then Irving got sore because they blamed him, and Mr. Rosenberg said, "You're the stronger, why should I blame Ben?"
I was present when the fight started: Ben came down the stairs and Irving made contact with him. Suddenly Ben became very angry, saying Irving had pushed him against the stairs, and he struck out at Irving, who counterattacked. Irving said he wanted to make Ben black and blue, beat him up and teach him a lesson. When Irving tried to desist, Ben would provoke a new attack. (This is common behavior. Irving gets terribly upset during these fights but Ben remains outwardly quite tranquil.)

So nothing has changed fundamentally. Everybody is upset, nobody has learned anything—no new information has been absorbed into the system and it can only deteriorate.

When Mrs. Rosenberg offers Irving food—the symbol of her Jewish motherhood—he crushes her by preferring soda pop. Irving is afraid of his mother's care now, and he doesn't want to give her a chance to "get her hooks" on him—as his father says about people who do you favors. He mistrusts her solicitude, for behind it lurks a "demon":

Once, while Mrs. Rosenberg was hurrying the kids to get ready (for the graduation ceremony), she came into the dining room and went over to Irving, smiling. When she left the room he turned to me and said, "She was smiling, but it seemed to me she was a demon," and he imitated a demon.

Irving has a dread of trust because in this house solicitude is associated with entrapment (recall Irving's offering Ben orange juice). In this view Irving paradoxically emerges as the ethical (though entirely unappreciated) hero of the ménage, for by doing nothing for anybody he lays no traps for anyone! It is this view—that solicitude is encirclement, that caring is crushing—which is the major dilemma of schizophrenics, and of our time. Because Irving rejects favors as traps, he can accept favors best only when he *extorts* them, as from his brother; the only absolutely safe gift is tribute. Hence the unpopularity of the spontaneous gift—the gift that is not a repayment for anything—throughout human history; hence our suspicion of it even today, and hence our willingness to accept it only from those nearest and dearest.

Since the time Irving locked himself in the lavatory I have been discussing the relationship between the boys and their parents' entanglement in it because when the parents are home it is not possible to study the relationship between the brothers separately, so small is the physical space within which the family moves; so easily do the parents, particularly the father, become involved with what the two boys are doing by themselves; and so readily may the consequence of what happens between a boy and a parent become transmuted and displaced into a happening between the boys. As a matter of fact, what goes on in the house at all is mostly a phenomenon of the children: nothing visible takes place in the relationship of husband and wife; it is a dead planet, and all the life of the family is in the boys; hence the compelling power of their existence. Thus another reason why what goes on between the boys has a magnetic attraction for the parents—particularly for the father, *who has outlived himself.**

Having offered some insight into the nature of the entanglement of the parents in the relationship between the sons, and having perceived how this entanglement leads to the parents' relationship having a quasi life, I turn to the last observations of the behavior of the boys without the parents.

(Saturday morning.) Since it was eleven-thirty and very quiet, I thought the boys must be outside, but they weren't. I found them in the living room watching a Navy recruiting program on TV. At the same time, Irving was also reading a newspaper. This division of attention is characteristic of both boys: they rarely give their attention completely to anything—although I have seen Irving concentrate on his homework.

The boys did not go outside all day, even though the weather was beautiful.

(Sunday.) Before Irving went to visit Abe, he left instructions with Ben to watch the Yankees on TV. Ben said he wanted to watch the Mets, so Irving told him again to watch the Yankees. Ben said he would, at least for a little while, but I don't think he did.

(Later that day.) The boys were sitting together watching TV. Irving occasionally hit Ben, as usual.

* See Jean-Paul Sartre's *Nausea* (New York, New Directions, 1949).

My record of the relations between Irving and Ben ends almost as it began. It reveals the bond between them as they sit close, watching TV, within the narrow space of their home; it shows Irving giving orders to Ben and beating him. But this time there is no provocation at all—there is no visible reason why Irving should hit Ben, and Ben, while remaining glued to his brother, neither protests, strikes back nor defends himself. The paradox of their relationship is thus made clearer than ever: it is held together by its tendency to split apart; it is sustained by its tension.

Summary of the Relationship between Irving and Ben

Imprisoned in the house by their problems, cut off from other children, Irving and Ben have little chance of adapting fully to American boy culture. Having created a kind of fraternal ghetto, in which they act out ungratified needs on each other, the brothers Rosenberg have increased their isolation, for not many could adapt to *them*—to their peculiar requirements. *No family should develop modes of gratification that cannot be matched in the outer world,* for then they will be without friends; but this is precisely what has happened between Irving and Ben. Ben is mother, slave and wife to Irving, to whom acquiescence is submission, and solicitude merely a veiled attempt to exploit. A selfish boy who cannot wait, who wants to exploit before he is exploited, Irving calls his use of others "efficiency"—a very nice statement of a general cultural value.

In response to what has been essentially a life of lovelessness and sham, the brothers have developed in different but complementary directions. Ben has come to acquiesce in nearly everything, while appearing to see through nothing; Irving has learned to resist everything and to be fooled by nothing. So in this house Ben has turned weakness into strength, and Irving's strength has become his vulnerability.

Though Ben enjoys being beaten by his brother, it is not clear that in enduring Irving's hectoring and beating Ben is merely masochistic, for he is learning to overpower and exhaust his brother, and in a full-fledged trial of endurance and strength Ben is usually the victor. This is the reverse of masochism; yet, by maintaining the appearance of submission, Ben has his brother dependent on him. Hence the value of sham; and hence its consolidation as a value.

As the boys fight—Irving always hitting first, Ben somehow conveying the idea that he is submitting, while usually giving a good account of himself; as Irving commands while Ben serves, always managing to avoid doing much of what Irving would like—the brothers achieve some sense of effectiveness and some gratification of needs never met by the parents. Ben ministers to Irving's need for mothering without domination; hovering over him to see that he is fed, running out to the store to buy a ball or French fries, allowing his brother to snuggle close at night, Ben is the embodiment of a maternal presence—benevolence without domination.

Feminine trends in both boys are a reflection of the fact that the only consequential person in the house is the mother.

Irving is the metaphysic of Ben's existence, for Irving's dependence and even his tyranny give his brother a reason for being. Irving is Ben's flight from nothingness. In his relation to Irving, Ben expresses the yearning for Irving which the mother had but could never gratify; and in his dependence on Ben, Irving expresses a yearning never gratified by the mother. Thus mother and son, in search of each other, meet in the youngest child: Irving and his mother are two blind souls, groping toward each other in love and hope, while condemned forever to screaming imprecations. The brotherly beating of Ben by Irving is the symbol of the despairing relationship between Irving and his mother.

Although Ben has a strong symbiotic feeling for Irving, sometimes even talking about his own needs as if they were his brother's, Irving has no such feelings. Irving struggles against acknowledging his dependence on Ben by hitting him and by belittling or ignoring Ben's mothering, and by attempting to put much of what Ben does for him on the basis of tribute.

In these various ways the boys combat feelings of loneliness, ineffectuality and anxiety. Ben is still much a *shtetl* child, but Irving has rejected all the *shtetl* ideals. Irving is proud, while his brother shares the parental characteristic of pathologic pridelessness. While Irving may get some sense of worth in the outer world through being captain on the student patrol, he cannot really enjoy it because his corroding selfishness leads him to interpret this position as "involuntary servitude." Perhaps he obtains some satisfaction from high grades and from looking down on his teachers as "garbage pails." Ben, however, has no such sources of self-esteem and is therefore all the more dependent for it on Irving and his parents. This involves him in double-dealing with his brother, and when Irving is under pressure from the parents, Ben does not take his part nor offer sympathy, but plays the goody-goody and deserts his brother in order to hold on to his mother and father. The night that Irving wept so bitterly in the lavatory, Ben did not confess that he really enjoys the fights, nor did he try to help Irving in any way. Instead, he pretended to care by telling his mother he would buy Irving a new *Mad*—a very ingenious piece of sham indeed.

In this violent encounter—in the blows, the ambiguity of the struggle itself, the intervention of the father, the despairing confusion of the mother as she tried to ameliorate what her husband had done (although she did not think that he was to blame), the treason of Ben and his sham solicitude, the distorted version of the fight given the engineer—is summed the reality and ambiguity of the boys' relationship and the parents' entanglement in it.

On Anger and Quarreling in the Rosenberg Family

> Her rages were the only reality
> in her life.
> —EDITH SITWELL,
> *Taken Care Of*

In reviewing what I have written I find I have not said that the boys are angry with each other. Only in the last fight—the one on the staircase— have I given any indication that they are, and, as a matter of fact, I have even repeated that Ben enjoys the fights. Of the last fight I say: "Irving gets terribly upset in these fights but Ben remains outwardly quite tranquil." On the other hand, in collisions of Irving and the father, both are said to be angry; Irving is even described "in a mounting rage." Since my studies were made before I developed my ideas on the phenomenology of anger and quarreling, I was careless about recording the nuances of anger and so must speculate* about how Irving felt during fights with Ben.

Since Irving is upset, probably because his brother's failure to do what he wants makes him feel powerless-frightened-angry, Irving attacks him. Ben's laughter and apparent enjoyment, combined with Irving's fatigue and real inability to overcome, seem to affect Irving as follows: on the one hand he gets some satisfaction out of pounding Ben, but on the other he sees that Ben enjoys being pounded. Meanwhile, as Irving is worn down by the but- tock thrusts, by Ben's falling on top of him, by a headlock or by his brother's greater endurance, Irving realizes that he cannot really subdue Ben. Thus as the fights drag out, Irving's feelings change, so that anger becomes mixed with fear and a growing sense of impending defeat. I think this is what I see when I say that Irving is terribly upset. So he tries to move away from the fight, but having acquired the American value of stubborn cour- age, the ability "to take it and dish it out," Irving has to return when Ben provokes him by a blow or by calling him "chicken." Eventually, however, Irving is compelled to withdraw. Confronted by his father's accusations— which must seem absurd in the light of what he has just been through—he is so overwrought that he blows up.

The fights must leave Irving with a sense of gnawing defeat and anger, which then goad him to beat his brother again, and he is able to do this over and over because Ben, though willing to accept a great deal of punishment, rarely hurts Irving in fighting back. When it is all over, Irving gets into bed with Ben, thus acknowledging his dependence, his arm around his neck— the aftermath is emotional repair—and the next day the brothers fight again on the same basis.

Ben, though always the target, never really complains, except in the last fight, where Irving shoved him against the wall, saying he wanted to beat Ben black and blue and teach him a lesson. What lesson he wished to teach him is not clear, but the lessons Irving might *want* to teach Ben are (1) not

* Since "clinical" case studies do not show an awareness that there are such nuances, I am not paralyzed with embarrassment over having to do this.

to cut him out with the parents by being goody-goody; (2) not to resist Irving—including letting himself be beaten up.

Irving's feelings appear to be on the surface, but Ben's are hidden, and though Irving seems to attach an almost desperate importance to the battles, Ben does not really seem to need them, for he never strikes the first blow. The fact that Ben's feelings are more hidden than Irving's should be emphasized, because in general Ben is less open, and in this respect, more *female*. In an encounter all he lets be seen is pleasure, and this is threatening to Irving because it implies that in the very act of trying to have an effect, Irving is ineffectual. The child who cries when his parent beats him is likely to be favored above the one who laughs, for the parent will take the laughter for scorn and return it with heavier blows. I think this is what makes Irving so ingenious in his attacks—screwing a knuckle into Ben's ribs, hitting him with his elbows, beating him with a shoe, and so on.

In every human relationship there is some expectation of *emotional complementarity*. Embracing a woman, a man expects her to respond with passion, not with a remark on the weather, and in a quarrel a person hopes that his anger will produce counter-anger, tears or at least an effort to calm him down—not a burst of laughter or a remark that he has food on his chin. Such incongruities create rage or desperation because they make him feel ineffectual just when he needs most to feel effective. *In one form of pathological relationship, there is a persisting lack of complementarity between one person's feelings—whether in love or in quarreling—and the other's.* The nature of the complementary response is culturally defined, and we have to know this wherever we go, whether here or abroad, lest we misunderstand the nature of a person's response to our feelings and cause offense. Beyond this, it is likely that for every individual there is a preferred response. In love, some women may crave the experience of being crushed, and others may want a gentler man; some men may need a woman who will swoon away in flaming passivity, others may want the searching lips of insistent desire, and so it goes. And so with rage: some want to demolish the opponent; some wish to see him run away; another wants his antagonist to fling back his obscenities with interest so that he can mount to the summit of rage. I do not think that Ben now gives his brother the response that Irving prefers. In this way Ben, to a degree, withholds gratification.

Irving is anger-prone because that is when he experiences his most intense states of selfhood. Only when pouring out his sense of irritated nothingness does Irving seem to feel like something in this house. And it is safe to pour it out on his brother because Irving knows he will not lose him and will not be injured. Though pitched battles must now leave Irving with a large residue of self-doubt, it is better for him to fight as he does—half winning, half losing—than never to fight at all.

At the same time, the fights express the brothers' unbreakable entanglement. Because Irving attacks Ben when he doesn't do what Irving wants him to, it may look as if only Irving has a goal. Yet, though the immediate causes are drummed up by him and a fight appears to serve his motives, actually, once it is in swing, the combat itself is rewarding for both brothers. As a matter of fact, the last time I saw Irving hitting Ben—on the sofa, as they watched TV—there was no visible trigger and Ben did not strike back or move out of reach.

A quarrel can occur only if there is resistance and assertiveness on both sides, and this condition is met most of the time in the relation between Irving and Ben: since Ben will not play the perfect slave, Irving tries to force the issue. Blame, then, is always one-sided: Irving blames Ben for crossing him, and in his view Ben deserves to be punished. What is so striking is the exclusively internal, personal definition of the relationship, and Ben's failure to take a strong stand against it. Since Ben does not rise up and shout, "You have no right to order me around," because he has much to lose if he does, Irving continues in his attitude and is outraged when his father challenges him. Were Ben to stop being a "slave"—or half slave, half free—it would be a catastrophe for Irving.

In this family Irving has become the point of discharge for blame: he attracts it, but Ben is blamed only by Irving. Between Ben and the parents, however, there is an unspoken agreement that he will not blame them for anything if they do not blame him, and this means he will leave them free to blame his brother. The counter-understanding is that if Ben blames them, they will blame him. Around themselves these three have drawn a *circle of innocence.* Thus in pathology, blame tends to become polarized, focusing on the family member exhibiting most plainly the consequences of the parents' own disturbance. It is the problem I have mentioned before— that *we punish most those we have wronged the most because they show in a most annoying way the effects of that punishment.* Of all groups we in America punish the Negro most because he suffers the most flagrantly— through poverty, disease, disorganization, etc.—from the consequences of our own unsolved internal problems. The very spectacle of his misery is insulting! We punish people when they show too clearly the consequences of the past punishments we have inflicted on them. And so it is with Irving; since he displays more irritatingly than Ben the result of having been reared in this punishing environment, the parents punish him most— largely by withdrawal, covert ridicule and blame.

Irving is not to blame. It is the whole family tragedy that is to blame. While Ben represents the family's need for some sort of feminine object different from the mother, *Irving stands for its need to express the hostility boiling within it; for its need to punish somebody for its deprivations; for its fear of being used.*

In discussing the phenomenology of anger, I said:

If, in any situation, a person is uninvolved, unassertive, has great tolerance for the anger and resistiveness of others so that he can put up with it without resorting to counter-assertion, and has a general low tension level, is wary of other people while being nonvigilant for triggering cues himself, he will not quarrel. If, in addition, the culture—family or general—disallows quarreling in the family while nourishing narcotizing attitudes within it, the chances of a person's ever getting into a quarrel are nil.

Irving is taut with anxiety and contained rage; he is assertive, has no tolerance for the resistiveness of others and gets deeply involved in whatever he wants. Under these circumstances the slightest interference makes him angry. Ben has a low tension level, but since he is counter-assertive— however mildly—he easily triggers Irving's anger. In addition, he triggers it inadvertently, by missing balls, for example, or being slow at chess. In the fights, however, there is no rancor and hence no apparent carry-over. There is no insult—no attack on the other's self, embittering and destroying the relationship. Hence there is no alienation in the aftermath, but instead reunion in bed, and the boys can pick up the next day where they left off. When the father is around, the relationship is even better protected because what rage might develop in Irving is displaced to him. Neither boy goes grousing to a parent. If the fights were serious, Ben would avoid Irving, and surely he would kick him out of bed—but he doesn't. It is the anger between the parents—mainly the father—and Irving that always goes unresolved; that is where we perceive post-conflict drift, and that is where the fundamental conflict lies. There is, therefore, always residual anger between Irving and his mother and father, and guilty efforts by them to appease *him* as he constantly finds ways to goad *them*.

Irving

There is a great deal more to understanding Irving than we have been able to grasp while watching him with his family. The reader should know everything the parents said about him, and I will present that material just as it comes from the notes. Then I will examine the meaning of resistiveness in Irving's life and end with an analysis of Irving's position between the family and the relatives.

Less Than Half a Loaf

Irving is constantly belittled by his parents in favor of Ben, who they say is very bright. They refer repeatedly to Irving's timidity. For example, they say Irving crawls into Ben's bed every night, and sleeps with his arm around Ben. If he has to go downstairs to the lavatory in the middle of the night he will wake up Ben to go with him. Irving, they say, makes a slavey of Ben, who does his tasks for him.

Once when she remonstrated with Ben about this, he said, "I like to be Irv's slave." Ben always makes his bed and puts things in order before he goes to school; if Irving does not, he will tell Ben to do it and Ben will go upstairs and do it.

Either Mr. or Mrs. Rosenberg said that Irving likes to talk big and pretend to be very masculine, but that basically he is very frightened. Mrs. Rosenberg says he draws well—and writes poetry.

I observed that Irving slept alone last night, and when I remarked on it to Mrs. Rosenberg, she said, "It is probably because you are here." (She said this on another occasion, too.)

Mrs. Rosenberg told me that Irving says his parents like Ben better than him. She wondered why he said this, and I said, "Don't you like Ben better than Irving?" Instead of answering this question she took off on the subject of what a nice boy Ben is and how selfish Irving is; that Ben always does things for people and is easygoing, while Irving is always kicking up a fuss. She can't figure out how Irving knows they like Ben better. It puzzles her and Mr. Rosenberg tremendously. What do they do, she wondered, to let Irving know they like Ben better than him? After all, don't they treat them both alike? Anything they do for Ben they do also for Irving. When I pressed her she would not say directly that they like Ben better, but she kept on saying how you can't help but like Ben because he is such a nice boy.

Mr. Rosenberg told me that he is very worried about Irving; that he behaves very much like Abe. I said it might be a good idea to take him to the Agency that takes care of Abe, but Mr. Rosenberg brushed this off almost as if he hadn't heard it. He said that Irving's "weapon" is his respiratory difficulty. If you provoke Irving too much, he said, he gets sick, so you have to be very careful with him. He says Irving is very violent.

Mr. Rosenberg told me that Irving always tries to be a big shot, but is really very mean and selfish. Mr. Rosenberg again spoke belittlingly of Irving.

The Rosenbergs think Irving is smarter than Abe, who was too inflexible. They admire Irving's cleverness and his skill at subterfuge. Mr. Rosenberg said Irving has been getting more nervous since he was about twelve years old.

The parents' love for Irving is a sham and he knows it. But Irving does not try to act as if he loves his parents, and he often shows he despises them. He still hopes, however, for a little from his mother, but even as he hopes, he distrusts what he gets and resents it as an effort to trap him, or as an expression of guilt, intended to calm *them* rather than to help him. His parents reveal their unlove to Irving but they do not think they do, and they cannot face the fact of their unlove. On the one hand they think they deceive their son, but since they feel that no deception is involved because they have to believe they love him, they feel wronged and trapped when Irving shows his hostility openly and violently. They feel wronged because, since they imagine they love him, they feel he has no right to treat them as he does, and they feel trapped because he has found them out. The parents, especially Mrs. Rosenberg, feel guilty also because while they believe they are obliged to love their son, at the same time they ridicule and degrade him behind his back because he is "mean" and "selfish" and because they want to disown his "queerness" as not part of them.

To Mr. and Mrs. Rosenberg, Benjamin is an equal, but not Irving, for the fact that he is unloved, mean, etc., degrades him in their eyes; but on the other hand, the fact that he knows they are pretending degrades them in his eyes.

Resistiveness, Effectiveness and Freedom

Though Ben acquiesces in most things, Irving acquiesces in nothing— not even for his acquiescent brother:

Ben was trying to read the paper and Irving had the TV set on so loud that it made Ben nervous. He went into the living room, scolded Irving for keeping it on when he wasn't even looking at it and turned the set off. But Irving turned it on again and continued *not* to look at it.

Since the TV set is often on when nobody is watching it, Ben really had no cause for complaint on that score. Instead of scolding, he could have said, "Irv, do you mind if I turn down the TV?" But, waiting until he was exasperated, Ben was forced out of his pleader role, with the result that Irving fought back. In this we are all very much the same, especially children. In different families, however, the same acts have different meanings, and here, when Ben scolds Irving, he not only violates his role as suppliant but erupts as the nagging mother, when his role in the family has been designed as a benign and acquiescent mother. If we did not know the family we might interpret Irving's behavior as an expression of his "struggle for autonomy."

On the fourth day of my visit I had my longest talk with Irving—when he was alone outside the house throwing a ball against the stoop, missing it, running after it and coming back to finish a sentence. We did not look each other in the eye because Irving kept throwing the ball and chasing it. Under these conditions, he was not easy to understand. Besides, he was at no pains to answer my questions directly, and the business with the ball gave him a chance to think. What was clearest was his hatred of Sol and Burt, two teen-age cousins who come to the house and with whom he sometimes plays. Although he protected his mother and blamed his father for not caring about things, for insensitivity and for hitting him, a story he told of his "quiet riot" was about a fight with his mother, which ended with his pinning up bits of paper with insults on them all over the house. The one I remember called his mother a Hitler. Irving said that this blowup was his "great rebellion" and that he was going to do it more often; he wants to be independent and not have anybody push him around. "People" are always "ganging up on me and beating me."

The fact that Mr. Rosenberg cannot leave Irving alone provokes the boy to rages and to paroxysms of resistiveness in which Irving's very life seems to be at stake.

I don't remember what Irving was talking about, but his father deliberately switched the conversation to Hebrew school—which he knows Irving abhors with venom. Mr. Rosenberg's attitude was: "Why talk about something like that, let's talk about something Hebrew" (which Mr. Rosenberg detests.)

Irving expressed intense satisfaction that Hebrew school would soon be over. Mr. Rosenberg then asked why he was so happy that school was over—didn't he like to be educated? Irving immediately became tremendously excited and began to yell. His father said that Irving should appreciate getting an education because he—Mr. Rosenberg—didn't have any. Irving said he didn't care what his father had, and that he needs a vacation, because if he doesn't get one, he'll collapse. His father retorted that education is important; why does Irving talk about vacation so much? All Mr. Rosenberg's arguments were easily destroyed by Irving.

Although Mr. Rosenberg knows that rages are bad for Irving, he cannot resist "turning his son on." The result is always that Irving becomes wild and demolishes his father's arguments, which can only make his father feel bad and want to get back at Irving some other time. Mr. Rosenberg's provocations are the counterpart of Ben's—father and younger son provoke Irving, and Ben gets beaten physically while the father is bruised psychically.

Actually, since Mr. Rosenberg has a streak of anti-Semitism in him, there is something unreal in his insistence that Irving continue Hebrew education. In other words, he acts as if he cared but there are good reasons to believe that he really does not.

Since resistiveness, of which rage and other forms of fighting are phases, is the only form of autonomy available to Irving in this house, it represents freedom. Hence rage is freedom, selfishness is freedom, and so on.

Resistiveness and Deprivation

While Mrs. Rosenberg was making dinner Irving sat in the kitchen talking to her. He first talked about an announcement Mrs. Rosenberg had received from some organization of which she is a member and which is trying to raise money for Israel. On the back of the announcement was a statement about how much will be charged for the fund-raising festivities. Irving read it over very carefully and came to the conclusion that too little food was offered for the money. So he took off in a violent denunciation. His mother argued that the money was for Israel, but Irving said he didn't care about that—all he cared about was what he was going to get out of it. Then he delivered a long diatribe against restaurants that charge high prices and a cover charge, and his mother sided with him. They talked about restaurants that charge a dollar for a cup of tea. (Apparently they had once been taken to such a place by a wealthy relative.) Meanwhile Ben entered and chimed in on the subject of expensive restaurants, and the three seemed to have a good time.

While we were waiting for dinner Irving kept screaming for food.

. . .

Irving, Ben, Ralph and Joe* were playing ball in the usual game: two players throw and catch the ball and two others run bases. Irving cheated twice—once interfering with a catch and once knocking the ball out of Ben's hand. This resulted in a loud altercation between Irving and the other boys, but particularly with Ben. Irving kept yelling and yelling and Ben eventually gave up.

Fear of deprivation appears under many forms in Irving's rages. It emerges here in his calculation of how much he might get in return for a contribution to a charitable cause, in his attack on restaurants that charge high prices, in his screaming for food and in his cheating in the ballgame. He cannot stand losing, because losing means deprivation and a threat to his shaky self-esteem. When he lost at chess with me he wanted to quit. Of course, he has been deprived so much that his self-esteem is almost non-existent—even his blood is nothing but "pop" and "bubbles." Fear of deprivation is the hidden dimension of Irving's fear of exploitation and of his resistance to being "pushed around." The motto of essentially deprived persons is, "Hold fast to everything." Their tragedy is that when they need us most they are most obnoxious, that when they appear most selfish and even dishonest it is because they are empty inside, that when they are contemptuous and humiliating it is because they have been treated like garbage.

Most people, without knowing it, follow Buddha's principle that though one cannot blame the cobra for his venom, it is not necessary to love him.

* Both boys are in the same age bracket as Irving and Ben. Joe is a neighbor, and Ralph a cousin.

And so it will be with Irving and "the world"; some may understand why he is selfish, contemptuous and dishonest, but few will sympathize. Since his parents cannot know the sources of these qualities, they maintain a façade of solicitude and even of love while behind his back, in their minds, they tear him down. Questioned on the subject, Irving answers guardedly, protecting them:

I drove Irving over to meet Abe, and on the way I said that he certainly gets a lot of nagging and he replied that he is used to it. I said, "I wonder why your parents seem to nag you more than they do Ben?" and he replied that he guessed they picked on him more than Ben because he is the older and supposed to be more responsible.

Though this answer protects the parents, it protects Irving too, for he avoids the pain of admitting that they nag him most because they love Ben best. He resists letting me see—or letting me see again—how much he suffers from nagging. It also enhances Irving's self-esteem if he believes that he, rather than his brother, is held accountable by the parents. Thus, out of the very deprivation Irving extracts—or seems to extract—a reward, and this, perhaps, is what makes it possible for him to carry on; it is the metaphysic of exceptionalness—of "being chosen to suffer because of being exceptional"—the mind's way of deadening the pain of rejection, its working out of the *dialectic of pain.*

Irving between His Family and His Relatives

Without the relatives the Rosenbergs could not live as well as they do; they are an important aspect of the Rosenberg living standard and even of their health, since the relatives' money pays for Mrs. Rosenberg's medical care. The relatives must be conserved; whatever the Rosenbergs might feel about them, they cannot be alienated, and resentment must be covert and quiet; an outburst would be threatening. So when Irving, offended that they had not been at the Hebrew school commencement,* talked against them, he was breaking an unwritten taboo. On the other hand, neither boy was aware that the relatives had not been invited!

At supper tonight Irving burst out in an attack on all the relatives who had not been present at the graduation ceremony. He said it made him feel very bad, and he went on and on in this vein and became very excited. His mother and father tried to make excuses. Mr. Rosenberg said it didn't really make any difference to him whether the relatives were there or not. This brought a tremendous attack from Irving, who said his father didn't care about anything and didn't have any sensitivity at all. "Mother has some sensitivity, but you don't have any!" Occasionally Ben chimed in on Irving's side: "Look, Dr. Henry has just been here a couple of days and hardly knows us, and he went to the ceremony but our relatives didn't." The only thing I remember Mrs. Rosenberg having said was, "You have to get used to taking many disappointments in this life. We have had mostly disappointments." Irving countered, "Yes, but how many of them could have been avoided? That's the point I'm making."

What Irving was trying to say was that what happened at the graduation

* See p. 124.

ceremony could have been avoided—as with many of the disappointments the family has endured. Irving laid the blame on his parents for the relatives' not coming.

This went on for a long time, Irving getting more and more excited. Mrs. Rosenberg ascribed the fact that Irving did not do his homework this evening to this excitement. She said he was so excited she did not want to press him.

While Irving was attacking the relatives he repeatedly said, "You wait until Saturday when they're all here and then you'll see some heads roll"—meaning that he would bawl them out. He repeatedly said he wanted to find out why they didn't come.

While Irving was carrying on, Ben quietly disappeared from the table.

Mrs. Rosenberg told me in private that this was just talk, and that Irving will do nothing to the relatives ("He just talks big"). She said that if I hadn't been present, Irving would have cried at the supper table. Later on Mr. Rosenberg told me that he deliberately had not invited the relatives because Irving's bar mitzvah had taken place a short time before. All the relatives had given him presents at that time—a total of a few hundred dollars—and Mr. Rosenberg was afraid that if they were invited to the graduation they might think they were expected to give presents again. As we were talking, Mrs. Rosenberg passed by in the hallway and briefly scolded Mr. Rosenberg for not inviting the relatives.

. . .

The next day when I raised the issue of the graduation with Mrs. Rosenberg, telling her what her husband had told me about his fears regarding the relatives, she said she had not invited them because graduation day was a working day. She then said her husband is always afraid people will think he wants something from them. She told me he has often said that if he had the money he would pay back everything that had been contributed to the house.

I told Mrs. Rosenberg what her husband had said: that the only reason Irving wanted the people to come was so they would bring him gifts, and she answered that Irving wanted them to come because he wanted them to come.

Certain things are clear from this account, and others are not, partly because I never cleared them up, partly because in a mendacious culture* nothing ever gets cleared up. It is clear, however, that Irving and Ben were angry because the relatives did not come to the ceremony and that Ben disappeared from the table in the heat of the argument. It is also clear that because they did not want the relatives to come—though husband and wife gave different reasons—they conspired to keep the relatives away but did not tell the boys, and that then the wife scolded the husband for doing what they had agreed to do. Of course, it is not clear exactly why the boys wanted the relatives, what the "real" reason was for not inviting them, why the boys were not told, why Mrs. Rosenberg scolded her husband *in front of the observer,* etc., etc. Meanwhile the parents, each ascribing different motivations to Irving, discuss the dinner-table argument as if it revolved entirely around him, though Ben was involved too. Thus the conflict, though developing out of a plot hatched by the parents, came to a focus in Irving, possibly because it was his bar mitzvah that made the parents reluctant to invite the relatives, but surely because it was Irving who made the biggest

---

* There are three kinds of cultures: (1) the veridical: cultures in which people always tell the truth—as in a monastery, perhaps; (2) the pseudoveridical: cultures in which people are supposed to tell the truth but lie a great deal of the time, as in our culture; (3) the mendacious: cultures in which people generally do not tell the truth, as on Alor. See Cora Du Bois, *The People of Alor* (Minneapolis, U. of Minnesota Press, 1944).

fuss. It seems to me that we can extract something like a "law of ambiguous causation and blame" from this tragicomedy. Let us say that when the true causes of an injustice are difficult to trace, those who are really responsible will manipulate the situation so as to make the victim who protests the most appear to be the culprit. This formula can be applied equally to anti-Semitism, racial discrimination, student demonstrations, etc., and to Irving.

Before I go further with the analysis, the reader should note how the father "turns his son on" with the ineffable, and insensitive, irrelevance that it didn't make any difference to *him* whether the relatives were there or not. "But," the reader may argue, "there is much more to what the father said than some vague 'instinctive' capacity to turn his son on." There is *the self as explanation of the world,* a kind of metaphysic of the self which states that what is good enough for me, what suits me, is eternal truth—a common enough failing. I agree. I remember, for example, that in the dispute with Irving about continuing in Hebrew school the father argued that because *he* didn't have an education Irving should value it highly enough to want to go to Hebrew high school; and in his discussion on Saturday night with his sister Leah about how much sleep people need (not reported here), Mr. Rosenberg argued that six hours is enough for anybody—and that's what *he* gets. True: by taking himself as the sole reference for understanding everybody else he makes communication with them impossible.

If only the parents had explained to the boys ahead of time! Were this a family where parents and children are mutually accessible, the argument would not have occurred. But with Irving's personality, he probably would have blown up if they had tried to explain. Or it may never have occurred to these parents that the matter could be ironed out in advance, for they do not face issues frankly.

Thus, behind all these lesser phantoms stands the greatest phantom—the dread of truth. In our culture, everyone in his right mind knows that existence must be a lie, only not too much so, for there must be enough truth in it to make it possible for trains to run on time, for schools to open and close on time, for merchandise not to be too far below the advertised quality, for contracts to be kept, and so on. Every culture needs some truth and reliability in order to get its work done within the tolerance limits of culturally prescribed inefficiency, and in any culture the mature person knows that in all of life there has to be a tolerable amount of fakery. Problems arise, however, when the cultural limits of dishonesty are passed, or when, because of his peculiar life circumstances, an individual rejects truth altogether, failing to perceive that one ought not reject all veracity but merely a good part of it. In our culture we call such a person a pathological liar, but really, he has merely an exaggerated dread of truth. Such are the parents Rosenberg. Since their whole life has been a sham, for them the greatest dread is revelation, the removal of the mask (as in Mrs. Rosenberg's dream), the overturning of Truth's Rock to reveal a snake underneath. Truth is a Valley of Dread; hence the *dread of truth,* hence the *flight from truth,* hence the fact that for them life is a rack on which they are tormented by the truth; hence their *flight from life*—their flight from their children.

But how many parents know how and when to tell their children the truth? It is so much a tradition in our culture to conceal the "ugly side" of life from children, that it takes intelligence, sensitivity and even training to communicate realities to them. It also requires respect for children, a nice estimate of their cognitive capabilities and an awareness of how the truth may affect them. It takes shrewd judgment, in a culture that is not naturally open and that provides many opportunities for concealment, to estimate the subjective relation between children and the truth. It takes parents who are not ashamed of their own motivations; parents who are aware of their own motivations. We expect children to tell adults the truth but since it is next to impossible for parents to tell children the truth, we take it for granted that adults will lie to children. Mr. and Mrs. Rosenberg simply have particular difficulty in this respect because their life circumstances, from birth to the present, have deprived them of the equipment with which to deal with the problem of truth. They have learned, too well, perhaps, to use truth *against* people rather than *for* people.

In the present instance, meanwhile, mother and father are so dependent on relatives, so ashamed, perhaps, that they are comparative failures among their more successful kin, they have taken so much from them already, that they feel under constant pecuniary surveillance—afraid and ashamed that they may be accused of trying to exact money. Hence, in mortification, they do not inform the relatives of the commencement, and out of fear they do not tell the boys what they have done.

Since the father has no use for Irving, it is not surprising that he says the only reason Irving wanted the relatives at the graduation ceremony was to get something out of them. But why conceal the truth from Ben? Because probably Ben would have told Irving. Thus distrust of Irving leads to distrust of Ben, and the dialectic of distrust plunges on. The effort to avoid an argument at the outset has merely turned upon the parents, destroying all hope of pleasure in the graduation. (Remember the cousin's ruckus at the synagogue, trying to push himself in where he had no business? Remember Irving's earlier rage when his father needled him about going to Hebrew high school?) In such a context the mother's use of a metaphysic of disappointment ("You have to get used to taking many disappointments in life") is retrospectively correct and also prophetic, for it is partly because her life has been and continues to be a sham that it has been and continues to be a disappointment too; it is because she and her husband made the relatives' relationship to the commencement into a sham that it turned out to be a disappointment, and it is because husband and wife fly from the truth that their life *will be* a disappointment. But Irving, the perceptive and resisting one, will not acquiesce in a metaphysic of disappointment as *his* explanation of life. He passionately believes that the family failure, of which he knows himself to be a consequence, could have been avoided. Yet with all his gifts he had not perceived that even as he sat there in such a fever, he was a phantom fighting in a phantom cause. The wrong he attacked—the relatives' refusal to come to commencement—didn't exist, and the explanation of life as disappointment was irrelevant because disappointment was not the issue, but rather his parents' duplicity.

In trying to evade difficulties with the children, the parents created difficulties; but at the same time, in shifting blame from themselves to the

I asked Leah what happens when she gets aggravated, and she said she gets sick.

Leah takes her turn at Irving, but really more at her brother, for having handled the matter in the wrong way, i.e., not as well as she might have. He should do as she does—take the child quietly aside and threaten to get sick (be "aggravated") if he does not obey. Behind the appearance of an attack on his son, Leah is accusing her brother (who secretly ridicules his sister for not knowing how to deal with *her* children) of not knowing how to handle *his* children.

On the porch after dinner, Irving was again the star—or target.

Irving said that our culture (I don't remember whether he said our "culture"; he probably said our "country") is crazy and not as good as Europe. When asked why he thought our country was crazy, the only things he could think of to mention were Bermuda shorts, jeans and rock-and-roll music. In the course of Irving's disquisition, the engineer, instead of trying to find out more about what Irving was thinking, attempted to refute him, saying that Bermuda shorts were not invented in this country but in Bermuda or England, and rock-and-roll music has spread all over the world. The engineer and the other adults are constantly trying to defeat Irving.

Thus the evening was in no small part an extension of the Rosenberg parents' effort to contain and put down Irving: the parents used the relatives to diminish the stature of their son, and the relatives were willing to oblige—within their powers, which, however, are always at a considerable disadvantage in coping with Irving's mind. The extension of the parental effort to reduce Irving involves the same devices Mr. and Mrs. Rosenberg use at home—sham, ambiguity, half-truth, secret mortification and flimsy argument. However, just as Irving is belittled behind his back to the relatives, so do the relatives, behind one another's backs, demean one another. Meanwhile, status and argument are undermined and contradicted by secret understandings, asides, half-truths and delusions; the evening with the relatives is a view, through the wider kinship, of an illness that afflicts the system as a whole. It is a system without compassion for the soul; destructive and even cruel; yet at the same time affording the Rosenbergs a measure of security.

Irving on the Ball Field

I said that Irving and Ben are poorly co-ordinated, that inability to enter easily into American-boy athletic culture contributes to their isolation, and that girls stay away from Irving, even though he is handsome. Here are some observations of Irving on the school playground.

I could hear voices of children at play in the schoolyard a block and a half away, so I walked over to see what was going on. Since it happened that Irving was there playing ball, I stood watching for about half an hour. Irving was not the only one with mediocre co-ordination; as a matter of fact there were one or two children more poorly co-ordinated than Irving, who, I would say, was about average in that setting. Of course, there were a couple who were very, very good, but it seemed to me they were in the minority. I saw Irving hit the ball rather robustly once and saw him catch a fly.

A couple of times there were close decisions about whether a kid was safe on first, and Irving joined the other kids in yelling.

. . .

I walked over to the playground on the chance that Irving might be there playing ball, even though he had told me he would not be, and sure enough, there he was. It was his gym class. Irving was way out in center field, where the ball was never hit. He was nowhere near any other player. He may have been assigned that position by the captain, since he is not good. During the game he isolated himself from other children even when his side was at bat. He did not take part in the horseplay that was going on and did not talk to the other children, but threw pebbles aimlessly, often with his back to the others. The girls were roaming around provoking the boys, but no girl came near him. Nobody approached him. In playing there was absolutely no comparison between his co-ordination and the other boys'—they were all far superior to him. The couple of times he was at bat he connected weakly and was out.

This seemed to be a gym class where boys and girls were mixed and the girls were playing softball with the boys. The girls constantly approached certain boys they seemed to feel attractive, put their arms around them and even pressed close to them. The boys made no overtures, merely appearing to accept the girls. The boys were interested in the game, the girls seemed more interested in the boys.

At supper that night, talking about how the girls on the playground pursued the boys, Mrs. Rosenberg turned to Irving and said they were after Irving, too, and he smiled as if they were.

Irving can make a go of it when he is with kids with the same disabilities, but it may be that at other times he is at such a disadvantage that he may make his position even worse by turning his back on everything. Where the other boys are much better than he, Irving is cast off—a difficult thing for anybody to take—and he reinforces this by a radical withdrawal. Such experiences must make him very reluctant indeed to seek friends among peers. Being the underdog, Irving does not attract these very aggressive girls either, in spite of his good looks, and since they need no overtures from boys in order to tackle them, there must be something special about Irving that keeps them away from him.

I am not convinced by any means that Irving's isolation is due to athletic incompetence only. After all, he is an exceedingly difficult boy, selfish and unyielding and prone to try to get his way by yelling, cheating and hitting. Many a boy who can neither hit a ball nor field one is tolerated by others if he is good-natured. What we see in this second observation, however, is ostracism, resembling, as in a caricature, Irving's position in his own family. There, however, Irving has Ben; here he has nobody. What is really missing in my research is a study of the children's attitude toward Irving, for after all, regardless of what happens to Irving in his family, it is the outer world that will, in the long run, determine whether he will be treated as "normal" or "disturbed."

Ben

> . . . Time was for her but an empty round between night and night, a repetition of sad nothingness, like the beat that sounded within her dress of dust; for her, the moments dropped like sad and meaningless tears.
>
> —EDITH SITWELL,
> *Taken Care Of*

Somewhere, through the years, the parents lost Ben, for though they are fond of him, he is cold to them. Father fondles him, saying tenderly, "Bennie, Bennie." Ben is submissive, but he is unresponsive. He seems to be the only thing the mother can care about in that house, yet he is aloof. How much she prefers him to Irving was made clear many times, but at no time was it demonstrated so well as at commencement.

When the graduates came down the aisle Mrs. Rosenberg said to me, "There's Ben," but when Irving came by she was silent.

Harsh words rarely pass between Ben and his parents, for he is acquiescent, but in refusing to withdraw from Irving, as his parents have done, he resists them. They hate Irving's sleeping in Ben's bed—he lets him; they cannot stand his being Irving's "slavey"—he submits; they resent Irving's beating him—he enjoys it. Ben does not really live unless Irving is around, for in this house it is his brother that is meaningful to him. Let us see how he treats his mother.

I had just about finished my breakfast when Ben came down. His mother called some loving remark and he approached her, but before getting to her, he turned on his heel and said, "Oh, I have to get the paper," and ran outside. When he came back he had his nose deep in the paper and did not go near his mother. The fact that he turned his back on her and went and got the paper shocked his mother, who remarked on it in a laughing way. Ben kept his nose in the paper, looking at all the baseball scores while he was eating. In order to reach him in some way, his mother made some comment about one of the teams. Ben, absorbed in the paper, neglected his breakfast, and his mother kept urging him to drink his orange juice, then milk, and to eat an egg.

What is most significant in the relationship between Ben and his mother is her reaching out and his identification and withdrawal. Ben has many female traits, but he is cold and hostile to his mother. Such a combination of identification and rejection is probably characteristic of many pathological relationships. Though becoming an acquiescent mama's boy has done nothing to warm the emotional life of mama or papa, it made it possible for Ben to survive and become "adapted"—to his family. Acquiescence made Ben acceptable to everybody but walled him off from other inner possibilities. In our Western culture, acquiescence, or perhaps better, resignation, may sometimes make existence comfortable for those who resign and for those who exact resignation, but it impoverishes both. *The central intellectual paradox of Western civilization is that while it requires disobedience in order to endure, it punishes disobedience ferociously. It therefore produces both "overconforming" and rebellious people, and swings cyclically between epochs of acquiescence and epochs of revolution.*

Emptiness

Ben has learned to give in, has filled himself with the needs of everyone else but has become empty to himself, and this emptiness afflicts him like an illness. Everywhere man strives to balance his own inner needs against the inner needs of others, so that he will not give more than he can or less than he should, and so that those around him will not exact more than he can give. Since no society can strike a perfect balance in this respect, the imbalance has been an evolutionary force, compelling *Homo sapiens*, because of the misery arising from failure in this regard, to search for social organizations that might provide equilibrium. In the Rosenberg family we see how the search has become a catastrophe—Irving giving nothing and Ben giving so much that he has nothing left for himself. Let us see how he spends his time when his brother is not present to order him around, to overcome him in games or to beat him up. The following illustrations are typical:

(Second day.) When Irving left he told Ben to "do the dishes as you always do." I asked Ben what he does with his spare time, and it seems he does nothing with it. He says he gets very lonesome in the house. Though I asked him about it, it was not clear why he did not go out with other kids. He watches TV sometimes, he says, but he is sick and tired of it. He has nothing to read. Apparently he is not much interested in reading. Besides, he says, the school library is closed.

Ben and I went into the living room. He got out two old issues of *Mad,* and we sat close together on the sofa for about half an hour while he went over them, calling my attention to items.

At last I got rather sleepy and went upstairs and took a nap. When I said I was going upstairs he said "Okay" and went into the kitchen to do the dishes, but when I came down a little later the dishes still had not been done.

I just came back to my room from a half-hour of watching TV with Ben. He turned to various channels and at last turned on a crime picture. It's obvious that he didn't get much out of the picture because he spent so much time looking away, but when it got intensely exciting it caught his attention. At one point he said, "Only six more hours to go," meaning that there were only six more hours to the graduation ceremony. Sitting there with Ben, I had the impression of oceanic boredom and of his hoping that time would pass.

(Third day.) After lunch was over and Irving had left, Ben wandered around in a do-less, aimless way, first fingering his marbles and then putting them on the floor and playing with them in a half-hearted, not very competent way. I offered to play with him but he refused.

I sat down in the living room and after a long time Ben asked me if I played chess. I said, "yes, but not very well." He beat me in the first game. He plays planlessly, like me. When I beat him in the second game, the effect on him was spectacular. On his face there appeared an expression of great tension, though he said nothing and did not offer to play a third game. Neither did I, and he turned again to TV.

Now, at two-fifteen, Ben is just moping around the house. He got out the cantata the children had sung at their graduation; when I asked him what it was about he did not tell me. He was going over the cantata to put down the names of the kids who recited the different parts. He did this on his copy and on Irving's, and when Irving came home he told him what he had done.

(Fourth day.) After lunch, at one forty-five, I found Ben sitting downstairs on the sofa in the living room staring into space and twiddling with his glass marbles. He had about a dozen and a half in his hands and was rolling them around. Then he got down on his knees by the ottoman on which there was a newspaper open to an ad for some dry goods or drugstore and he read that. The TV was on but he had his back to it. This is a common situation with both boys, but particularly with Ben because Ben is home so much and alone for so long. He went to the door and looked out. He twiddled with his marbles. He got down on the floor, rolling some of the marbles toward one another in some sort of game. (The reader will note that Ben did not aim and shoot the marbles, which is what an average boy would have done. There was no sign that he had mastered this technique.) I did not offer to play with him because he had refused yesterday. While rolling the marbles, he would occasionally say something unintelligible. The TV was on to a big-league game but Ben was not watching it.

At two-fifteen I went out with the idea of going to the market to get some lox and bagles for the family and some stationery for myself. As I got into the car I turned and saw Ben watching me from the door and when I asked him if he would like to come along he said yes with alacrity.

When we got back Ben took to twiddling with his marbles again and watched a ball game on TV.

When Ben is alone he aches with time; only when his brother comes home does this pain leave him, for since he cannot stand freedom-in-time, his bondage to his brother is sweet. So, in the dialectic of his relation to time, Ben is relieved from the pain of it, paradoxically, by the punishment he gets from his brother, and his bond to him is strong partly because his ties outside do not exist. Of the tiny space that is their house the brothers have made a jail, and to each other they are fellow prisoners. Imprisoned in the house, they are imprisoned also in each other's sickness.

Everywhere, whether on the ice of the North, in tropical rain forests or on ancient prairies of Kansas and Missouri, the culture of tribal man has provided something for him to do on those extremely rare occasions when he is alone. So Ben's suffering is due also to the fact that he cannot use the means our culture provides for twelve-year-old boys to fill in time when alone. He does not read, he has no interest in music, TV can hold him now only when it passes his excitement threshold; and he does not do those things which boys his age do to fill in time alone: he does not whittle, make things, play with model airplanes, autos, trains, etc.; he does not know how to play against himself: shooting marbles skillfully, bouncing a ball off the stoop; he is afraid to go out alone. He has been drained.

Ben knows how to do only one thing well—acquiesce—and when there is no one around to acquiesce to, he has nothing to do. Since time, space (the little house) and acquiescence flow together in *Irving*, Irving is existence, and when he is not present Ben does not exist as a self. When his brother comes home Ben must undergo pain, but he has learned to transmute physical pain into psychic pleasure. Ben has become an acquiescent and empty boy, but since emptiness makes time an unbearable burden for him, his tendency to acquiesce is strengthened, because acquiescence in what his brother does gives Ben pleasure and relieves his intolerable boredom. However, since physical pain also somewhat negates this tendency to acquiesce, Ben is trying to find a way to acquiesce without overdoing it. In *resisting*, Ben has to lose some of the pleasure of *acquiescence*, but he compensates in the new pleasure of *overcoming*. In this way, as he struggles toward autonomy, transformation of a largely masochistic adaptation to a sado-masochistic one is accomplished through *the dialectic of pain*.

Thus, resistiveness is Ben's way to freedom as well as it is Irving's. Resistance requires courage, and while Irving's takes the form of standing up emotionally and intellectually to adults, Ben stands up to Irving's blows. That this has been a gradual process is substantiated by his mother's observation that

you never know how people are going to turn out. Ben, who is now brave, used to run from strangers and hide under the table and suck his thumb.

We also know that he is able to face the phantoms of the night on the way to the bathroom. So, gradually, cautiously, using his brother as a kind of testing ground, Ben is experimenting with courage. Until the age of eight he still moved his bowels in his underpants and went to bed with bowel movement still in them. Now Ben is not afraid of the toilet.

So we see that it takes pain and courage to become a self, and that this boy, who only four years ago had such low self-esteem that he gave in to his bowels at once, metaphorically and literally "crapping on himself," is now becoming a person. And this may be the deeper reason why his reaction to being defeated by me at chess was so overwhelming and why he refused to play when I asked him on another day—he could not bear to have me "defecate on him." Only from his brother can Ben accept being defeated because it is part of the total pattern of subordination and acceptance. It is defeat without shit.

There is so much *as-ifness* in this family that before going further, I shall summarize it.

1. The parents live together as if their marriage were not a sham—as if they were not "emotionally divorced."
2. They talk as if they love Irving but they do not.
3. The family treats Ben as if he were a girl.
4. Ben acts as if he were Irving's mother.
5. Irving acts as if Ben were his slave, while Ben acts as if he were conforming to Irving's wishes much of the time, but he does not.
7. In the fights Ben acts as if submitting but does not, and Irving acts as if superior but he is not.
8. The father interferes in the fights as if Irving were on top but he is not; as if interfering solely to protect Ben but he is not.
9. Irving acts as if he were not to blame.

What has kept the fights between the brothers going? What is the underlying family situation of which they are an expression?

We know that the relation between husband and wife has been ambiguous, providing little basis for loving children. Ungratified, the boys work out its consequences *on* each other, as they try to meet, *through each other*, dependency needs not met by the parents. The parents' preference for Ben also helps keep the fighting going. But this preference is not based on Ben's more acquiescent disposition only, for of great significance is his femininity—he has been chosen by the others to be a girl.* They need someone with the gratifying capabilities of a woman, without Mrs. Rosenberg's nagging and violence. Mrs. Rosenberg needs someone to keep her company and to relieve her of the burden of being a woman; someone to help her take care of the family and of the house. The following puts the issue clearly:

> Mrs. Rosenberg came home about three o'clock. Through the window Ben saw her approaching. He went to the door and called out, "Hi, Mommy!" or something like that. The first thing she said as she entered was: "I have news for you—Mrs. Pzaric has had a new baby girl after having had three boys." Mrs. Rosenberg was very relieved about this because Mrs. Pzaric was tired of having boys and thought she would have one more try to see whether she could have a girl. Ben showed mild interest. . . . Then Mrs. Rosenberg said she was very happy with her (Mrs. Rosenberg's) boys.
>
> She asked me how I was and I said Ben had taken very good care of me, and she said, "Sure, he's Mama's boy," and that she likes what he does. I said, "He took very good care of me."

Mrs. Rosenberg relates to Ben as to another woman; his father likes to touch his buttocks and thighs as he snuggles up to Ben, and we know what the pattern of contact is between Ben and Irving.

Here is another example of Ben's erotic valance:

> Mr. Rosenberg was sitting on the sofa and next to him was Ben, his buttocks against his father's thigh, the father's arm around Ben.

"Underlying the bristling façade of negativism," says Hilda Bruch,† writing of Eric, one of her patients, "an all-pervasive fear of impotence and ineffectiveness could be recognized. . . . Though Eric possessed good capacities for thinking and acting as an individual, he had failed in the past to find help and encouragement for developing them and testing them out." In the Rosenberg family Irving fights his fear of impotence and ineffectiveness with negativism, and Ben fights the same feelings with acquiescence and imitation of his mother, because she is the most effective person in the family. In this way Ben saves himself the suffering that negativism entails, gains a foothold Irving does not have, and gets some sensation of having an effect; he does do things; he obtains some recognition from his parents, and he makes Irving dependent while enjoying the sweetness of accomplishment and physical closeness. Everyone in the Rosenberg family tries to be effective there, but is incapable of it without distorting himself and others.

* I owe this insight to Professor Magoroh Maruyama of San Francisco State College.
† In "Effectiveness in Psychotherapy," *Psychoanalytic Quarterly*, Vol. XXXVII (1963), pp. 322–39.

Abraham

I shall not attempt to answer the question "What made Abraham ill?" because it is not the purpose of this book to answer that kind of question. It would be impossible, anyway, since I came on the scene long after the damage was done and when the child was no longer at home. Every once in a while he would call up and ask Irving to visit him. Since this happened when I was there, it gave me an opportunity to see how similar the relations of both boys were to the parents; my purpose now is to illustrate this. I begin by giving a little of Abraham's life history as obtained from his mother.

She told me that "when I held him in my arms, the world was mine." A relative said, "Abe is baked in your heart." He was a "genius" and everyone took turns educating him. When Abe was two years of age his grandfather was teaching him Hebrew and he could read the labels on boxes he saw in the grocery store. At three he performed "mental miracles." His mother bought him an encyclopedia and would have put him on television except that she was warned that the publicity would "interfere with his rest." In elementary school he became a showpiece because he could do arithmetic several grades beyond his own. As time went on, however, he grew more and more resistive, refused to do anything anybody wanted him to and finally lost all interest in studying. His mother also told me that when he was two years old she was already beating him with a strap. She said that Abraham always believed she and her husband had secrets from him—that things were going on behind his back—and even today he feels that anything done for him is just for the purpose of taking advantage.

When Abe called up and asked Irving to come and see him, his mother confided in me that she believed the only reason he wanted to see Irving was to "pump" him. This is what took place a couple of days later:

(Fourth day.) This evening there was a long telephone conversation between Abe and his father, during which Mr. Rosenberg said to Abe again and again, "Why does a father have to have a purpose in calling his son?"

The issue, as I got it from Mrs. Rosenberg, was that since Abe was not expecting a call from his father until Sunday, he wanted to know why he called up now. I asked Mrs. Rosenberg why and she said her husband just got lonely and wanted to talk to his son. At present I am so suspicious that I feel as Abraham did—that his father must have had some ulterior motive.

In reading what follows it is important to bear in mind that Abe had already expressed a desire to see Irving, that all arrangements are made for Irving's visit, and that the parents are afraid Abe is going to "pump" Irving.

(Sixth day.) It was time to phone Abe but Mr. Rosenberg didn't want to or wanted to call it off but his wife went to the phone immediately and got Abe. She does this sort of thing to her husband; that is to say, she puts him in a position where he has to act. When Mr. Rosenberg had Abe on the phone the conversation proceeded something like this: Mr. Rosenberg asked Abe how he was and the boy said "All right." Mr. Rosenberg then said Dave (a teen-age relative) had gone to Palmerston. He asked Abe whether anything had happened at the Center, was there any news. Apparently Abe wanted to know what he was asking about and his father said he just wanted to know if there was any news. Then he asked Abe whether he knew that I was here, and apparently Abe said yes. He then gave Abe (according to my explicit instructions that he do so) a pretty straight-forward account of why I was there—that I was studying the families of these children in order to find out as much as possible. I don't remember what he said in this connection: as much as possible about what? At any rate, Abe seemed satisfied.

Mr. Rosenberg (although the matter had all been settled!) asked Abe whether he wanted to see Irving alone or with Dave or Burt (another teen-age relative), to which Abe apparently answered he wanted to see Irving. . . . Just before the conversation ended Mr. Rosenberg asked Abe, "Do you trust me?" and apparently Abe said he did.

It is important to have this rigamarole down because there was only one reason why Mr. Rosenberg called Abe, and that was to find out whether he still wanted Irving to come. We have to notice some of the subterfuges he uses: he introduces the entirely unimportant news that Dave has gone to Palmerston and then asks Abe whether he would like to see Dave or Burt, too. All this, before coming to the point.

These chronically frightened parents don't want the older boys to see each other alone. Once Mr. Rosenberg tried to pump me after suggesting I have a talk with Irving about the family, and Mrs. Rosenberg wanted me to check up on Ben and Irving while she was away at work. A day before Abe and Irving were to get together, Mr. Rosenberg, still working anxiously to head off a private meeting, remarked to me that it might be a good idea if the boys got together at Dave's house, but I was against it.* Now he is still bent on blocking them; he thinks if he can get Abe interested in Burt, with Burt there, Irving and Abe won't talk. Talking to Abe on the phone, he first says Dave is out of town and then asks Abe if he wants to see him. Finally he asks Abe if he trusts his father!

((Seventh day.) I drove Irving over to the Center where Abe is, and left him. When I returned to the Rosenberg house, Mr. Rosenberg immediately began to pump me on what had happened, and even though I said I simply left Irving there and drove away, he did not believe me, but continued to ply me with questions. So I had to tell him again that I simply left Irving there and came back.

At two-forty Irving returned and refused to say anything to his father about what had happened between him and Abe. Mr. Rosenberg says that Irving will never tell him what went on. This time when the father asked Irving the boy merely tuned out.

Later the father again tried to pump Irving. Irving said they had played ping-pong. His father didn't know what ping-pong was, so Irving explained. He then said that Abe asked whether his mother and father still nagged and that he answered yes. Mr. Rosenberg asked whether Abe knows about my presence and Irving said yes.

Having turned the culturally determined predisposition to distrust the outer world against their own children, Mr. and Mrs. Rosenberg view Abraham and Irving *as if* they were outside the family. A strong basic distrust, probably present before marriage but aggravated because the marriage was a sham, predetermined the marriage to catastrophe. The irony of their life has been that two such distrustful people should have married for ambiguous reasons. The main problem in the Rosenberg family now is that the

---

* He proposed the idea to me as if asking my opinion.

children see through them. The irony has been that these pathetically frightened parents, who lack the skill to do it, try to pull the wool over their children's eyes. How much better it might have been for everybody, if Abe and Irving had been stupid!

Now a question: Are Abraham and Irving "paranoid," or is distrust merely a natural adaptation in this family? Paranoid schizophrenia, the disease of distrust and resistance, is one adaptation to an environment of deception and unlove; blind acquiescence is another. Behind them both is the culture—or more realistically, our people in their millions—part honest, part dishonest, sometimes to be distrusted, often not; willing to exploit the naïve; blandly ready to flip-flop into transient honesty when it suits certain ends or if deception fails.

What has made the difference between Abraham and Irving on the one hand, and Ben on the other? What has brought it about that two resisted and one acquiesced? Is it that Ben analyzed the situation, perceived the suffering of his brothers and decided that resistance brought only misery? After all, there *is* a human brain, powerful even in babies; there *is* a great capacity to think as well as to feel, even in babies; and we know that children alter their behavior toward parents in the light of their judgment about how to get along with them. The first order of business for all children, as judgment takes form, is to figure out how to get along with other people. Some children, like Irving and Abraham, make the decision not to get along with other people. In order to avoid blows, scolding and scorn, however, all one has to decide is that acquiescence is best. This is Ben. If a child does not acquiesce, it must be only because the broader consequences of acquiescence seem to him worse than the punishment he escapes by giving in. In the dialectic of pain, one often can only make a choice between different forms of it, and the victim will always choose the form that seems easiest to bear. Under such circumstances, it can seem that it is worse to acquiesce than to resist.

The process of choosing whether to suffer and become a self or to suppress the self has not been analyzed for children,* and it is surely different for different children.

In the case of the brothers Rosenberg, Abraham and Irving refused to deny their selves and so suffer the *agony of affirmation*, while Benjamin did deny his and so enjoys the relative comfort that comes with denial of self—a comfort which most people in our culture value even above our standard of living. We have observed, however, that Ben is beginning to change. We have seen this in his relationship to Irving, and we will presently observe it in relation to his mother, where it emerges most clearly in connection with food.

* Of course, Søren Kierkegaard has examined the role of suffering in this process, but only for adults.

Food

Although in the usual household a mother's primal function is to feed the family, in kosher Jewish homes her responsibility is particularly heavy, for not only must she guard against infraction of the elaborate food taboos, but she must also minister to everybody's food idiosyncrasies—even to serving them distinct meals—and feed them at different times. Because everybody's peculiar tastes must be served, a Jewish home can become a kind of alimentary merry-go-round, everybody wanting something different, everybody examining his food meticulously, everybody wanting to eat at a different time, so that mother, constantly in motion, rarely has a chance to sit down in her own kitchen, and if she does, sits on the edge of her chair. She saves the day for herself and keeps her husband and children quiet if she is a good cook. Mrs. Rosenberg was the worst cook I have ever encountered. Thus, in addition to being unable to meet the emotional needs of her family, she couldn't feed them properly. Though some readers may, perhaps, feel overwhelmed by the mass of food detail I present in the following paragraphs, it is necessary to include all of it in order that the reader perceive how food can be used in family pathology, and how badly prepared food, even when abundant and of good quality, can be characteristic of extended families, so that within the family network there is no escape from tormenting food. A detailed account of a "food madness" as part of general family psychopathology has never been presented before in the literature on psychopathology. In the following pages, I show how these conditions flow together.

(First day.) Dinner was first of all that soup which is standard in kosher households, and one knows that this chicken soup has left behind it a desolate, stringy chicken which someone must eat sooner or later. Then came another dish which is standard in kosher households: beef that has first been boiled and then roasted. This was accompanied by canned peas, lemonade, rolls and a mixed salad without dressing. In other words, with a few American trimmings like canned peas and garden vegetables, I recognized the standard kosher cooking from the *shtetl*.

(Second day.) At about seven-fifteen the next morning Mrs. Rosenberg called out to Ben to get up, and immediately made an omelet for him. It looked beautiful, but she made it so far in advance that I'm sure by the time he got down and began to eat, the omelet was cold.

I discovered something about the soup; it is not Mrs. Rosenberg's chicken soup but a packaged soup.* It doesn't seem to have anything in it but flavoring. The boys are very much opposed to this soup; Ben refused to eat it altogether and Irving ate it under protest, saying it was merely water.

At dinner Ben had steak and Irving said he wanted meat loaf, but when his mother started to serve it to him he refused, saying he had asked for steak. There was quite a hubbub over this. Mrs. Rosenberg was very upset that there had been this change of signals, but at last Irving accepted the meat loaf.

Irving kept calling for food. When he had come down after his bath he kept

---

* The following is the composition of one kosher packaged soup as stated on the envelope: "Pure egg noodles, salt, wheat starch, dextrose, hydrogenated vegetable oil, monosodium glutamate, spices, flavoring and turmeric."

asking for food. Mrs. Rosenberg said, "I like hungry little boys." At the table Mrs. Rosenberg got into some sort of anxious discussion with Ben over his having been drenched because the shower nozzle was turned in the wrong direction—when he turned it on, his bathrobe got soaked. They were anxiously discussing this while Irving was waiting for food, and he called out to his mother that he was hungry. So she stopped the discussion and got out some meat loaf. First she offered me a huge piece, but I said, "You should serve Irving first." She insisted on serving me first. Then I said I wanted only half of what she offered me; in addition to the meat loaf there was a baked potato and the usual canned peas and sliced-vegetable salad—very dreary food. Irving talked about how much he loves tomatoes.

(Fourth day.) In addition to beef tenderloin there was, as usual, the repulsive canned peas, the usual sliced cucumber, lettuce and tomato, and mashed potatoes. Only Mr. Rosenberg and I ate some of those salad things. For dessert we could have either frozen strawberries or watermelon. I chose strawberries. Mrs. Rosenberg asked her husband what he wanted, and when he said he didn't care she gave him canned applesauce.

While his mother had been preparing dinner Irving complained that he was hungry, and accused her of not caring about his being hungry. He kept screaming for food. She said that he wouldn't have to complain if he learned how to cook and have everything ready when she came home.

Ben began to talk animatedly about how much he liked to go to a certain place for a chocolate milk shake and French fries, and he described huge plates of French fried potatoes. This gave his brother the idea of getting some from Joe's, a restaurant nearby, so he told Ben to go and get some, and his mother supported the idea. Mrs. Rosenberg asked Irving why he hadn't gone to the store for the French fries and he made some laughing excuse. Ben, who seemed very eager to go, was given money and ran all the way to the restaurant and back. By the time he returned, we had sat down to dinner.

The business with the French fries made Mrs. Rosenberg very anxious because she made a huge mess of mashed potatoes, flavored, I think, with chicken or goose fat, and quite good. But the boys ate the French fries. Their mother remarked frequently on the foolishness of spending money on French fries when she had made so much mashed potatoes. Mr. Rosenberg said nothing.

(Fifth day.) The mother and Irving having sent Ben off to buy a ball for the boys to play with, the family sat down to dinner and was half finished before Ben got back. Mrs. Rosenberg said Ben doesn't like soup, anyway. When he came in, he sat down at the place left for him at the table and immediately said he didn't like any of the meat because it looked cold and because he didn't like the color of the gravy. Mrs. Rosenberg had put a huge pile of chicken and roast beef on the table, but Ben left the dining room and went into the kitchen and took a piece of roast beef out of the pan. It was exactly like the roast beef on the table, although it was probably warmer.

Mrs. Rosenberg bemoaned to me the fact that her family won't eat vegetables, but I would say that it really is impossible to make the vegetable much worse than she does. Those horrible canned peas have been the only cooked green vegetable on the table so far. I asked her whether she ever tried dressing on the salad and she said the boys won't touch it. She said she doesn't think that stuff is good for you, anyway.

Irving took both chicken legs, and that was all he ate for dinner. As a matter of fact, it seems to me that these kids eat hardly anything but protein and cake. I believe that the first time I saw either of them eat anything else was last night after the parents had gone to bed, when Irving ate half an apple.

(Seventh day.) Mrs. Rosenberg is making *milchiks** for lunch. She is going to make fried perch with mashed potatoes, but Irving wants meat.

The boys at last came to the lunch table after being urged. Since they wanted to continue watching TV, the mother said, "Well, you can come to the table and watch TV at the same time." Irving brought along a magazine and read it at the table. His mother asked him to put it away, and after some urging, he did.

Because of where his mother was sitting, Irving could not easily see the TV, so he asked her to move. But when she did, she was in Ben's way, and he told her to get out of the way. She got up angrily and turned the TV so that nobody could see it, and Irving said he wouldn't eat. He got up and turned the set toward them, and they ate their lunch and watched TV at the same time. The lunch was completely dominated by TV and nobody said anything. Only the boys were watching it.

Since we were having *milchiks,* Mrs. Rosenberg was very eager to get everybody to eat up the mashed potatoes. Because these potatoes have been mashed with milk they cannot be eaten with meat and she would have to throw them away, she said. She kept urging them on everybody, but although she and her husband and I had some, the boys would not touch them.

While others ate the fried perch, Mr. Rosenberg, who had previously told me he did not like herring, was eating herring from a jar. Mrs. Rosenberg asked Ben whether he would have some mashed potatoes, and he said "Maybe." She asked him this while he was eating (canned) tomato soup. When she asked him why he said "Maybe," he answered that, well, he was eating his soup now and didn't know whether he would want potatoes until he was finished. He didn't take any.

These notes were made at five o'clock. Mrs. Rosenberg took a nap and has now been up for about half an hour. When she got up she immediately went into the kitchen to prepare dinner. The boys were howling for food and were very angry with her. They are still howling for food because they ate practically nothing at lunch. It seems to me that anyone living in this house has to hold his capacity for experiencing a taste sensation completely in abeyance. (At lunch the fish was only half cooked and was terrible, anyway, and the potatoes were almost as bad. Then there were those dreadful canned peas, which are eaten by nobody but the mother. On this occasion even Ben was in a bad mood. When his mother asked him why he ate so little he said, "I don't like the fish, and the potatoes were regular potatoes and I like fried potatoes." Ben had completely rejected the fish and made himself a salami sandwich.)

After raving about not getting anything to eat, Irving was at last served a plate of packaged noodle soup and then some leftover beans. He also ate a little chicken. He wanted cake, but his mother said he would not get cake unless he ate more. She was very angry and they were yelling at each other. She threatened to give him no food if he gets hungry tonight. (Later in the evening, however, not long after this, the boys got a glass of milk and a piece of chocolate cake. When his mother threatened Irving, he said, "You're always threatening me.")

Ben quieted down after a while and sat sulking at the table. At last his mother set food in front of him but he became very angry because he didn't like the color of the gravy. He said it should be dark brown instead of yellow and green. He ate a salami sandwich. As the boys expressed their anger, Mr. Rosenberg kept telling his wife to let them alone.

In the course of the altercation with Irving about his eating more and not getting up from the table unless he ate more, Mrs. Rosenberg yelled that she had rushed around to get supper for him and this was all he ate. She said, "Take a

* Dairy foods, as distinguished from *fleischiks,* meat foods, and *parve,* foods which are neither. *Milchiks* and *fleischiks* must not be mixed, but *parve* can be mixed with either.

roll; they were gotten especially for you. You don't like them hard, so I warmed them up and now they are soft." So Irving said, "All right, I'll take a bite to please you." So he took a roll, tore out a piece and ate it, and that was all. As a matter of fact, though these rolls look good, they are practically tasteless. (Sham rolls!)

The dinner was leftover beef and chicken that had been warmed over two or three times and were relatively unpalatable, or, putting it mildly, were relatively tasteless. As Irving was very angry, his father told him to go and watch TV.

Finally, just to show how the relatives become involved in the network of food troubles:

In the course of our conversation, Irving said that his mother's sister's family has taken maybe a hundred meals in their house, but he has had only three or four in theirs. (His aunt's children are Sol and Burt.)

There was beef tenderloin tonight and everybody ate it except Mrs. Rosenberg, who had leftover meat loaf. Sol came in when they had all sat down to dinner, but he was left standing there, not even offered a seat, until the whole family had eaten. Then he was given leftover meat loaf, which he ate alone.

· · ·

Sol was again present this evening (at the gathering of the relatives), and while everybody else was eating beef, chicken, and other things, he was given lox and bagel. This is the second time he has been hovering around while others eat better food. This time, however, he said he wanted to eat something that had not been bought on Saturday, so he sat at the corner of the table and ate lox and bagel that had been around for several days.

· · ·

In discussing the relatives, Mrs. Rosenberg referred to them as "they," and she mentioned the enormous pressure "they" were putting on the Rosenbergs in regard to being kosher. Most of this pressure comes from Sol and Burt. Whenever they are in the house, she says, you have the impression they are spying on you. Burt stayed at their house for a couple of days for some reason, and every time she returned from shopping he would go through the bag and ask of everything whether it was kosher. "They" also object to the light being on in the refrigerator on Saturday because you're not supposed to turn on a light on Saturday. So she always has the feeling that both boys are spying on her in order to find out whether she is being completely Orthodox and kosher.

· · ·

Leah, Mr. Rosenberg's sister, arrived with a cake she had baked. She brought what she called a strudel—a leaden affair with only the faintest resemblance to any strudel I ever saw or tasted—and cookies that were heavy, with little sugar or shortening.

It is clear that the family pathology has penetrated the food complex; instead of being won over by delicious food, the boys feel a resentment over food that flares nearly every time their mother feeds them. In the first place she's a terrible cook, and in the second, she can't learn to do away with things her family doesn't like—to at least change the soup and get something else in place of the canned peas—maybe frozen ones. She won't experiment, try one thing and another, until she finds something everybody likes. She just says the boys don't like vegetables. She's marooned in a sea of packaged soup, trapped in a can of peas! She doesn't realize that her beautiful omelets are cold by the time the boys come down in the morning. Even her willingness to serve Irving one thing and Ben another turns against her because when the boys are picky she explodes. So at mealtimes they really punish her—there is no trouble about the food when she's not at home. What makes Mrs. Rosenberg especially vulnerable is her very effort to be a good mother. She wants her children to eat. She tries hard, but the boys use her best efforts against her: they suddenly change their minds, refuse a special tidbit, even complain about the color of the gravy, until, provoked beyond endurance, she flies into a rage and becomes a bad, angry mother, which only proves to the boys that she was a bad mother in the first place. "You're always threatening me," says Irving. If only she were a good cook she might at least have Ben on her side.

Saturday lunch was a nightmare. The food was awful, the taboo on mixing *milchik* and *fleischik* made Mrs. Rosenberg anxious about the mashed potatoes, and the boys treated her like dirt when she got in front of the TV. Meanwhile Mr. Rosenberg sat quietly (innocently!) eating his herring (which he presumably dislikes!) and didn't lift a finger while the boys were pushing their mother around about the TV. Later he was on the boys' side again when he told his wife to stop yelling at them, but he canceled himself by advising Irving to watch TV, because this is nothing to tell a boy who is screaming for food.

The boys' hostility and disrespect for their mother pours out so easily at mealtimes because that is when she materializes as the embodiment of all they never had from her, because she is most vulnerable just where she is trying hardest to be motherly and because they can defend themselves against her by not eating. It is precisely when Mrs. Rosenberg tries to be a *good* mother that the pent-up anger against the *bad* mother erupts and makes it impossible for her to be good. Thus in psychopathology, values become traps and people die by values instead of living by them.

Ben resists, letting his hostility show, because to acquiesce in eating this food is sometimes even beyond *him*, and because his mother is weakest, and on the defensive, in her role as feeder. Even in the TV incident he is stronger than she: since she gave the boys permission to watch it during lunch, she has no right to interfere. So where Ben is strong, and pushed to the limits of his endurance by bad food, he becomes his brother's ally against the mother. Here she changes places with Irving, for although he is often thrust to the family periphery by the hostility of his parents and the defection of his brother, here she is excluded by the hostility of the children and the desertion of her husband. The father's silence and his advice to leave the boys alone isolates her further. This is a family of shifting coalitions, and the only person who is never excluded from any of them is Ben.

In fighting his inner battle against his mother, Ben moves cautiously. Since he is only twelve years old and very dependent, he must be careful not to go too far in asserting himself. He must resist only where his mother is most vulnerable, when he does not have to fight alone, and in the right manner—he must not scream or appear violent, like Irving. In encounters with the mother over food, Ben has his brother on his side and then the *mother* cannot go too far because the boys will refuse to eat. Thus the boys are able to take advantage of their mother's wish to be a good mother—for she could tell them to go to hell when they are making things difficult.

The fact that Irving and Ben treat their mother with harshness and contempt suggests that the desire to be this kind of good mother was not al-

ways so strong in her; that she is changing because beating is no longer
possible.

What struck me first when Irving said his mother didn't care about his
being hungry was that as he sat there famished, as only a boy of his age can
be, blaming his mother for not caring, she did not reply, "But I do care, and
I'm rushing. *Here, take something for a minute,*" but answered Irving with
a counter accusation, raking up his history of doing nothing in the house,
filling his belly with blame. It is true that sickly as she is, having been up
since six o'clock, possibly having spent a bad night, having worked all day
downtown and fought her way home on the public transportation system—
probably standing all the way—perhaps Mrs. Rosenberg dreams of finding
everything ready when she comes home. It is dismal enough to walk day in,
day out, right from the job into the kitchen, there to expend one's remaining strength without help or appreciation. But then to be accused, by a
person who doesn't help, of not caring is beyond endurance. As a matter of
fact, considering this situation Mrs. Rosenberg handles herself with great
restraint; some might have had a tantrum. Nevertheless, her response
seems only to have enraged Irving, for he continued screaming for food.

My ruminations on Irving's not helping are contained in the following
note to myself:

Since Irving never sees his father do anything to help his mother, it is natural
that Irving should not do anything either. If, as Irving may see it, his father
exploits his mother and sits around and does nothing while his mother is working,
why should Irving do anything different?

Why didn't his mother say something like "Look, Irving, I get up at six
o'clock so I can make breakfast for you and get everything ready for your
lunch. Remember, I work all day, and when I come home I'm tired, and just
as hungry as you. Have a little patience!" Over and over again the observer
is struck by the fact that in critical situations the obvious is never said. We
are all very much the same. In the present instance the relationship is so
disturbed that a simple human approach is no longer possible for Mrs. Rosenberg.

Turning at last to Burt and Sol: the Rosenbergs detest them, but the boys
are able to get back at the Rosenbergs by using the food taboos as their
environment of attack. In a closely knit group of relatives, pathology may
be a *network of pathology;* the pathology of one family is likely to extend into related ones, not because they share the same bloodstream, but
because they have been exposed to similar social conditions. If related families see one another often, rely on one another much, and are deeply involved in one another's affairs, there is a high probability of involvement in
and expression of one another's pathology. And the converse is probably
true also: the more involved families are in one another's pathology, the
greater the probability that they will be involved in other ways and will see
one another often, even if underneath it all and behind one another's backs,
they tear one another to pieces. This must be true because they are the only
ones who will tolerate one another's eccentricities.

LAST SCENES

Sunday was my last day with the Rosenbergs; I left after breakfast on Monday. It seems to me that it would be well for the reader to see the last paragraphs of my record, because they evoke the atmosphere of this home, convey much that is significant in it and reveal the impression it made on the observer.

(Monday morning, the eighth day.) I was downstairs with Mrs. Rosenberg after having had breakfast. When Irving came down she called a cheery "Good morning" to him but he did not respond. She went into the hallway to kiss him, and as she kissed him he shrank away silently. He came into the kitchen and ate his scrambled eggs without a word. He went upstairs, dressed, came down, read the paper without a word. His mother told him to do his homework instead of reading the paper, and after a while he did. In all this he was completely silent. Ben came down at seven-fifteen and had his breakfast wordlessly, his nose in the paper. Then he went into the living room and continued to read. His mother called out, "Ben, are you busy?" but there was no response. About five minutes later she called out again, telling Ben to come and "drink your milk." He said, "Wait, I just have to finish the last page." She called back, "You'll have to rush!" He turned the paper over, glanced at the last page, went into the kitchen and drank his milk. Meanwhile Irving was doing his homework.

It was five minutes to eight. As the mother left for work she kissed Irving good-bye and he turned and kissed her on the cheek too. Ben could not close his briefcase, so he asked his mother to do it. He has a lot of paper, which the children take from him when they don't have any. He said one kid owes him twenty sheets, which he expects to get back today.

Mrs. Rosenberg left and Irving remained downstairs doing homework, while I went upstairs to get ready to leave. When Ben went off to school he actually said good-bye to me, which astonished me. I guess it's because he knows this is my last day here.

I have in my notes the following:

Mr. and Mrs. Rosenberg have never been able to fight back against the world and so they fight their children. Mr. and Mrs. Rosenberg have always been at the bottom, and this is the first time in their lives they have ever had anyone *under* them, i.e., their children. This is the first time in their lives there has been any human being around in a weaker position than they. That is to say, their own children are the only people in the world who have ever been weaker than Mr. and Mrs. Rosenberg, and so they fight the children.

Summary of the Rosenberg Case

We must not underestimate Mrs. Rosenberg: she is an energetic, orderly, determined, responsible woman who does not confront her misfortunes in rage and anxiety only, but also in sorrow. She keeps the house running, and in true Jewish tradition, she is mother to her husband as well as to the children. We do not know what crushed her, what made her intellectually inadequate, but in her organizational powers and occasionally in her observations on her own condition, there are signs that something was there. In spite of the fact that she is a sick woman she does her duty by her family firmly and grimly. She has a conscience, and even the fact that she clearly despises Irving does not prevent her from trying to do her duty by him. Somewhere, as she did her duty by her children, the harshness, iron and blindness of her character turned her children against her and turned her, in rage against her children, so that in trying to be a good mother she became a bad one. Even today this paradox—that in trying to do good she does evil—is used by her children against her, and it emerges with ferocious irony as she tries to get the boys to eat unspeakable food, and as they trap her in the kitchen and punish her there.

Mrs. Rosenberg, like so many of us, believes that existence is a sham and a disappointment, but there is a difference between her life-in-sham and that of most of us: she has been compelled to sham deep feeling—to sham some feeling—for her husband while belittling him, and some love for her children while finding it impossible to love children begotten on her dutifully by a man she could not love. Her life has thus become a chaos of duty, anger, pretense and longing. We must not forget that she has a longing— the longing to be loved—at least by her children, or at least by Ben, and perhaps even by Irving. Her histrionic kissing of the boys, her greetings to them in the morning—the display of lovey-dovey clichés arranged to gull the observer—merely dramatize what she wishes her life really were. The very maneuvers she employs to mislead, her very shams before me, express the emptiness of her life. At least the boys, in spite of coldness, are somewhat closer to her than to their father.

Mrs. Rosenberg knows what struck her: "You have to get used to taking many disappointments in life." So when one son becomes very severely emotionally disturbed, another becomes almost unmanageable and the third is acquiescent but sly and cold, it is all part of life's disappointment; it is in the very nature of existence to be disappointed, dealt blows by an impersonal force, the pervading, malificent *mana* of the universe, as palpable as the Melanesian's conception of *mana*, the invisible, formless, indwelling power in every star and planet, in every stream and rock, in every living thing. So that Irving's cry that disappointments could have been avoided must have sounded to her like the thought of an inexperienced child—perhaps just another expression of Irving's intransigence, a veiled attempt to pin blame on his parents. In Mrs. Rosenberg's view, existence is governed by luck also, and one merely accepts passively what luck turns up. Her husband was no luck, but on the other hand, in spite of the fact that Benjamin was an accident she did not want, he "turned out to be a good boy."

The notion of "turning out" has a complexity all its own. When an artist says of his work, "It went poorly for a long time and caused me a lot of trouble but it turned out all right," he doesn't mean *literally* that the work has a life of its own that dominates him and moves the brush, the pen or the chisel, because all along he knows that the work is his own creation and that saying "it turned out all right" does not really impute an independent stomach, heart and brain to the work. But when Mrs. Rosenberg says that Ben turned out to be a good boy, she implies that he has an inherent tendency to develop and that she has had little or nothing to do with it—not an unusual idea among uneducated people by any means, and not strange to many who should know better. A metaphysic of chance makes disengagement from a child that turns out "bad" easy.

Mr. Rosenberg's rationale of disengagement is more complex than his wife's. By ascribing his sons' condition to his wife's mistreatment and to a "queer" strain in her family, he too avoids responsibility. The explanations of husband and wife project the inimical outside themselves: she assumes it to be inherent in existence and he assumes it to be inherent in her and her whole family (who, we must remember, have been so good to him). Both explanations conform to the Rosenbergs' unresponsible life configuration, in which dependence on relatives is the dominant element.

Mrs. Rosenberg does not say that Ben turned out to be intelligent, warm, loving, of a sunny disposition; she says he is good. This means he does what he's told and doesn't cause any trouble—an attitude we frequently find when we interview people who are not highly educated on the question "What would you say is a good child?"

In my study the Rosenbergs were the only parents who made a point of belittling their children to me, but even as Mrs. Rosenberg was contemptuous of Irving in private, she was eager to prove that *she* was solicitous. And even as she was making clear to me her low opinion of him, she wondered how he knew that they cared more for Ben than for him. It may seem puzzling that a mother can imagine that a child will not know her true attitude, unless we bear in mind that most people think they can pull the wool over a child's eyes and unless we realize that children are usually smart enough to let their parents think they do not see through the parental shams. Irving was unable to do this, and in tearing away the screen, he threw these extremely vulnerable and terrified people into a panic that led to a desire to be rid of him.

It is easy for Mrs. Rosenberg to speak well of Ben—she is fond of him— but of her husband she *tries* to speak loyally, though she regrets him. Just as in speaking of Irving she alternates between contempt and betrayal on the one hand and an effort to present an appearance of solicitude on the other, when she talks about her husband she tries to praise him, but she is trapped into blame by the resentment bred of the emptiness of her life with him. Still, even with her *shreds* of loyalty, she has more of it than he.

Mr. Rosenberg presents himself instantly as a self-effacing, passive man who asks for nothing. He seems to say, as he comes toward you, inside his worn and baggy clothes, "Look at me! I'm a nice, quiet, harmless man; and I don't want anything from you." Beaten as a child, a slave to heavy, unrewarding work much of his life, uneducated, a poor ghetto Jew, he comes by this attitude, atmosphere and appearance legitimately. He seems calm as he sits with you and hangs around the house, but he isn't; the lava of nothingness boils in his guts and once paralyzed him with a gastrointestinal ailment. Though he seems to make no demands, he has been cared for by his wife's family and is taken care of at home while doing nothing to help his sick and heavily burdened wife. His innocuous appearance is contradicted by his behavior, as he tells the observer the "whole truth" about his wife, runs down the character of his two eldest boys, plans effortlessly for sham, acts it out, and provokes Irving, who he knows is susceptible to severe respiratory difficulties if enraged.

Nothingness is thus not the negative one might imagine. The concept is a model, an ideal type, perhaps only a metaphoric way of talking about the consequences of a cruelty to the body and soul of a human being that leaves him merely physically alive. As long as a human being lives he cannot be literally nothing; a fact discovered only recently in mental hospitals, where even the neglected denizens of the chronic wards, the waxy-flexible ones who used to sit all day on the floor, against the walls in their rat-gray uniforms, were found to be *something* when a new psychiatry, not accepting the paradox of a human being existing as nothing, got them off the floor and gave them something interesting to do.

So, though Mr. Rosenberg is far from mad, neither is he exactly nothing, nor is that something that he still is really possible to live with. He still needs to feel effectual but can express it only in a pathological way—attacking Irving, belittling most of the people he knows, caressing Ben almost sexually. The only constructive things he does for the family are to work regularly for a modest wage and to trim the shrubs around the house. It is fortunate that he has little energy—he is so destructive when active. Although Mr. Rosenberg has largely abdicated as father, he causes trouble when he tries to be one. Playing the role of peacemaker—a phase of perfect innocence—he darts in where it is not necessary, interfering with the boys and undercutting his wife when she has her hands full with them. Yet his peacemaking activities endear him to no one, largely because of their ambiguous goal. Thus the dialectic of nothingness yields the definition that *nothingness is a state in which he who is nothing is constantly propelled by an intolerable misery into active negation of himself.*

Perhaps they talk things over in bed, but in my presence Mr. and Mrs. Rosenberg never conversed. There was little discussion when Irving locked himself in the lavatory, and when they did talk during that incident it was because they were scared. In my presence the parents never called each other by name, and in speaking to me about each other, it was always as "my husband" or "my wife." Sham, an empty life, and a thousand secret angers in which disappointment in and contempt for each other caused the worst anger of all, even overshadowing their feelings about the disaster of their children, have all but eliminated communication between them. Thus, even from the beginning, husband and wife lived in the shadow of the dread of truth. Not trusting each other, they did not trust their children, and fearing each other, they came to fear their children.

There is a wall, or rather, an electrically charged barbed-wire fence, between parents and children, and although there is some fun, moments of relaxation quickly give way to quarreling. The funmaker—as well as the biggest troublemaker—is Irving. Most of the communication that takes place between children and parents is acrimonious; and even when not explicit, there is an overtone of protest in what the children say. Tension and bitterness, of course, are expressed most often by Irving, not only because he has suffered most but also because he is most articulate—the town crier of the family misery.

The mistake his parents made in getting married in the first place is now expressed with greatest anguish in Irving, after Abraham had become ill. Since Irving suffers most visibly, he has fallen under the iron law that he who has suffered most will be punished most, and since he has become the embodiment of the inimical, the family distress appears to center in him. In their relationship to Irving the parents are as if confronted by a nemesis, and it is he whom the father assails with his remnants of courage—this father, who, having been crushed, has not dared to challenge even his wife, attacks the son, the metamorphosis of *his* father's and mother's wretchedness and delusions. Thus in an unimaginably paradoxical way Irving has almost raised up this paternal Lazarus, because his own spectacular suffering, taking the form either of resistiveness and rage or of selfishness, either of a bad respiratory difficulty or of weeping, has driven his father, one of the causes of it all, into a quasi existence in which the father arises to fight what he himself has created. Let us be clear on this: having approached but not quite plumbed nothingness, Mr. Rosenberg is dragged back into existence as he tries to protect, to bring domestic peace to the house and to establish himself in the affections of Ben. The tragedy, of course, is that in his very effort to become something, such a man can only cancel himself and others.

As I studied the individual relationships between Irving and his parents I saw that although hostility and contempt stand between them and their son, there is a difference in the underlying feeling between Irving and his mother and between Irving and his father. I felt that there is no real bond between Irving and his father—that the father enters the son's sphere only as an intruder, whose right to trespass derives solely from the jural fact that they are father and child living under the same roof and subject to certain culturally determined rules. As far as Irving is concerned his father does not exist, except as a sudden painfully provoking obtrusion, and as far as Mr. Rosenberg is concerned, the mere sight of his son stirs him to rage. It is a very different matter with the mother. Her efforts to feed Irving well, to get him to do his homework, to take a bath, to tempt him with a goody, to lure him out of the lavatory, and so on, all suggest that in spite of her anger and contempt, she would still like to have him. I felt the same way about Irving's attitude toward her: his statement that in contrast to his father, she has some sensitivity, his occasional seeking her out spontaneously for conversation, his once-in-a-blue-moon going to meet her as she comes home from work, all taken together suggest that that relationship, harrowing as it is, is not entirely dead and could be revived. What moves her to action is not Irving's resistiveness, but a steady, though often woefully distorted yearning to be a real mother.

Much of the malice in her feeling toward Irving is now an expression of his rejection of her. Of course, she cannot see how she has caused it. Doesn't she treat Irving as well as Ben? Doesn't she try to be nice to Irving? But by this time he is so distrustful that her efforts seem bait. "She smiled," he says, "but she seemed a demon." Now that he is adolescent, resistiveness and distrust have an expanded meaning, for what was in earlier childhood a mechanical resistance to aversive force now symbolizes freedom and power. Thus early survival responses become transmuted by later experiences with the culture into standardized motivations: childish negativism, poured into the maturational mold, turns into resistance to all controls and then becomes a drive for total freedom and the control of others. Irving's attempt to rule Benjamin is not only a distortion and imitation of what his parents do, not merely exploitation of Ben's acceptance of the role of an acquiescent mama's boy, but also the trying out of his drive to dominate everything—and, incidentally, to make submission of others a phase of his drive to freedom. And this, after all, is just one, rather common expression of the wish to be free—a desire that others be one's prisoner, for the subservience of one confirms the liberty of another.

And just as Mr. Rosenberg erupts into a fugitive and ambiguous effectiveness by attempting to rule Irving, so Irving tries to feel effective by dominating his brother. Though Ben does not yield entirely, he yields enough to take the edge off Irving's hungers, while cautiously moving toward a less submissive position himself. Meanwhile, he clings like a pilot-fish to Irving, without whom he is nothing. To lie on the floor watching TV and the street until his brother comes home, to gaze vacantly, to play aimlessly, to count the hours until Irving returns—this indeed seems to me to be a nothingness that can be filled only by the return of that beloved person. And because this is so, Ben will put up with his brother's beating and hectoring and even enjoy it—within limits. The limits are set by the fact that he is not a little fellow any more, that a beating is not undiluted pleasure for him and that for anyone who has delighted in subservience, the very punishment he receives gives him a peep over the wall into the gardens of the free, into the possibility of reversal, into the bliss of doing the same thing himself. The paradox inherent in the dominance-subordinate relationship is precisely this: he who has been subordinate may yearn for the time when he can turn the trick. And this can be true even if he enjoys subordination for its advantages.

The symbiotic relationship between Ben and Irving causes Ben to think of his own needs in terms of his brother's. But meanwhile, also, such clinging to Irving does not blind Ben to his position with his parents, and when the going gets rough, Ben is silent; he is just as interested in defending his appearance of innocence as they are in defending theirs. The value of loyalty appears in this family in Irving's loyalty to "his" baseball team, in his mother's loyalty to his father, when she feels herself on parade; and in Mr. Rosenberg's loyalty to his uncle—the one person of whom he always speaks well.

In the brothers' relationship to each other, Irving does not respond as Ben does; he does not phrase his wants in terms of Ben's. It is true that to do so would interfere with his thrust toward independence, yet we know enough about the capacity of the organism for paradox to realize that a thrust toward independence does not rule out symbiotic dependence either. Still, independence goes more smoothly if one does not lean too much on the person from whom one seeks to be free. The symbol of Irving's dependence on Ben is the position in which he sleeps with him.

At the present, Irving is in a precarious state in the family, while Ben is growing stronger, for not only are Ben's acquiescence and quietness assets, he is beginning to wear his brother down. Thus Irving's possibilities seem threatened, as he is attacked from all sides, while Ben's possibilities seem to increase. Everything depends on whether Irving can hold out against his parents and whether he can transfer the gratification he gets from Ben to some other object. Meanwhile he blows up easily and vents much of his chronic irritation and anxiety on Ben. I don't think he punches Ben only because it is *Ben*, but also because he needs to hammer on something relatively responsive to punishment. He needs something that will respond to pain, that will keep him company while he suffers too; something that he can abuse in relative safety and see squirm a little. And thus through the dialectic of his own misery, Irving drags his father and brother out of nothingness, but also turns them both against him, as his father blames and his brother resists: as Irving drives people out of nothingness, they try to drive him into it.

Cut off from other children by their entanglement in each other, by their awkwardness in sports and by their special emotional needs, the brothers have become imprisoned in each other. The separateness and privacy our culture values so highly facilitate the isolation of Irving and Ben in their self-created fraternal ghetto. Our cultural configuration of space, which supplies each individual with a small capsule out of which he must break on his own initiative and under his own power, is such that unless one forces one's self out, one can rot in one's privacy. Depending on the culture, space is an environment where isolation is inconceivable—as in many tribal cultures—and where insistence on it is punished, sometimes even by death; or an environment like ours where adults are "private citizens" and have to break isolation in order to become socialized. Thus the Rosenberg "private house" has become a hothouse where Irving's and Ben's pathology flowers because there is so little interference with their mutual stimulation. In this narrow space, furthermore, *their* conflicts collide persistently with their parents'—particularly the father's—because all the Rosenbergs stay home so much. As the boys act out on each other, they inevitably arouse their parents' underlying disturbances: the father hurls himself into the boys' fights to provoke Irving and get him away from Ben, his love object; and the mother, perceiving and treating Ben almost as another woman in the house, inadvertently makes him a libidinal object for the other males. Lacking a truly feminine figure in the home, Irving and his father have turned to Ben, whose qualities of yieldingness and softness are lacking in the mother. Thus, in his curious and distorted way, Ben makes living in this house possible. While Irving is everything the parents fear and despise, Ben symbolizes what everybody longs for. In the *shtetl* they say that marriage is with the husband but the love affair is with the son; between them Ben and Irving have what is missing in the husband: Ben is responsible, Irving is vigorous, intelligent, prideful, literate and ambitious. He may be even more desired by the mother than Ben—yet he has put himself beyond her reach. The bitter paradox for Mrs. Rosenberg is that all her life what she really wanted has been beyond the reach of love. Thus the parents and children have become mutually inaccessible to one another and practically all communication that is not wrangling has dried up.

In conclusion, let us look at the parents' values. *Sham*, a value that has carried human, and particularly Western, culture to wealth and power unequaled in history, a value with titanic potential for the building of fortune and empire, for the promotion of almost everything significant in the culture of the West, has merely wrecked the Rosenberg family, because instead of using it appropriately against the outer world, they have turned it against one another. Though sham is an essential ingredient in political speeches, in the governing of men, in the promotion of advertising, the rigging of prices, the waging of wars, etc.—and anyone in his right mind will grant that such wholesome activities cannot be carried out without sham—sham is of limited value in the home. The parents Rosenberg not only practice white sham beyond the point of intelligent usage, they use black sham to trap Irving.

Exploitation, the use of others—wryly and perceptively called "efficiency" by Irving, the black sheep—is another important Western value that has become a trap in the Rosenberg household. Ben is valued too much for services as a domestic, and Irving is hated too much because he refuses to render them. Relatives are valued exclusively in terms of what they contribute to the Rosenberg household, but Mr. Rosenberg and his wife resent dependence. At the same time, however, they so need to use the relatives that instead of defending Irving against them, they expose him. Exploitation, extremely useful for expanding wealth and power but of negative value in intimate human relations, has been made to work as a unifying principle in the Rosenberg household, but this is a contradiction. Exploitation is naked in the relationship between the brothers but is dressed up as love in the relationship between the parents and Ben. Ben uses his willingness to be exploited to bind the family to him.

Pride is an important value here because, since nobody in the family is aware of it, Irving's assertion of the right to pride is strange and threatening. He wants to feel puffed up, big, proud. What right has he to this where father and mother have been ground down? Irving just talks big, his parents say, and this talking big is not accepted as natural in an adolescent who wants to be something, but every grandiloquent word is felt by the parents as a personal threat.

This is related to Irving's need to be dominant and strong in a household where dominance crosses the pathway of the mother and threatens the father who, in his very appearance and approach—in his entire life—expresses passiveness and acceptance. Yet Mr. Rosenberg still tries to dominate Irving, the indomitable. Insignificant—almost to nothingness—as he is, Mr. Rosenberg will not let his son push him around; asserting his self against Irving is his last claim on selfhood, and far from giving it up, he often turns Irving on, even though he knows it is bad for the boy. While between Irving and his father the attempts to be dominant and strong destroy the relationship, between the brothers these attempts maintain the relationship. Ben almost gives Irving the gratification of dominance, and Irving rescues Ben from being nothing; Ben provides Irving with the quasi satisfaction of ambiguous control, and Irving provides Ben with the reality of dependence. Fundamentally, therefore, Irving gives—always without knowing it, of course—as much as he gets of those pathological distortions of gratification that bind the brothers to each other, and which they cannot duplicate in the outer world. Between Irving and his father there really is neither dominance nor submission—each drives the other to further anger. When the boys fight, what anger arises passes quickly and is obliterated in bed. Between Irving and his father there is no reconciliation at all.

Mrs. Rosenberg is an overworked and badly treated domestic whom the boys persecute and ridicule almost at will as they pin her to the wall with her own inadequacies. Because of their ingenious malice, sustained by the abomination of her food, she has no redress; she cannot force them to eat, and she is anxious when they will not. So she swings between anger, anxiety and despair, while they punish her for past abuses with this tailor-made instrument—her motherhood-anxiety.

There is no value the Rosenbergs have not turned against themselves; as in all pathological families, values have become weapons the family members use against one another and against themselves. Even the value of "motherhood" or "maternal solicitude" is a disaster, in spite of the fact that Mrs. Rosenberg still tries, to the point of emotional and physical exhaustion, to be a good mother. Yet it is only this determination, this doggedness, this despairing effort, that keeps the family going. Where would they all be if she died?

PART III

The Metz Family

When the man of hope would
have a future which can have
no reality for him, or the man of
memory would remember a
past which has had no reality,
then we have the essentially
unhappy individuals . . . for
though the hoping individual
does not hope for something
which has no reality for him,
he may nevertheless hope for
something which he himself
knows cannot be realized.
—SØREN KIERKEGAARD,
Either/Or

INTRODUCTION

Messages of Love

If a man says, "I love you," to a woman, she may wonder whether he means it, whether he loves only her, how much he loves her, whether he will love her next week or next year, or whether this love only means that he wants her to love him. She may even wonder whether his love includes respect and care, or whether his love is merely physical. "I love you" is surely an ambiguous message. The woman may come to the conclusion that his idea of love is not hers and that the kind of love he has to give would not make her happy. So in spite of his caresses and in spite of the fact that she enjoys the man, the woman refuses to marry him and breaks off.

If Joan says, "I hate you," to Joseph, she may just be in a transient rage; "I hate you" may be her manner of speaking when she is angry. Joseph may be used to it, or perhaps he thinks that "all girls talk that way." The proof may be that although Joan says, "I hate you," on Saturday, she will be sweet to him on the phone Sunday. But if Joe says to Bill, "I hate you," it is a different matter, because men do not usually say, "I hate you," to each other even when they really do. The word "hate" passes more readily across the sexes than between two men.

Everything depends on who says what to whom and how he says it, and human beings scan each other's utterances to see what lies behind the words.

The Dialectic of Utterances

In the dots and dashes of telegraph messages there is no ambiguity—a sound on the wire is *either* a dot *or* a dash, and it is not necessary for the sender to reassure the receiver that he really means this dot or that dash, nor does the receiver have to ask the sender whether he really intended that particular dot or dash. An electric pulse does not have the capacity for ambiguity, falsification or self-contradiction. The burden of clarity is carried perfectly by the apparatus. A dot in Morse code always, invariably, implies "not dash." The telegraph signal is so clear that it automatically excludes its opposite. But in everyday human communication there is no such possibility. I can even say, "Plants grow from seeds," in such a way as to make people doubt that I really mean it. I may smile, give a peculiar modulation to my voice, look out of the corner of my eyes in such a way as to make people think that the whole idea is fraudulent or at least that I do not believe what I am saying.

Without knowing it, we comment on every utterance we make in order to make people understand that we "mean" what we say or that we do not; that we feel it deeply or that we do not; that we are honest about it or not. A parent can say "I love you" to his child so as to make clear that it is not true—that "I love you" really means "I can't stand you, you make me sick." But at the same time the parent can hold his child to it, can insist that the child act toward him as if he were really loved. Thus, though the child detects within his parent's message its own negation, he cannot act as if he did. He must act as if the parent really *meant* what he said. The child is thus in a *double bind*.

What is said of utterances is equally true of actions. Every kiss between lovers must carry with it a comment of how it is meant. People who have had many affairs become experts at interpreting the meaning of kisses and embraces, and may grade them according to warmth, sincerity and intensity. "He kissed me as if he meant it"; "She put her whole soul into the kiss"; "His embraces became more and more distant" express the physical comment our bodies make in the act of embracing. Kissing with the eyes open is the worst comment on a kiss, because in our culture it makes clear that the lover does not love. On the other hand, we kiss our children with our eyes open; if a man kisses his daughter with his eyes closed we think of incest.

The problem of the human message, then, is that it must always carry with it a comment that gives the intention. In our culture a most important sign of adulthood—not maturity, necessarily—is to have learned how to communicate about love, and usually by the time adulthood is reached, men and women have learned. When two become lovers they have read each other's messages aright, up to a point, mostly because they have grown up in the same culture, read the same books, seen the same movies, etc. But for an infant the problem is different. He has two lessons to learn: what his parents mean by all the things they do and say to him, and the kind of response they want from him.

Normally a baby who is contented with his mother lets her know it by the way he moves when she approaches, by the way his eyes follow her, by the way he smiles, by the way he relaxes in her arms, by the way he kicks about, gurgles and coos when his diaper is changed. And since the mother, by responding with smiling, cooing and the movement of her eyes and body, rewards the baby, he keeps on giving off signs of contentment, which we call happiness; he has learned how, without knowing that he is doing so, to show his mother that he is happy, and the mother shows the baby she is happy too. "Normal" mothers are supposed to have an intuition that tells them when all the signs of baby's happiness are right, although it seems, from the fact that there are baby books, that these criteria are not quite as intuitive as one might think. At any rate, in the normal course of events a happy baby learns, from his mother's responses to its messages, that all is well between them—that he is giving his mother something she needs.

"In the normal course of events" in our culture, the contentment messages are substituted by "love" messages. We do not know when or how this transformation takes place, but at that point there is probably much greater variation in the messages—love messages are no doubt much more variable than contentment messages, and probably every mother teaches her baby a different way to show love. Everything hinges on the outcome of this education for love: the mother must show the baby how to love her, and "in the normal course of events" in our culture, the baby learns and the mother is happy. Between the baby's inherent tendencies and the mother's requirements, a code is worked out. "Normally" all this takes place with neither mother nor child knowing that anything is being learned or taught. When the mother hugs the child, kisses him, says, "I love you," sets him on her lap and smiles, she does not know that she is teaching the child to show his own love for her by hugging, kissing, coming to sit on her lap, saying "I love you," and so on. The mother accepts this as natural love and is very happy about it.

In psychopathology many things can go wrong in these "communication systems." In the earliest months a mother may expect too much—perhaps expect the smile sooner or more often than the baby can give it. She may even expect, somehow, that the baby give signs of loving her when he can show only an animal contentment, and she may therefore become depressed and even angry with the baby. The problem might deepen in the second year: perhaps the mother is histrionic, overdemonstrative, capable of giving "oceans of love," and expects the child to respond with similar demonstrativeness—and the child cannot. However, as the child gets a little older, perhaps he actually responds histrionically, and this would be fatal, because the mother would think that the child was "putting on an act." Once we enter the area of psychopathology the possibilities for disturbances to arise in this area, on the basis of love expectations, increase.

Man is distinguished from all other animals by the fact that he speaks; and by the fact that he must surround whatever he says by a blaze of lights so that it may be viewed from all sides and finally confirmed to mean *one* thing and not another. We walk around a statue in order to see all sides of it; we go close to a picture and then step back from it in order to grasp it. An intention—a word or a movement—is like a statue around which we walk to see what it really signifies. It follows that if we train children to look at meaning from only one side, they will be easier to manage. But if all our behavior—including what we say—is ambiguous, then what we say is something like an oil painting framed in glass: there are so many interfering reflections and refractions that we cannot clearly grasp the picture. Parents who talk in riddles have children who painfully examine what is said, or who reject out of hand what is said, or suspect what is said, or rush headlong into meaning in the sense that they simply take everything at face value without asking what is really meant. This may be a comfort to parents who talk ambiguously, or they may become very angry because their children take them literally.

Redundance and the Love Code

In information theory, *redundance* refers to the clarity of a message. If I say "I like," the message is not clear because it lacks redundance—i.e., adequate definition of the message. When I say, "I like animals," the message is a little clearer because something has been added that defines what it is I like. When I clarify the message further by saying, "I like warm-blooded animals," the message is better, and when I say, "I like mammals," the message is getting still clearer because I am progressively defining what it is I like. But the sentence will not be clear until I say, with sufficient redundance to cover all cases, what animals I really like. The best, the most redundant—and the most boring—sentence is probably "I like fur-bearing, harmless, four-footed mammals and marsupials," for then it is unnecessary to say that besides rabbits, squirrels, baby ocelots, dogs and cats, I like kangaroos, wallabies and opossums too; and it is unnecessary to say that I *dislike* hyenas, lions, tigers, leopards and cheetahs, as well as birds, fish, frogs and armadillos. Merely at the logical level, a "best" sentence rules out all opposites by virtue of the redundance.

In social life a restless search for redundance is a function of vulnerability. Extremely vulnerable people never seem satisfied with a statement, but want endless elaborations. When you talk to them you can never finish what you have to say because they interrupt constantly for clarification. They can also think of all the reservations to what you say. There is never a sentence redundant enough to quiet them. On the other hand, they may do just the opposite: react against their feelings of vulnerability by accepting without inspection barefaced lies and counterfeits. The more vulnerable a person, the more easily he is deceived in love and also possibly the more suspicious.

A child born to an excessively vulnerable mother is in trouble the moment he leaves the womb, for without his knowing it, his mother will demand proof that he loves her. The baby is like someone pleading a case in a court whose rules of evidence he does not know and of whose statutes he is ignorant, and by the time the child is aware of what is expected, he may have broken his mother's "laws" so many times that he is condemned without knowing it. Suddenly, perhaps at two or three or four, it dawns on him that his mother is against him. Why? He discovers from hints or from outright accusations that it is because his mother thinks he does not love her. How can he prove now that this is not true? How can he escape the dreadful punishment of her anger by proving he loves her? The issue now is not whether he really loves her—whatever that may mean—but that he must escape her rage. It is clear that every gesture toward proving his love can only be counterfeit because now it is not based on love but on fear and pain, and his mother cannot but perceive the hypocrisy. Her child then appears a monster, a fake who is trying to "take her in." The child was badly off before he knew what was going on; now things are even worse, for to the insult of not loving his mother as she desires, he seems to add the injury of fakery.

In our culture, therefore, the most important task for a child is to "crack his mother's love code." If his mother is able to teach him the kind of love language that conveys to her that the child feels the kind of love she needs, all is well. But if for some reason—perhaps because the mother herself never had the kind of love she now wants from her child and therefore does not know how to teach the code to him—the mother is not able to teach her child this language, then she will hate him. She will hate him because she thinks he does not love her the way she feels she ought to be loved by her child. What is most shocking about this is that "Honor your father and your mother" may become a justification for hating a child for not loving. Though the Fifth Commandment is millennia in our past, we live with it as if its literal Old Testament meaning were still socially possible.*

Love and Kinship

It is easier to be a parent than a loving parent; easier to be a child than a loving one; and the law, in its wisdom, does not require that a parent love his child, merely that he support him and not be so cruel that the mistreatment comes to the attention of the police. A good law establishes what is feasible for everyone; and that is what our laws pertaining to childhood do, leaving it to the folk to work out, in their own homes, the subtler "laws" of parenthood and childhood, not enforceable by the jural process because the folk prescriptions are too vague and too arguable. How do you prove your mother loves you? Or your son? Such folk legality is constantly at work, and evidence is accumulated day after day, bearing on one side of the case or on the other. At any rate, since it is easier to be a kinsman only, rather than a kinsman and a lover too, the overwhelming number of the cultures of the world have settled for kinship and have left love out as a jural imperative in the relationship among kin. That is to say, they promise loyalty, responsibility and approval to kin, including children and parents, but they do not, on the whole, speak of love. They say, "I do so and so for him because he is my son," not "I do so and so for my son because I love him." Thus, though *Homo sapiens* has from time to time combined love and parenthood, most of the cultures of the world have settled for loyalty.

Since the very nature of love leaves it unclear and surely difficult to enforce by jural means, it must constantly be reaffirmed in every relationship where it is supposed to be present. It follows that breakdown of love in kinship should occur often. The hazard for all of us is that since love is not readily expoundable—like laws—we must trust to intuition. It is natural that since love is not a jural matter, it should be private, but since it is the most difficult aspect of the relationship to children, we ought to have constant advice on it. It ought to be possible for people to say to one another, "It doesn't seem to me that your child is getting much love from you." The only reason the proposal seems ridiculous to everybody who reads this is that since the isolation of our cultural existence makes it difficult for us to talk to one another, it has also deprived us of sureness about children. If we reflect, however, that formerly people thought "bad" children were that way because they were born so, while today we recognize that such children are "emotionally disturbed because they never had enough love," we will see that we are moving in the apparently preposterous direction of which I speak; that is to say, in the direction of being able to tell one another that we are not loving our children right.

* While the Fifth Commandment says "honor" and not "love," its modern meaning has become the latter, and is just as much a commandment.

Love: Wanting, Getting and Giving It

To be available for love must mean that there is some sort of balance in the soul between wanting to be loved and wanting to give it. I remember a man who said just after his baby was born, "When I see that baby I know I can take all the love I can get. I know that I can absorb a lot of love." He had nearly zero capacity to give love, yet imagined he had a great capacity to absorb it. All he was doing was identifying with the baby! It was not long before he was complaining that the baby disturbed him at his work. He had the capacity to absorb love as *he* perceived love, at times acceptable to *him*, in dosages he could tolerate of the right prescription. One thinks of his desiring a love shower-bath, which he does not have to trouble to turn on. When he is finished he dries himself off and retreats to his study, leaving the shower running—in this case, the child. The same would apply to his wife. If the shower is not working that night, there will be shouts, tears, silence and alienation.

Saints in remote eastern deserts may be able to imagine a blending of two souls in love, but other people experience love as getting and returning ("requiting"). The image of annihilation-in-the-other, which derives from Kierkegaard—this image of total, trancelike union—is not for most of us.

Since to love is to get and requite, and since getting and requiting must always occur, absolutely, on two people's individual terms, there has to be a common agreement on what the terms shall be. But this agreement is rarely present on the day of marriage; and if the marriage is to succeed, each partner must master the other's unconscious conception of what he wants "in return for what he gives." He must, indeed, learn whether the other has any conception at all of giving. A paradigm for the misunderstanding possible in this situation is the wife who, when her husband hands her flowers, bursts into tears and cries, "You don't love me!" because though he can give flowers, he won't listen to her conversation, which 90 percent of the time is at least as interesting as his.

Love-in-our-time is supposed to arise and endure when the man and woman are able to give each other what each wants. Let us unite in compassion for the person chosen on such a basis, for the assumption that whoever is wanted will necessarily be loved is false. Statements like "He was stable, I was flighty, so I married him"; "I was lonely and she seemed a woman who would take care of me"; "He was respectful and considerate and I had always been pushed around, so I married him"; "I always wanted a woman who could do things on her own, so I married Betty" illustrate the point at issue. We always find ourselves drawn to what we need, in the illusion that that is what we love. Yearning and overwhelming need often cover up the problem of love. Finding the "right" person and having a happy marriage are not necessarily the same and sometimes may turn out to be mutually exclusive, for the qualities admired can become so inflated in the light of the need that the *person* may be overshadowed: that "stable" man may also be a cold, immovable bore. Yet in man-woman relations we are more likely to perceive what we need than what is good for us. Put another way: when we are deprived in a certain way, we inflate what we require because we tend to be blind to what is not related to the depriva-tion. Thus deprivation imposes its own perceptual configuration.

The psychoanalysts, however, may put the matter this way: what we seek consciously in a partner merely masks an unconscious need. Of the woman who marries the "stable" man, they might say that unconsciously she needs a man who will treat her coldly.

There always has to be some kind of balance between what a person needs and what those around him need. When a child cries and his mother says "Shut up," his needs are not the complement of hers, for although he needs some kind of comfort, she feels no need to give it. When a woman is in love and needs to express her love by sheltering another person, she will not be able to love a man who is self-sufficient. If a person really has the capacity to pour his love on the world, the world will reject him because our world has no capacity to absorb that much love. One can even imagine the case where a withdrawn mother has a responsive child*—he would merely frighten and enrage her; she would be frightened by her inability to re-spond and enraged because she was frightened. One can imagine the case of a mother able to love only when she is giving but unable to cope with the reciprocal love of her child. Loving the child as an infant, she is repelled by the child when it is two years old because she cannot cope with what she has taught the child to expect. A man who has taught a woman to love him because he knows how to appear to be tender may be frightened when the woman takes him at face value.

Loving is patterned, and everybody who wants to be loved has to make love within that pattern; if not, he will not be understood. The danger lies in that the patterned expression may lack the feeling implied in the ges-ture, yet the other person often cannot know that the patterned movement is an unlit fire. Every gesture of love implies that the person who makes it wants something. That is to say, the expression "I love you," the hand laid tenderly on the neck, the fingers smoothing the hair, the voice, while con-veying a certain message of love, also convey its dialectical meaning, which is "I need something," but what exactly is needed is never really communi-cated in a love message. As they say in information-theory jargon, the mes-sage lacks redundance: it is unclear: everything is implied and must be inferred. Two people then discover themselves in bed with a set of despa-rate expectations: the needs of one are not complementary to those of the other.

The fundamental problem of mankind is to develop a culture where the needs of the individual are always complementary to those around him; a culture in which a child is not slapped for crying; a culture in which sorrow always is met by the complementary need to be compassionate; where fear is always met by the complementary need in others to give reassurance; where the need to be loved is met by a need to give love in the way it is wanted, at the time it is wanted and as much as it is wanted. This is not an American view, for the American makes conflict into a god; and although sociology swells its chest with a thousand "conflict theories," it has none on compassion. Because, in the chesty American view, which sociology con-

* Mrs. Portman in Chapter 9 of my *Culture Against Man* (Vintage Books; New York, Random House, 1963).

tinues to express in a supine and opportunistic way, conflict is the source of all progress. Life without conflict seems stale to the American élites; and compassion, which is a low-paid motivation, has been relegated to the fringes of the low-paid segments of the culture, and has never been a subject for research.

All needs are affected by time; what I needed when I was nineteen I may not need now that I am, let's say, thirty-five. So the image of the one I loved becomes deflated. The arrow of time has driven through the youthful image. What now? What was available for love in me when I was nineteen is no longer there. Can I love the memory? Well, I can try, and in this I will follow many others who love in memory the spouse they once loved in hope. But sometimes, I think, these miserable two can come to an unconscious agreement, which states: "Neither of us will try to remember our hope if the other acts as if the past were still repeating itself." So they can hold hands and look the other way. Hope then is like an ancestor long dead who yet exercises a ghostly influence in the present. The present beings then have a ghostly quality—something like the two shades in Sartre's *Les Jeux sont faits*.

Vulnerability and Gratification

The story of Eve and the serpent is a tale of the dangers of pleasure, and the present state of sex in this country proves the proposition that whenever gratification is safe, people will seek it if they are interested. It also suggests that where pleasure seems dangerous, people will take it if they think they can escape punishment. It implies, further, that when gratification seems dangerous, people will take what is safe and try to live with their frustrations. But the implication here is that where safety is chosen over pleasure, the joy renounced remains in memory and is experienced as a hope.

> Whoever seeks unsanctioned joy
> God or the State will soon destroy.

And the history and literature of man-in-the-West, from the Old Testament to Freud, records this dialectical interplay between renunciation, safety and strength on the one hand, and gratification, danger and weakness on the other. The theme is not unknown even among tribal peoples: my old friends, the Kaingáng Indians of Brazil, said that any man who spent too much time in sex was vulnerable to his enemies. When I was in elementary school I learned that the reason the Continental troops crushed the enemy at Valley Forge was because the British and the Hessian mercenaries were having such a good time that the Americans, half frozen and stealing over the ice on bleeding feet, were able to fall upon them unawares.

It is likely that there is a true association between renunciation and invulnerability because it is so hard to be alert while enjoying oneself, and drunkenness and sex, the two greatest pleasures, really make us most vulnerable. Since in history gratification and safety are all too often antagonistic, every human being ought to have a reasonable sensitivity to the dialectic; prudence suggests that we do not make love while driving sixty miles an hour. In disturbed people, the antagonism between gratification and safety may become disturbed also, so that some renounce too much and others too little. Normality in any culture consists in part in following the culturally determined mean between gratification and danger; every era and every culture defines it differently.

In all of us there is a tendency to want to have a good time and a tendency to see good times as, perhaps, leading to danger, but as long as the latter element is relatively weak, we can enjoy ourselves. In our culture, most people can take their pleasures without fear most of the time. Disturbed people, however, are likely to perceive all pleasures as dangerous, or not to see the danger at all. Suppose a disturbed person starts to enjoy himself—his heart may beat so fast that he gives up this pleasure, or perhaps he gets so depressed that he has to put it off, or he may become depressed in the midst of enjoyment. At some point in his life, pleasure has been so punished that he is afraid of it.

In our culture we most often encounter disturbances of the former type —the person who fears pleasure, especially sexual pleasure. This is more characteristic of women than of men because women have more to lose in ignoring the dangers in sex, not only because of the risk of pregnancy but also because of the danger of choosing a man who, though sexually attractive, is "not the right man to marry." Choices made in favor of safety then leave a bitter memory of pleasure lost and a hope of pleasure to be found "someday"—in the sky, perhaps. Our sympathy, thus, for the man who has been chosen because he is safe—for the woman who has chosen him will never forgive him for depriving her of pleasure by offering her safety. The motto then is, "I cannot stand my husband because I chose him," for the husband is blamed for the wife's loss of pleasure. And so with the husband: "Lulu was passionate, but she was too beautiful and too flighty, so I married Mary." Poor Mary!

Some Functions of Delusion

Though man has been forced to do what he prefers not to, to end up where he would rather not, to lead a life he would rather not and to renounce what he wants, he has the ability to form delusions that compensate. Though delusion is a weak rebuttal to the disappointments of life, for many people it is better than nothing.

In his *General Introduction to Psychoanalysis*, Freud relates the case of a middle-aged woman who accused her husband of having an affair. It turned out, however, that though her husband was not having an affair, the wife was actually unconsciously in love with their son-in-law. The lady's feeling about her husband's "affair" was intense and real, and she became extremely jealous. Freud called this a "delusion of jealousy," and argued that this delusion was a compensation for her unconscious guilt over her love for her son-in-law: if her husband was having an affair, Freud argued, it would not be quite so bad for her to be in love with her son-in-law. Her son-in-law was as unaware of her love as she was unconscious of it.

This delusion was the product of the antagonism between gratification and danger—in our culture one does not go to bed with one's son-in-law. In some tribal cultures, social arrangements* make even marriage with the son-in-law possible, but to us, fear of social punishment for an affair with the son-in-law makes pleasure with him unthinkable. Hence the lady's delusion was born of a collision between pleasure and danger, and was a compensation for her "evil" thoughts; a compensation for love forgone; a kind of accusation of the world, having the form, "All you men are secretly having affairs, but to me love is denied." Many delusions, then, are accusations. In this context, delusions of irresistibleness can turn out to be compensations for love renounced and for accusations against one's husband or wife for not giving what one needs.

If the lady with the delusion of jealousy had kept quiet, things might have gone on without too much disturbance. She would perhaps have appeared somewhat withdrawn and hostile, but this might all have been brushed aside as "characteristic of her period of life." The matter was brought to Freud's attention because the lady kept accusing her husband and made the family's life miserable. But not all delusions annoy and upset other people, for most of them are quiet—unseen expressions of inner misery, tolerated because they do not bother society. Thus another quality of delusions: some are tolerated, or even unnoticed, by society, but others are not; hence, a corollary: all societies have certain tolerances for unreality. Who shall say what they are? And furthermore, since delusion is an expression of disappointment and of the struggle between pleasure and danger, who among us has the right, or even the capacity, to reveal delusion for what it is?

Kierkegaard says that the unhappiest man is the one all of whose hopes are memories; I dare to suggest that the unhappiest person is the one all of whose desires have become delusions so that life itself is a delusion—a delusion of extrication. When life has failed a person, he can extricate himself from it by imagining that he is not in it.

Time and Delusion

It follows from what Kierkegaard says that the self is involved in time, and that when a man is involved in many delusions about himself, he becomes involved in a delusion of time. If he is living as a hope that which should be a memory, and living as a memory what should be a hope, then he will be confused about time. Since what should be hope is but memories of vanished possibilities, he will think himself old when he is still young; still hoping for what should be a memory, he will think himself young when he is old. Time will appear to have passed when it is still to be seized by the forelock, and time may still seem to have much in store when it has actually passed. One day he wakes up feeling lively, and by the time he has

---

* Some tribal cultures have no taboo on a man's marrying his wife's widowed mother; the Kaingáng Indians do so even when the father-in-law is alive. Among the Ashanti of Ghana a man may take the responsibility for his father-in-law's family when the father-in-law dies. Sometimes his mother-in-law becomes his wife.

brushed his teeth he feels old; on another day he may wake up feeling all aches and pains, but something trivial happens and he feels young and ready for anything.

Hope engenders delusions of time, for ambition compresses time and there does not seem to be enough of it, and the greater one's ambition, the less time one seems to have. It follows that where ambition is grandiose, there is no time at all. Hence the conclusion that the perception of time is related to what one wants for oneself. The man who desires to be Caesar says to himself, "It may be too late," but the man who has no hope says that time has never been or that there is too much of it: time is a void echoing his nothingness. For the ambitious man, time is a plaza ringing with cheers, for he experiences his success before he has it. A man without hope already endures his despair tomorrow as he does today and as he did yesterday.

Toynbee says that Leonidas wanted to monopolize the defense of Thermopylae in order to reap all the glory for the Spartans. Ambition that combines death and glory seizes time "before it has arrived" and treats it as if it were "here"; it captures time and compels it to do duty in the future. Imagination fired by glory dragoons the future into the present. But in hopelessness the future forces itself into the present and magnifies despair, because hope is not there to transform it. Thus the expression "seize time by the forelock" expresses the active attitude toward time of the hopeful and ambitious man, while there is no phrase in our language for the passive attitude of the hopeless toward time. Yet there are many passages of poetry that express the feeling:

> Time's the king of men
> He's both their parent and he is their grave,
> And gives them what he will, not what they crave.*
>
> * * * * *
>
> Mis-shapen Time, copesmate of ugly Night,
> Swift subtle post, carrier of grisly care,
> Eater of youth, false slave to false delight,
> Base watch of woes, sin's packhorse, virtue's snare;
> Thou nursest all and murd'rest all that are.†
>
> * * * * *
>
> Unfathomable Sea, whose waves are years;
>   Ocean of Time, whose waters of deep woe
> Are brackish with the salt of human tears!
>   Thou shoreless flood, which in thy ebb and flow
> Claspest the limits of mortality!
>   And sick of prey, yet howling on for more,
>   Vomitest thy wrecks on its inhospitable shore;
> Treacherous in calm and terrible in storm,
>   Who shall put forth on thee,
> Unfathomable Sea? ‡

Here despairing man is prostrate before time, but *time* is active and threatening.

Man's inner experience of time is determined by hope and memory in all cultures, even where, to the superficial observer, all of life seems charted

* Shakespeare, *Pericles*, ii, 3, 45.
† Shakespeare, *The Rape of Lucrece*, l. 925.
‡ Shelley, *Time*.

from birth—as in most tribal societies—so that hope seems unnecessary, and memory is of ancestral ways and a form of bookkeeping in which one keeps an account of the yams owed or the wife promised.

If we consider that the self lives on hope and memory, and experiences time in them, it follows that anybody who remembers and hopes must have a self. Many deny that tribal man has a self; he is "submerged in the group," they say. Since all men hope and remember, what is it that organizes life around hope and memory? It must be a self, or, as some prefer, an ego.

When hope is defeated, time is thick with pain. "O aching time! O moments big as years!" cries Thea as she stands over the defeated Saturn in Keats's *Hyperion,* and a way to bear this pain is to narcotize it with illusory hopes:

> "Search, Thea search! and tell me, if thou seest
> A certain shape or shadow, making way
> With wings or chariot fierce to repossess
> A heaven he lost erstwhile: it must—it must
> Be of ripe progress—Saturn must be King.
> Yes, there must be a golden victory;
> There must be Gods thrown down, and trumpets blown
> Of triumph calm, and hymns of festival
> Upon the gold clouds metropolitan,
> Voices of soft proclaim, and silver stir
> Of strings in hollow shells; and here shall be
> Beautiful things made new, for the surprise
> Of the sky-children; I will give command:
> Thea! Thea! where is Saturn?"

Saturn, the fallen King, hallucinates empire recovered; mortals must imagine other things. Whether Saturn or mortal, delusion is rooted in a memory which has become transmuted into hope. In the midst of his hallucination, Saturn suddenly says, "Thea! Thea! where is Saturn?," for he has come to himself—his new and undesired self—or selflessness.

> I am gone
> Away from my own bosom: I have left
> My strong identity, my real self,
> Somewhere between the throne, and where I sit
> Here on this spot of earth.

Thus, if a man is sane he is aware, even in the midst of his delusions, that he has lost his self and that the delusions are not reality.

In the Negro ghettos of this country, among those who have been irrecoverably deprived, who have never known a family as the middle class knows it, who have lived on doles amid vermin, we can study the pathologies of hope and memory. There, hopes are illusions and are acted out in despairing ways through sexual exploit, conning, drinking, taking drugs, boasting and pretending. Where adaptation is an accommodation to extreme deprivation, one can perceive all the dreams of the dethroned Saturn degraded to the level of those compelled to live in filth and despair. Among these people, reality is often inseparable from delusion; because pain is so intense only the greatest variety of delusions strongly held can narcotize it.

So, for an adolescent girl, a trip to the suburbs in a boy friend's hot rod is like a trip to Europe; a cheap hamburger at a drive-in becomes a steak; a third-rate neighborhood movie, a seat at the opera; and an ice cream cone a full meal to a girl who has had nothing to eat all day.* From this we learn something else about delusion—that when the deprivation is extreme, trivia will be magnified out of proportion by the delusional process. We also learn that extreme deprivation leads one to give what one has that is real in order to capture a delusional joy. As an even exchange, these girls have sex with the boys who give them a ride, buy them a burger or a cone, or take them to the movies. The average middle-class girl, on the other hand, still values her own sexuality so highly that she must give it for nothing, if she is to enjoy it. The ghetto girl magnifies the material trivium, while the middle-class girl inflates her own image.

* For supporting documentation, see Lee Rainwater, "Crucible of Identity: The Negro Lower-Class Family," *Daedalus* (Winter 1966), and my "White People's Time-Colored People's Time," *TransAction* (March–April 1965).

THE METZ FAMILY

Kurt and Gertrude Metz are in their forties. Neither has had much education. He travels about the Eastern city in which they live, selling printers' materials, and his wife stays at home, keeps house and watches over their fourteen-year-old daughter Myra. Their seventeen-year-old son Albert was in an institution when I was studying the family.

NOTE TO THE READER

The Metz family has been the most difficult to write up, because Mrs. Metz, who dominates the picture, has been the hardest for me to understand and because some of the most illuminating material, her creative endeavors, cannot be reproduced, for to do so would reveal her identity to those who know her and thus violate her privacy. I therefore follow a somewhat different procedure in presenting this case: I start with a brief and partial description of Mrs. Metz, instead of letting her picture emerge from the total discussion, for I believe that this will make it easier for the reader to find his way through the analysis.

Imagine a woman who wants to be a kind of Gypsy Rose Lee, to go on the stage and always to be the center of it, and able to get what she wants because she is beautiful, talented and willing to lead an unconventional life. Imagine, on the other hand, a woman who has the same obsession but who is exceedingly conventional and far from beautiful, and who never attains her ambition but retains an illusion of herself as, somehow, "on stage." She cannot give up the wish to be in the limelight. She has the longing of the footlight personality but no footlights, and her scenery—her life—is the monotonous commonplace reality of the lower middle class. This is Mrs. Metz.

Mrs. Metz has had little education, but she is very intelligent. She has composed "lyrics," one each for her children, Albert and Myra, when they were just born, and others dedicated primarily to her husband and parents. Altogether there are only a dozen or so, and she stopped writing a long time ago. The "poetry" is a combination of the commercial Tin Pan Alley love songs of the thirties and forties and the kind of sentiments one finds on anniversary, birthday, Mother's and Father's Day cards, and such. Something of the same spirit, but with more originality, appears in the ingenious and amusing announcement Mrs. Metz made up for the birth of Myra, her second child, now in her early teens. From these writings, it looks as if, in the first years of marriage, and with the birth of each infant, Mrs. Metz was swept by a new wave of hope and illusion. The disappearance of efforts to write, however, and the absence of any "lyric" about the children after infancy suggest what marriage and childbearing have meant to Mrs. Metz. The fact that she keeps all these mementos and shows them to me suggests also how much she lives in memory and illusion. Hope, memory, illusion and disappointment constitute major themes of her life—as they do for so many of us—and it is around these that I have largely constructed the analysis of the Metz family.

Mrs. Metz

The most important thing that occurred during my week with the Metzes was the arrival of Albert, allegedly psychotic, home for a visit from the Institute. Since what happened to him that day cannot be understood unless one knows something about his mother, I begin this account of the Metz family with her, telling just enough at the outset to enable the reader to comprehend what she did on that occasion. I call the visit "the most important thing" because it bears on a simple problem, clearly defined, that can be studied in *all* cases of home visits of "disturbed" people: what happens to them when they cross again the thresholds of the homes from which they were expelled. What makes people "break down" is an enormously complex problem, but what happens to them when they come home for a visit can be recorded quite simply. The interpretation of what happened is difficult, but recording the events is much simpler: all that is necessary is that an observer be on the spot.

Eyewitness accounts of such visits are extremely rare,* but reports that include observed evidence of the mother's feelings, her preparations several days in advance and her subsequent behavior, do not exist. The first part of my account will be a description of Mrs. Metz as she appears in my notes.

The First Meeting

(From my notes.) I had been told by the Institute that the Metzes would accept me this week, but when I telephoned, Mr. Metz tried to put me off until next week. When I asked whether I might start today, he consulted his wife and then said I could come. Since the Metzes had changed their minds once before, I felt they were evading again and that I had to insist. Mrs. Metz took the phone and said cheerfully, "Oh yes, come on out for dinner." She said she wasn't feeling well— I believe it was some "woman's trouble."

Since Mrs. Metz had suggested that I come after lunch, I arrived about three o'clock. The Metzes have an apartment in a lower-middle-class neighborhood in a small city. Mrs. Metz, a large woman, came to the door sloppily dressed. She was wearing no make-up, and the dark rings under her eyes were quite noticeable. As she greeted me she said she had been in the bathroom because she was feeling very, very bad. Although she gave every sign of wanting to go back or lie down, she offered to get me something cold to drink. She suggested I go sit on the porch.

* I have never seen one, but since there may be one somewhere, I do not say "unheard of."

There she switched on the TV to a soap opera and I waited while she made limeade, which she is very fond of. I thought that after she had given me something to drink she would retire to the bedroom or bathroom, but when she came out onto the porch with the limeade, she turned off the TV, sat down next to me on the sofa and talked. She said right away, and without questions from me, that she was in menopause and that every month she had terrible pains. She pointed to her abdomen and indicated it was swollen. "When I menstruate," she said, "it's worse than when some women give birth." She was wearing a housecoat that was inadequate for her size, so whenever she crossed her legs most of her thighs were revealed, and she repeatedly scratched them in an apparently unselfconscious way.

At dinner that night she said, in the presence of her husband, that all her life she had had dreadful cramps during her period, that she had been examined by many doctors, x-rayed, and so on, but that they had found nothing. On the porch, over the limeade, however, she had talked mostly about Albert.

Spontaneously, with great emotion and often seeming on the verge of tears, she gave me his case history. Love, love, love, love, love ran constantly through all she said or showed me: everybody in the family loves everybody else—her husband and she, their parents, their friends.

On the living-room wall are two photographs of Albert at different ages. There is no picture of Myra.

When Albert was three years old, Mrs. Metz gave birth to Myra, now fourteen. (She first said, "When Myra gave birth to me.") She was very sick with Myra but insisted on trying to nurse her, even though she didn't have enough milk ("I tried to be a cow, but I couldn't"), with the result that she developed abscesses on the breast and had to be operated on. A little later she had other serious operations, which resulted in Al's being removed from her for three or four months.

On the day Mrs. Metz delivered Albert she was doing the floors, and when the pains started she rushed to a beauty parlor to have her hair set so she would look nice. One of her troubles, for which she later underwent an operation, started just after Albert was born—pregnancy caused it, she said. After he was born, the pain was so severe that sometimes she blacked out. One doctor said it was psychological, but after many tests—and she gave me all the details of every test and x-ray—they discovered what it was. But for three years, until after Myra was born and she had had surgery, Mrs. Metz was tormented. Now that she comes to think of it, *she realizes for the first time that Albert must have known she was in trouble.*

Until he was about eight years old, Al was perfectly normal and healthy; then one night, during a severe storm, his room and an adjacent building were struck by lightning. Enormous quantities of debris fell into Al's room. Though the house was strewn with debris and broken glass, she ran to her son's room. Her husband remained in bed, frightened, she said. A few reassuring words to Myra from her mother calmed the daughter, but when Mrs. Metz got to Albert's room she could hear his heart thumping "from six feet away."

Mrs. Metz told the story with great agitation. Although she ran barefoot through the rubble and broken glass, she was not scratched because her dead father's spirit intervened. She ascribes all such escapes to him: once she put her hand through a plate-glass window but was not cut; another time she fell down two or three flights of stairs but remained unhurt. She mentioned several miraculous escapes she or the children had had, all due to the intervention of her father's spirit. When her father died she did not mourn, but said to her mother, "Mother, I'm so happy he passed away in this way," because he just had one heart attack and died. At this very moment she feels her father is sitting with us right there on the sofa on the porch where she is talking to me. Her father had always told Mrs. Metz that she was the richest in the family, because though she was not well-to-do, she has the greatest love.

Ever since the night of the storm, Albert began to act strangely; she mimicked precisely his distorted speech, facial grimaces and disturbed motility. It was really ghastly to see her do it so well. She consulted doctors and psychiatrists, and at last Albert was admitted to a hospital, where he was rehabilitated in about two years and returned home. Though the doctor said he needed no further psychiatric attention, Mrs. Metz heard this with much misgiving because, in her opinion, "a child who had been through what Albert had been through" needed psychiatric care. However, he did rather well, and everything went fine until the seventh grade, when he was put on the departmental grade system in school; this meant that instead of having one teacher all day for a whole semester, he had six. Then he became disorganized and slid back. He began to tear his clothes, he ran around touching things with his finger and in general behaving in such a disturbed way that his teachers decided that he should be taken out of school. Mrs. Metz choked back tears several times as she told this story.

Albert explained that he tore his clothes because they made him feel hemmed in, but once he called up his father and asked him to please come home because he was tearing things up and didn't know why and couldn't help himself. He went around putting his finger on people in church because, he said, they had spots on them. I asked Mrs. Metz what she did when he began to act up and she answered that he began to behave in a very nasty and vulgar manner. I asked again and she said her husband scolded him and took away all his privileges for a week. She also beat him with a strap. They went to psychiatrists, who tried to find out whether she and her husband were happily married and if their sex life was all right. When she was told she "protests too much," meaning she protests too much about how much she and her husband love each other, she said, "You can talk to my husband," and they got the same story from him.

Albert was admitted to the hospital a second time, but the doctor felt that he could not be rehabilitated there and the Institute was recommended. This upset his mother terribly. Throughout her story of Albert, Mrs. Metz mentioned her husband only in passing, mostly to point out that he was terribly frightened the night of the storm. Mrs. Metz suddenly referred to Albert as dead, caught herself and apologized to me—or sort of excused herself.

She was much stricter with Al than with Myra and kept him closer to her because "boys like to have more freedom" than girls. He was toilet-trained by the time he was nine months old because when he was six months old she began putting him on the potty for fifteen minutes every hour on the hour. Her pediatrician said it was okay. While Albert was on the potty, she would say "*S-s-s-s*" and turn on the faucet. Once, when Albert was two and a half, the train they were on was three hours late and then she had trouble getting a taxi. Albert had to urinate but although she begged him to make "sissy" in his pants, in his diaper, he would not. At last she got a taxi to her mother's house, and as soon as he got on the potty there, he urinated. It was such a tremendous relief to *everybody,* and his grandmother remarked, "What a neat child you are!" At nine months he could no longer tolerate moving his bowels in his diaper. He has a remarkable memory.

, Albert hated eggs from the very beginning, but since the doctor recommended them, she went to great lengths to get him to eat them—telling him stories, amusing him, spending hours with him trying to make him eat eggs.

The story of Albert was interlarded with affirmations of her love for him and of his love for her. For instance, he would not run to his father when he came home from work without her permission and he was always with her, never with his father.

The entire story came out with no prompting from me.

Love and Verse

On the porch, which used to be Albert's room, was a large folder with hundreds of greeting cards—the kind that can be bought anywhere, with the standard verses and sentiments. There were no deliberately funny or "sick" cards. Mrs. Metz also brought out a box in which there was a huge mass of greeting cards for birthdays, Mother's Day, Father's Day, wedding anniversaries, Valentine's Day, etc., going back for more than twenty years, and all mixed up with photos, old bills, receipts, letters from relatives, and such. Mrs. Metz went through these things very intensely, mingling all she said with expressions of love. She expressed love for her family and described how everybody loves everybody else. As I sat there with her on the sofa looking at the mementos, Mrs. Metz kept slapping me and touching me on the leg and thigh, until I shrank into a corner. (She would do this when Myra was around, too.)

Mrs. Metz raved about her husband, about their love, about what a sweet and wonderful man he is—that he is not the kind who comes home from work and sits back and lets his wife do everything in the house just because he has worked all day—and this is true, as I saw.

All greeting cards, says Mrs. Metz, should be signed by at least two people and addressed to two. One sent from the Institute by Albert to his mother on her birthday is signed by Myra and Albert. (If a card is sent by two people, how can you tell who sent it?) There is some exception to this rule, but I have seen only one card—from Albert to his mother—that is signed by and addressed to only one person. The cards Mr. and Mrs. Metz send to each other are signed "I do."

Mrs. Metz is proud of her ability to write and wants to do a book about her mother. She recited several bits of her "poetry," as she calls it; her verse is full of love for everybody.

(Second day.) I have not seen as much kissing and, in general, affectionate demonstrativeness in any other family I have studied. Myra kissed her mother when she left to go to a party and again when she went to baby-sit, saying, "Do you love me?" Mr. and Mrs. Metz kissed when he came home tonight; and she reached out and held his hand as we sat on the porch after dinner. When Mr. Metz called up to say he was just leaving work, Mrs. Metz would say, "honey," "darling," and "dear" a great deal. She says Albert could never understand why she never called his father "Kurt" or why he never called her "Gertie"—why they always called each other "dear," "darling" or "honey." He resented it. Once, when Albert was five, he got lost, and when his father found him, the police said they couldn't get his father's name from the boy, because when they asked him what it was he said his father's name is "dear" and his mother's "honey."

Just after dinner Mrs. Bauman, Mrs. Metz's mother, called up, and there was a lot of "dear" and "darling" over the phone and Mrs. Metz sent her mother a kiss. It is impossible to convey the sugary quality of Mrs. Metz's voice as she talks to her mother. But when she hung up, she read me a couple of her mother's letters, mimicking her mother's way of speaking and calling my attention to misspelled words. She was impressed by the tender sentiments—"God bless you . . . May you always be happy . . . May God watch over you," etc. She had a good time telling me how crazy her mother is. Once her mother could not find a corset she wanted to wear to church, but since Mrs. Bauman had been arranging things in the oven, Mrs. Metz looked for it and found it there. Mrs. Bauman is the kind of person, says Mrs. Metz, who cannot find the sugar because she has put it in the refrigerator. Mrs. Metz says she is just like her mother.

Mrs. Bauman gave a demonstration of odd behavior when I was visiting the Metzes. Mrs. Metz was speaking to her mother on the phone. Mrs. Bauman asked her daughter for a phone number and immediately, without saying good-bye, hung up, and had to call back. Mrs. Metz told me her mother had said, "What an idiot I am," etc.

When Mrs. Metz was a child, her mother sometimes took her and her other children to the movies, and right in the middle of the picture she would suddenly remember she had to fix supper and dash out, leaving the kids behind. They would just laugh, knowing that sooner or later she would realize she had left them there and would come back.

When Mrs. Metz talks about her father she uses the standard, posthumous, religious, affectionate expressions, but when she talks of her mother she belittles her, while saying what a wonderful and loving mother she is.

As Mrs. Metz was getting dinner ready, the radio was blaring rock and roll. With her back to me, she made agitated movements in time to the music. A couple of days later she did it again, making sure this time that I would notice her, by calling my attention to her derrière.

Mrs. Metz is histrionic and would like to be sexy. You can never be sure of what is going on with her. She acts sick but her sickness seems to disappear instantly if something interests her. On the phone she is loving to her mother but not after she hangs up. She talks of love as if she were its very image: she loves her husband but does not hesitate to tell the observer the very first day that as she skimmed heroically over the floor on the night of the great storm, protected from the splinters and the glass only by the magic of her dead father, her husband lay abed frozen with fear. She talks about her disturbed son with tears in her voice and in her eyes, yet mimics his symptoms terrifyingly well; and instead of describing how happy she was when he was pronounced cured by the psychiatric service of the hospital, she says she did not believe it; and she refers to him as dead. What is the meaning of her collection of greeting cards—that collection of mass-produced clichés? Is it evidence to prove that she is loved? Or that she loves! Of what is she afraid? She reacts to me as if I had come to the door to ask, "Do you love anybody or are you a fraud? Show me your hands!" Thus, in my first moments in her house, she stated her life problem: getting and giving love.

But the scenery was destroyed the day Albert came home for a visit.

Albert's Return

(Third day.) While I was sitting in the kitchen with Mrs. Metz and Myra, the phone rang. It was Mr. Woodson from the Institute to tell Mrs. Metz that they were going to let Al come home for a visit on Sunday. He would arrive for breakfast and would spend the day with the family. . . . This threw Mrs. Metz into demonstrations of what seemed to be genuine happiness. She acted tremendously excited and immediately began to lay plans for Sunday.

She felt she had to call up her mother and tell her, and wondered whether she should invite her over to see Al, but at this point my conscience prodded me into an effort to keep *this* disturbed person out of the picture because of the danger to Al, so I said, "I think definitely your mother should not come." She said, "I wonder whether it would be too deceitful not to tell Mother?" but I kept silent. Then she said, "No, I guess I better tell her, because if I don't, she'll find out from somebody else." So she called her mother and said Al was coming home but that it was just going to be an affair of the immediate family. Apparently, Mrs. Bauman accepted this very well.

When Mrs. Metz hung up she imitated her mother's speech, though she sounded very affectionate on the phone, as usual. Myra had asked to talk to her grandma, and when she said good-bye, blew her a kiss over the phone, after a preliminary hum. She told her grandma she missed her.

Mrs. Metz called her husband and told him the news. Now she began to plan what she would fix for Albert. Since he is crazy about French toast, she is going to make it. Without asking me, she decided that her husband and I should go out and pick up Albert in my car. She has fitted me into the family so easily: I have a car and can take her wherever she wants to go—a very, very different way of treating me from other families I have studied.

Myra felt she had to tell her friend Mary that Albert was coming home because Mary is crazy about him.

Mrs. Metz showed me pictures of Albert and the family taken the last Sunday they saw him. His expression seemed that of a normal, cheerful boy. Of course, the Metzes are careful to take pictures of people smiling. Mrs. Metz showed me pictures of Myra and Albert together when they were much younger. In one picture Albert's arms were around Myra and she was looking at him coquettishly; in the other she had her back to him. I feel that all Mrs. Metz's demonstrativeness about Albert, all her excitement and happiness are real.

When Albert called up, his mother sounded sincerely affectionate, but talked to him as if he were a small child. He wanted a pair of jeans. When she said good-bye she kissed him *after* she hung up. In the evening she mentioned the call to her husband and told him she wanted to get something really nice for Albert; even though he might not be permitted to take it back to the Institute, she would keep it for him at home.

(Fourth day.) Mrs. Metz came into the dime store where Myra and I were wandering around, and showed us what she had bought Albert: the jeans he wanted, and two very unattractive shirts, which she said were beautiful, one of them reduced from $3.99 to $1. As we walked around the dime store looking for something for Al, she said, "I want to buy some junk for Al." She bought some cheap candy.

The meat Mrs. Metz bought for his lunch tomorrow was the cheapest hamburger she could find.

The Homecoming

(Fifth day.) I was supposed to pick up Mr. Metz at nine-thirty, but when I got there at nine-twenty, he was already waiting in front of the building and came running toward me. Mrs. Metz came outside to greet me warmly. Mr. Metz and I drove to the Institute in about half an hour, and found Albert waiting, talking to a woman. When he saw his father he called out, "Hi, Dad!" and got into the front seat with him and me. His father kept his arm around him all the way home.

At this point I am reminded that during the day, whenever either his father or mother tried to kiss him, Albert resisted, sometimes even violently. Privately, however, he told me he wanted this visit. I cannot blame him, for having had a glimpse of the inside of the Institute and having seen that it is like a prison, I say to myself, "Who the hell would want to be in there?" Albert is certainly caught between wanting to get out and the difficulty of putting up with his parents.

On the way home Mr. Metz repeatedly ignored what Albert was saying and Albert had to call his attention to it. Mr. Metz would either ramble on, talk about matters not related to what his son was saying, or talk to me. Albert was fidgety, had a tic on one side of his face and switched rapidly from one subject to another. He was preoccupied with the fact that he was a tenderfoot scout, and in his hip pocket he carried some printed matter about the Boy Scouts, which he brought out every once in a while. He talked about wanting to go to Harvard. However, I shall not spend time on what he talked about but rather concentrate on family relations. Mr. Metz's lack of interest in what Albert was saying had nothing to do with its intelligibility, because most of the time what Albert was talking about was perfectly intelligible and intelligent. He was much involved in a five-mile hike he was going on soon, with the fact that he had been swimming four times, and with looking forward to dancing with a blonde on Wednesday night.

When we got home his sister greeted him first, kissed him and seemed happy to see him. Then he and his mother kissed. Mrs. Metz sat us all down at once to eat. Frequently during the day Albert told his mother he really loved her, but I don't remember whether she told him she loved him too. A couple of times during the day Albert grabbed her roughly, kissed her and said, laughing, "I love you. You know I love you, Mumsy."

Home

Almost from the moment Albert entered the house Mrs. Metz, yelling in a very irritated way, interfered with practically everything he did. She was so destructive that I kept looking for signs of the effects of her behavior on him; by the end of the day Albert was depressed, his facial tics had increased and he was biting his wrists. It is difficult to remember the many times his mother blocked or attacked the boy, but I shall try to describe what I can recall.

When Albert came in, you could see from what he said and did that he wanted to soak up the house. He wanted to go around and look at all the rooms, to sit on the porch and relax, to go into Myra's room, etc., but his mother would not let him, insisting that he sit down to breakfast because everybody was hungry. When he was sitting on the porch—formerly his room—just soaking the place up, she dragged him away, scolding. He wanted to try on the new pants but she said no, he must eat his breakfast. He wanted to go next door to see the neighbor's dog but his mother said the neighbors were probably still asleep, although it was almost eleven o'clock. Albert wanted to take lunch and go to the beach right after breakfast, but his mother said, "Let's eat here." He wanted to look in one of the closets on the porch, but his mother told him not to open it and scolded him for poking around in closets. He asked what was in there but she wouldn't tell him. (I heard her tell a neighbor that the top of the closet was very disorderly.)

Albert had arrived wearing a pair of very badly wrinkled chino pants, a white shirt and a pullover. The shirt collar was turned up and his mother insisted he turn it down, even though Albert said all teen-agers wear their collars up these days. She finally got the collar down. She was a completely transformed person the minute her son set foot in the house—she became irascible, hostile and destructive. Once during the day, when she was scolding him, Albert sang under his breath, "Oh, why was I born?" All day long he kept singing, "Are you looking for trouble?," which seems to be a line from another song. A couple of times when his mother bawled him out, Albert lowered his head and said, "All right, Mom, all right."

As he prowled around the house, Albert constantly used current teen-age lingo —called girls "cats"; kept saying "Dig that jive," sometimes when it was irrelevant, and kept calling things "cool." "Dig that jive," "It's cool" and "It's gone" about exhausted Albert's vocabulary of lingo, and he used the same expressions over and over again. This so amused his mother that she talked about it to one of her neighbors out the back window of the porch.

My impression is that the boys in the Institute do everything possible to maintain connection with the outer world, and that the lingo is a medium through which they can feel they are in contact with it. For them, using the language really means they are literally, pathetically, "with it."

The seating arrangement at breakfast was Albert and Myra on one side of the table, Mrs. Metz opposite them and Mr. Metz at one end. There was plenty of very dry French toast, which, nevertheless, Albert seemed to like. His mother quickly lost interest in him, and turning to me, talked of other matters. In the middle of what Albert was saying, she would change the subject.

After breakfast Albert roamed in and out of the rooms. He could not sit still, and his mother bawled him out for being fidgety. He was eager to see his friends Mary and Jane, and he and Myra went to invite them to go to the beach. When Mary and Jane arrived they were very quiet, and Mary, who likes Albert very much and wants to go steady with him, looked at him intensely, but he was skittish, stand-offish and shy.

While we were waiting to go to the beach there was a lot of activity in the parents' bedroom. The record player had been brought in there and rock-and-roll records put on, and a couple of times Albert danced a few steps but seemed unable to continue. It looked as if he might get off to a good start, but nothing ever happened. He would not dance with anybody, so Mary and Myra danced with each other. At one time the three girls, Albert, Mr. and Mrs. Metz and I were all in the bedroom, but Mrs. Metz told us to go into the living room, where the same kind of dancing, etc., continued.

When Albert first went away, he had left his records at home and they were together with Myra's in a record box. He was very anxious—I say anxious, rather than eager—to take some of his records back with him to the Institute because there is no music for the party they are going to have, but Myra objected and his mother reprimanded him. By begging, he managed to get four. It was quite pitiful. (After we had taken Albert back, his mother told me he was in the wrong. "After all," she said, "he gave those records to Myra and it is just Indian-giving to want them back.")

Albert wanted to ride his sister's bicycle, but his mother vetoed that on the grounds that he would hurt his "groin." According to the way she explained it to me, she actually seemed to believe this, yet it is difficult to see how a boy could hurt himself in the "groin" on a girl's bicycle.

Albert "accidentally" walked into the bathroom while his sister was preparing for a shower, and I heard him call out, "Why don't you draw the curtain?" She complained loudly and his mother got after him to get out of the bathroom. She also drove him out of his sister's room, but I don't think Myra was in there at the time.

The Beach

Mrs. Metz did not want to go to the beach and played a long-drawn-out delaying game which made Albert anxious and fidgety, but at last she gave in. She didn't want to go because she looks terrible in a bathing suit, she said, because there is no shade at the beach and she would be miserable in the sun, because she is tired and because there is no ladies' room there. At last, after delaying and delaying for about an hour, she went along in an ordinary dress. When we got there, Mrs. Metz sat at the top of the stairs leading to the beach, on the platform, where there was shade. She found an old woman to talk to, and, as she said, the two of them "yakkety-yakked."

Albert splashed and ducked the girls, but mostly his sister. I was surprised at this, expecting him to duck Mary and Jane more. The kids had a very good time and Albert's tic disappeared. He was proud of his swimming and said that since he was able to rescue people from drowning, we shouldn't be frightened if there was no lifeguard around. Actually, he seemed able to swim only about ten very crude strokes. I got out to the kids before Mr. Metz did, and Albert asked anxiously where his father was. When I said he was up on the beach, we set out to find him and met him about fifty yards out from shore on his way to us. Albert put his arm around his father and made as if to drag him into the water, but did not. I got the feeling he was trying to boss his father. Mr. Metz stood there in amiable inactivity; then he, Albert and I formed a "side" and splashed the girls. Mr. Metz cupped his hands, and using them as a stirrup, tossed the girls. On the whole he was amiably in evidence, but not much use. He cannot swim. Once or twice the kids made as if to duck him, but did not.

In the water the girls' play revolved around Albert, who was noisy. He was trying desperately to convey some idea of masculinity, but was badly frightened. The following is a good illustration: the bottom was very irregular, sometimes the water was shallow, then it would deepen—but never over our heads—and then become shallow again, and none of us was bothered by it except Albert. As he and I walked toward shore, he looked very anxious, so I said, "It's all right, it doesn't get any deeper and soon it will be shallower," and he calmed down.

Back on the shore, Jane started to bury Albert in the sand but did not get very far, while Myra and Mary sat on a blanket and fixed their hair. Then Albert ran over to the base of the platform where his mother was seated and did a cartwheel.

In order to get to the platform from the beach one could either mount the stairs or climb up to it on the supporting structure. When Albert climbed up, his mother bawled him out, and scolded him again when he tried to go down the same way. His father blocked him, too. Mrs. Metz complained to me about Albert's being a show-off—doing cartwheels and climbing up to the platform instead of using the stairs. Once she reprimanded him in front of the entire group for showing off.

On the platform were Mr. and Mrs. Metz, Myra, Albert, two other girls about Myra's age and a couple of strangers. In front of them all, in a loud and irritated voice, Mrs. Metz said that Albert's swimming trunks did not adequately cover him in the crotch and that he must not wear them again without a jockstrap. Albert showed no reaction.

Albert boxed a little with his father, but his boxing had the inchoate quality of his dancing. He would take a boxer's stance, lash out at his father two or three times and then quit, laughing. The boxing was amicable, and Albert kept his hands open. He slapped his father a few times but not very hard. Because of the stance he took, I expected Albert to box expertly, but suddenly his boxing form would collapse totally. The whole display occurred in a series of such fast frames that all I had was an impression of his starting, stopping, and then coming back to start and stop again. A couple of times Mr. Metz went for Albert's head in a wrestling or rough caressing movement, but Albert avoided him and at last asked why he did it.

I went with Albert to buy Popsicles with money provided by his mother, and since we were alone, he asked me what I had been talking to her about, and I said I asked about the causes of his illness. He wanted to know what she said, and when I told him about the lightning, he said, "My psychiatrist thinks that's a lot of crap." So I asked twice, "What do *you* think?" and each time he said something unrelated to the question. There was an undertone of scornful belittlement in whatever Albert said to his mother or mumbled under his breath. Out of earshot, he ridiculed her appearance a few times.

When we went into the water a second time, matters were different. The first time Albert had thrown himself into the play, but now, having in the interim been cut down a number of times by his mother, he was withdrawn; he hung back quite a ways as we walked into the water, and participated little in the play. Most of the time Mr. Metz was on the platform with his wife. When we finally left the water, we found Mrs. Metz with a neighbor's daughter. Mrs. Metz was playing with the daughter's baby and raving over it.

Supper and Evening

When we got home Mrs. Metz prepared supper of scrambled eggs and bologna, leftover tuna fish, frozen fish cakes which she had thawed earlier, leftover cottage cheese with pineapple, a freshly prepared salad, leftover canned franks, corn on the cob, pickles and bread. Since it took a long time to throw this together and the kids were very hungry, Albert came in and took a piece of fish cake, and she snarled at him for picking food off the table before things were ready. But Albert came back again and again, and it seemed to me that he did it because she snarled.

Several times during the day he had offered to help his mother in the kitchen, but she had refused. She told me Al was very considerate, that ever since he was a small child he had offered to help and had helped in the kitchen, but that Myra does not. While Myra, at her mother's request, was helping her mother get supper, Albert walked back and forth between the kitchen and the porch. He simply could not sit still; he would sit on the porch for a few minutes, get up, go and sit down in the kitchen, then go back to the porch. Once I saw him tapping his fingers on top of the head, and when he came into the kitchen, he asked me whether it doesn't sometimes seem to me that when you tap the top of your head it's just like snare drums.

Supper was served on TV-dinner trays, which looked exactly like institutional or army trays, and Albert remarked, "I come *home* and this is the kind of plate I get." Mrs. Metz was pleased that I had said her cooking was the best of any family I had visited and told this to Albert, and when he checked on this with me, I said it was the truth. He said, "You probably say that to all the mothers," but I denied it. When he was served the odds and ends at supper tonight, he kept saying under his breath, "My mother is the best cook." *He didn't have a decent meal all day.*

We had limeade and when Albert remarked that his mother never made enough or that there wasn't enough, she said, "Oh yes, there is," but it turned out there wasn't. Albert drank a great deal of it. Later, when his mother saw him prowling around looking for a cold drink, she said they would make more limeade, so his father made it from a can of concentrate but added such an enormous quantity of water that it was flat. He said, "I think I put too much water in it," but gave some to Albert, who made a nasty face and rejected it after a sip. Albert, Mr. Metz and I ate supper in the kitchen, and Myra and her mother on the porch, but after a while Myra went into another room and Mrs. Metz was alone. Albert started to bring her a corn on the cob but dropped it on the kitchen floor. He said, "Is it all right to use it? Can I wash it? Can I give it to you?" and his mother said okay. But when he got to the porch with it, he dropped it at her feet. She said it made no difference to her and that she would eat it, anyway.

Myra was told to wash the supper dishes and did, her father having cleared off the table, put the food away and stacked the dishes in the sink to soak. After everybody had finished, Mrs. Metz sat on the porch, still eating corn on the cob, with which she was having difficulty because of a loose front tooth. She was alone and kept me there. The kids were out in the yard playing croquet, and Mr. Metz had disappeared. I sat with her for a while and then left because I wanted to watch the kids.

When the game broke up, they spread a blanket, and Albert, Myra, Mary and Jane lay down on it. A couple of times when Albert teased his sister she called out, "Mommy, he's slapping me"—or something like that—and her father would go over and say, "Now, what's going on here?" All of a sudden Al stood up, bent over his sister and slapped her hard on both cheeks. She yelled to her mother, and when Albert lay down on his stomach Myra slapped him hard on the back and buttocks. The whole thing passed over. Mrs. Metz said that though they tease each other, one won't let anybody outside say anything against the other. Mary came and sat on Albert's back. He protested, and after a while he got up and said, "I'm going to dance with a blonde on Wednesday night." As Mary left she said, "Write and tell me about your dancing with a blonde." His mother told me the kids don't see anything wrong with Albert. The last I saw of the blanket episode, Albert was lying down and Mary had her head on his chest. When she said she was going to write him, Albert became anxious and asked everybody to be sure to send the letters Mary gives them for him.

We went into the living room and Albert was wearing his new jeans, which he said were beautiful, but the fly was open, and his mother called his attention to it and he zipped it up. He is obsessed by rock music, and he wanted to sing, but just as he got the idea his sister turned on the record player. He scolded her and his mother tore into him for trying to take the limelight. "You're not the boss around here," she yelled. I had gone into another room to get something, but I heard the yelling and Mrs. Metz told me what had happened. An almost identical situation developed a few minutes later when Albert started to sing again: his mother scolded him in a loud, irritated voice for always trying to be in the limelight, for singing rock and roll instead of other kinds of songs, and for trying to imitate the latest singers. When he started to sing, his mother showed distracted attention and interrupted to criticize. He ended up not singing at all. He sings without pitch, like his sister, but his mother says he once had a very beautiful voice.

Often, throughout the day, Albert said, "Oh, I wish I had a guitar." He said he really can't play but just likes to hold one—if girls see you holding a guitar they flock around you. When his mother mentioned classical music to him sometime during the day, Albert said, "Mommy, I'm a teen-ager now and teen-agers are not interested in that."

Good-bye

When we were about to leave to take Albert back, his mother said she had to have a shower. Since the Institute is rigid and punitive about re-entry hours, Albert was terribly, terribly anxious all the way back and afraid he would not be able to get a milk shake—something he desired intensely.

He kissed Myra good-bye before getting into the car, and sat gazing out the window all during the return trip. He looked very depressed and remained almost completely detached from what was going on in the car, which was mostly his mother talking. His father sat in front with me and Albert was in back with his mother. She was on the left side and Albert sat pressed into the right-hand corner. There was no physical contact between them. Albert had a bagful of stuff that consisted mostly of cheap supermarket cookies.

Albert asked his mother to please have some new article of clothing for him every time he came home, but she said that it was impossible. He said, "Myra has everything," but his mother snapped, "Myra works for everything she gets" (she earns money baby-sitting). Of course, what Albert really meant was that in the Institute he has nothing, while by contrast Myra, since she is at home and free, has everything. He wanted to know what her allowance was, and when Mrs. Metz said $2.37, he asked, "Why the thirty-seven cents?" and there was some discussion of the money that I can't remember. We arrived five minutes before the deadline and asked the man at the door if we could go and get something from the stand, and he said okay. Since we had this reprieve, Albert got the idea that instead of just having a cone, he would get a milk shake, but his father said, "Oh, there won't be time," which was not true. Mrs. Metz asked her husband to get her a cone, but he bought himself a cone and got her a chocolate sundae. This irritated her, and when he asked her, "What did you want?" she answered, "What you're eating."

On the way home Mrs. Metz asked me, "What do you think of my boy?" and after thinking a moment, I said, "I think he's not in very good shape." She said, "I think he's wonderful," and I replied that in my position I could not say what a neighbor might, but had to give an honest opinion. "Well," she said, "I know very well he is in bad shape and that it will be a long time before he can come home. Anybody can see he's in bad shape." I said, "I think people like him. He is really a very appealing boy," which is true. "Yes," she said, "that is what Mr. Woodson at the Institute says—that he is very appealing."

While getting supper, Mrs. Metz complained of being exhausted, but when we came back from the Institute she took a long walk with a friend. She was in excellent spirits, laughing and talking. She said repeatedly that she was looking forward to Albert's next visit.

Anger Unresolved

Albert and his mother are alienated by unresolved anger and blame. He ridicules her behind her back, and even as he makes affectionate gestures. She makes no pretense to him of affection, but humiliates and attacks him publicly: she is a hurricane of self-righteous anger, and almost every move Albert makes stirs it up. Only when he is out of sight is he beyond the reach of her anger, though he must always feel it inside him. Only when he hit his sister did his mother fail to intervene.

Though Albert may rage inwardly against his mother, it has to be bottled up, to come out as mocking "affection," as ridicule behind her back, or in words like "My mother is the best cook" mumbled under his breath. Anxiety and depression were the aftermath of the day-long attack to which he was exposed, while for his mother, the aftermath was relief.

His mother's anger was destructive, but since Albert was almost totally unassertive, there was no quarrel;-he hung his head and said, "All right, Mom." All he could do was acquiesce. Furthermore, he had no backing from anybody in the family. The livelong day nobody stood up for him: his father was silent or supported his mother, and his sister said nothing. Finally, we have to reckon with places like the Institute where patients are often degraded and compelled to be submissive. When an inmate learns not to be a "troublemaker," he has taken the first step toward release. If Mrs. Metz reported to the Institute that her son had been "difficult," had "acted up—been insulting and hard to manage," they would have concluded that he was sicker than they thought, and would defer his release.

I have told this story mainly from my notes, so that the reader could see for himself the difference between Mrs. Metz's acting and the reality of her relationship to her son. I have been careful to let the reader see how I was taken in; how Mrs. Metz's performance of the loving mother at first comes convincingly across the footlights. However, under the stress of hostility that she cannot control, the scenery folds, the houselights go up and Mrs. Metz stands before us, without make-up or costume, in the ordinary clothes of a mother who cannot stand her child. I do not have in all my notes any more convincing proof of the value of firsthand observation.

Showing Off and Erotic Contempt

The main themes are clear from the notes; yet since so much occurred in the few pages I have thus far presented, I want to go over them to give the reader my impression of the significance of what happened. I deal first with the problem of Mrs. Metz's menstrual pain and menopause.

For the first two days of my visit Mrs. Metz complained of severe, sickening pain, yet when something interested her she became light as a feather. Talking to me, she said, made her forget her pain, and when, on the second day, a traveling grocery store parked across the street, she was up, out the door and away, even though a moment before she had acted half dead.

She walked around inside the traveling grocery store, almost as if it belonged to her; she slapped the owner on the back, but he paid no attention. She met a couple of neighbors too. It was very hot outside, and while we had been waiting to enter, Mrs. Metz kept calling impatiently to Tom, the proprietor, though everyone else was quiet. This reminds me of something she told me: when she was eleven years old she received a one-year scholarship for study of "dramatic art," but her mother (note: not her father) would not permit her to accept because she thought the scholarship a come-on—that at the end of the year the school would try to get her daughter to continue and the family to pay. Mrs. Metz is very much interested in dramatics and so is Myra. "Secretly," says Mrs. Metz, "I always wanted to be an actress."

Mrs. Metz needs to be the center of attention; even her public attacks on Albert—rebuking him publicly for what she called his too-brief swimming trunks and for showing off—call attention to herself. This attention-getting is often tinged with sexuality: in her touching my leg and thigh, in calling me, the milkman, and other accidental males, "babe," in flaunting and scratching her thighs, jiggling herself in front of me, slapping the owner of the traveling grocery store on the back—in all these flouncings and flauntings she employs the sexual to communicate. On the other hand, in this woman's life, love (or at least the affirmation of it) and sexuality have been devices for degrading people; and if she is to accept love, as we shall see, it has to be on her own complicated terms. Witness how she ridicules her mother, though she talks to her with sugary affection, and how she publicly castrates Albert.

Much of what happens between her and the world outside the family becomes a means of display—the milkman appears and she calls out to him, "Bring in everything you've got!" A traveling grocery store becomes a stage, where she is actress and producer; she walks about in the little trailer store as if she owns it. The main attraction of the store is not that she can buy something, but that she can go on stage there.

My impression is that because of a loveless childhood and adolescence, the theme around which Mrs. Metz has organized her life drama is oceanic love. She told me only two incidents of her early childhood, but two incidents, without prompting, selected from a great range of possibilities, tell much, because spontaneous choice of *just these* suggest their symbolic importance in the life of the teller:

1. The first has already been told—it is the story of how her mother would jump up from her seat and leave the children at the movies.

2. Mrs. Metz told me she was a very quiet baby, and in order to illustrate, she told the following story. One day, when she was two, her mother had to leave the house at about ten in the morning and left detailed instructions with her father on how to take care of her. When Mrs. Bauman returned at about five o'clock, she found the baby's diaper dry.* Thinking her husband had taken very good care of the baby, she complimented him, whereupon he exclaimed, "My goodness, I completely forgot about the baby." He had not fed her, nor given her anything to drink. The point Mrs. Metz made was that she was such a good baby she had not made a sound all day to remind her father of her existence. Mrs. Bauman became so enraged that she took red pepper and rubbed it on the *baby's* mouth. Mrs. Metz thinks that may be why she talks so much now. This tale was told to Mrs. Metz by her mother.

We do not have to believe this story, though it may be true, but it reflects Mrs. Metz's feeling that she was neglected, overlooked and accidental, that she was unjustly and irrelevantly punished, and that if one is quiet one will be forgotten.

Thus inflation of the love theme is both a reflex and a camouflage of childhood neglect.

_____
* Not an absolute impossibility if she—like her own son at two—was in absolute terror of going in her diaper or pants.

Giving and Getting Love

Mrs. Metz came to have excessive cravings—not so much, perhaps, for love's solemn and profound reality, but for its outward show; and while she wanted love, paradoxically she had to distrust it when it seemed to her like show.

What Mrs. Metz exacts, even from a young organism, is illustrated by the following encounter with her two-year-old niece Lucy:

(Sixth day.) Mrs. Metz's brother was here with his wife and their daughter, Lucy, who talks fairly well. Everybody was absorbed with Lucy, trying to get her to do something: to count, to dance, to sing, to remember what various people did, to remember what happened to her. Mrs. Metz kept telling Lucy how much she loved her, and over and over again snatched her up and kissed her. Mrs. Metz said that often when Lucy thought her mother wasn't going to come over to her Aunt Gertie's house, she would start to cry. Mrs. Metz tried to get her sister-in-law to promise to leave Lucy with her sometime next week, but the sister-in-law begged off. At one point during the visit Mrs. Metz said, "I'm blessed in one thing: everybody—men, women, young and old—loves me." She tried to get Lucy to say she loves her.

Mrs. Metz was just "eating up" Lucy with love, and expecting Lucy to match her declarations and demonstrations; yet at the same time, much of what Mrs. Metz was saying must have been incomprehensible to Lucy. Nevertheless, from watching Lucy, I get the impression that she genuinely likes Mrs. Metz: she goes to her spontaneously and puts her little hands on her face.

Mrs. Metz told me her brother has been doing very poorly financially but has a heart of gold and is full of love, like everybody in her family.

Imagining herself capable of giving oceans of love, she wants the world to give her oceans in return. I started the description of her with the love theme because she brought it up: as soon as I crossed her threshold she had to show me right away that she radiates love. The phantasmagoric episode with Albert, however; her love messages over the phone, coupled with constant harassment of the boy; the fact that she did not give him a decent meal all day—the very least one can do for a person, not to mention a son, who comes home from an institution; and the fact that she would not let him take any phonograph records back with him, illustrate the brutal contradiction in her between her image of herself—what she wants the world to think of her—and what she really is. Mrs. Metz constantly fails before our eyes: wanting love, she cannot get it because she does not know how to give it. In love she makes enormous demands, and she wants a display of love, but, paradoxically, she distrusts it when she sees it, because it awakens frightening reminders of her own playacting.

I opened this section with the complete record of Albert's homecoming and closed it with a description of how Mrs. Metz goes about getting a child to love her and how she displays her "lovingness" so the world can see how love-magnetic she is. It seems to me that Lucy and Albert illustrate the contradiction in Mrs. Metz: on the one hand the adolescent son burlesques his mother's love because he does not believe it, and on the other, the baby niece succeeds in responding to Mrs. Metz as she seems to want it. Perhaps

Lucy intuitively perceives what Albert may never have been able to—that beneath the frantic histrionics is a real hunger for love.

Courtship and Marriage

My story of Mrs. Metz's courtship starts with a hangnail.

(Second day.) At lunch today* Mrs. Metz began to tear at what she called a hangnail on a finger on her left hand. She tore at it and tore at it and tore at it in a way that really upset me, until she at last tore a piece of skin away and was satisfied that she had gotten it; it turned out that *she hadn't gotten the piece of cuticle she wanted*. By evening the finger was causing her a great deal of pain, and when I remarked on how persistent she had been in tearing at the hangnail, she said, "Just as persistent as I was in going after my husband."

So the equation is husband=hangnail=self-torture—and you don't get what you want, after all, in spite of the pain. Continuing:

I asked her about the courtship and she said that when she had first met Kurt and a friend of his, she came back and told her mother that there was one "who is just like me and full of the devil, and then there is another one who is very quiet and very much a gentleman." Mrs. Metz told her mother she was going to marry the "quiet gentleman"—Kurt—and her mother spat and said, "You're crazy!" It took Mrs. Metz five years to get him, but at last she succeeded. As I see Mr. Metz now, it *would* have taken an exceedingly aggressive woman five years to overcome his shyness.

When a woman says a man is "very much a gentleman" she often means he does not make unwanted sexual advances—or she believes he won't. This is the dilemma, perhaps, of women more than men: whom shall one marry, the most attractive or the least threatening?

Kurt's friend was "full of the devil," like Gertrude, but Kurt was pure and a gentleman. It was worth waiting five years for him.

(Third day.) I reminded her of what she had said about how long it took her to land her husband, and she said it took five years only because he didn't have any money. He was earning very little, and he was taking care of his family. Gertrude and Kurt would have gotten married sooner if he had had the money. Then she told me the whole story of the courtship:

Kurt was very reluctant to take her out; he seemed to want to take out any other girl rather than her. I asked her why, and she said he didn't care how he spent the time with other girls, but he thought that when he took *her* out, it always had to be some place where he would spend money on her. Kurt and his friends had formed a club; she was the only woman included in their meetings. They often came to her for advice and all sorts of things. After a ball game they would all go out to eat some place and would invite her along—six or seven boys including Kurt. "Kurt was always with me and I was with Kurt." She would walk around the house singing a song, something like "Kurt, Kurt, when are you going to call me up?" or "Kurt, Kurt, when are you going to ask the question?" She

* Mr. Metz was at work and Myra was not there.

wanted him so badly because he was so polite, so gentlemanly and so considerate. He was just the opposite of her: she was always "in the limelight," singing and dancing.

For five years she waited for this passive, poorly educated man with low earning power, who avoided being alone with her. When they met it was usually in the company of numerous other boys, who provided Mrs. Metz with the necessary staging—the "limelight"—and, I think, protection, for the more numerous the gathering the less the danger of a sexual confrontation with Kurt. Being the only female in a men's club, she was the center. But she could also choose from among the men, and the fact that they brought their troubles to her gave her further opportunity to select; yet she clung to Kurt. Kurt was thus an obsession—nobody was like him; her imagination inflated the qualities of this very ordinary man. As she flounced around her house singing her courting song, his image was before her, radiant with virtues. For this fanciful paragon, this saint, she renounced another suitor, Arty, the reality of a dynamic man.

Arty is now wealthy. He gave her a tremendous rush, and after knowing her for only a few hours asked her to marry him. What impressed Arty about her was that she didn't smoke or drink, and she walked out of a party when people began to tell dirty jokes. He followed her out of the room and asked why she had walked out. She answered that they were talking about things in there that didn't interest her, and that when it was all over she'd go back and dance.

Arty gave her such a rush that it frightened her. When I asked why she got scared she said, "Well, I couldn't imagine what he could see in me after only a few hours." Nevertheless, this went on, and there was a time when she was going out with Arty three times a week.

Arty was very domineering. One night she went out with somebody else and Arty tracked her all over town until he located her in a café, walked right in and asked what she was doing there. He said, "I thought you didn't drink," and she said, "Look what I have." When it turned out to be ginger ale he apologized and asked her to leave with him, but she said, "How could I, with these other people?" He followed them all the way home, and afterward she told him it couldn't go on like that, and he apologized.

Once Arty took her to a wedding and introduced her as his fiancée. She didn't deny it there and then, but later told him that he had made a complete fool of himself—that he had no right to say it, that if anyone were to know, her parents should know first, and that she really didn't think she should go out with him any more. All the while she had in the back of her mind that she absolutely had to have Kurt.

Kurt knew her for three years before he dared kiss her, he was so respectful. I said, "Well, wasn't Arty respectful, too?" but she switched to the matter of his wanting to marry her after knowing her only a few hours. I said, "Doesn't that show a great deal of respect?" She talked as if she thought that if she had continued to go out with Arty he would have broken through her sexual defenses. She didn't use such terms, but the implication from much of what she said was precisely that. She did say that if Arty had kept it up, he would have worn her down—meaning that she would have consented to marry him. At that time, unlike Kurt, Arty already had his own business.

At last Kurt proposed to her, first asking her father for her hand. Her father said, "Take her hand, take her foot, take everything, but just take her." He was only joking, of course, said Mrs. Metz. When Kurt proposed he got down on his knees.

It seems to me that Gertrude was afraid of Arty; she distrusted his ardor; he was tempestuously possessive, domineering and supremely aggressive—the classic picture of a man in love. But when she compared him with Kurt, Arty lost. Kurt—slow, uncertain and frightened—was the opposite of Arty. He went out with almost any girl but Gertrude; she longed in vain for Kurt to call her, while Arty was insistent and always in evidence. He breathed fire; Kurt exhaled damp indecision. So Kurt was the man for her! He would not try to break her down; she could have it or leave it alone; *she* would dominate him, not the other way around. Arty represented everything she feared in maleness and became a phobia; Kurt symbolized the opposite and became an obsession. Arty was pleasure and danger; Kurt was nothing and safety. Kurt would never threaten her; Arty would threaten her everywhere: he would take the limelight, be sexually demanding, run her life. But she wanted to run a man's life. If she married Arty he would have to be the center of *her* life. He would dominate her, eat her up, engulf her, sexually exhaust and maybe even dirty her. The very existential mass of Arty —his living, breathing, masculine adequacy—was too much.

Marry her after only a few hours? *She* knew all about such histrionics. Arty was clearly not for her. Better to have a man whom *she* had chased across the desert of his reluctance, for only what was exacted could be real. And furthermore, who could love a woman like her, forgotten by her parents, a burden whom her father was eager to give away: "Take her hand, take her foot, take everything, but just take her."

She may have wondered what would become of her after Arty married her and discovered how little she had to give, how little to return for this ardor. That, I think, was the root of her fear of him—that someday he would wake up beside her and ask himself, "Whom have I married?" I believe that deep down she must have felt that the question was less likely to come up if she married Kurt. Inwardly she must have feared that she was only half a loaf—and known that Kurt was half a man.

Mrs. Metz said she would wait and wait for Kurt to call her up for a date. She turned down many fine invitations just waiting for him, and often he did not call. She told of the time he sat on the fence outside her house watching her go out on a date with Arty and step into Arty's swell-looking car. She felt pretty wonderful to be able to do this in front of Kurt.

Such tricks suggest that the affair with Arty might have been mostly to build a fire under Kurt—who was so ardently refusing to burn!

She would use tricks to stimulate Kurt. She would walk past his house to the drugstore to get an ice cream cone. He lived close by, and on hot summer nights she knew he and his family would be sitting outside the house. When he saw her walk by to get a cone, he would go into the store and pay for it. Their favorite treat was to divide a sandwich and a bottle of pop between them. She speaks of this courtship with great pleasure and gets tremendous enjoyment out of telling how she went after Kurt. She talks about Arty with considerable fright as she emphasizes how domineering he was. Anyone who ever saw Kurt thought him wonderful because he was so kind, considerate and courteous.

So Gertrude pursued Kurt persistently—one might even say relentlessly—for five years until he gave in and, on his knees, she says histrionically, asked her to marry him.

A word is necessary about how I feel about Mrs. Metz's description of Arty. Even if she romanticized him and exaggerated his ardor, even if what she describes is his image, remembered, adorned with yearning and lined with her own fears, it shows us her inner reality. I have treated the story of Arty as if it were true because I believe it represents the inner truth of Mrs. Metz. I believe also that it represents the truth for many women in our culture who, like Mrs. Metz, have been deprived.

Renunciation of Life

And so Gertrude and Kurt were married:

(Third day.) Mr. Metz told me that on their wedding day Gertrude did not appear at the appointed hour. He went to the beauty parlor where she was supposed to be; when he did not find her he went looking for her and discovered her in a restaurant having brunch with some friends. He asked, "Do you know what day this is?" and she said yes, but she had completely forgotten the time. At this point his wife took up the story, which she told in order to show how completely relaxed she was!

Everyone was nervous at the wedding, she said, but she went around straightening the men's ties and the girls' dresses and *delayed* things in that way, while people said to her, "You are the one that is supposed to be straightened up, not the other people." As she walked down the aisle she winked to this one and that one. According to her, the whole thing was carried off as a lark and her husband got the impression that *she tried to make a joke out of the whole business. He thought it very amusing.* Both were in raptures over the wonderful wedding ceremony.

The wedding performance dramatized Gertrude's obliteration; it was a last display before, making a mockery of herself, Gertrude threw herself away in a marriage that seemed ridiculous to her, but which she had to go through with because, buried in *this* marriage, she would never be found out, would never betray herself. The wedding dramatized her full renunciation; it was a kind of execution, and on the way to the scaffold she put on a brave front. Actually, though, it was also a kind of play—it really wasn't there. The audience were the real players, and that is why she straightened them up. Because Kurt was not what she wanted, Gertrude could still say to me that three years later, shortly after giving birth to Albert, she "gave up everything" when she left her parents to join her husband, who had gotten a job in a different town. Going to join Kurt at that time was a second and final renunciation.

On Delusion and Unreality

A delusion is a compensatory distortion of reality that arises when an unconscious idea or impulse is impossible to endure. Mrs. Metz, never really loved by her parents, develops the delusion that she is rich in love and irresistible. A delusion is one possible outcome of an unbearable unconscious truth. Think of what it would mean to Mrs. Metz were she really to perceive the meaning of her father's having forgotten about her and her mother's having rubbed red pepper on *her* mouth instead of on her father's? She would have to hate them both. By believing she is rich in love, she can continue to repress hatred of her parents. Thus, as we have learned from Freud, the delusion is at the service of repression. And if Mrs. Metz can imagine herself a great actress, the center of all eyes, an erotic vision, she can deal with the reality that as a child she was ignored.

Mrs. Metz makes a performance and an illusion of the solemn occasions of her life. When her father died, she did not mourn; she was "happy" because he passed away with a single heart attack. Now he watches over her and sits next to her on the sofa! Her son was driven mad by a bolt from the sky, and as she flitted over the debris to his side, she was guided and saved by her father's spirit! Myra was not a birth, she was a production!

One characteristic of a show distinguishes it from all other human events—it isn't real: it is "only make-believe," "only a movie," "only a dream." What is only a show may not really count, because it will soon be over; it may be an illusion that will pass. If life is just a play or an image on a screen, its pain as well as its pleasure is unreal. But one suffers because of the impossibility of maintaining the delusion; marriage really is contracted, the misery of lovelessness is really in the flesh; and an unloved child remains, somewhere between actuality and memory ("Albert is dead") to torment and to be in torment.

To live as if life were one's special show, however, is narcotizing, for not only does the delusion tend to put reality to sleep, but since acting itself is exhilarating, it quiets pain. Walking about, a prima donna on the stage, the pain is forgotten in the stimulation of the performance and the noise of the applause—or the imagined applause.

After the wedding came the honeymoon:

(Sixth day. On this evening I drove Mr. and Mrs. Metz and Myra over to a nearby waterfall.) Most of the time when we were admiring the falls, Mrs. Metz talked about their honeymoon, nearly twenty years before. They had a week at a "theatrical" hotel where they saw many famous people. She was delighted with the way they had given their party the slip, and she talked at length about the good time they had during the honeymoon week. She spoke of the plays and movies they saw, the vaudeville singers they heard and the place they went to on New Year's Eve. Myra asked, "How much did your honeymoon cost?" and Mr. Metz said he didn't remember, but his wife remembered the exact figure. She said they imagined nobody at the hotel knew they were newlyweds, "but how could they not know we were newlyweds when we came down to breakfast at two o'clock in the afternoon?" Myra wanted to know how that showed they were newlyweds and Mrs. Metz said, "You don't have to know everything."

So they had a week at a hotel where Mrs. Metz could be among *other* actors, and where she could imagine herself gazed at and admired. And, of course, everybody in the hotel must have known they were newlyweds, for what else did the help have to do other than notice when Mr. and Mrs. Metz came down to breakfast? (What hotel serves breakfast at 2 P.M.?)

Why does Mrs. Metz tell me all this? Why so sexy, especially in front of her daughter? Why, after nearly twenty years, does she try to recover, on this particular night, the experience of her honeymoon? Why does she tell me about the theatrical personalities merely vaguely present in her life so long ago? What meaning does time have for this woman, who lives on fantasy, whose every hope is a memory? What is a place? What is the nature of the objects in the space she occupies? What are people? Where is Mrs. Metz in the hierarchy of our society—high, low, exalted? And if she imagines herself a queen of the theater, does she ever "come back to herself"? And if and when she does, what does she feel? Does she still hope "to *be* something"?

I think Mrs. Metz does not merely wish to "impress" me and her daughter by the story of her honeymoon. I think she wants us to believe that she is glamorous—that somehow she really is a theatrical personality. The longing to be what she never was able to be is still so strong that even now she projects the wish as a reality. Somehow she is what she has wished to be and she draws sustenance from the image. On this summer night, at the falls, she remembered the hotel where long ago she had almost been able to touch what she wanted to be. In some respects time is what Mrs. Metz wants it to be, and its images are determined by the intensity of her longing. Mrs. Metz's longing to be what she never was is so piercing that when she fantasies herself-in-theater, past and present become one and she is what she always wished to be. *Longing paralyzes time:* then we are what we have never been, and what we wish to be, we are. We become like the Spartans and the Sioux, who projected the story of their own death so vividly and lived their glory before they died so intensely that death, when it came, deprived them of nothing. In fantasy, they had already died gloriously and heard the survivors praise them. The living dignity of many Sioux was that of men already gloriously dead; who, though alive, were made proud by the voices they could imagine glorifying their brave death. To be "resolute before one's death," as Heidegger has put it, one must be able to imagine, while alive, the panegyrics on one's death, and be willing to die, and even feel obliged to die, because of them.

When Mrs. Metz thinks about herself, or rather, fantasies herself, time is no more and she is a theatrical personality, glamorously irresistible. Yet she can see that she is an aging, no longer attractive woman. What of glamour then? The theatrical images defend her against the realization of her present condition, and so time is canceled again. Space is a stage, people are an audience, the play is always a success, Mrs. Metz is at the top of the profession, her name is in lights, and the observer—as she has insisted for years —has come to write a book about her.

Mrs. Metz is not always in the clouds; most of the time she acts like a wife and mother, but any happening that seems to provide opportunity for public display will start her off. She has a tendency to react to events in terms of whether or not they can be used to dramatize herself.

Husband and Wife

One hazard in observing is to fail to record what else is going on while something is happening. What was Mr. Metz doing each time his wife scolded Albert? Where was he? What did he do when his wife complained of pain? When she was talking about a fight with the lady upstairs, how did he react? When Mrs. Metz was entranced with a TV quiz show, was Mr. Metz asleep, watching, smiling—or what? No matter how conscious one is of the importance of knowing what is happening when something else is occurring, one sometimes forgets. The more intense the action in one sphere, the greater the danger that the observer will overlook all others. Mrs. Metz had the ability to focus attention so intensely on herself that in spite of my being an experienced observer, I sometimes lost her husband among the multitude of her activities. Here are some notes from the first day:

> Mr. Metz is a very sweet guy who gives the impression of being very ineffectual in this house. He says he is very highly valued by his employers, for whom he has been working many years. He thinks the world of them and they think the world of him.

The reader should notice that I said he "*is* a very sweet guy," not that he *seems* to be a sweet guy. First impressions are important because they show the nature of our mistakes, of our predispositions and of our guilt. I wanted to believe that everybody was sincere and really loved everybody else, because I wanted to defend myself against the accusation that I was biased, and because of a possible predisposition to "place charges" against the parents of disturbed children. One might say, then, that I had a tendency to let myself be deceived in their favor. Let us look at the record.

On the second day Mrs. Metz decided that she, Myra, Mary and I would go in my car to the shop where Mr. Metz worked when he was not traveling for his job, and bring him home.

> Myra and Mary were dressed in bathing suits with little blouses over them. Mrs. Metz did not approve, but that's the way they went into the shop. Mr. Metz did not object; as a matter of fact, he said, "Oh well, let them relax for a change," and his wife was amazed because usually he is so strict.
>
> Mr. Metz seemed relaxed and smiling—as he generally seems to me—when we went through the shop, starting with the retail outlet, which is Mr. Metz's responsibility. His wife says he had previously been a supervisor* but that she had compelled him to give it up because of the strain on him. . . . In his explanation of how the shop functioned, he was delightfully brief. The kids were wandering around and at one point Mr. Metz said, "Be careful, don't get any dust on your clothes."

First impressions of Mr. Metz are of a "relaxed," pleasant sort of man, living quietly and ineffectually with his dominating wife. Yet, it is worth looking at my additional notes. As I drove back to the house from the shop, Mr. Metz guided me.

> His wife suddenly got the idea that she would like to go to a drive-in movie tonight but her husband said, "No, no"; and at a certain point on the road the kids wanted to get some doughnuts, but although his wife said okay, he said, "We can't turn off here." But I did manage to turn off and the doughnuts were bought. My impression is that Mr. Metz is a basic kill-joy. He didn't want to play croquet either and said lamely he thought it could be played only by two

---

* This is not confirmed by other records, which indicate that he had a semiskilled job, and was earning rather modest pay. Surveys have repeatedly shown that respondents usually upgrade themselves when asked about jobs and pay.

people. When I suggested I take the family to dinner he vetoed that, too, and as he and I were sitting on the porch and his wife suggested we go into the yard where it was cooler, he said, "Dr. Henry and I are perfectly happy here."

A kill-joy kills joy, and one reason he does is because he is depressed and therefore finds pleasure—indeed, almost any action—antagonistic. A depressed person mourns the loss of one beloved or of himself. Another interpretation of Mr. Metz, however, is that nullity expresses itself most perfectly as negation. What can a person who is nothing contribute to existence but its negation? Hence a major activity of such a person is interference. Even when he seems to be doing something positive, as when Mr. Metz, against his wife's wishes, let Myra and Mary go into the shop in swimsuits and blouses, the positive act was the consequence of a negation. Positive, giving acts, unmotivated by negativism, do occur in Mr. Metz's life, but they are few, as we shall see.

Behind his bland, smiling, relaxed exterior lies depression. Mr. Metz withdraws from life, helped, perhaps, by the driving qualities of his wife, who flees from her own feelings of despair and nothingness by thrusting herself into existence. Mr. Metz married a woman who, by the intensity of her entrance into life, would make it easy for him to withdraw from it, or, rather, make it easy for him to continue on its margins.

The Communications of Love

Kissing, fondling, tender words—love messages—often passed between husband and wife.

When Mr. Metz called up to say he was leaving, she kept calling him "honey," "dear" and "darling."

They kissed when he came home tonight and she held his hand when we sat on the porch.

Mrs. Metz has just come back from visiting some out-of-town relatives, and she and her husband protest that this will never happen again because he could never stand being without her that way.

She says that when she was out of town a week or so ago, her husband, who was driven so desperate by her absence that he could not fall asleep, tried the same technique of turning on the radio and relaxing in bed that she uses, but the large bed was so empty that he could not go to sleep. I said, "Well, he missed you," and she said, "Of course, that's the idea." She added that he said he'll never let her go away again without him; and I heard him say that too.

We were on the porch right after dinner, Mr. and Mrs. Metz sitting on the sofa about three feet apart. Their arms were stretched along the back of the sofa and she fondled his. This seemed to embarrass him very much—possibly because of my presence—and he ended up sitting way over in the corner of the sofa.

After finishing the dishes, Mrs. Metz came out on the porch and sat on the sofa with her husband. They were about four feet apart but stroked each other's arms and held hands. Mr. Metz did not withdraw but sought his wife's hand sometimes. Mrs. Metz told me this morning that she had said to her husband, "If Dr. Henry saw the way you said good-bye to me he would have told you to stay home."

. . . .

It was close to seven o'clock when Myra and her mother thought Mr. Metz would be coming home, so we all went outside and Myra saw him in the distance. I could not see him but Mrs. Metz imitated his walk, leaning sharply to the right, his right arm hanging down. When I caught sight of him he wasn't leaning at all. Mrs. Metz and Myra walked toward him, but his wife reached him first and walked back to the house with her arm over his shoulder. Part of the time, I think, they were holding hands.

. . .

When Mr. Metz finished washing the dishes he came and sat down on the sofa and it wasn't long before he was lying with his head on his wife's thigh and she stroked his head.

Mrs. Metz gave me a detailed account of their sleeping behavior today. Last night she and her husband had tried sleeping in various parts of the house, but she got practically no sleep. The reason she wanders around is because his snoring keeps her awake—she does not know how she has stood it for so many years. At any rate, last night she started out in the living room, tossed around and couldn't fall asleep. She and her husband were lying on the floor (no doubt to escape the heat). He dropped off to sleep but she couldn't, so she got up carefully and tiptoed away, but he discovered she had left and followed her into the bedroom. He fell asleep, but she got out of bed and went to sleep on the porch. He discovered she had left, so followed her, and joined her on the sofa. But this time —the third time—she escaped by waiting until he was really in a very deep sleep, so that she was able to escape back to the bedroom and get two and a half hours' sleep before he discovered she was not with him and came and lay down beside her.

She says that when he sleeps he has to have his arm around her abdomen and hold her very tightly there, and she has gotten so used to it now that if it isn't there she's uncomfortable.

He says he cannot sleep without her and she said, "How did you manage when I was away?" and he replied, "I went through hell; I just didn't sleep."

When she gets up to leave him she feels very guilty. She used to toss around a great deal when she was a child, but then for a long time she slept with her aunt, who pinched her every time she shoved against her aunt, and this trained her to sleep without moving. . . .

She does not need much sleep and when she makes up her mind to sleep, she does. She says her husband snores so violently that he practically saws through the bed, but when she wakes him up he is very sweet about it. I wouldn't be surprised if this is one of the reasons why Mrs. Metz constantly complains of fatigue and has such enormous black pockets under her eyes.

What is the meaning of her love communications, when she compares her husband to a listing ship and her marriage to a sore and throbbing finger, to punishment she inflicted on herself? It may mean that she denies inwardly what she affirms by appearances; it can mean that half a loaf is better than none; that it is better to live half alone than all alone; that the sham and sorrow of life are covered up and compensated somewhat by other things, like having a home and somebody to sleep with.

Two people holding hands may be two souls clinging to each other in despair while looking out of the corner of the inner eye at vanished hopes.

This is not necessarily deception. Mutuality in depression and despair can be a kind of union, even though it is not what sorority girls think love should be. It seems that in despair one can have this mutuality even when there is mutual belittling, for there *is* the despairing union of those who live in self-contempt. Courtship itself can then become a search for another who matches one in self-devaluation; and the pain of the dialectic—that they must necessarily ridicule each other—is dulled by the narcotic of mutuality in despair. This is my feeling about the "love communications" between Gertrude and Kurt.

Let us study sleep. The behaviorist would say of the way Mr. and Mrs. Metz sleep together that Mr. Metz simply found it rewarding to sleep with his arm around his wife, that her abdomen is the conditioned stimulus necessary to Mr. Metz's sleep, and that therefore he cannot sleep without the abdominal grip and wakes up when his wife isn't there, pursuing her until he finds her. An ordinary human being—i.e., a nonbehaviorist—however, would have to ask, "Why can't Mr. Metz show some consideration and give his wife a chance to get some sleep?" The behaviorist answer would be that the response pattern has become so strongly "reinforced," so firmly linked to the sleep "drive" that it overrides everything else, even such things as his wife's comfort. Then our next questions are, "Why hasn't a wish (or drive?) to bring comfort to his wife been just as strongly reinforced?" and "Why doesn't a desire to let his wife sleep affect his own sleep drive?" The behaviorist answer is, perhaps, that the so-called "wish" of which I speak is only my invention, and furthermore, that it is a purely "social drive"—and biological drives take precedence. But don't people forgo sleep in the interest of such "social drives" as success, for example? And furthermore, isn't consideration for one's wife related to love and isn't love a phase of the sexual drive, which is also biological?

Now, surely there is such a thing as love—I believe even behaviorists would admit that they marry for love and not for reinforcement! And surely considerateness is part of love, so we still have the fact that Mr. Metz's desire for sleep overrides consideration for his *wife's* sleep, and we wonder why. Or, in the language of behaviorism, we wonder why considerate behavior was not reinforced in all the years Mr. and Mrs. Metz have lived together. In dealing with rats it is always clear why, of all possible behaviors, one in particular is reinforced—for the simple reason that the experimenter controls it. And the statement about why one behavior was reinforced implies the reasons for *not* reinforcing others. In the laboratory the explanation of why a rat was fed when he turned to the right and not to the left, or why he got food when he leaped at a white card rather than a black, is given in terms of the *conscious goals of the experimenter*. But in human life there are no such explanations. So the questions "Why was sleep reinforced to the exclusion of consideration?" and "Why did Mr. Metz seem unable to show concern for his wife's sleep?" cannot be answered. But we do know that his sleep took precedence, to the degree that he seemed to hound his wife into sleeplessness. So really, the behaviorist explanation leaves us nowhere—it takes us off in a leaky theory and leaves us marooned on an island of unsolved problems. But all I have to say is that Mr. Metz did not have enough consideration for his wife, and the examples still to come document this.

Another question is, "Why of all possible responses to his wife's presence just before sleep was that particular response reinforced?," i.e., why did that *particular* act of gripping his wife tightly put Mr. Metz to sleep? At this point reasonable people—those not brainwashed by graduate work in ex- -perimental psychology—would probably think that there was "something inside Mr. Metz" * that responded especially to that position and to no other, but, and above all, that maybe his wife had something to do with this existential "experiment" in ·operant conditioning. Since at this point the argument passes into the realm of discourse of ordinary citizens, I leave it and go on to more important matters.

While the sleep, entanglement deprives Mrs. Metz of rest and her hus- band of independence, it gives Mrs. Metz an absolute, though dearly—and possibly unconsciously—bought control over her husband, and makes her indispensable. The sleep pattern persists by virtue of its rewards, and while Mrs. Metz dare not break it definitively, though she does make efforts to evade it, her husband cannot even attempt a break; he does not have the power or the desire to. Though when awake he may have dreams of being free, when asleep he knows it is impossible, so the grip expresses at once his panic and resentment. The deepest insight comes to us from Mr. Metz's as- sertion that he will never again let his wife go away on vacation without him, and from her assertion that a serious accident she had on a previous vacation was due to her having gone away without him: thus she atoned for wayward thoughts. By accepting the grip and the sleep-destroying snoring, she atones for the catastrophe of the marriage and makes *it* impossible to destroy. Her sleep is ransom for the marriage.

Considerateness

It seems inconsiderate of Mr. Metz to keep following his wife so that all she gets is two and a half hours' sleep; yet Mrs. Metz married Kurt because ·he was so thoughtful and considerate, and *he* says he is too. Let us look at occasions when he might have shown it.

Although Mrs. Metz's finger was obviously causing her a great deal of pain, her husband showed no interest in it, changing the subject whenever she brought it up. When she suggested putting a Band-Aid on it, he did not move a muscle to get it. When she suggested a cold compress, he made no effort to get ice water. He did not suggest going to the drugstore to get something either. (Myra, who was sitting there, showed no reaction.)

---

* Here the behaviorist really has us, he thinks, because this "something" is merely fuzzy-mindedness of the canaille: if we cannot specify our "something" it really isn't there; what is unknown has no bearing on scientific argument. But the point is that that "something inside Mr. Metz"—which we cannot name, because it is in the nature of all historic phenomena to be lost if they are not written down—is precisely that black box of motivation which, in a transaction between Mr. Metz and his wife, de- termined that the grip would be the response selected.

But furthermore, the argument that unknowns cannot enter scientific argument is incorrect. The history of science is precisely the opposite, viz., that when the survey of a given universe has suggested the probable presence of a phenomenon, it must be taken into account in all reasoning and will be confirmed when the theory and method have been developed for verifying.

Mrs. Metz complained of pains in her thighs, saying it was probably due to the change in the weather. Her husband said, "Well, I should trade you in for a new model," and she replied, "Then you would have to trade the new model in for the old one again." When she complained about her finger again he did not respond but went right on talking about what he had been talking about. (Myra was not present.)

Sometimes Mr. Metz does the dishes, but otherwise little suggests that he is thoughtful and considerate—except his withdrawal. Since he leaves practically all of the family management to his wife, there are no arguments, and his *abdication thus becomes the measure of his considerateness*. Giving in may be interpreted as thoughtfulness by a person determined to have his—or her—own way, or by a person *condemned to accept leeway for love*. The slogan of a parent who does this to a child is: "I can't love you but I can let you get away with murder"; and the slogan of a wife or husband is something like it: "I can't really love you but I can let you have your own way—and I shall always hold it against you." Mrs. Metz accepts yielding in place of love, and that, I surmise, is why Kurt was so intoxicating, while Arty scared her. Resistance to Gertrude's wishes would seem coldness or worse to her, and therefore the more a man gives in to her, the greater his love (and "consideration") would seem to be. This is merely the reverse of the more usual sexual confrontation in our culture, where feminine yielding is so exciting to some men that they mistake their own exhalations of dominance for love's sweet breath. At home, the direction of existence has almost become Gertrude's monopoly.

As we observe the marriage today, Kurt seems the bland, relaxed, undemanding person his wife describes, the opposite of Arty and the ideal consort for her. He is relatively unassertive, almost absent; she is volcanically present and domineering. It seems, however, that underneath this exterior, Kurt is in mourning for himself; he is a kill-joy because joy has been killed within him; and since he tends towards nullity, he exercises himself most often in negation, which is the predominant expression of his effectiveness in the home. Although he supports the family, Mr. Metz engages in few other positive acts in anybody's interest; though he is physically present, he acts as if he had a *delusion of absence*—a delusion of extrication—so little does he attempt to affect the life around him. As his wife's fear of being nothing drives her violently into life, she helps expel him from it, and in this sense they complement each other; her entry is the complement of his withdrawal.

In Kurt, Gertrude mistook withdrawal for consideration; mistook inability to express a wish for deference to her wishes; mistook apathy toward all wishes for accommodation to hers. She thus mistook absence of *any* attitude for a positive one, and in marriage this negative attitude, this inhibition of his own existence, became an indifference to her needs; what she took for consideration functioned in daily life as inconsiderateness. At no point does Kurt enter the life of another person in a giving way; it is almost impossible for him to stir, although he will often do what he is asked to by his wife. He is indifferent to her pain—but he is indifferent about what TV show he watches also. Kurt does not exhibit empathy for any person nor identify with any course of action. Wrapped in his depression and apathy,

he carries on at his little job at a very modest wage, comes home, eats
supper, watches whatever TV channel his wife chooses, never touches his
daughter unless she touches him first—and goes to bed, where his aspiration and his panic are expressed in the iron grip on his wife's belly.

This vigorous woman, with her lively, though banal intelligence, is her
husband's protection against the world; and this, as we shall see, includes
his daughter. He is afraid of being cheated and afraid of confronting issues
himself, so uses his wife as go-between. He turned his children entirely
over to her, and even communicates with them about important matters
through her. He did not address me spontaneously, and though he kept
asking his wife, "What is Dr. Henry after?" would not ask me. He is like a
lonely hillock of sand on which the random footprints of transient seabirds
are quickly obliterated by the wind.

The Relationship between Myra and Her Parents

What Mrs. Metz called consideration, but which is really abdication-in-
unawareness, has destructive affects in parents' relationship with children.
We saw that when Albert came home from the Institute, his mother, with no
intervention by his father, did what she pleased with him, and she has told
us that when he was little he would not go to meet his father without her
permission. The frequency with which a person lets such things occur
seems a measure of this kind of "consideration." We have to study Mr.
Metz's behavior over a wide range, however, in order to be sure that abdica-
tion-in-unawareness is not part of a coalition against Albert, not simply an
outcome of his depression and his wife's determination to monopolize the
children.

(Second day.) This evening there was a wonderful demonstration of how a
child's inner propulsions can crystallize and make evident the patterns of feeling
and behavior in a family, in spite of what the parents might wish to show an
observer. At about a quarter to nine the Metzes and I were on the porch watching
TV when Myra suddenly raised the problem of an increase in her weekly allowance. She gets $2.37 a week and wants $3.75. She said her mother had promised
her this, so she asked her father. Her father put her off, saying, "Let's talk about
it. Let's think about it." She said, "I need the money," and he said, "I do, too."
Mrs. Metz said yes, she had agreed to a raise, but added that she didn't say
when it was going to take effect. I think she said it would probably be when
school began again, but Myra insisted that she needs it now because it costs her
so much to go to the movies—because of the combined carfare and admission
price. In order to get her father to consent to an increase, Myra threw herself on
him, kissing him and throwing her arms around him vigorously and persistently.
He laughed and pushed her away; although he kissed her once, he refused to
give in. She then turned on her mother and assailed her in the same way, but her
mother did not yield either. Mother and father told her to go into the kitchen and
get some ice cream and finish drying the dishes—they punctuated their commands with a certain amount of laughter and irritation—but Myra was oblivious
to their wishes. At last she did yield and went into the kitchen, but from there

she kept up a drumfire of demand for an increase in her allowance. Her parents told her to keep quiet, but she did not. Once she smiled at me slyly when she thought her parents couldn't see her, but her mother noticed it and told her to stop laughing. Her father, who had been sitting on the sofa, moved over to the chair closest to the TV.

Myra came back to the porch and her chief preoccupation then was to get her mother to say that she loved her and liked her. Her mother told her to go get her father some ice cream. She brought it to him, but in handing it to him, she let it fall on the floor. She picked it up, took it back to the kitchen and came out again with another ice cream stick. Myra continued to try to get her mother to say she loved her and liked her, but her mother, half laughing, half serious, refused. It is difficult to characterize the interchange. Myra constantly threw herself against her mother, nuzzling her, lying on her, throwing her arms around her, kissing her, snuggling up to her. When I left at ten o'clock the mother had not yet yielded, although Myra had been at her between forty-five minutes and an hour.

In her onslaught Myra showed a mingling of anxiety, hostility and playfulness. Hostility was evident in the persistent attacks, and playfulness appeared in the changes of expression on her face. Every once in a while Mrs. Metz would throw Myra off rather violently, and once she slapped her on the bottom. She tried to spank her, but Myra resisted. All this was done in a fairly good spirit, but Mrs. Metz absolutely refused to give Myra what she wanted, which was to say that she liked her. The important thing here is that Mrs. Metz makes a distinction between loving and liking. She says she always loves her children, but when she is angry with them, she doesn't like them. So it was more important to Myra for her mother to say she liked her than to say she loved her. Myra covered her mother's face with kisses, but her mother did not kiss Myra until just before I left.

While Myra was behaving this way. her father was watching TV, but every once in a while he would turn around and snarl and tell her to stop, but she would not. Once or twice her mother called upon him to interfere, which he did not. There was no doubt that the mother was Myra's principal target and that her father was shut out.

What has happened? In front of a stranger, Myra asks her parents for a raise in her allowance and accuses them of not keeping a promise. (This is a public degradation of her parents—if one wants to see it that way!) Myra tries to win her father by making love to him, but fails. (This is a public demonstration of strength and distrust by her father.) Next Myra throws herself on her mother, but her mother does not yield. (A public demonstration of strength and distrust by her mother.) We understand that one reason why both parents resist is that they assume the observer knows that Myra's histrionics have nothing to do with love or affection in any fundamental sense.

Following her failures, and perceiving that her parents are angry, Myra tries to reconstitute herself with her mother, but Mrs. Metz will have none of it. Myra does not try to be reconciled with her father. He is angry, ashamed and withdrawn.

The next day Mrs. Metz told me she was very much annoyed, and the neighbors were outraged at Myra's behavior: they could hear her.

There are several more points to be emphasized:

1. Myra rarely goes near her father, yet when she wants more money she throws herself on him.

2. Though Myra sees the pecuniary possibilities in my presence and tries to turn them to account, she miscalculates; she gambles and loses. Then,

using the very means ("love") she had employed to get money, she tries to redeem herself. It is as if a counterfeiter were trying to pay his bail with the money that got him in trouble.

3. Myra is extremely sensitive to her mother, but she does not attempt to reconstitute herself with her father. He makes no attempt to reach her either, but snarls and withdraws to TV.

4. In spite of everything, the parents do not really go to extremes; they do not try to shame Myra, though she tries to shame them. They protect her.

5. The like/love contrast is a disciplinary technique, but also a tease.

Under what conditions can a child try to put his parents on the spot like this in front of a stranger? Under what conditions can he exploit love? Under what conditions is a father isolated, as we see him here?

When a parent's power is not assured and when keeping up appearances begins to take precedence over family order, a child can attempt to embarrass its parents in front of a stranger. In an exploitive society, where people are also vulnerable because they want love, and love can be used to use them, a child—or anyone—can exploit love to get what he wants. When love begins to take precedence over order and discipline in the family, the entire structure of power is altered and the child's power can increase.* When the father, in general, is not involved in children's affairs but they are turned over to his wife, he will tend to be isolated from the children. This would be "structural" isolation. But there is also "manipulative" isolation, where, though fatherly involvement is possible, he is excluded through complex maneuvering. This is the situation in the Metz family, and I shall discuss it at some length later on.

The love-but-not-like ritual is not unique to the Metz family; it is normal, middle-class pathology and belongs to the large category of rituals called "Held in Purgatory for Love," in which somebody keeps somebody else in torment until the latter regains the former's affections. Yet, though the ritual is familiar, I have the impression I witnessed an exaggerated form of it, and I believe it took that form because of years of rehearsing and because Mrs. Metz is as anxious about her daughter's love as her daughter is about hers.

When, three days later, I took the Metzes to dinner and then for a drive, I had further opportunity to study the relationship between the three.

(Sixth day.) I took the Metzes to dinner at a restaurant in the neighborhood this evening. Mrs. Metz had filet mignon; Mr. Metz and I had veal cutlet. Myra and her mother got into a long-drawn-out discussion of whether she should order turkey or chicken. There was some kind of involved logic here, some of it having to do with how much Myra could eat. But she ended up ordering half a chicken. Since she could not eat it all, part was eaten by her father and the rest was left. Throughout the dinner, when Myra had anything to say, she talked to her mother. Mr. Metz talked briefly about his job and how successful he is selling desk blotters. We had a very pleasant time. There were no arguments, no flare-ups—ac-

* Though love can be used to control the child and even rob him of independence, I believe it is true that in our culture, the shift in the ideology and structure of parental control from order and discipline, backed by authority, to control based largely on exchange of love between parents and children (exchange of libidinal supplies, as psychoanalysts have put it) has placed a new instrument of power in the hands of children.

tually, when Albert is not around, everything is much quieter, on the whole. Mrs. Metz went through half an enormous sweet potato, ate plenty of bread sticks with butter and had a rich carbohydrate dessert. I believe she was supposed to start dieting today. She and I ordered pastries from the pastry tray, and Mr. Metz and Myra had ice cream. Myra was very quiet, and once when she raised her voice a little, her mother scolded her. She was really very ladylike, without seeming stiff. Mr. Metz was his usual smiling self. After dinner, Mrs. Metz and Myra went into the furniture store next door to look at a green chair, but weren't there very long. Mr. Metz and I waited outside. I cannot remember what we talked about.

When the women came out we got into my car and they asked me where I would like to go, since Mrs. Metz had been talking before dinner of showing me the town. I said I had seen everything in town, and that it was up to them, I would take them wherever they wanted to go. So, she suggested the falls, which was vetoed by Mr. Metz, who said, "It's too late." But Mrs. Metz and Myra wanted to go, so I said, "Well, what shall we do?" The females said, "Let's go to the falls," and Mr. Metz was silent. So we drove out.

As we stood watching the falls, Myra was close to her mother, I was next to her, and her father was standing on the other side of me. (This is the evening when Mrs. Metz spoke about the honeymoon.) Myra took her mother's arms and put them around her own shoulders; during the evening she also hugged and kissed her mother. Their relationship is obviously a very close one; I would even say warm. Myra touched her father only once—when, in talking about needing her mother and father, she dropped her mother's arm and went around to her father's side as we walked along. . . .

On the way home Mr. Metz sat in the front of the car with me and mother and daughter sat together on the back seat. . . .

Several times during the evening Mrs. Metz referred to the Bauman family as full of love, or maybe she said, "We Metzes are full of love."

Mrs. Metz and her daughter did not, because they could not, abandon their entanglement just because an observer happened to be present. Why should they? Is there anything wrong with love between mother and daughter; anything strange in a daughter's preferring her mother? And isn't Mrs. Metz obviously irresistibly love-valent, anyway? And isn't Myra, by devoting herself simply to her mother, proving this to the observer? And just because an observer is there, can Mr. Metz suddenly erupt out of his domestic exile to fling himself between them? What more natural than when a daughter has anything to say she should say it to her mother—while her father "talks business" to the visitor? The evening was a mother-daughter evening: Myra discussed with her mother what she should eat; at dinner, if she had anything to say, she said it to her mother; when she talked it was her mother who decided that it was too loud; it was Myra and her mother who went to look at the chair without even asking the father to come along; the women decided, over the objections of the father, that we would go to the falls; and all through the evening Myra stuck close to her mother, except for one moment when she went around to her father to show him she needed him as well. Her mother did not command Myra to stick close, but Myra doesn't need orders any more, for she has learned that until she is married, life is to be very much a love affair between her and her mother.

(Seventh day.) After dinner, when Mr. and Mrs. Metz and I went onto the porch to watch TV, Myra came out and sat next to her mother, then she lay down and put her head on her mother's thigh. She took hold of her mother's hand, put it on her own head and asked her mother to scratch it. When Mrs. Metz got tired of this, Myra pulled her hand back and also ran her fingers over her mother's arm, until Mrs. Metz became irritated and complained that Myra was beginning to act up again. She asked her husband to put a stop to it, so he told Myra to stop bothering her mother.

The second time Mrs. Metz used him as a disciplinarian was in order to get Myra off the phone, and he did. When Myra got off the phone she came and sat down on the sofa, away from her mother, and began a long yarn about wanting to sleep at a girl friend's house. Although her father was there, Myra addressed herself to her mother and the two locked horns in a long wrangle until at last Mrs. Metz became very angry, yelled at Myra and told her to go to bed, and off she went in a huff, saying "All right!" Her mother threatened to spank Myra and continued to talk angrily after Myra had gone to bed. She told her husband she thought the whole thing was a cock-and-bull story. Myra overheard and protested it was true . . . Mrs. Metz told Myra she was not going to sleep at her friend's: "That's the end of it." Mr. Metz just listened.

(A little while after Myra had gone to bed Mr. Metz, at his wife's request, sat next to her on the sofa and then put his head down on her thigh, without request.)

Mr. Metz is usually merely a spectator of the activity of his wife and daughter unless he is ordered into action by his wife when the tension gets to be too much for her and she wants to straighten Myra out. Only when his wife asks him to intervene does one discover that he really has been listening; otherwise, he seems as involved as the furniture. What can be the content and response of such listening? How does a person manage to sit by for years, knowing what is going on but doing nothing? He manages because he has been pushed out of life or withdrawn from it; and it must be that such a person hears as from far away, as his family breaks upon his ears like the sound of distant surf.

In the observations I have just been discussing, Mrs. Metz twice asks her husband to control Myra. Why didn't he do it without being asked, and when he was asked, why was he so obedient? Since I never asked Mr. Metz, I can attempt only a cautious answer. I think it is obvious that he stayed out of the situation because what was restraining him was stronger than what might attract him. The restraints were, first, his tendency toward detachment, and second, the obsessive relationship between mother and daughter, which draws a circle around them. On the other hand, since nothing had occurred during my stay to suggest why he should be attracted into a discussion or dispute between his wife and daughter, I am reduced to saying that although from my observation I can see what *restrains* Mr. Metz from taking part in mother-daughter activity, I cannot, for the life of me, see what might *attract* him! What, then, makes him respond at once to his wife's request to intervene? After all, if he can say no to eating out, to the movies, to going to the falls, to sitting in the backyard, to buying doughnuts, etc., why doesn't he say no to this? The minimal answer is that he is more willing to discipline his daughter than to do most other things.

Actually Mrs. Metz takes most of the responsibility for disciplining Myra, and what she says in the following reflects what really goes on:

Mrs. Metz does not believe that mother and father should punish the child differently, and she deprecates mothers who leave punishment to the father. She says it isn't fair because it always puts the father in a bad light. If there is any punishing to be done in the Metz family, she says, she does it, if the child's misbehavior occurs when she is present. When Albert was behaving very, very badly and they did not yet know he was sick, she called his behavior to her husband's attention and he did the scolding. (While I was with the Metzes, nothing occurred that I would call punishment, just scolding, and Mrs. Metz did almost all of that.) It isn't fair to the husband, she says, to put the burden of punishment on him. Some of her friends, when the husband comes home, will go to him and say, "Oh, Johnny gave me such a terrible time today"—and egg him on to punish the children. She doesn't feel this should happen.

In the present instance Mrs. Metz gets very annoyed with Myra for tormenting her, to the point where Mrs. Metz calls on her husband to put a stop to it. It is reminiscent of a child's calling on a parent to stop his brother or sister from persecuting him. "Save me from Myra," she seems to be saying, "because I cannot do it myself!" And Mr. Metz does.

This is the second time we have seen Myra use the outward show of affection in a hostile way beyond affection's true meaning. In trying to get an increase in her allowance, Myra employed "love"; and afterward for nearly an hour, she badgered her mother to say, "I like you." In the present observation, Myra leads her mother to think she wants caressing, but she really wants to annoy her.

When *awake,* Myra sometimes shows a tendency to mix something hostile in her love communications with her mother, and while her father is *asleep* he does the same thing—gripping his wife hard and pursuing her when she tries to escape. It is not that the Metzes do not love each other, but that their love is baneful, too. And who is capable of "pure" love? Who among us has not at some time been hurt or hurt others by baneful love, by love mixed with contempt, by love polluted by deception, by love made weak by reservations, by love embittered by nothingness, domination or rage?

Aware of such contamination, Freud considered the mingling of opposites a characteristic of some "instincts," such as the sexual urge, for example. That love is often poisoned is a common-enough observation, yet I do not believe that such pollution is inherent in human "instinctual" organization, but rather that it is a product of culture, a residue of the irritating day-to-day experience of people with one another. Love-with-contempt, love-with-lies, love-with-reservations, love-with-nothingness, love-and-anger—a menagerie of phantasmic sensations—are the product of a culture that cannot let love die but lacks the ability to keep it alive; a culture where the ideal of love subsists in a mythology that never expresses more than a hope. In a culture where people are bred to feel contempt for themselves and taught that to lie is to survive; where they so fear exploitation that relationships are hemmed in by reservations and where people struggle constantly against nothingness and anger, for many the effort to love is a forlorn hope; and what is achieved by most is an amalgam of what they feel about themselves and what they hope for from others. The phenomenology of love yields merely the understanding that for many, love is a dear myth rotted by culture. If a person seeks the ontology, the absolute of what love *is,* he finds first *himself* and then, too often, the catastrophe of his hope. This is central to the relationship between Myra and her mother.

Myra and Her Mother

INTRODUCTORY OBSERVATIONS

(First day.) Myra came in with Mary while Mrs. Metz and I were sitting on the porch. Myra is charming and has a very, very sweet and appealing manner. I took to her right away. I think the first thing Mrs. Metz said to Myra was, "Oh, your teeth are yellow"—apparently because Myra had been eating potato chips. This did not appear to faze Myra, who, by the way, has a reputation for letting everything roll off her like water off a duck's back. For example, according to Mrs. Metz, although an emotionally disturbed couple that used to live around the corner upset Albert terribly, Myra seemed unruffled. She apologized for coming home late. She had been expected home at three-thirty, and here it was a quarter to four. She explained why she didn't call up and her mother said, "Well, fifteen minutes isn't very late."

Apparently the reason Myra explained her fifteen-minute tardiness was that Mrs. Metz, like so many people in her city, is terribly afraid of muggings, rape, etc., so that she insists that her daughter keep in close touch with her. If Myra is supposed to call up at a certain time, she must call, no matter where she is. (During my week at the Metzes', Myra never called up to say she would be late and I did not hear her discuss the matter with her mother again.)

Soon after Myra came in, her mother asked her to remove the glasses from which Mrs. Metz and I had been drinking limeade, and Myra did, without protest.

She and Mary sat with us on the porch chatting quietly for a long time, partly with Mrs. Metz, partly with each other, and occasionally with me. Mrs. Metz calls Mary her adopted daughter and kept interfering in her affairs as her own mother might.

Mrs. Metz complained that Myra's lipstick was put on badly, but as far as I could see it was all right. Myra now borrowed a cosmetic from Mary that covers lipstick and used it to cover her lips entirely. Mrs. Metz began to worry that the stuff was poisonous and would harm Myra—maybe she was allergic to it or something. So Myra calmly wiped it off and the original lipstick emerged.

Then Mrs. Metz upbraided Mary for wearing lipstick because Mary's mother does not let her unless she is going out. Mrs. Metz told her emphatically to wipe it off, and Mary did.

Myra was going to a barbecue in the evening and would not be home for dinner, and she was not going to baby-sit.

On first meeting, I found Myra quite appealing. In the presence of the stranger—the observer—Myra shows that she loves and respects her mother. When Mrs. Metz acts with authority, Myra obeys. Myra takes the reference to her yellow teeth impassively, and obediently wipes the "poisonous" cosmetic off her lips. Through such hints, Mrs. Metz suggests to Myra that she needs her mother to guide and protect her. Both girls are very quiet and Mary permits Mrs. Metz's intervention as "adoptive mother," though her own is at home and well.

Mrs. Metz says her children are always models, always very well behaved and would never do a thing without asking her. They never broke anything in the house, not even a little bit of bric-a-brac.

Arrangements were made for Mary to sleep over tonight, after the barbecue.

The kids had a musical-comedy record on the phonograph. Mrs. Metz asked them to play it loud enough for her to hear, but they turned the volume up so high that she asked them to turn it down a bit, and Myra came in and asked very solicitously whether it was all right.

In toning down the record Myra acts thoughtfully—something her mother longs for. But even more: Myra does it in front of an audience—the observer. So while her mother protects, Myra reciprocates with considerateness and obedience; and the two enact for me a production entitled "How Myra Loves and Respects Her Mother." Myra is sensitive at this point to her mother's wishes, fantasies and hopes, and when it suits her she can, without a word from her mother, perform as she has been taught—as she has been sensitized to react.

Mrs. Metz showed me the gift *she* had just bought for Myra's birthday—a silver locket. It was very handsome.

It takes care, thoughtfulness and affection to pick out a nice gift, especially when you are like the Metzes, who do not have much money; but though Mrs. Metz got a pretty gift for Myra, what she bought for Albert was ugly and junky. Myra has a large room all to herself with pictures on the wall of rock-and-roll singers and movie and TV personalities; Albert slept on the porch. Albert calls his sister "the Queen"—and the queen belongs to mother. Note that Mrs. Metz didn't say *she and her husband* shopped for Myra's gift or that *they* enjoyed picking it out. What comes to Myra comes as from her mother, even though her father provides the money.

(Second day.) When I got to the house this morning the record player was going, and Myra and Mary were still in bed and having a wild time under the covers. Mrs. Metz told me this is typical. The kids stayed in bed until about ten-thirty, until Mrs. Metz, very irritated after repeatedly trying and failing to get them up, at last routed them out. She also got them to fix up the room, after complaining, with considerable annoyance, because they hadn't done it properly.

During this time Mrs. Metz, in spite of the fact that she said she wasn't feeling well, went down to the basement and got the clothes off the line and washed the breakfast dishes.

At last the kids emerged, all lipsticked and carefully dressed, and they went about preparing their own breakfast very efficiently. They had apricot juice, scrambled eggs, toast and chocolate milk. Mrs. Metz sat at the table with them and they talked.

The atmosphere at breakfast was very pleasant. Mrs. Metz sat chatting with the girls, seeming to take pleasure in having the kids around. There is some kind of balancing here: Myra's kisses, perhaps, take the place of real concern for her mother. The fact that Mrs. Metz can sit and talk to Myra about feminine—and youthful—things and that Mrs. Metz can be hospitable to Mary, her "adoptive daughter," helps make life possible for Mrs. Metz.

Myra wanted to take out Mrs. Smith's baby today for two reasons—because she wanted to make some money and because Mrs. Metz wanted her to go to the store, and if she took out the baby she could use the carriage for the packages. So she called up Mrs. Smith but Mrs. Smith said she didn't need her today. Myra offered to take out the baby for nothing, but that didn't work out. The result was that Myra wouldn't do the shopping.

Here's the way this works. Today is Dollar Day on Broadway and Myra wanted to go up there with Mary and Mrs. Fuller, because Mrs. Fuller wants to buy some school clothes for Mary. Since Myra was going to Broadway, Mrs. Metz wanted her to buy a few things, but Myra refused, telling her mother to go to the corner grocery store. Mrs. Metz accepted this without protest.

While the girls were finishing up the bedroom, Mrs. Metz, who had just finished washing the other breakfast dishes, now washed theirs.

Mary went home and Myra changed her clothes. She came back into the kitchen wearing a shirt that was tied up so that her midriff was bare, and asked her mother if she could go to Broadway like that. Her mother said no, so Myra went back and rearranged the shirt to cover her midriff. When she left the house, she kissed her mother good-bye.

Myra fixes up her room, like many kids her age, only after being badgered by her mother; she adjusts her clothes to suit her mother; leaves the breakfast dishes (she never washes dishes); refuses to shop for her mother, but kisses her mother good-bye. Myra is willing to meet her mother halfway; if she could have taken out the Smith's baby, she would have gone to the store for her mother. As a matter of fact, she was willing to take out the baby for nothing just to accommodate her mother. Such egoistic solicitude, where one's own comfort is in the forefront, is identical with pragmatic ethics and evaporates when the would-be giver sees nothing in the transaction for himself. This is simple common sense in our culture, or as Fromm puts it, "socially patterned defect."

Since Myra seems to be a relatively average American girl, rather well adapted to a corrupt culture, one of our objectives should be to explore the problem of adaptation to corruption.

I have reviewed some observations which show Myra giving in to her mother on some points and not yielding on others, and since this raises the general question of acquiescing and resisting, I examine it in the next section.

ACQUIESCING AND RESISTING

Under what circumstances does a child resist his parents and under what circumstances does he give in? (1) A child will resist his parents most when they intervene most in his life; if parents do not intervene, the question of resistance becomes irrelevant. For example, Pilagá Indian parents will intervene in marriage choice but never in the child's sexual life before marriage; therefore the question of acquiescing to parents' feelings about sex before marriage is irrelevant. (2) A child will resist his parents most when they interfere with impulse gratification, but will resist least when his parents want to help him along. (3) A child will resist least what the parents want him to do when it improves the child's self-concept or raises his status (which amounts to the same thing), and will resist when no enhancement of self is involved or where it is actually degraded. (4) A child will resist his parents when, though resisting causes the child's inconvenience, he sees no advantage in acquiescing. (5) A child will resist when he has little to lose but much to gain by it. This seems a general social law that applies to everybody. (6) A child will resist his parents when it seems to him that what adults want him to do is more for the benefit of the adult than the child. This separation is most likely to occur in cultures where mutuality of adult-child interests is being lost, and/or children distrust adults.

Among the Pilagá Indians, parents do not intervene much in their child's life after the cataclysmic intervention of weaning. The child's sex life is not blocked, he may eat when he pleases if there is food, go to bed and get up when he pleases, play with whom he pleases, and so on. No feeding* or sleeping problems among them! When food is scarce a Pilagá child cannot take what he wants and may be compelled to give some of what he has to other members of the family. All through childhood, all through life, there is constant insistence on sharing food. On the other hand, nobody intervenes when children attack one another.

A baby in our culture will reject the bottle, want to feed himself and be happy to "go" on the potty, instead of in his diaper, when these accomplishments give him increased value in his parents' eyes.† Yet the drag of infantile pleasures holds back the upward pull of status and approval and may make it difficult even for biological maturation to assert itself. There is a period in a child's life when a way has to be found to prove to it that "upward mobility" and enhancement of his image in his parents' eyes are more gratifying than ministering to his infantile impulses. Adults—the adult world—has to demonstrate to the child that in growing up there is something in it for him. Much of the difficulty in getting a child of our culture to do what we want derives from the sheer magnitude of adult intervention in his life and from the fact that that intervention seems to take away pleasures without adequate compensation. It seems perfectly natural for a child to resist an adult demand when he sees nothing in it for him if he yields and feels he has nothing to lose if he does not. This is the economic calculus of self-interest, when love is not strong enough to win the child to the parents' point of view.

If a child is given unconditional love or none, he has nothing to lose by resisting; and he has nothing to lose if he can erase the ill effects of his opposition by some specific act—like showering his mother with kisses. Where love, or its outward gestures, can buy off *all* parental complaint, a child can do what he pleases. This rarely occurs, even in the Metz family; yet, as we have seen, and as we shall see further, the display of love enables Myra to do a great deal.

In every culture the dialectic between one's own needs and the needs of others works out in a different way, and in our culture every family has its own particular form of it, its own variant of the general cultural dialectic. In the Metz family Myra is almost completely freed of the requirement to be demonstrative to her father; yet, though demonstrative to her mother, Myra does little to meet her mother's deepest need—for the kind of love and understanding that would reach past Mrs. Metz's complex inability to express her own yearnings. Only a sensitive psychoanalyst could do this—it certainly is beyond Myra. At the same time, adaptation to our culture requires that Myra—perhaps any child—turn her back on her mother's deep-

* See J. Henry and Joann Boggs, "Child Rearing, Culture and the Natural World," *Psychiatry*, Vol. XV (1962), pp. 261–71.

† In his *General Introduction to Psychoanalysis*, Freud credits Lou Andreas with the insight that in the anal stage a child "first" learns to renounce instinctual pleasures for the sake of adult approval. Though I do not believe we know when a child *begins* to give up infantile pleasures in order to "achieve value" in adult eyes, I do believe that this kind of exchange is the fundamental factor urging a child toward social maturation.

est unmet needs in order to achieve her own goals. It also stands to reason
that if Myra had the capacity to really help her mother, if she had that
necessary insight, Myra would be unfit for those feats of egoism so necessary to a consuming culture of shallow personal involvements.

The problems to be examined in the relationship between Myra and her
mother have now been outlined: to examine the interplay between yielding
and resisting; between disciplining and giving in; between sincerity and
façade; between selfishness and solicitude. Studying them in the relationship between Myra and her mother, we approach some central problems of
mankind.

STRIVING TO BE MOTHER AND DAUGHTER

Needs of the self and needs of others. An ideal life for an average person
in our culture is one in which he gives others what affection and approval
they need and, in return, gets the affection and approval he needs. This is
perfect equilibrium in a pecuniary culture. Let us consider what happens in
the more usual case—when the equation does not balance. If a parent feels
that he gives more to his children than he gets from them, then in whatever
he does for them, he may express the attitude, "You don't deserve it"; and
they may reciprocate with the feeling, "My dad does it grudgingly," or "My
mother thinks I owe her my life for whatever she does for me," or "What
my parents give me with one hand they take back with the other." A parent
who feels he is not compensated for what he gives may decide to give minimal affection, or he may wait for gestures from his children before giving
any sign of affection himself. This would be pretty serious pathology, and in
such a family, communication may be reduced to recrimination. It is also
possible to deny that one bestows affection while in the very act of giving,
in order to avoid the pain of no return. Then acts of affection appear as
accidental, so that the one who has given can understand why he gets nothing back—the other person did not know that affection was intended. The
danger here is that the one who gives may not quite accept the fact that he
concealed his intention so well, and therefore not forgive the other person
for not perceiving it. "Couldn't you *see* I loved you?" is the unspoken reproach.

Another difficulty is that a parent may be unable to teach his child the
precise value he places on what he does, the precise currency in which he
hopes to be paid, or even the very idea that he expects to be repaid. If I fling
myself in love on my child, how does he know he is supposed to do the
same to me? If I give him love, how is he to know, unless I tell him, that
what I want in return is not only his kisses but his kindness? If I "slave" for
him, how does he know I want him to love me for it? Why should he "naturally" make this interpretation? Some people think their love messages
carry their own decoding key. Children have to be taught to decode, interpret and generalize their parents' messages of love. What I get in return for
what I give is partly a function of my own comment on it. Unless, as a
parent puts his arms around his child, he lets him know in some way that
he wants the child to do the same, the child will remain limp in his arms,
until the child, in its primordial search for meaning, deciphers the parent's

message, which is, "Please embrace me, too," and reciprocates. While it is true that babies embrace their parents, the world around, it is not because they want to pay their parents back for parental embraces or because they perceive that the parent needs it, but because the *baby* needs it. But if the baby does not feel that it needs the parent *in that particular way*, there is no reason why it should do it spontaneously.

What we all search for in the communications of others is some sign of the intention of the communication, regardless of what it is about. The first time a friend called me "pea brain" I was angry and perplexed, but I soon realized that this insult is a masculine way of expressing affection in our culture. My friend expected me to know that such insults belong to the class of "nonsexual, masculine, affectional, joking relationships." How does a child discover that a hug "belongs in the class of gestures signifying love and should be returned in kind"? And how does he ever learn that hugging, kissing and words of affection ought to be requited with *solicitude* for the person hugging and kissing him, provided that the person is *next of kin only*? How does he learn that the hug which makes him feel good because *he* needs it expresses the other person's need to get a hug from him?

Partly because of such complexities, giving and getting affection in our culture get mixed with the ambiguity inherent in the process itself. Since in our culture we cannot help expressing emotional needs within our economic framework, and since all systems suffer the disabilities of their own paradoxes, we do too, in emotional life, and we call these disabilities *ambivalences*. If we give but feel incompletely requited, if we do a minimum in expectation of not being adequately repaid, if we are paid in the wrong currency for the "commodity" we have "delivered," then hostility ensues. Hostility develops also if we provide a false or adulterated product, if we deliver a commodity but hide it under a misleading label, if we do not deliver the expected merchandise but claim payment as if we had, and so on. These do not exhaust the possibilities of the economic analogy, but they do serve to illustrate the calculus of feeling in a capitalist culture, under the heading of "needs of the self and needs of others."

In the pages that follow, I study further the relationship between Myra and her mother and there we shall see that, as Kierkegaard has said, "existence is striving." * While encounters between Mrs. Metz and her daughter usually express Mrs. Metz's efforts to be a good mother, and while it is less clear that Myra is striving to be a good daughter, I wouldn't rule out Myra's willingness to be a good daughter, nor would I urge that she is much different from other fourteen-year-old girls of her social class.

Between Myra and her mother it is always Myra who starts the hugging, kissing and snuggling. It is therefore understandable that Myra should be edgy—always on the verge of smashing the image of the affectionate child, and that her feelings are likely to find expression in hurtful disregard of her mother. I think that much of Myra's demonstrativeness comes from anxiety —that since her parents are not spontaneously demonstrative, she is worried. Mrs. Metz, apparently so outgoing when dealing with other people's

* In *Concluding Unscientific Postscript*, trans. by D. F. Swenson and W. Lowrie (Princeton, N.J., Princeton University Press, 1941).

children, has her own daughter come to her. The reader already has had one example of this in the love affair between Myra and her mother at the falls. Here is another:

On the way back [from Mr. Metz's place of work] Myra had her arm around her mother, and at a certain point, Mrs. Metz had her hand on Myra. Myra sat with her arm around her mother, and, I think, at one point snuggled up to her. When we got home Myra snuggled up and kissed her father.

I find that when Myra leaves the house my record always reads that "Myra kissed her mother good-bye."

In the account of the relationship between mother and daughter that will follow, other opportunities arise to examine the accuracy of my impression that Mrs. Metz waits for Myra to start the expressions of affection. Meanwhile, here is one more observation:

Myra came into the house and sat down very close to her mother. They kissed, and Mrs. Metz stroked Myra several times; they seemed to enjoy the physical contact very much. A little later Myra moved away about six inches. It seems to me that they were genuinely affectionate to each other.

This is the only record I have in which Myra and her mother seemed to turn toward each other *together;* as always, the overtures were made by Myra.

The best illustration of the complexity of the relationship between these two comes from the four-hour-long shopping tour the day before Albert's visit.

The Significance of Shopping

(Fourth day.) I arrived at the Metzes' this morning at about eight-fifty. The arrangement was that I would get there at nine in order for us to have an early breakfast and then leave so that Myra could go shopping with us and get back in time to go to the beach this afternoon. When I got there Myra still was in bed and her mother said, "I thought I would let her sleep this morning," but shortly after I arrived she woke her up. I heard Myra say, "Tell me you love me." "I don't love you." "Tell me you like me." "I love you." Then there were sounds of kissing.

Mrs. Metz had had a bad night; the pain in her thighs had gone but she couldn't sleep, anyway. She wasn't hungry and didn't eat breakfast.

Myra was so long in coming in that her mother called out to ask what was taking so long, and Myra answered that she was having a hard time setting her hair. At last she emerged, wearing shorts and a shirt with a flowered pattern. She had so much lipstick on that her mother got very annoyed and demanded that she wipe it off. She wiped some of it off.

(Myra decided to make "egg in the hole"—an egg fried in the hole of a piece of bread.) She gave one to me. It was pretty good and her mother made me another. Myra always gets up and leaves the table as soon as she is finished eating, no matter whether other people are finished or not, and this breakfast was no exception. . . . Somewhere along in here Myra went and sat in her mother's lap and nuzzled her. . . .

(We left the house to go shopping somewhat after ten and our first stop was the dime store, where a number of purchases were made.)

All the purchases were put into a bag, which Mrs. Metz carried. (She carried all the packages we accumulated.) We went into two ladies'-wear stores, and each time, Myra put her purse on the floor next to the packages her mother had been carrying. When we left she took her purse but not the packages. Mrs. Metz picked them up without protest.

In the five-and-ten Myra and her mother got into a long argument about what a lollipop is. Mrs. Metz said she wanted to buy something she could suck on at home or in the movies; and she found round candy which was a "pop"-something-or-other. This set off a discussion about Mrs. Metz's having sent kids out to buy lollipops when they had a scavenger hunt some time ago. All came back with suckers, but these round things were really what she had wanted. Mother and daughter had quite an argument about this. Mrs. Metz bought five of what she called lollipops and then was disappointed that they were so much cheaper at Miller's, a big supermarket.

(After the five-and-ten we went to a store to buy a pair of jeans for Albert.)

Next we went to a ladies'-wear store where Myra wanted to buy a coat of simulated fur. Her mother warned her repeatedly that she would have to pay for it out of her baby-sitter money but Myra said, "Well, you will add something to it," and Mrs. Metz said she would. Myra went about looking at the coats, without intervention from her mother. The coats were obviously made for women much older than Myra, for when she tried them on she looked like a little girl dressed up in her mother's coat, but Mrs. Metz thought them beautiful. Myra picked a dark one and it was set aside for a $3.50 down payment. The full price was something like $60. Mrs. Metz said to me, "Myra knows what she wants."

The transaction was carried out in a businesslike way, with Myra running the whole thing, Mrs. Metz sitting in a chair waiting for Myra to come and show her how she looked. When the order had been written up, Mrs. Metz said, "Well, that's all," but Myra wanted her to go to Fantan to see something Myra had looked at before. First Mrs. Metz said no, but Myra wheedled her into going by saying, "I just want to show it to you—I won't even try it on." Well, the obvious happened. We went to Fantan and stayed there about half an hour while Myra tried on a whole lot of stuff but ended up with nothing. Mrs. Metz kept protesting to me and Myra how little money she had.

When we finished there, we went to Miller's. Myra behaved like a small child, asking for all kinds of things that caught her eye. She wanted a special kind of cookie her mother refused to let her have, but which I decided I would get for her. She wanted a number of other things, only some of which I can remember—Hawaiian Punch, for example, but her mother turned it down because it cost thirty-seven cents a can. She said she liked black olives but her mother refused to buy them; there were a couple of other things Mrs. Metz did buy but would not have bought if Myra had not picked them out. Myra roamed about, showing very little interest in what her mother was buying, but looking at the shelves at random to see if there was anything she might like. Myra asked for some cheese and her mother bought it, saying it was a real luxury. As we passed the toilet-paper counter Mrs. Metz said to me, "I can never pass this by," and bought some toilet paper.

We got home with five huge bags full of groceries. I was in a quandary about what to do about all these bags, because although I probably could have carried them in all by myself, it would have distorted the family picture. So I carried in one bag and waited to see what would happen. Mrs. Metz carried in one. Myra carried in nothing, but went directly to the telephone to get in touch with Flossie, one of her friends. Mrs. Metz brought in another bag and then yelled at Myra to get off the phone. First she asked Myra to get off, and when Myra didn't she screamed, and Myra screamed back but got off. Mrs. Metz wanted Myra to help her, and Myra went toward the door with her and then said, "I can't carry that stuff," so Mrs. Metz carried the last bag while Myra held the door open.

Later I asked Mrs. Metz, "Is Myra a strong child?" and she acted as if she didn't understand what I meant. I said, "Well, is she a strong, heathy, normal child or is she weak?" Mrs. Metz replied, "She is a perfectly strong, healthy girl," so I asked, "Well, then, why didn't she help you carry in the groceries?" First she said Myra expected me to carry in the packages, but Mrs. Metz had explained to her that maybe I was the sort of man who couldn't carry heavy things—lots of men can't carry heavy things. Then she said Myra often helps her when she comes home with things. She added, "On the other hand, I wouldn't let her carry anything very heavy," but she ended up by saying there is no doubt that Myra is spoiled. I explained to Mrs. Metz why I didn't carry the packages—because I am studying the way the family would be living without me. Mrs. Metz understood and said she wanted things to go on as if I were not there.

Mrs. Metz was very tired, hungry and irritable when we got home, but she put everything away herself. During most of this scene Myra was simply not in evidence—I don't know where she was. Mrs. Metz wanted Myra to carry two very small packages of detergent to the basement, and Myra snapped, "What do you want?" and when Mrs. Metz told her, Myra said she would do it, but although her mother reminded her twice, Myra did not do it. She was just about to go out the front door when her mother called out, "How about taking these things down to the basement?" Myra grumbled in a very disagreeable way, and her mother said, "Oh, go ahead, I'll take them down."

While her mother was putting things away, Myra came into the kitchen and nibbled at some of the food we had bought and then said, "I've got to get going," meaning she had to get to her friend Flossie's house so that they could go to the beach together. She asked me if I would drive them to the beach and I said I would, but not before I had had something to eat. So Myra left by herself. All this time the atmosphere between mother and daughter had been charged, although after her outburst Mrs. Metz addressed Myra as "dear" and "darling," asking her if she wanted something to eat and offering her one thing or another. Myra was obviously very sore. I wondered what *she* was sore about.

After the argument had blown over and Myra was gone, her mother told me that she [Mrs. Metz] was very nervous because she was terribly hungry. She hadn't had anything to eat before we went shopping and we didn't get back until almost two o'clock, which means that she had been without food since eight o'clock the night before. She said she wouldn't be surprised if she started to menstruate again because she had carried the heavy bundles.

Myra begins her day by exacting from her mother an affirmation of love; thus repeating, where there seems to be *no* stress, the ritual performed the night (the second night of my visit) Myra made a scene about her allowance: as Myra extorts the affirmation, her mother is assured that she is the center of her daughter's life. Kisses, audible down the corridor (from Myra's room to the kitchen), are a necessary part of the ritual.

Before we went shopping, Mrs. Metz and I waited and waited in the kitchen for Myra to come out of her room, but since, in her social class, it is absolutely essential, at fourteen, that hair be set and lipstick be put on, Myra could not be concerned with the possibility that we might be hungry and waiting. My presence and the anxiety of going shopping on Broadway, where everybody would be looking at her, made it necessary that Myra look just right. All this seems so healthy. Who would expect Myra to behave differently? Lipstick or no lipstick is a constant struggle in the Metz family, as it is in many American families of that class with girls Myra's age, but it is one of the issues on which Mrs. Metz seems to be able to get Myra to yield without trouble. It is relatively easy to remove lipstick, and Myra can also always do what she pleases about it when she is out of sight of her mother, anyway. It is one aspect of her life where it is not too inconvenient for Myra to be obedient.

From the moment Myra is awake, the day becomes one long narcissistic trance. She keeps us waiting for breakfast; she shows no interest in what her mother is buying, but wanders around in the stores; she models dozens of coats and suits in the women's-wear stores. She is as if governed by beams radiating from food, clothing and cosmetics. During this day Myra shows she is aware of her mother only when her mother makes commodities available to her; but the moment she is challenged to do something for her mother, she avoids her. As Myra steps fastidiously around the packages her mother has deposited on the floor of the ladies'-wear stores, retrieving only her own purse, it is as though she is stepping around filth—or danger. Homecoming is a climactic moment when the entire reality—or unreality —of the relationship between mother and daughter threatens for one frightening moment to come up out of the cellar: when this girl, who begs her mother to say she loves her and sits so sweetly on her mother's lap kissing and nuzzling, shows her mother where her mother really stands. And where does her mother stand? She stands between love and lovelessness on the ambiguous line between pretense and truth, on the cutting edge between half a loaf and a whole one, where hope dissolves in inner tears, where tears dry in the warmth of hope and where despair is quieted a little by the gestures of love. So Mrs. Metz takes pleasure in her daughter; she likes to watch her model clothes—Myra does it so well, and she is so pretty. Myra "knows what she wants"—and, her mother should have added, she knows how to get it. Myra's trying on clothes is a small narcissistic dream for both of them: the daughter absorbed in contemplating herself, and the mother contemplating herself in her daughter. Otherwise, why did she sit there for half an hour? Why did she enjoy her*self* so much?

The argument about suckers and lollipops has the kind of content most likely to fascinate two such narcissistic personalities as Myra and her mother—oral content. But it is also an argument for our time, for it marks the outer reach of minds oriented toward impulse release, fun and orality. There are many similar debates taking place all around us: the virtues of sirloin over rib roast; the fundamental differences between Coca-Cola and Pepsi-Cola; the advantages of Joe's for hamburgers as against Steve's for pizza, and so on. Since the debate is about the quality of impulse release that gives the most fun, the argument between Mrs. Metz and Myra expresses the metaphysics of our time, for just as philosophers in epochs of aspiration have discussed the difference between forms of being, so people in epochs of impulse release and fun will split hairs over the difference between a sucker and a lollipop. In such exchanges of "ideas," mother and daughter reach an understanding at the oral level. This is the nature of a narcissistic involvement: mother and daughter complement each other in their oral cravings, in their love-with-demonstrativeness-and-reservations, in their interest in clothes—Myra modeling, her mother admiring. But such an involvement leaves the need for love unsatisfied, and thinly veils the hostility caused by lack of it. Hence the incident of the five shopping bags and its sequel. It was an explosion of selfishness and despair; the moment

Myra was asked to do something that was inconveniently and inescapably for her mother, she became angry and intractable. Myra's helping herself to food while her mother puts away the groceries Myra had refused to bring in is the quintessence of defiant resistance, selfishness, irony and gall, and proves how strong Myra really is in that house.

It is now necessary to speculate a little about the relationship between what happened during those hours and the fact that Albert was due home next day. Mrs. Metz was thinking about Albert all day long and he may have been a reason for her not sleeping the night before. Some of her purchases—shirts, "junk" candy, jeans, and cheap hamburger—indicate that she must have had Albert on her mind as she shopped. Weary from sleeplessness and lack of food; harried by the anticipation of Albert's visit; feeling guilty, perhaps, about her responsibility for his illness; worried lest she do the same thing to her daughter; anxious that she might lose her love, such as it is; remembering that Albert had always been more considerate than Myra; and aware that whereas Albert was deprived (she was "stricter" with him), Myra is spoiled, Mrs. Metz reached the limit of her endurance. All day long she was reminded of Myra's callousness and indifference, while being fearful of the consequences of her own temper. At last, however, the anger broke out of her when Myra refused to lend a hand with the packages. Yet the realization that the violence of which she is capable would alienate Myra, and might even injure her, restrained Mrs. Metz, so that she let Myra off with just a short, moderate outburst. When we consider that she might have continued to scream at Myra until she brought in the packages or took down the detergent to the basement, or even have struck her, and when we consider that she let Myra have lunch without badgering her, we realize that Mrs. Metz does not hound her daughter. However, we must also remember that the next day, the only point at which she did not interfere with Albert was when he was hitting Myra.

A Concerned Mother and an Unconcerned Daughter

The next selection from the notes shows that a source of Myra's strength is her mother's genuine concern for her.

(Seventh day.) Mrs. Metz was in the backyard, just having finished taking in her wash. She said she was very tired because she had spent the day washing. Myra was sitting on the porch, in a long housecoat, underneath which, according to her mother, she wore a flimsy little nightdress of chiffon. Myra felt sick today, and she had a rash which her mother thought she got from the dirty water at the beach or from the sand thrown on her. Later in the evening her mother offered to give Myra a physic but Myra rejected it. Myra bounced around every once in a while, giving no indication of being sick, and when the Metzes and I were looking at TV, Myra carried on a very animated phone conversation for about half an hour.

Let's follow her through. She sat on the porch slumped in one corner of the sofa; the TV was on but Myra was not looking at it. Part of the time I think she was just sitting, and part of the time she was reading one of the magazines she had brought out and put in a pile on the floor by the sofa. Her mother hovered around rather anxiously. Myra didn't want any supper, only a piece of cantaloupe, but when we came to dessert, which was banana cake, she wanted some. Mrs. Metz brought her a slice of the cake and ice cream, but Myra snarled that she didn't want ice cream. Her mother expressed fluttering distress.

(This was followed by Myra's taking her mother's hand, having her scratch her head and irritating her mother by running her fingers over her arm, etc., as recorded on pages 235–36.)

Why does Myra pay back her mother's offer of ice cream with a snarl? Why does she reward her day-long solicitude by putting herself in the position to be caressed (her head on her mother's thigh) and then annoying her? Since Myra has this tendency to aggravate her mother to the point of anxiety and exasperation even when a situation seems to call for affection, and since her mother never annoys Myra this way, it is obvious that Myra's anger toward her mother is less under control than her mother's hostility toward her.

Mrs. Metz is not showy with her husband and children; it is a front she puts on for the outside world. But she does require a child to be showy with her. What I see in Mrs. Metz, in spite of the front, are despair and anger rather than shallowness: anger and despair because she starved for love and never got it; and because she was never loved, she did not know how to awaken it in her children. You cannot teach children to love you if you were not a loved child because in order to teach, you have to know. You don't teach children to love you out of a textbook of greeting-card clichés. Mrs. Metz, as we saw when she was with her little niece Lucy, can go through a love-gesture-getting performance in which she lets the other person know what *she* wants—or rather what she thinks she wants—but he will learn only what she is able to teach, and give *that* back in return. Although she never learned through her own flesh what love is, she picked up some notions about it from popular songs, greeting cards, movies, and so on. Her enormous collection of greeting cards is her encyclopedia of true love, and her jingles express the conviction that love will come to her as presented in the mass media. I think that by the time she gave birth to Myra, however, Mrs. Metz was beginning to understand that she was not going to have love according to the mass media, and when she understood that, she stopped writing jingles.

While it may be true that Mrs. Metz shows only a superficial sensitivity to the feelings of others, this is a quality shared by millions.

Because Mrs. Metz does not want the world to ask whether she has love —the question she most fears—she shows off love, "protests too much." She is as a timid child declaring his bravery while begging with his eyes to be protected.

Identification, Hope and Memory

Mrs. Metz worries about the way Myra puts on lipstick and she would not let her walk up Broadway with her midriff exposed. The following is another example of such maternal prudence:

Myra was on her way to the beach and came out on the porch wearing a man's shirt with the tails tucked into the bottom part of her two-piece bathing suit, so that it looked as if she had nothing on under the shirt. This enraged her mother, who told her to take it off, but though Myra answered back angrily, her mother said she couldn't go out that way. So Myra went to her room and come back wearing a cute little dress with a very short skirt that had many narrow pleats. Myra said, in an irritated way, "All these pleats will be destroyed in a few minutes," or words to that effect.

Mrs. Metz exclaimed to me that the way Myra was wearing that shirt was disgraceful and that she was afraid Myra might be assaulted—she had had a narrow escape once before. Myra is a very attractive little girl and this sort of thing is a provocation to men, her mother thinks. I must say I can't blame Mrs. Metz for making Myra take off the shirt; she did look very provocative.

Let me remind the reader now of Mrs. Metz making agitated movements to the rock and roll; telling me that she said to her husband, "If Dr. Henry had seen the way you said good-bye to me this morning he would have told you to stay home"; saying that the hotel help must have known she and Kurt were newlyweds because they came down to breakfast at two in the afternoon; touching me on the leg and thigh in front of Myra and calling me "babe"; putting her arm around the shoulder of the owner of the traveling grocery store, etc., etc. With a mother like that, a fourteen-year-old girl is likely to try to be extremely provocative to men. Of course, Myra picks up the lyrics from other girls her age, but the music is her mother's. Myra, in responding to the repressed in her mother's personality, behaves like many daughters who, without knowing it, act out for their mothers, and who, like Myra, may be scolded, or worse, for their enthusiasm. Yet Mrs. Metz has the good sense, because she wants to be a good mother, not to try to experience too much through Myra.

Myra is her mother's surrogate in life, her understudy in all the dramas of existence she never played. Myra is the dream image projected along the wastelands of her mother's life, where the hands of broken watches point to immobilized time. If Mrs. Metz is "marooned in time," to use Freud's powerful figure, Myra is her mother's "dreamboat" which, in fantasy, will rescue Mrs. Metz from the shoals where life left her stranded. A lyric she wrote and dedicated to Myra was like a real lover's lyric, and she has remained faithful to the hope expressed in it. So even as Myra does the "wrong thing," offending her mother's sense of propriety by doing just what her mother tries to do, thus stirring up her mother's sexual fears and yearnings, Myra also does the "right thing," because, by her behavior, she affirms that her mother's delusion is "reality," that the past is not over. The stories Mrs. Metz poured out—the affair with Arty, her charm in the old days, the romantic honeymoon—show how she repudiates the present. Myra is permitted to be exquisitely selfish to her mother because Myra has meaning beyond herself: she is the embodiment of her mother's memory and hope.

Earlier I asked, but gave only a partial answer to the question. In what do children acquiesce? Now the answer can be expanded. Myra acquiesces—or rather appears to acquiesce—in being the vehicle by which her mother denies her own condition. Myra has "consented" to be as self-centered as her mother was, and to try to act out her mother's unexpressed sexuality. It is through responding intuitively to the parent's innermost desires, his memories and hopes that a child becomes a "successful" son or daughter—

not so much successful in the world as in the family. But since it is a renunciation when a child learns to become more the parent than his own self, he will hold it against the parent. It is in becoming the acquiescent expression of a parent's delusions that sons and daughters of disturbed parents achieve a kind of success as children, though they fail their selves. In this we are all much like them, both as parents of our children and as children of our parents, and from this renunciation, from this desertion, this abandonment, this persecution and imprisonment of the self, and the ensuing rage against the parent, rather than from the Oedipus complex, comes the "nameless guilt" of which Freud spoke, and which he thought "afflicts all mankind." What *nameless* guilt we share with mankind derives in the first instance from having betrayed our *selves,* and in the second instance from our rage against the one who forced us to it.*

Yet, even as a child tries to act out his parent's unconscious wishes, the parent may still hold him in check, for the unconscious wish embodies both the wish and the *fear* of it. If the girl whose mother wants to be promiscuous actually becomes promiscuous, she might be punished by her mother and abandoned, but be admired by her mother if she were merely provocative. What we see in the interplay between Mrs. Metz and Myra is on the one hand the mother's suspicion, anger and anxiety that Myra tries to express the impulses her mother has fostered, and on the other, Myra's anger at being prevented from acting on them. In this, again, we are all very much alike.

The Coalition

Myra has acquiesced in her mother's drawing a line between her and her father. Although this has not happened without some collaboration—withdrawal, "considerateness" (?)—on his part, the evidence suggests that Mrs. Metz is a determined, dominating woman who, from the very beginning, possessed her children. What we see today is a one-sided coalition between mother and daughter.

The evening I took the family to dinner, Myra, her mother and I were waiting for Mr. Metz outside the restaurant and

Myra said, "We can take Daddy in and show him my coat." Her mother replied, "I don't think we will," but Myra insisted, "I want to. As long as he is going to pay for it, he should put in his two cents' worth. I don't mean it exactly that way, but . . ." and her voice trailed off.

When Myra suggested it at dinner her father said no, he didn't want to look at it, he'd look at it when she wore it. This upset Myra; it made her look sort of sad.

This reveals, most vividly, the long-standing agreement between mother and daughter to exclude the father. But there is something else involved: Mr. Metz acts as if nothing suggested by the females is for his benefit, and this feeling is, perhaps, another reason for his killing joy—it is *their* joy.

---

* Just to keep the record clear, I want to point out that most of us have many good reasons for feeling guilty—all the way from the ordinary hypocrisies of life to acquiescing in the murder of helpless peasants.

Mr. Metz is out of their circle, not only because of the obsessive relationship between his wife and daughter but also because of what goes on behind his back. How can he live with it? Or does he die with it? Mrs. Metz, having become the unique source of love, manipulates the family so that she will remain so. But does she succeed? Who loves her? Everybody needs her, but do they love her?

Intercepting Kurt's fatherhood—a maneuver made easy by his general withdrawal—Gertrude deprived him of a link to manhood and diminished him as a member of the family. Myra, however, acquiesces, by her own withdrawal from him: she helps to desocialize her father, to metamorphose him into something between petulant old man and child. But if, when little, Myra had flung herself on him like Norma Wilson (see Part IV) on her inert father, and had not permitted him to drift away, she would have had to contend with her possessive, dominating mother. Though Mrs. Metz separated Myra from her father, she also weaned Myra from herself, for a parent who tries to make a child his property merely delivers the child, narcissistically, to the child. The child experiences a parent's jealous possessiveness as a rejection, because the child feels that he is not valued for himself but as his parent's creature. The inner existence of the child is thus denied. While this wounds and antagonizes him the parent's love gestures make it impossible for him to protest or free himself. Furthermore, it restricts the child's freedom to love; in Myra's case she was shut away from her father— to such a degree, indeed, that Mrs. Metz is like an emissary between father and daughter.

This isolating encirclement, this binding of Myra so that in the family she has become her mother's satellite, has brought it about that Myra oscillates between affection for her mother and hostility, and often expresses both at the same time. Hence the affair on the sofa when Myra got her mother to stroke her head and then annoyed her. When her mother's guard is down, Myra wants to hurt her because she cannot stand her power. Or we can look at it this way: when Myra is impressed with her mother's power she is affectionate, but when she feels her mother is weak she is not—or is even hostile.

So Myra acquiesces in always being the one to start the affectionate demonstrations. Mrs. Metz wants her children to come to her (remember how Albert did it, but always showed his contempt?). Sitting on her mother's lap, putting her mother's arms around her, seeking her mother's side (rather than her father's) and always kissing her mother good-bye (except after the fight over carrying the groceries)—Myra does what is expected.

Cultural Factors

The dialectic of the Metz family could not develop in a culture where a child's fundamental social relations are with a broad social group rather than with a small family of parents and children, for while in the small family the roots of a child's emotional life are entangled with those of his parents, in the other case they spread more widely.

When a woman's life is set for her before she is born, so that all she has to do in growing is to fulfill the requirements that are traditionally hers, there can be little question of powerful private ambitions frustrated; and where there is no prescription for unconditional love between parents and children—all that is required of parents being care and education, and all that is required of children being reciprocity and learning—conflicts such as that between Myra and her mother cannot arise. In tribal societies, though parenthood is nearly everywhere modified by sentiment, the *rights* and *obligations* of fathers and mothers are much more strictly and widely prescribed than in ours. There is, with really only moderate variation, one way to be a father or mother, and within that role the prescriptions of responsibility are usually stipulated with considerable precision—the conditions of residence, rights to inheritance, obligation to provide a spouse for the child, and so on. Unfatherly, *idiosyncratic* abdication, purely arbitrary monopolizing of the children by the wife, could not occur in such societies. Furthermore, since family affairs are usually open to the view of neighbors, relatives, and other villagers, the relations between parents and children are constantly under scrutiny, and family deviations are publicly criticized.

The tantalizing distinction between *love* and *like*, which leaves a child spinning around at the end of the verbal thread, is also peculiar to our linguistic and cultural tradition. Such gradations of intensity of feeling (*love* versus *like*) about the desired object are strange to the exotic languages and cultures I have studied in the wilderness of South America. Not only the language is involved, however, but the range of associated feeling as well, for were the feeling not there, the capacity the language gives us to make the distinction would be irrelevant. At any rate, the existence of this configuration of word and feeling is used by Mrs. Metz to refine, to give nuance, to communicate fear to her relationship with her daughter and impel her to climb the thread of speech to her mother's affection—thus storing resentment as she climbs.

The complex feeling that controls Myra and her mother is the product of a culture where, since between parents and children little is determined by law and much can be demanded and expected at will, nuance of feeling has become the primary control of behavior in the family. Since there is no law, except the law of feeling, to compel solicitude, imperviousness to others enables one to ignore their needs without suffering *legal* consequences. But in cultures where ramifying concern for others is compelled by law, such withdrawal is impossible. In our culture, where all a person has to keep him from insecurity, loneliness and contempt is the caprice of feeling, extreme narcissism is so threatening that it is considered pathology. In the other cultures of which I speak, however, jural regulations determine not only what a parent must do for his child but vice versa; what a person must do for his father's sister or mother's father and vice versa; who shall mourn at his funeral; who shall feed him when he is sick; who shall bring him his pipe or kava bowl, and so on, down through the details of social relations.

Between Myra and her father there is a void. Her turning away from him is facilitated by the fact that in our culture no legal regulations compel her to show him concern, and by the fact that no law interferes with Mrs. Metz's determination to bind Myra to herself.

Mother and daughter pay for turning away from the father with impoverishment of their own lives, because normally, in our culture, a father's

affection for his child deepens his feeling for his wife, while a bond between him and his child enriches the existence of both. Actually Mrya is
contemptuous of her father; the little speech about putting in "his two
cents' worth" is proof enough of that, so that her turning from him, although related to her tie to her mother, is related also to contempt for her
father.

Mrs. Metz's monopolizing strategy, in combination with her husband's
withdrawal and negativism, helps seal Myra within herself, so she has become extremely self-centered, and she is just as callous toward her mother
as her father is: when her mother was complaining about the pain in her
finger Myra said nothing, she let her mother handle the heavy load of groceries, carry all packages, and so on. Myra's extreme narcissism is the consequence of her mother's *inability* to awaken love in a child. Since she had
no love herself, her ideas about it come from greeting cards and the media.

In this family nobody's deeper needs are met; everyone gropes like a
figure in a dream, but the mother gives the clearest sign that she *knows*
what is lacking in her life. Hence her despair and rage are most apparent,
and hence she protests the most—and that is too much. Since mother and
daughter do not know how to help each other, their encounters are tinged
with discontent that comes out in teasing and anger. As for the father—
Myra seems scarcely aware that he has needs; walking over to his side on
the night we went to the falls is the single example I have of some awareness on her part that he might have some feelings about her. Yet, since he
never caresses her spontaneously, although he is quick to discipline her, he
gives the observer no sign that he wants to get anything from her. All her
life she seems to have been merely "over there" to him—one for whom he
has a parental responsibility but no feeling.

In spite of discontent, there is a bond between Myra and her mother, for
although Myra is without solicitude for others and aware only of her own
needs and of the importance of treating her mother with prudent amounts
of demonstrativeness, Mrs. Metz tries to be a good mother.

Study of the relationship between Myra and her parents has shown that
while there is a complex, strongly ambivalent relationship between Myra
and her mother, Myra and her father seem to be largely absent from each
other's lives. In their relationship to their daughter Mr. and Mrs. Metz appear to have an agreement—that he will leave the child to her. We see that
this father does not reach out to his child at all, but rather waits for a signal
from his wife, or for some gesture from his daughter, before making a
move toward her. As we see him now, Mr. Metz has no capacity to satisfy
anything inward in Myra, not only because of his own make-up and the
coalition between mother and daughter, but especially because Myra's personality has been molded so much by her mother; because Myra is so much
a product of the *emotional culture* established by her and her mother. In his
relationship to his daughter Mr. Metz is like our Department of State trying
to understand an average Chinese. Mother and daughter have created a
milieu of feeling in which they function with intuitive ease, but which an
outsider comprehends only by careful study. Myra and her mother manipulate each other but conspire against the father. The dialectic of this is that
since he is shut out, he reacts like a shutout, or to use the contemporary
colorful figure, like a "dropout" from fatherhood.

The Bond between Mother and Daughter

Though Mr. Metz spoke little, I think that one of his failings is lack of feeling for make-believe. He seems a solid, down-to-earth, no-nonsense person, and since he does not have the capacity for delusion and fantasy his wife and daughter have, he is useless to them for communicating what is closest to their hearts.

While we were having dinner the record player was blaring out rock and roll. Myra and her mother enjoyed it very much, but not Mr. Metz, who at last asked Myra to turn it off, but she didn't. Nothing much happened at the table—the loud noise was too deafening. I remember well how many times Myra said she loved one song or another. Mr. Metz told of having been to the movies with Albert, and remarked on how intensely Al watched the picture. Mr. Metz thought it awful because it was full of violence and crime, and bad for teen-agers.

I have argued that although Myra and her mother disappoint each other at the level of deep feeling, there is something more positive between them as well because Mrs. Metz tries to be a good mother: she watches over Myra and is not afraid to discipline her. There is a bond between them also because they can talk so absorbedly about inconsequential things—especially the feminine kind. Mrs. Metz is an encyclopedia of trivia, and her knowledge and wisdom in this sphere correspond well to the world in which Myra will live. Thus, though the household lacks a masculine figure and so, I think, made Albert's becoming a man difficult, it does have a female model in Mrs. Metz. She is vigorous, colorful and protective; she knows her own mind and she sets limits. In addition she knows about the fustian world of women of her social class because she is part of it, and her head is full of what a girl has to understand to take her place in the culture. A few more examples illustrate the point.

Close to ten o'clock in the evening Myra came in with Mary, saying they had a big problem: Myra wants to wear dressy shoes to go shopping with Mary tomorrow but Mary doesn't want to wear heels, though they had agreed they would. Another problem is that Myra doesn't have any other shoes to wear, except those with heels, but Mary doesn't want to wear heels because they hurt her feet. This business about the shoes went on and on and on and on, Myra sometimes showing great irritation with her mother. Mrs. Metz went and found a pair of black flats Myra could wear; meanwhile Mr. Metz had fallen asleep on the porch. The upshot was that the kids would go in flats. I mention this only in order to illustrate the extreme normalness of Myra and her mother.

Mrs. Metz presided over the dispute and solved the problem wisely, by "discovering" what she and Myra must have known—that Myra had a pair of flats. Mrs. Metz decided in favor of her "adoptive daughter's" feet, rather than of her own daughter's inclinations to look provocative and "older." Situations like this one occur in most families in our culture. Women's ability to take the "problems" seriously, to listen carefully and answer, and to be on the alert for a flaw in an argument or to make a telling point make them good mothers. Only a child who knows her mother is concerned enough to watch what heels she wears when she goes out the door would bring the matter up at all. So from one point of view the dispute over heels versus flats belongs to what intellectuals consider "the world of pseudo values," but from another, it involves a relationship of concern and respect. Beneath the issue of the heels lies the deeper one of the relationship between mother and daughter, between mother and friend, and between friend and friend. In this confrontation Myra displayed her selfishness, for she didn't care about Mary's feet but the mother did: In a dispute over a trifle, Mrs. Metz was able to communicate an ethical principle.

I did not realize at the time how momentous this scene was; perhaps if I had I would have tried to remember more. I wish there were more; I wish I had in my notes more of Myra's argument and of her mother's; something of what her mother said to irritate her. The methodological principle that one should try to remember everything and put it down was not enough. What was necessary was awareness that mothers educate daughters through arguments, and over issues the intelligentsia consider trivial.

Discussions between parents and children in any culture are practically standardized. The debates we have so far observed between Myra and her mother—over flats versus heels, over the allowance, over whether Myra can or cannot have certain clothes, over how provocative she can look, over whether she should carry the parcels, etc., occur almost everywhere in the United States. They are patterned communications through which children learn the culture, and through which parents and children express mutual regard or disregard. Since the arguments I have analyzed are standard vehicles of communication between parents and children and express relatively fixed relationships among objects, institutions and people, they are inevitable. An adequate parent communicates with his child in the framework of the cultural banalities, and without half trying, affirms their eternity.

The following are further illustrations:

Myra and Mary came in. They had been shopping, and Myra had bought a pretty pair of shoes for $3.98, reduced from $7. Mary displayed a box of really nice things she had bought for a total of $44. The three females discussed Mary's clothes—the price, style, and so on. They also talked about the attitude of Mary's parents toward her clothes and Mary said she knows how to handle her mother; her mother will say yes but her father will probably say no. Soon Mary left. (At dinner Myra said she had picked out Mary's clothes and when I asked why, Mrs. Metz said, "Because Myra has much better taste." I looked at Myra and she said, "Mary asked me to pick them out.")

After Mary left, Mrs. Metz, Myra and I were in the living room, and mother and daughter talked about clothes for a long time.

Then Myra described how she tried to get away with not paying full fare on the bus. When she gave the conductor the half fare, he said she had to pay full fare, and Myra said, "There's no harm in trying." The conductor told her, "You can be sent to juvenile court for that," and Myra answered back very sharply. Mrs. Metz took Myra's part. She was also on her side in the discussion about the price of admission to movies. Myra's point was that there should be a graded series of prices: one for children under a certain age, one for teen-age students and one for adults. She complained about how much it cost to get into the movies and raised the question of her allowance, but her mother got irritated and said, "I'll talk about it when school opens."

Discussion of Mary's clothes naturally becomes an affirmation of the feminine plot against male resistance—a spontaneous female ritual exalting the values of female culture and accompanied by display of clothes, the ceremonial objects of female cult, surpassed in sacredness only by babies. The process of feminine identification progresses in this way.

After Mary's departure, the rule that it is all right to beat the system is affirmed and stressed again in Mrs. Metz's approval of Myra's trying to get away with half fare. Everybody who has his head screwed on right tries to cheat public utilities (who in his right mind turns in the money to the company if the pay-station phone accidentally returns it?), and Myra has a mother who knows what is innocently illegitimate. Mrs. Metz plays an important moral role in certifying our folk conception of legitimate transgression. Whether it is merely innocently illegitimate to let Myra talk behind her father's back about putting in "his two cents' worth," however, is another question; and that question marks a boundary between what is innocently illegal in the outer world and crime in the family world. It is an illusion that one can practice chicanery in the outer world and keep the family free of it. Yet who can be honest in "the world"?

Thus Mrs. Metz gives Myra moral guidance. There is a fundamental difference between Mr. Metz's no and hers, for his is usually based merely on personal feeling—no doughnuts, no malted milks, no movies, no trip to the falls—while for the most part her negatives are directed to the moral education of Myra. Mere, apparently arbitrary, cancellation of family pleasures can only make a parent appear a kill-joy, whereas the setting of limits —killing joy—has a different effect because it involves responsibility for the child's welfare. While Mrs. Metz sets limits, she also pushes for pleasure—eating out, going to the falls or to the movies, etc.; Mrs. Metz expresses the "pleasure principle" in life. But she expresses the "reality principle," too, by setting limits—the ideal condition for the formation of a superego, as we understand these more or less flabby things in contemporary culture.

In interfering with the "pleasure principle" in Myra, Mrs. Metz rarely puts her own convenience first. But the sacrifice of her own comfort, when she is feeling bad or hungry, has adverse consequences for the relationship between mother and daughter, because there is a limit to how much most people can sacrifice their own comfort for someone else without turning against him. Putting up with Myra's self-centeredness—a self-centeredness that is sometimes even cruel—must turn her mother against her.

Anger between Mother and Daughter

Mrs. Metz got angry with Myra about seven times while I was there: when Myra acted up about her allowance, when she talked too loudly in the restaurant, when she refused to help carry the groceries, when she kept running her fingers over her mother's arm when her mother wanted to stroke her, when she told an alleged cock-and-bull story so she could sleep at a girl friend's house, when she and Mary wouldn't get out of bed, and when Myra tried to dress too provocatively. But Mrs. Metz does not hound Myra, as she did Albert when he came home, and each outburst at Myra seems to have a specific and reasonable cause. Actually, with the exception of the incident of the shopping bags, none of the anger between mother and daughter was alienating, on the face of it.

Nevertheless, the fact that Myra constantly protests her love, and begs her mother "Say you love me" or "Say you like me," makes it appear as if between them there exists a continuous, though inaudible and invisible quarrel; as if mother and daughter live a continuous aftermath and are constantly making up, even though, on the surface, nothing has happened; as if the two are in endless emotional repair, though openly they fight few battles.

When two people act *as if* they are constantly quarreling and making up, we have a form of pathological quarreling. Even though not much appears on the surface, one has the feeling that inwardly they are fighting each other continually.

Myra is always on the defensive, and her mother self-righteous. Mrs. Metz is always right, never in doubt, and Myra is without recourse—the stereotype of the relationship between matriarch and child. Yet, even when she is most incensed, Mrs. Metz never really forces the issue; she does not keep piling an outburst over one thing on top of another outburst over something else: her anger is not cumulative, because she stops the dialectic short.

Angry outbursts usually come from the mother but most of the time these do not cause a quarrel, because Myra does not resist, and since there is no quarrel, there is no visible need to make up. On the surface, anger between Myra and her mother usually flows in one direction—from mother to daughter—and has the consequence of emphasizing Myra's immaturity and her mother's power. With Myra, on the whole, Mrs. Metz's anger is corrective, limiting, morally toned. Since it is not humiliating, it has an inherent rationality, a quality lacking in her anger with Albert.

Considering that their relationship is frustrating and ambiguous with a tendency to store resentment, it seems to me that mother and daughter do remarkably well. On the occasions when anger flared, they held themselves in check, and one decisive symptom of pathology—hypervigilance for slights—was entirely absent.

Myra—A More or Less Normal Teen-ager

Myra compensates her mother for her husband, acting out somewhat her mother's sexual cravings and unfulfilled hopes. Acquiescing in more than she knows—her mother's need to have her all to herself, to have recompense for her husband, to have a child that seems to express what she could never have—Myra has her mother more dependent on her than she is on her mother. Both are anxious that the other may let her down; yet in striving for reassurance Myra is really the stronger, for whereas she has a lot of friends her own age—and one best girl friend, Mary—with whom she goes to the movies, the beach and shopping; at whose homes she sometimes sleeps, and who sleep at hers; and whereas she spends much time at Mary's during the day and visits Mrs. Smith, her mother is limited largely to the family (while I was there no friend of Mrs. Metz's phoned). Since, therefore, Myra can escape the circle of dependence, while her mother cannot, her mother needs her more than she needs her mother.

The fact that Myra can escape, that her mother has not closed the ring of dependence altogether, is a sign of her mother's health and of a good prognosis for Myra. Mrs. Metz wants to be all things to Myra in the family, but Myra is free to have friends outside. She has always allowed Myra more freedom than Albert:

> She told me she was much less strict with Myra than she had been with Albert, because Albert is a boy. When I asked her what she meant by that she said, "Well, boys like to have more freedom." She kept Albert much closer to her than Myra; he was less self-reliant than Myra, she said.

In this section I want to stress the "normal" in Myra, and show how different she is when not directly entangled with her parents, particularly with her mother; how she breaks her dependence; and how she extends her relationships to people outside her family.

> (Second day.) Mrs. Smith came over with her baby and asked Mrs. Metz whether she could leave him with her. Mrs. Metz showed little interest in the baby. She tried to a couple of times, but never could keep it up for more than a minute. She attempted, in various ways, to stimulate the baby but he did not show any enthusiasm, nor did Mrs. Metz, who preferred to talk to me.
>
> The contrast between her and Myra was marked. After we had been sitting there for about half an hour, Myra came along and the baby responded to her immediately. She knelt before it and kissed it over and over again, playing with it in a warm and absorbed manner.

The baby is certainly crazy about Myra, and although Myra's behavior is reminiscent of her mother's with Lucy, and of Myra's displays of affection at home, it would be wrong, on the present evidence, to suggest that she is not fond of the baby. What she does with it seems to fit the standard female pattern. In the next illustration, Myra and Mary look more normal than the adults.

> This evening after dinner the Metzes, a couple visiting them and I played croquet. The outstanding characteristic of the game was the behavior of Mrs. Metz, who broke rules and loudly protested them when things were not going her way. She did not play in the second round and the visiting lady took her place. Mr. Metz said repeatedly of the decisions made by Myra and Mary that "they make up the rules to suit themselves," although the kids knew the rules of croquet.

Dramatizing her frustration, Mrs. Metz becomes a figure of comic despair, while her husband says the children are cheating. Overwhelmed by little failures, the adults reveal the shaky framework of their souls. The croquet molehill has become a mountain of personal disaster for these people, who are so vulnerable.

In the next example, where Myra and Mary are together, Myra seems a very "normal" girl.

> I went to pick up the kids at the beach, as had been arranged, and found Myra and Mary waiting for me with a boy who looked about fourteen or fifteen years old. Before she said good-bye Myra kissed him on the cheek and gave him her

phone number when he asked for it. She told me she likes him very much and
has been seeing him for a long time—three years.

On the way home we stopped at a delicatessen because Mary complained of
being very hungry. She said she has to have seven pieces of bread every day with
her milk or she will be hungry, and today she did not. But she bought bubble
gum and Myra bought two bars of candy, which I paid for. Myra ate the candy
and Mary chewed her gum. I don't remember what we talked about on the way
home.

There was more average behavior on the way to pick up Mr. Metz:

Myra said we should go one way and her mother said another. It turned out
that Myra was right, but only after we had first gone in the direction Mrs. Metz
insisted on. . . . On the way the kids talked about other kids' personalities and
looks, about cute boys and unpleasant girls—maybe once or twice about pleasant
girls. They also talked about the price of clothes. Myra said she had seen a wonderful suit for $5, reduced from $10. Her mother said she didn't think it could be
a very good suit at that price.

Conversation about the superficialities of boys and girls, with special
venom for girls, is standard proto-adolescent* girl behavior in our culture.

I had very little opportunity to be alone with Myra, but when I was, there
was nothing extraordinary about what she did or said.

(Third day.) I picked up Myra at the beach today at five o'clock. I went around
looking for her and couldn't find her, but she saw me and came over and we got
into the car and drove home. (She spoke only when I asked questions.) When I
asked whether she goes on dates she said that she does, but not at night unless
she goes to a party. She does go to the movies with boys and girls in the afternoon. Sometimes when she goes to a party she stays out "real late"—until midnight. I asked whether Pete—a boy I saw her kiss yesterday—was at the beach
today and she said he had been there twice but finally left to go somewhere with
his mother. She answered my questions readily and pleasantly. There is nothing
hostile or withdrawn in Myra's interaction with me.

Myra is quiet, like a good fourteen-year-old girl; she speaks when she is
spoken to, and not too much or too little. She listens to her mother, remaining within the middle-class norms of sex conduct for girls her age. Her
mother makes no serious complaint. Myra does not try to boast, either—
does not spin yarns about doing things her mother would not want her to
do. Midnight is still "real late" for her. All this shows that Mrs. Metz sets
limits and holds Myra to them—that she cares; and it shows that although
Myra is a selfish little kid, she is a "good" kid, too. She is a "good," "clean,"
"decent" lower-middle-class kid, and even though she tries to be too sexy at
times, she stays within bounds, and she does not "worry her mother sick,"
as some kids do. She obeys her mother in most things, is home on time and
does not roam around the street. This is a comfort to her mother; maybe
we'd find out that it is to her father, too, if he talked.

Here is the other instance of Myra's behavior alone with me, in her parents' bedroom.

After her mother left the room Myra invited me to sit on the bed, where she
was stretched out reading the paper. I sat there for about five minutes and then
joined her mother on the porch.

* See my *Culture Against Man* (*op. cit.*) for this term, which I use to designate
children between thirteen and fifteen (pp. 218–20).

It seems to me that Myra's behavior is "within normal limits" here, too. She is experimenting with the older man, trying herself out and trying him out, too: conventionally seductive.

The next day I spent an hour and a half at the beach, observing Myra with her friends.

(Fourth day.) Myra was with nine other girls about her age. She was playing cards with a group of about four; the others were either sitting around staring into space, or lying down getting a tan. On the edge of the gathering were two boys, about fourteen, playing cards. At first they did not seem to belong to the group, but later they began to talk to the girls, so I got the idea that maybe they were members. I watched from a distance of about ten or fifteen feet. Myra had noticed me and waved. Once she looked around to see if I was still there. After a while she and a companion, I think it was Flossie—the girl with whom she had gone to the beach—got up and went to the refreshment booth and bought some stuff. I watched the group eating potato chips, candy and Eskimo pies, and littering the refuse around. Later Myra and her friend Flossie went into the water together. Flossie is much more developed than Myra. Flossie pushed Myra down and Myra splashed in a typically childish way. The two had not been in the water long when they were approached by the two boys, who were interested in Flossie. They pulled her toward the water and tried to drag her in for some horseplay. They paid no attention to Myra. However, she was not to be left out, so she went to Flossie and tried to pull her away from the boys, even hitting them—all in a typically coltish way. This went on for quite some time, and then Flossie and Myra sat at the edge of the water and talked to the boys, laughing and joking. The boys chased them up the beach. Finally Myra and Flossie went into the water with the boys, now touching, and met three other girls in the water.

What could be more normal in our culture than a group of proto-adolescent girls sunning themselves and playing cards while a couple of boys hang around on the edges? And it seems normal too for a couple of girls, one taking advantage of the maturer sexual development of the other, to separate from the group to attract the boys. Myra's relationship to her parents is not so disturbed, her tie to her mother not so close that they prevent her from having a good time with girls her age. All that proto-adolescent-girl culture asks of Myra is that she dress right, laugh at the right crack; be involved with the boys without going too far, be quiet, like or hate what the culture prescribes, and be absolutely trivial. Myra obeys these laws intuitively because she has a mother who trains her right.

Picking Flossie to go into the water with is good strategy in sex; and in refusing to let the boys ignore her just because Flossie excites them more than she, Myra shows strength and sexy know-how. Instead of being crushed, as some girls might be, because Flossie arouses the boys right away and she doesn't, Myra executes a maneuver that gets her into the play in a nice way. She does not "act cheap," she does not try to be provocative beyond the limits of proto-adolescent culture, but she does let the boys know that she would like to be considered available, and they respond. Thus the sexual stimulation Myra gets from observing her mother helps weaken Myra's tie to her, because sex makes Myra look for boys and pushes her into friendships with girls interested in the same thing. This is all very different from the Rosenberg family (Part II), where the sexual configuration made it impossible for the boys to break out of the family.

Myra is never out of touch with other kids; well or sick, awake or on the verge of sleep, she picks up their signals. Like any normal American girl, she cannot be alone.

(Sixth day.) When we got back to the house at about ten-fifteen after the trip to the falls, the phone rang and Myra answered it. It was a friend of hers. The two were cooking up a party and they hung on the phone for about half an hour, but her parents made only feeble efforts to get Myra to hang up. Once, when Mrs. Metz got irritated with Myra because she was talking so loudly, Myra almost yelled back, "What do you want me to do?" in a sort of whining inflection. This passed off immediately, however, and her parents let her finish without further prodding.

Once in a while Mrs. Metz may become irritated by the amount of time Myra spends on the phone, but on the whole, she doesn't interfere. Were Mrs. Metz to tell Myra to get off the phone, she would be doing it only for her own benefit, not for Myra's, and she avoids this. Furthermore, it would be a kind of hounding, and she avoids that, too. Mrs. Metz's renunciation of anger, therefore, gives Myra more freedom; freedom in the sense of being free to follow the pattern of adolescent group conformity; freedom in the paradoxical sense of being free to subject herself to another form of constraint.* Obviously there is nothing about Myra's group life that frightens her mother; it has a sheltered character that is the obverse of liberty. Giving in, i.e., renunciation of anger, by Mrs. Metz, is a condition for letting Myra go; Mrs. Metz's holding back is the dialectical condition for Myra's going out, and the final product, the synthesis, is Myra's incorporation into the tyranny of the group, a new form of subjugation. Mrs. Metz tries to be a good mother while rarely following her own personal interests in disciplining Myra, and this helps Myra give in too, especially when her mother's personal needs do not interfere with her own.

The pathway to Myra's cultural conformity, i.e., to sanity, seems to be the following: Step 1. A mother who tries to be a good mother. Step 2. A mother who, while making herself the center of the child's life at home, is able, Step 3, to release her to the prevailing adolescent ways and groups outside the home. Step 4. A mother who provides, as primary criteria of existence, the standardized cultural interests, its ideas of correct behavior and its goals. Step 5. A mother who does not put her own needs above those of the child. Step 6. A mother who does not hound and overwhelm her child with angry outbursts.

The evolution of human society shows that the existence of Homo sapiens has two fundamental components: activity, obligations and rights in the family, and activity, obligations and rights in the outer world. Since there is no society in which both components are not deemed necessary, no society in which both are not expressed with constant insistence, we must conclude that the drive to social activity in the outer world is an inherent tendency of Homo sapiens. It follows that the parent who enables his child to be actively incorporated into the outer world, unburdened by the parent's personal inner needs, is following a biosocial law. Since Mrs. Metz obeys this law, her daughter appears to be relatively free of serious emotional difficulties.

* My indebtedness to Eric Fromm's great book Escape from Freedom is evident here.

Mrs. Metz Alone

> Boredom depends on the noth-
> ingness which pervades reality;
> it causes a dizziness like that
> produced by looking down into
> a yawning chasm, and this diz-
> ziness is infinite. The eccentric
> form of diversion . . . sounds
> forth without producing an
> echo . . . ; for in nothingness
> not even an echo is produced.
> —Søren Kierkegaard,
> *Either/Or*

The Dialectic of Personality

Whatever a person does reflects his personality, but ambiguously: he may be mad in some respects but not in others; if he seems aggressive he may sometimes be passive. While it is not correct to say that nobody is all of a piece, it is true that what one is, is the outcome of dialectical processes that make people merely *seem* contradictory. For example, if a person is rude and arrogant to his family but quiet outside, this quietness may reflect the fact that he views the outer world as too powerful to be attacked and his family as too threatening to be let alone. At the core of his aggressive-ness-passiveness duality is his fear of powerlessness.

There is some madness in the sane, there is often a good deal of sanity in the mad, and neither madness nor sanity can mobilize the personality com-pletely. The strong have weaknesses related to their strength, and the weak have strength related to their weaknesses. This is due to the existence, in *Homo sapiens*, of evolutionary options, in the sense that a supreme flexibil-ity inheres in the *personality*: it cannot integrate only one set of adaptive responses, and circumstances call forth its adaptive capabilities. This in-herent inability of the personality, even in madness, to harden in one atti-tude alone, is due to a unique dialectic quality that enables *Homo sapiens* to harbor, simultaneously, a personality characteristic and its opposite. Fear lurks in the shadow of courage, so that even when we are bravest we may long to run away. Resistance lurks in the shadow of acquiescence, so that even as we acquiesce we often wish to resist. Self-indulgence lurks in the shadow of austerity because we become tired of self-denial, and so on. *Homo sapiens* is the dialectical animal.

To understand Mrs. Metz it is necessary to explore the dialectic of per-sonality.

The sensation of the imminence of social punishment. Once we have passed the age when we delight our parents simply by moving our bowels in the potty, by finishing our milk or by speaking a complete sentence, we receive no applause for merely doing what we are expected to do but are, rather, punished for not doing it. Adults do not receive a medal for stopping at a red light but get a summons for not stopping, if a traffic policeman happens to see them. Since, by the time we are six, we are more likely to be punished for violating convention than applauded for observing it (who pats a six-year-old on the back for not "going" in his pants?), all of us suffer from a feeling of vulnerability to culture's laws—the sensation of the imminence of social punishment—and take no pleasure in obeying them (what idiot enjoys obeying the law?). Most people can cope with this sensation; since they have developed sources of gratification outside the culture's system of recognition and persecution, they are able to forget, as a matter of everyday coming and going, that society is ready to club them if they violate its conventions. Society establishes broad norms, including its laws, and allows us to seek gratification within them. That people happen to love their spouses and children is merely a hopeful development within the conventions of marriage, and society does not really care if the members of a family drive one another mad, as long as broad conventions are observed. If you enjoy good books, that is a mere improbability of the system of compulsory education, and once you are out of school, society does not care a fig what you do with your literacy, as long as you do not use it for criminal purposes.

Society could not care less about what gratifications you derive within the framework of its conventions; it merely punishes you if you break them. You might think that this is rather irresponsible on the part of the demon Society, but let us try to regard even society with some compassion and understanding. To anthropomorphize society—and the police—for a moment, let us say this: having laid down his norms, the demon is content to go to sleep and, like Argus, close all but one of his thousand eyes to what you do in trying to have a good time. His single eye looks only at his damn norms, and he does not care much what else you do.*

The foregoing suggests the following law: the more I am likely to be punished for what I do wrong, the worse I feel if there are no rewards for what I do right. The parent or teacher who keeps punishing a child for wrongdoing without giving him some blessings for getting things done right will have a depressed, secretive, evasive and angry child on his hands.

The relation of this law to Mrs. Metz is as follows: when an individual like her feels the imminence of social punishment because his life has few gratifications, he tries to free himself from this pain. But lacking courage, education, imagination and financial means, what can he do, especially if he has a strong sense of responsibility?

(1) He can overconform, in the sense that, out of fear, he will do nothing to challenge anything or anybody. (2) In imagination, he can give to his ordinary conventional acts a quality of unconventionality, taking a secret and even erotic pleasure in commonplaces. (3) He can live in a fantasy world of broken conventions while living the most conventional life. Let us call this the "Star Rover" syndrome.† (4) If he is somewhat more

---

* This is characteristic of capitalist countries only, for Communist societies assume responsibility for gratification as well as for punishment.

† After the powerful novel by Jack London about prisoners in brutally tight strait jackets in solitary confinement, who put their bodies to sleep so they would not feel

daring, he can deliberately commit slightly unconventional acts—legitimate misdemeanors—and try to conceal them. In these ways a person lacking a really gratifying life, and therefore oppressed by the sensation of the imminence of social punishment, can try to compensate. These problems lead us to consider the relation between painful and gratifying experience.

Gratification and pain. Just as there is a sort of calculus of conformity and nonconformity that has an outcome I have called the sensation of the imminence of social punishment, so there is a logic of gratification and pain that has an outcome I shall call "negative expectations"—the feeling that whatever happens is bound to be bad.

If a person's life has been mostly miserable he will expect it to continue to be so. Many who have lived miserable lives attempt to avoid further misery by shunning all new—strange—situations, but live in a wonder world of fantasy. Often they blind themselves also to the pain in any situation. On the other hand, a need to compensate for negative expectations might generate false optimism—false because behind a façade of optimism is the conviction that it is no use—and even a readiness, therefore, to accept exploitation as friendship or love. They tend to avoid anything that does not guarantee immediate gratification, and this means sticking to the familiar, once it has proved safe. Thus negative expectations can be a cause of immobility as well as of false liveliness, for if we expect things to turn out badly, we will stay where we are: better a familiar, friendly street in Middletown than the unknown, the strange boulevards of Paris.

Big and little things. In ordinary life, a big thing might be deciding what occupation to choose, planning for a new baby, deciding whom Jane should marry, etc., and a little thing might be deciding who makes the best French fries, Joe's or the Big Barn; whether the snow shovel should be kept in the right or left corner of the cellar; whether geraniums or tulips look best on the porch window, and so on. While it is true that at any moment little things can become major issues, this does not destroy their essential difference from big things: big things have to do with serious issues of human welfare, and little things do not. In the calculus of feeling, the more one's life is detached from concern with big things, the more little things enter to fill it, and the "little things of life" seem to be obsessions. If there is little of import in a person's life, trivia will become preoccupations, and just as whole folk philosophies enter into a decision about what occupations to choose, marrying off a daughter or welcoming an infant into the world, so metaphysical systems are constructed around trivia.

Little things can come to fill all life and take on the appearance of bigness, and in such cases a person may give the impression of being under enormous tension to get his business done, though it might seem trivial to us. When a person's life has no significance to him even though he may be unaware of it, trivia may drive him on as matters of life and death.*

It is in order to explore the dialectic of personality that I consider commonplace (everyday) aspects of Mrs. Metz's behavior, away from immediate contact with her family. I look first at her housekeeping.

---

the pain, and in that condition traveled in dreams through time and space to previous existences, all fantastic, wonderful and shimmering.

* For description of such a personality, see the novel *Oblamov*, by Ivan Aleksandrovich Goncharov.

Kitchen and Market

A HIGH-STATUS MEAL

(First day.) The dinner was to be of beef tenderloin, mashed potatoes made from a package mix, and canned wax beans. Mrs. Metz asked how I wanted my steak and I said, "You prepare them whatever way you want." She said, "I put garlic powder on them," and I said that was all right. She made the steaks with onions and mushrooms and they were quite good.

I sat in the kitchen while Mrs. Metz very efficiently went about preparing dinner. Her kitchen is very well ordered. The closets are not in as good order as you might expect, considering the rest of the house, but the kitchen was immaculate, possibly because she was expecting me.

One thing Mrs. Metz says she can't stand is people messing up the salt shaker, and this is something Myra does all the time. When Mrs. Metz put the salt shaker on the table, she had to wash it all around because Myra had smeared grease on it by picking it up.

Mrs. Metz held the onion in her hand and cut it with the knife drawn toward her. I remarked that when my wife cuts onions she puts them on a board, and Mrs. Metz said, well, she doesn't and she doesn't cut her hand.

She also said she was running out of kitchen knives, and I expressed surprise, wondering how one could run out of kitchen knives. She showed me how she nicked the edges of knives by using them to open packages.

There is nothing bizarre about this scene: Mrs. Metz knows that in our culture you serve an important guest high-status food, like beef tenderloin on the first night, and not hamburger or frankfurters, and you always ask a guest how he wants his steak. She understands that in our culture the most important part of a meal is the meat, and the vegetable is secondary. She is aware that in her social class in her part of the country you do not serve turnips or rutabaga to a high-status guest. In her *class* and *section* of the country a bizarre meal for a guest would be pig's ears, rutabaga and cornmeal mush. Thus Mrs. Metz grasps the relation between food and social status, the difference between right and wrong; the morality of the dining room!

It would perhaps have been more appropriate to serve a seasonal fresh vegetable or frozen rather than canned beans, but since she does not have a car, frozen foods might thaw on the way home from the market. The mashed-potato mix can be set down to the corrupt American taste, which can no longer distinguish between a genuine food and a chemically treated one. Similar considerations apply to the beans: since most Americans never taste a garden-fresh vegetable, they cannot draw a distinction between one kind of packaging and another. Thus in the very corruption of her taste, Mrs. Metz is normal. This suggests the law that a normal person is corrupted in the culturally approved ways.

Since Mrs. Metz's kitchen is in good order, her strong feeling about the messy salt shaker seems like a normal housewifely desire to keep things in proper condition.

Many women take unnecessary chances, cutting an onion held in the hand, and it may have something to do with not wanting to dirty a dish or wash a cutting board.

Mrs. Metz is somewhat careless about knives, but in a culture of abundance where knives are cheap, probably many housewives keep them in poor condition and use them for purposes for which they were never intended. Actually, since it is so often difficult to open a package, the use of a cutting tool for prying is merely another aspect of *Homo sapiens'* ingenuity in employing for a variety of purposes whatever tool he happens to have! Thus in her sense of order and condition there is nothing abnormal about Mrs. Metz, and she manages the food system well.

A FINE DINNER FOR KURT

Confined to kitchen and market, we find life dull and try to squeeze novelty out of it; to build fantasies on what look to us like commonplaces, making them into something fey; to convert everyday happenings into exciting events. Thus the dreariness of the days can, hopefully, be transmuted. On the third day of my visit Mrs. Metz was enthusiastic about making a fine dinner for her husband, and she and I went shopping on Broadway.

(Third day.) I parked the car and Mrs. Metz fished in her purse for some change for the meter, which I took because I didn't have any. I indicated I would remain in the car but she asked me to go with her. As we crossed the street she took my arm.

We went first to a butcher shop about which she is very enthusiastic, and after discussing whether or not she should buy capon and telling the butcher just what she was planning to do, she settled for chickens. The butcher "weighed" the chickens: he didn't wait to see what the weight really was but dumped each bird perfunctorily on the scale, took it off and told her the price when she asked.

On the way to the supermarket where Mrs. Metz would do her "preliminary" shopping for the week—she will do her big shopping tomorrow*—she talked enthusiastically about the wonderful supper she is going to cook: chicken soup and roast chicken. That's why she bought two chickens, one for soup and one for roasting; but she also said that when you dip boiled chicken in gravy, it tastes just like roast chicken.

In the supermarket Mrs. Metz, without asking, cut a test slice off a rotten-looking watermelon and was about to buy it. Having been sensitized to the tendency of schizophrenogenic women to buy spoiled produce, and not wishing to eat rotten watermelon, I pointed out that the melon she was about to buy was overripe. Several times, rather insistently, she asked the clerk in charge of fruits and vegetables whether he had any more watermelon, but he didn't answer. At last he got another melon and cut it open, and she bought a piece, though it was just a shade better than the first.

Mrs. Metz bought very small cans of things—cans that would not even serve two people. I would have bought larger ones, but the point is that she puts at least half a dozen different things on the table, so you end up having enough to eat. She bought canned mushrooms, saying she puts mushrooms in everything. She calls little cans "little pieces" and says that Kurt is so fond of little pieces.

After the supermarket we went to a bakery. Mrs. Metz said a number of times that she was going to make either blueberry or corn muffins, but then it turned out that she was going to buy them. She took a number in the bake shop, but on being told by a clerk that there were no blueberry muffins, she left, and went to another shop where, I think, she bought corn muffins. Next we went to the five-

---

* See "Striving to Be Mother and Daughter," p. 245.

and-ten, where Mrs. Metz bought paper and envelopes for thank-you notes to some out-of-town people who had entertained her. Mrs. Metz joked and was hail-fellow-well-met with the clerk behind the counter.

Last we went to the shop where Mrs. Metz's radio was being fixed, and when she discovered that it cost over $9 to fix her $20 radio, she was so upset that she called her husband. However, from looking at her you couldn't tell that she was agitated. Mr. Metz apparently was annoyed too. We all thought she had been overcharged. On the way home she said she couldn't live without her radio, and when we arrived she asked me to plug it in in the bedroom. (Later when we went out again she left it on.)

So now we were home and the radio was plugged in and Mrs. Metz was in the kitchen making soup. She cleaned the inside of the chicken, taking out the coagulated blood, like so many women. She washed it thoroughly and put it on to cook. First she put an onion in the water and let it boil awhile; then she put in the celery and carrots. The other chicken she set aside for roasting.

Mrs. Metz is setting great store on tonight's dinner. She said they usually go out for dinner on Friday, and when I asked why they didn't today, she said they just felt like having dinner at home tonight. I asked whether Myra was going to have dinner out and Mrs. Metz said no, she wanted Myra to have dinner at home tonight. [I left to pick up Myra at the beach.]

When we got home, everything was ready. Mrs. Metz had two kinds of muffins in the oven—a corn muffin and one made with raisins. She expressed anxiety that her husband had not called and she remained anxious until he did; after all, she was making him a big dinner and she wanted him home on time.

Sometime before her husband came home Mrs. Metz sent Myra to her neighbor friend's and to Mary's house with some muffins.

The first questions are: Where does Mrs. Metz behave like a good citizen and where does she misbehave? She is a fine and upright citizen in allowing herself to be cheated by the butcher and the supermarket, but she seems too brash with the clerks. (I think she was too brash with me, too.) Every nice, clean-cut, law-abiding American must allow himself to be cheated rather than make a scene in public. You simply don't say to the butcher, "Hold it there, let me see how much it weighs! How much did you say it costs a pound?" And only shameless people compel a clerk to get them a melon that isn't rotten! Mrs. Metz has behaved beautifully, and it is only because I press her that she practically disgraces herself by refusing to accept far-gone produce. She quickly redeems herself, however, by taking a piece of melon almost as bad. Mrs. Metz shows her willingness to submit to the laws of pecuniary chicanery as well, by not complaining to the radio repairman about being overcharged. She is quiet, keeps her anxiety and anger to herself and merely telephones her husband, who does nothing either. So far, so good, for these fine citizens!

Mrs. Metz has shown her strength again—strength in the sense of being cowed, of having the culturally determined vulnerabilities, of having enough sense of decency not to resist the brazen exploitation of the pecuniary culture. This is mental health! I will go further: Mrs. Metz, in *not noticing* that the melons were not fit to eat, has demonstrated something of the normal American's inability to perceive what he is buying. After all, it is not only these watermelons that are not worth buying!

Mrs. Metz says she puts "mushrooms in everything." This is a kind of kitchen recklessness, a cutting loose, a sort of painting-the-kitchen-red with mushrooms; a kind of devil-may-careishness by a bored housewife. She can, perhaps, do nothing with her life but she can "put mushrooms in everything." There is something of this in buying "little pieces," so that half a dozen fruits or vegetables go on the table instead of one.

But let us not go too far: Mrs. Metz *is* doing *something* with her life; she is holding her family together. And putting mushrooms in everything, being hail-fellow-well-met, and so on, prove that she is still prepared to face life with a certain vigor.

Having built her dream of Friday on the dinner, Mrs. Metz worked hard, and as far as I could see, she did everything "normally." The only trouble was that she didn't check the time precisely, with the result that dinner was ready over half an hour before her husband came home, and had to be reheated—a kind of disaster. But all of this is within normal limits. The nice neighborly gesture with the muffins shows once more that Mrs. Metz has good social sense.

Although everything Mrs. Metz did in market and kitchen was "within normal limits," all in all I am left with the feeling that she seems a little strange. Taking my arm familiarly when she knows me not quite two and a half days, being bluff and hearty with the clerks, letting herself be sold overripe melon and charged a high price for the repair of her radio without asking questions suggest that all is not well with her: she is just a shade off on too many things. Does she have to be cheated on the chicken, the melon *and* the radio? Isn't she a bit too passive and conforming in some things; a bit too forward in others? Behind her hearty exterior, isn't there a fright? A fear of the world?

Since in Mrs. Metz's life there have been few rewards, she feels she has nothing. Besides, life in backyard and kitchen is boring. She will therefore seize on some things and try to transmute them. She will glorify a Friday dinner, "put mushrooms in everything," make her jingles into a "book of poems," make her honeymoon a "theatrical" production, and so on. The clerks in the stores become conquests. Mrs. Metz has no better way of lessening the pain of the real blows she has received in life.

Since she is anxious, oppressed by the sensation of social punishment, she overconforms, unable to do battle with the vegetable man, the butcher and the radio repairman, which would save a little money and give some sense of selfhood. Because Mrs. Metz swings between small glory and big conformity, she yearns for something novel, something a bit out of the ordinary, something, perhaps, even slightly off-color that might provide that minimal function of deviation in a conforming, empty life. I think this dialectic accounts for much of Mrs. Metz's behavior in the outer world. When she is with her family, she cannot free herself to be a little bit wild.

I think that all who are able to exist in our culture without falling into too deep a depression, without being eaten up by dissatisfaction, are able to do so because the gratifications they are able to extort from the culture compensate for the pain of conforming social life. There are many, however, who are able to continue also because they compensate their pain by exaggerating the significance of the gratifications, weighing them inwardly so that they balance out misery.

The potentiality for gratification inheres in enjoyment of our selves. If I were to say that "my self is like Mozart's music," people might forgive me on the ground that I was mad, which would be true because I would have combined in one intolerable image the sacredness of Mozart's person and the greatness of his music. It is clear therefore that culture compels me to restrict my conception of my self. *My culture would rather that I think myself a swine than that I think myself Mozart!* My culture clearly permits me to degrade myself—to think of myself as stinking, so that I have to use deodorants, to eat like a pig, etc.—but it will clap me in a lunatic asylum for inappropriate autoelevation. It follows that our culture makes it easier to feel degraded than elevated. Hence another reason for depression.

But things are not that simple, you say; the point is the literalness of one's self-conception. If I thought I was literally a pig—grunted, wallowed in the mud, ate garbage,* etc.—I would be put into an asylum just as surely as if I thought myself literally Mozart. Very well; a point has been partially won. But consider this: suppose that in neither case my conception was literal. In the first case I act as if people recognized genius in me, which I do not have; in the second I act as if people recognized merely a barnyard animal in me; in the first case I act as if people were at my feet; in the second I act as if I were at people's feet. In the first case I act as if people owed me homage. Which is more acceptable to society? Clearly the second, for, as I have said, it is easier to tolerate the man who thinks he is nothing than the person who gives himself airs. We thus are encouraged to develop the selves most acceptable to society, and if we cannot strike the balance society considers perfect—have an "integrated ego," be "authentic," "autonomous," have a "sense of identity," etc.—it is better, from society's point of view, to err in the direction of nothingness than in the direction of inflation. A clean, decent person automatically underrates himself —at least publicly.

Although the ability to enjoy our *selves* is a necessary condition for the enjoyment of life in our culture, the insistence that selves adapt to principles of social acceptability creates immense difficulties in perception. How does one sharpen the inner eye in order to develop a self which society wants but which will also be able to enjoy life? Since most people are overwhelmed by the task, they become inwardly degraded. We are like those minuscule bureaucrats inhabiting the Pentagon, for whom it is safer to stamp a document of no strategic importance "Top Secret" than to release it to the press: they can be punished for releasing the document, but never for holding it back. Society will whip me for puffing myself up ("Who the hell does he think he is?") but leave me in peace with my feelings of self-abasement.

Mrs. Metz is, perhaps, a rather extreme case of the latter. Since there is really nothing she enjoys about herself, she invents things—like being irresistibly lovable, for example. She also magnifies little satisfactions into big ones and even creates occasions for gratification out of nothing. Mushrooms are the fields of Camelot! Freedom is in the traveling grocery store— the Arabian caravan of cabbages and grapefruit. In apparent pain and depression because of menstrual cramps, in an instant she is off and away when Sindbad's whistle blows. She lives a constrained life and therefore feels of almost anything she can *choose* to do: "This is freedom!" Since death is the ultimate imprisonment, a little freedom is a small escape from

---

* The filthy, garbage-eating-pig image is a product of Western culture. Pigs living among primitives are free of such dirty habits.

death, and one who feels almost dead will snatch at any liberty—even de-lusional—to escape for a moment from the sensation of being dead.

A FRANKFURTER ON A SUMMER AFTERNOON

I have argued that Mrs. Metz extorts big gratifications from little things, that minor diversions from kitchen and market are construed as libera-tions, and that Mr. Metz is a kill-joy. Put these together and we get the conditions for a high-keyed expedition with the observer, in quest of a very special frankfurter.

(Second day.) Around noon Mrs. Metz finished preparing the soup for to-night's dinner. When we were shopping this morning she had expressed a strong yen for hot dogs for lunch, and I suggested, "Let's come over here and get some later on." I think she said, "Well, we can have lunch at home, too," so we came home and brought all the groceries. Now she asked, "Well, what would you like for lunch, Jules?" She repeated it a number of times, and I answered each time, "Whatever you would like to have; whatever you have lying around." At last I caught on and said, "Let's go out and have hot dogs," and she thought that a wonderful idea. All the time we were having them she kept saying, "This is a treat; this is great!"

The hot-dog place we were trying to find was a very special one. Mrs. Metz didn't like the first one we saw because the woman there served warmed-over French fries. There was a very special place, which was really a "dump," Mrs. Metz said, but they had wonderful frankfurters and wonderful French fries. We drove around for a while and at last found this little joint, but it turned out not to be the place she had in mind. She could tell because the place she had in mind had rolls with poppy seeds but this one didn't. Mrs. Metz was disappointed, but we stayed there. She thought the French fries were warmed over, but then de-cided they really weren't. She said, as we were waiting, that her mouth was water-ing.

Mrs. Metz had a frankfurter with mustard, relish and piccalilli, and I had two frankfurters with mustard and relish but no French fries. Mrs. Metz is wild about them.

We didn't talk much in the joint.

This quest for liberation, novelty and excitement is enveloped in oral fantasies and an oral metaphysic: a combination of principles about frank-furters. Fundamental components of the metaphysic are, first, a proposi-tion from folk myth that treasure is often concealed beneath a modest, even forbidding exterior, and that it is often found by blundering upon it in commonplace, even degraded surroundings. The best frankfurters are therefore to be found in "dumps." This particular dump, however, has a distinguishing sign—the poppy-seed roll—that reveals its truth. There are places that look like true dumps but are deceptive, and reveal themselves by the fact that the French fries are warmed over. Here we have determin-ism with roots deep in our cultural past. Since deception is everywhere, a person has to search among all likely places until, always mindful of trick-ery, he comes upon the right, the honest one. Somewhere there may even be a witch—like a woman who serves warmed-over French fries.

The frankfurter is in two worlds—the ordinary one of home and kitchen, and the holiday world of bowling alleys, amusement parks, drive-in movies, big baseball and football games, and so on. Thus, if one cannot have a real holiday, one can absorb its spiritual substance in a hot dog. If you can't go around the world, you can go around the corner for a frankfurter in a seedy joint where you can imagine yourself on the docks of Piraeus or in a dive in Istanbul. A hot dog is lower-middle-class shishkebob.

In her feeling for frankfurters, in her choice of pathway to liberation, Mrs. Metz shows she is normal. Just as she understands the *issue* of the difference between lollipops and suckers and draws nice distinctions between them, so she has an intuitive awareness of the realities of the frankfurters. Hers is the pathetic scholarship of the empty and the bored, and with this immense company she has her closest intellectual kinship.

I now attempt to bring together the discussion of lollipops and suckers (see page 245) and the expedition in search of the right frankfurter place. Since both matters require careful distinctions between right and wrong choice, they involve a kind of morality, basically a morality of the palate. There is embodied in these two also a kind of perfectionistic outlook—if you are judicious, perceptive and experienced, perfection will be achieved. Thus, as in all moral systems, right and wrong are related to a perfectionistic theory. We have here also a theory of the absolute: the absolutely perfect candy, the absolutely perfect frankfurter. Many people do nothing more exciting with their spare time than drive around looking for the absolutely perfect restaurant. In this way you can have the illusion of the primordial human quest, while all the time you are in the intellectual gutter of existence. At the same time, eating the absolutely perfect meal can be a transfiguring experience, so that all week long a person who has encountered the absolute may seem to exude gastronomic spirituality. We all know such people, those who have enough money to spend on expensive restaurants: they smile with a quiet inwardness derived from remembering the last dish.

In spite of longing for a hot dog, Mrs. Metz did not let emotion drive her to transgress the boundaries of propriety. Patiently, with restraint, and only indirectly, she maneuvered until I remembered that I had proposed going for frankfurters. Mrs. Metz did not accept my first invitation but suggested instead that we eat at home. Having made the appropriate gesture, she then managed me so that the idea of lunching out would again appear to come from me. Since I repeated it—even after she had suggested lunching at home—how could she not defer to my wishes without violating propriety? Since the perfect woman makes it appear as if her wishes come from the man, Mrs. Metz scores perfectly here!

Throughout her days, sometimes in fantasy, sometimes in reality, now quietly, now boisterously, there is an interplay in Mrs. Metz's personality between conventionality and deviation, between novelty and boredom, between freedom and constraint, between friendship and isolation, between selfhood and self-rejection. This is, perhaps, a description of Average Man's and Average Woman's days in our culture: they fluctuate within this dialectic, urged inwardly to break the narrowness of life but restrained by fear, stretching out their arms to others but held back by inner admonitions, seeking novelty but wanting also the security of sameness.

Dealing with Others: Concentric Circles of Feeling

Closeness. Who are these others? They are family, friends, relatives, servants, clerks in stores, bus drivers, milkmen, postmen, garbage men—dozens of service persons who are here for a moment and then gone. (In the life of a student there are teachers and fellow-students, principals, coaches, and others—perhaps the service personnel in the school cafeteria.) To all these people we behave differently. From our families we want much of one kind of love, from our friends another. From servants and service personnel we expect no love at all, and surely from utter strangers we expect nothing, not even a smile, unless we happen to bump into them, gently and by accident. We greet each kind of person differently; possibly an expression of love for members of the family in the morning; for friends we have a different greeting; and service personnel we might not greet at all, depending on the situation; in a suburb one knows one's mailman fairly well and the greeting to him has a certain warmth; the suburban garbage man is more distant than the postman. Servants should be treated with some measure of prudence nowadays: we don't expect their love and they don't expect ours, but nevertheless, since this is an age of equality, servants cannot be slighted. They should even be courted because they are scarce. And so it goes. Were we to construct a model of the diffusion of attitudes, whether of love, circumspection, confidence, effusiveness, etc., with our family as the center of a series of concentric circles, our friends next, our relatives thereafter, and so on, for every attitude we could chart the differences as we went outward from the innermost circle. Though such models are not studied in the schools, we all learn them by experience, and a measure of savoir-faire—i.e., of mental health—is our ability to have the right attitude and to act right in each of the circles: not to be too familiar with the milkman; to be circumspect with servants and to be properly warm to the postman, depending upon where we live, etc. With Otto, the milkman, Mrs. Metz seems a little too familiar:

(Fourth day.) Mrs. Metz was all dressed to go shopping and was running back and forth from the kitchen to the backyard watching for the milkman, who seemed to be very late. She said he was probably talking with some of the housewives down the line.

Eventually, after breakfast, the milkman arrived. When she saw him she called out, "Bring in everything you've got, Otto. I want white milk and chocolate milk and butter and eggs." Then she gave me the rundown on Otto while he was getting ready to come in, telling me about his family and children.

Otto seemed like a nice, sweet-looking person, and, of course, Mrs. Metz treated him as hail-fellow-well-met. She asked about his family and lamented with him the fact that his wife wasn't feeling well and that the doctor bills were so high. Mrs. Metz treated Otto with great familiarity, the way she does almost everybody. By the way, she calls not only me "babe," she calls Otto "babe" too. She calls a lot of random people "babe."

Otto would have remained and talked indefinitely but she shooed him out. She suggested he go to his religious charity for financial help, but he said that would only be a last resort.

I am going to try to clarify this matter of friendliness and familiarity by studying Mrs. Metz's attitude toward the Barneses, her neighbors.

On the second day Mrs. Metz and I were on our way out to the hot-dog joint for lunch.

On the way out she asked Mrs. Barnes if she would like to have one brought back, and Mrs. Barnes said yes. I said I would pay for all the hot dogs, but Mrs. Metz wouldn't let me pay for Mrs. Barnes's because Mrs. Barnes didn't know me, and besides, the Metzes and the Barneses have a relationship, she said, where they account for everything exactly. The relationship between the Metzes and the Barneses is a neighborly one, not a friendly one, and Mrs. Metz was very careful to explain that to me. They come in and have a cup of coffee with one another every once in a while, and the Metzes keep Mrs. Barnes company when her husband is away, but this has not developed into a friendship between the families. Myra spends a lot of time at the Barneses'; sometimes she sleeps at Mrs. Barnes's when her husband is away. Mrs. Barnes's daughter, now married, was like a sister to Myra and like a daughter to Mrs. Metz.

I should have asked Mrs. Metz, "Why don't you consider your relationship with the Barneses a friendly one?"; "What would it have to be like for you to call it friendly?"; "Why didn't it ever become friendly?"; "Look, you say that the Barneses' daughter was like a daughter to you and a sister to Myra; isn't that friendship?"; "Isn't it a friendly relationship when you sit up with a woman whose husband is away?" But since I didn't ask these questions, I don't know what restrained Mrs. Metz from calling the Barneses friends. What I can say, however, is that in spite of many exchanges between the families, Mrs. Metz does not want to be considered a friend of the Barneses. And I can say also that although the Metzes act toward the Barneses as if they were friends, Mrs. Metz denies that they are. The same applies to Otto: though he is treated familiarly and is the object of Mrs. Metz's (apparent) solicitude, he is really a stranger. Thus there is considerable as-ifness in Mrs. Metz's behavior toward people outside the family.

Anger and contempt. Though it would be possible to draw a model for "familiarity" like the one for love, one cannot be drawn for anger because the expression of it depends on different factors. In our culture, these are primarily *status, power, propriety* and *payoff*. When someone is frustrated, he is most likely to express anger when the person who frustrates him (the irritant) is lower in the social scale and weaker;* but the probability of someone's having an angry outburst is affected also by the chance that it will pay off. Even if the irritant is low-status and powerless, the likelihood that the frustrated person will show anger is not great if he feels that he won't get anything out of it—if he feels there will be no improvement in the situation or in the person who is frustrating him, and that there isn't even the possibility of injuring him in a self-satisfying way, like firing or humiliating him. But even if the status, power and payoff conditions are propitious, anger might not come out if it is inappropriate. It might, for example, pay off to scream at the children next door for trampling your irises, but it would be inappropriate because in suburbs one does not scream at the neighbor's children: your irises are hostage to public relations. In most cases the payoff is strongly affected by culturally determined, intuitive feelings of propriety.

---

* A sweeper or a machine operator is lower in status than a foreman or a boss, but foreman and boss must act circumspectly because although the worker is lower, he is far from powerless nowadays, since the union will back him up.

These considerations are relevant to what happened between Mrs. Metz and Bertha, the woman who was sent from the employment agency to do Mrs. Metz's ironing.

(Second day.) When I arrived at about nine forty-five, Bertha was there. She had never worked for the Metzes before. Mrs. Metz wanted her to do the ironing, and although Bertha said she didn't iron, Mrs. Metz paid no attention. When we got down to the basement and Bertha saw all the work she had to do she repeated that she didn't iron and said that she even sent her own laundry out—she was a cleaner, not an ironer. Mrs. Metz tried to persuade her to do the ironing; Bertha kept insisting she never ironed.

Mrs. Metz took all the wash off the line and piled it up on a table and Bertha set up the ironing board, announcing, meanwhile, that she never did any ironing. Then she said she didn't want to iron in the basement because the floor was dirty. Mrs. Metz told her that it was nice to iron in the basement because it was cooler, but if Bertha didn't want to iron there, she could do it upstairs.

All the while that Bertha kept saying she was a cleaner and not an ironer, Mrs. Metz was very conciliatory.

I carried the ironing board upstairs, and then the business started all over again—Bertha saying she never did any ironing and Mrs. Metz trying to persuade her—but at last they decided Bertha wouldn't work there. Mrs. Metz got on the phone and told the employment agency that she had specifically asked for someone who would iron. Then Bertha got on and said she had told them she was a cleaner, not an ironer.

Bertha left, the agency promised to send someone who would iron, and at eleven o'clock Esther appeared. Mrs. Metz told her what to do and Esther did an excellent job.

The three of us had lunch together, but Esther was on a diet and could not have anything with salt in it, could not have cheese or anything frozen or canned. Mrs. Metz kept giving me the wink, as if she were very skeptical of Esther's diet, but it seemed authentic to me—she had gotten it from the Clinic.

At any rate, Mrs. Metz, with no sign that there was anything about Esther's color that was unusual, served us all, and we ate the same food, with the exception, of course, that Esther stuck to her diet and refused cheese.

It seems to me that the argument between Mrs. Metz and Bertha was merely a normal kind of wrangle. Although Mrs. Metz was quite annoyed that the agency had sent the wrong kind of person, she was very decent to Bertha, and so was Bertha to her. She asked Bertha if she would come and clean sometime and Bertha kept saying, "I don't iron." From the time Bertha left until Esther arrived Mrs. Metz was quite upset. It might have been related to the fact that she was in her third day of menstruation and still had severe cramps.

Mrs. Metz was also irritated by the fact that Bertha had sat down and smoked a cigarette before starting to work. Mrs. Metz told me she gave Bertha breakfast, though it was not part of the deal.

The fact that Mrs. Metz showed no anger, although Bertha is a Negro and a domestic and therefore of very low status, suggests that she was restrained by a sense of propriety, that she did not view Bertha as powerless but as likely to retaliate, that she might not even have felt her to be of lower status and that she saw no chance of a pay-off anyway, even if she had gotten angry.

Considering how Mrs. Metz might have behaved, she did very well. She did not shout, did not become visibly agitated and did not scold the agency. It is true that she gives the impression of having been too insistent with Bertha, when a solution to her problem was obvious and easy; but still, she was merely absurd, not bizarre. She tried to force the issue, and that was absurd; but if she had shouted accusations at Bertha, that would have been so far outside the bounds of propriety that it would have bordered on the bizarre. Furthermore, it would not have done any good. To be ruled by these considerations requires normal restraint and a feeling for the culture. In our culture, "reasonableness" cannot be legitimately transgressed by emotion, especially with strangers, for we set intuitive limits on what we allow emotion to compel us to do. We are not like, let us say, the Alorese of Dutch New Guinea, who let anybody shriek almost anything—even permitting small children to call down immense curses on their parents—when they are angry. In our culture, but in some ethnic groups more than in others, unreasonableness under the influence of strong feelings is not so bad in the family, but with outsiders ("to reveal yourself like that in front of strangers") it is shameful.

Since Mrs. Metz would only have looked ridiculous to Bertha if she had gotten angry, restraint preserved her social image. Such sensitivity to the vulnerability of one's image in the presence of different kinds of people is a necessary component of a sense of propriety and hence of normality. Furthermore, and finally, nice people must not shout at all, except, perhaps, when deeply offended.

In every culture there are criteria of emotional expression, felt intuitively by everybody, though they may never be able to put them into words, and people feel when the criteria have been violated—when emotional expression is not appropriate to the situation. Such a folk intuition is the only basis for the notion of "inappropriate affect," considered an important symptom of schizophrenia, by those who believe their own expressions are appropriate. For such firm reasons I feel Mrs. Metz behaved normally.

I now consider the problem of Mrs. Metz's having given Bertha breakfast. In our culture it is necessary to feed domestics who work by the day, because since they are at the bottom of the occupational scale and therefore receive the lowest pay, they are also subject to that most primitive of all wages, "payment in kind";* hence food is included in the pay. Because they will be working intimately around the house—also a primitive economic form of labor—feeding them also helps break down boundaries between them and the employer. Furthermore, since the worker may have had little or nothing to eat before starting, it is good to give coffee or breakfast; he may work better. Mrs. Metz therefore shows good sense and a sense of propriety. It may be, however, that she persisted in trying to get Bertha to do the ironing *because* she had given her breakfast and let her smoke a cigarette, for if Bertha went away without doing the work, Mrs. Metz would have lost part of the hidden wage she had already paid her. In spite of this frustration Mrs. Metz met the situation well "within normal limits." She even washed Bertha's dishes, i.e., *she worked for Bertha, and without pay!*

---

* All wage systems that are still in the most primitive stage include payment in kind. At the bottom of the occupational scale in a developed capitalist economy, we therefore find vestiges of the earliest wage systems.

Not to have gotten angry with her under such circumstances was an achievement.

Now consider the following, from the next day:

Mrs. Metz kept up a steady stream of chatter. She talked about the time she lost weight dieting when Albert was having such a terrible time. She had shown a great deal of will power and refused to break her diet even under great provocation. As an instance, she told of having gone to a party given by an extremely wealthy relative, and described in heroic terms the quantity and variety of delicious foods served. Yet all she had was a bit of cantaloupe, black coffee, and one or two other things. . . . The second time Albert broke, however, she ate everything; I guess to keep herself from going mad. She just kept eating and eating. Now, she says, she doesn't have the will power to keep to a diet. The pills that are supposed to reduce appetite, she says, simply give her all kinds of allergic reactions.

Perhaps if Esther had not insisted on her diet, she might not have been offensive to Mrs. Metz. Dieting has very disturbing overtones for Mrs. Metz, because when she thinks of dieting she associates it with her son's psychosis. When she talks about dieting it is as if she were saying, "The first time Albert broke, I had some hope, but the second time I lost it." And, even more speculatively, "When his mind broke, so did my will, and so might I."

Distortions in Communication

Mrs. Metz's behavior fluctuates gently between convention and deviation, but sometimes her language diverged sharply from conventional speech. It was not extensive; only from time to time a sudden alteration caught my ear.

When she was talking to me about the collection of mementos she was showing me, she wanted to comment on their great age and said, "They are yellow with pages" (instead of "yellow with age"). When she wanted to say she was lying down with her eyes closed, she said, "I was lying there with my eyes folded," which I presume is a telescoping of "eyes closed and arms folded."

Mrs. Metz spoke about a relative who bought up land in a town for $14 a "share"; by which I presume she meant "acre" or "lot." She mentioned another relative who collected "compensation" when the wonderful market he owned blew up. I presume she meant "insurance."

The confusion of "share" with "acre" or "lot," and of "compensation" with "insurance," may not be merely instances of poorly schooled normality, but further examples of her telescoping ideas through her use of words. The thought that the relative was able to make a nice profit on land bought at $14 an acre might have suggested to Mrs. Metz that she would have liked to have a *share* of it; and collecting insurance might have reminded her of her husband's eligibility for *compensation*, as an employee, should his place of work blow up.

As Mrs. Metz started to take the shopping bags out of the car, she said, "I guess we'll have to take them out singularly," meaning "one at a time."

She referred to small cans of pineapple juice as "pieces of pineapple."

Her mixed-upness, however, goes much further, because sometimes she seems to be saying just the opposite of what she means. [Nothing specific in the record on this.]

Sometimes it was hard to tell whether Mrs. Metz was confused or whether she was avoiding the truth. The following example illustrates the problem.

A QUESTION OF TRUTH

(Second day.) The Metzes are invited to a dinner on Saturday night and I asked Mrs. Metz if she could bring me along as a houseguest. She said "Definitely no," because these were all "young couples."

Since the Metzes are in their forties, one could hardly call them a "young couple" but I have the idea that she still thinks of her self and her husband as a "young couple."

(Two days later.) Mrs. Metz is still quite upset about the problem of going to visit their friend tonight. She said the man is about the same age as Mr. Metz and the woman about her own age—she wasn't sure about this. So I said to Mrs. Metz, "I thought you said they were a young couple?" This startled her and she said, "Well, er, I mean they married later than we did, they've only been married nine years."

Perhaps Mrs. Metz lied because she could not think of a way to explain me to her friends. Proof that she lied would be that she equated chronological age with length of marriage, for if the friends are "young" because they have been married only nine years, then the Metzes are "old" because they have been married twice as long, and therefore have no business at the party. On the other hand, since Mrs. Metz still finds herself in memory rather than in hope, since she still yearns for the unreality of her youth and the excitement of courtship and honeymoon, since the past is remembered as colorful and the present is drab, she may cling to the memory of herself when young. Thus she compresses time because she has to forget the present.

Let us come straight to the point: Mrs. Metz did not want me at the dinner party, so gave me a song and dance, and the reason she calls herself and Kurt "young" is merely because women in our culture have to think themselves young—especially as they become menopausal. But it seems to me that this would be to assume that I had the view of her she had of herself.

Continuing with the data:

Mrs. Metz didn't want to go and it was not clear whether her husband wanted to, but these friends have been putting tremendous pressure on them to come. I said to Mrs. Metz that apparently she wanted to go in order to please them, but she replied, "I want to go because Kurt needs to get out." She told me that these people love to eat. They have no children and are forever going to restaurants. Once the Metzes went out with them on some sort of excursion and they ate constantly. The four of them ended up in a movie, but Mr. and Mrs. Metz had eaten so much that they couldn't enjoy the picture. She is afraid of the enormous quantities of fatty foods they will put on the table. When I left today Mrs. Metz was still not sure whether they were going, and I was to call at six o'clock to find out. [They went.]

We are back again and comfortable in middle-class sham. Neither Mrs. Metz nor her husband wants to go to the party, but do so because of "pressure" and for other reasons their hosts might not like to hear. She never said she was fond of these people. We note that evenings and outings with them have strong oral components—an extremely important aspect of middle-class sociability—and that although the Metzes are afraid of the food, they eat it anyway. Take a person who rarely goes to a fine restaurant and set before him, in immense array, viands he has never, or rarely, eaten before, and he may well eat himself sick. It seems to me that Mrs. Metz showed a good healthy fear of eating too much.

I believe that Mrs. Metz's behavior was within normal limits. Even saying she insists on telling the truth is strictly within normal limits, representing, perhaps, the best expression of normality—for how many among us know when we lie? As a matter of fact, one who is *perfectly* socialized to the corrupt system moves between truth and falsehood as if there were no difference; all that exists for him is expediency.

Perhaps expediency was behind the following series of contradictions:

While Myra and Mary went into the doughnut shop with Mrs. Metz, I told Mr. Metz that he shouldn't think that I wanted to go to the movies simply because I offered to lend my car if they wanted to go to a drive-in. He said no, that hadn't occurred to him, but he doesn't like to go out during the week. As a matter of fact, he said, he doesn't like movies at all, although his wife *used to be crazy* about them.

. . .

I mentioned to Mrs. Metz that her husband had not wanted to go to the movies the night before. She said that he is not a moviegoer, and that the poor man is so tired when he gets home from work. "Why should he drag himself out to the movies?" She spoke without irritation.

Perhaps Mrs. Metz thought that if she told me she and her husband were fond of the movies, I might offer to take them. But if her husband is tired at night, why should she wish to drag him out? Perhaps she thinks it would be good for him to get out of the house. Perhaps, perhaps . . . Then, on the other hand, while I was there she never watched a movie on TV, always preferring game shows. As a matter of fact, at home she had made the airwaves completely hers: when the family is around, she determines what they shall watch; and the only radio in the house is hers—it is on her side of the bed.

Mrs. Metz said she is like me—she cannot stand subterfuge,* must always say exactly what's on her mind and insists on telling the truth.

Speaking of her children, Mrs. Metz says that

she disciplines them by saying, "If you have done anything wrong, come and tell me, because I would rather hear it from you than from other people."

Demanding the truth from children while giving one's self the privilege of concealing it from them is another indicator of Mrs. Metz's normality,

* My word for her idea, the wording of which I do not remember exactly.

for in our culture this privilege is an expression of the legitimate exercise of superior power and therefore a proper maneuver to conceal one's shortcomings. It is hard to imagine how our culture could carry on otherwise. Were parents to reveal to children what *they* had done "wrong," it would destroy that precious parental image, that image so necessary to the maintenance of childish illusions about the parents, to the formation of character, to the constitution of the superego. Were the parental image damaged by parental confession, it could never be swallowed, i.e., introjected by the child. Better an illusory image than none at all. Another score then for Mrs. Metz on the "cultural normality test." But as we all know, children's heads are full of involuntary parental confessions anyhow. The average child is able to deal with this, using his hidden knowledge to outwit the parent and maneuver in the outer world. The child who goes mad has found the involuntary confessions too devastating to master.

The gigantic, normal fraud that parents in our culture are *compelled* to perpetrate on their children is at the same time a burlesque. To be forced to present one's self to one's children as the embodiment of moral perfection is comic, tragic and without parallel in tribal society. Since we feel that some catastrophe would occur if our children knew the truth about us and our feelings about them, our culture slams an iron door between parent and child. Basically, then, there is a moral fraudulence at the very beginning; not in the sense that people are morally fraudulent, but in the sense that since the essence of domestic morality is a fraud, to tell the truth is wrong. What other civilizations have had to live with this? Peasant China, I believe, and peasant India. Fraudulence between parent and child is thus an accomplishment of the Great Civilizations. Hence those who live in them naturally expect it of their statesmen, too. The political function of parental hypocrisy is to enable us to endure lying politicians and even to love them.

Thus, in dealing with Mrs. Metz's truth, we learn that it is a mixture of middle-class shams, conventions, memories, hopes and vulnerabilities, and since this is truth for most middle-class people, we must enter in her case history: "Conception of truth: within normal limits."

Sometimes, as I analyze Mrs. Metz's "truth functions," I think that I am not dealing with a generally mixed-up person, but with one who is somewhat fuzzy because she does not have to split hairs with a professor everyday. Consider the following:

(Fourth day.) She announced that she is not going to be around on Monday because Mondays she has a special appointment and spends a lot of time downtown. Wondering what the appointment was, I asked her whether she gets psychotherapy, and she said, "Why, do you think I need it?" And I answered that I had no idea, but that the reason I asked was that many people don't like to say that they are in therapy, so when she was mysterious about it, I thought she was going to psychotherapy . She said no, she goes to see her girl friend every Monday and takes care of her children: she likes to get out of the house this way.

Now came one of those curious mixed-up statements Mrs. Metz makes. She says the reason she didn't say where she was going was because (and I'm not sure this is what she said) sometimes her girl friend might not like (I'm sorry, I really can't remember the mixed-up reasons for not saying where she was going). But I think other people must have trouble figuring out the relationship between her explanation of what she does and what she is really doing.

I had no proof of the last sentence, and as a matter of fact, I had little difficulty following most conversations in the family. That there was such ambiguity in the family relationships is clear, but when Mrs. Metz was talking to her family, there usually was no mistaking what she was saying.

The following example seems to be clearly one of confused perception:

When the game show ended, the next program on the same channel was what looked like a very interesting picture of Africa, but Mrs. Metz said, "Oh, this is one of those costume things. Turn to something else. Maybe you can get a game show." She doesn't like anything with costumes in it, she says, but she wasn't able to give me a good reason why; she just thinks they are silly. But she once named a number of "costume" movies she had enjoyed.

Lack of interest in Africa is lack of interest in the strange (i.e., the unconventional), and since costumes express strangeness, a picture of Africa is a costume picture. Furthermore, as she indicated to me, she is afraid of almost any place in the world except the United States.

My minimal net conclusion, which applies equally to the date with the heavy eaters, the date with the girl friend downtown and the incident of the TV is that Mrs. Metz has tendencies to impenetrability which make trained observers wonder whether she isn't just confused at times. This surmise gains support from her more obvious distortions of language: "yellow with pages," "I was lying there with my eyes folded," etc. Yet, in spite of occasional *impenetrability*, Mrs. Metz shows a normal grasp of fundamental cultural frames of reference, including sham. Her main difficulty with sham, of course, is that it has become entangled in her family relationships.

To help the reader draw his own conclusions I summarize other distortions I discussed earlier:

1. If Albert were to ride his sister's bicycle he might hurt his "groin."
2. "Myra gave birth to me."
3. Mrs. Metz "gave up everything" to join her husband in the distant town where he was working.
4. Albert is "dead."

Perhaps some might prefer to call these "distortions in thought." In that category, then, belongs her behavior on her wedding day: her failure to appear at the appointed hour and her treating the ceremony as if it were a play in which she was the producer, readying the cast to go on stage. This line of reasoning, however, leads us to ask whether putting her arm around the owner of the traveling grocery store, calling me "babe," being hail-fellow-well-met with clerks, thinking herself sexy, and so on, are not also distortions in thought. And if the answer is affirmative, we are led necessarily to ask whether much of her life hasn't been lived according to disturbed thinking.

Summary of the Metz Case

Today the Metz household is so dominated by Gertrude that it is easy to write the story of the family as if Kurt were not there. He comes home from work, cleans up and sits down to eat his supper, and then, if nothing is going on with Myra to excite his interest or irritation, he watches TV. One struggles to insert him in the record. Forgetting him is made even easier by the fact that he does not talk readily to the observer. As I write this summary, as I wrote the report, I am constantly troubled by the fact that I seem to be including Mr. Metz only as a necessary part of my description of his wife. He enters the story not so much in his own right but as the man his wife married; not as a parent of these children, but as a person who is also there, who must from time to time be taken into account, because he has a jural right to say yes and no and because he earns the money.

In my presence Mr. Metz never said he loved his wife, and his behavior is a mixture of indifference to her pain and complete dependence on her. Myra plays up to her mother's need for demonstrations of love, while at the same time she is tantalizing and callous. She joins her mother in a tight little coalition to which the father has no entry. This exclusion is a powerful factor in the solidarity between mother and daughter. Mr. Metz simply lets it go on; it is a phase of his withdrawal from life.

Gertrude married him because she felt she had little to give and because she wanted to have things her own way; because she needed a man who would not overwhelm her with demands beyond her potential. She ran away from a man who was too passionate, too determined, too positive, too domineering for her. Yet she still imagines that man with longing. Arty really had what Mrs. Metz could only dramatize as if she had it. He took her to be the costume she wore, but she knew better. What she renounced by marrying Kurt was merely a theatrical part she played; and I trace Mrs. Metz's dislike of "costume things" in movies and TV to this disparity between what she acts out and what she really is. When she turns away from costumes she turns away from her own inner failure; every costume she sees reminds her of the costumes she would have liked to wear and of the façade she wears now.

Although Gertrude pursued Kurt for five years, when the wedding day came she failed to appear at the appointed hour, and then she tried to carry the ceremony off as if it were something between a joke and a show. She tried to extricate herself by the delusion that it was not real, that it was not happening to her.

Buoyed up by many compensating illusions, sustained by a hope that marriage, or at least children, would give her everything she wanted, Mrs. Metz was unable to awaken in her first child a capacity which, though she did not have it herself, she needed to find in him—the capacity to give oceanic love. Her inability to make Albert love her was aggravated by the fact that for three years after his birth she was seriously ill. And then too, though her husband was a temperate, responsible person, he lacked warmth and masculine character. Mrs. Metz never mentioned her husband to me in connection with her illness, never said he had been considerate or had lightened her burden, or taken care of the baby. But she did say she never let Albert go to him without her permission.

Albert was unable to make his mother happy and was isolated from his father. When I spoke to Mr. Metz about Albert's early days, all he mentioned were some minor accidents Albert had incurred.

During Albert's visit at home, the observer could witness the contradiction between what his mother had said about her feeling for him and what it actually was; between her protestations of love, at first so convincing, and the actuality of her hostility. On my trip to market with Mrs. Metz the day after she was informed that Albert was coming home, the day after she spoke sweetly to him over the telephone, I witnessed the lack of consistency between the mother's expressions of affection and the reality of her coldness.

A SPECULATIVE CHART OF THE EMOTIONAL SOURCES OF ALBERT'S PSYCHOSIS

1 *What Mrs. Metz thinks*	2 *What Mrs. Metz is able to give*	3 *What Mrs. Metz does to demonstrate love*	4 *What a child would do to reciprocate*
Love should be oceanic and demonstrative; full of hugs, kisses, love words.	Not very much.	Short, sporadic outbursts of hollow quality.	Moderate, short-lived, sporadic demonstrativeness having a hollow quality.

5 *Mrs. Metz's reaction*	6 *Child's reaction to this*	7 *Mrs. Metz's reaction to this*	8 *Child's reaction*
Anger: "The child does not love me; he is hypocritical."	"Mother is always angry with me." The child becomes withdrawn and "unloving."	Increased hostility.	Effort to save himself by hollow demonstrativeness.

Columns 5–8 are a self-reinforcing vicious circle, which may lead to mounting, disorganizing rage in the mother and psychosis in the child. The child feels he is being punished for a nameless sin and is made to feel guilty and worthless for reasons unclear to him; the mother, in a constant state of self-righteous anger, feels she has spawned a monster, who does not deserve to live. Failure to love his mother deprives the child of the right to exist. Matters are worse if the mother feels she does not have the right to be loved nor the power to attract it, for she can only hate the being that confirms her worst fears about herself. Getting the child out of the house, then, is not so much removing a disturbed person as removing the evidence of her own lovelessness, of her own inability to awaken love, of her own nothingness.

Mrs. Metz tries to be a good mother and wife. For many years she has endured her husband's snoring and his grip. She holds his hand, caresses him, invites him to put his head on her thigh, tries to make good meals for him and keep a good house. She watches over Myra and steers her on pathways to conformity. She takes interest in Myra's clothes, and when Myra is ill, hovers over her. She grants a great deal of independence to Myra, does not hound her and does not impose obligations that would be purely for her own benefit. In anger she is forbearing. Thus, though Gertrude has accepted a marriage that did not bring what she had hoped, though she has to live with all the unrealities she herself creates, and though she feels unrewarded, tied down and more fearful of society's punishments than hopeful of its rewards, she has managed to emerge, at last, as a pretty good wife and mother.

PART IV

The Wilson Family

INTRODUCTION

Availability in General

In *Life with Picasso*,* Françoise Gilot says that Picasso's mother told Olga Khoklova, his first wife, "I don't believe any woman could be happy with my son. He's available for himself but for no one else." This was not entirely true, for he was available to those he *chose*, in terms of the fantastically convoluted complexity of his character, at particular moments and for as long as he could tolerate them. Françoise relates that every morning after the birth of her first child with Picasso, she had to go through the exhausting ritual of overcoming his depression—of making it possible for him to get out of bed. Before Picasso could settle down to work it was midafternoon, for in the morning his art had no attraction for him. Françoise implies that without her, Picasso might not have been able to go on, that it was her invasion of his depression that made him available to her and to the world.

Some people are available spontaneously, others have to be made available, and some can never be made available at all; but between availability and inaccessibility there always has to be someone willing and able to exert the necessary force in the direction of the former.

Had Françoise not loved Picasso and he her—in his way—she would not have taken the trouble to help him, for it was repetitious and exhausting to go through the same struggle every morning. If she had spent a bad night she had to bring him to life, anyway. But what was there to bring her to life? Obviously Picasso's need of her; surely Picasso himself.

If Picasso had not felt the love in her resolve, would he have responded?

People are made available to others through the love and determination of those who make themselves available—and the process of bringing to life has to be repeated every day because all the fundamental tasks of existence are repetitious.† In our culture an infant will become a self only if he is urged on by love, and nobody can become a human being alone. To become human an infant needs the intervention of an available person who will compel him to become human if the child does not have enough energy (a "quiet" baby), or who will help him become human if he has. Quiet babies can be looked at romantically as not having a strong desire to be human—as not having a strong *élan vital*, or they can be viewed scientifically as having "high thresholds of response to inner and outer stimuli." This simply means that a quiet baby can put up with great discomfort from within, like a pain in the stomach or hunger, or from without, like a cold draft or mosquito bites, before he will utter a sound, while a noisy one will

* Françoise Gilot and Carlton Lake (New York, McGraw-Hill, 1964).
† On this point, see Søren Kierkegaard's *Repetition: An Essay in Experimental Psychology*, trans. and ed. by Walter Lowrie (New York, Harper, 1965).

cry at the slightest discomfort. But whether one's outlook is romantic or scientific, the primal requirement is the availability of another person. Only another person can transmute the baby's possibility of being human into an actuality. A quiet baby, left alone, does not cry, but a "noisy" one does, as if he could not breathe except in the presence of a member of the species— especially one who feels, sounds and smells like his mother. If a quiet baby is born to a quiet, withdrawn mother—one who needs to have somebody fling himself on her to get her to respond—she will not go to the baby, except to do the necessaries. "It was easy to stay away from Donald," said Mrs. Wilson, "because he never cried." But if a noisy baby is born to the same kind of woman, he may cry enough to drive her to him. A baby is not a Françoise, however; and not having the strength of an adult, he often cannot persevere until his mother's inaccessibility is broken down. But a mother who is available (not a "quiet" mother), who finds it hard to stay away, will be there often, even without a peep from the baby. Science knows nothing about the quiet babies that have been born to supremely available mothers; because those babies are compelled to join the human race by the loving energy of their mothers, they never come to the attention of doctors or psychologists. Finally, even a noisy baby born to a quiet mother may become autistic, never become human, because he never got the necessary social stimulation. Mrs. Jones in this book* and Mrs. Portman in my *Culture Against Man*† are withdrawn mothers who do not go to noisy babies. In such situations the pediatric folklore advises against spoiling the child by too much attention, counsels the mother to teach the baby "who is boss," diagnoses prolonged crying as mere "fussing," unworthy of concern, and explains that the baby is "only crying for attention." All this supports the mother‡ who stays away from her baby. No other culture has invented so many excuses for keeping a mother away from her infant.

What is a quiet baby—these infants, from newborn to a year, who do not cry? No scientist has ever described *one*, let alone an "adequate sample" of them. A sound, whether it be a baby's crying or highway noise, is obviously relevant to a pair of ears. At the Center for Advanced Study in the Behavioral Sciences at Stanford, where everything imaginable is done to facilitate our work, the noise from the highway, several blocks away and about a hundred feet below us, bothers me, but my next-door neighbor does not hear it. Some mothers, at the faintest peep out of their infant, go in to see what is going on, and some even have amplifying devices in the baby's room to carry his cries to her; others seem not to hear the baby until it is choking with paroxysmal crying. We know nothing at all about the sensitivity of different mothers to babies' crying. Psychologists do not seem even to be aware that the problem exists, yet they have formulated the "theory" of the quiet baby. The quiet baby may be a myth invented by mothers who wanted to get themselves off the hook, in league with psychologists who wanted to get *themselves* off the hook. The quiet baby is somewhat reminis-

---

* See Part I.
† *Op. cit.* (Vintage Books; New York, Random House, 1963), Chapter 9.
‡ It is not essential that it be the *mother* who provides the baby with the necessary social stimulation to prevent it from going mad—social stimulation can be given by anyone.

cent of the *windigo** psychosis among the Ojibway Indians of the Lake Superior region.

The cause of humanness is the availability of another person, for a human being has his being in the availability of love. I want to make clear that I am talking about our culture only, for the self has many forms, depending on the culture. In our culture one cannot be a self without love. I distinguish between being a self and being merely nonvegetable, an entity that can perform the roles society assigns him. Mere attentive availability, without persecution and ambiguity, is enough to generate language and acceptable social behavior in a child, and in any culture, these alone are sufficient to make it possible for him to survive. In our culture, however, we do not think it's enough if people can merely talk and do what they are supposed to do. Only love can provide the rest—the rest of what it is to be human.

Each day the whole world reveals itself more and more as a medieval torture chamber. On the streets of great cities, in the jungles and villages of underdeveloped countries, in public or in the secrecy of prisons, on the ground and from the sky, millions are killed, mutilated and burned on a scale without parallel in history. In such a world, particularly in the West, where adults grow detached from one another and where children, therefore, feel more and more the impact of this detachment—witness, for example, the child murders† by parents and the use of teaching machines—adults now attempt to evade responsibility for the emotional disturbance of children; and psychology, always eager to develop rationalizations to fit current needs, relieves parents of blame for their autistic children, by applying the theory of the "quiet child." How strange that a mother should need a child's cry in order to have enough contact with her baby to prevent him from going mad!

A terrifying aspect of the psychosis called primary infantile autism is its quietness: since the baby' is conveniently quiet, since such babies are "good" babies, parents think everything is fine. Either the baby "was born quiet" or, though noisy and annoying at first, he stopped crying, just as the pediatrician said he would, when his crying was ignored. At two years the baby does not talk. Well, the parents are told, some babies are late talkers. Sometimes the full horror is not perceived until a nursery school teacher says the child seems "retarded" and does not get on with other children. Deprived of social stimulation, the child has "obeyed" his parents' wishes—he has grown indifferent to society.‡ The wish that the child be quiet has become the magic jest—the child is quiet forever.

It is no more cogent to speak of a quiet or passive mother than of that kind of child. A woman who is quiet with one husband may not be so with another. Often one does not know a woman's capabilities for noise or activ-

* According to accounts of it, a person afflicted with *windigo* saw people as beavers and wanted to eat them. In the voluminous literature on the subject, however, there is nobody who actually saw a case. All writings are based on hearsay accounts by Indian informants. It is a psychosis often described but never seen.

† In this connection, see Elizabeth Elmer, "Identification of Abused Children," in *Children*, Vol. X (September–October 1963), p. 180.

‡ For an excellent summary of the destructive effects on the brain by deprivation of social stimulation, see Mark R. Rosenzweig, "Environmental Complexity, Cerebral Change, and Behavior," in *American Psychologist*, Vol. XXI (April 1966), pp. 321–32.

ity until she divorces the husband who put a damper on her. Compelled by her husband to stay away from her infant, a woman can appear passive, withdrawn, quiet. A mother's availability to her child is always affected by her relationship with her husband, and in pathology, her availability to the child may be incompatible with her availability to her husband. As we saw in the Jones case, if a man needs his wife as *his* mother, he will not tolerate her being the child's. Since, in general, people do not know that *isolation alone* can impair the mind, only tradition, as in tribal society, or love, as in our own, makes a parent available to an infant for the necessary length of time. A father interested only in himself—"available only to himself"—who thinks only of his own need, can compel a troubled mother to withdraw from her child. In my experience one of the most striking qualities of the mothers of autistic children is that they are not bizarre, and although their later* children may be troubled, they are far from psychotic. The relationship between husband and wife, however, was bad; and in all but the Wilson family, the relationship was clearly miserable during the time when the child was becoming autistic. But I think that Mrs. Wilson concealed the reality of the relationship in the early days.

Availability in Particular

> "Everybody has the same energy potential. The average person wastes his in a dozen little ways. I bring mine to bear on one thing only: my painting, and everything else is sacrificed to it —you and everyone else, myself included."
>
> —PABLO PICASSO †

One can tell next to nothing about a person's availability unless one has had a chance to observe him over the whole range of his behavior. Mr. Wilson was available at all times to his clients—they would even come to the house. He was a lively and intelligent conversationalist and seemed to pursue his law practice with pleasure and élan, enjoying its responsibilities and battles. But with his family he was a log. Available mainly to outsiders, he was, according to his wife's description, better now than when Donald— their autistic child—was a baby. Perhaps it was partly because the shock of having an autistic child had altered him, as it does the parents of all autistic children; perhaps it was partly because their second child, Norma, threw herself on him—invaded him—in spite of his lethargy; perhaps it was because she was a girl and very pretty; perhaps it was partly because Mrs. Wilson had made herself available to Norma when she was an infant and so had made Norma available to the world.

---

* Most autistic children are first-born. See Bernard Rimland, *Infantile Autism* (New York, Appleton-Century-Crofts, 1962), p. 6, and Bruno Bettelheim, *The Empty Fortress* (Glencoe, N.Y., The Free Press, 1967), p. 422.

† As quoted in Gilot and Lake, *op. cit.*

Some people are available only to their families, others only to their jobs, still others to boys but not to girls; some are available to adults but not to children; some are available in sex but at no other time, and so on. Nobody is available to everyone; everyone, except some psychotic people, is available at some moments and not at others, and everyone is limited by his personality. In the course of evolution only those cultures could have survived in which mothers or their surrogates were adequately available to infants. Societies must disappear which place such burdens on people that there is not enough time for sufficient interaction with infants to make them human; hence today only those remain which achieved the proper balance.* It is axiomatic, therefore, that a culture must give children enough social contact to enable them to learn to talk and to become socially acceptable. But beyond this, what a culture requires of the individual is unique to each culture. Ours has made an issue of being more than simply socially correct, and we have placed on love most of the burden of developing it. Cultures constructed like the Jones family in its early days, when Tommy was neglected, or like the Wilsons, would disappear not because infants would not be fed, but because infants would go mad. Every culture has to strive to make adults available long enough to keep children sane, and the existence of infantile autism in our culture proves that the struggle has not been completely won. In contemporary society, though a parent may drive a child mad through isolation, he cannot be "held" for "cruelty" as long as the child appears fat, round and clean, because a cruelty of isolation, without starvation, without welts, without blood, is merely an invisible cruelty that is only of the mind.

Allocation of Resources

In a culture like ours, engaged in international trade, in economic competition, in the maximization of production and in the using up, replenishment and allocation of resources, people feel comfortable thinking about personal relations in economic metaphors, and the formulation of libido theory is the most illustrious example of this. The notion of the economics of libido took root easily because our culture formulates all of existence in pathetic analogy to economic† and because in all society *Homo sapiens* has to achieve a working relationship between what is required of him and how much time and energy he has. Since society and the individual are a continuous system, no system can work if its demands are so great that people become exhausted. The housewife who falls apart because she is unable to balance her own strength against the needs of four children, making love with her husband, keeping the house orderly, maintaining a social life, etc., is typical of the inherent tendency of all social systems to make exorbitant demands. Throughout his historic course *Homo sapiens*

---

* In the eighteenth century, when missionaries visited the Mbayá Indians of Paraguay, they discovered that the tribe survived largely by adopting babies from the Chané, because the difficulties between men and women had reached such a point that not enough children were being born or surviving.

† A colleague of mine has a marginal-utility theory of friendship.

has fought this; yet there is no social system known to me which man has been able to control so that it does not threaten him with excessive physical or emotional demands. Hence the expression "allocation of resources," despite its ugly, gritty, economic connotation, does apply to a primordial, unsolved problem.

Most of us are able to distribute our energies and our selves among the requirements of existence so that we do not become overwhelmed, yet for many of us, allocation is an unsolved problem. Consider keeping house: a woman in our culture has a choice, roughly, between taking care of her children most, taking care of the house most or taking care of her husband most. In a sensible and loving family, a woman with, let's say, four children, would probably "let the house go" while giving herself to her husband and children. Under stress she might diminish attentiveness to her husband in favor of the children; and if difficulties increase—perhaps two or more of the children come down with the flu—in a sensible family the husband will "take over" and even forget sex for a while. Allocation is a social thing, and what we must do with our energies must always be considered in relation to others; however clearly a person may see his own problem, the other may not see it that way because he has problems whose solutions are inseparable from the resources of the first.

In psychopathology a person either allocates his resources the wrong way, or he underestimates or overestimates them. A man gives too much time to his business affairs and not enough to his wife and children; a woman gives her "very existence—her all" to her children and neglects her husband. Other troubled people are in a constant state of psychogenic exhaustion and have energy for nothing. They drag themselves out of bed in the morning or have to be dragged. They swallow vitamins; they get injections; they take tonics. They consume quantities of coffee. At the end of the day they "fall into bed," even when the amount of necessary work they did is very small. On the other hand, some overestimate their resources and become exhausted by giving themselves to every cause and to everybody. This overestimation may be pure fantasy, so that though mountains are moved in fantasy, nothing happens in reality, while the person becomes exhausted by imaginary exertions.

The allocation of resources may be a question of power. The natural inclination of a confused or troubled wife, for example, can be distorted by a threatening husband who may demand that she ignore her child in favor of him. In psychopathology each member of a family may attempt to monopolize the family's resources of affection and solicitude—often without knowing he is doing it. On the other hand, some people cannot use the resources their family has.

There is power in weakness too, and power in memory and in hope. If one family member is physically ill and weak, he subtracts resources from the others. If he has become psychotic and been removed from the home, the guilt and yearning he may leave behind exercise a phantom power over the rest of the family, for the memory of him draws on the resources of those remaining, preventing their giving one another what might otherwise be possible. Hope actualizes resources that are latent: if I have hope for my child I can become active in his life, but if I am without hope—like a Negro slum parent, sunk in his own degradation and hopelessness—then whatever possibilities I might have for helping my child are never actualized—my resources are not made available to him. What a parent is to his children, what energy and enthusiasm he can awaken in them, is related to his hope. It is this, above all else, which makes it possible for the parents of some psychotic children to change and have other children who do not go mad. The shock of the psychosis is a blast that admits them to new galleries of power.

Can a Man Build a Life? *

How can any middle-class man in our culture build a life for his family? Aren't there middle-class men oriented toward *death-in-a-career* instead? Aren't business and the professions mostly a matter of dog-eat-dog or, at best, a matter of getting ahead while dying to one's self? No one trains a man to think of enriching his family life, yet many instruct him in how to avoid failure in business or profession. I wonder how a man manages to have a decent family life?

How can an average man credit an infant—wordless for over a year and then only slowly, almost word by word, becoming more articulate—with any life but hunger, pain and primitive pleasure? How can an average man imagine that a child of two, three or four years has any brain at all? After all, babies seem to have no ideas. To some men they seem boring. Can one really expect the average man to understand how much is going on inside a child's head—how profoundly he is thinking? In most cultures of the world, even children of six are not considered to have any personality at all; why should the average father in our culture have a different attitude? I know that many fathers do, but I cannot explain why.

What conditions does our society create that make any father want to be with his infant? One condition it tries to create is an ambience of love. Loving the mother, we say, a father will want to be with his child, but considering the life a man has to lead, this is a fragile thing to rely on. Pressure for a career, fatigue, depression and anxiety created by the job, as well as the need for relaxation and pleasure, interfere with a man's closeness to his child, and love and a feeling that he needs the baby must be strong enough to overcome all that tends to separate the two. A baby more or less *has* his mother; it seems to me that he has to *fight* to capture his father, and the immense decision of whether to charm him, whether to win him by acquiescing or whether to attempt to overpower him by protest, is the baby's. In all of this the baby gets some help from his mother, under the best conditions, but how he makes his decision in favor of one tactic or another is a mystery.

So, since our society seems to create the conditions for separation of the

* Since the Wilsons are upper-middle-class, what I have to say under this heading applies to that class. Yet the reader will perceive that the problem of how a man builds a life exists in all classes, though in different forms. It is seen in its most desperate form, of course, in the lower-class Negro male. In this connection, see particularly Chapter 4 of the famous Moynihan Report, i.e., *The Negro Family: The Case for National Action*, Office of Planning and Research, United States Department of Labor. Reprinted in full in *The Moynihan Report and the Politics of Controversy*, by Lee Rainwater and William Yancey (Cambridge, The M.I.T. Press, 1967).

middle-class father and child rather than for their union, the relationship of these fathers to their children puzzles me, and though there are many "warm, good" fathers, they seem improbable.*

We have to consider the dialectic of the factors—ambition, fatigue, depression and anxiety—that seem to make it difficult for a father to be close to his child. Ambition often pushes a father toward his child: he wants his son to be athletic and strong, so he plays with him and roughs him up, or he wants his son to be smart, so he prods him intellectually or helps him with his schoolwork. When the father comes home from work anxious and depressed, he may find relaxation and solace with his child; and the father is helped to be close to his child by the fact that the changing roles of men and women make it easy for him to be more "maternal" if he wants to.†

Much has been written about parents who make excessive demands on children, but little about the plight of a child whose demands exceed his parents' emotional resources and therefore seem excessive to them. Inseparable from love is an understanding of people's limitations, and exorbitant demands may make love seem irrelevant. In the Wilson case, Norma has learned to ask of her parents only what enables her to get along with them. She, as any six-year-old must, has assessed her parents, so that she neither asks too much nor gives too little or too much. She does not overwhelm her parents with affectionate embraces. A capacity for *emotional assessment* is inherent in *Homo sapiens;* it is a biological function, enabling him to adapt to his fellows.

Activity-Passivity

An upper-middle-class man should be active (not "passive"), "adequate," vigorous, ambitious, able to realize his potential and not afraid to compete. Fathers who are not are reputed to be bad for their children, and case records of disturbed children are littered with notations like "Father is passive, inadequate, withdrawn. *Nothing is known about fathers so labeled whose children are all right,* because those children do not land in child-guidance clinics, and nobody even knows how many such fathers have disturbed children, anyway. Each of the fathers labeled as passive-inadequate that I have studied is different. Mr. Wilson has a delightful little girl, Mr. Metz's daughter is charming and gets on well, but the Rosenberg boys are in trou-

---

* Some explanation of what I mean by "improbable" is necessary. When we understand that the origins of life came about through the chance combinations of lifeless chemicals, and that earliest life developed through an incalculable series of single-cell organisms, first into plants, then into something between plant and animal, and so on up through paramecia, invertebrates and vertebrates to man, it seems so unlikely that the entire sequence could have occurred that we say man is improbable. *Similarly,* when one takes into account all the factors necessary to produce "good" fathers in our culture, such fathers seem improbable.

† I have discussed the alteration in the pattern of closeness between fathers and children in Chapter 5, "Parents and Children," of my *Culture Against Man* (*op. cit.*). On p. 132 I say: "Deprived in his work life of personality aspirations, the American father reaches deeply into the emotional resources of his family for gratifications formerly considered womanly—the tenderness and closeness of his children; and his children reach thirstily toward him."

ble. It is clear that passivity, inadequacy or withdrawal in a father is not in itself enough to make a child mad.

These passive-inadequate men are fascinating to watch—if you can remember they are there. At home they slump in chairs; they are remote; they talk little; they are aloof. Absorbed in the activities of the rest of the family, the observer suddenly wonders where the father has been. Perhaps he has been silent and immobile; perhaps he has quietly disappeared, gone to sleep in another room.

American intolerance of inactivity is measured by the pennies thrown at alligators in zoos. We cannot stand such complacent lethargy; let us rouse the alligator! It is a tribute to American restraint that visitors to zoos throw only pennies at the alligator. The hard-skinned, somnolent reptile is like the remote father who refuses to stir from behind his newspaper, beer and cigar.

This labeled class of men is not homogeneous. Some are "passive" and "inadequate" at home but not at work; others are passive and inadequate with their children, and inadequate with their wives but not passive. Some alternate between periods of passivity and sudden bursts of activity, often pathogenic. Some take no responsibility because their wives are happy to do it all; others take responsibility but with a net pathogenic outcome. Some, like Mr. Metz, will become active when their wives ask; others are never asked. Some are passive with their children because they have no empathy for a young organism; others are passive with their children because they have no feeling for their wives; still others are passive because of depression. A man may be an active businessman but a passive father whose only ambition at home is to be left alone so he can dream of his business.

In every case the impact of these labeled fathers on their families is different. The presence of an inactive person is a problem only when he is expected to be active but is not. Is it pathology if a scholarly, contemplative, Old World Jewish father is relatively inactive in his child's upbringing—except perhaps to listen to his son's lessons, or to scold him or even switch him if his mother complains too bitterly about his naughtiness? Surely adaptations to these fathers took place which enabled the children to grow up sane. The same applies to the traditional Chinese peasant father. Is the problem, then, that of the failure of the American family to adjust to the "passive" father? Is it that a certain kind of American woman, married to a certain kind of man, cannot bring up her child undamaged? Is it that such a father facilitates pathology? Perhaps he is a man who tries to push the mother away from her child, or who forms a focus of active rejection in the family, or who gives the mother so little that she is in a constant state of desperation and maybe even turns from her child. Perhaps it is a mother who expects too much from a man, or who loses interest in her child if her husband shows none. A man is always passive, inadequate, etc., relative to culturally determined expectations others may have of him, and always in reference to a certain kind of wife. It is hard to imagine that there is anything inherent in "excessive" paternal passivity which makes a child emotionally ill; everything depends on the total family configuration.

In our culture the pathogenic potential in a certain kind of passive father derives from the fact that he is a ruined person, while the emotionally re-

mote Jewish or Chinese father was what he was supposed to be. Because of
her upbringing, the wife could deal with that kind of husband as well as
her child with that kind of father around. We can see from the studies of
Mr. Rosenberg and Mr. Metz that it is not passivity alone that is the pathogenic agent, but specific destructive activities. No able-bodied, sane person
is inert, and a problem in a clinically "passive" man is that the little activity
in which he does engage is often pathogenic. Only if he is observed at
home, in his natural habitat, can one perceive what is pathogenic in his
activity.

Availability-Passivity

Unavailability and passivity stand for different ways of looking at the
same thing. The virtue in discussing availability and passivity as if they
were different is that in doing so one sees different aspects of the same
phenomenon. When I talk about availability, I am concerned with how a
person distributes his resources among various people and activities; when
I discuss "passive" fathers, I am examining a psychiatric cliché. Availability is a concept of universal applicability; passivity is a culture-bound notion, murky with connotations that have made a shibboleth of activity: the
word has become so saturated with cultural meanings that it cannot enter
clearly into scientific discourse.

THE WILSON FAMILY

Mr. Wilson is a corporate lawyer. His wife, who has been to high school, keeps house and takes care of their six-year-old daughter Norma, who is in elementary school. Donald, diagnosed autistic, was about ten years old when I studied the family, and was in an institution. Mr. and Mrs. Wilson are in their mid-thirties.

Origins of the Tragedy

The evening of my arrival I saw the difference between Mr. and Mrs. Wilson.

Norma went to play with a friend. The Wilsons and I sat in the parlor, and Mrs. Wilson did 90 percent of the talking. She spoke with enormous intensity about Donald, their autistic child—mostly about her guilt. She said she had neglected him, and this neglect seems to stem from about the second or third year of his life. She did not go in when he cried; she paid no attention; she left him alone in his playpen. She said that under these circumstances one could never expect a child to grow up normally. He never had a chance to see anything, to interact with anybody, to learn how to deal with human beings. She grasped at straws in an effort to explain his condition according to causes other than neglect, but she really felt that fundamentally it was all her fault. She described, for example, the time when she and her husband went off for a couple of days and left Donald with a sitter, and when they came back his face was all black and blue. The sitter said Donald had fallen off the toilet seat but Mrs. Wilson did not think that would have done it. She doesn't know what happened, but ever since then he stopped singing. Before that he used to sing beautifully. He used to stand up in his crib, shake the crib and sing.

She said a doctor had told her Donald needed to have his tonsils and adenoids removed; and when she took him to the hospital the anaesthetist clapped the mask over his face and then the operation was performed. After that Donald began to run back and forth.*

She described numerous trips to various physicians in order to find out what was the matter with Donald. She told the same story many, many times: his experiences in nursery school,† the way her pediatrician told her to leave Donald alone, her trips to specialists, the neuroencephalograms performed on Donald, and so on. All of this was told with tremendous guilt; I had the feeling Mrs. Wilson was about to cry, but she did not.

---

* Autistic children have bizarre, stereotyped movements. A common one is to run back and forth, always in the same way, and often even along the same pathway.
† Which I, inexplicably, did not put in the record!

Mrs. Wilson was sitting on my right in an easy chair and Mr. Wilson, as always, sat as far away as possible, at the other end of the room. Every once in a while he would interrupt his wife and say he was of a different opinion—that he thinks Donald's condition is constitutional.

Suddenly Mrs. Wilson flew into an absolute—I won't say frenzy, but intensity of feeling about her husband. She said that when she was pregnant with Norma she was very much annoyed with her husband because he was forever going out to play cards with the boys, leaving her alone. She was very angry about this, and the night she began to have labor pains he was also out with the boys and she had to call him to bring him home. On the way to the hospital Donald was in the car with them because they wanted to leave him with his grandmother (or his aunt). Mr. and Mrs. Wilson quarreled because she was furious at the way he had neglected her, and she thinks this quarrel may have had an effect on Donald.

Mr. Wilson took all this quite calmly. I had a very strong feeling that he considers himself above it all. Possibly this attitude is expressed best in something he said to me as he drove me back to my hotel: "I think you are doing Mrs. Wilson a great deal of good, because she has all this feeling about Donald churning around inside her, and nobody to tell it to."

It doesn't do *him* good because he doesn't have all that feeling churning around inside him. Yet, as we shall see, he is not so far above it as he might at first seem (from time to time, possibly because of his wife, he feels some guilt too), and he works hard, he says, to earn the money to keep Donald in an institution.

Mrs. Wilson—who never studied psychology and who never attended college—has such fine insight into the causes of primary infantile autism that I sometimes think I may have gotten my own theory of it from her. Her description of Donald's isolation—of his general "stimulus impoverishment"—also describes my view of the cause of this disease perfectly. And because she believes it, because she blames herself, guilt is a devil riding on her back; she gets very little sleep, even with the aid of pills. She blames herself for leaving Donald alone, for following the directions of the pediatrician and for leaving him for two days with the sitter. Meanwhile her husband brushes all her explanations aside, as he does his own guilt. He is calm; she is almost beside herself. If he is calm when she is so upset, what must his condition be when a person is merely sorrowful or ebullient? Notice that the entire recitation of disaster was by his wife; his only entrance into the drama was as a feeble one-man chorus, denying her reality.

I summarize the dynamics: she talks intensely; he is mostly silent. She takes blame; he evades it. She, with no higher education, shows scientific insight; her husband, far more formally educated, shows none. She supplies the details of Donald's existence, not her husband. She accuses her husband of neglecting her; he does not deny it. She sits near me; he sits far away from both of us. (His characteristic, rather, his inflexible, position in the living room was as far toward the end of the room as possible, at the left end of the sofa, near the TV set.) He says my being there will do *her* a great deal of good (not him!). *She* has nobody (this must include him) to talk to.

As I talk with the Wilsons at our first meeting the picture of remoteness is already beginning to assume form; the principal lines of force are becoming distinct. This is always the case: the general outlines appear during the first hours of a visit. Mr. Wilson is at the periphery of the family's existence. He is where his family is in *space,* but where it *lives,* he is not. Its life does not claim him—he is barely available; his wife's anguish falls on his ears like distant weeping. I wish I had had sense enough to record where his wife's eyes were during the first encounter in the living room, but this may be an indication:

(I had just arrived, having been brought to the Wilson home by Mr. Wilson, who picked me up at the hotel.)

As soon as I sat down, Mrs. Wilson began asking very anxiously about Donald (whom I knew at the Institute, briefly) and I repeated what I had told her husband when he asked me at the hotel: that I'd only seen Donald a little while, that he had the flu when I left, and that he was still a very much withdrawn child.* Mr. Wilson took a seat at the far end of the room on the sofa, looking at TV and listening to us at the same time, until he got up and turned off the television set.

This observation suggests that Mr. Wilson's senses are not oriented toward his family; that he is tuned out; that "The Wilson Family" is not "his program"; that he is insensitive to his family; that he is, perhaps, sensitive to them only when they are plugged into his legal business.

Let us now look more closely at the character of Mr. Wilson.

Observations on the Character of a Remote Father

(First day.) Norma got up and greeted her daddy. It seems to me that she just said, "Hello, Daddy." He didn't snatch her up, throw her up in the air, fondle or caress her.

After dinner we all went into the living room, and shortly after that Norma was put to bed. She went without trouble, though there was a little by-play between her and her mother, Norma lying on the floor, laughing very hard, trying to delay going to bed. Then her mother *told* her to go over and say good night to her father, so she went over to him playfully and squatted between his knees. He raised her off the floor, trying, in a kindly way, to get her to go to bed. I felt he was keeping the kid at a distance. Although he tousled her hair, I didn't have the impression of a father who easily fondles his daughter.

At last Norma went off to bed in gales of laughter, her mother smiling indulgently.

(Second day.) Norma had been watching TV and decided to stop. She then sort of threw herself down near her father, who grabbed her and fondled her very tenderly and slapped her on the behind a number of times; this went on for maybe ten minutes. They both seemed to be enjoying themselves. This is the most demonstrative I have seen him, but it is interesting that she has to provoke him. He is very phlegmatic and has to be provoked to be attentive to Norma, but when she does, he seems to enjoy it up to a point. For example, today while Norma and I were outside collecting bugs, he went to sleep. When we came in, Mrs. Wilson, having decided we ought to go to the park, tried to wake him up, but it was Norma who was more aggressive. It made him grumpy, and he told her, rather

---

* When I told this to Mr. Wilson at the hotel "he frowned and wrinkled his forehead"; the rest of the way home he chattered animately about the town and his practice.

sharply, to stop. She then went into the bathroom and came back with a wet rag. She was going to put it on his face, but he grabbed her firmly but tenderly; she fell on the floor and he put the rag on her. She enjoyed this immensely, laughing uproariously, and they both went on this way for a couple of minutes.

In the park Norma was completely divorced from her father during the whole afternoon, spending her time either with her mother or alone on the swings. When Norma walked on the little wall that runs along the edge of the lake, it was her mother who held her hand; it was Mrs. Wilson and Norma who went into ecstacies over the ducks—which Mr. Wilson insisted on calling white swans.

It is interesting that I haven't seen Mr. Wilson interact with Norma when he wasn't sitting or lying down. He likes to go to the ball games by himself.

When we came into the living room after dinner, Norma was watching TV and her father was at the other end of the sofa. Mrs. Wilson sat down between them and carried on a lively conversation and interchange with Norma about one thing or another while Mr. Wilson read the paper.

(Third day.) Again today before going to bed, Norma snuggled up against her father; he caressed her and patted her bottom as he usually does.

When her mother came in to take her to bed, Norma "fell asleep" on her father and he picked her up and said, somewhat sternly, "Now, Norma," meaning that it was time for her to go to bed; so her mother started to take her out of the room and then she slumped over on me and I rumpled her hair.

As usual Mr. Wilson did not go into Norma's room to say good night.

As Norma went off to bed Mr. Wilson and I were alone in the living room watching a horse opera. He sat slumped way down on the sofa, as usual, almost supine, his legs on the floor, just his head and neck against the back of the sofa. When Norma was sitting next to him—or, you might say, lying next to him—she had taken exactly the same position.

Well, he and I watched one horse opera, making so-called humorous cracks to each other about the show, and when that program was over we watched another. During both programs Mr. Wilson was in and out of the room taking business calls.

(Fourth day.) When Mr. Wilson came home this evening Norma was in the backyard and did not go to greet him. Later, when I was playing ball with her and he came into the yard with his newspaper and a glass of beer, she did not go to him, nor he to her. (She did not go near him until after dinner, or rather after TV, when she rolled on him in her usual way of saying good night.)

Mr. Wilson was sitting in the yard, facing Norma and me, holding his glass of beer, with his newspaper up to his face. There he remained until dinner was announced, except that at one point, when Norma was becoming very excited, he called, "Norma!" as if to tell her to calm down, but she kept right on.

At dinner Norma asked him whether he liked something she was doing and he said no.

After dinner Mr. Wilson, as usual, went into the living room, sat down in his usual place on the sofa, turned on TV and began to read the paper. Norma sat down on the floor somewhat removed from him, first sticking a pencil into his paper. Neither of them watched TV, although it was going full blast.

She told her mother and me to take numbers; I took seventeen, her mother took nine. Each number was supposed to stand for something. Mine stood for something bad, which she whispered to her mother, and her mother told her not to say it aloud. Then she said I was a flower and her mother a duck. She asked her father to take numbers. He was reading the paper, and each time she asked him he would mutter a number and then go back to the paper. The first number he picked turned out to mean, "You are a bad father"; the second, "You are poor," and the third, "You are stubborn as a mule," and Mr. Wilson said, "That's right." He did not acknowledge the first two numbers even with a grunt. As a matter of fact, one might say that Mr. Wilson has organized his home life in terms of minimal response.

A client of Mr. Wilson's came in; they sat on the sofa talking about his business while Norma sat on the floor looking into space. (Mr. Wilson had almost fallen asleep before the client arrived; and I thought, once, while he was sitting in the corner staring into space that he looked just like Donald dreaming off. My marginal note here reads: "But Mr. Wilson always looks like this when he's sitting on the sofa.")

Mrs. Wilson was in the kitchen washing dishes part of the time. . . . .

After the client left, Mr. Wilson came and sat near me in the other easy chair, at the other end of the table, and we talked briefly about the client. Meanwhile Norma sat in a corner of the sofa, not in the one her father usually occupies, and watched TV. She kept firing questions at Mr. Wilson about the picture and he would answer only if she asked the question a couple of times; and then the answer seemed to me so mumbled that she couldn't have heard it very well; I, for one, could not understand what he was saying, even though he was only a few feet away.

As I was returning to the living room from having said good night to Norma, Mr. Wilson went to her room to say good night and he bent over and kissed her and fondled her bottom. It was unusual for him to go in to say good night to Norma; I've been here four nights, and this is the first time he has done it.

It makes immediate sense to any man in our culture that, though only half alive when his child is talking to him, Mr. Wilson should be a burst of electric charges when a client calls. What is more important to a man—his children or his phone calls? What makes more sense—the "vacuous" chatter of a six-year-old or the concrete, remunerative, self-image-enhancing conversation of a customer, client or colleague? Isn't it true that we talk to our children to indulge them, because we *ought* to, but to colleagues, customers and clients (the three sacred C's!) because they are absorbing? Isn't it obvious that a person can perceive at every moment whether he is building his image in the eyes of his colleagues but hasn't the faintest idea what he is building in the eyes of his child? And does it matter? If Mr. Wilson is a "bad father," what does it matter? It does not affect his practice in the least, Norma cannot go away, and her childish protest is not even felt. Norma has sized up her father (assessed him): she knows under what circumstances and to what degree he is available. Perhaps she has watched her mother and learned from her father's response to her mother that his rousability is minimal. Perhaps she remembers from her earliest childhood and from watching him with Donald that to try to stimulate him beyond a certain point and outside of certain times only results in anger. Thus her father has his peculiar cycle; he is accessible at specific moments only, and Norma's adaptation to the cycle is marvelous. Something has happened to her that makes it possible for her to accept this lethargy; yet though she has grown practically independent of her father, she does not give him up because when she treats him right and acts in her charming way, she can get a tender response out of him. What took place when she woke him up and threatened to put a wet rag on his face is a good example. She has learned —they have learned together—that under certain conditions a little tenderness can occur between them without exhausting him; that under certain conditions, because she is what she is—a charming little girl—she can transform his anger into tenderness.

This is the issue, with her: to pick the strategic moment and the right tactic when his ready irritation can be transmuted into love. Somewhere— or rather, at some time—she learned how to do it, not by distorting her self or her sex—like Ben Rosenberg—but by being truly *female*. At some moment in her life she discovered that her father cannot resist her charm; that although he seems inaccessible, she can make him accessible, *under his conditions*. She learned what would make her father emerge for *her*. The tragedy of many children is that since they cannot make this discovery, they lose their parents; and they cannot make the discovery because the inaccessibility of the parent so upsets them that they can react only with rage and sorrow, which makes the parent even more inaccessible. Some children, for some reason, solve the problem of such a parent; we need a handbook for babies on "How to Reach Your Inaccessible Parent."

Since Mr. Wilson does not try to fake an interest he does not feel, there is no sham feeling between him and Norma. She is not compelled to feel, when he is playing with her, that he would rather be with his newspaper and TV, so she does not have to act as if she believed he was a willing part of her play, while she is wishing all the time that he would go away, knowing all the time that he would rather not be there, though unable to send him away.

Imagine a sham relationship in which there is a little girl, whom we shall call Betty, and her father. Betty wants to play Little Red Riding Hood, but her friends are all at home and her mother is making dinner. Her father has just come home from work, tired, irritated and anxious, as usual, but Betty drags him into a game. He would rather read the paper or watch TV and Betty knows it, but she does want to play Little Red Riding Hood and she wants her daddy. He plays at being the wolf and pretends to enjoy it, and Betty tries to enjoy the game, even though she can feel that her father would rather not be in it. Since she feels this frustrated reluctance in him, she would rather not have him play with her; yet she wants him and she loves to play Little Red Riding Hood, especially because in that game she abreacts her fear of and hostility to her father. So she acts as if she believed he was a willing part of her play, while wishing he would go away . . . etc.

There is a certain honesty about Mr. Wilson. He does retain a corner of his soul for his daughter, and even though she is not a client, she is able to yield him just that amount of emotional income he needs to keep his self alive; he does not try to cheat her—to make her believe he wants to do what he would rather not do. If he took more from her he would have to pay back more, and if he tried to give more, he would only feel resentful. Hence, perhaps, his irritation when she seems to want to prolong the game of going to bed is partly due to the fact that he feels his limitations.

Norma has to work to keep her father in contact, and she can get at him only when he is able to emerge from retreat, which is at the moment of her definitive departure: she never comes back. Their contact has to be ritualized—they do not caress at random; there has to be a reason. And the temporal framework has to be rigid, with *mutual escape*, as she retires into her bedroom, into which he rarely follows her. Norma makes no physical overtures to her father unless she is going to bed, because *these are the conditions he has taught her;* or, these are the conditions that have emerged in the interplay (nowadays called "transactions" *) between them over the past five years. She has learned to give him the contact (perhaps love?) he has taught her to give him; at other times she can barely provoke him from behind his paper, and then it is not worth the trouble because his response is feeble and his communication unintelligible. At bedtime, however, when she will be gone from the living room in a few moments, he will move to caress her rather sensually. He is one of that large class of parents who are able to caress their children, even the young ones, on ceremonial occasions only—occasions when parent and child, in any culture, come into one another's awareness, with special vividness, as an affirmation of the relationship. Arrivals and departures are such times; in our culture bedtime is one, and in many families, bath time; or, sometimes for the mother, getting the child up in the morning. But Mr. Wilson and Norma have reduced mutual ceremonial affirmation to a minimum. When he comes home from work, sometimes there is not even a greeting. In the yard, he sits down, takes his beer and puts his paper up to his face, and only when Norma utters an irritating little shriek of excitement does she seem to float into her father's awareness for a moment, and then vanish. But who knows; maybe he is renewed just through feeling her presence; maybe she is glad to know her daddy is there and facing in her direction. Who really knows how one gets resonance out of lethargy? Perhaps young turtles can discern faint, signaling tremors in the vibrations of their mother's shell! Still, since Norma calls him "lazy," "bad father," "poor" and "stubborn as a mule," it does not seem as if such vibrations are enough for her.

The only way Mr. Wilson can become available to Norma is by her direct physical onslaught. Words and games are no use; he responds below the level of intelligibility; vocalizes but says nothing. Norma does not communicate with him as a verbal creature; he does not care what she has to say, but cares only for the physical pressure of her body. And he is available to her through his body only. He has no interest in intervening in her activity —except, perhaps, to call out to her if her noise disturbs him or to urge her to go away, to bed. When she collects bugs, he goes to sleep; when she is having fun in the park, he talks to me; when she plays, he reads the paper or watches TV. When he responds to Norma it is as if from far away, and as he emerges he looks over his shoulder to the retreat he has left. He has come up out of a great distance, where isolation, the forgetfulness of newspaper, TV and Mighty Mouse fantasy are like a quiet cabin in the woods. When he returns from retreat, he enjoys the few moments with Norma just about as long as he can sustain it; eager to drift or dream off again. He is a dream-off addict, waiting for the needle of detachment. When his wife wants Norma to go to bed he does not try to prolong contact with his daughter "for just another second," but urges her away; nor does Norma usually try to prolong it either. There is no coalition between father and daughter to

* John Dewey and Arthur F. Bentley, *Knowing and the Known.* This book, now in paperback, was first published in 1949 (Boston, Beacon Press). It is there that Dewey and Bentley discuss, at great length, the concept of transaction, which recently has become a social-science cliché.

frustrate, for just one moment, the mother's desire to get Norma to bed. It is not that his wife "steals" Norma from him but that he is unavailable. By experiment, Norma has discovered the single moment when he will respond humanly.

The Test Theme

Uncertainty is the root of testing another person, and uncertainty is the cause of testing in love as well as in everything else, as people, unsure of each other, use tricks to see who can be trusted. I shall speculate about bedtime as a testing ground. In the bedtime play, Norma and her father test each other and themselves. Mr. Wilson waits, apparently lethargic but on the alert, to see if Norma, in saying good night, will prove that she loves him; and she flings herself on him to see whether he, by responding, will prove that he loves her. She tests herself to see whether she has the power to make him respond; and I will guess that when he does not go in to say good night to her, he says to himself, "She doesn't care, anyway," or "If she really cares she will come and say good night even if I don't move." Each time his wife has to say to Norma, "Say good night to your daddy," is evidence that his daughter does not love him, so he stores up proof.

Night after night Norma stirs her father to lovelike animation, but the reason he responds at all is that they both want to be loved; because Norma needs to test herself by testing her father; because Mr. Wilson tests himself by testing Norma; and because Mrs. Wilson works to build the relationship. But when a relationship is always subject to testing because people are unsure of themselves and of what life will give them, existence itself becomes a test, and people become shopkeepers of life, biting each coin.

Drifting Off

There are people for whom contact with others is almost too abrasive, so that they are always on the verge of drifting off, back into themselves, and there are others who cannot maintain contact at all and do drift permanently into themselves. These latter are madmen. Many people fight the battle between presence and nonpresence all the time: contact is made and sustained with the head, and even as they converse they are thinking of other things. Such a person has to concentrate on what the other is saying, while wishing he would stop talking. He has to convince himself that what the other is saying is interesting, inwardly ridiculing it all the while. He has to compel himself to play with his own child, and he has to be forced into an embrace by overwhelming charm. But even this may be fleeting, a hard pull away from the forces dragging him back into himself; thus, even as a man is telling himself how delightful his child is, he wishes the child would go away. This is Mr. Wilson, so it seems to me.

Those who drift back into themselves but are not psychotic can be made to respond truly to others only under strong force. Perhaps only sex will do it, yet in passion's aftermath they smoke a cigarette and drift away again, far away from the person lying in their arms. Perhaps only a kind of public appearance enables them to respond, when, excited by their own point of view, dramatizing themselves, they appear vivid and even appealing because they have rehearsed the whole thing so many times in fantasy, because in their detachment they have studied other people, without half trying. Perpetual Toms, peeping at life of others from behind screens, they understand. Perhaps alcohol brings them out, but as they get older, the strain of contact under any conditions becomes too great. Sex has died down, and dramatizing themselves has become tiresome because it is always empty; the effort is not worth the return. Almost any attempt to make them accessible is futile, and they become available only to the necessities of physical survival itself. For the rest, they are pictures hanging on the wall.

These are people for whom all but the most essential contacts are the negation of a wish—to return within themselves. Behind the mask, the wish; behind the wish, the despair; behind the despair, nothingness.

Without knowing what they are doing, they often become obsessed with one thing because it prevents them from losing contact entirely. So they throw themselves into work, have affairs or get drunk because they really do not want to retreat—real isolation terrifies them—but since any extensive contact with the world does too, they are always anxious. Mr. Wilson hates to travel, and though he drifts off at home (or perhaps because home is the place where he can drift off), he is eager to get there; like all those I have been discussing, he wants the world to "be there," but at arm's length.

Inner Exhaustion

Mr. Wilson's efforts to drag himself back to and keep himself "in the world" exhaust him; he seems to lack energy for anything more than is necessary to keep himself and his family alive and at a good middle-class standard of living.

We happened to be talking about the fact that people follow a certain personality line of functioning, and Mr. Wilson mentioned himself. He said he plans very methodically. He said that the best tennis players do not run up and down the court the way he does and become exhausted, but plan their play very carefully.

. . .

Mr. Wilson repeatedly refers to the fact that he's getting old, though he is only in his thirties. He says he's too old to play tennis. He says that as one grows older one changes one's ideas about things. He feels old right now.

Slumped on the sofa in front of TV every night, he is a picture of inner depletion. He cannot have fun with Norma unless he is suspended by his occiput from the back of the sofa. Psychogenic exhaustion is a reflex of depression, and depression is often a reflex of inner rage. When I told Mr. Wilson that a mountain-climbing colleague of mine called all mountains "rascals" and fought his inner demons by triumphing over them, he liked that idea and said, "I fight my inner demons when I fight my cases."

Mr. Wilson told me the kind of fishing trip he likes. He wants the weather to be warm so he can sit in the canoe, drink beer and doze. Fishermen usually refer to good fishing weather as a time when the fish will bite; Mr. Wilson talks about it in terms of how comfortable he is. His favorite form of fishing is to leave a baited hook out overnight.

He said he really likes his work because of all the fighting it involves, but, he says, when he is not working he sleeps.

All the time I have been here Mrs. Wilson has done the housework herself. Today she washed the dishes while her husband either read the paper or slept.

Fighting, exhaustion, sleep. Fighting to stay alive in the business world, fighting inner demons, getting exhausted, sleeping, withdrawing; Mr. Wilson likes to go to ball games alone and he does not like picnics with the family.

I asked Mrs. Wilson whether she and her husband ever go on picnics and she said, "No, he doesn't like picnics," and when she and Norma go to the park and take lunch or go to the amusement park, they go alone, because Mr. Wilson stays home.

Fighting, fear of losing, success, exhaustion, sleep, joy in thoughts of victory, counting his medals, revival, the battle again, strength. Mr. Wilson loves horse operas, maintains a spectator interest in athletics, admires men of powerful physique and boasts that he can hold his liquor, though he definitely is not a drinking man.

Mr. Wilson likes to tell stories of his successes—there are none of failure, of course.

Mr. Wilson talked about some of his exploits. He enjoyed provoking his professors. He wrote one essay attempting to show that orthodox contemporary economics was just a phase of Marxist economics, and his professor blew his stack. He provoked another professor by attacking Justice Holmes.

* * *

At dinner Mr. Wilson talked with great animation about his job—how he had saved a firm money. He described how he had called the bluff of parties who were trying to browbeat him. He took a great deal of pleasure in telling me how as legal adviser he saved various people money, and as a matter of fact, he sounded very ingenious and analytical to me. His wife was very much interested in what he was saying and supported any idea he had.

* * *

During one of the horse operas Mr. Wilson repeatedly remarked on the strength and size of the leading character.

* * *

After a client left, Mr. Wilson told me his legal advice had practically saved this man from the gutter, and how the man now has a big contract from the city. Mr. Wilson is very proud of this, and the man's whole family swears by him and even calls him up for advice on intimate personal matters.

But all Mr. Wilson's accomplishments—his saving people from disaster —are outside the family. He has little conception of how he might cause disaster inside his own family, nor much of an idea of saving anybody in it.

On the third day I invited the family to dinner at my hotel; and Mr.

Wilson absorbed me in conversation about legal matters so that I could not take much account of what was going on with his daughter and wife. Norma went to the ladies' room a couple of times and lost her sweater.

We looked high and low for the lost sweater. Mrs. Wilson went into the ladies' room a couple of times looking for it and I called the housekeeper; she and I spoke to the manager, but no sweater. Mrs. Wilson remained calm; her husband took no part in trying to find the sweater but was phlegmatic and detached.

At last we got into the car and Norma was quite upset. The first indication of how bad it was, was when she refused to sit next to her mother and said she wanted to sit next to me (note: not next to her father). Norma pushed herself into a corner of the car, as far away from her mother as possible. Then she began to talk about losing the sweater and being afraid of a spanking. She started to cry, but her mother said, "That's foolish! Who do you think is more important, you or the sweater?" With that, she scooped Norma up and set her on her knee, and Norma stopped crying. Meanwhile Mr. Wilson said jocularly, "You're going to be spanked," but Norma ignored that. Her mother continued to soothe her, saying, "Anybody could lose a sweater; that's the way you learn." I said, "This is the first time in my life I've ever been able to hold on to a raincoat for a year." * Mrs. Wilson was grateful for that and said, "You see?" Before I mentioned my raincoat, however, Norma had already quieted. . . .

When we got home Mr. Wilson and I sat down in the living room, and Norma was taken off to bed by her mother, without protest and after *saying* good night to her father and me. Mr. Wilson, as usual, did not go to Norma's room to say good night, but after talking with him for about ten minutes I decided to go in. I found Norma actively abreacting the sweater affair. She talked mostly about people being spanked and ended up laughing, saying, "Instead of the child being spanked she spanked the sheet and the blanket."

Mr. Wilson is his wife's opposite: she is energetic all the time; he has energy only for his practice. Working hard as a responsible husband and father, he provides a home, but he can barely give his family anything emotionally. During the sweater episode, when Norma was afraid that she might be spanked—or that, at least, her parents were furious with her—he withdrew; he had no comfort for her.

Mr. Wilson can avail himself of Norma if and when he wishes, because his wife takes responsibility for her. This is a case where any more attention from this father would be more than Norma could tolerate, because he would be giving more than he could tolerate. We do not have to assume that everybody has some potentiality for being called into life which will never be realized unless he has a child. This is elementary; yet many adults who do not have the potentiality have children anyhow. Looked at another way, Mr. Wilson does not appear to need Norma very much; and let us give him his due—he does not try to act as if he did.

---

* My anxiety over Norma's intense anxiety was so great that I was moved to help allay the child's feeling. It may have helped Norma understand that I did not think of her as a bad girl either.

Mrs. Wilson and Norma

Bringing Up a Middle-Class Girl

INTRODUCTION

Certain issues are so prominent in the relationship between Mrs. Wilson and Norma that I discuss them before analyzing the relationship itself. Those issues are *presence;* the *psychosomatic system* (adoption by a child of the psychosomatic sensitivities necessary to get along in his culture); *insatiability, protectiveness* and *blame* (the part played by blame in the relationship between parent and child).

On being present. In order for a parent in our culture to "do right by his child," the child must, at the very least, be completely present to him. If a mother is depressed because she has a child like Donald, it may be difficult for her to put her "heart and soul" into bringing up a second one. Though the first child is in an institution, he is, nevertheless, present in memory and there may be a constant inner interchange between the mother's conscience and her activity every moment, particularly as she plays with and does things for the healthy child.

The inner conversation is covered by the wish "If only *he* were here!" When she throws a ball to the healthy child, she is throwing it to his spectral brother also; when she feeds the healthy one she is passing food to his absent brother too; when she puts the healthy one to bed she draws the covers over the absent one also; in the bed is an insubstantial presence, asleep beside the corporeal one. A parent might attempt to eliminate, with the new child, all the things he thinks led to the illness of the first. If he thinks it was neglect, he may intervene constantly in the new life; if he thinks it was harshness, he might be extremely gentle; if he thinks he pushed the first too hard, he might not push the second child at all. But the illness of the first child conditions the existence of the second. This plays a very important role in the relationship between Norma and her mother. She is present to her mother through the lens of her vanished brother.

The psychosomatic system. The process of regulating a child's mind and body to suit the cultural pattern begins right after he is born. Regulation of the child's psychosomatic system includes teaching him how and when to eat and eliminate, and how to think and feel. People speak of the role the child's autonomous "ego" plays in this, but when we consider that babies everywhere adapt to their own culture—Pilagá Indian babies grow into adult Pilagá, American babies turn into American adults and Javanese babies become Javanese adults, etc.—we understand that adults have the upper hand. *Cultural differences exist because the adults win,* and what remains of child autonomy is only the ability of each little Pilagá, Javanese, American, and so on, to be somewhat different from his fellows.

One of the first social tasks of an infant is to allow himself to be captured by the culture. Like an exemplary prisoner, he has to smell out his captors' preferences so that they will treat him right. In all cultures the secret of freedom is to adapt body and mind to the bars. This is psychosomatic autonomy.

There is a fight for the infant's mind with every mouthful of food he takes, every time he moves his bowels, in the toys he plays with, in how and where he sleeps, in how he is held, etc. The necessary intervention of the adult in infancy, merely to defeat death, immediately begins the destruction of "autonomy." When an infant is driven by hunger, he does not stop to ask whether he is being fed according to his preferences; and the timing of his feeding, what he is given to eat and how he is fed are at the will of the adult and accepted under the lash of hunger. Nor does the baby have any say about whether his mother holds him loosely or tightly, lets him sleep or wakes him up to be fed, swaddles him, tucks him into her parka, carries him around or hangs him in a cradle board from the limb of a tree. Different babies do react differently to what adults do, but these are idiosyncratic adaptations to major, inescapable adult decisions: Pilagá Indian babies, breast-fed on demand, cannot scream for a bottle and "demand" a schedule; American babies, bottle-fed on schedule, are powerless to "demand" the breast or to demand to be fed "on demand." American children from, let's say, three to eight can fight bedtime, but among the Pilagá there is nothing comparable to those (usually losing) battles; since compulsive bedtime does not exist, there is a total absence of bedtime battle.*

Among ourselves there is scarcely a point where adults do not intervene. The contrast between our fussiness and "tribal" permissiveness has been pointed out many times. In school the teacher's intervention is added to the parents'. The net result of all adult intervention is to produce an organism which will respond psychosomatically according to the requirements in that culture, and which will feel the difference between "right" and "wrong" as a moral contrast and a *bodily sensation*.

Insatiability. On page 14 of *The Structure of the American Economy*† there is a table entitled "Effect of Level of Consumer Expenditures on the Direction of Expenditures," which projects the size of consumer expenditures at different levels of national income. Discussing the table, the authors state:

> The most striking feature of Table III is the apparent lack of any indication of a limit to any of the [consumer] wants reflected in the items [in the table]. At the highest level of expenditure, for every one of the separate items there would be a great increase in expenditure over the lowest . . .
>
> For each major category of consumption, the structure of wants appears to be such that a big lift in consumer expenditures would create a greatly increased domestic market for every broad class of products. (p. 15)

The table and the comment are momentous, for the implication is that since there are no limits to consumer wants, Americans as consumers are insatiable. I present the following news items in support of this analysis:

---

* See "Child Rearing, Culture and the Natural World," by Jules Henry and Joann Boggs (*op. cit.*), *Psychiatry*, Vol. XV (1962), pp. 261–71.

† Ed. by Gardner Means (U. S. Government Printing Office, 1939). I have written about the economic roots of the insatiable character structure in *Culture Against Man* (*op. cit.*) and in "A Theory for an Anthropological Analysis of American Culture," *Anthropological Quarterly*, Vol. XXXIX (1966), pp. 90–109.

DATE OF ARTICLE	HEADLINE OR CONTENTS OF ARTICLE IN THE NEW YORK TIMES . . .
August 7, 1962	Bigger engagement rings and bigger jewelry sales were forecast. There is a trend toward bigger engagement rings.
November 12, 1964	"The man who has everything really doesn't unless he owns such necessities of life as thermometer cuff links, a martini scale and an executive foot massager." "A phenomenon among the eccentric new products currently being merchandised is the creations that do absolutely nothing."
January 26, 1965	More than $300 million was spent on hunting clothing and boots in 1963 alone.
June 14, 1965	Bean bags for business executives to toss around in the office; cost, $2 to $5.
August 15, 1965	Per capita consumption of beef has risen 40 percent in the last seven years.
November 19, 1965	". . . Liberace recently sold his Cadillac limousine, which was upholstered to resemble a piano keyboard, and now owns another limousine, whose exterior is adorned by diamond-studded candelabra. Mr. Presley has his own diamond-studded Cadillac."
November 25, 1965	"When the average American family sits down to its Thanksgiving dinner tomorrow, enough food will be on the table to feed an African or Asian family for seven days."
December 19, 1966	"3,000 Tree Ornaments and 6 Months Work Go Into Designer's Party."
	. . . AND FROM THE SAN FRANCISCO EXAMINER
September 11, 1966	In the $2 million castle built on a Nevada hill by Charles Steen, his 18-year-old son Andy has a $10,000 "circular bed that is flanked by gadgets and luxuries. . . . The closets in the boys' rooms look like men's stores with dozens of pairs of shoes, suits, sports jackets and sweaters.
	"The oldest boys have 50 sweaters each. The sweaters cost $50 each."

Such items are not strange to us, but it is good to be reminded of them, I think, so that we do not forget that we are members of a historically insatiable culture. The expression "rich as Croesus" carries the perspective on insatiability back about three thousand years.* The question is, however, "How does a tradition of insatiability get into the body and soul of each generation of children?"

In answer to the question, "What do you like most and what do you like least about your mother/father?" † children gave, as the principal reason for liking or not liking a parent, the fact that he or she "let" the child do something or refused: "He lets me go to Plankeville . . ."; "She lets me go to visit my friends often. She lets me invite them over"; ". . . he doesn't

---

* The time estimate is based on Herodotus' description of Croesus and his wars. Surely insatiability goes back further!
† See my *Culture Against Man* (*op. cit.*), Chapter 9, pp. 134 ff.

believe in letting me go to the show"; "She usually lets me do what I want"; "He won't let me wear lipstick"; "She lets me help her fix supper." The answers describe only a little of the massive parental intervention in children's lives. When a child has to get permission for a number of things, many wishes become seeds of potential frustrations. Furthermore, beside the wish granted there is often a permission partly withheld. If a child is given an ice cream cone, he may often want another but can't have it. A child may get permission to visit a friend but be prevented from staying as long as he wishes. A thirteen-year-old girl may be allowed to use lipstick but not whenever she wishes, nor is she ever permitted to put on as much as she wishes, etc. Since satiety is often prevented, a condition is given for insatiability—and theft. It would take an extremely warm, loving, "giving" parent to overcome the insatiability that comes from this infinity of partial satisfactions.

While the family is the place where personality is formed, it is also the place where the processes of decomposition are installed, or, let us say, where the processes are set in motion through which personality is maintained in that state, halfway between autonomy and disintegration, which we *call* personality, or, let's say, where personality is maintained in that particular state of dissolution necessary to our particular kind of culture. One of the ways in which personality adapts is by becoming insatiable.*

I have about a thousand short compositions written for me by teen-agers in answer to the question "What are your main personal problems?" In virtually all the responses the parents are, overwhelmingly, the principal personal problem—second only to sex. The essays document the intervention, the belittlement, the punitiveness, the pushing—among other "personality solvents"—which are compensated by insatiability. The stresses set in motion in the home are, as can be seen here, reinforced in school and in the interplay between what happens to the child there and his parents' reaction to it.

In the literature on child psychiatry, emotional deprivation is held responsible for insatiability.† It is hard, however, to see how any child in our culture could not feel so deprived. In spite of parents' love, in spite of efforts to make the child "feel wanted," the very idea reflects the difficulty of loving. Meanwhile, by an *attitude* of loving, many parents who are unable to give much awaken in the child expectations that cannot be fulfilled; and a child, in seeking the love he is led to believe is there, may be disappointed. We therefore have the following train of consequences; the child goes after what he is led to expect, but he does not get it: he seeks satisfaction in various forms of displacement (compensation, sublimation); he does what contributes to maximizing the culture—consumes, becomes am-

---

* In the lower orders of mammals, satiety is controlled by the ventromedial hypothalamic nuclei. In man, cultural factors play such an important role in the regulation of satiety that the thalmus does not have the overshadowing role it has in lower animals. See "Regulation of Food Intake and Obesity," by Jean Mayer and Donald W. Thomas, in *Science*, Vol. CLVI, No. 3773 (April 21, 1967), pp. 328–37.

† My wife and I have written on the relationship between emotional deprivation and greediness among a tribal people. See Jules and Zunia Henry, *Doll Play of Pilagá Indian Children*, Monograph No. 4, The American Orthopsychiatric Association (1944); and Jules Henry, "Cultural Determinants of Hostility in Pilagá Indian Children," *American Journal of Orthopsychiatry*, Vol. X (1940), pp. 111–22.

bitious, achieves and envies. Meanwhile he may secretly accuse his parents of promising more than they give, and the result is a freezing in an attitude of accusation.

Protectiveness negates death. Driving off death can dominate the world view of a culture consciously, as among the Kaingáng Indians whose theory of the universe revolves around death and the flight from it, or unconsciously, as among ourselves who endlessly elaborate the theme of death in industry (armaments), international affairs and fantasy (movies, television), while believing we are a life-and-fun-loving people. When a culture is in flight from death, the pall of death hangs over even the relationship between parents and children. The Jones family flies from death by acting as if it were not there—as if it were already negated; hence, they live close to danger, sometimes without knowing it.

It is difficult to separate our own culturally determined feelings about death and danger from our judgment about a parent's protectiveness. Mrs. Wilson seems to me very protective of Norma—some might say she is overprotective; on the other hand, Mrs. Jones (in Part I) seems underprotective with Harriet. The Joneses believe danger should be faced, and faced *down* —a common American attitude; Mrs. Wilson has a different attitude. Whether a parent moves at once from the perception of danger to an intimation of death itself so that he permits no risks, or whether, perceiving danger, he feels it is not *that* serious, depends on his temperament and what his culture has taught him to think about death as well as how he feels about his child.

Blame. Since blame develops out of the wish to determine the source of harm, and since such discovery contributes to survival, *Homo sapiens* must have a strong inherent tendency to blame. Yet each culture follows its own pathway to discovery. Some, using divination, blame sorcery, and some, the gods. In some cultures the causes of illness are largely impersonal, as in ours; in others it is always a malevolent *person* that is blamed. In some cultures a child cannot blame a parent for his own misdeeds or ill fortune; in others, like our own, for example, parents can be blamed for almost anything done by a child and compelled to defend themselves. Blame is patterned by the social structure of vulnerability, and the more vulnerable a person, the more likely he is to be blamed and the less right he has to blame others. A good example of the social patterning of vulnerability is the white man's past "right" to blame the Negro for the degradation of the Negro that was forced on him by the white man.

This brings me to the relationship between blame and deprivation, for a tendency to blame others is an expression of deprivation. Deprived people tend to blame others for whatever happens to them. Their blame puts others on the defensive and may make them more giving. Unless blame has been driven underground by terror or glossed over by a compensating, saccharine attitude that the world is wonderful, the tendency to blame others is in direct proportion to one's feeling of deprivation. An accusing child is a deprived one, though it does not follow that the absence of accusation indicates that the child has not been deprived.

I turn now to the analysis of the relationship between Norma and her mother.

Remembering, Guilt and Despair

> Life has become a bitter drink to
> me, and yet I must take it like
> medicine, slowly, drop by drop.
> —Søren Kierkegaard,
> *Either/Or*

A preliminary study of Mrs. Wilson's absorption in Donald is necessary in order to portray her sorrow and in order to show how Donald's shadow falls on the relationship between mother and daughter. I start with the record of my many conversations with Mrs. Wilson about Donald.

The Wilsons practically never go out. Mrs. Wilson says she doesn't like to because people always talk about their children and it makes her feel bad about Donald. I said, "Why should you feel bad? Look at what a jewel Norma is." And Mrs. Wilson said, "Yes, but you know, a man who has only one arm cannot forget the time when he had two." She says Donald weighs on her mind constantly. She used a very extreme expression I cannot remember, but I inferred from it that Donald is an obsession with her; there is no doubt, from the way she talks about him, that he is. I think she said she'll never forget him as long as she lives. She mentioned that the last time she saw Donald at the Institution, Donald looked at her glassy-eyed, as if he didn't know who she was.

. . .

Mrs. Wilson says the pediatrician told her she should teach Donald who's boss when he cries, and not give in. "And," she said, rather pathetically, "he learned." But I am sure, from watching Mrs. Wilson with Norma, that she generally shows Norma who is boss.

Mrs. Wilson said Norma keeps thinking of Donald all the time and yearning to have him back, and she feels very bad having to explain to Norma that she has to wait. Mrs. Wilson is in very great anguish that Donald is away. She says she really lives only for him. When I asked why she never had a third child, she said she had a miscarriage and she thinks it was because she is really completely wrapped up in Donald. She said, "I really live for Donald; I live for something I cannot have."

Mrs. Wilson said a number of times that she would prefer Donald to have died, rather than be living as he is now. Now he is alive, never having had any of the pleasures a child should have, and suffering. At least, if he were dead he wouldn't be enduring all the suffering he is now. Then she hastened to add that she doesn't want him to die.

. . .

Mrs. Wilson said that during the first year of Donald's life she not only spent a great deal of time helping her husband, but kept running errands constantly for her own family and for her in-laws. She would go shopping for them and help out in many other ways. She told of having gone to her mother-in-law's house with Donald and having stayed there very late to wash the dishes, while her mother-in-law's sister, who lived nearby, went home. Though Mrs. Wilson lived a long distance away, she was the one who remained to help clean up.

She says her own mother was insensitive to her needs with respect to Donald. Once, when she was going out of town to visit Donald in an institution, her mother called and said, "While you're in that city, please buy a present for Millie" (an aunt). This was amazingly insensitive, Mrs. Wilson thought. How could her

mother think of such a thing at a time like that? She wasn't going out of town
for fun, but to visit a sick child.

She was always the one on whom her mother made constant demands. The
other children in the family acted only in their own interests. I asked her who her
mother's favorite child was and she said she didn't know, but my inference is
that she didn't think *she* was.

Talking about Donald, she said repeatedly, "Why didn't I see what I was doing? Why was I so stupid?" So I asked, "Well, why didn't you see what you were
doing?" But she said she didn't know.

People haven't any idea of what real trouble is, she said. She went to a child's
birthday party, and the mother's eyes were red from weeping because she had
badly dented her brand-new car. Mrs. Wilson said, marvelous, healthy child, having a birthday party for it, and she was weeping about an automobile! She doesn't
know when she is well off." Mrs. Wilson hates to go to parties where she sees
other children happy.

Mrs. Wilson feels her husband has written Donald off and that only her drive
keeps Donald in the Institution. She says that she and her husband never talk
about him.

Mr. Wilson told me that his wife's whole attitude toward troubles has
changed. In former years she would have been tremendously upset on
learning that her nephew had broken his hip, but now she doesn't care—
she knows that in a few weeks he'll be up and running around. "Formerly
she would get terribly upset about shopping, but now these things don't
bother her at all."

Mrs. Wilson said that people don't want to listen to your troubles and
turn away when you talk about them; you're expected to be strong and bear
everything yourself and keep it all in. She has learned to do that. "But," she
said, "as far as Donald is concerned, I'll never give up."

Since only Søren Kierkegaard puts such loneliness, alienation and despair into universal language, I quote him instead of trying to use my own.

From *Either/Or*, Vol. 1*

The unhappy person is one who has his ideal, the content of his life, the
fullness of his consciousness, the essence of his being, in some manner outside of himself. He is always absent, never present to himself. . . . The unhappy person is consequently absent. . . . Now, there are some individuals
who live in hope, and others who live in memory. These are indeed in a
sense unhappy individuals, insofar, namely, as they live solely in hope or in
memory. . . . (p. 20)

Memory is emphatically the real element of the unhappy. . . . In order
that the man of hope may be able to find himself in the future, the future
must have reality, or, rather, it must have reality for him. . . . (p. 221)

. . . the unhappiest man will have to be sought among the unhappy individuals of memory. (pp. 222–23)

Our age has lost all the substantial categories of family, state, and race. It
must leave the individual entirely to himself, so that in a stricter sense he
becomes his own creator, his guilt is consequently his sin, his pain remorse.
. . . (p. 147)

* *Op. cit.* (Anchor Books; New York, Doubleday, 1959).

Sometimes when you have scrutinized a face long and persistently, you seem to discover a second face hidden behind the one you see. This is generally an unmistakable sign that this soul harbors an emigrant who has withdrawn from the world in order to watch over secret treasure, and the path for the investigator is indicated by the fact that one face lies beneath the other, as it were, from which he understands that he must attempt to penetrate within if he wishes to discover anything. The face, which ordinarily is the mirror of the soul, here takes on, though it be but for an instant, an ambiguity that resists artistic production. An exceptional eye is needed to see it, and trained powers of observation to follow this infallible index of a secret grief. (p. 173)

From *Concluding Unscientific Postscript**

But suffering as the essential expression for existential pathos means that suffering is real, or that the reality of the suffering is real, or that the reality of the suffering constitutes the existential pathos; and by the reality of the suffering is meant its persistence as essential for the pathetic relationship to an external happiness . . . the persistence of the suffering guarantee[s] that the individual remains in the correct position and preserves himself in it. (p. 396)

Mrs. Wilson cannot be entirely present either to Norma or to herself because of tormenting memories of the autistic son, because of her grief, which she bears alone, since her husband drifts away and the world does not want to listen—and the world does not have to listen because "our age has lost all the substantial categories," which, through ties of kinship, *would* listen and mourn not only because compelled to, but because, when there are "substantial categories" of kin, a loss to one is a loss to all. Mrs. Wilson perceives Norma through memories of Donald, in the light of hope for Norma and Donald. Norma is two people—Norma herself, and Norma as a restitution for her mother's injury to Donald. Thus Mrs. Wilson's "secret treasure" is Donald, and "the path for the investigator" is backward, through Mrs. Wilson's recollection of Donald and through her suffering.

The reality of her life—what "so permeates [her] being as to constitute [her] controlling necessity and destiny"—is Donald. Her suffering relates her to existence and to the possibility of becoming a self; if she brings Donald back, she can go on from there. But looking backward at Donald, she finds it difficult to see the present, which is Norma.

Putting One's Self Last

Mrs. Wilson, like so many people, has never been able to resist the demands of others. But in always yielding, some sacrifice themselves, some sacrifice others: they are unable to make decisions among the kind of competing demands that *Homo sapiens* has had to make in order to survive; they are unable to "put first things first." But what is "first"? What are the criteria? If we "normal people" can perceive what is "first" in the lives of the Mrs. Wilsons, whose inability to decide causes disaster, why couldn't they? Just as she was placed pathetically between her child and her hus-

* *Op. cit.* (Princeton U. Press, 1941).

band by his work, and between her child and her family by their demands, Donald is now between her and Norma because of her memories—very much memories of work she did not allocate properly. She is one of those many who, by wrong choices or through feeling forces to be irresistible when they are not, or being unaware of their own rights, cut themselves off from the roots of existence. Lacking a strong-enough inward involvement in her son, Mrs. Wilson yielded to external demands that were obvious and insistent, and since Donald was weak—especially since he was quiet—he could exert no compulsion. Even now her husband seems always slipping away emotionally. Even had he not demanded that she do his clerical work, his tendency to become inert compels people to throw their last pennies of energy at him. Besides, since he is a human being in the living room, not an alligator in a zoo, his inertia seems a constant reproach ("You don't care; you don't pay attention"). Her other families—her mother's and her husband's—used Mrs. Wilson as a servant because she let them. You will only allow yourself to be treated as a servant when you cannot justify your self in any other way; everybody's rights seem superior to your own. Between her husband and the need to claim recognition from her other families, Donald was sacrificed—and he did not know what was going on. His attitude toward her was unknown; he was inarticulate and too small and weak to express his opinion of her or to assert *his* rights: he lost—and so did she.

Mrs. Wilson could not make a decision in her own favor, because of the way she felt about herself. She had never stopped being a child who had to prove herself to her mother, so that even after she was married and had a baby, she felt she had to yield to her mother's demands. And it wasn't enough to prove herself to her husband, either; she felt she had to prove herself to his family as well. This compulsion overshadowed all other needs. There was no independent self with the *right* to decide in her favor, because her self was the prisoner of those others and of her own feelings of nothingness. But in the effort to *prove* her self she *dis*proved it, by failing with Donald: when nothingness acts, it can only destroy. Yet in disproving her self—in failing her self—she eventually freed her self, because horror at what she had done gave her strength to break prison. Sitting in horrified judgment on her self, she now sits in judgment on those others, and can act in accordance with how *she* feels. Now she is bringing work and self together by proving herself in Norma.

Mrs. Wilson is making Norma her work. What appears in my observations is not hugging and cuddling, but work, for what love Mrs. Wilson has for Norma is expressed largely in acts of transformation, of bringing out possibilities, of projecting the image of the child into the future. I think all this is due to the fact that work is an overshadowing compulsion in Mrs. Wilson—which she now devotes to this child—and to the fact that Norma must be the annulment of the harm done to Donald. Donald's mind died, Norma's must excel; she did not work on Donald, she will work on Norma; Donald had nothing, Norma must have everything; Donald is past, Norma *shall* be. And so shall her husband work *for* Donald; she says the only reason she stays with him is to make sure he works for Donald. And so, at last there is a *commitment*, for the disaster of Mrs. Wilson's life is that, feeling compelled to do too much, she was committed to nothing.

Letting Go and Holding On

Norma is timid—a little too afraid of being injured, falling, getting lost.

(Second day.) We went to the park, where Norma was interested in going only on the swings and the teeter-totter. It was her mother who took her to these things, while her father talked to me. Mrs. Wilson did not hover over Norma; once having gotten her started on one swing or another, she left her alone. I watched Norma and saw that she was very cautious on the swings. She gave herself only a slight push, but if someone pushed her higher, she accepted that too. She sat very solemnly on the swings; whatever excitement there might have been was inward. The contrast between her and other girls her age was striking: they went sailing way up in the air under their own steam or pushed by others, and while they laughed and called out, Norma was silent and solemn, propelling herself on the swing, but very gently. Either her mother or father said, "Norma is very cautious."

(Third day.) Mrs. Wilson suggested that we go to a nearby park where there are swings, a sandbox and teeter-totters. So we walked about a quarter of a mile to get there. On the way Norma stuck close to her mother, often holding her hand, sometimes running a little ahead, but always coming back.

Not long after we arrived, a little girl Norma's age but looking much firmer and stronger called out, "Hello Norma!" and Norma recognized her at once as Peggy. The two girls set out together. Peggy would "pump" freely and lie down on her tummy on the swing, but Norma maintained her usual frightened posture. The first thing Peggy suggested was that they go on the teeter-totter and Norma thought that a good idea. Norma would not sit on the end of it but about two feet in, and while Peggy pushed herself vigorously up from the ground, Norma did not. She seemed afraid of losing contact with the ground, for she hung over the seesaw, one leg hanging down, looking very frightened, until she at last gave up and got off.

Norma was constantly wandering away from Peggy—I think because Peggy was too vigorous and self-confident for her. It seemed to me that she really had no attachment to Peggy and she said nothing nice about her. She didn't think Peggy was pretty and said she rubbed a lot in school—erased instead of crossed out. When I asked her if she liked Peggy she said yes. Peggy was much more the American semi-tomgirl of that age, full of confidence, of laughter, of interest in other things going on around her while enjoying the activity, whereas Norma was so absorbed in the mere mastery of the mechanical devices and seemed so absorbed with her own timidity that she could only concentrate on the apparatus.

There were two types of swings ("baby" enclosed swings and the open type for older children) and Norma wandered between them. She went down the slide a couple of times and walked away from that. She ended up in the sandbox; before very long she was surrounded by children, but she shrank off into a corner of the box all alone.

She went over to the baby swings, and after pushing some of the children, got into a baby swing herself.

(Fourth day. Norma and her friend Abby were taken to the park by Mrs. Wilson.) At each street crossing Mrs. Wilson tried to get Norma to look carefully, but when there was a green light Mrs. Wilson talked so much about watching the light that Norma really didn't know what to do so she just waited for her mother to give the signal and we all crossed.

On the way Norma stuck pretty close to her mother, coming back every once in a while to take her hand. In the park, however, both kids ran pretty far ahead and Mrs. Wilson did not try to call them back.

The kids went immediately to the swings. Since Abby didn't know how to "pump," either, they repeatedly asked me to push them, saying, each in her turn, "I want to go very, very high," but not really wanting me to push them high, and I stuck to their instructions. Norma was very gay today and didn't seem nearly as scared as on the previous day. She really made me push her higher than before. Her mother, however, would not push Norma as high as Norma wanted. Mrs. Wilson also noticed that Norma was less timid than in the past.

Once Mrs. Wilson insisted on pushing them, although the kids kept yelling for me. I felt she did it because she was afraid I would push them too high. Of course, when Mrs. Wilson wanted to push, I made no move to.

"Mrs. Wilson," run my notes, "says that since she was two years old Norma has had a tremendous drive for independence and has insisted on doing things by herself as much as possible. For example, Norma would try and try to lace her shoes, and when she couldn't, would blame her mother for not telling her how." Then Mrs. Wilson went on to say, "Once Norma ate a lot of cookies and vomited and blamed me for letting her do it."

It looks as if independence is not exactly a pleasant idea to Mrs. Wilson, and the behavior of mother and child does not suggest an untrammeled joy in freedom. Norma is quite afraid of being hurt and of being out of reach of her mother's hand. As Norma begins to get excited about going way up high on the swing, her mother will not push her hard, and when Mrs. Wilson thinks I am pushing the swing too high, she steps in. Considering Norma's general caution on the equipment, it seems as if she had not been exposed much to swings or teeter-totters. Whatever drive for independence Norma may have, it certainly is detached from *physical* independence.

Norma is afraid of strange children too, for in the sandbox, instead of trying to make friends, she shrinks into a corner. Peggy overwhelms her; too much freedom, too much free-swinging *body;* too much separation from, too much scorn of, the *ground.* It was startling to hear Mrs. Wilson say to Norma, "When you swing it's like flying; it's like being a bird," when Norma was afraid to move and her mother was afraid to move her. The tension between permitting and refusing—between holding on to Norma and letting go; between affirming and negating, affirming Norma's growth and negating it; between freedom and constraint; between acceptance of life and fear of death—causes Mrs. Wilson to hold Norma back while releasing her. She urges her to duck her face in the backyard wading pool but not to get her hair wet; when they are crossing the street, Mrs. Wilson talks as if Norma might do it on her own, but confuses her so by the anxious push of speech that Norma has to rely on her mother; she lets Norma play with bugs but is so repelled and even frightened that Norma feels them crawling on her when they aren't there.

(Second day.) Shortly after lunch Norma came in, announcing that she had caught some ants and put them in a jar and that she wanted her mother to come out and see. After her mother had gone and come back, Norma returned and announced that she had caught some more. Her mother went out again, and so did I, but her father was uninterested and said so. When I suggested that we put leaves and grass in the jar, Norma thought that a wonderful idea, so she and I put some in.

Then Norma and I began collecting ants and other bugs and had a wonderful time, but her mother got very squeamish and soon went inside. Norma was very active catching the bugs, always picking them up with a leaf, however, for she would not dare, as I sometimes did, pick up an insect with bare fingers. She showed no horror, but rather an indefatigable interest in collecting more and more.

We kept collecting bugs until I got tired and said I thought we had had enough. Norma brought the jar inside and her mother took it, but screwed the cover down very tight. She told Norma not to take the top off because the ants might get out and into her bed and crawl all over her. Shortly after that, Norma, lying on the floor of the living room, said ants were crawling on her, but she didn't seem very serious about it, and after scratching herself for a couple of minutes, forgot all about it. Nobody took her feeling very seriously.

The next day the jar was out of the house, on the steps; Mrs. Wilson said she had found a bug crawling around on the table.

Her mother hasn't made Norma afraid of bugs; yet there is little Norma is able to enjoy without her mother imparting some anxiety, without raising in Norma's mind some question about what is safe and what is dangerous, whether what she is doing can or should be done, whether what she is about to do does not contain within itself its own contradiction—like ducking one's face and keeping one's hair dry, or flying like a bird without leaving the ground. Norma and her mother are the living expression of the rhyme:

> Mother, may I go out to swim?
> Yes, my darling daughter;
> Hang your clothes on a hickory limb
> But don't go near the water.

Hence Norma's fear of freedom—as manifested in her coming back to take her mother's hand.

People must learn what to enjoy and what to fear, but they must also have their pleasures free enough from fear so that they can enjoy them, and have their fears free enough from pleasure to prevent them from being irresistibly attracted to danger.*

Pathways to Insatiability

Mrs. Wilson had told me of the time Norma vomited from eating too many cookies. Here are other examples of anxiety about "pleasure eating":

After dinner Norma said she was hungry, and with some misgivings, her mother went to the kitchen and brought back two bowls of fruit, one with apricots and plums and the other with grapes. Mrs. Wilson set the former next to Norma and the larger next to me, whereupon Norma said, "I want that bowl," and her mother said, "You can't have it." Then she said that when Norma eats too much she gets a stomach ache and blames her mother for letting her eat too much.

---

* I saw an Italian movie with a hero who could not make love unless it was dangerous. On the one hand, he had to break into his own wife's room like a prowler and act as if raping her, and on the other, he was irresistibly drawn to make love to other women when it seemed very dangerous. In cultures with a true warrior tradition, fighting is of course a dangerous, self-destructive pleasure.

Mrs. Wilson repeated this. Norma objected fairly strenuously to having the bowl taken away, but her mother insisted.

. . .

Mrs. Wilson stopped Norma from eating cookies, saying, "That's enough." I can't figure out why she did. Then Norma asked us how many we had had. I said, "I don't know, I didn't count them. Maybe I had three." She asked her mother, and her mother said three, and Norma said, "You can't have the same number as he," so her mother said five. Then Norma said she had had four, which, with her mother's five, made nine. So Mrs. Wilson obliged Norma to add them all up, and after one mistake she got it right—twelve—and her mother praised her.

The point about the fruit is not that Mrs. Wilson might have brought the grapes especially for me, but that by putting two bowls of fruit in front of—but *not* in front of—Norma, she contrived a paradox. But when you set up such paradoxes, you are actually inviting a child to eat too much, because the child is tempted and deprived, both at the same time. It is the "tree of knowledge" syndrome.

Norma didn't like being told to leave the cookies alone, so she got even; frustration was sublimated in power as this miniature tyrant compelled us to tell how many cookies we had eaten but denied us the right to tell the truth. The moment she assumed power, with our consent, she brushed our reality aside; deprived of cookies, she took away our freedom. Much of Western civilization was re-enacted in this minute drama of the cookies!

When, through superior counterpower, Mrs. Wilson introduced her countermeasure, her countercontrol, commanding Norma to add up the cookies, the little dictator was dethroned but rewarded for renouncing the cookies, for handing control over to her mother, and above all, for transmuting love of cookies into successful arithmetic, for giving up reality (cookies) for obsession with achievement and work. But Mrs. Wilson had a special triumph, perhaps, for I was there to see *her* Norma add, and I could see Norma obedient. In Norma's yielding and counting, I would see with my own eyes that she really "loved" her mother!

There was an exchange of freedoms here: we gave up ours to Norma in order to pacify her and retain her regard, and Norma gave up her freedom twice in order to placate her mother and retain her mother's regard. Meanwhile the sweet, edible reality of the cookies disappeared; cookies, eating and the true number of cookies vanished in the combined, blinding glare of the personal relationship and the obsession. *This is culture:* mutual renunciation and exchange of freedoms, pacification, placation—and truth (the cookie) transmuted into illusion and obsession for the sake of solidarity and value.

While culture is *Homo sapiens'* reality it also conceals it, for objects having unchallengeable denotations (a cookie is a cookie is a cookie, sweet, edible, crumbly and small) and acts having clear outlines (eating) become enveloped in interpersonal meanings and obsessions. It is better, of course, to say that culture envelops the bare reality of object and act in its own reality, which is the configuration of interpersonal relations and traditional obsessions. Normality—reason itself—consists in choosing this "higher reality." Reason, therefore, does not, as philosophers have stated, consist in piercing through the immediate evidence of the senses to some immanent, self-subsisting "truth," but precisely in accepting as truth the figments with which culture, including philosophy, presents us. Thus, in the long run, it will be better—"truer"—for Norma to be praised for arithmetic than to have cookies, for it is the quintessence of bourgeois existence, of being middle-class, to be deprived of goodies in the interest of furthering achievement. In the alchemy of drive-transmutation, what Norma loses at home, in cookies, she will gain in school, for cookies lost are A's achieved. Let us note, however, that the transmutation—the sublimation—is not spontaneous, but occurs in the alembic of the parents' personalities, over the flame of their obsession.

I have suggested that one source of insatiability* is having our pleasure constantly cut off in the middle. Another is mixing anxiety with pleasure, for if we cannot have pleasure without anxiety we become insatiable, because anxiety gets in the way of satisfaction. Since dissatisfaction consequently increases, we are always unsatisfied, and end up insatiable.

Let us look at Norma's fantasy for just a moment.

Almost throughout dinner Norma chattered incessantly and very charmingly about everything under the sun. Now, let's see: she said she would like to own the school, the whole world and Dr. Henry. She talked about her dollies, and particularly about Lucy, her new dolly, which has earrings and high heels. She said her daddy was lazy.

I do not say that *Norma* wants everything; I merely say she wants everything *just like so many other people in our culture.*

Observations point to many small, subterranean streams feeding Norma's anxiety: her mother urges her on but makes her anxious, makes it difficult for Norma to decide what is safe and what is dangerous, and injects ambivalence into Norma's pleasure. Numberless little indecisions, holdings back and anxieties contribute to an underlying insatiability—in Norma as in any other normal American child. In the next section I explore further sources of her restlessness and dissatisfaction.

Sword and Sandals of the Middle Class

Adults try to control the mind of a child by pointing out what is right and wrong and by making what is right an obsession, so that there is no room for contradiction; so that, waking or sleeping, the mind is so preoccupied

---

* Insatiability, like the ocean, is fed by many streams, some of them poisonous. According to Suetonius, Caligula, emperor of Rome, was a monster who committed all crimes for his pleasure, including murder, incest and the torture of innocents. Even as a child he enjoyed watching executions and torture, and when he became emperor, was able to command them at his pleasure. Since, in the psychoanalytic view, the repressed is essentially criminal, it would follow that many today would do as Caligula if they had his absolute power and, like him, believed themselves divine, for absolute power has no external restraint and the conviction of divinity eliminates guilt. Ordinary people, lacking absolute power and restrained by guilt, must express the repressed in more conventional pleasures, which, however, because of the force of the repressed, are sought insatiably.

I would disagree with this formulation in one respect: I do not believe that only "evil" is repressed, for much spontaneous infantile goodness—the tendency to love widely and let oneself be loved by many, the tendency to give away what one has, the tendency to tell the truth—must be repressed also, because it is too threatening to society.

with the cultural obsession that contradiction is necessarily excluded; so that what is contrary is merely repulsive—an obsession in its own right. In order to create an obsession it is necessary to give a great deal of attention to the details of a child's life, rewarding correct expressions of the obsession, and punishing deviations. Since parents and other adults in the culture have the obsessions, their reactions to a child's successes or failures in this regard are like reflexes. When we consider the relationship between institutionalized obsession and love, we perceive that obsession can engross love to the degree that love may be expressed through establishing obsession in the child. With what warmth and indulgence a parent in our culture can say, "Johnny is such a darling little finagler—if he can get around you, he will," or "My little Tillie is a real little moneybag; she saves her money and tries to figure out how to get her inheritance out of the bank before she's twenty-one." When obsession engrosses love, a parent's very acts of love may become mere expressions of it. An illustration I often use that suggests this sort of thing is the Dakota Indian father who says to his son, his hand on his shoulder, "My son, it is time for you to die," because he wants his son to go on the warpath and become glorious. The myth of Theseus is another example: when Theseus' father, Aegeus, king of Athens, departed Troezen, he left a pair of sandals and a sword beneath a stone for the day when Theseus could lift it and retrieve them. Young Theseus labored, strengthening himself by exercise, until he moved the stone. Then he sought his father, who made him his heir. The myth contains two elements important for us; the first is that the parent, in his very gesture of love, interest or concern, cultivates the culturally necessary obsession in the child, and the second, that the child, in order to be worthy of the parent, must become obsessed too.

The marrow of the obsession of the American middle class is the combination of achievement, competition, monopoly, accumulation, high-rising living standard and insatiability. I give below further observations on how Mrs. Wilson builds this marrow in her daughter's bone, and how Norma exercises to lift the stone, to retrieve the sword and sandals of the middle class.

Another example of Mrs. Wilson's domination of Norma's mind is her attempt to control the game Norma had set up for the two of us. When Norma and her mother are together, whether playing or in any other way, Mrs. Wilson constantly attempts to get Norma to count or spell. For example, today when Norma and her mother were playing ball, Norma said, "Right now," and her mother told her to spell "right" and "now." This, it seems to me, is sometimes a way of preventing Norma from arguing or thinking. When Norma seems about to start an argument, in order to side-track her, her mother gets her to spell the last word she said.

. . .

Before we sat down to dinner Norma was reading the greeting cards that were in a bowl on a small table. The cards—valentines, birthday cards and Christmas greetings—appeared to have been there a long time. As Norma read them her mother watched carefully to see whether Norma read correctly, and was pleased when she did. There were valentines which Mr. and Mrs. Wilson had sent to each other.

. . .

Her mother wanted to show me the summer panty pajamas Norma was wearing and pulled down the bedcovers for me to see, but Norma pulled them back. I said that my daughter, who is in college, wears pajamas like that, and Mrs. Wilson said to Norma, "You see—college."

. . .

On the way home Norma was very tired, especially when we were walking up a hill, but her mother pooh-poohed that, and insisted that Norma not act that way, indicating to her that such signs of weakness were unbecoming.

Because Mrs. Wilson's compulsion keeps Norma counting and spelling, the achievement drive is thrust unrealistically into the middle of the game of catch. Real achievement in a game of catch—fielding difficult pitches, throwing straight, retrieving fast, and so on—is thrust aside, and the irreal*—spelling—takes its place. The game and its pleasure, including being with one's mother, are muddied by the imposed lesson, and while the eyes are following the ball the mind is following words, honing the cutting edge of the middle-class achievement drive. *Perception* is distorted under orders from "above": "You are commanded not to perceive this activity as catch but as an achievement in spelling." The process continues in elementary school, but there spelling is converted into "spelling baseball" † and arithmetic into a variety of other competitive games. The humiliation and depersonalization of the child in school, of which we see something even here, in the Wilson home, consist in the fact that the impulses to play, to know and to understand are subverted, and used to shove the cultural drives down the child's throat. This is the ultimate treachery and the ultimate indignity. But the paradox is that only through this treason can he become loyal (to the culture), and only through failing himself (his inherent drive to *know*) can he succeed in the culture.

Because Mrs. Wilson perceives Norma not only as a loved daughter but also, rather obsessively, as a bundle of conventional possibilities and as justification of her self, it would be difficult for Norma to be clear about her relationship to her mother. What is she to her mother and her mother to her? How does she perceive herself in relation to her mother?

Can she perceive herself? In Norma's life, things often change before her eyes, as in a surrealist movie. She touches a cookie and it springs out from under her hand, or out of her mouth, a problem in addition; she tosses a ball and in midflight it explodes into an array of compulsive words that have to be spelled. The sentiments on greeting cards are not what is important—they are not expressions of the thoughtfulness of others but tests of reading skill; nor is Lucy a doll that expresses somebodys' love for Norma: "Granma gave you this dolly," or "We bought that for Norma when we were downtown." One moment Norma is a little girl being put to bed, the next she is a grown girl made to think of college. She is about to sit down to dinner and it turns into a quiz. There are no simple combinations of things —like milk and cookies, or cookies as opposed to candy, or even no cookies versus some cookies, which are the kinds of oppositions, contrasts, combinations and negations we imagine children learn. The ordinary phenomena of her life become conditions for the expression of the achievement drive— lessons through which Norma must prove herself to her untiring, because driven, inquisitor and trainer.

* I have selected this variant of "unreal" or "not real" in order to express the illusion-like quality of the association between catching a ball—or any obvious act of clear outline—and an underlying compulsion.

† See my *Culture Against Man*, (*op. cit.*), Chapter 8, pp. 297–301.

Mrs. Wilson began to talk about Norma's restlessness and about her ability to make friends with anyone under the sun: with children in kindergarten, with children her own age, and even with older children. She added that Norma must always have something to do; I said that most American kids are that way and that they cannot stand being alone. This reassured Mrs. Wilson a good deal.

Mrs. Wilson likes harsh taskmasters for Norma:

This morning we talked about schools, and I described some suburban schools as permissive, using the "brink of chaos" method of discipline. Mrs. Wilson said it is very different here—the teachers are very strict. She described Norma's new teacher, of whom all the children were very fond. When the teacher becomes exasperated with a child she shakes her, threatens to cut off her head, and threatens to cut off her hands if she doesn't write the way she should. "But," Mrs. Wilson said, "all the children love her." When Norma had to write a composition at the end of the term, all she wrote was: "Dear Miss So-and-so, I love you very much. Signed: Norma." It was clear, from the way she talked about the teacher, that Mrs. Wilson likes strict discipline.

And Mrs. Wilson doesn't believe in giving in too easily.

After Norma and Abby had gotten out of the pool, Norma asked her mother whether they could go and dress up. Mrs. Wilson hemmed and hawed until Norma said "Okay!" and dashed into the house with Abby. I said to Mrs. Wilson, "It seems to me that Norma interprets your delay as permission." She said that she often delays giving consent immediately; she feels she shouldn't give in too easily in order that Norma may value more what she gets through having to struggle to get it.

. . .

Norma told her mother a number of times that she wanted to go to the park again and go on the swings, and her mother kept saying, "All right," but each time she also said, "Do you really want to go?" and Norma would reply, "Yes, I want to go," but nothing would happen. We sat there on the lawn for about forty-five minutes before we left to go to the park, with only about forty-five minutes to spare because Mrs. Wilson had to be back to fix dinner.

And, of course, if Norma will value more what she has to struggle for, it follows that she will value most what is "hard to get."

I shall summarize the analysis up to this point by looking at Mrs. Wilson as having left Donald so alone that he became autistic. I want to try to answer the question whether there is anything about her now that suggests the possibility of her having been a person who could leave her child completely alone. Is there anything about this woman, who now projects herself in every aspect of her child's existence, that at all hints at the opposite?

I believe it is present in the following: (1) Obsession with achievement, competition and wealth. At first this involved Mrs. Wilson so deeply in her husband's practice that she neglected Donald. Formerly the obsession was expressed through her husband and she neglected her child; now she makes the obsession and the child, Norma, one. (2) Commitment to discipline and to making things hard to get. This commitment, as we shall see further, is attenuated now, but though the early attitude has "spent its malice," its "stored thunder" can be heard today. In dealing with an infant, her attitude of not making things too easy would come out in her not making herself too readily available to it. (3) Mrs. Wilson's overshadowing need to achieve conventional goals and to prove herself. Formerly she hoped to do this through her husband, and through the work she did for him she helped get him established. But by doing this she neglected Donald. However, now that convention and proving herself to the outer world come together in her daughter, the underlying trouble appears—*she does not see Norma in the child's own light* but very much in the light reflected on Norma by conventional aspirations. Donald was scarcely a child at all; Norma is a child and not a child, because her mother is not able to distinguish between what is good for Norma and what, in Norma, is her mother's aspiration and obsession. In this, we are all very much like her. (4) Injecting a contradiction into what she does, so that she is able to feel strongly a reason for not doing what she intends to do.* I think, in Donald's case, the negative got the upper hand; a reason for not going in to him would arise every time she started toward him, and since she had the backing of the pediatrician, and her husband required that she do his work, the negative won. It was easy for this to happen because Mrs. Wilson's pleasures are so mixed with fears: the pleasure of going to Donald would be muddied by fear that she might be spoiling him, that she was neglecting and offending her husband, that she was undermining the family's future by not taking care of her husband's work, that she might be letting her mother down by *indulging herself* with the baby instead of being at her mother's house doing chores, and so on. (5) The primacy of work. Being obsessed with work—work for husband and work for family—filled the obsessive need. What unacceptable, unconscious impulses Mrs. Wilson harbored that had to be bound by compulsion were most readily bound by work, and the compulsion was more readily shifted to people who demanded than to a quiet baby who seemed inherently no work. What follows is very speculative indeed: with the advent of Norma, Mrs. Wilson was able to shift her compulsion and make Norma her work. Donald was known to be seriously ill; Mrs. Wilson now believed it was damaging to leave a baby alone, and Norma was a noisy baby. Mrs. Wilson says that when Norma was born she gave her a great deal of attention in order to keep her quiet so she wouldn't wake Donald, and even now, in the middle of nothing at all

a number of times at the table Norma has said, in a very low voice, "Now don't wake the baby! Don't make so much noise, you'll wake the baby." I think this is related to the fact that her mother used to tell her to keep quiet so as not to wake Donald.

But how do you keep a baby quiet in our culture? Why, you carry him around, pet him, talk to him, give him the bottle or breast, coo to him—are *there*. Thus, in the very act of making certain that Donald would be quiet—asleep—and making sure that Norma would be quiet too, so that Donald would be quiet, Mrs. Wilson became active and thereby gave Norma the social contact she needed.

There are many ironies in Mrs. Wilson's reason for giving Norma a lot of attention. What if it were true that Mrs. Wilson had never held an infant in her arms much, and learned how it really felt from holding *one* in order to keep the *other* quiet? What if she learned to love Norma because keeping her quiet was a kind of "work" she was doing for Donald? What if she felt that since she had to keep Donald asleep she had a good reason for giving

* This phenomenon is familiar as a symptom of obsessively compulsive people.

attention to Norma? What if she really loved the baby girl from the very start but needed an excuse for spending time with her? Sleep is sacred in the family—it is a dimension of life that is ceremonialized. Isn't it strange that Mrs. Wilson cannot say, "I loved Norma so much that I loved to hold her," but has to say, *as the only thing she says,* that she gave Norma a lot of attention *in order to accomplish something?* Think of all that she might have said—but she picks out that *one* thing! *Does she have to have an excuse for giving attention to her own baby?*

Love and Death

From the first day I thought that Mrs. Wilson loved Norma, though the only times she was tender to her was when she put her to bed and when Norma lost her sweater. Mrs. Wilson was mindful of Norma, was never humiliating, often took her to the park, played with her and protected her. Mrs. Wilson is not demonstrative, yet it is hard to say whether she is not a demonstrative person or whether the phantom presence of the psychotic child holds her back. She may be the kind who, as I pointed out, can express involvement in a child only through training him in the cultural obsessions; she may be self-contained, able to come out of herself only on ceremonial occasions (like bedtime) or in emergencies (like the sweater incident). At any rate, I give below my observations of affectionate expressions.

(First day.) While Norma was talking Mrs. Wilson looked at her the whole time, her eyes glowing with pleasure, and her father looked at her, smiling indulgently. She is quite a clean child; and she was wearing a becoming little blue oufit, on which there did not seem to be a single stain.

(Third day. Mrs. Wilson was putting Norma to bed.) Her mother pulled back the covers and Norma crawled in and the two embraced very tenderly—Mrs. Wilson obviously "eating up" the child, and the child enjoying it.

While bidding me good night, Mrs. Wilson began to talk about what Norma would sometimes say to her when being put to bed: "You must be just like an angel," or "You're a beautiful flower." Mrs. Wilson says that if she laughs when Norma says a thing like that the child becomes very upset because she means it from the bottom of her little heart. Mrs. Wilson was very ecstatic about her relationship with Norma.

Though Norma may call her mother "flower" and "angel," I did not hear Mrs. Wilson call Norma by those names, nor did mother and daughter kiss outside of the bedroom. Norma never threw her arms around her mother, and she sat on her lap only when her mother put her there after she had lost her sweater. The next extract—from the notes on the fifth day—reflects a good part of my feeling about the two of them.

We went into the backyard and Mrs. Wilson reclined on a chair I set up for her. Norma kept saying how much she loved the cowboy doll (which I had just bought her) and something about its going to heaven. Then she said she'd like to die and her mother asked anxiously why, and Norma said because she'd like to go to heaven. Her mother said, "Well, we want you here." It seemed to me that

Norma was provoking her mother by talking about dying, that Mrs. Wilson's absorption in Donald must lead Norma to frequent provocations, and that her strong expressions of love may be a function of her mother's absorption in Donald. It is also clear now that Norma's absorption in Donald is a function of her mother's guilt absorption in Donald. Both share the absorption in Donald. Norma shows, on the one hand, an effort to free her mother from Donald, and on the other, an effort to identify herself with her mother's love for Donald so that her mother can love her equally.

Most people—not Mrs. Wilson—think that "children don't understand death—don't know what death is," and when you point out to them that children see it on television and in the movies, see dead animals, hear about the death of relatives, of people being killed in accidents, dying of cancer or perishing on battlefields, and that parents constantly protect children from being killed by automobiles or germs, they say, "But they don't *really* know what it is." * And some of them resist the belief that children understand death even when you tell them that many children of Norma's age and less ask, "Mommy [or Daddy], will you die?" or point out that children play at dying in nursery school.† For such people Norma's remark can have no significance.

The doll is Norma. She loves it the way she would like to be loved, perhaps. If the dolly died she would feel bad, but, she wonders, would her mother feel as bad if Norma died and went to heaven as Norma would feel if her dolly died? When she answers her mother's question by saying she'd like to go to heaven, she is really asking one of her own: "Would you feel just as bad about losing me as I would if my dolly died?" And her mother's expression of her love for Norma provokes a positive response.

The very least that children perceive of death is that people called "dead" are as if permanently asleep and that they disappear. Since children sleep and see others asleep and know that dead people disappear, there is no reason why children should not think they might easily fall permanently asleep and disappear—die. Donald has disappeared and Norma is preoccupied with not waking the baby. Perhaps she thinks Donald is dead.‡ Her parents tell her Donald is sick, away somewhere—why should she believe them? Parents and others repeatedly say things that are not true (see infra); why should *this* be true? And if Donald has died, why shouldn't she? Why does her mother seem so sad? Some of her mother's grief must

---

* Important works on children's attitudes toward an understanding of death are: Sylvia Anthony, *The Child's Discovery of Death: A Study in Child Psychology* (London, Kegan Paul, Trench, Trubner & Co., Ltd., 1940); John Bowlby, "Grief and Mourning in Infancy and Early Childhood," *Psychoanalytic Study of the Child*, Vol. XV (1960), pp. 9–52; and Alexius T. Portz, *The Meaning of Death to Children*, Ph.D. dissertation, U. of Michigan, 1964.

Most research, however, is based on questioning children and is therefore of limited value.

† See my "Death, Fear and Climax in Nursery School Play" (*op. cit.*), in *Concepts of Development in Early Childhood Education*, ed. by Peter Neubauer (Springfield, Ill., Charles C. Thomas, 1965).

‡ Let me remind the reader of the following facts: (1) Mrs. Wilson is constantly grieving for Donald. (2) Mr. Wilson "has written Donald off." (Further, he says, according to his wife, Donald "has died to me"—see p. 362.) (3) Mrs. Wilson says that she would prefer that Donald had died rather than exist in his present condition. (4) Mrs. Wilson says that she does not want Donald to die. Without her parents' wishing it, the aura of death that surrounds Donald may very likely communicate the idea to Norma that he is indeed dead.

be communicated to Norma: why should Norma not ruminate about death? On the (dangerous) swing, perhaps, or on the teeter-totter? Or crossing dangerous streets? Maybe her dolly isn't merely inanimate but dead. Why should she not then be worried that her parents might die? The anxiety and depression an adult feels when he thinks someone close to him might die is the sense of loss through death, and when a friend loses someone he loves, the adult, normally, experiences a sense of loss, sympathetically. A child Norma's age might be sensitive only to what she might lose through death, but there is no reason why, sensing how she would feel should her mother die, she would not be aware of, or wonder about, how her mother would feel were she to die.

Since a sense of death in the social sense* is not only awareness of how people feel when someone close dies, but includes also the capacity to grieve with them if they are close, sorrow defines relationships even more sharply than affection. When those with whom I grieve and those with whom I share affection are the same, when the circle of my affection overlaps the circle of my sorrow, then the relationship is intense indeed. If, as an adult, I cannot truly grieve with a person—feel his sense of loss—I do not love him.

The capacity to feel loss is universal.† It is, perhaps, the capacity to feel the loss of persons other than one's parents, or of others equally close, and the capacity to sorrow at another person's bereavement that mark the difference between young children and adults.

Mrs. Wilson's anxious response to what Norma said about dying is very good. It might have been better, perhaps, if she had gotten out of her chair and hugged Norma, without even a word, perhaps, but we know she is austere. Still, she is not like pathogenic parents, absent when most needed. When Norma was in distress about the sweater, her mother was emotionally present, her father absent; and here, when the child thinks of death, her mother does not ignore it or brush it aside. She takes her daughter seriously; she treats her with respect and replies to what she says as if it meant something. To her mother, Norma is *never* a subject for jest. This kind of negative has a *positive* outcome, and enables us to see that it is not only what a parent does for or to a child that contributes to or cancels its selfhood, but also what the parent does not do. Mrs. Wilson is restrained and rather compulsive, but she is always *there;* she knows when to step in to help; she is never humiliating, and Norma is a real person to her, not a doll, a bunny rabbit, a puppy, or worse.‡ True, I feel that because of Donald, the real Norma is not quite *there* to Mrs. Wilson; that she sees Norma through the glass of sorrow and guilt, and that this adds to her inherent restraint; yet she is in contact enough to make herself real to Norma when needed. If Norma did not know that her mother was available, was in-

* The sense of death is an important component of Martin Heidegger's existential analytic, but it is completely self-centered, in line with Heidegger's narcissistic metaphysic. That being a person could have any reference to being sensitive to another person's bereavement would be a contradiction in a solipsistic system.

† Perhaps infants raised in large households where several women regularly take care of them, and more than one give them the breast, do not feel the loss of the mother as irreparably as children in our culture.

‡ In pathogenic metamorphosis a parent may think of his child as a human garbage pail, a "Mister Magoo," a "monster," etc. See my *Culture Against Man* (*op. cit.*), Chapter 9, the Portman family.

volved in her, she would not have said that she wanted to die and go to heaven. On the other hand, it seems to me that Norma tests her mother in this way too, and I think she does it because she wants to be sure that her mother, who is so preoccupied, really cares about her.

Accusation

Accusation is a kind of testing. Norma repeatedly accuses her mother in little matters, even seeming to pluck things out of the blue. Since Mrs. Wilson remembers these accusations for years, since she is wary of Norma, and since she tells me of her fear of being accused, accusation must be a persisting irritant in the relationship. I have already discussed Norma's blaming her mother when she vomited because she had eaten too many cookies and for not teaching her how to lace her shoes. Below I give the accusations I observed.

As we were leaving the park Norma decided that she would go one way and we should go another. Her mother said Norma always wants to do things differently from everybody else. Norma had apparently got it into her head while she was on her way that we would meet her as she came out, but we waited about a hundred yards from where she did and she came down to us. She was very angry that we had not come to get her, and when her mother explained that we did not know we were supposed to, Norma said, "Oh yes, you did; you said you were going to do it and you didn't do it." So I suggested that her mother and I walk down to where Norma had been and come back and meet her. On the way Mrs. Wilson said to me, "We are going to meet 'the queen' now."

(When we got home Norma asked me to come into her room and play with her, and we started to cut some things out of heavy cardboard with a rather inadequate pair of scissors.) The cardboard was awfully hard to cut, and I showed her the impression the scissors had made on my hand. She then got sort of angry and went in to her mother and said, "We are hurting our fingers trying to cut the cardboard." So her mother came back with a huge pair of scissors, which she gave to me, and Norma used the smaller one I had been working with.

What can we say of these accusations? In the first place, we have established that they occur, which means they are permitted to occur; this suggests that in some way accusation is rewarded. In the second place, we can say that Norma is ready to accuse her mother—out of the blue, as in the case of the scissors. But what does "out of the blue" mean? It must mean that Norma feels her mother as a *presence* who is responsible for everything, and whose fault it is if anything goes wrong. When Norma is frightened and angry because we fail to appear at the park exit, it can't be because she said nothing about meeting her; rather, our failure to appear is transformed by her fright into violation of a promise. Since, if we had made the agreement and stuck to it we would have been there, and she would not have been frightened, it follows that since she was frightened, an agreement must have been made and broken: a cause is invented to fit a consequence. The same holds for the scissors: my ("our") painful fingers become a consequence of maternal failure because if her mother had done what she should have—provided adequate scissors—"our" fingers would not hurt. It makes no difference that her mother was unaware of what was really going on.

Behind these inventions lies the assumption of a *malificent* omniscience,* responsible for pain; in inventing illusory malificent power to account for misfortune, Norma resembles us all. But not merely this. Norma has an accusatory *attitude* toward her mother, as if she held her responsible for some great underlying failure; as if the audible accusations were but surrogates for an inaudible, because graver, accusation. Her attitude does not imply that her mother did anything out of malice, but rather that her mother *was not there*.

Norma not only feels her mother's distance; she also senses her guilt but uses it to construct her own existence; she uses her mother's guilt to get her involved in her. Mrs. Wilson's guilt—about Donald—is the complement of Norma's accusations.

Imagining and talking out loud about her own death, Norma makes herself vividly alive to her mother. She involves her mother in her by negating herself ("I might die") or her mother ("You failed"). Mrs. Wilson feels as if in bondage to Norma ("the queen"), and Norma has this power over her because of Mrs. Wilson's guilt, her anxiety, her need to prove herself, her achievement drive and because of her determination to make Norma a shining jewel—to show the world—and to give her a good life.

In our culture people can become actualized to one another in three ways: through acts of negation, through acts of affirmation, or through some combination of these. The first makes use, largely, of guilt accusation, fear, and fear of death, provoking what does not comes spontaneously; the second does not need to do this because love gives naturally; in the third, affirmation and negation alternate painfully and querulously. I think in Norma and her mother we have the third case.

Learning to Disbelieve and Cover Up

I have said that although her parents tell her that Donald is away because he is sick, there is no reason why Norma should not believe instead that he is dead, since she sees and hears many things that do not quite square with the truth.

I asked Norma how old she is and she said seven—or rather, I said she was six and she "corrected" me. This is "curious": she entered school at five, instead of six, so now the principal tells everybody that Norma, who is in the second year, is seven years old. So Norma is mixed up about how old she is.

Another deception in which Norma is involved has to do with Donald. She has been told that he suffers from rheumatic fever so severely that he was taken out West to a place that has excellent facilities to help sufferers from this disease,

---

* Though Piaget has made us familiar with this *type* of childish thinking, in which everything must have its motivated cause—see Jean Piaget's *Language and Thought of the Child* (Meridian Books; Cleveland, World Publishing, 1955)—the complex social interrelationships of this "finalism" are not discussed by him. Assuming that at Norma's age children in our culture tend to ascribe events to final causes, Norma's *accusatory attitude* still cannot be dismissed *simply* as finalism, but must be understood as her unique expression of it, in relation to her mother.

and that's where he is. In fact, that is what everybody has been told. When children ask Norma where her brother is she always answers that he's away because he has rheumatic fever. The teachers say, "Well, there are other children who have rheumatic fever and they are still here. How is it that your brother is away?" And Norma says he's just away. It's not easy for the children to accept the fact that her brother is not around.

      . . .

At lunch today Norma asked me whether I would marry her mother if her mother wasn't married and I wasn't married. Mrs. Wilson's anxiety would not permit Norma and me to straighten this out—she jumped in and battered Norma with arguments. They ran something like this: "How do you know—look at all the women there are in the world! If Dr. Henry didn't have a wife—well, he would go around looking all over the world and finally end up with the wife he has now, because that's the girl he wants." Norma listened quietly to this and at last told her mother, in exasperation, that her mother simply did not understand.

I said to Norma, "I know what you're after—you want to know whether I like you, and I certainly do. And you want to know whether I like your mommy, and I certainly do." But Mrs. Wilson explained, "No, Norma really wants to find out whether you would marry me," and Norma said yes. I told her, "Well, I really don't know," and stuck to my guns, adding, "How can you try to get me to answer a question when I really don't know?" And that's where I left the matter.

I was quite struck by the strength Norma showed in standing up to this battering. I think the dialectic is as follows: Mrs. Wilson's practice of stimulating Norma to think, on the one hand, and trying to prevent her from thinking, on the other, sometimes confuses Norma and sometimes defeats her mother, because the very forces of thought her mother uses to stimulate Norma, the child also turns against her.

This afternoon Norma mentioned a girl who has very large lips and her mother said immediately that it is probably because she sucked her thumb until her lips turned out. Then Norma said the girl uses lipstick, and her mother said she probably does to make the lips feel better.

      . . .

When Mr. Wilson came into the living room, Norma, who was half watching *Robin Hood*, became absorbed in her doll, and then wandered off into another room. As usual, her father turned to a horse opera. When Norma came back she asked whether *Robin Hood* was on and her father told her it would be over in ten minutes. Norma became confused: she didn't know whether she was looking at *Robin Hood* or not. (Of course, *Robin Hood* was being shown, but on a different channel, and would be over in ten minutes.) He kept Norma thinking she was looking at *Robin Hood* and at the same time not looking at it. After ten minutes her father said, "*Robin Hood* is all over; now its time to go to bed." Norma looked completely nonplused and befuddled and I must admit that I was confused too.*

While we were out on the lawn in front of the house a cat came along, and Norma, after stroking it, tried to get it to do something. When it wouldn't obey she chased it, and her mother said, "Oh, you're training it!"

      . . .

Mrs. Wilson said Norma suspected a man they knew of having an affair with a neighborhood girl, but Mrs. Wilson had said with a frown, "Norma, why do you say such a thing?" and Norma answered, "Well, I think it's true." Mrs. Wilson denied that anything like that was possible. Norma's reason for thinking as she

---

* Mr. Wilson's distortion, in the interest of getting his own way, does not contradict what I have said earlier about his not deceiving Norma emotionally; about his not pretending a love he does not feel, not exacting feelings he does not reciprocate.

did was that the man talks so sweetly to the girl—and Mrs. Wilson mimicked the way Norma had imitated him—but doesn't talk sweetly to his wife, and Mrs. Wilson had answered, "Of course not, she's around all the time." This is a fine indication of what Mrs. Wilson expects from her husband—or from any husband, for that matter.

Norma must often be skeptical of what her mother says; she must doubt her parents' ambiguous definitions of what is right under her nose; and, in general, doubt what adults tell her. She ought to be rather resentful of being treated at times as if she were dumb.

The skepticism of others about where Donald is may force Norma to wonder where he really is, and she must sense evasiveness when she asks her parents about it—an evasiveness that probably appears when she asks them about death too. If they are evasive about the disappearance of dead people—as most parents are*—and evasive about the disappearance of Donald, whom she seems to remember best as being asleep—then her conclusion that Donald is dead is a logical step. The rather speculative syllogism is simple:

> People are evasive and avert their eyes
> when you ask about dead people.
>
> My parents are evasive and avert their eyes
> when I ask about Donald.
>
> Donald is dead.

When I was saying good night to Norma in her room, the same day she had asked me at lunch whether I would marry her mother, she said she wished I were her daddy and her mother smiled as if to say, "Well, this is just a child talking," but she did reprove her mildly.

Norma is perceptive, sees to the heart of things. It is natural that she should want me for her daddy because I played with her and responded to her—made myself available, while her real daddy did not—but I think there was more to her question than that. Feeling that her mother sensed something in me that she could not get from her husband, at lunch Norma had articulated her mother's need as well as her own; hence her mother's anxious horror at Norma's question—it struck too deep. At bedtime, however, Mrs. Wilson had control of herself, and besides, Norma's remark was less dangerous—just about a daddy and not about a new husband.

Since Norma's questions about factual things compel adults to be evasive, she can infer the presence of deception, even though she may not be able to discover the truth. She cannot force reality to appear, but she can compel deception to admit it is a lie.

In the light of this, what shall we say about the girl with the large lips? First off, Mrs. Wilson is worried about Norma's continuing to suck her thumb at six. It is true, of course, that many parents try to scare children out of habits the parents don't like, but I think children don't believe them.†

---

* In *Childhood and Society* (*op. cit.*), Erik Erikson cites the case of a three-year-old boy who mocked his parents when they told him that his dead grandmother was no longer home because she had gone to Seattle. See p. 23 of the 1950 edition (New York, Norton).

† We need evidence for this.

The threats have little effect because the immediate pleasure of the habit is so intense that it cancels the distant possibility of retribution. So Norma may pass over the thumb-sucking bogey, but being intelligent, how could she ignore the nonsense about the lipstick. At any rate, the problem is, Why did Mrs. Wilson make lipstick into medicine? I believe it was to defend the girl against the implied accusation that she is "bad" because she uses it, and because she doesn't want Norma to think nasty, bad, gossipy thoughts. Norma does say things that are not nice. It was not nice to say that Peggy is not pretty and that she "rubs" a lot. When we were picking various numbers for Norma to interpret, the meaning of my number was so unpleasant that Norma whispered it to her mother and was told not to say it out loud; and all her father's numbers signified unpleasantness. Norma's thoughts about the married man and the neighborhood girl were not nice, and her mother tried to cover that up.

Mrs. Wilson is sure that her daughter accepts distortions, because like practically all adults, she will not recognize the fact that children think. If adults did, however, how would they be able to cope with their own sham or with their need to deceive people, including their own children? In a mendacious culture you try to fool your own children and believe you can fool them, but this is impossible if you accept the fact that they think. And in a mendacious culture normal children learn to give the impression that they are fooled.

History suggests that we are always trying to destroy our culture;* and we want to destroy it because we hate and despise it.† Since children, however, are defined as "innocent," blind to chicanery and incapable of hate, it is immoral to think that they can sense our own world-historic hatred or that they can hate too. Middle-class parents want their children to believe that parents are incapable of hate, in a world without hate—saving, of course, the convenient and approved hatred of Negroes, Jews or any other inconvenient group. And even hatred of the Negroes is covered up by honey in the South, where white people claim they really love the "nigras" as long as they stay in their place. The Southern case proves the point—that middle-class people don't want to be associated with hate. Nevertheless, children in our culture show they despise the world, even though they don't know they do. Like Norma, they have a mean streak and say nasty things about people; they distrust parents; they are competitive and they are cruel ‡—in other words, well trained. In the schizophrenic child the hatred and fear that come to him from adults—and often from other children too—have overwhelmed him, while other children are able to cope with their fear and hatred.

There is a difference between Mrs. Wilson's deception and her husband's. She deceives Norma because she is anxious and because she wants

---

* Some might argue that we try to destroy other people's cultures only. Is there a difference?

† In an argument with me about the moral responsibility of scientists, a man who played an important role in the development of plutonium said he felt no responsibility at all because "mankind isn't worth saving."

‡ William Golding's *Lord of the Flies* is an excellent statement of these characteristics of children in our culture. I don't think he left girls out of the book because he believes little girls are made of "sugar and spice and everything nice," but just to simplify telling the story.

to protect her. She tries to be a good mother, and in our culture a good mother tries to fool her child with these "white" deceptions. But Mr. Wilson's deceptions strike at perception itself and he scrambles signals. Furthermore, rather than being protective, his deceptions are purely egoistic, as he talks to Norma unintelligibly from behind his paper, and scrambles the signals in the *Robin Hood* affair. His deceptions are intellectual tricks; his wife's are mindless protective acts.

Why did Mrs. Wilson say Norma was "training" the reluctant pussy cat? Why couldn't she have just ignored the whole thing? An imperious child, an impervious cat—what could be more commonplace? I think saying it expresses Mrs. Wilson's compulsion to intervene; a compulsion to dominate Norma's mind, to give a significance to whatever she can. Action must preferably have some kind of "goodness significance"; phenomena must strain toward goodness, and toward niceness too. Hence the lipstick is medicine, chasing the cat is training, eating cookies is arithmetic, and so on. The "absolute" Hegelian reality is a ceaseless flux of things becoming other, more perfect things.

So the matter of the neighborhood girl and the married man is a benign deception—a benign American middle-class deception. Norma must be protected against sex and against wrong ideas about marriage, and she must be protected against people's thinking that she is a nasty little girl who has wrong ("bad") ideas about marriage and is a gossip. In the very act of trying to convince Norma that an extramarital affair is unthinkable, however, and that all marriages are somehow good, Mrs. Wilson's wording lets Norma see that Mrs. Wilson's own marriage is not.

I think, based on evidence from my observations below, that another reason why Mrs. Wilson tried to cover up in the case of the lipstick and the affair is because she is rather prudish—perhaps extremely so.

I decided to go in and see Mrs. Wilson put Norma to bed. . . . I think interesting that just as Norma was taking off her underpants, Mrs. Wilson came around and stood between me and Norma, on the pretext of getting Norma's nightgown out of the dresser. She did not take anything out. Norma was unabashed in getting undressed in front of me.

. . .

I left the living room and went into Norma's room to say good night. She was sitting naked in a chair, and as soon as her mother heard me coming, she ran around in front of her, saying it was wrong of me to see a little girl that way. I don't remember her exact words.

Norma got the idea, and when her mother uncovered her to show me her pretty pajamas, the child pulled the covers back.

Since it may be that even after five days, almost any good middle-class American mother would continue to hide her child like this from the eyes of a middle-aged scientist, father of a daughter himself, I draw no conclusion from her behavior, but point out that it is in harmony with Mrs. Wilson's definition of lipstick-using girls and her effort to cover up the affair of the married man and the girl. It may all be just a virtuous middle-class cover-up and Norma a covered-up little middle-class girl. A really nice old-fashioned middle-class girl is not a cover girl but a *covered-up* girl.

Let us look for a moment at what Mrs. Wilson says about Norma and niceness.

When her mother was telling me that Norma always wants to be different from other people, she said that when Norma is asked, "How are you?" she says, "I'm nice," instead of "Very well, thank you." Norma says she does this because she feels that as far as she's concerned, she just feels nice.

All cultures must introduce a certain amount of intellectual sabotage into education, otherwise children would see through sham and challenge underlying assumptions. What science does not now know is at what points and by whom the sabotage is introduced. We know, of course, that in our culture, school does a great deal of it, but the process has not been analyzed empirically; in public school it all happens naturally, with the unconscious verve of tradition.

A great deal of sabotage occurs in the home, preparing the ground for the more systematic sabotage in school. In Norma's home, "niceness" is an important instrument of intellectual sabotage; the achievement drive is another. What is not nice is distorted and made nice, and what might conceivably contribute to the achievement drive—the cultural obsession—is twisted and compelled to serve it. Through unremitting intervention adults, without half trying, push the child's existence into the value obsessions of the culture, so that he cannot see the world in other terms. The instant he starts to think, or to perceive, perception and thought become amalgamated with the obsessions, or rather, they never are other than these, because there is no difference between "mind" and culture. On the one hand, culture makes thought and perception possible, and on the other, it negates perception and thought because it always introduces something not really "there." The intellectual history of mankind is a constant process of trying to free the mind from previous—and fiercely held—beliefs, but all the mind can do is move from one incomplete, false or sabotaged conception into another. What makes change and discovery possible in our culture, however, is just those kinds of irritating nonsense we see foisted on Norma and which she cannot believe. Our culture has always provided some outlet for the intellectual distrust generated by nonsense, and so we have been discharged, slowly, and through much suffering, from one ignorance after the other.

Power, self-interest, acquiescence and reward also play a role, however, for the child believes because of adult power, because it is to the interest of both the adult and the child that nonsense be believed and because the reward for acquiescing in the sabotage of one's intellectual capabilities is great and punishment for refusal fierce. Yet in our culture, little by little, the power to think escapes sabotage. All of this proves that Mrs. Wilson is a good mother, for she not only introduces the correct quality of intellectual sabotage into Norma's thinking but does not punish her when she rebels. It is the millions of anonymous Mrs. Wilsons and their children who make the intellectual quest possible while holding it back. Let us rear a monument to them—a mother shielding her child's eyes from the sun; and let us call it *Culture*.

What is at issue in all education* is the detachment of subject from predicate,† and emphasis on the latter. When Norma is in bed and her

---

* Some might prefer to use the term "enculturation," a word introduced into anthropology by the late Melville Herskovits.

† I think this expression originated with Hegel, but is best known to psychiatry,

mother shows me her pajamas, the prettiness of the garment is forgotten because suddenly college comes up and Norma has to become a *college girl*. What is important about the cookies is not the eating of them, or even that she might get sick from eating too many, but that they stand for *achievement = arithmetic*. In no culture is a child merely a child but someone *representing the cultural values;* and this is true of every observation and event also. The girl with the large lip is not merely a girl with an unfortunate ugliness; she stands for the *wrongness* of thumb-sucking and lipstick. Whenever an object is underscored, not in terms of its obvious outer (denotative) characteristics, but in terms of some transcendent cultural preoccupation, we can say that a predicate has been emphasized.

A further note on sham. From all this I conclude that if a child in our culture has not begun to believe that sham is truth by the time he is six years old, he will be in serious difficulty with adults.* Indeed, the "latency period" is not so much a period of repression of child sexuality as a period of repression of the impulse to truth. When a child "enters latency" in our culture, he learns how to present a sexless façade to adults, but more important, he rapidly learns that they are shams—and that, if he wants to survive, he must be one too.

Sexuality begins to assert itself with its full power in adolescence, but in our culture adolescence is also the time when the impulse to truth often bursts forth again with renewed force and shakes the adult world. At this point, however, teen-age culture obligingly does the truth-repression work for the adult world, because teen-age "fun" represses the impulse to truth. For example, the impulse to intellectual searching is often put to sleep by sex. Sex and truth were once companions in the prison of repression; now sex is freed—to become truth's jailor.

The Dialectic of Protection

Mrs. Wilson protects Norma from physical, social and psychic harm. She does not push her high on the swing, and, until my arrival Norma had not been on the big swings at all. When Norma walked on the wall that runs along the edge of the lake at the park her mother held her hand. Norma sticks close to her, constantly returns to her when they are walking along the street, and she tells Norma about crossing streets and how to watch out for the lights. She watches Norma to see that she does not overeat. Mrs. Wilson protects her daughter against having unkind thoughts and against exposing her body to the eyes of a man. When Norma seems to need emotional support, her mother is "there." Sharpening Norma's mind by pushing her to count and spell is also a kind of protection. The dialectic of social life, however, drives protection in the direction of fear, control and acquiescence; and perhaps because of my temperament, perhaps because I am an

---

perhaps, from E. von Domarus' essay "The Specific Laws of Logic in Schizophrenia," in *Language and Thought in Schizophrenia*, ed. by J. S. Kasanin (U. of Calif. Press, 1944).

* I have developed this theme in "Sham," *North American Review*, Vol. CCLII, No. 3 (May 1967).

American and "don't want nobody pushin' me around," perhaps because of a certain compulsiveness about Mrs. Wilson, my observations frequently express my feeling that fear and control overshadow protectiveness. The examples I give below reflect this.

Another example of the battle for Norma's mind is Mrs. Wilson's reminding her of something that happened two years ago. When Norma was four years old she walked off with a younger relative in the direction of Mrs. Wilson's sister-in-law's house, and disappeared. Mrs. Wilson at last learned where her daughter was when she got a frantic phone call from her sister-in-law. Mrs. Wilson went and got Norma and gave her a hard spanking, and Norma has never forgotten it. For me, the issue here is that Mrs. Wilson is constantly reminding Norma of it.

I cannot escape the feeling that repeatedly Mrs. Wilson projects herself into Norma's mind in order to guide her every thought.

. . .

Mrs. Wilson says that when she is around she lets Norma play in front of the house because she can protect Norma from the traffic, but when she's not around Norma has to play in the back.

Mrs. Wilson said she would not permit Norma to go to the playground alone because of the streets she has to cross, although she will leave her at the movies alone.

When Norma came to the [lunch] table, her mother asked to see her hands, and they weren't very clean. She tried to get Norma to wash them but Norma refused, and because I was there, I think, her mother did not force her but said, "Well, if you want to get germs, it's up to you." Quite a number of times Mrs. Wilson has tried to make Norma scared of germs. As a matter of fact, there is a continuous process of subjecting Norma to mild frights. I think this is important, in view of the fact that Mrs. Wilson thinks people can be permanently damaged by frights.

. . .

While Norma and Abby were playing, Mrs. Wilson left them strictly alone. However, I do remember that at one point Norma stepped into a box of leaves and grass at the base of a tree, and her mother yelled at her to get out of it because that was the box into which I had emptied an insect zoo a couple of days ago when the insects had all died.

Charlie (a little boy, fond of Norma) had not been there for more than a minute when he told Mrs. Wilson that Norma had crossed the street. Mrs. Wilson looked very grimly at Norma, but then said that she could cross the street on this block if she looked to right and left. Norma seemed upset that Charlie had told on her.

Protection, fear and control are inseparable. It is impossible to protect a child without inspiring a fear of danger in him and without controlling his mind and body. Making a game of chasing Harriet, Mrs. Jones did not teach her about fear and did not control her—for what control may have been implicit in chasing Harriet toward the road was masked by the pleasure and the gaiety—so Harriet, not knowing fear, was not protected and narrowly escaped death.* Because fear and control, since they negate death, become part of existence in the normal course of staying alive, the question is not, Shall there be fear? but rather, Fear of what? How much of it? and What is its quality?

* See the Jones case, p. 34.

Protection tends to take pleasure out of life or, under certain circumstances, substitute the pleasure of "nestling" for the fear of encounter. Protection is also inseparable from acquiescence, for in order to be protected a child must acquiesce. It follows from all this that the more a child is protected, the more he is controlled; the more he fears, the more he must acquiesce; and there is inherent in protectiveness a tendency to cancel independence. There is also a tendency, especially in the middle class, for protectiveness to increase without limit,* because when a child is imbued with fear he tends not to want to stir without a signal, and because parent and child get so much out of nestling.

Although in many ways Norma seems a timid child, she also shows signs of coming out of it. The first time we went to the park she was scared of the swings, but when she went the next time she was less afraid, and even preferred that I push her. She comes looping back to her mother when walking along the street, but she cuts away in the park. She is not afraid of bugs. When Norma gives her mother a sip from her bottle of pop, her mother always tears off the part of the straw that was in her own mouth, but her mother's fear of germs does not impress Norma.

Norma isn't afraid of being seen naked by me, for if she were she would have tried frantically to cover herself instead of being unconcerned. Norma is not afraid to think out loud about sexual matters, either: my marrying her mother and her notion about the affair suggest curiosity about sex, not fear of it. My notes say that I thought Norma a rather immature six-year-old, but I really know very little about how average middle-class six-year-old girls act with their mothers around. It was summer and many kids were away, and Mrs. Wilson said she usually does not spend that much time with Norma. Still, during all the time I was there, Norma was not out of her sight. It looks to me as if Mrs. Wilson was just beginning to let go of her. After all, this is Norma's second year in primary school and she will spend a lot of time there—not only because of the daily five-hour grind but also because she "is in everything at school," as her mother says, and she is among children a year older than she. Yet, though kids her age in the park were swinging free on the big swings, she held back. In such things she seems too scared. Shrinking away from the other kids in the sandbox might have been due to fear of being hit, but she didn't leave, and that took courage. Intellectually and emotionally, on the other hand, she seems much surer of herself. She has charm, and nobody is charming if he does not expect it to have an effect. Unafraid, she keeps up her onslaughts on her father. She accepted me after the first day and she has a close friend, Abby, and a sweetheart, Charlie. She is full of laughter and she's a barrel of giggles; though she can be nasty and cruel, she can also be gentle.

---

* The tendency for protectiveness to decrease without limit seems more characteristic of disorganized, lower-class families, and of disorganized families in general. In well-organized lower-class families, extreme forms of protectiveness may appear because of real dangers in the environment.

Power and Illusion

Mrs. Wilson got angry at Norma only once while I was there:

Mrs. Wilson wanted Norma to get two chairs so Norma and Abby could put their towels on the chairs while they were in the pool, but Norma said, "You're the one who said we should go swimming," and her mother said angrily, "Well, if you think that's the case, then you can put on your shoes and you can't go swimming." But things didn't go any further because Abby got the chairs.

Norma tried to turn the real situation inside out; she tried to make having fun in the pool look like something her mother made her do—as if she were doing her mother a favor by getting into the pool. It almost seemed an accusation: "You made me go swimming, so at least you ought to take the trouble to get the chairs. It isn't my *fault* that we are going swimming, so you should help out." Trying to make having fun in the pool look like a chore expresses Norma's attitude toward her mother and reveals one of Norma's stratagems. When Norma runs into a difficulty she tries to make it appear her mother's fault; and then, taking advantage of her mother's guilty vulnerability, she blasts her with accusation. Behind it is Norma's chronic discontent. But her mother really is to blame, because she is austere and because much of her heart is elsewhere. Norma has merely learned to take advantage of her mother's weakness, which is something every normal child learns to do. Isn't it perfectly obvious that every normal person in our culture should take advantage of other people's weaknesses? In the immediate instance, however, the accusation was so absurd that Mrs. Wilson felt she had the right to get angry—Norma could not browbeat her this time.

In the reign of Claudius, the two brothers Petra were executed because one of them had a dream that was interpreted as a wish for the emperor's death:

> . . . the ostensible charge . . . was a dream in which he [Petra] had seen Claudius wearing a wheaten wreath with inverted ears. This Petra had interpreted as portending a corn shortage. The wreath was otherwise described as whitening vine leaves, predicting the emperor's death in the autumn. In any case, it was certainly a dream which destroyed him and his brother.*

The story of the Petra brothers' death suggests that under proper cultural conditions one can be blamed—and executed—for anything at all, and that culture determines the nature of the blame and the selection of accuser, accused, sentence and executioner. It is clear, from the *Annals*, that accusation and execution were matters of relative power; nobody anywhere dares accuse if he knows he will be crushed, and I therefore conclude that Norma is in a strong power position relative to her mother. I conclude also that knowing whom to accuse of what is a necessary characteristic of normality in any culture. You would certainly be hurried off to a lunatic asylum nowadays if you accused people of having unkind dreams about you, and if you physically attacked a person because someone told you that per-

---

* In Tacitus, *Annals of Imperial Rome*, trans. by Michael Grant (Penguin Classics; Baltimore, Penguin, 1956), pp. 226–27.

son had had a foreboding dream about you. But being emperor in Rome entitled you to execute your subjects for their dreams.

I am not done with the matter of the wading pool yet, for I am confused to hear Norma and her mother call wading and splashing "swimming." Is it all right to do this? Is it of no significance? Or perhaps, does calling it "swimming" make Norma half believe she can swim?

Mrs. Wilson wants Norma to take swimming lessons because she thinks a child should know how to swim. So at lunch I said, "My daughter is a good swimmer; she can swim far," and Norma, who can't swim at all, said, "I can swim further." (I have no record of what her mother answered.)

Does Norma really think she can do things she cannot? Does she half believe she can (or is she "merely fibbing")?

At the hotel we saw a wonderful little donkey made out of plant fiber, and when Norma laid eyes on it she said, "Oh, anybody could do anything like that."

Is this the way six-year-olds think, or do parents somehow help them along? If chasing a pussy cat when it won't obey is training it; if dragging one's feet on the ground while sitting frightened in a swing is flying; if eating cookies is a kind of arithmetic, and a horse opera is *Robin Hood*— why isn't splashing = swimming? In other words, I would not dismiss what Norma says about this as mere childish fibbing. Until we know more about the daydreams of "normal" six-year-olds, and until we record more conversations between children and their parents who encourage them to believe that they know how to do something they don't, I will not quite know what to say about Norma's statement that she can do something I know she cannot.

Adults do not take a child's boasting seriously. I remember—or I seem to remember—that when I was about four or five years old, another little boy and I bragged to each other about the size of the cake of ice we could get (it was summer in New York). He made a tremendous boast—I no longer remember what it was—I challenged him to produce the ice, and when he went home and came out without it, I hit him. In those days I too must have half believed I could do what I could not, because I wanted so much to be able to. Evidence I have from nursery school observations and from my daughter's growing up shows that children in our culture often do not accept one another's boastful pretensions; yet Norma persists in hers. Her mother does not let her get away with all of them.

When I was playing ball with Norma, she said everything I did was wrong; and when I sang a little bit of "When You Wish Upon a Star," Norma said that was wrong too. But her mother said, "No, it isn't wrong; let's see if you can sing it." Norma didn't get it right, so her mother said, "Why did you say it was wrong?"

Such a challenge to Norma's illusions of superiority and excellence occurred only once while I was there; usually her mother fostered such illusions, like any good middle-class American parent.* Since it was obvious that I knew the song, Mrs. Wilson felt she had to intervene, but why did she demand that Norma sing it? Why did she insist on driving her into the

* It is my impression that this does not occur below the poverty line, except among the socially mobile.

ground, so to speak? She could merely have said, "No, it isn't wrong." The answer goes beyond my data, yet raises an important question that faces middle-class parents: What illusions to foster in children, and for how long?

What is the dialectic that governs the fostering and challenging of illusions? Do the weak foster illusions in the strong, or do the strong foster them in the weak? Do the weak cultivate it in themselves, while the strong have no need of it? Does one person foster illusions in another, or is it a conspiracy in which one induces the other to foster the illusions in him because he needs them, and the first perceives that the other needs the illusions and will, perhaps, reward him for fostering them? Does a parent foster illusions of excellence and superiority in his child because he fears he may lose the child's love if he is frank, or because the parent perceives, or thinks he perceives, some weakness in the child that will prevent him from facing the truth? One weakness the middle-class parent thinks he perceives is the child's inability to face his own immaturity and incompetence. But the real point is that the adult is embarrassed by the child's performance—let's say a drawing—because he is not able to see it simply as an expression of the child *at his age*—let's say two or three years. The problem of the squeamish, fraudulent, yet sensitive middle-class adult is that though he perceives that by adult standards the work is incompetent, he dare not communicate this to the child for fear of hurting him. Hence he covers up, becomes a sham, and in the very act of protecting the child, becomes his enemy. It is treachery in the nursery; a fantastic treason of love. Meanwhile the child is unaware of this, or he may sense the sham but not know why the adult is dishonest.

The middle-class parent becomes a sham, in this case, because he cannot understand the child's work—the child's reality—and because he suffers from his own feelings of weakness and incompetence. Thus the child's *un*reality is fostered because the parent has to turn away from his own reality: vulnerable parents foster illusions in vulnerable children, and the children are vulnerable because their parents cannot understand them, cannot understand the nature of their accomplishment.

Middle-class parents suffer so from their own feelings of inadequacy that when they see their child's work, often all they can think of is that they do not want to hurt the child as they have been hurt; and the child, insatiable for parental approval, may learn to accept the sham. Hence there is a conspiracy between parent and child, the terms of which are that the child will accept the sham if the parent will love him, and the parent will continue to foster the illusions if the child will love him. Yet the dialectic moves on, and a point is reached when the parent begins to perceive that illusions are not good for the child and that in order to protect him he must break them; he must become the child's enemy a second time. This is the point at which Mrs. Wilson steps in and confronts Norma with the fact that she does not know the song. We conclude that to the degree that he fosters illusion, a good middle-class parent first becomes his child's enemy while trying to be his friend, and then, later, in order to destroy the illusions, becomes the child's friend while appearing to be his enemy. It is not only the illusion of Santa Claus and the Blue Fairy that the six-year-old loses, or begins to lose, but the illusions he had from his parents about his own excellence. School helps in the destructive process, but it also fosters illusions where there is no clear "pass" or "fail," as in "art." A child may be awful in spelling and arithmetic, but he can still get a phony "That's fine, Timmy" from the teacher during "art." *

Identification

Pathways to identification, pathways to becoming *like* another, pathways to becoming *that* other, pathways to becoming *other than* one's self, pathways to becoming a mixture of self and other, pathways to becoming one's self; pathways to identity, to authenticity; then becoming one's self; giving up one's self; diffused identity, concentrated identity; losing one's self and finding one's self, choosing one's self and rejecting one's self. Introjection, imitation and rebellion also fit in here. As children seem less willing than ever before to copy their parents, money and brains are concentrated on the problems of "identification" and "identity"— while society more and more prevents the consolidation of "identity" because it wants youth to hold itself in readiness for the role of killer, which means no identity at all. Faceless, docile, brutal killer-sheep is the perfect nonidentity for mechanized armies of imperial guards.

Identification, resemblance, or whatever, occurs through the basic components of contemporary existence: love, death, aspiration, hope and illusion. It is useless to examine identification unless we know what the underlying values of culture and family are, whether parents and children love one another and the quality of that love, what the feeling is about death and what a person aspires and hopes for, for his self and his children. We must also know what the attitude toward children is—whether they are valued and whether it is expected of them to identify with—resemble— their parents. Consider the following:

As late as the seventeenth century, in *Le Caquet de l'accouchée,* we have a neighbour, standing at the bedside of a woman who has just given birth, the mother of five "little brats," and calming her fears with these words: "Before they are old enough to bother you, you will have lost half of them, or perhaps all of them." A strange consolation! *People could not allow themselves to become too attached* [my italics] to something that was regarded as a probable loss. This was the reason for certain remarks which shock our present-day sensibility, such as Montaigne's observation: "I have lost two or three children in their infancy, not without regrets, but without great sorrow," or Molière's comment on Louison in *Le Malade imaginaire:* "The girl doesn't count." Most people probably felt, like Montaigne, that children had "neither mental activities nor recognizable bodily shape." Mme. de Sévigné records without any sign of surprise a similar remark made by Mme. de Coetquen when the latter fainted on receiving the news of her little daughter's death: "She is greatly distressed and says she will never again have one so pretty."

Nobody thought, as we ordinarily think today, that every child already

* Based on many years of systematic direct observation of elementary school classrooms.

contained a man's personality. Too many of them died. "All mine die in infancy," wrote Montaigne.*

Since parents play a crucial role in the formation of a child's self and since what they do with him is so important in determining whether his character will resemble theirs, where children "don't count" and have "neither mental activities nor recognizable bodily shape" the role of the parents in the shaping of identification will be very different from what it is where children do count and where they do have recognizable mental activities and bodily shape. Furthermore, where, as in our middle class, all children are expected to survive, the emotional investment † of parents in their children is likely to be greater than in a society or in a social class where the survival rate is low; hence the entire problem of identification will be different. If one lives constantly in the shadow of death—as in a headhunting culture; or in one in which men restlessly seek glory through war; or where sorcery is a constant, brooding and imminent threat; or where the whim of absolute power, as in imperial Rome, can destroy a person and his whole family at a blow; or where plague strikes suddenly and often; or where one is always likely to be carried off by the lonesome ghost of a dead relative; or where one is drilled constantly in the idea that life on earth is merely preparation for an eternal afterlife—then identification with the living becomes possible only in relation to death, for in resembling them one has to mirror their conceptions of death. In such cultures it is not simply a matter of learning about death—something everybody has to learn—but the adoption of an attitude (often very gloomy, often terrified) toward one's own existence. It is not, as in the United States, that death is simply one possible event in life, but that death permeates thought constantly. Then the adults can recognize a child as a member of the same culture—even as being "my child" when it develops those very important attitudes toward death. Then death itself becomes an affirmation of life itself; it is through one's feelings about death that one asserts a claim on life; it is through one's feelings about death that one can assert a claim on *love* (only if a Dakota Indian or a Spartan boy demonstrated readiness to die had he a right to love.) ‡ In "sorcery cultures" § no child careless with "dirt" ** could be tolerated, much less loved. In cultures dominated by concern with death, death can so absorb conversation that people talk exclusively about who died, what killed him, why he died, what the latest divinations and omens of death are, and so on.

Obviously the opposite can be the case also: cultures where there seems no reason to fear death, where people take it as a matter of course and where the death rate is not high because life is relatively safe. I have never

* *Centuries of Childhood,* by Philippe Ariès, trans. from the French by Robert Baldick (Vintage Books; New York, Random House, 1965), pp. 38–39.

† Since in the deprived classes the death rate is several times higher than in the middle class, this may play an important role in restraining emotional commitment to children.

‡ In our culture a remote parallel would be the case of a young man, a friend of mine, rejected by his parents, for being a conscientious objector.

§ An offhand expression for cultures dominated by terror of black magic.

** A translation of a term, common in Melanesia, for anything that can be used to sorcerize an enemy because it has been in contact with his body: food, nail pairings, feces, a sleeping mat with his semen on it, etc.

heard of such a culture, but it may exist. The more usual case, it seems to me, is the one in which death is denied through emphasis on life, which usually turns out to mean emphasis on sensuous pleasure, for the fear of death is excluded most vigorously—canceled—by intense physical experience.* In such a culture a child identifies with his parents through perceiving their fear of death through their emphasis on pleasure, and senses their fear of death in the midst of their eating and drinking.

In the sections on "Love and Death" (page 326) and "Power and Illusion" (page 339), there is much that suggests Norma's identification with her mother; it shows that she is trying to be what her mother, aware or unaware, wants her to be. Neither she nor her mother embrace each other except at bedtime, and the morbid presence—or absence—of Donald seems to affect them both. Norma also reflects her mother's wish to have a different husband. I think that Norma also identifies with her mother's feelings about niceness and with her fear of physical injury.

Achievement, etc.

Being "right." Anybody who is going anywhere has to look right, act right, "relate to people," know how to get along and be bright, alert, sparkle. Here is Norma:

Norma is very bright, very pretty and very well put together. She is very outgoing and quite difficult to resist.

Norma sat down at the table opposite me. The idea is that in her usual place she can look at herself in the glass door of the china closet. Her parents say she likes to sit there so she can look at herself while she is eating.

. . .

The Wilsons were my guests for dinner tonight at the hotel. Dinner was set for six-thirty and they arrived exactly on time. Norma and her mother came in first. Norma looked lovely in a yellow little dress, with a flaring skirt, and she was carrying Lucy, her favorite doll. She came toward me and I walked rapidly toward her and stopped. I said, "You look very pretty tonight," and I said to her mother, "You look nice, too."

It is easy to see that Norma likes herself; and this her parents have done for her. Since her parents do not like themselves or each other, it is obvious that Norma does not "take after" either of them in this respect: she does not "identify with" her parents' self-hatred. Her parents'—mostly her mother's—great achievement has been to cancel themselves out in Norma in this respect, to destroy the possibility that she will hate herself. It was horror of what she had done to Donald that reversed Mrs. Wilson's behavior and made it possible for her to *withhold part of her self* from Norma—to renounce the possibility of seeing this part of her self in Norma while giving her self. Knowing what she had done, hating her self, but sound enough, controlled enough to be able to love, to be able to give to Norma,

* In "White People's Time—Colored People's Time" (*op. cit.*), I discussed this issue in bottom-of-the-barrel Negro ghetto life. See *Transaction* (March–April 1965), pp. 31–34.

she avoided infecting her child with her own feeling about her self. Because of Norma, and because I know what happened to Donald, I am impressed with the strength and intelligence of Mrs. Wilson. Norma's "being right" is here, in considerable part, an expression of her mother's being wrong and knowing it.

But Norma's "being right" is also an actualization of Mrs. Wilson's own unrealized possibilities, for though Mrs. Wilson never had the chance to become what Norma is, she is able to bring to actuality in her child what she never could be. Because she had some hope for her self at one time, and because that hope was never killed, it remained in memory. It is that hope, which remained a memory, that Mrs. Wilson was able to reconstruct, resurrect and realize in Norma.

Accumulation, getting ahead, etc. I have given the view that Mrs. Wilson expressed her love for Norma through driving, and pointed out that Norma was pretty insatiable—that she wanted to own the school, "Dr. Henry" and the whole world. Here is more of the same:

When Norma came down I reminded her that she had promised to show me her dolly with the high heels and earrings, so she went and got it. It was made up more or less like some sort of jazzed-up Hollywood character, with painted toenails, high heels, green-silvered dress and earrings. She put it in my hands in a completely offhand manner and asked me to guess its name. She said it began with L, and, of course, I guessed wrong. Then she said it began with L-u, and I guessed wrong again. Then she said it was L-u-c and when I said, "It's Lucy," she said that was right, and her mother expressed pleasure that Norma could spell it.

Mrs. Wilson said Norma wants to go to college. When she sees a waiter she says, "Look, he doesn't know anything, so he has to be a waiter." Once when a man came around to sharpen knives, Norma said, "Look, he hasn't been to college, so he has to sharpen knives." She says Norma is very sensitive to things like mink coats and has promised to buy her one. Mrs. Wilson told me about Norma's attempt to get her own money out of the bank. Norma cannot take it out until she's eighteen, so she hatched the idea of getting one of her older friends, who is eighteen, to take it out. Mrs. Wilson explained to Norma that the bank doesn't have her signature because when the money was deposited Norma could not write. Mrs. Wilson was delighted that Norma had gotten the idea of having a friend take the money out for her.

. . .

Mrs. Wilson asked Norma, "Who would you rather marry? Suppose you had a nice man without much money and a man who was not so nice but had a lot of money—who would you marry?" and Norma said she would marry the one with a whole lot of money. This embarrassed Mrs. Wilson, and she said to me, "That's not the way she answered once before; once before she said it would be nice if both men were nice."

The question and answer about the nice man and the poor one harmonize with mink coats and jazzed-up dollies. Mrs. Wilson would have preferred the evasive answer, even though it amounts to almost the same thing as the other, because it is nicer and she would prefer that Norma cover up. Ready to swell with pride at a nice (sham) answer, Mrs. Wilson was put out by candor—it is all so *healthy!* Since Norma is only six, her mother is merely indulgently embarrassed, but if the child talks like that at ten, she will be reprimanded, as in any healthy middle-class household! Mrs. Wilson is contradictory: on the one hand, right in front of Norma, Mrs. Wilson, like any middle-class mother, is proud and happy that her daughter should love her enough to want to buy her an expensive gift, and pleased that Norma could figure out such a smart little trick for getting her money. On the other hand, she doesn't like it when Norma is open about the kind of (money)-man she wants to marry. Why the difference? Mrs. Wilson is frank about mink coats because mink expresses the moral imperative of the high-rising living standard and conspicuous consumption, and she is delighted with Norma's scheme to get money out of the bank because it reflects the key beat-the-game value, without which our culture could not survive. But she feels it is wrong to admit openly that you want a rich husband because that contradicts the people-should-be-loved-for-themselves value.

Through adopting her mother's values, Norma loves her mother back and identifies with her. Norma shows the result of good upbringing, for Mrs. Wilson, in teaching her daughter to think this way, is being a very good American mother. No—let's say, rather, a very good *civilized* mother.

How can a child of our culture know when to be frank about his parents' values and when to cover up? I think he can learn only step by step, through experience with each value, because nearly every value has a yes, a no and a cover-up. It is right to love things connected with money, but we must not be obvious about connecting love of people with money. To steal outright is bad, but to cheat on taxes, to steal in any other legitimate way, like misrepresenting merchandise, is not bad. We should be honest, but not if we might lose money. Killing is wrong, but not killing anybody defined by Big Brother as "enemy." All men are equal, but not Negroes, and in the North one does not admit it. And so on.

With each yes, with each no and with each cover-up we must also acquire the appropriate psychosomatic reaction. We must learn to "feel good" when we have been conventionally honest, to "feel like a fool" if we do not steal when it is legitimate, and to "feel embarrassed" if we spill the beans about our true feelings about honesty and dishonesty. We must learn to *feel* miserable if our sweetheart is poor, to affirm that "money makes no difference," and to feel ashamed if our true opinion becomes known; in the North we must be taught to affirm the equality of the black man while not inviting him to our house, and to feel like a fool if we allow our real attitude to be seen. Unless we acquire the corresponding psychosomatic state along with the value—its affirmation, its denial and its sham—our value system is unstable. Since, in children, the somatic reaction proper to each value has not yet become inevitable, their values can be more readily altered than those of adults. I surmise that the reaction becomes stabilized at different ages, depending on the value, so that at different ages one value can be changed but not another. I also surmise that it is easier to change the objects to which the values are attached than the values: a person might start out oriented toward money as an object, but shift the achievement drive to academic kudos.

I must have been moved when Norma handed me her dolly in that "offhand" way, though I did not put it in my notes. It is so easy for her to get along with adults! Then she involved me further by having me guess the doll's name while she spelled it. And her mother was delighted to see her turn the encounter into an exercise in achievement, in which Norma could show off. But her mother doesn't approve of everything Norma does in order to come out on top. Here is something she definitely disapproved of:

> (Norma and Abby were in the park with Mrs. Wilson.) At first Norma hogged the only swing there was and Abby was looking very unhappy, but Mrs. Wilson obliged Norma to give up the swing to Abby. In the park Norma and Abby stuck close together.

Here is more of the same, *not* disapproved:

> On the way to the park Mrs. Wilson stopped and bought a bottle of orange pop for Norma and Abby, and they both drank out of it at the same time with straws. I had the impression they were sucking violently so neither would get more than the other.

The realm of play. I have discussed insatiability earlier (see pages 319–321). Insatiability is a phase of the achievement drive: you can't expect children to want to get ahead without expecting them to want to get ahead of everybody; you can't expect them to want to accumulate without their wanting to accumulate everything; you can't expect them to be competitive without expecting them to want to win in everything. Very well—but everything in its place and in a nice way. No hogging of swings, especially from friends; you shouldn't let your achievement drive get in the way of love and friendship. And that is the issue: the achievement drive should be contained by friendship but let go without restraint among non-friends. The dialectic of achievement requires a *realm of play*, as the opposite of the area of self-restraint. Loot, burn and rape among the enemy, but not among friends. Jezebel plundered a neighbor's vineyard (unnatural behavior); the tragedy of the Balkans was that they were a realm of play for powerful, alternately plundering, unfriendly neighbors (naturally!). The tragedy of imperial Rome was that in the imperial city and within the imperial families the boundary between friend and enemy, between the realm of play (for the achievement drive) and the area of self-restraint, was lost: Nero had his brother Britannicus poisoned and continued his dinner while Britannicus was in his death agony. Later he arranged the assassination of his mother. Napalm for the enemies of achievement (naturally!), but the welfare state at home (naturally!): the realm of play versus the area of restraint. Two little girls sucking hard on the ends of straws in a bottle of soda pop, each trying to make sure the other doesn't get too much of it—this is the destiny of our culture. When these children are older, however, they will have learned to renounce the soda pop in each other's interest, *to defend themselves against the wish—against the repressed wish to go over the boundary.*

Which brings us back to the teachings of Freud, which I dare paraphrase and gloss as follows: the culture of the in-group is the repressed and sublimated expression of the desire to transgress. Is it nothing more? Is there nothing in life in an achieving culture but constant war—war against the outside as the fullest expression of the drive, and war on the inside to contain and transform it? The grisly history of achieving cultures does not permit anything but the affirmation: No, there is nothing more. Though the inner and the outer war continue, the outer has so far been most successful, and the history of the achievement drive shows that *Homo sapiens* has been dying of success and will probably fail as a species because of it.

Is it *nothing* more? Well, who would say that life under any obsession is nothing more than expressing it and repressing it? After all, you say, look at the tranquil gardens in the suburbs, the innocent babies toddling on the lawns and along the quiet sidewalks, followed by loving mothers and watched by solicitous neighbors. Look at the happy families pitching tents in Yellowstone and in the Grand Tetons! Observe the Sunday barbecue, the church picnic, the whatever! Remember Phidias, Bach, Michelangelo and Dylan Thomas! Very well, life does extort some possibility from the achievement drive, and I love and appreciate what is extorted. But I know those babies already are little achievers, driven on, now gently, now harshly, by achieving parents; that those suburbs are ugly because of achieving realtors; that Yellowstone, the Grand Canyon and the Grand Tetons are pathetic salvage from the concessionaires and from the lumber and cattle men; that the church, where Christianity is lost, is an achieving church, complete with TV and support of war; that Phidias' sculpture is the expression of imperial Athens, that Michelangelo was the property of a warring pope and that Dylan Thomas was a lost soul in a driven culture.

The hogging of the swing and the sucking on the straws are the immature expressions of identification with parents. Why, then, are parents horrified by it? Isn't hogging a natural expression of the achievement drive, of wholesome competitiveness? Where, after all, is the line between wanting "the world," or even a mink coat, and wanting a swing all to one's self? In our culture the problem of parents' objecting to hogging is not that they have "conflicting values," but that in the immaturities of their children they confront the naked, horrifying reality of the achievement drive in themselves. *Unless people are horrified* the "conflict" does not appear. Where is Christianity in the presence of napalm? Barely visible, because man in America is not horrified. Hence the crime of Redwood City.* The logic is simple: no horror, no conflict.† But there is no horror until the drive turns against us. If Mrs. Wilson had let Norma hog the swing and do similar things, Norma would have lost her friends—and Mrs. Wilson herself would have had to bear Norma's appetite.

Being feminine. Norma's identification with her mother is implied by restraint in affection, by expressing it through achieving, imagining and talking about achievement and by transforming encounters into occasions for expressing the achievement drive, by thinking about having a different daddy as her mother desires a different husband, by being concerned and sad about Donald, and by "being right" and nice. But the most significant identification of all is in being feminine: Norma doesn't fall in with Peggy's tomboyishness; she is neat, clean and well dressed; she keeps Lucy and a crowd of other dressed-up lady dollies neatly arranged in her room.

Norma has a whole lot of toys, and although her room is not chaotic, it is not as neat as I would have expected, considering her mother's compulsive character.

---

* See *Ramparts* (August 1966) for an article on the failure of the protest against the manufacture of napalm in Redwood City, California.
† It may be construed as the most general law of an existential dialectic that the thesis moves into antithesis only when real people, with power to act, become dismayed, horrified or enraged by present circumstances.

Norma had all her dolls lined up. There was a very large doll, all dressed up as a bride, flanked by smaller dolls. I didn't see any stuffed animals.

And Norma even prepared a meal for us:

When Mr. and Mrs. Wilson and I were sitting in the living room, Mrs. Wilson left suddenly because there was a noise of dishes rattling in the kitchen. She returned shortly, saying Norma was preparing lunch for all of us.

I went into the kitchen, and sure enough, that is what was happening. Norma had found some hard-boiled eggs, had peeled and cut them and put them on plates and was now setting the table. She wanted us to eat there, but her mother said no. Norma dumped the shells very carefully into the garbage can, and her mother was delighted that Norma had been able to do this without getting herself dirty. She made a couple of passes over Norma's chest to get a few crumbs off Norma's shirt.

Norma's best friend is a girl but she keeps a swain around, and when she was in the park little boys pushed her on the swing. Norma's play with Abby (see also page 324) is feminine, and so is the way she treats Charlie. Here is some more material on being feminine:

[At my hotel for dinner] Norma headed toward an enormous enclosure, a combination store and showcase. They sell fancy souvenirs and jewelry there, and Norma wanted to know at once whether the things were for sale to children. She pointed to a doll she would like to have.

. . .

I gave Norma a gift—the tiny bearded cowboy she had admired the other night in the store in the hotel lobby. She immediately wanted to take off the hat, but her mother and I said this was not the kind of doll you can take the clothes off.

Examining the doll, Norma soon discovered what she called a cut on the doll's forehead, but her mother said, "Those must be the wrinkles to match the nose." The cowboy had a red tomato-of-a-nose. It stood about four inches high. Presently Norma discarded it to play with a cat, but not for long. She came back to the doll and wanted to take off the coat. She was very, very happy about the cowboy—she's a good child to give a present to. She appreciated it a great deal; she kept kissing it and hugging it all evening. At dinner she said, "Do you know what its name is? It's Jack Wilson—that's my daddy's grandfather's name." Her father showed no sign of emotion whatsoever.

(This is the doll Norma said was going to heaven.)

Norma went next door to show Charlie her doll and brought Charlie back with her. He sat very close to her when Norma was sitting on the reclining chair with her mother. When Norma kissed the doll, Charlie tried to kiss it too and then tried to kiss Norma, but she pushed him away.

Soon Abby came over and the two girls, as usual, teamed up against Charlie and went into the house. There was quite a struggle, physical as well as verbal, between Norma and Charlie because Norma wanted to shut him out. At last, with the help of Mrs. Wilson, Charlie got into the house but was soon ejected. He showed Mrs. Wilson where Norma had scratched his arm. Mrs. Wilson kept hovering around, telling Norma to be nice to Charlie, but when he was finally expelled, she said, "Well, that's the way it is."

There is no doubt that this feminine little girl can be quite savage. Her mother told me of another occasion when Norma had beat up Charlie, but Charlie had been aggressive. Mrs. Wilson told this story with considerable satisfaction.

After Charlie had been sent home, Norma and Abby decided they would like to go into the little wading pool in the backyard. Norma asked Abby which suit she would like, the one with the pictures or the blue one, and Abby said the one with the designs, so Norma let her have it. The two of them went indoors and soon came out in suits, Norma looking very charming.

Wouldn't it have been bizarre if Norma and Charlie had embraced and kissed each other or had gone off behind the house with the doll to play "husband-wife-and-child" like some other little savages? But being cruel to Charlie (making him sad!), keeping him around when convenient and discharging him forcibly when he is inconvenient, is not bizarre. This is "natural" little-girl-and-boyhood in our culture, we say. And this is femininity too. But this is only one side. There is also another; on the other side, children from the age of three or even sooner, perhaps, become sweethearts. Perhaps such love affairs tend to vanish at six . . . who knows? At any rate, this dimension of child life is not present here.

Little girls are Norma's in-group and little boys her out-group, and what hostility is pent up in her—from the achievement drive and from all the other sources I have spoken of—gets directed against little boys when they are vulnerable. So being cruel to little boys is a direct expression of being *female*, but is not necessarily an expression of identification with *mother*, though mother probably had a hand in it somewhere along the line, as her pride in Norma's having beaten up Charlie suggests. Being feminine includes being cruel to other little girls too,* just as little boys are cruel to one another. In childhood, in our culture and in many others,† the consequence of childhood vulnerability is torment at the hands of other children; in our culture, girls cut each other down and boys beat up one another, particularly in big cities.

Perhaps we ought to say that Norma is capricious and callous rather than cruel. She goes and gets Charlie and casts him off when it suits her. Depending on her needs at the moment—the need to tease someone, the need to have someone to show her doll to—she uses Charlie. He is like an employee, like a domestic, like nonunionized help! Poor Charlie—and it is all his fault, really, for being so vulnerable!

In connection with the relationship between Norma and Charlie, I said he loves her, and Mrs. Wilson said yes. I talked about the deep feelings of which children of that age are capable, stressing the relationship between little girls and boys. Mrs. Wilson, however, said she could not remember having a single boy friend when she was a child. Then she switched to talking about Norma's drive to independence. . . .

I stressed the deep involvements of little boys and girls in one another, but this invoked nothing in Mrs. Wilson. She began to talk about Norma's suspicions about the relationship between the married man and neighborhood girl.

Since what I said about love affairs between little boys and girls is countered by stress on independence, by a story of illicit sex and by denial of any childhood love affair of her own, I infer that children's love affairs, independence and illicitness are somehow related in Mrs. Wilson's mind.

---

* See my *Culture Against Man* (*op cit.*), although there I deal with children no younger than twelve years of age.

† John Whiting's *Becoming a Kwoma: Teaching and Learning in a New Guinea Tribe* illustrates this well (New Haven, Yale U. Press, 1941).

From this I derive the conclusion that Mrs. Wilson's attitudes encourage lack of involvement with little boys—and that Norma's stand-offishness is another aspect of identification with her mother's restraint. What is so interesting is that although she was proud that Norma had beat up Charlie, she had nothing positive to say about his feeling *for* Norma. She might have said, "Yes, poor kid, he is in love with her, and she treats him worse than a rag doll." But you cannot talk like that if you have missed out on love yourself. Mrs. Wilson's accounts of her relationship with her husband, of being a kind of Cinderella to an insensitive mother, of never having had a little boy friend, suggest that she has lived in the ashes of life. It is a victory for her that she has been able to respond warmly to Norma.

It is all Charlie's fault for being so vulnerable! If he did not need Norma she could not treat him as she does. In this encounter of children we see, crudely expressed, a fundamental pattern of relationships between men and women in our culture; only in their case, folklore has it, the pattern is reversed, and the callous man exploits the vulnerable woman. At any rate, there it is: wanting love, in our culture, makes one vulnerable, and callousness can exploit it. This has been Mrs. Wilson's lot: to need love and to let herself be exploited for it. Hence, when I speak of love, Mrs. Wilson talks of independence.

Norma was crazy about the cowboy doll: she hugged it, kissed it, named it after her great-grandfather. What a pleasure it is to give something to a person who really *can* show she appreciates it. What a little girl! No ifs, no maybes—she *can* adore something and she *can* let it be seen. No concealment, no second thoughts! So one feels the full impact of Norma's capacity to appreciate some things immediately "from the heart." Isn't this an asset —in our culture? Isn't this something this mother has done for this child? And isn't this something that will make Norma liked, especially by adults? No calculation: just primordial responsiveness. She overflows, has to give the doll a name right away, has to take it next door to show somebody—to show Charlie. Her pleasure propels her right into other people—she can't keep it inside herself: *her pleasure immediately becomes social.* So Norma has a great capacity for pleasure and for socializing it too. She had a great time playing with Abby, and she was nice about letting Abby have her choice of bathing suits: she was a proper little hostess.

Norma and Abby played happily in the pool for quite some time and at last decided to get out and get dressed. They went into the house, and when they came out Norma had on an entirely new costume, which included a pretty skirt and a fetching blouse with beading sewn on. Naturally, I admired it. Norma stroked Abby's hair, saying it was nice and curly.

Imagine flattering a friend's hair, admiring her hair, at six! Have they or haven't they absorbed the culture, these pretty, showcase hostesses? And the beaded blouse!—won't Abby ask her mother for one if she doesn't already have one? How these babies provoke each other to the values of their class, socializing each other like mad! Shades of *Dick and Jane:* a complete new picture wardrobe with each episode.* Could Norma possibly want a

---

* The *Dick and Jane* reader series for the lower primary school grades has the Dick and Jane family appear in entirely new outfits in each story. They are so tasteful, by middle-class suburban American standards, that, looking at them, one is convinced that a stylist must have been hired to make the illustrations.

friend who didn't appreciate her clothes, for whom she couldn't dress up for *real*?

I would not say that Norma figures out on whom she can best exercise her propensities for achievement-in-friendship; but rather that her feelings make it impossible for her to be comfortable with any little girl—perhaps with anyone—in whose presence she cannot express those propensities. She wouldn't feel right with girls who didn't like proper clothes and who didn't care about how she felt about their hair. Does this mean that Norma doesn't like people "for themselves"? No—we always like people for themselves, which must always include their class-determined characteristics. After all, what is a self? I mean, what is the self, when you get away from Kierkegaard, Heidegger, Sartre, et al.? Why, it is mostly the bundle of class-determined characteristics. If it weren't, how could you ever have a *society*, or even a social class? How could you ever *have* a society, with a mob of unique selves floating around like so much jetsam, with no common class ballast to make them stay upright and steer right? Who are our friends? They are people with the same class-determined characteristics, from their clothes to their inner conflicts, their hopes, their memories of hopes, their values and their shams.

Leadership. Notice that suggestions for play come from Norma. Is it that Norma has "leadership qualities," that Abby is tactful enough to let ideas come from Norma, or that Norma picks friends who will let *her* do the suggesting? I have evidence that implies the latter. First let me remind the reader of the expressions of Norma's drive to be on top that have already been discussed: monopolization of the swing; saying I was singing the song wrong, when I was right; saying that she can swim farther than my daughter, when she cannot swim at all; having her mother, father and me guess the objects she associated with numbers; control of games; having us tell her how many cookies we had; wanting to own the world; shrinking from the superiority of Peggy. Now consider the following in addition:

Mrs. Wilson and Norma were out on the front lawn throwing a ball back and forth. I asked whether I could play and got into the game, but was expelled in about five or ten minutes by Norma for infraction of rules she had set up. Mrs. Wilson says she always makes up rules to suit herself. So I just sat and watched mother and daughter have a good time.

Later, in the park, Mrs. Wilson found a ball-point pen she could not bear to discard, so she gave it to me, but I gave it back to her. She gave it to Norma and Norma dropped it and her mother frowned. Norma picked it up and gave it to me. She wanted to know whether I had a ball-point pen of my own, and when I showed mine to her she thought it so beautiful that she wanted to exchange it for the one she had given me, but when I refused she said hers was more beautiful than mine.

When we got home from the park Mrs. Wilson ordered us to relax. Norma wanted me to go into her room and play with her, so I did. First she had the idea that we should play "Look and See," and she got a kaleidoscope and had me guess what color she saw. I was right two times out of three, so Norma said, "Well, let's stop now." I think I was guessing the colors too accurately for her, which really wasn't very hard, because I think all there were, were red, yellow and green.

Next she got out a cardboard on which had been pasted paper pictures of "medals" for going to bed early, one for achievement, one for eating, and so on, and each medal had a little printed ribbon to go with it. Norma's idea was that we were to cut out the medals, punch holes in them and hang them on her pegboard. I was to close my eyes, she was to remove some of the medals, and I was to guess which ones. Even though she might have learned the *idea* in school, the transfer of the concept to the medals seemed to me an ingenious idea and well organized. . . .

Norma cut through the cardboard very fast, and though she mangled the medals somewhat, she did a very good job. I took longer and was much more careful than necessary. At last all the medals were cut out and Norma tried to hang them on hooks on the pegboard, but of course she couldn't do it because the medals had no holes and she couldn't puncture the medals with the pegs because they were too dull. So she said, "Mommy has a hole-punching machine," and she went and got it and punched holes in the medals. A number of times the holes were punched so near the edge of the medals that they were not holes but scallops. I showed Norma that she had to push the medals farther into the machine, and then she did it well.

The whole thing was very well co-ordinated—the work of an intelligent and active child.

We got all the holes punched but couldn't do any more before lunch. Just when lunch was announced Norma discovered she had only nine medals instead of ten, and she got rather anxious about finding the tenth one, so she told me to go and wash my hands first. By the time I was ready, she had found the missing medal.

And immediately after Abby left, the day they were playing in the pool,

Norma asked me to play ball with her. She made up the rules, never giving me a chance to do anything she didn't dictate, and saying everything I did was wrong.

Norma has to be on top all the time and when her position is threatened she feels anxious and resentful. Abby seems a little girl who is not a threat to her. Norma is so intelligent and well co-ordinated that she will be able to go far and perhaps achieve much, if she doesn't lose friends—and lovers— because she is so determined to be on top. Perhaps we can say that while Mr. and Mrs. Wilson made Donald into nothing, Norma is becoming too much. It seems to me that there should be some give, some point where Norma does not compete, feel deposed, thrown down if the other person is good or has something good she doesn't have. But how can there be? For Norma has an obsession where there should be love, or love and the obsession are so amalgamated that they are practically one. We could not say, *simply,* that in her achievement drive, Norma "identifies" with her parents —particularly with her mother. The achievement drive in Norma is so intense because she does not really *have* her parents. The fact that she begrudges superiority to another person in anything reflects a dissatisfaction, a gnawing sense of not having what she really wants. And because she does not have it she will never get it.

I have spoken of Norma's illusion of superiority, but I wonder now whether this is really the way to put it. Perhaps it would be better to say, an illusion that if she is not superior—to everything—she will be lost. Her mother wants her to be superior, flawless, even if Norma drops a pen her mother frowns. But *is* it illusion? Wouldn't she lose her mother if she were not superior? What is the point at which the *obsession with* superiority becomes *conviction of* superiority? What is the point at which the obsessive *need* to be on top becomes the belief that one *is* on top? What is the point at

which dissatisfaction, combined with goading to be on top, is transformed
into the illusion that one is *there*? It is transformed because a constant fear
of inadequacy or failure, in somebody else's eyes, creates the illusion of
superiority, as a defense. But the illusion of superiority is the illusion of
being the *best*. And since illusion is a paper house, whoever lives in it feels
anyone's excellence as a threat.

Albert Camus has given us a play entitled *Caligula*, in which the mad
emperor really believes himself divine; yet though divine, he is unable to
accomplish supernatural things. And here is little Norma, with her illusion
of being the best, unable to swim and even unable to sing a little Walt
Disney song. How can she bear it?

Calculating the odds. Norma used the paper achievement medals to set
up a game in which her drive to be on top was exquisitely realized in control over me and over my chances of winning. One aspect of success is
control, isn't it? And the way to success is often through control. Thus the
idea of success, the implied message of the cardboard panel, achieved logical expression in the game Norma proposed. Against the backdrop (the
panel) of achievement, the ideal itself was given expression in the guessing
game: a child's sound intuition put together success, control and guessing.
Norma is training herself in "figuring the odds." She wants me to guess
what medals have been removed from the pegboard, what color she is looking at in the kaleidoscope and what her doll's name is, according to probabilities assessed by her, and if I win easily she quits.

Life in our culture is figuring the odds; all the way from passing a car on
the road, to taking a job, to courting, it is trying to arrange and select situations so that you cannot lose. The mathematical theory of probability brings
together self-interest, mathematics and the achievement motive. While "the
concept of probability . . . [is] one of the fundamental notions of modern science and philosophy of nature," its origins are in commercial insurance, legal procedures and games of chance.* But that phenomena are
merely probable—that an event depends on certain contingencies—is a
fundamental human experience, which, however, mankind has always
tried to control, often by magic. Magic is the primordial attempt to deny
probability. An aspect of this is to try to put the control of probability in
your own hands—as in Norma's games, for example. In these childish
games, therefore, I see not only an expression of the wish to deny probability but also the essence of our culture, for war, the total expression of the
achievement motive, is a game in which one side tries to control all contingencies in order to destroy the other's possibilities of success. In gambling
casinos "the house" sets the conditions so that the players will lose, on the
average. The difference between friendly games and others is that in the latter one side determines, or tries to determine the odds, and only the winner
gets a reward.

One source of Norma's game is her mother's making her count and spell.
Accusation is also a game, but while in counting and spelling Mrs. Wilson
determines the conditions of play and the reward, in accusation Norma has
control and always wins unless she slips by making the wrong kind of accusation. In spelling and counting Norma is rewarded by praise, and her
mother is rewarded by Norma's performance, but only Norma gets any-

* *Encyclopaedia Britannica*, 1965 edition, article on "Probability."

thing out of accusation.* Accusation is not a friendly game, and from this I conclude that Norma feels that she and her mother are in some way arrayed against each other. This feeling of being arrayed, of being drawn up for combat, is a component in all Norma's relations, and accounts in part for her tendency to convert encounters into games in which she controls the chances. Perhaps, in this, we are all very much alike.

Summary of the Wilson Case

I have written many pages about the Wilson family but have not reached the end, and now, in order to move forward it is necessary to look back at what I have said.

I now turn again to the study of Mr. Wilson's character, to his relationship to his wife and to the relationship of both of them to the children. It may seem to the reader that what I say now belongs at the beginning of the study of the Wilson family; yet there is an advantage in separating the analysis of the adults in this way, for by the time he has read my lengthy discussion of the relationship between mother and daughter, the reader might well have become vague about the role of the father. Discussing him again here puts him more clearly in the picture.

In his remoteness, in his tendency to drift away, in his lack of interest in what is going on in the family, in his general unavailability, Mr. Wilson is reminiscent of an autistic person, but merely reminiscent—he suggests the idea of autism, though he is far from mad. He is a metaphor of autism, whose reality is Donald. This metaphor became actual and real in the autistic child through the unavailability of both parents to the baby, and the baby at last became unavailable to the parents: the dialectic outcome of the father's tendency to drift away is the son who did. And this occurred partly because the emotional resources expended on keeping the father present were withdrawn from the child. Mrs. Wilson's problem was different, for she had to prevent others from drifting away from her: running around to do chores for her mother's family and her husband's, doing her husband's work at home, she tried so hard to make herself present to those others that she became absent to her son. Husband and wife had the same problem ("They don't care about me"), but it was expressed in opposite ways and through different disposition and actualization of resources: Mr. Wilson, fearing exhaustion, expended his resources drop by drop where he thought there would be a pecuniary payoff. His wife dissipated hers where she felt insecure, and she felt insecure everywhere—everywhere when there was

* I do not deny the existence of minor phases of the achievement drive in which the control of probability plays little or no part. To play an instrument well or to paint well seem to belong here. When, however, an artist is "playing (professionally) for keeps," he calculates the odds. If he is a musician he puts himself under a "famous name," and when preparing to play in public, he chooses a program that "will go over." If he is a painter he studies *Art News* and "cases" the galleries to see what is selling. Achievement "in the world" is impossible without some control of probability. Only the great, only the original artist can flout its laws. The same considerations apply to the sciences—especially to the social sciences.

power to threaten her. In talking to me, she covered up her relationship with her husband during the first years of marriage almost completely, but she did imply that in order to hold him, she gave herself to his work. While this helped them achieve success, she left her baby alone—he could not hold her, for he lacked the power to threaten her.

Though not clinically mad by any means, Mr. Wilson is *maddening*—his daughter alternately woos him and calls him names, his wife upbraids him; even in the middle of a discussion of Donald he turns on the TV. He is at the periphery of the family's existence—he is in its social space but not where it lives. Norma seems to understand her father well and she does not make emotional demands he cannot meet; she touches him briefly before going to bed, and that is all; all he can tolerate. Yet, in her name-calling, playful approaches and attacks, we see that she still hopes to get more out of him. Her father is there, but largely as a negation of himself which enables and compels her mother to be paramount in her life. This negative, which once forced Mrs. Wilson to turn away from her other child, now has the opposite effect, because of the *horror* at what she did before. Now she turns away from her husband and toward her child.

Because of Donald, Mrs. Wilson has experienced despair in the true existential sense of a regenerative power. Having come into her self, she has found her self in Norma. Of course, this self is the middle-class, achieving self, but it has the essential meaning of vindication, lustration and rebirth. Since Norma is expiation for Donald, however, she is partially deprived of love even while seeming to get it wholly. She has love, but mixed with serious family problems. Furthermore, Mrs. Wilson is an austere person who never caresses Norma except at bedtime. Her unspoken motto seems to be, "Norma—my love—my work; Norma—work—and be loved." Since she cannot stop proving her *self*, she imposes this on her child, and almost everything Norma attempts becomes an effort at self-proof.

Norma identifies in most ways with her mother, but since her mother has protected her from self-hatred, Norma likes her self and is able to like others, though she can be cruel too. She has a self-confident way of going about tasks, but she begrudges the success of others, has to be on top and even seems to have delusions of being on top. A chronically accusatory attitude is Norma's repayment for the love which is offered but is partly withheld, and accusation is the complement of her mother's guilt. Yet, on the other hand, accusation is also a reaction against the implication, in her mother's drivenness, that "you'd *better* be smart; you'd *better* go to college!" Though Mrs. Wilson may have her daughter's good at heart, her compulsive focus on achievement rides Norma. While driving Norma toward achievement, Mrs. Wilson is afraid to let her go. Hence the "don't go near the water" syndrome, in which she urges Norma to action while at the same time restraining her. She wants her to think—to be smart—yet is constantly projecting her mind into Norma's: interrupting her thinking, she tries to bind her mind. In physical things also Mrs. Wilson seems to say, "Go ahead but stop."

Compulsive restraints on independence make a contribution to Norma's accusatory attitude also, for whoever intervenes in everything will be blamed for frustration. Since her mother is in everything, anything that goes wrong must logically be her mother's fault. Since her father is in nothing, he is blamed for nothing, but by the same token, gets credit for nothing. When he does intervene *spontaneously* in her activity, it is not lovingly. The best example is his "joke" about spanking Norma because she lost her sweater.

Norma's metaphysic must be something like this: behind everything lies an omniscient and omnipotent being—mother. In this competitive and achieving universe, people are pitted against one another, and one who is on top might lose out at any moment. The underpinning of the universe is not stable, for the omniscient and omnipotent being is not fully present at all times, but has to be actualized, sometimes forcibly, by accusation. One may think one's self capable of an act, but at any moment may discover one's self to be incapable. Life itself is not certain either, for if Donald disappeared—died—so might Norma. Meanwhile the being makes confusing interpretations of reality and may transform it into irreality.

Out of all this comes Norma the gambler, Norma the miniature tyrant—the woman-who-would-be-emperor—who tries to control everything, who tries to prevent the world from slipping away, who so needs to control the world that she must control her friends. But she is gay, and she laughs a lot and is able to have a very good time, if she can be in control. Her father's toleration and her mother's love, mixed up though it is with her mother's own problems, have made it possible for Norma to have fun, to go readily toward adult strangers, to thoroughly enjoy presents and to give pleasure to others when she is pleased. She can socialize her good feelings, an important ingredient of good relations in our culture.

Husband and Wife

STATUS HUNGER

Mr. Wilson's status sensitivity was acute and though his own house was modest, the urban landscape with its sometimes luxurious apartments provoked him to envious sarcasm. A Chrysler Imperial encountered at the door of the hotel as we emerged from dinner led him to ask, "Is that the kind of car you have?" And when I said I had a Chevy he said he was going to trade in his four-year-old car for an Olds. There is no doubt that he suffered from "acute status deprivation," and that status deprivation, being somebody's lackey, was a nightmare.

Status deprivation is like food deprivation: a man's soul becomes wasted and meager and he thinks in a meager and wasted way; for a man thinks with his status; and it is with status that he sees and hears. Deprive a man of status, and he is as if mentally retarded. Who talks the most and most confidently—even if absurdly? People with status! Who are spiritually fattest and sleekest? Who gleam with spiritual opulence, talk with words most ringing? Perceive with insight? Carry most authority—even for nonsense? Those of highest status! So a man will wear himself out, drain himself and his family to get it. Status is palpable: perceive how Those-of-High-Status wrap themselves in status, like Caesar, in a mantle of imperial purple! It has a soft and silky touch—like mink, like the Golden Fleece. But in our culture each man sails *alone* to Colchis—without fifty heroes to back him.

Sometimes at meals, often when alone with me, Mr. Wilson spoke enthusiastically and intelligently about his practice, discussing his successes, never mentioning failures, pointing out how those who rely on him succeed —whereas those who do not, fail. He told me stories of outwitting people and gave me free-wheeling advice on how to handle my expense account— advice, incidentally, in which his wife joined. Sometimes Norma was present while he was discussing his exploits, and once, during a long story, she kept saying, "I talk too much."

Fighting in his competitive world was a pleasure, a necessity, an obsession and a release for Mr. Wilson: when he came home, he slept—or as good as slept, dreaming off with newspaper and TV.

This evening I was just outside the kitchen door talking to Mrs. Wilson when her husband came home. She was preparing steaks, and he said—as a matter of fact, it was the first thing he said—"You see what a short-order cook my wife is?" Then, after talking briefly to her, he went into the living room and slumped into his usual position on the sofa.

(He was quite disturbed about all the unpleasant things he was having to do to people in connection with his practice.)

. . .

Before I sat down to dinner I asked Mrs. Wilson for a glass of water; it seems they don't drink water at meals—she never puts it on the table. She said, "Oh yes, I remember, you're a water drinker." Her husband said she's a poor waitress, because a good one would have had the water on the table. She didn't like this, but did not show it much.

This led her husband to say he doesn't like to travel because then he gets waited on, and he can't stand it. He can't stand to be brushed off at the barber's either. He mentioned that he remembers that in *The Brothers Karamazov* somebody blackened somebody else's boots. I was struck by the fact that of all the things to remember about the book, he selected this. Obviously his fear of being a lackey is strong.

Mr. Wilson does no chores at all in the home. When he comes home from work, he dreams off with TV and newspaper. His wife says, jokingly, that he's an authority on TV.

Perhaps in many troubled families husband and wife first ridicule and then hate each other for the very reasons they marry each other. A woman marries a man because he is a hard worker, then ridicules him because he cannot think of anything but his work, then hates him because he neglects her and the children. A man perhaps marries a woman because she will "take care of" him, and then ridicules her for being a "waitress" or a "short-order cook," or "just a servant." The reason this occurs is that marrying a person because he *was* this or could *do* that covers up an unmet wish for a spouse who could really love, and since marriage soon reveals the mistake, the original attribute becomes hateful. None of this, however, enters consciousness. The irony in what Mr. Wilson says to his wife here is that he belittles her for the very reason she was most useful to him. Of her work for him he said merely that she is a "perfectionist," and that she had been Girl Friday to "some very important people." Even this, however, did not tell me that she worked for *him*, and I would not have known it if she had not said so. In all the conversation I had with him he never mentioned what to her looms as most meaningful in their early relationship. Even if he suppressed it because he could not face the fact that it had played an important role in bringing on his son's illness, the fact remains that today he appears to be unaware of something that had played a most important role in establishing their marriage. What must have been the reaction of this man, who aches with mortification when he has to be waited on in a restaurant, to a wife who served so diligently?

My record of the dinner we had at the hotel illustrates dominating trends in Mr. Wilson's character, as well as my own reaction to them.

Mr. Wilson and I talked a good deal about business and business operations, and I was able to do it because of my reading. So he and I spent practically the entire dinner hour discussing his business interests, while his wife took care of Norma, whom she let fill up on bread and pop.

Just before we entered the posh dining room, I had told Mr. Wilson he could be sure that if I were entertaining on my own funds, what I could offer would be much more modest. I did this because I was worried about his possible sensitivity to being taken out to dinner in a fancy place like the hotel, and I wished to put him at ease through making it clear that the money spent was not my own.

I ordered a bottle of wine, which turned out to be very good, the best part of the dinner. At first Mrs. Wilson refused emphatically to touch the wine, because even the slightest bit gives her a headache the next morning, but when I said, "Oh, please take a little bit so we can drink to the happy outcome of our hopes," she accepted immediately and sipped some for our toast. Mr. Wilson and I downed three glasses. At first he said he didn't want any, and he had refused cocktails also, saying he's not much of a drinker, but soon he began to talk about his experiences in drinking. He said that no matter how much he drinks he never loses his head, but told of having drunk a great deal at a wedding, so that he had to be taken out for a walk. I paralleled this with a story of having drunk too much at a wedding myself.

For general and particular reasons I told a number of stories to make myself small. The general reason was awareness of Mr. Wilson's status sensitivity, and the particular reason was his reference to Dr. Phillips, who runs the rehabilitation center. Dr. Phillips had told him he was going to give a paper somewhere, and Mr. Wilson considered this to be patting himself on the back. He mentioned this a number of times in a deprecatory way. He is very sensitive to anyone's effort to build himself up in the eyes of another.

I am reminded, immediately, in this context, of a short interchange between the three of us when we got home. Mr. Wilson, as usual, immediately sat down, picked up the paper and began to look over the TV offerings. He saw the announcement of the movie *Trial at Nuremberg* and we talked for a while about what a wonderful movie it was. I mentioned *The Secret Life of Walter Mitty* and said I had enjoyed it, but neither of them had seen or read it. I explained that it was a movie of a man who daydreams and imagines himself in some wonderful capacity—a great surgeon, great war pilot, etc., and I said, "All men like that story because all men have dreams of being something wonderful." Mr. Wilson agreed with me emphatically.

Since Norma must hear a great deal from her father about competition, about being on top or on bottom, and so on, her competitive drive is come by legitimately—from both sides of the family. Meanwhile, here at dinner, in an indirect way, Mr. Wilson continues to display his characteristic withdrawal from his family while plunging into what really interests him— dreams of superiority—for during the entire evening he talked to me, because with me he could discuss what means most to him.

His wife's account of the role achievement played in their lives is illuminating.

Mrs. Wilson and I had a long talk about Donald and her husband. I started the whole thing by asking her about the relationship between her and Mr. Wilson during the first year of Donald's life and immediately after the marriage. She stated quite firmly that the relationship was good. She said, however, that she left Donald alone a great deal—she left him absolutely alone because she had to work on her husband's material. She said he insisted that she do it because she was the only one who could do it perfectly. Now that she realizes how stupid she had been she does the work only at night, and sometimes she works very late at it. She used to do it during the day, but she changed after Norma was born. She kept saying how stupid she had been to do such a thing and that she can't forgive herself. She didn't know any better, she says, but "not knowing is no excuse."

Her husband's insistence that she do his work led me to ask whether he had felt secure in his relationship with her immediately after marriage, but instead of answering directly she said she had had a suitor, a professional man, considerably older than she, whom she had given up in order to marry Mr. Wilson, and her mother was disappointed that she had not married the other man. She claims she married her husband because she loved him.

Mrs. Wilson said that although Mr. Wilson's father was lower-class and miserly, she admires his mother, a strong woman.

In Mrs. Wilson's family there are highly educated people, but her husband's is far down on the social scale, and he has never ceased to compare himself with people of higher position. Mr. Wilson still feels his mother-in-law is very critical of him—even though she may say nothing, he feels that, inwardly, she is criticizing him. I said that considering the differences in social conditions, it would be difficult for him not to sense this gnawing at him constantly; that for a man in our culture—though I did not use these exact words—it is hard not to be continually measuring one's status against that of other men.

It is impossible—or rather, next to impossible—for anybody in the Wilson family to act, to come to life, whether in talk or action, without bringing in status, achievement, money, work—or any of the components of the success drive. Thus, when Mrs. Wilson talks about Donald, his fate gets entangled with work, and when I ask about her husband's feeling secure in his relationship with her, she talks about his status problem instead of talking about love and acceptance. Their relationship was good in the early days, she says, but in the next breath she says she left the baby alone to do her husband's work. Her perceptive analysis of his status problem, given without any question on the subject from me, suggests that the issue overshadowed their lives from the first.

Mr. Wilson could not discuss Donald without bringing in achievement considerations:

He would not talk about anything personal unless I led him around to it elaborately. He did say that when Donald was born, he was struggling to get his feet on the ground in his law practice and the first time he got a phone call he went streaking out of the house. His wife still remarks on it and laughs, but he doesn't think it's anything to laugh about.

I gave him many opportunities to talk about strains that may have existed between him and his wife over Donald in the early days of marriage, but he did not respond. As a matter of fact, I don't think he knew what was going on. I gave him the chance to talk about his own dependence on his wife during this period, but he would not talk about that, either.

I asked Mr. Wilson whether he had ever wanted to follow some other occupation, and he said that his sisters had been willing to send him through architectural school but he declined. . . . He complained that he got no help from his wife's family in paying for Donald's medical care.

. . .

When Mrs. Wilson wanted to give up the pediatrician who was recommending that she stay away from Donald, her husband said two things; first, "If you give him up you'll hurt the doctor's feelings," and second, "Look how many hundreds of people go to him—he must be good." The doctor was the uncle of one of Mr. Wilson's important clients.

"Well," Mr. Wilson seems to be saying, "I'm outside the whole thing. When Donald was a baby I was trying to get my feet on the ground . . . so what could you expect?" or something like that. "But in spite of everything," he seems to say, "I'm taking full responsibility, financially." On the one hand, he tries to clear himself of guilt* for the illness, and on the other, he protests that he is taking more than his share of responsibility for the cure. His bourgeois values, however, obtrude in both pleadings. As happens with many of us, his child is all tangled up with his dollars and his ambitions.

His wife's account of the early years of marriage as conventionally happy-loving, is contradicted by her statement that when her husband learned Donald was psychotic he turned away from her.

She said that after two or three years, when her husband discovered what Donald's condition really was, he practically abandoned her. He wouldn't sleep in the same room with her and wanted a divorce. She would have given it to him but for the fact that if she did, she would not have been able to do anything for Donald—he would have lost her husband's financial support. It was only when her husband went with her to visit Donald and saw the terrible condition of the children there that he experienced some feelings of humanity.

At this point she burst into tears, and after a while said that this was the first time she had cried in a long time. I gave her some Kleenex—that's all I did.

When her husband discovered Donald's condition he turned away from her, she said. He has often said, "You married the wrong guy."

In explaining why Mr. Wilson almost completely ignored Donald, she said Mr. Wilson never had a real father, so does not know what the role of a father is. When he came home, Donald would rattle his highchair to attract his father's attention, but Mr. Wilson would not go near him, saying, "Oh, he's only a kid, he doesn't understand anything." He would tell her to leave Donald alone—that pampering would spoil him.

The tragedy of Donald was not one they shared in love and despair—it was fate, a malfunctioning at birth. Donald was his wife's responsibility—and in some way even her "fault." Mrs. Wilson told me she lives almost entirely on pills, which she said were a stronger form of aspirin. They make her feel relaxed and she can fall asleep. She is repeatedly awakened by nightmares. Mr. Wilson seeks escape by sleeping in a separate room and wanting "a divorce" from her (and Donald). He has to defend himself

---

* On p. 298 I pointed out that he tends also to attribute Donald's illness to a condition he was born with.

against any kind of implication that he had a hand in Donald's illness. He has, like Mr. Rosenberg, a *hunger for innocence;* that is why he spends so much of his working time getting people out of the clutches of the law.

Mrs. Wilson feels that her husband has written Donald off, and she thinks it is only her drive that keeps Donald in the private institution. She and her husband never discuss Donald.

She says her husband has shut Donald out of his life, and that he said to her, "He's died to me." He cannot stand strong emotion, she says, and when his own mother was dying, he could not bear to go to see her, but would tell Mrs. Wilson to go, and she would go and spend time with her. Mrs. Wilson was the only one who went near her when she was dying—everyone else deserted her.

Mr. Wilson is a man who sent his lackey to his mother's death watch. The dialectic of this tragedy is that while Mrs. Wilson was away from home at her mother-in-law's deathbed she was, by withdrawing from her child, merely continuing the activity that had brought about a kind of death in her own home.

Though Mr. Wilson is depressed by the fact that Donald is not normal, he feels no sorrow for the boy, only contempt for his incompetence.

Mr. Wilson is very, very vague about the whole problem of Donald. He knows he is not a normal child, but when he talks about the genesis of Donald's illness he talks about Donald's being slow, taking a long time to walk, and things of that kind. When I press him he comes to the conclusion that Donald was born that way. He says that Dr. Reade says they ought to have another child, but he is worried—he's afraid they'll have another Donald. I mentioned a family that had an autistic child but three nonautistic ones. He said there is also the expense of keeping Donald at the Institute.

When Norma was twenty months old she already knew by heart the names of a whole bunch of records—something Donald never knew, Mr. Wilson was quick to point out.

Though there is a lingering doubt in Mr. Wilson's mind about whether Donald's condition is due entirely to constitution, he tries to push the whole thing out of his mind and feels it is useless to talk about it.

Mr. Wilson and I went for a walk, and after talking generalities for a while, I said that although his wife talks constantly about Donald, he never does. He said, "What can I do? There is nothing I can do, so why talk about it?" He said that all he can do is try to make the money to keep Donald in the private institution, and hope he will get well. He said that he tries to forget his troubles at work. I asked what troubles, and he said, his feelings about Donald. He remarked that his wife keeps blaming herself for what Donald did (*sic!*) and added, "Well, what's the use of talking about it, even if it was our fault?"

Yet his interest in the child is not very deep. While Mrs. Wilson asks her questions out of anguish, he asks his out of curiosity; and when she asks whether my study will do Donald any good, he merely wonders why an anthropologist is doing such a study.

Mrs. Wilson asked whether the study would help Donald and I said, "It is not at all sure that it will help Donald, but what is certain is that it will enable us to learn something about the genesis of autism and to help parents in the future." I also said that this is the first time anybody has ever taken the trouble to study families in this way. Mr. Wilson wanted to know why an *anthropologist* was doing it, and I said that anthropologists are the only ones trained to observe people living their natural lives.

Why and how do they live together? This is the most difficult question of all to answer. One would think that there was nothing between these two at all; yet the bowl containing the greeting cards had valentines they had sent to each other—how old, I do not know; and valentines can be a sham. One day she called him "dear," and I was startled, but she did it only once. He never called her "dear" in my hearing. Though he belittles her housework, he lets her order him around:

It was about nine twenty-five in the evening now and I said that I would like to leave, and they both indicated reluctance to let me go. I offered to take the bus back to the hotel but they would not hear of it. Mrs. Wilson said, "Oh, my husband'll be glad to drive you back; he would only watch TV, anyway," and he agreed to that. On the way his main topic was how to invest your money.

. . .

When I suggested to Mr. Wilson that we go for a walk, his wife said immediately, "He'd love to go out for a walk."

They did not touch each other in my presence—there was no warm exchange of any kind. The house did not look as if love were expended on it to make it beautiful. They had nothing good to say about each other, except that she did remark that she was perfectly satisfied with her husband's income: "After all, we're not in want."

And so they were living together when I met them; perhaps it was in the interest of their daughter—it certainly did not seem as if they had much interest in each other.

Reflections

I would not say that the achievement drive destroyed the Wilsons' chances of happiness, but what I would say is that given the personality handicaps with which they started out, their achievement drive was too much for *them*. Considering the fact that family, school and friends drive us with whips and chains to be successful, it takes a strong personality indeed not to succumb to the success drive itself. Only if we have love can we avoid getting sick in struggling to achieve. I hope I am making myself clear: the achievement drive must be installed in the psyche of middle- and upper-class people with such torrential fury that they will drive on. But how is the fury contained at all? Look at war—the ultimate expression of the achievement drive: it is not turned against our own society, because it *is* ours, because we are taught that this is the area exempt from war attack. But society is a metaphor of love, and as Freud made clear, we contain our egoism with love. And so, if we are loved enough in our family, we have love within us to so hold our achievement drive in check that we do not destroy our family, and in destroying it, destroy ourselves. I think that neither Mr. nor Mrs. Wilson had ever been loved enough to be able to manage their achievement drive so that it would not destroy their possibilities for happiness.

In this context Mr. Wilson saw Donald as a sign of *failure*, and since, for him, there could be nothing worse, he turned away. Mrs. Wilson's attachment to Norma is by love-achievement, and Norma must toe the mark of success, take off and never stop running.

PART V

The Keen Family

INTRODUCTION

The Miracle of Tenderness

In this book we see much cruelty and little tenderness. It is time for a general discussion of the miracle of tenderness—particularly here, because in the Keen family there is cruelty but practically no tenderness. To me, tenderness is a miracle in our culture; though it is easy to account for cruelty, it is not easy to account for tenderness. As I look at the cruelty of the world—around me, now, and throughout history—I find it nearly impossible to account for the survival of tenderness in human culture.

It is easy to understand why there are cruel people in our culture; a competitive, achieving, power-hungry, greedy culture creates cruelty, almost by definition. The armed forces, school, organizational life (including business), sports (football, hockey, boxing, wrestling, hunting, fishing) are institutions in which people and animals are treated cruelly and in which people learn to be cruel. Thus cruelty has an *institutional structure* that sustains, teaches and may even glorify it. But where are the institutions—the organizations—that sustain and teach tenderness? The most that can be said for government is that it attempts to alleviate problems at home by pragmatic means, but government is not tender, and often, in its repressive functions, it is cruel.

Freud explained the occurrence of the "social impulses," among which he would have to include tenderness, by the action of the erotic on man's "boundless egoism." The limitless evil of which humans are capable, he said, is purified by eros. Yet this theory leaves the socializing thrust of eros itself unaccounted for.

Egoism must be held in check in order for man to have any society at all, because if he gives full rein within his own society to his tendencies to cruelty, selfishness, etc., he will be without friends and will soon be murdered. Even if he is a Caligula or a Nero, his enemies will eventually get through his bodyguard. Hence a nearly universal characteristic of *Homo sapiens* is solicitude at home and cruelty abroad, care for members of one's own society or caste, and hostility and even death and torture to outsiders. In many cultures, however, solicitude is expressed simply through reciprocity, in mere conventional support in domestic matters, in backing up relatives in quarrels, in taking part in warfare, etc. In our culture, on the other hand, mere reciprocity is despised and in its place is put the ideal of tenderness.

Tenderness does not emerge out of the necessities of social living, for it is beyond society. In tenderness, *Man* is beyond *Homo sapiens;* in being tender, man is more than a mere social animal. It is possible to have a society without tenderness, but *Homo sapiens* has never been able to survive without cruelty. Hence I say "the miracle of tenderness."

When we are tender we want to touch the other, and touch is gentle, caressing and slow. We tend to be gentle and slow also with those who are vulnerable. Since vulnerability is related to neediness, we are often tender to those who seem to need us and in the presence of whom, paradoxically, we feel our own need. Those who live in the delusion of strength cannot be tender, and do not awaken tenderness in others.

Tenderness can emerge only when people are sensitive both to the inner and outer needs of others. Awareness that an infant needs protection, feeding, and so on, is not enough to make us feel tender toward him, but the perception of the infant's *inner* need elicits tenderness—and the same applies to tenderness between man and woman. In our culture, men may not show tenderness to one another because of the myth of masculine strength; on the battlefield they can be tender to wounded buddies, for the wounded man need no longer, in our battle culture, maintain the delusion of strength. His intense pain gives him the right to acknowledge weakness, and his buddies the right to be tender to a vulnerable man: they move him gently and slowly; he expresses the eternal vulnerability of all of them. "And they laid him tenderly to rest" may be said of a man who never, in his lifetime, was shown any tenderness by his fellows.

Man in our culture has felt the close association between vulnerability and tenderness, and though in his philosophical and literary works he has never put the matter in so many words, from time to time his feeling about the general relationship has come through, in what poets and others have written in passing. Thus one of La Rochefoucauld's Maxims:

> We readily console ourselves for the misfortunes that befall our friends, when they serve to actualize our tenderness for them.*

And again in William Winter's poem to I. H. Bromley:

> . . . every grief that mortals share
> Found pity in his tenderness.

Tenderness also is a way of loving ourselves. When a man strokes a woman's breasts and she responds with longing and need, he can be tender only if he feels that her response is a part of him. "There never was just a single creature in the world," says the Angel in Giraudoux's *Sodom and Gomorrah;* "it was a pair. God did not create man and woman, one after the other, nor one from the other. He created twins, united by bonds of real flesh, which he severed, in an access of trust, the day he created tenderness." † And so, also, in fondling a baby, we can be tender to him only if we feel the baby's response as part of our self, and only because we trust him.

Such symbiosis, however, is as culturally determined as forms of marriage and parenthood, and can occur only in cultures where the ideal of love is mutual assimilation. Hence tenderness is antagonistic to that kind of "independence" of which Sartre has spoken. Whoever wants to be a detached particle cannot experience tenderness.

* *Nous nous consolons aisément des disgrâces de nos amis lorsqu'elles servent à signaler notre tendresse pour eux.*

† *"Il n'y a jamais eu de créature. Il n'y a jamais eu que le couple. Dieu n'a pas créé l'homme et la femme l'un après l'autre, ni l'un de l'autre. Il a créé deux corps jumeaux unis par des lanières de chair qu'il a tranchées depuis, dans un accès de confiance, le jour où il a créé la tendresse."* (ii, 7)

Tenderness therefore requires special cultural conditions in order to come into being. Cruelty is present in practically all cultures, but outside motherhood, tenderness appears with great difficulty and is easily destroyed. All that is necessary for cruelty is the wish to triumph over other men, but in tenderness man must be beyond himself. Hence, the miracle of tenderness.

There is still the question of why, in this, man is able to go beyond himself. But before attempting an answer, I must point out that in being cruel, man is merely being himself. Man is, primordially, a predator, preying on wild (and now, on domestic) animals and on his fellows. Furthermore, in order to survive, in order to survive as a social creature, man has had to be cruel to—exterminate—other men, outsiders. Hence to be cruel is merely to be hominid. Meanwhile it is possible for him to maintain his own—his "friendly"—social system through reciprocity and through observing conventional protective measures toward others. This has been the pattern in most cultures. It follows that since social existence can be sustained in this way, *Homo sapiens* is not necessarily tender. Hence, in tenderness, man is beyond himself: he does not cease to be a hominid, yet he becomes man.

When I recall philosophers' reflections on the emotions, it seems to me that they have always held that if emotions were to get out of hand, they would destroy man; therefore, emotions must be brought under the domination of "intellect." Freud's system is but a variant of this, and his "reality principle" looks just like Spinoza's "intellect." Yet we know now that intellect is just as capable of getting out of hand, for it is the untrammeled functioning of the brain that has been, in part, responsible for the nuclear crisis and the crisis of the computerized world in which we find ourselves. Even if we urge that it is not intellect, in itself, that is responsible, but rather the fact that intellect has placed itself, as usual, at the disposition of people in power, it is still a matter of intellect's getting out of hand. Since intellect has the intoxicating quality of being usable against others, it paradoxically casts man back upon his primordial, predatory nature. But tenderness, an emotion, fosters others. Tenderness can never be used, in a predatory way, against other men and it can never be the instrument of power.

Since anthropoid apes and other nonhuman primates are tender to members of the same band,* man's capacity for tenderness is seen to be a persistence, in a species that is predatory, of a trait already developed in an earlier, primarily nonpredatory one. In these animals, tenderness is a necessary expression of their biosocial constitution, but in man, tenderness comes out only under special cultural conditions, partly because he does not need it.

As far as I know, the following is the only description in print of tenderness among males in a tribal society:

---

* As shown, principally in grooming behavior. See especially the chimpanzee and the bonnet macaque in *Primate Behavior*, ed. by Irven DeVore (New York, Holt, Rinehart and Winston, 1965). In this connection the following on the bonnet macaque is particularly striking: "Wounded monkeys present for grooming often and are often groomed. There seems to be a direct relationship between the seriousness of the wound and the amount of grooming activity. The subadult male with two slash wounds more than three inches long coupled with deep puncture wounds presented to monkey after monkey for grooming, and when one ceased grooming moved immediately to another." (p. 188)

Kaingáng young men love to sleep together. At night they call to one another, "Come and lie down with me, with *me*." Then there is a shifting and a
squirming so that Nggugn or Waipó or Kanyahé can lie down where he is
bidden. In camp one sees young men caressing. Married and unmarried
young men lie cheek by jowl, arms around one another, legs slung across
bodies, for all the world like lovers in our own society. Sometimes they lie
caressing that way in knots of three or four . . .* The basis for man's
loyalty to man has roots in the many warm bodily contacts between them.
The violent, annihilating conflicts among men in Kaingáng society were all
among those who had never shared the languid exchange of caresses on a
hot afternoon under the green arched shelter of a house nor lain together
night after night under a blanket against the cold. . . . The relationships
built on these hours of lying together with anyone at all bear fruit in the
softening of conflicts that are so characteristic of the Kaingáng.†

The Kaingáng illustrate perfectly a point made here, for though the men
were tender to men of their own extended families, they massacred the
families with whom they were feuding, often feigning tenderness to men
they intended to trap.

Since it is difficult to find a balance between cruelty and solicitude, and
since unrestrained tenderness in one culture would probably lead to destruction by other societies eager to exploit any sign of weakness, human
social organization has, on the whole, severely limited tenderness or blotted
it out, even at home. In the United States no legislation can be enacted on
the basis of tenderness, but must pass the "pragmatic" test of its contribution to survival and to the values of achievement, power and accumulation.

Man has a strong inherent tendency to substitute gifts of goods and services for the gift of the body (tenderness); instead of attempting to achieve
social harmony through caressing his fellows, he engages in reciprocal,
ceremonial gift giving and the tendering of mutual services. It is almost too
perfect a correspondence with this theory to observe that the Kaingáng are
among the poorest people on earth and have practically no ceremonial life.
The development of culture and the growth of populations have compelled
man to spend his time manipulating his property and his ceremonial life,
so that the dynamics of evolution have made their contribution to the elimination of tenderness. The issue is that the kind of caressing we observed
among the Kaingáng can serve to integrate only very small groups, for there
is a narrow limit to the number of people with whom one can be tender. As
it was, Kaingáng men spent their lives wandering around the forests in
an endless effort to show their affection for all who had a right to it. The
result was angry fallings-out between men who thought themselves neglected. Since, however, they had had long-standing relationships with one
another, these quarrels never amounted to anything within the same extended family.

In discussing love, Spinoza says

that spiritual unhealthiness and misfortunes can generally be traced to excessive love for something which is subject to many variations. . . .
We may thus readily conceive the power which clear and distinct knowledge, and especially . . . knowledge founded on the actual knowledge of

* There is no consummated homosexuality.
† From my *Jungle People* (*op. cit.*), pp. 18–19.

God, possesses over the emotions: . . . it begets a love towards a thing immutable and eternal . . . neither can it be defiled with those faults which are inherent in ordinary love; but it may grow from strength to strength, and may engross the greater part of the mind, and deeply penetrate it.*

From this passage I conclude that Spinoza believed we should love things for their eternal qualities, and from this I go on to the understanding that in our culture we feel spontaneous tenderness toward things that express universal, secret, ethical hungers—hungers which, in our culture, are so persuasive, so intense that we refer to them as eternal. We suddenly feel an overwhelming tenderness for the buddy who is hit, because suddenly he embodies the essence of humanity suffering the consequences of universal cruelty. We feel tender toward whatever baby we see, because by virtue of his shape and constitution, a baby expresses the eternal vulnerability of man and infancy; a baby expresses innocence—total freedom from the ambiguities, hypocrisy and cruelty of the adult; and a baby is eternal hope. Thus, we have incorporated in our tissues a metaphysic of infancy, and we feel tender without our knowing why.

In the subsequent discussion of the Keen case I examine the phenomenon of the miracle of tenderness and what happens when the metaphysic of infancy is not incorporated.

The notion of the "secret ethical hungers" is readily understood if we consider a period in history when ethics seemed to have largely disappeared from one population—the Roman, between the death of Augustus and the ascent of Vespasian. Yet during that period, when tens of thousands perished each year, not only on the imperial battlefields but also in Rome at the hands of executioners and in the Roman circus, and when men, women and children died by torture, by the sword, by poison, through treachery, the people of Rome, depraved and humiliated as they were, could still admire and praise an emperor for occasional clemency or honesty. What one perceives on the surface, through the eyes of a Tacitus or a Suetonius, is depravity, but the people, as Tacitus and Suetonius repeatedly make clear, also yearned for clemency and hoped for honesty and justice; hence the "secret ethical hungers." This is why, even as men destroy others, they can talk of bringing peace to the world. Hypocrisy it is, but its appeal lies in the fact that except for the most depraved, in our culture men have a secret ethics—a secret ethical hunger. This is what Spinoza meant, I think, by "the eternal qualities of man."

While the arousal of one's ethical hungers arouses tenderness too, the impulse to violate a person's ethical qualities—to humiliate him†—necessarily makes tenderness impossible. In the Keen family we will see why, because of humiliation, there was no chance for tenderness.

* *The Ethics*, ed. by James Gutmann, trans. by William H. White (New York, Hafner, 1953), Part V, Proposition XX.
† What Charles de Gaulle called "this strange passion for degradation," in his television speech of August 10, 1967. It ought to be read by every civilized person.

Can Adults Drive Adults to Psychosis?

We learned from psychoanalysis that parents are the principal cause of their children's disturbance, but once this was learned, all related learning stopped. We memorized our lesson as if we had been taught that *only* parents cause anybody's disturbance. Unconsciously we assumed the obverse of the proposition along with the proposition itself. While humans have a tendency to assume the obverse when a proposition has been stated, psychiatry has contributed to one-sidedness by being one-sided itself, never exploring the generality implied in the proposition "Parents drive children mad." Stated in its most general terms, the proposition is, "People drive people mad," and this must include, therefore, adults driving other adults mad, children driving one another mad, and so on.

The Keen case is an especially good one in which to examine these possibilities, because there it looks as if husband and children are driving the mother mad.

The notion that parents alone are responsible for their offspring's psychotic collapse—in childhood or in later life—implies that the psychosis would have come about regardless of any external circumstances; in other words, that the person was marked for a breakdown by his parents' actions, which rules out environmental influences outside the home. Proof that parental influence alone is responsible, however, has never been given. We know that psychotic persons have histories of parental abuse, but there is no systematic way of getting the early records of people with similar experiences who did not break down. On the other hand, since under proper environmental conditions a psychotic adult may be restored to sanity, why isn't it likely that under improper environmental conditions he may lose his sanity? Admittedly parental influence in the early years is overdetermining, but if a later environment can restore a person to health, why can't it also facilitate his going mad or prevent it? Granted that a child whose parents are very sick runs a strong risk of going mad as an adult, it seems logical that this will only occur if in later life he encounters conditions that are pathogenic for him. If a therapist can do him some good, why can't a mischievous, unfeeling or half-crazy spouse do him such harm that he loses his mind? It is illogical to assume that after childhood a person can be restored to health but not driven to a breakdown.

Sometimes we work with people who are a joy, and sometimes we work with people who are unbearable—picky, hostile, capricious, unreachable, etc.—to such an extent that when we come home at night it takes hours to get over it, and sometimes it even interferes with sleep. Fortunately we "don't have to live with them," but sometimes we are as badly off as if we were living with them—and we eventually quit the job or get transferred. Think of being married for ten years to a person you can't bear! Surely it is not impossible to imagine that you'd go mad, especially if as a child you were damaged by your parents. Freud has said that

> a woman who is brutally treated and mercilessly exploited by her husband
> fairly regularly takes refuge in neurosis, if her disposition admits of it. This
> will happen if she is too cowardly or too conventional to console herself with
> another man, if she is not strong enough to defy her husband, if she has no

prospect of being able to maintain herself or of finding a better husband, and last of all, if she is still strongly attached sexually to this brutal man. Her illness becomes her weapon in her struggle against him, one that she can use for her protection, or misuse for purposes of revenge.*

Freud talks about neurosis—but there is no reason why we should stop there. I presume that when Freud says "if her disposition admits of it," he means, in his system, either heredity or early "trauma."

The trouble with the oversimplified genetic theory of psychosis ("it all started in childhood") is that it diverts attention from the adult patient's immediate associates—from the role they play in creating the conditions for his illness. Overwhelmingly psychiatry, even the new "family psychotherapy," has directed its attention to the psychotic child as a phenomenon of parental ineptness, sickness, stupidity and confusion, with no attention paid to the psychotic parent as a victim of a cruel, insensitive spouse. Why the difference?

When a psychotic individual is brought to an institution, he is usually accompanied by a person who, compared to the psychotic person, appears "adequate," "stable," etc., and the contrast between the two is taken at face value. Furthermore, since the law requires that commitment be by a responsible adult who is not himself "insane," the suspicion that the person committing the psychotic person is himself ill, or is responsible for the illness, would raise problems. Thus the law protects a cruel spouse from investigation of his responsibility for the illness of the other. The law is hand in glove with the "genetic" theory. And all of this in spite of the fact that over and over again, when we deal with the family of a psychotic adult, we find the other members badly disorganized or insensitive to the needs of the sick person, or both.

Under the proposition that "he was doomed by his upbringing," we acquit all the institutions in our culture except the family of complicity in the destruction of the individual. One of my earliest experiences in a psychiatric clinic was being told by a psychoanalyst that school phobias have nothing to do with the school. My own opinion now, after many years' study of classrooms, is that considering what most schools are, what we have to understand is what makes it possible for our children to survive in them at all. At any rate, the money the National Institute of Mental Health has spent on "school mental health" demonstrates that the "inevitability" of the "genetic process" is no longer taken for granted.

The worst thing about the simple-minded form of the genetic theory is that it makes it unnecessary for the "sane" member of a pair to examine himself or be examined by others, thus leaving him untreated, a persisting pathogenic vector in the social system—so he can keep right on making others miserable and even psychotic—and that it exempts the pathogenic institutions of our culture from examination. It is like diagnosing cholera victims without analyzing the water they drink.

Emergence of the "family dynamics" theory of psychosis expresses our

* From *A General Introduction to Psychoanalysis* (Perma Books edition), p. 391. While the "paranosic gain"—the "gain from illness"—has been discussed by Freud in several places, notably in *On the History of the Psychoanalytical Movement; An Autobiographical Study; Inhibitions, Symptoms and Anxiety:* and *The Question of Lay Analysis,* this particular example, as far as I can find, was given only in his Vienna lectures.

hatred—and the psychiatrists' own hatred—of the contemporary family, and though the theory is a great step forward, it still diverts attention from the destructiveness of the culture as a whole, from the fact that it does not permit a rewarding life to most people. Through this theory we attack what is nearest, what has inflicted on us the immediate, the most memorable pain. The family, however, is merely the place where the general pathology of the culture is incubated, concentrated and finally transmuted into individual psychosis. Family therapy is a good thing, and "family dynamics" is a valid theory, but let us remember that the family merely distills into a lethal dose what exists in the culture at large.

A NOTE ON RESEARCH ON THE WORKING-CLASS FAMILY

There is a great deal of research on the "blue collar" family,* practically all of it "survey" and "interview" research by middle-class social scientists. The picture obtained is uniformly depressing. The findings agree that the working class uses physical punishment of children much more than the middle class. Husband and wife are remote from each other, and the wife is much less interested in sex than her husband is.† Working-class people, according to these accounts, live isolated lives; they see few people, go out little, stay glued to television. The mother spends the day—day after day— cooking, cleaning, washing, ironing, harassed by her children, whom she alternately loves and rejects. Life is stressful, boring, routine; there is no tenderness in her life and she is not sure of her husband.

From this formalistic middle-class research we get an almost joyless picture of the working class, somewhat relieved by outings and expenditures for hard goods. When the father comes home from work he is tired out and wants to be left alone—not to be bothered by the kids—and the mother is exhausted by housework and kids, but she cannot withdraw. Husband and wife feel inferior, lonely, alienated. Unfortunately the comparisons with the middle class are not thorough enough to make this research convincing. We are badly in need of an ethnography of the stable working class, with suitable comparative material on the middle class, and until we have it I fear we may be slaves of stereotypes that are, perhaps, a product of the myopia and the method of the researchers. Since the Keens are a "blue collar" ‡ family, I shall refer to *Workingman's Wife* from time to time, because that book contains the material most relevant to this study.

* Material on child training has been summarized up to about 1957 by Urie Bronfenbrenner in "Socialization and Social Class through Time and Space," in *Readings in Social Psychology*, ed. by Eleanor E. Maccoby, Theodore M. Newcomb and Eugene L. Hartley (New York, Holt, 1958). Two papers by Melvin L. Kohn should also be consulted: "Social Class and the Exercise of Parental Authority," *American Sociological Review*, Vol. XXIV (1959), pp. 352–66, and "Social Class and Parent-Child Relationships: An Interpretation," *American Journal of Sociology*, Vol. LXVIII (1963), pp. 471–80. A series of papers on aspects of working-class life is contained in *Blue-Collar World*, ed. by Arthur B. Shostak and William Gomberg (Englewood Cliffs, N.J., Prentice-Hall, 1964). A stimulating and rounded study is *Workingman's Wife*, by Lee Rainwater, Richard Coleman and Gerald Handel (New York, Macfadden, 1962).

† Mirra Komarovsky's *Blue-Collar Marriage* (New York, Random House, 1962) gives a different picture.

‡ How many factory and service workers, skilled, semiskilled and unskilled, really wear "blue collars"? Airplane and missile factories, for instance, are alive with workers in white suits—and in white (dust-free, air-and-temperature-controlled) rooms!

THE KEEN FAMILY

Bob Keen and his late wife, Alice, were close to forty years old when the study began. At the time of the observer's first visit they had three children —Paul, Mrs. Keen's son from a previous marriage, aged ten and a half; Frankie, three years old; and Carol, about eleven months old. Mrs. Keen was pregnant with her fourth child. Sometime after the observer left, Mrs. Keen gave birth to a son—Charles—and then she became acutely ill and died.

The Keens lived in a small city in the Northeast. Bob worked in a factory. Alice stayed home and took care of the house and children, usually dragging herself around barefoot, in blouse and shorts. She was anemic during her last pregnancy. Paul, her son by her first husband, had been diagnosed "retarded, with behavior reaction."

This is the only family in the book that I did not study myself. Susan, who did the study, was recommended to me as an outstanding child-care worker and I gave her some training before she studied the Keen family. She was there for a week, from seven in the morning until nine at night— about one hundred hours in all—and returned a few times, after her first visit, spending several hours with the family, which gave her plenty of time to get a feeling for the family. However, since this was Susan's first experience with this kind of work, and since I could not monitor her daily dictation, there are some gaps in her account—more, I think, than in mine. Nevertheless, there is so much that is valuable in her work that it ought to be published, and it shows that although new on the job, a sensitive observer can capture the quality of a family's life and make it possible for others to understand it.

We have here the only account of its kind in existence: a fourteen-hour-a-day record, for a solid week, of an entire family in which a mother is quite seriously disturbed: after she remarried, Mrs. Keen had two alleged nervous breakdowns* and she went to a psychiatric hospital again not too long after the observer's first visit.

Mrs. Keen hadn't had much education. When she dropped out of high school, she had stayed at home for a while, helping around the house, and then had various unskilled jobs as a service worker before she married. Her first husband had been unfaithful and drank too much. In contrast, Bob Keen was stable. He was also quite intelligent and read a great deal. In his job relations he did well, but at home he stumbled as husband and father.

I shall begin the account with long sections from the notes, in which the whole family can be seen together.

---

* Although the record indicates two breakdowns before the observations started, conversation revolved around only one hospitalization. Mrs. Keen may have had outpatient treatment for one of her episodes.

An Outing

(Fifth day.) Before we left, Mrs. Keen fed Carol a boiling hot lunch. I could see the steam rising, and when she spooned it to Carol, the baby started to whimper and screwed up her face. It was obviously too hot, and her mother finally put some milk in it.

Mrs. Keen began to get ready to go out, and changed her clothes. She had on a pink shirt and slacks and she looked very nice. I went into the kitchen and asked where we were going. She said she didn't know, but thought her husband wanted to go over to his mother's for a while. Frankie, the three-year-old, asked where we were going. She said, "Never mind, just get ready." There was some bickering over getting ready—so typical in this house—but I can't remember what was said. Mother and father always yell at the kids when they try to get them to do something.

Our first stop was Mr. Keen's mother's house. She was on the porch when we arrived and said right away to Mrs. Keen, "Let me have the baby, let me have the baby, let me have the baby," and tried to get Carol to walk. She put her against the wall and coaxed her to walk, but Carol wouldn't budge. Her grandmother kept saying, "Stand by yourself, stand by yourself," and she said to Mrs. Keen, "You know, Alice, what you should do is put chairs up so she can walk from chair to chair." And looking at me, she said, "That's how I taught my babies to walk." Meanwhile Mr. Keen stood off, away from us, near the porch. Frankie climbed around on it, asking about this, that and the other, and Paul just sat. Frankie went into the house, got himself a piece of candy and offered one to his father, who said, "No, give it to Susan," so Frankie handed it to me.

At last we left. [Mr. Keen drove around and around, in what seemed to the observer a pointless and even circular route.] We drove and drove. Every time Frankie got out of his seat or made a noise his father told him to sit down. At one point he was standing behind Mr. Keen and occasionally did make a noise that might have been irritating to a driver. Several times Mr. Keen remarked to his wife that children never mind any more. She was fairly quiet. We reached a spot where Mr. Keen said, "Can you see that building through there? That's Mount Rose." Since all I could make out was what looked like a roof, I said I thought I saw something, and he said, "Well, that's Mount Rose," and I said, "Hospital?" and asked Mrs. Keen whether that was where she went to have her babies. He replied, "No, that's where she went to have her nervous breakdown; it's a psychiatric hospital where people go to have rests."

Mr. Keen asked his wife a number of times to please hold on to Carol because he might have to stop suddenly, and his wife yelled at him that she *was* watching the baby.

We finally got out at a roadside restaurant and Mr. Keen ordered hamburgers for everybody. Somehow a fight started between Mr. and Mrs. Keen. When I say "somehow," I mean they can bicker at the drop of a word: there is a wall between them almost constantly and they can argue about anything. This time the fight started because she had set the baby on the table in the booth we took. "Look, Alice," he said, "don't let the baby up on the table—she'll fall off!" At this she got up and said, "Let me out! I'm not going to take this; I'm going out and sit in the car. Here, you can have her—I'll just leave her with you." And she set the baby down in the seat, and off she went to the rest room. He kept saying, "Ain't that something," but the boys didn't say a word. When she came back she asked Paul to let her back in [to her seat in the booth] and he did. She held the baby. Mr. Keen took half of Frankie's sandwich, saying, "Give half of this to your mother." Frankie objected but his father insisted.

Mr. Keen said we would drive back and have a look at the river, and there was a fight about that; his wife said, "Just go on and do anything you want; you think everybody is going to do what you want to do." We drove to a scenic spot but couldn't find a parking space. The boys were getting very anxious and wanted to get out of the car, but since there was no place to park, Mr. Keen suggested, "Susan, why don't you get out with the boys and go look at the river." We had hardly been there more than two minutes when Mrs. Keen called, "Come back, Frankie," so we returned to the car. Mr. Keen said, "Get in, so your mother won't have to be watching you," and announced that we were going home. When the boys protested and started to cry, their mother said there was no place to park.

On our way home the bickering got worse and there was more yelling about Frankie and Paul. Frankie was repeatedly told to sit down. A couple of times he was just sitting there and Paul would touch him or draw him into conversation, and Frankie would start to talk in his high-pitched voice and his father would tell him to stop. Once Mrs. Keen said she was going to beat Frankie to death if he didn't stop it, and once she threatened to throw him out of the car. Paul asked me what was the matter and when I said, "Nothing," he said, "Are you happy?" I countered with, "Are you happy?" and he looked at the floor. During the trip he kept saying, "Isn't this a wonderful day?" and "Aren't we having a good time?" and things like that.

When we got home we had Cornish hen and spaghetti for dinner. Paul wanted to leave before he had finished what was on his plate, so Mr. Keen told him to go to his room, but Mrs. Keen objected to this because, she said, he always ate well, and if he didn't want to eat his spaghetti this time he didn't have to. [The record does not say whether Paul went or how Mr. Keen reacted to his wife's objection.] Frankie just played with his food. Once he stuck his fork into it and said, "Ouch, there's a bone." At last his father took him outside in the yard to play.

Dinner on the Last Day

(Seventh day.) Mr. Keen drove up and got out of the car looking grim. Frankie ran toward him calling "Daddy!" and stopped midway. As Mr. Keen approached the house the first thing he said was, "What's this cup doing here?" (There was a cup by the porch stairs.) Then he looked at the walk, saw some gravel and pushed it off onto the lawn with his foot. Frankie said something to the effect that Myrtle (his little friend who lives down the street) had thrown it there.

When Mr. Keen went inside, I followed him into the kitchen and sat on a stool by the door. He wanted to add some cucumber to the salad, but his wife yelled, "You and your last-minute stuff—get out of here!" but she took the cucumber and peeled it. As he mixed the salad she stood there ready to slice the cucumber and he said, "Go ahead, put it in there."

Frankie came along with his flying saucer and said he was going to put it on my foot. Then he asked me what was on my foot and I said, "I can't guess; why don't you guess?" He seemed delighted with the game and coaxed me, "Oh, come on, you guess," so I told him, "I think it's a flying saucer." He asked, "Who put it there?" and I said, "You know, I don't know; I think it was some little boy." He laughed and his mother came along and said, "Stop doing that."

At dinner Paul had a pork chop and some potatoes on his plate and Mr. Keen asked if that was all he was going to eat. Paul said yes, but Mr. Keen suggested that he have some corn, and turning to his wife, said, "Alice, will you give him some corn so he can put some on his plate?" I passed the salad bowl to Paul, who sat there, bowl in hand, looking from his mother to his stepfather until Mr. Keen glanced up and said, "Will you stop playing?" Paul burst out, "I *will*," and his mother said, "Don't you scream, don't you be smart," so he finally took some salad. Frankie was playing with his food, and in the living room the baby was crying, but not very loudly. The dinner seemed to move quickly and it was rather quiet—there wasn't any real conversation. At one point Paul said he had seen Frankie with some candy and his mother said, "Do you always have to snitch?" Paul, in the time I was there, was never given money to buy himself a treat.

When Carol was brought in to be fed she was crying. She slid down inside the highchair and her father turned around, yanked her up and said, "Stop doing that!" She was crying very, very hard now and he said she was doing it on purpose. The baby was holding the bag in which the bread had been wrapped and Frankie said, "Look what she's got!" Mr. Keen took it away and she cried harder. Paul, the only one who attempted to comfort her, got up, went over to her and said, "Oh, Carol, don't cry." Mr. Keen told him to stop it, but Paul clapped his hands for the baby and said, "Carol, don't cry," and she was quiet for a moment. His stepfather repeated, "Don't do that," but Paul kept it up, saying something like "She's my sister and you don't have to pester her," and finally stomped off to his room.

The food Mrs. Keen brought for the baby was boiling hot, and I watched to see if steam was coming off the spoon too, but I didn't notice any and the baby didn't wince, as I had seen her do before, when I was sure that the hot food really bothered her. Mrs. Keen turned to me and said, "Look, Susan, I'm eating potatoes like you"—talking for Carol, as she sometimes does—and Frankie looked over and said to me, "So am I eating *my* potatoes." After asking me about the toys I had bought the kids, and who had paid for them, and getting the answer that I had bought them with money Dr. Henry had given me, he went outside.

I remained at the table with Mr. and Mrs. Keen and the baby, and she took Carol and held her over her head and tickled her. This seemed to bother her husband, for he said, "Don't! You'll drop her. Don't tickle her like that." [The record does not indicate whether she stopped.]

As Mr. Keen was opening his mail he found a little plastic puppet in one of the packages and began to play with it with the baby. Her mother laughed and it was really one of the sane moments—there are these sane moments. It was a joyful thing to see: Mr. Keen was dangling the puppet, the baby was smiling and laughing, and her mother was too. Frankie came into the kitchen with his shoes in his hand, saw the puppet and said, "Where did you get that?" Mr. Keen said, "Watch, watch—he's going to want this," and his mother agreed. Mr. Keen said he had bought the puppet. Frankie asked, "Who's it for?" and his father answered, "It's for Carol," and with that Frankie threw one of his shoes at the refrigerator. (He'd had his shoes off several time during the day.) His father took him into the boys' room and spanked him; when he came back his wife said, "Now, see what you've done! You knew he would want that; you were just teasing him, like you do everybody. I'm not going to stand for that screaming—you let him come out!" But he said, "No, he's got to learn to mind; he can't always think that everything is for him." What struck me was that he lied to Frankie when he said that he had bought the puppet and that it was for Carol.

At last Mr. Keen told Frankie he could come out in about five minutes if he quieted down, which Frankie did, and then his father let him go outside.

When Paul came out of his room Mr. Keen sent him to the store for cigarettes. This was the third time he was sent to the store, but I don't recall his ever being given money for himself.

Mr. Keen had gone into the living room and was reading the paper when I joined him, and he gave me part of the paper to read. Meanwhile Carol was fussing in the playpen and he finally took her out and set her on his lap. Mrs. Keen finished the dishes and then came in and read the paper too, but he went into the kitchen, and as usual at this time of night, had some coffee. He asked me and his wife if we wanted some. She said no, but I had some in the kitchen with him. He started talking about his job.

At one point during the evening while Mr. Keen was watching TV in the living room, Carol fell down in the playpen and bumped her head against it and her father said, "Get up, get up." Carol was crying a great deal in the playpen and there was much talk about what was wrong with her; her mother thought she was tired. Finally she took her up and started giving her the bottle but stopped for a while and started again, stopping and starting about three or four times because the baby didn't want the bottle. Mr. Keen said once, "She doesn't want it," and asked his wife why she was forcing her. She spanked the baby when she bobbed up and down and the baby cried.

Mr. Keen and I went into the kitchen again and he talked some more about his work. Among other things he said it was a thankless job and not really what he wanted. Then Frankie, who had been outside playing, came in, whining for a glass of milk, but his father told him to be quiet because *he* was talking.

Earlier in the evening Frankie had asked his mother for a glass of water and she told him to ask his brother, and later, when Mrs. Keen and I were sitting in the living room (I was telling her I had really enjoyed being in the house and thanked her for letting me visit), Frankie came along and asked her to put his shoe on but she said, "No, I can't now, I can't. Let Susan do it." But he begged, "No, Mommy, I want you to do it," and she repeated, "No, I can't." When Frankie started to walk away she asked me, "Would you please put on his shoe?" So I did.

After a while Frankie came in again, crying that his little friend had taken his toy, and his mother told him to go tell his father. Mr. Keen said, "You just go fight your own battles," so Frankie left.

Mr. Keen had spanked Frankie again for something I can't remember. He had spanked him hard and now went into the boys' room (where Paul was watching a TV program) and spanked Frankie again, so that by bedtime the boy was screaming. The boys started to get ready for bed about seven forty-five. They always go to bed about eight, though Mr. Keen has protested several times that it is too early. When I went to say good-bye to them, the boys were in bed and Frankie was still screaming, and crying for his mother. She sat in the living room with the baby and did not move.

This is a family in which, it seems, everyone is always separated from everyone else. After dinner Paul shuts himself in the boys' room with the TV set his grandmother gave him; Mr. and Mrs. Keen don't stay together very long in the living room: he usually goes into the kitchen when she comes into the living room to give the baby the bottle; and Frankie is in and out all the time. Because of their shifting around it's difficult to keep track of their movements.

The Keen Household Some Weeks Later

I arrived Saturday morning at ten o'clock and rang the doorbell. Mr. Keen called from inside, "Come on in!" and I saw him sagged in a comfortable chair in the living room near Carol's playpen, where, I noticed, there was a new pad. Though Mrs. Keen was now in the hospital, the living room was clean.

Carol didn't look very happy. When Frankie and Paul came in I saw at once the striking change in Frankie: he was much paler and had rings under his eyes. Paul didn't look happy either—he barely smiled and looked at me out of the corner of his eye. Frankie had lost some of his summer tan and wasn't nearly as peppy as he had been when I had visited with them a few weeks earlier, though he did smile when he saw me.

[Pretty soon Susan and the kids began to play, and they were still at it when Mr. Keen announced lunch.]

Mr. Keen called from the kitchen, "Come on, you-all!" so I said to Frankie and Paul, "Let's put away the game." When he called us again, I told the boys we could wait until after lunch to clear the game off the floor.

Paul and I went in first and Mr. Keen asked us to sit down. Meanwhile Frankie, who was still in the living room, called me a few times and his father kept telling him to come out.

Mr. Keen had set the table with paper plates and there was a hamburger on a slice of white bread on each, a second slice to make a sandwich, and some crackers. To the left of each plate was a bowl of soup and in the center of the table was a plate with some more hamburgers.

Mr. Keen asked me whether I wanted soda or beer, and I said soda would be just fine. When Paul got up and went into the living room his father, who was a little irritated by this time, said, "Come on and eat right now."

We all started to eat. Frankie sat in the highchair, eating very slowly. He took a few spoonfuls of soup and his father said, "Now, don't you touch your soda until you eat all your food." He told me that if Frankie drinks soda he won't eat. Frankie sat there pouting while Paul ate everything, and Mr. Keen, calling Frankie's attention to it, said Paul would get a star. When Mrs. Keen's mother stayed with them she gave a star to whoever ate his dinner. Mr. Keen urged Frankie to eat if he wanted a star now. Frankie took a few more mouthfuls of soup but continued to pout and refused to eat until his father said, "All right, do you want to go to your room?" Of course, Frankie didn't want to go, but a few minutes later Mr. Keen abruptly turned the highchair around and said, "All right, go to your room!" Frankie uttered a horrible scream and ran to his room. Meanwhile Paul was eating and called his stepfather's attention to the fact and Mr. Keen said, "I see, I see." After a while he called Frankie back. Frankie came in, saw there was a little soup in the bottom of my bowl and said I hadn't finished my soup, but his father said, "Yes, she has." When Paul finished he remarked that he had eaten all his food.

Mr. Keen got up and started to clear the table. All this time Carol was in her playpen in the living room and you could hear her gurgling.

While Frankie was in his room, Paul had said, "I wonder how Mom is feeling," and Mr. Keen passed this off with "I guess she's feeling all right." Then Paul remarked that everyone in the family except his mother has brown eyes and hers are blue, and he pointed out that mine are blue too.

The Relationship between Mr. and Mrs. Keen

The Iron Ring of Negation

I have given this section the subtitle above because iron symbolizes the unbreakable and because, in writing about warfare, writers speak of "closing the iron ring" on the enemy, implying his destruction. The relationship between Mr. and Mrs. Keen gives me this feeling. Negation involves denial, contradiction and cancellation—blotting out. So by "The Iron Ring of Negation" I mean to suggest that in this relationship someone is inexorably blotting out an enemy. Let us consider the transcripts from the observer's first visit.

(Second day.) I went into the kitchen and sat down at the table with Mr. and Mrs. Keen. She was reading the paper, stopping at the ads, while he was going over some insurance papers and bank statements. She came across a picture of a plastic swimming pool and exclaimed, "Oh, look, Bob, here's a swimming pool!" and he said, "Those are no good—you go right through the plastic bottom." She said, "But look at them!" and he answered, in a very irritated voice, "I *know;* they're no good." She went on and saw some shirts advertised on sale and said, "Oh, look, Bob, some shirts on sale—five for four dollars," and he said, "So what do I want to do with them?" She told him, "I thought you wanted a shirt," and he said, "I've got more than I can wear now." She continued to leaf through the newspaper and saw some pictures of women with fancy hairdos, and asked me if I had ever thought of getting a wig. I told her I had, and she said her husband had thought about getting her one but decided against it. He flatly denied it, but she insisted, "Oh yes, you did; oh yes, you did." He said, "I did not. What you really ought to have is a mask," and her reply was, "Why would I want a mask?"

A gradual change came over Mrs. Keen; she lost most of her irritability and nervousness and was joking with her husband; she seemed to enjoy this sarcastic banter. She giggled and seemed to become younger; at one point her chin was resting on the table and she acted girlish. "You said you were going to get a Negro girl," she teased him, and he answered, "Maybe I will." She said, "Well, go ahead—maybe you can beat her on the head and get some money."

Then he asked her, "What have you done all day? Nothing!" She looked at me and said, "See what I mean?" She had told me he would come home and say just that. He glanced around and saw the roses she had cut [on cutting the roses, Mrs. Keen expressed anxiety that he would complain because she had cut them] and said, "Who cut the roses?" When she answered, "I did," he asked, "What did you cut the buds for?"

She asked him if he wanted a divorce and he said, "Go ahead and file." They began to argue about who would take the children; he said he would and she said she was the one who bore them. He asked her how she would take care of them and she said, "Oh, you'd be surprised." She insisted that she wanted Carol.

Frankie came in and she remarked how cute he was. Her husband asked me if I was married and when I said no, he told me, "Take my advice, don't get married." He said I ought to eat crackers because I was too skinny, and his wife said she wished she were as thin as I. (Of course, Mrs. Keen was pregnant at the time.) Then he said to her, "But you know where all the fat is, don't you?" and gestured toward his head. She said, "Yes, but you *love* it."

The boys were watching television. Carol started to cry, so her mother gave her the bottle. The boys were pretty rowdy now and Mr. Keen thought they ought to stay up later but his wife said no, they needed to go to bed. She got them ready, yelling at them as usual, while her husband dandled Carol on his knee. Then she yelled at him as she was getting the baby ready, "Why aren't you going out? Why is this Friday night different from any other Friday night; you always go out on Friday night, why not tonight?"

They also fought about what she should wear the next evening [they were going out to a tavern to celebrate their anniversary]. He didn't want her to wear a certain dress because, he said, she looked like a blimp in it: "They might launch you tomorrow." Then she said she wouldn't wear a certain suit. The night was filled with bickering. It had lost its playfulness, and neither of them seemed amused any more. Finally he said, "I really don't care what you wear; wear whatever you want tomorrow night." To her sarcastic "It wouldn't matter to me if you did care," he retorted "That's what I thought—that's why I said it." At this point I got ready to leave. But just before I left, Mr. Keen said he was going out, and his wife said, "Well, go ahead."

(Third day.) Mrs. Keen said she didn't like Frankie's shoes—they were cheap and cost only $4, and the others she had gotten him were $7. Her husband looked at me and said caustically, "That makes sense—you pay four dollars at one place where you've paid seven dollars before, so they're cheaper." * This is what he tends to do—make sarcastic comments to me about his wife. Sometimes he uses the third person, making it sound as if that is the way *she* thinks.

They had been quarreling all morning long—there wasn't a moment when they weren't at each other's throats. They argued about the anniversary present for Mrs. Keen and about a frame she wanted for Frankie's picture. It was constant bickering without letup. She complained about the fact that she never went out but that he went out all the time. He said she complained all the time. He said she was nuts and she said he was. I went into the bedroom to take a nap and through the door I could hear them arguing. She asked him if he would take her out and he kept saying, "Where do you want to go? Just tell me where you want to go." I couldn't tell, from the way she talked, whether she really wanted to go out. Then I began to think about the fact that she hadn't left the house while I was there; I think the farthest she ever got was halfway down their yard to call to her neighbor, who was sitting on the porch. He kept saying, "Where do you want to go?" and she kept yelling, "You always go out." He said he would take her and the kids but that right now he wanted to wait until the beef stew [he was cooking] was done. Finally he said he'd turn off the gas and take her out.

More bickering occurred at lunch, and when Mr. Keen went into the living room his wife walked in and out of there eight or nine times to tell him, "Just go and do what you have to do; just go on and do it; just get out of here," and he kept saying things like "I don't have anything to do."

There was a question of a barbecue pit. He had thought of buying one and then decided against it, and thought he would borrow his sister's. For some reason his wife didn't like the idea and told him, "Just go out and buy one." He said something about getting it at a discount, and she said, "Just go out and get it," and he said, "Do you want to go? I said I would take you." At last he stomped off to the bathroom, saying, "I never saw a bigger nag than you."

I asked Mrs. Keen how fights like this get started, and she said they really aren't fights, just disagreements, and that she wasn't going to let any man get the better of her: "He's always going out and I don't think that's right."

Mrs. Keen then fed the baby, giving her alternately spoonfuls of peas and plums. The baby gagged and spat out the food. Once she jerked her hand and made her mother spill some of the food and Mrs. Keen said, "Now, don't do that!" and hit her, making her cry.

Mr. Keen said he wanted to go to see his mother and they began bickering about that. Mrs. Keen said she didn't owe that woman anything and why didn't he go tonight instead of tomorrow, because she didn't want to go, especially "when she sends spies to spy on me at school when I have Frankie and Paul with me, or at the picnic. I don't need those spies. I don't need anything to do with anybody like that." Mr. Keen left the room and I asked what picnic and what spies, but she didn't respond. After a while she repeated she didn't want anything

---

* Susan says about this exchange that she thinks Mrs. Keen was emphasizing the cheapness of the quality, and her husband was thinking only about the difference in price.

to do with that woman. Apparently someone who saw the kids at a school picnic had told Mr. Keen's mother they had acted up, and she repeated it to her daughter-in-law. Mrs. Keen said to me that kids usually run wild at picnics and that she didn't need anybody spying around. She said this emphatically, looking squarely at me.

(Tonight is the Keens' anniversary and they are going out.) Mrs. Keen was all dressed up: high heels, make-up, lipstick and the cheap earrings her husband had brought her in a paper bag. She looked really attractive. She opened the door and her husband said, "Don't do that, Alice, you'll let in the bugs." This reminded me that when he had gone into the kitchen after dinner for a cup of coffee, he said, "Look at all those crumbs under the table. Did you sweep the floor?" She said yes, and he told her, "Give me the broom and I'll do it. You know what happens if they are left down there for a long time."

Out of the blue Mrs. Keen's mother (who had come over to baby-sit) said when we were all in the living room, "Did you hear about the fourteen-year-old girl who sucks her thumb?" Mrs. Keen and I had seen the article in the paper and had been talking about it. Mr. Keen said, "That's the third time I've heard about it today," and his wife remarked, "You know, they say thumb-sucking comes from emotional problems." (The day before, she had said it comes from insecurity.) Mr. Keen replied, "Well, I don't know anything about it, Alice." She said, "Maybe that baby [Carol] has emotional problems," and he said, "Maybe you have emotional problems."

(Fourth day.) A couple of times Mrs. Keen announced that she was going to bed but she stayed around. Finally she stood up and said she was going to bed, so, as usual, I phoned for a cab to take me home. I thanked them for a nice day and Mr. Keen said he didn't think it had been very nice, adding, "We'll go for a ride or something tomorrow." Then Mrs. Keen said, "I'm not going; you go where you want," and started to berate him ("He tells me I'm nuts and I tell him he's nuts. I don't have to take that"). I asked her if she felt nuts and she said no, and her husband kept saying, "Why don't you tell her the whole story?" I asked, "What's the whole story?" but the taxi came and I left.*

On whom is the iron ring closing, and who is closing it? Who are the enemies, and *are* there enemies? Since it was Mrs. Keen who broke down, the ring closed on her, it seems. Yet, if she had not become so ill, all we could say would be that existence had dealt with both of them so badly that they could only express obsessively the negative component of it, and that the iron ring was the circle of *mutual* attack.

Since this is like an ancient tragedy, in which actors express the pathos† of the characters, I imagine two Greek choruses: Chorus One, articulating mellowed experience and strong sympathy for the wife, and Chorus Two, symbolizing inexperience and siding with the husband. In the following verses they present two opposing views of the case. During the debate the

* Researchers' subordination to time and money—even when they know there is money to back them up at every point—has killed many an important research opportunity. Susan could have given the driver a dollar—or even two!—for his trouble, and called another cab later. The Keens were usually all in bed by ten o'clock or sooner. Susan is extremely intelligent and quite beyond belief in her commitment to the research. Yet even she was trapped by the delusion of the inevitability of time!

† *Pathos,* as I understand it, is the inner expression of one's fate. In this sense, the *pathos* of Clytemnestra was hatred of Agamemnon, sorrow and despair over the death of her daughter Iphigenia, love of Aegisthus, jealousy and hatred of Cassandra, and determination to kill Agamemnon—a horrid mixture of emotions that constituted her essence and drove her to her fate.

choruses sometimes become angry with each other, self-contradictory and even insulting—showing how even "sane" people can become vague and angry. As the argument wears on they repeat themselves and sometimes even seem to switch sides—another characteristic of "normals" in heated arguments.

First Chorus

Since he's a man of little education,
Inclined to strike back hard at what annoys him,
Why should he be much different with his wife?
You really think that he could see the harm,
Where others, so much smarter, never have?
If he's like me—brought up in city slums,
And taught to teach her fellows with her claws—
It ought to take him many years to learn
That there are other ways to manage what
You happen not to like in people close
To you. Besides, the man has troubles
Of his own. Perhaps a dreadful infancy,
A childhood even worse; and treated with
Contempt. He broods about this bickering,
But there is nothing he can do. He knows,
And so does she, that they are making life
Unbearable—not only for themselves
But for the children too. Does tenderness
Come naturally?

Second Chorus

I think it does. All men
And women have an inborn need to get
And give solicitude and tenderness,
But it requires nurture in the home.
But then . . .

First Chorus

But then if some are pushed aside
And do not get that nurture, tenderness
Will be impossible for them—to give or to
Receive. They're beaten things—half rage, half fear,
Distrusting even—mostly!—those most close
To them. Stretch out your hand and touch them once—
They look at you, suspicion in their eyes.

Second Chorus

You mean they even might reject all signs
Of tenderness? That's horrible! You make them seem
Like porcupines or frightened cats with fur
On end, with legs drawn up and arched back.
But how explain the courtship—married for
Some years, two children, and she's pregnant now,

If there is nothing in their lives but hate
And fear?

FIRST CHORUS

Did I say nothing else? There still
Is hope in them, I think, that they will get
Some tenderness from someone, who might, through
A miracle—and that is what they want—
Revive, make real again, the distant time
When they received that modicum of care,
Of watchfulness, which, throughout history,
Has kept the race alive.

SECOND CHORUS

They live on hope?

FIRST CHORUS

I think that's what I mean. It seems to me
That every marriage is a hope, and each
Successive child regenerates the hope.
George Hegel said that history
Is spirit emptied into time, and I
Believe that marriage is the infant's hope
Externalized and emptied into someone else—
I mean, of course, the infant hoping in
The adult memory: and if you cannot feel
The other person's hope, you are divorced
Without a writ.

SECOND CHORUS

Such elevated thoughts!

FIRST CHORUS

We've gotten far away from Mr. Keen
Who seems to me inhuman—or shall I say
Insensitive? The word's too weak for him,
And has a suffocating bourgeois smell;
It covers up, like many bourgeois terms,
An older, killing trait—it's *cruelty*.
I think that Mr. Keen is cruel. He cuts
His wife, who holds herself together by
Sheer will, who's only fighting to stay sane,
To shreds. Bob ridicules his wife in front
Of Susan, he does not spare his sarcasm,
He tries to make a fool of her. He "turns
Her on." What else? He is without remorse;
He cannot let her just blow off, although
He clearly feels that he's the stronger of
The two—not "nuts." He wraps the ragged,

Stinking, filthy, vermin-covered cloak
Of sanity around himself and puts
Her down, when he should hold her up. His wife's
An individual who cannot weep
But fights instead. You know, some fight when they
Should weep; some weep when they should fight; and some
Stay silent. But who do you think could move
That Calaban? Tears do not stir this man:
When Carol cries he says she's doing it
On purpose! What perfect irony it is
To hear him say he fights because when she
Fights back it helps preserve her sanity!
I really think that she is such a threat
To him, he cannot feel compassion, for
He feels so weak himself: "There by the grace
Of God go I!" Perhaps he wants to rid
Himself of her. It almost seems as if
He wants to drive her mad—a horrible idea.
How else do you explain the fact that Mr. Keen
Calls Alice "nuts," "disturbed," and tells her she
Has fat between the ears? What did he have in mind
The time he pointed out Mount Rose—so far
Away, it took, I think, a really grim
Determination to imagine it
Was there.

SECOND CHORUS

You have such horrible ideas
I think you'd better keep them to yourself.
They're wrong and only do a person harm.
And who could stand that constant badgering
From such a nagging wife?

FIRST CHORUS

He only makes
Her worse by hitting back; and she's the sick
One. She deserves consideration; she
Has broken twice and has the children to
Take care of all day long. Suppose she breaks
Again—what then? They'll take her, and the kids
Will suffer more than anyone. You know,
A mother may look terrible to us,
But to the kids—well, she is all they have.
Her husband is without compassion; no
Capacity to feel, no self-control.
He's like a child: when angry, he lets fly.

SECOND CHORUS

But who could live with such a shrew? You think
He's superhuman? He is just a man—
A high school education's all he's had,
And all he knows, outside the streets and bars,

Is factories, machines and punching time.
So what do you expect—a paragon
Of "virtues middle class?" Who has them? Not
The middle class! They write them down and try
To make the virtues they don't have, but wish
They did, a guidance clinic Testament!
Believe me, only St. Elizabeth
Could stand her—it's an ancient loony bin
In Washington, where she has never been.

First Chorus

You simply show yourself insensitive
As Bob. No jokes! It's people like yourself
Who laugh in psychiatric rounds; who in
The eighteenth century paid a franc
To see the miserable lunatics
Exhibited. I could not live with such
A man. Could you, and keep your sanity?
But on the other hand, it seems to me
He's just like everybody else: he makes
Her mad and treats her with contempt because
She's mad.

Second Chorus

       Such unremitting bickering
Goes on in many homes: since love has gone
The man and wife express their discontent
Obsessively by senseless quarreling.
Why blame it all on Bob? She probably
Was pretty sick before he married her . . .

First Chorus

In other words, he merely finished her!

Second Chorus

. . . She spanks the baby when she cannot eat!
Well, only lunatics and bitches do
That to a helpless babe.

First Chorus

       If you had such
A husband you would do the same. Naïve!
You simply do not know, have no idea
Of what it is to live with such a man.

Second Chorus

Though I am inexperienced, I know
When married to a certain kind of wife,
A man's a certain kind of man. His wife's
What makes him. Do you know what Mr. Keen
Would be if Alice were a different kind

Of wife? She's mad, she's always been insane
Or getting ready to go mad. She's no
Fit company for any man.

First Chorus

And you—
Who are not married, never nursed a babe
Yet rattle on as if you understood—
How do you know what Alice might have been?
When married to a certain kind of man,
A woman is a certain kind of wife.
I've read how husbands keep their sanity
By driving wife and children mad.
Insanity is not a thing, wrapped up
Inside of people's heads, just waiting to
Come out. There's absolutely nothing known
About the men and women saved by love—
Men and women who, depressed, confused,
Lashed out and hurt those close to them, but who,
Nevertheless, because the others loved
Them and could understand their suffering,
Were helped—reclaimed. The very ones they seemed
To hurt, embraced them warmly, held them close,
Explained, endured and felt no rancor—just
Perplexity and yearning. I believe
That all you need to save a mind is love,
Intelligence and skilled advice . . .

Second Chorus

That's fine!
Saints and philosophers, or men who are
Saints and philosophers rolled into one,
Might help a child like Mrs. Keen. I hope
Someday I'll have the luck to find a man
Like that—I hope that every woman will!

Like any two people who disagree over an important issue about which they feel strongly, the choruses repeat themselves and are sometimes contemptuous of each other. But the Keens argue and are contemptuous mostly over *nothing:* or rather, over what is nothing on the surface but which goes back to the unspoken fact that they cannot satisfy each other. Even when there does seem to be an issue between them, one has the feeling that the argument is not about that but about the lack of mutual satisfaction in their lives. Paradoxically, then, their fighting is about their basic *agreement*— that they get little from each other. The iron ring tightens around both of them, closed by their own hands; and since Alice broke under the pressure, she must be the weaker. It follows that had Bob been a different kind of man, she would have become a different woman.* Perhaps if they had had a trained therapeutic visitor for some time, they might have been saved.

---

* Obviously this argument is not intended for those who believe psychosis to be genetically determined; nor is the entire book, for that matter. Those who believe disturbance to be of biological origin are exempt from the duty of understanding it.

There has never been a culture without hostility, nor one in which all husbands and wives satisfied each other's emotional needs, but outside the "high" cultures of East and West, husband and wife are not so imprisoned with each other. If, as in many tribal cultures, Mrs. Keen could have made her own living without much trouble, or have left her husband and been readily cared for by her own family; if she could have taken lovers and if her husband could have had several wives at once, matters would not have been so desperate for Mr. and Mrs. Keen. If everything she wanted, from love to a wading pool, had not depended on her husband alone; and if, with several wives, he had not had to come home to the same one every day, much of the stress would have been removed from their lives. Human culture has often permitted the potentiality for love in man and woman to die; to die quietly, on the whole, because it was not overly aroused. But our culture, having aroused the need and hope of love, has shut men and women up with each other—with the breath of hell outside, compelled them to seek love from each other and made it difficult to separate when the hope was lost and the need unsatisfied. In our culture there is either love or negation, or an alternation between the two; but negation with *no exit* is madness—is hell, as Sartre dramatized. When two people compulsively cancel what they both seek* in the very act of seeking it, they are as good as mad, even if only one of them becomes "officially" so. There are many occasions when, though Mr. and Mrs. Keen reach out toward each other, one of them is rebuffed: when she asks him what she should wear on their anniversary night, or, as we shall see later, when he is "in one of his lovey-dovey moods," when she is playfully badgering him as he reads the paper, and so on. But these gropings are canceled into bitterness by the bitterness in each of them.

An American Working-Class Tragedy?

> "He looks like he'd do what he wanted to do."
> —From *Workingman's Wife*†

Since some of the characteristics of the relationship between Mr. and Mrs. Keen may come from the fact that they are of the working class, I give below material from *Workingman's Wife*‡ that seems to bear on the issue.

> . . . the woman is deeply uncertain of her "place" in the husband's life . . .
> Yet these women frequently feel isolated from their husbands . . . and retain lingering doubts as to their "hold" on their husbands' affections. They frequently appear afraid to act openly in a fashion contrary to their husbands' wishes, lest a permanent alienation of affections results.
> The working-class woman sees men as dominant and controlling. . . .

---

* As in Samuel Beckett's *Waiting for Godot,* for example.

† Response to one of the famous Thematic Apperception Test (TAT) pictures. Rainwater, et al., *op. cit.,* p. 79.

‡ These quotes are from Chapter IV, pp. 77–88.

She is hopeful that her . . . husband will be benign toward her, but she counts it as a blessing rather than her natural right when he is. She is grateful when she has such a husband, and she often does, for not every working-class husband is as assertive as his wife's preconceived image would have him. Her expectation, nonetheless, is that men are likely to be controlling in ways that may hurt her. She is inclined to see them as insensitive and inconsiderate, sometimes teasing, sometimes accusing, sometimes vulgar, and always potentially withholding affection.

[From a wife's response to a TAT picture]: "The third guy is the one she thinks most about; [he] asks her opinion. She loves him."

It is also clear [from the responses to the same TAT picture] that one cannot expect much from most men. The storyteller is quite content that she finds a man who asks her opinion.

To a picture showing a woman's head against a man's shoulder, we find some stories that indicate expectations along this line [of response to her needs and wishes]:

"Looks to me like he's tender and loving, which is something unusual for a man. Looks like a nice way to comfort one another."

"Tenderness, care, affection are exceptions . . ."

She seems unable to free herself altogether from the view that men are quite independent and can easily leave.

[And from a TAT picture]:

"Looks like she is trying to explain something to him. He doesn't want to listen to it. That's all."

"He looks like he'd do what he wanted to do."

The sense of inferiority to the male is marked. . . . No real independence of action is attributed to the female. The man has the strength and the control over the situation.

The working-class woman feels that she has to put up with brusqueness and inconsiderateness. Sometimes she also feels that she has to accept rough behavior from her man in order to hold on to him.

The actual frequency of such behavior cannot be judged. What is important . . . is that these women anticipate its possibility.

The working-class woman feels her relationship to her husband is subject, or at least potentially vulnerable, to great ups and downs. Her own feelings are unpredictable; men are unpredictable. She believes that husbands usually do not want to feel that they are at all controlled by women, particularly by their wives. . . . Men are seen as self-seeking and pretty much able to have their own way.

Despite such problems with the husband, he means a great deal to her. Most often, she would like to have more contact with him rather than less. . . . She may be somewhat resigned to, but she is not pleased with, the extent to which he can move out of range of her. Still, her own capacity for intimacy . . . is not great. What she wants is to have him around more and show interest in her, rather than any more intensely emotional relationship.

These women show a great deal of anxiety about their acceptability to men, and a tendency to feel they must give in, or at least not respond assertively if they are to have a chance with the man they want. At a very deep level assertiveness signifies to them alienation from men, and thereby loneliness. . . . She feels that men as a group cannot be stood up to, and the necessity to do so in the give-and-take of marriage is a tense business because of this.

[Since the wife is isolated and has few outside interests, she is] excessively dependent on her husband for contact and attention, and has a fairly steady sense of frustration and disappointment because his interests are such that he does not provide these.

Submissiveness is another way working-class wives deal with their husbands. Where the wife does try to get closer to her husband and his activities, she usually does it in a submissive way. That is, she simply goes along with him, doing what he wants to do, or often simply watching him do what interests him.

Mrs. Keen is very assertive, and if it is true that the way to get along with a working-class man is to "give in" and be "submissive," then she does not handle her husband right. She seems to have a predisposition to breakdown —stemming, probably, from a difficult childhood, yet she is unable to do the very thing she needs to do to prevent breakdown—not to fight it out with her husband "at the drop of a word," not to make her life a prize ring. In her compulsion to fight back, to let practically nothing pass and even to start fights, she does everything that is likely to

make her *place* in her husband's life uncertain;

feel *isolated* from her husband and unsure of her *hold* on him;

render her husband anything but *benign;*

provoke her husband to *hurt* her;

render her husband *insensitive* and *inconsiderate;*

diminish his *tenderness* and *affection;* etc.

As we see him today, Mr. Keen actually has all the negatives that working-class women expect in a man, and his wife hurls herself against them until she breaks. She would rather go mad than let any man get the better of her; yet she is so pathetically weak that she might be better off submitting.

Mrs. Keen just seems to get more and more into herself. She dresses sloppily most of the time. Her hair looks uncombed and her face wan and bedraggled.

Mrs. Keen seems to need lots of reassurance, which she does not get from her husband. He is very callous to her and acts as though it's all he can do to *bear* her presence.

.   .   .

I thought about how Mr. Keen orders her to do things, like getting napkins for the table and telling her to do this and do that, and how she depends so much on him for direction. Then it began to strike me how much support she needs. She often asked me what I thought about this; if I liked that; how I cleaned my floors, if I vacuumed my hardwood floors. She asked me what kinds of skirts I wear, what detergent I use, if I do a lot of cooking and if I like to cook.

Mr. Keen is troubled by their constant fighting and ponders what to do to help his wife; yet even as he talks to the observer about her problems, he talks down to his wife and hurts her feelings in other ways. He does not talk about changing himself. Meanwhile their difficulties are increased by Mrs. Keen's confusion, but this might be a consequence of the unrelieved tension in the home.*

* I do not overlook the following explanation of their difficulties: she is "paranoid," distrusts her husband and accuses him when he is innocent. He hits back and gets her upset, and the vicious circle is on its way.

(Third day.) Mr. Keen said to me, in his wife's presence, "I don't know what it is, but we just don't get along." I asked, "You and Mrs. Keen?" and he answered, "Yes—we have different views about things." He said she didn't like to go out with him. She had thought of joining the Ladies' Aid but had wanted him to join the church ushers. Meanwhile she was saying things like "You're always going out," and he responded that he considered going to a union meeting a night out. She replied, "I'm just not going to have it," and "It's not going to be that way." Her husband said repeatedly that she'd say she wanted to go out, but whenever he asked her where she wanted to go she couldn't tell him.

I asked her what she would like to do and she answered that she would like to have a new house. Then he said she didn't realize that you have to pay a real estate company when you sell the house and might lose some of the money you paid out on it. She didn't say much to that. When I asked her if she really liked to go out, I got an evasive answer. I also asked if there was something she didn't like about going out.

When Mr. Keen said he had encouraged her to take a sewing course, a discussion started about his mother. He said his wife didn't like needlepoint or anything like that, because his mother did it. He could understand why someone might not want to do needlepoint because it was old-fashioned and did take a long time, but his mother could do it and watch TV at the same time because she had been doing needlepoint for years and years.

He got on the subject of material goods and said his wife was more interested in material goods than he. He began to talk about religion, saying he had gone to religious schools and hated it: the rich kids got good grades and nobody cared about the poor. He said he had wanted Paul to go to some church instructional function. They had a beautiful school and everything, and they sent him a letter telling him it was his duty to get his child enrolled, but when he told them Paul was in "special education" [education for below-average children] he never heard from them again. They stand up in the pulpit, he said, and say all those gorgeous things, but nothing happens. Churches are a bunch of show.

[Mr. Keen gave an acute and very bitter analysis of the behavior of organized religion. Then he said] he thought his wife needed education and that highly educated people, like great scientists, don't believe in God. He wondered about the phrase "God is dead," and said he sometimes thinks he really is. This disturbed his wife, who said, "You're not going to start that again, are you?" I asked her how she felt when she heard it and whether she thought that God was dead, and she said she didn't know but that "as long as He puts food on my table I think He's alive," and she repeated it several times.

Once during this conversation she got very giggly and the bickering became less caustic.

Mr. Keen said his wife was searching for her youth again and that's why she was interested in material goods. She said she did feel young and that she is young. I asked her how old she felt and she started giggling again and said fifteen. I asked if it felt good to be fifteen and she said it did. Then I asked what she was doing when she was fifteen—if she was in school—and she said she was working.

[There is a long discussion about their bad experiences with counseling, and Mr. Keen turned the discussion to Paul and the Institute.] I asked him why they had gone to the Counseling Institute and he said, "Oh, it was her idea—she just wouldn't accept the fact that Paul is retarded," and she said yes. I noticed that while he was going on this way and when she said yes, she was looking down at the table. She didn't look at me or at her husband very much. It seemed to me, however, that she had calmed down a little bit, because at the beginning of the discussion she had taken a knife and was picking dirt out of the crack in the table, and he said several times, "Do you have to do that now?"

I mentioned the clay figure I had seen, which she had made in the hospital, and asked her if she had ever thought of going on with work like that, and Mr. Keen said, "I should think the figure would be a reminder that you didn't want to go back in the hospital." Then he added, "You did do some painting," and she laughed and said, "I did not," and he said, "Yes, you did."

A couple of times he would say things like "I'm not perfect but you've got to face up to reality, and she just doesn't want to do that." I asked him what he thought she did all day and he said, "I know she cleans the house but she talks on the phone and listens to all her silly girl friends' talk." He said she accepted as fact whatever her girl friends told her.

I asked Mrs. Keen if she felt that the problem of the arguments was the problem of both of them or whether one person was always responsible, and she said "Both" right away; but he said to her, "Now *listen* to what she's asking you; just listen."

Mr. Keen discusses his wife with the observer as an insensitive parent might discuss his child in front of the child's teacher: he refers to her while she mostly listens in silence. He offends her religious feelings and hurts her by the way he talks about Paul—as if he were her child, not his; as if he had never developed fatherly feelings for the boy. I do not understand why Mr. Keen makes constant references to "going out," but it is obviously a problem he is unable to solve. Since Mrs. Keen is unable to tell him where she wants to go when he asks her, one would think that if he really wanted to go out with her, he would have experimented with ideas himself, but none appear in the notes. When he really wants to go, as on the day they took the bewildering drive to the river, he goes. The following suggests that he really does not want to take her out:

(Fourth day.) When I came into the kitchen, Mrs. Keen asked me if I had heard them fighting. She had gone into the yard, where her husband was barbecuing, and I had heard them yelling but couldn't make out what they said. Mrs. Keen told me she had asked to go to a drive-in movie—but what she said wasn't entirely clear. It seemed, however, that he didn't want to go.

Even in talking about needlepoint, Mr. Keen is negative to his wife, for he describes what an expert his mother is. Whatever he touches on is a negation of his wife: she doesn't understand about his union meetings or about what is involved in buying a new house; his mother is great at needlepoint but his wife can't do it at all; churches are fake and God is dead; Paul, *her* child, is retarded; she should stop picking at the table; she doesn't face reality, he does. He even tells her to listen to the observer, as if she were incapable of listening herself. In a moment of apparent sensitivity he says, when the observer mentions the clay figure, that working on that sort of thing might remind his wife of the mental hospital; yet that's hardly enough when we consider that he keeps calling her "nuts," reminds her of her psychosis by pointing out Mount Rose Hospital during the outing, and when he engages in discussions like the following:

(Seventh day. Mrs. Keen and the observer are talking about her stay at the hospital when she had Carol.) She said she had wanted to stay a week but had remained only five days. Mr. Keen thought she was talking about her stay at

Mount Rose, so they got into an argument because he could not understand why she would have wanted to stay a week. He said that he had worked sixteen-hour shifts but that the money was going out as fast as it was coming in to pay for her hospital bills.

They got into a discussion of Mrs. Keen's hospitalization for her nervous breakdown, and he talked at length about how much the shock treatments had cost. Although she tried to get a word in a number of times, he kept interrupting her and monopolized the conversation. Then she talked about a friend of hers who had had a shock treatment, had gotten some kind of shot beforehand and keeled over. She said she herself had been frightened at the first one she had. They couldn't find the mouthpiece; she got scared and thought it was the end of the world. I asked what shock did and he said, "They make you so you can't remember. Sometimes you remember most of it afterwards." He said over and over again that she didn't remember. When she said, "I remember how scared I was at that first shock treatment," he told her, "Oh, you don't remember." . . . He said that when she was in the hospital she would say things like the lady next to her was a spy. He said that when he took her out of the first hospital, because she got worse, she said people were following her. . . . She said she got scared when they took her into that room for the treatments. . . .

As he talked about her notion that people were spying on her, he laughed. I didn't laugh, and he said, "It's not really funny, but when you get to thinking about it, it's funny." In general, he seemed very callous about the whole situation—unempathic, to say the least. He seemed more worried about his own position than about his wife's.

At one point she asked him whether he could have stood the shock treatments —that he couldn't. But he said, "Oh yes, yes," very sarcastically. He often speaks to her this way, and "Oh yes, yes" is a common expression of his.

He said to me that he had told his wife to send their curtains to the cleaner's but she had put them in the washing machine. He said the curtains tore to shreds in the washer and that she had cried a lot about this. He said he could explain it better because she didn't remember, and that I had to understand his position.

Mr. Keen feels no sympathy or sorrow for his wife, just resentment tempered by ridicule, and he pushes her back toward illness again by humiliation, by reminding her of how much she cost him, of her symptoms, of her incompetence and of her forgetfulness. He dominates: *he* tells what happened; electroshock wasn't his wife's experience because she can't remember it; what matters is what he has to say about her experience. He implies that if the observer wants to know the facts, she should listen to him.

As for electroshock, the busy private practitioner or the harassed resident often give many shock treatments in a morning—seriatim. Patients may be quite fearful, but frequently there is little time to calm their fears. Often the regular "shock team" of nurses, attendants and administering physician is suddenly incomplete because somebody is absent, and the team has to find a substitute in a hurry. The patient is placed in the apparatus, the electrodes are attached to him, and the mouthpiece—to prevent his biting his tongue during the electroconvulsion—is inserted. The patient is supposed to have amnesia for the actual shock, but entrance into the situation is frightening, and for some it is terrifying. Even in the "best" hospitals there may be no psychological preparation of the patient at all, if for no other reason than that the hospital is understaffed, and even when an attempt is made to prepare the patient psychologically, he may be so confused that he cannot understand. Emergence from shock is *the* time when maximum loving care must be given. I have seen nurses tenderly feeding patients who have had "their morning shock," but I have also seen patients wander terrified in the corridors, not knowing where they are. Even in the "best" hospitals the nurses may be so busy with other things—like charting, preparing medications, getting patients to x-ray, and so on, that there is no time for the patient. When the supervisor comes around she can tell whether the place is clean and the charts are filled out, but she cannot count how many patients have received tender care. I have seen patients remember their fear right there in the hospital, and when a patient comes out of his convulsion, the doctor who threw the switch is usually not even there. So I have profound sympathy for Mrs. Keen.

One of the most important "problems" in psychiatry is what happens to a patient when he comes home from the hospital. But it is a problem mainly because no trained person is there to observe him and because often nobody really cares. Nobody would have known what was happening to Mrs. Keen if the observer, a research worker hired by a chance scientist, had not been present. Yet the treatment a patient receives after coming out of the hospital should be more than half the therapy. It takes little psychiatric brains to prescribe shock, but it requires intelligence and feeling to handle a patient after he leaves the hospital. In this "very good" hospital there was no aftercare, so Mrs. Keen was thrown back into the bitter environment that had contributed to her madness in the first place.

Yet, in spite of his callousness Mr. Keen does what many men, with a whole lot more money, might not do for their wives: instead of dumping her in a state institution, he sends her to a private hospital for her breakdown and works sixteen-hour shifts to pay the bills. For her confinement, he also gets her good medical care. He sometimes shows consideration in little things too: he tells her to get out of the sun because he knows it is bad for her; he offers her a snack. On the one hand he tells her to wear her maternity clothes when she comes out of the hospital, but then turns around and buys her a new wardrobe. For their anniversary he takes her out and buys her a pair of inexpensive earrings. There is no evidence in the notes of his wife's ever showing similar consideration for her husband. In discussions of his wife's problems, even when he talks down to her and says things that hurt, he is thinking of ways to help her. It does not seem as if he really wants to get rid of her; he reaches out toward her, in barely discernible ways, and when the chips are down he does for her the best he can. He can get into a "lovey-dovey" mood, but then his wife may turn her back. She has no way of using, for her own salvation, what potentialities her husband has for considerateness. *The greatest problem that confronts all disturbed people is to be able to use the healing properties in those that have contributed to their illness;* yet the dialectic of emotional illness has this very fatality: the person who has fallen ill searches out in others what harms him most, so that in the process of being harmed he is driven away from what is beneficial in the other person. We see that with all his harshness, Mr. Keen is groping for a way out and that he has possibilities for good; yet his wife is unable to use these—indeed, if she could she would not be ill. And that is one of our problems—to be able to show the (labeled) sick person that those who contribute to his illness have good qualities also.

ANALYTICAL SUMMARY

This is an "American working-class tragedy," since it occurred in a working-class family. Yet, although qualities attributed to men by working-class women are evident in Mr. Keen, they might appear in any class. Perhaps this kind of circular, mutual attack without remorse, without insight and without reconciliation occurs more often among people of little education than among the more enlightened strata of our society, but this we will not know until the research is done.

The main outlines of the tragedy are clear, and such misery is tragic even if no one breaks down. Since the Keens cannot satisfy each other's needs, they fight and never seem to make up. They tear at each other constantly and there is no effort at emotional repair. Both are callous and both react violently to provocation. The iron ring is closing on both of them, because they have practically become enemies. For these people, isolated in their little house and its patches of yard and lawn, our form of society provides no escape except divorce.

The greater responsibility is Mr. Keen's, for since his wife has been very seriously ill, it is now up to him to "submit" to her provocations and try to be gentle, but this would be to renounce the very core of himself. Furthermore, to his general dissatisfaction is added the burden of a wife who is "nuts"; and to him, her being "nuts" is not a stimulus to compassion but a further occasion for harshness. Many surveys have shown that the lower the educational level, the more intolerant people are of mental illness. Mr. Keen is not good for his wife once she became ill; in his abuse he attacks her ego—the worst thing he could do.

Finally, I blame our society, which gives practically no education about mental illness, a medical profession that provides inadequate care before and after electroshock, and a system that spends too much on war and not enough on hospitals, while educating its citizens to mercilessness so that they will be impersonally cruel in war. Is it surprising that this cruelty should be turned against the cruel?

Mrs. Keen Feeding her Children

The Parameters of Infancy: Metaphysical or Biometaphysical?

Normally, in our culture, we have a profound empathy for an infant's unutterable helplessness and vulnerability, and because we think of him as weak and dominated by biological urges, we do not attribute calculated motivation to him—he is innocent. Helplessness, vulnerability, weakness, innocence and subjection to overwhelming biological urges are important parameters of our thinking about infants, and they are present in the mind of the average parent in our culture, regardless of what his own baby signifies to him. The *meaning* of a baby to his parents is different in every family, but in the average person—the person not so distorted by inner troubles that his relation to his child is distorted too—the *parameters* are transcendent. The metaphysic that defines infancy in our culture includes also *incomprehension*—the baby doesn't understand; he has a certain, nonstigmatizing, infantile stupidity. Precisely what it is that a baby supposedly does not understand varies from person to person, but in general—and everywhere—people believe that at first a baby cannot understand speech, and then, very gradually, learns to understand a few words. We believe also that an infant does not know our motivations, though we think we understand, more or less, his urges. So, for the first year or less, almost universally, the baby's urges confront adult motivations, and the baby's version of the culture begins to emerge here in the dialectic resolution of the confrontation. Normal parents do not insist that a baby has motivations that must be consonant with the parents' urges, but taking their own overwhelming power into account, allow the baby his urges and try to bring their own motivations into line. Thus we have to add infantile absence of motivation (infantile motivationlessness), incomprehension and impulse domination to the other metaphysical parameters.

The metaphysic that surrounds and defines a baby becomes so much part of our bodies, as well as of our minds, that we are unable to act counter to it, and we are filled with pity, rage and anxiety and even feel sick if we see it violated. On the other hand, perceiving the principles observed, we have a feeling of well-being—as if heaven had affirmed itself: a baby's signs of contentment are the only proof on earth that any metaphysic has any validity at all.

Unlike most metaphysical systems, which do not bother with the human consequences of their principles, the metaphysic of infancy exacts certain behaviors. For example, in dealing with infants, we must hold our own strength in check and use it only for solicitude, and we must be vigilant that the infant not be hurt. Since the baby is dominated by impulse and is innocent, we do not punish him, or as they say at law, we "hold him harmless," for an infant can do no harm and cannot even wish to.* Finally, since infants are relatively inaccessible to speech, we do not talk to them expecting a reply, and since they are uncomprehending, we do not reason with them. Looked at in this way, infancy turns out to be not merely a biological state of the organism but also a biosocial relationship governed by certain principles. These *principles*—which we absorb without knowing it—compel us to perceive infants in a certain way, and, naturally, have the reverse consequence in compelling babies to perceive *us* in a certain way. If we see a mother treat her baby badly, i.e., violate the principles, we think, "What's wrong with her? She cannot understand (perceive) that that baby is utterly helpless," or "She talks to the baby as if he understood her," and so on.

In our culture the metaphysic surrounds and protects the baby, even far

* Other systems challenge this. Certain denominations hold or have held that since the child is born in sin, we must begin very early to extirpate the evil, and psychoanalysis argues that all infants are swept by tornadoes of destructive, cannibalistic, "oral incorporative" drives. Such beliefs prove that our present metaphysic is not biologically determined altogether, that even in the history of our own culture this metaphysic changes—as do all of them—and that even among ourselves one metaphysic may be more compassionate than another.

into childhood, with a vast exemption from accusations and punishments; but the metaphysic is more important still, for it forms, throughout modern culture, a foundation for *general* exemptions and it enters into ethical codes and relationships among all peoples. The metaphysic penetrates international relations also, affecting such notions as "aggression" and "small helpless nations," and is used to justify "foreign aid." What I have called the metaphysic of infancy is, therefore, but a reflection of the multiform legality of states, and thus the claims of infancy rest on the metaphysical foundations of the contemporary world. They are a metaphysic of compassion and even of survival, and whoever violates it attacks underlying principles of our ethical system. This is the reason why, when we perceive a violation of it, it is as if a stone had hit us between the eyes. Let us be clear about this: when we see a mother mistreat her baby, we react—*not only*—because we "identify with" the baby or because we "want to be mothered" or because of our own "oral predispositions," but because—or *also because*—what is being challenged is the ethical foundation of our world.

Helplessness, vulnerability, weakness, innocence, incomprehension and subjection to overwhelming urges seem to inhere in the biology of infancy,* but it does not follow that what looks inherent to us need be accepted by all people, and furthermore, what we dismiss—that the baby is inherently evil or cannibalistic—as improbable may be truth in another people's system. With these considerations in mind, let us study Mrs. Keen feeding Carol.

Feeding Carol

> These women find that "life around little children" is one perpetual battle. . . . And sometimes, "They don't want to eat," so that the mother must "fight" with the children to get them to eat.
>
> —From *Workingman's Wife*

#1

(First day.) Mrs. Keen sat in front of the highchair and forced the food into Carol's mouth, spoonful after spoonful, barely giving the child a chance to swallow. At the end of the feeding, since the mechanism of the tray was broken so that she could not remove it, Mrs. Keen tried to pull Carol out of the chair and seemed upset when the child's foot got caught and the leg got twisted so that it hurt as Mrs. Keen kept pulling, and the baby cried.

#2

She put Carol in the highchair and started to feed her as rapidly as she had before. The baby had a look of dismay on its face but her mother kept feeding her faster and faster: as soon as she took the spoon out of the baby's mouth she put it in again. Toward the end of the feeding the baby began to spit out, and her mother yelled that there was no reason for doing that. Then she forced milk

---

* Throughout history, somewhat the same characteristics have been attributed to women in our culture.

on the baby in a small plastic cup and you could hear her gulping. When the baby sort of choked, Mrs. Keen said, "I bet you think Mother's trying to strangle you," and laughed. Then the baby threw up all over the tray. Mrs. Keen was very upset about the mess on the tray and about the fact that Carol's dress was also a mess. Again she took the baby out of the highchair without moving the tray and the baby's foot got caught again.

Mrs. Keen put Carol on the floor and began wiping up, saying Carol had got the vomit down into the seat of the highchair by the metal rungs where it was hard to clean. This seemed to disturb Mrs. Keen. She took a cold cloth and wiped the vomit off the side of the baby's dress and then let her crawl around on the floor for a while.

#3

Mrs. Keen went and got the baby and brought her back. She hurt her jamming her into the highchair without raising the tray, and the baby cried. She then fed her in the same very hurried manner and took her back to the playpen and began cleaning up.

#4

(Second day.) Then Mrs. Keen fed Carol. She jammed her into the highchair and her foot got stuck. She cried, and Mrs. Keen said, "Now you've *really* done it." Finally she got the baby into the highchair and fed her very fast.

#5

(Third day.) The feeding was rushed again. The baby had part of an egg yolk and some cereal, which she gagged on. Mrs. Keen said she thought the baby was gagging because the cereal was too thick. The baby took about half the bowl of cereal and a little milk and was put in the playpen.

#6

Mrs. Keen fed the baby, alternating between peas and plums, first a spoonful of one and then the other. Carol gagged and spat out the food. Once she jerked her hand, causing Mrs. Keen to spill the food, and she hit the child, saying, "Don't do that." Carol cried. The feeding was rough and ended in her pulling the baby out of the chair. Every time Mrs. Keen takes the baby out of the highchair she gets the baby's leg caught in it.

#7

(Fourth day.) Mrs. Keen got mad at Carol because she wouldn't take her bottle, and spanked her. The baby cried. I asked if spanking helped, and Mrs. Keen said that sometimes it does. Carol grabbed her mother's hair and she said, "Ouch, Carol, you're pulling my hair." I wondered why Carol pulled her hair, and Mrs. Keen said, "It's just her way of showing affection."

#8

(Sixth day.) Mrs. Keen was feeding the baby at nine-twenty, twenty minutes later than she is supposed to, according to Mrs. Keen. Carol is always left in the crib until it is time for her breakfast.

At breakfast Mrs. Keen mentioned that she had five washes to do, and when she finished eating she went right downstairs, put in a load, came up and began to feed the baby in the usual hurried manner. Carol fussed, as always, spat out some of the food, and her mother asked her why she did it. I have asked Mrs. Keen several times why she thinks the baby moves around so much and she always answers with "She's teething," or "She gets into these states sometimes."

#9

She came in to feed the baby. She put her in the highchair and prepared baby food—vegetables, chicken and fruit. The food was steaming hot. The baby took three or four spoonfuls without objecting. Then she started to cry and spit out the food and to scoot down in the highchair. Her mother said, "Carol, don't do that! Stop jumping around in your chair. What are you trying to do to me? Honestly!"

Finally the baby was spitting the food all down the front of her dress* and her mother said she would have to change her clothes.

Since the baby was crying, her mother took her out of the highchair and sat with her. Raising the baby to her face, she said, "Oh, I'm sorry, I'm sorry baby, I'm sorry." The baby stopped crying. Then she abruptly set Carol back on her lap and told her she was naughty. The baby just sat there, but when Mrs. Keen said, "Bad, bad," the baby started to cry again. Her mother started to laugh, lifted the baby to her face, and said, "I'm sorry, I'm sorry," and set her down again. She said, "The funniest thing is, you're not even crying," and then she said, "Bad," and the baby started to cry. She took her on her shoulder and again said she was sorry. Then she set her back down on her lap and did the same thing over again.

Then she started playing very roughly † with Carol, the way she does, and the baby laughed, seeming to enjoy it. Mrs. Keen made faces at her. She had her standing up and sitting down and nuzzled the baby's chest. The baby seemed to like it.

#10

(Seventh day.) Carol's feeding took place in the middle of the ironing, at about nine forty-five in the morning. It is striking how much time the baby spends behind bars—either in the crib or playpen. She has been in one or the other almost all morning every day, except for the one or two occasions when her mother took her out on the porch. Of course, she is taken out from behind bars to the highchair to be fed.

Feeding was over in five minutes or less this time. The food was steaming hot —I could see the steam but the baby didn't put up much of a fight, so maybe the food wasn't as hot as it looked. As Mrs. Keen fed the baby, the baby spit out and carried on as she always does. Feeding seems to be a very anxious time for her because her mother feeds her so fast.

Then Carol was put in the playpen and that is where she was when I was in the living room with Frankie and his little friend Myrtle.

Biometaphysics and Feeding

Our metaphysic of infancy is obviously not part of Mrs. Keen's consciousness; she does not even hold the baby harmless but blames her for being "bad"; and the stream of aversive language ("Now you've *really* done it"; "Carol, don't do that! Stop jumping around in your chair. What are you trying to do to me?") implies that she does not comprehend that the infant cannot understand her; she puts her own motivations in the forefront and demands that the infant comply. Mrs. Keen does not perceive Carol as a "true" baby—as a baby is culturally defined—but has instead metamorphosed her into a kind of adversary who, though too weak to overpower her physically, so vulnerable she cannot even eat without being urged to, is yet

---

* It is not clear from the notes whether or not Carol was wearing a bib.
† No description of this in the notes. In a letter the observer says, "Maybe it just seemed to me too rough for after-feeding play."

capable of defeating her by tricks. In this fantasy of a thing-that-tries-to-destroy-its-mother-by-not-eating, we see an extreme expression of a common attitude in our culture—that babies will not eat spontaneously but have to be maneuvered into it, lest they die. Perhaps this reflects the belief that babies are so weak and vulnerable that they will not even eat by themselves. Another folk attitude that comes out here is that "you've got to show the baby who's the boss," and that parents will become their babies' prisoners if they don't fight back.

Since Mrs. Keen perceives the baby's distress as perverse, she cannot use Carol to look into her self; like many parents, she is opaque to light emanating from her child.

In spite of apparent insensitivity, Mrs. Keen does seem aware that often she is more than the baby can stand. When, for example, Carol gulped the milk and "sort of choked," Mrs. Keen said, "I bet you think Mother's trying to strangle you"; and in feeding observation #9, the teasing alternation between "I'm sorry" and "Bad" suggests that Mrs. Keen feels she has been forcing the baby. Yet she cannot change. Just before her third breakdown Mrs. Keen wept over the phone to the observer and said, "I cannot be a good mother to my children."

A striking feature of this abuse is that the baby does not resist absolutely, does not keep her mouth closed, does not refuse to take milk from the plastic cup (she does refuse the bottle), and does not even turn her head away, as many babies do. Perhaps Carol is compelled by hunger.

Since the observer says that Mrs. Keen feeds Carol "spoonful after spoonful, barely giving the child a chance to swallow"; that "her mother kept feeding her faster and faster"; that "she then fed her in the same very hurried manner," and so on, we can see that Mrs. Keen violates the observer's sense of time; that Mrs. Keen has her own private, onrushing, internal clock. All cultures have their own pace for everything, and people feel it when someone breaks it. Yet biological constitution sets limits too, and whatever the observer's feelings about speed may have been, there was a point where the baby clearly reached her biological limit, gagged, spat and vomited.

Vicious Circles

This misery is a consequence not only of Mrs. Keen's failure to see Carol truly as an infant and to recognize ordinary limitations, but also of her tendency to easily and quickly become more insistent and even violent when things don't go her way and of her inability to discern alternatives or plumb reasons—she can't even master the problem of getting Carol in and out of the highchair. For her, there are only two ways to meet resistance: insistence and force. And she has only one reaction to resistance: rage-despair—feeling-of-helplessness. So when she can't remove the tray from the newfangled highchair, she jams the baby in and drags her out in a rage. Failing to perceive Carol as she really is—or unable to act on this perception—Mrs. Keen acts *as if* the baby were strong, capable (not helpless) and able to assimilate the food as she is given it. Since Carol is not capable, her

organism resists; and since her mother cannot solve the problem but reacts by forcing, yelling and hitting, matters become worse—with a result
that might lead some to say, "She hates the baby"; yet, since this behavior,
which looks like an expression of hatred, can be explained by an alternative
hypothesis—combining perceptual failure, inability to discern alternatives
and a tendency to react to frustration with rage, bullheadedness and violence—we have a respectable alternative to a theory of hate; an alternative
which, though still placing the burden of psychopathology on Mrs. Keen,
acquits her of hatred and death wishes toward her baby.

Here is what *Workingman's Wife* says about the working-class woman's
anger and violence:

> In comparsion with the middle-class woman, the working-class woman's
> emotionality is not well organized or easily controlled. . . . This immedi-
> ate emotional responsiveness to stimulation bespeaks a lesser degree of
> inner self-restraint. When a working-class woman experiences some emo-
> tion, she is more likely to be carried away by it than is the middle-class
> woman. Further, strong feelings can be elicited by less intense stimula-
> tion, as compared to the middle-class women. A middle-class person look-
> ing closely at the working-class woman would be somewhat inclined to
> judge that she does not have a sense of proportion in emotional matters.
> This may be illustrated by [the] stories [stimulated by] a picture showing a
> woman with her hands at the neck or head of another person. . . . In the
> population at large . . . two main interpretations of the picture occur in
> the stories . . . : (1) the woman is attacking the other person; (2) the
> woman is helping the other person. . . . In our study, the working-class
> women markedly interpret the picture in the first way; the middle-class
> women in the second.*

This interpretation of the difference between the two classes of women,
even if valid, is vulnerable to the criticism that the middle-class woman is
"hip" to what is going on in the test and knows how to conceal her true
feelings, while the working-class woman does not. Furthermore, the proof
has never been given that people who give a "violent" response to a picture
are necessarily violent in real life. Another problem I have with this quote
is that though it stresses attack, *Workingman's Wife* makes the point elsewhere that these women think constantly of helping others.† At any rate,
the possibility must be borne in mind that Mrs. Keen is only an extreme
example of a general working-class female explosiveness.

The Highchair: Prison and Torture

In the domestic culture of the Keen family, anxiety about survival has
become transformed into a jural principle: it is illegal for the children not
to eat what their parents say they should, and they are punished if they
don't. The difference between father and mother is only that he is more
lenient with the *baby*—more "average." The following illustrates the difference:

* *Ibid.*, p. 68.
† See *ibid.*, pp. 57 and 65, for instances.

(First day.) Mrs. Keen was trying to give Carol the bottle and the baby obviously didn't want it. Mrs. Keen was spanking the baby rather hard and telling her she had to take the bottle. The baby cried. Mr. Keen had been taking a bath; he came out, heard the spanking and said, "Alice, why are you spanking the baby? She doesn't want the bottle, so don't force her." That seemed to calm things for a while.

Mrs. Keen went into the master bedroom, lay down with Carol and told her that if she didn't take the bottle she was going to punch her good. Then she put her in the crib, came in, sat down with her feet up and said she was tired and was going to bed.

(Fifth day.) Mrs. Keen was trying to give Carol the bottle, but she did not want it. Mrs. Keen was going through the usual spanking and the baby was crying. Mr. Keen said, "Alice, she doesn't want the bottle." When Mrs. Keen hits the baby while feeding her, all Mr. Keen does is say that Carol doesn't want the bottle. At lunch today, when the mother was feeding Carol hot food, her husband was standing right there, saying not to rush the baby, but he didn't seem to notice that the food was hot. He said Carol's teeth must be bothering her or something. [Some months later, when Mrs. Keen was in the hospital, suffering from the ailment from which she was to die, the observer watched Mr. Keen feed Carol, and he did it fast. Carol did not spit out or vomit.]

Mrs. Keen's way of jamming Carol into the highchair and dragging her out would make you think that she has not the slightest conception of a baby's vulnerability. But this behavior raises other points too: she doesn't seem to be able to relate the dimensions of the highchair to the configuration of a baby's body and she seems to have no capacity to relate her *own* body to the configuration of the highchair—specifically to the space between the rigid tray and the rigid back of the chair. We can't even be sure that she perceives the highchair as rigid, for she acts *as if* it were rubbery and would stretch to accommodate the baby's body! Thus: she acts *as if* some things were flexible when they are not; she acts *as if* some things (food) were not hot when they are; she acts *as if* the baby were strong (not helpless) when she is not, *as if* the baby were motivated against her when she is not, and could not be, and so on.

When I imagine myself with Carol in my arms in front of the highchair, from which the tray cannot be removed, so that Carol has to be fitted into a rather narrow space, I know that I would somehow slip one arm around her legs and gently maneuver her so that she would fit in; and taking her out, I would do the same, so that her feet would not get hooked in the rungs. This involves having a certain image and perception of the way a baby's body *is* and what has to be done to it to adapt it to an object which cannot be adapted to the baby. I have to assess the size of the aperture and the configuration of the chair below the tray, and this involves an ability to put myself in the baby's place. All these perceptions stem from an understanding of the baby's helplessness and vulnerability. Only if I know what a *baby* is—perhaps only if the baby is *me*—will I trouble myself to perceive the character of the chair and to act on that perception. Chair, baby and I, in the fullness of my consciousness, are one social and perceptual system. The fact that I perceive the chair in a certain way is inseparable from the way I see and feel about the baby.

While Mrs. Keen blames the baby for unreasonably rejecting the food, material from observation #8 (page 399) suggests that I may have over-simplified.

Though Mrs. Keen does not seem to think that her difficulties with Carol come entirely from the baby's unreasonableness, she still behaves as if they had little or nothing to do with herself. Perhaps, in calmer moments and under questioning by an outsider, Mrs. Keen is able to recollect herself enough to realize that the baby is not purposely crossing her, while when she is on the highchair-feeding–firing-line, the baby becomes her enemy and she quickly falls back on hostile interpretations.

In observation #9, when the feeding is going badly and Carol is crying, Mrs. Keen takes her out of the highchair and alternately nuzzles her, saying, "I'm sorry," and sets her down abruptly on her lap, saying, "Bad." While acknowledging that Carol is crying, she also denies that she is— (". . . you're not even crying"). Without apparent cause, but with a gener-ally jocular façade, the mother shifts from niceness to nastiness. What we see in the mother is a spirit of play; what we see in the baby is dead ear-nestness. We can't tell to what extent and in what the mother is serious, but we can see that the baby takes each change in her mother's behavior as a reflection of a truth: when she is held to her mother's face she becomes quiet because this seems to represent acceptance; when she is called "bad" she cries because this seems a rejection and scares her. The mother con-fronts the baby's innocent acceptance of surface meanings with her own ambiguity and callousness. With the pathetic incomprehension of infancy, the baby misinterprets her mother and is trapped, but the mother never misses a prediction about what the baby will do. The power is the mother's; the weakness is the baby's.

Workingman's Wife, again on the basis of the Thematic Apperception Test, reports that working-class women are fond of their children and find fulfillment in them. On the other hand, the wife of the blue-collar worker

> has some tendency to regard children as though they were a combination of animated toy, stuffed animal, and sparkling bauble. A child is for her, in one of its major aspects, a passive object to be hugged close, or to deck out in appealing clothes, or to be enjoyed for its antics. Though she knows that children have minds of their own, she does not always have this fact clearly fixed in her own mind. . . . These women tend not to see chil-dren as already being persons—individuals with an integrity of their own and worthy of respect. They are not greatly interested in a child's individuality except perhaps for his entertainment value.*

The observer felt that Mr. and Mrs. Keen had the same attitude toward Carol. Yet the alternation here between reassuring and frightening is not just an interest in antics—it is an interest in pain; and this puts Mrs. Keen well beyond the area of merely class-determined behavior.

It is impossible to deny that this alternation between nuzzling and scar-ing Carol looks like punishment for not eating and that the mother seems to enjoy it, but I think that it also expresses the underlying quality of relations in this family: the parents cannot easily permit joy, and when delight in each other or in the children appears, the urge to cancel it comes ravening

---

* *Ibid.,* p. 97. That these attitudes are predominantly working-class is open to serious question.

behind. In the next example Mrs. Keen again alternates between being nice and hostile to the baby:

Mrs. Keen asked her husband to let her sit in his chair. He finally got up, rather ungraciously, and she took Carol and began to give her the bottle. [The observer twice left the room for a few minutes and when she returned, Mrs. Keen was still giving the baby the bottle.] Carol didn't want it and had become stiff as a board. Mrs. Keen kept saying, "Don't do that," and when Carol cried, started to play with her. Then she said, "I'm going to pinch you," and added that in a few years Carol would give her mother a fit running off along the sidewalk and perhaps even going around the block once she got started. As she played with the baby both of them laughed.

While we focus on the baby and the mother in the foreground, the relationship between husband and wife can also be discerned, like a gray backdrop, which perhaps explains the misery of the relationship between mother and baby. Yet, since they are in the foreground, we notice that even as Mrs. Keen appears to take pleasure in playing with Carol, she threatens to pinch her and dwells on the trouble she will have with Carol when she is big enough to run around the block—like any adventurous two-year-old. I think she means to prevent that—and we will examine the evidence later.

Freud has spoken of the "pleasure principle"; and "beyond" it, he says, is the impulse to destroy.* Yet in serious pathology the one is not beyond the other but always at its side or mixed with it, so that the impulse to destroy rages wherever there is pleasure; so that the impulse to be tender is often instantly transformed—as in schizophrenia—into destructiveness. The compulsion to kill pleasure, however, is an undiagnosed illness, endemic in Western culture, emerging now in one form, now in another. In some people it occurs only at Christmas time or at birthdays—this is the intermittent form of the illness; in others, in those more disturbed, it is fairly constant; in psychosis it is always present, canceling all possibility of human relationships and interfering with therapy. It is in terms of this endemic illness that we can understand the compulsion of Mr. and Mrs. Keen to crush joy.

ANALYTICAL SUMMARY

Forcing Carol to eat while ignoring her biological limitations, Mrs. Keen compels the baby to reject what she most desires, and at the same time punishes her for doing it and prevents her escape. This is the commonest form of pathogenesis, and the most lethal, for not only does it split the personality in half by introducing a tormenting contradiction, but it does so at the *biological level*, where the organism literally lives. The outcome of any compulsion is that the object is obliged to behave differently from itself. On one side it results in culture, on the other in *counter-culture*, i.e., rebellion and revolution. Culture is a consequence, in which an individual becomes different from himself but as the culture wants him.†

In feeding and playing with her baby, Mrs. Keen acts as if all the advice

---

* In *Beyond the Pleasure Principle*. A somewhat different formulation appears in his "Thoughts for the Times on War and Death."

† The objection to circular reasoning is an unexamined prejudice based on a culturally determined antipathy to traveling in circles.

she ever heard about babies had passed her by. Thus her incomprehension bestows on her a kind of innocence, and thus she is, in her way, somewhat of a baby too. Like a baby, she is impulse-driven, flaring into a rage when things don't go her way. What surprises us is that the baby eats at all, for Mrs. Keen acts as if she were determined to destroy the wish to eat, even as she whips herself into a fury in order to preserve it. Behind this fury is perhaps the anxiety that she can't be a good mother, and what we see is perhaps not really rage but anxiety-rage, a product of despair and frustration. Because we feel compassion, and because alternative explanations are at hand, we do not say that she wants to hurt Carol; yet there are times when we are compelled to wonder. Perhaps there is a point where a baby, forced by a sick mother, drives her mother to such a compounded despair that the mother not only acts as if she hated the baby, but really does. How else can we explain the "sorry-bad" game and the threats to pinch and punch? All Mrs. Keen really longs for is that Carol should eat, but since Mrs. Keen does not know how to get her to, the baby objects. In this we are all very much the same: we often try to get our children to do what they want to do and what both of us recognize is fundamentally necessary, but since we often do not know how to manage, these foundations of existence escape us. In extreme cases parent and child fight each other fiercely in the very act of trying to get for each other what they want for the other's benefit —as in the case where a parent wants a child to eat and the child would like to eat for its own sake and for the parent's, but simply cannot bring itself to.

A FINAL REFLECTION ON CALLOUSNESS AND CRUELTY TO BABIES

Shortly after Mrs. Keen's death, the observer returned for a visit. Carol was now thirteen months old, and there was a new baby boy in the house. Mrs. Keen's mother was helping out, and she said that one of the jobs she did not like was feeding the baby.

The grandmother started to give the baby the bottle even though it was too hot, saying, "If this were the only bottle the baby ever wanted, it would be good," and laughed uproariously.

Mr. Keen put Carol in the highchair and gave her a small glass of soda, which she gulped down, making gasping noises after each long drink. Her father told her to slow down. . . .

After she'd had her soda she was let down, and she came over to me and made motions to get up on my lap. She whined, raised her arms toward me and raised her leg to my knee. When I picked her up, she first stood on my lap and then sat down facing her father. Then she climbed down. She got up and down a number of times, sometimes going off into the living room. Her father kept telling her to stop getting on and off my lap, and told me she would drive me crazy, but I said she wasn't bothering me, which was true. Her grandmother said, "Maybe Carol just wants a little loving. You told me to give her some loving!" nd he said, "Yes, but she shouldn't bother other people. It's all right if she bothers us; it's not all right if she bothers other people."

The fact that Carol was getting up on my lap seemed to annoy her father. He told her to stop bothering me, and when she came over again and leaned against my leg, he said, "Now, Carol, don't do that any more. Do you want me to get the ruler?" They had mentioned this before in connection with Carol; the grandmother said that all she had to say to Carol was, "Do you want me to get the ruler?" and Carol knew what that meant.

Mr. Keen got the ruler off the top of the refrigerator and pointed it at Carol, who started backwards out the kitchen door. Even when she bumped her head against the doorjamb, it didn't stop her retreat from the kitchen.

I present these data in order to show that Mrs. Keen was not merely disturbed or "sadistic." When we see that Mr. Keen and his mother-in-law threaten Carol with the ruler, we are forced to surmise a cultural factor—either in working-class culture or in the subculture of this little family network. If we set aside our humane feelings for a moment, we realize that it is not metaphysically necessary that babies not be struck, even by "normal" people. All that is biosocially necessary is that they not be struck so hard that they are injured. If we assume that the best way to train a child is by blows, that he must be shown very early "who is boss," that he must not be spoiled and that he should not interfere too much with the convenience of adults, then the way is clear to strike him. And if we further assume that children are born evil and have to be purified by discipline, or merely that some children are born ornery and have to be corrected ("All my kids were little pests from the minute they were born"), then the way is opened for conscientious harshness, for innocent—or even exalted—cruelty. Carry the idea further, to the "institutional sanity" of government or of organized religion, and you have the basis for "moral" and "holy" wars, the "conscientious" torture of heretics "to save their souls," etc., etc.

The grandmother says, "If this were the only bottle the baby ever wanted, it would be good," and laughs uproariously at her own "joke"; we know from this that the baby is going to have a very rough time with his grandmother—perhaps as rough as Carol had with her own mother. So we can repeat that although we feel, from the way Mrs. Keen fed Carol, that she was pretty sick, she was not *merely* sick, not *merely* "sadistic," but was perpetuating pathology with which she had been infected by her own mother.

Coupled with these observations of callousness and harshness toward Carol, we have the attitude that counsels love. Mr. Keen's telling his mother-in-law to "give her [Carol] some loving" suggests that if a grandmother has to be told to give her dead daughter's child "some loving," these people are strange indeed, by middle-class standards. *Mrs. Keen was part of an environment in which tenderness toward children is an afterthought.*

These remarkable follow-up observations—unique in the history of psychiatry—cast light on Mrs. Keen's relationship to Carol, for we see here that her harshness was not *merely* an expression of her feelings about *that* baby, but was also an expression of a *milieu* in which people are insensitive. When we consider that, for all his callousness, Mr. Keen was the person most aware of Carol's physical discomfort, and that he told the grandmother to "give her some loving," he stands out almost as a mountain of compassion.

Feeding Frankie

This section ought to be appraised in the light of the contemporary argument around who's to blame when children are disturbed. Defenders of parents argue that it is more or less the children's fault because they were born so difficult, or even deviant, that the parents could not cope with them, a vicious circle developed, and parents and children became more and more disturbed. Those opposed to this view insist that the parents were so disturbed to begin with that they made the child ill. Twenty years ago the debate scarcely existed, and it has developed partly because some in the human disciplines feel the need to escape the accusation of having, perhaps, damaged their own children. But the main reason the dispute continues is that there are no good observations of family life. In the absence of more data of the kind presented here, the argument will continue, fruitlessly.

There is the helplessness of a being *in itself* and there is the helplessness of a being in relation to others; the latter is the more variable. An infant is helpless *in itself* because he is feeble and can do little for himself, but he is also helpless in relation to the superior power of adults and older children. The more an adult chooses to exert power, the more helpless the child; and the longer an adult exerts power, the longer the child remains helpless. In this way Frankie is made to appear helpless.

(First day.) Frank kept saying he wasn't going to eat his lunch. Mrs. Keen sat down next to him, took up the spoon and forced him to eat his soup. Frank would push away her hand and the hot soup spilled on his chest. He kept saying it was burning him and she said, "No, it isn't," and kept putting spoonful after spoonful into his mouth. He had eaten some ham and wanted more, but his mother said, "No, not before you eat your soup, you're not going to have any more ham." Frank had a helpless look on his face. He said things like "Mommy, don't," and she kept screaming at him to stop touching her hand and to eat his food. At last he said, "Let me do it; let me feed myself," and she said all right and he fed himself. He looked at me and said, "I bet I can beat you." I said, "I bet you can't." His mother remarked that I had probably noticed he was a terrible eater, and really, it was hard to get him to eat.

Frankie finds a way out of his trouble by proposing that he feed himself; at three he can suggest an alternative his mother is unable to. A person in pain is more likely to think of ways to escape it than the one who inflicts it on him.* A person will try to overcome his helplessness when it is painful but may be content to remain helpless when it is sweet. The secret of an enduring tyranny is not only that it makes rebellion painful but that it makes submission rewarding.

It is good that Mrs. Keen lets Frankie escape and feed himself, for it is the binding into duress that is lethal. So in this case, Frankie and his mother show a potentiality for health. Since her actions express her compulsion, she has to drive on; yet, as Frankie's resistance mounts, perhaps she tires, longs to change and is actually relieved to accept a suggestion.

* Consider the ingenious ways victims of torture found for committing suicide, in Tacitus' *Annals of Imperial Rome* and Suetonius' *Twelve Caesars*.

Mrs. Keen is trying to be a good mother, but her anxiety about the children's not eating becomes part of the nightmare she creates for them. Perhaps in her dreams she starves; perhaps in the dreams of working-class people *they* starve, for they are extremely vulnerable to the economic system.* Perhaps, on the other hand, Frankie feels, even in his mother's onslaught, a concern for his welfare. Perhaps when a child feels that his parent's harshness is in the child's own interest, it is more difficult for him to hold it against the parent than when the harshness is solely in the parent's interest.

Underlying Mrs. Keen's forcing is our folk belief that, in children, hunger is an unreliable regulator of feeding, and that the inherent processes of development cannot alone be counted on to cancel helplessness. Mrs. Keen is merely extreme. In our culture it seems to take enormous strength just to let a child go without food until he decides he wants to eat. When a child refuses to eat, doom seems to fill the house. That life must be preserved! The child must be strong to resist disease, etc. Other fears enter: a mother's feeling of being rejected, of being unequal to the task assigned to her, of failing as a mother. Basic fears crystallize on that little spoon: the nightmare of failure, the nightmare of deprivation and weakness, and the nightmare of being unloved. By that spoon hangs the question, Are the dreams right or wrong? And the child must eat to prove them wrong!

(Second day.) Mrs. Keen had a loaf of bread and the Braunschweiger on the table and told me to make a sandwich. She served me some soup and started to give some to Frankie. She had told him to eat his lunch or else go to bed, and that was "it," but he said he didn't want anything. When he said he wouldn't eat his soup she said, "All right, I'll eat it then." She took a piece of bread and a piece of cheese and folded the bread over it and said, "Here's your lunch." When Frankie said he wanted to take it outside she said no, but he did, anyway.

Frankie came in and announced that his sandwich had gotten dirty and that he had given it to the dog. His mother said, "It's not good enough for you but it's good enough for the dog."

Since these parents' anxiety about their children's health is mixed with the concept of power, every time a child swallows food he validates that power, and if he refuses he threatens it. But we see that Frankie is bringing about a shift in the balance of power, for his mother accepts alternatives to forcing—shams which enable her to imagine that she retains power, while she is aware she is relinquishing it. They also let her imagine that Frankie thinks she has power, while she knows Frankie is aware she is giving it up. As power declines it becomes gesture. In our culture, parents first relinquish power in feeding. It is probably true that everywhere parents first give up their power over children's biological functions.

Since Frankie has the courage not to eat his soup and to go outside though his mother objects, it is obvious that she must have been giving him

* For contradicting data, see Rainwater, et al., *Workingman's Wife* (*op. cit.*), and "Marketing and the Working-Class Family," a paper by James M. Patterson in Shostak and Gombergs, eds., *Blue-Collar World* (*op. cit.*). Their data were obtained from surveys and do not probe deep terrors. The sudden waves of layoffs and strikes introduce just that element of uncertainty and anxiety into working-class life which causes such dreams.

leeway. However, the general outline of the forcing pattern remains the same as it is for Carol.

(Second day.) Stubbornly, whimpering, Frankie refused to eat the fish, and his mother got very upset and yelled at him to eat it. When he still refused she said, "Do you want me to get the belt?" So he started eating but did not finish.

She accepted a gesture of compliance. The many observations of feeding Frankie show that his mother is often willing to give in to his wishes, and that, as compared to Carol, she gives Frankie much more freedom during meals.

In the next two examples Frankie uses food against his mother. In both he badgers her to *give* him food, which is a reversal of the usual transaction, in which she badgers him to take it.

Then Frank asked for jello, but his mother said she had told him before that he should wait until everyone else had been served and then he would get some. Over and over again he said he wanted jello and his mother kept telling him he couldn't have any and that she would spank him hard if he didn't stop. So he sat on the floor and pounded her legs and kept asking for jello until she hit him.

. . .

Frank went to the refrigerator and took out a carton with frankfurters and cheese, brought it into the living room and said he wanted to eat. His mother kept yelling that she would fix his lunch after she finished folding the clothes. She was telling me that she really didn't mind folding diapers (the baby uses about a dozen a day). Frank tipped the carton and most of the cheese and franks fell on the floor. His mother yelled at him to take it back. He did not move and neither did she.*

Then he brought in some jello and started eating it with his hands. She glanced at him and then looked away. Finally she realized what he was doing and started to yell at him not to make a mess with the jello. Then she forgot it for a while. Frank took a handful of jello and rubbed it on the little table in front of the chair, and this really put her in a rage. She jumped up and got a cloth from the kitchen and told Frank he was really going to get a beating and that sometimes she could just kill him. He looked tearful and went into the bathroom.

Mrs. Keen's forbearance is most interesting. She does not hit Frankie as soon as he starts pounding her legs and she does not hit him for smearing jello on the furniture, even though it "really put her in a rage" so that she "could just kill him." The most surprising fact that emerges from comparing the feeding of Frankie with the feeding of Carol is that the baby is struck more often than the three-year-old, *reversing the universal human pattern, according to which the punishment of children increases with age.* Another surprising finding is that while in Frankie's case objective provocation—like smearing jello—sometimes seems great, punishment is mild, while in Carol's case objective provocation seems nonexistent but punishment is severe. This means, of course, that Mrs. Keen perceives provocation where we see little or none, and vice versa.

This leads to two hypotheses: (1) Disturbed people in any culture tend

* The notes do not say what finally happened to the food.

to reverse universal human patterns. (2) In any culture a difference between disturbed people and others is in what they consider provoking.

When we talk about such a thing as "objective provocation," we have nothing to go by but intuition, which usually boils down to a feeling that "if this happened to me I would get angry." * In all cultures, intuitive standards determine for what, how and by whom a child shall be punished for minor transgressions; and violation of the standards marks abnormality. When Mrs. Keen says she "could just kill" Frankie, I think she is normal, because he deserved the scolding and because I discount the threat to kill as a verbal flight by a harassed mother; but when she hits Carol and yells at her for not eating, I consider that abnormal in our culture.† Both judgments are purely intuitive.

Having actually seen Frankie fight his mother with food, we can, with hindsight, say that since she attacks the children while feeding them, it is to be expected that they use food and feeding against her. Yet Frankie can counterattack in this way only because his mother has a weakness, and that weakness is, paradoxically, a streak of restraint. The child's counterattack with food recalls the prophecy, "He who takes up the sword shall perish by the sword," but both go back to an inherent tendency in *Homo sapiens* to use the enemy's weapon, or one superior to it, against him.

ANALYTICAL SUMMARY

Mrs. Keen tries to feed Frankie the way she feeds the baby, but since he is three years old, since she is not entirely merciless and since she is perhaps getting a little tired of fighting two children, she allows him more leeway.

Surely this pattern of feeding by forcing is created by the mother; surely it would be absurd to argue that both children are such defective eaters that she has to feed them at great speed, with food that is too hot. Could a child be born with the need to get fed with food that burns him, born with a need to be fed so fast he cannot take it? Surely in this case naturalistic observation of the same mother feeding different children makes it clear where the fault lies: it is the mother's. However, it is not possible to say, from the evidence, that she does this because she hates her children or because she wishes them dead. We do not accuse her of wickedness; we merely describe her behavior and show it to be a pattern she imposes on the children because she cannot help herself. We even show that under certain conditions she is able to modify her behavior, that she can learn, that she—like many thousands, I am sure—does not fit the stereotype of the unchangeable disturbed parent. What observation indicates is that since her own child can show her the way to change, it is possible for a therapist who knows what is going on to suggest changes too. What we see before our eyes is that this mother, on the verge of an alleged nervous breakdown, is able to take lessons from her own children when the lessons are not too threatening to learn, and when the mother is ready for them.

In all of us the rate of speed at which we function expresses a relation-

---

* Not all provocations are hostile.

† It seems to me that it is biologically inappropriate in any culture, for a beaten baby cannot eat.

ship to an inner (psychic) clock, and to an outer one—the clock that times the routine events of the culture. The inner comes into relation with the outer largely on a basis of feeling, and often drives us on so that we tend to perceive the temporal urgency of what is outside distorted by what is happening inside. Our inner clock is wound during infancy and childhood, and depending on later experience, remains in harmony or out of joint with life around us. The way we feel time acts as a compulsion, so that we may try to force our own feeling on others, regardless of conditions. Incorporated into our bodies, the culture's pace, combined with our own special training and experience, acts like a physiological thing—as if, when we walk down the street, keep an engagement, feed ourselves or our children, and so on, we do it not only by the use of our muscles and nerves but also through a second body—time. *I am a Siamese twin and my other body is called Time! There is one heart of me that beats the biologic rhythm, but the other beats the subjective one; there is one stomach in me that responds to objective deprivation, but the other responds to Time. I have a pair of kidneys that purifies my blood and drips urine in my bladder; the other kidneys handle the wastes of Time.*

Time is not only a perception but an emotion as well, not only an idea but also a need. We have to fulfill our relation to time almost as we need to assuage hunger or sex; time can become as imperious a want as any appetite, so that if time needs are not met we feel worse than if we are merely temporarily in need of a meal. Unless a child she *feeds* eats at asphyxiating speed, Mrs. Keen, who is extreme, of course, is beside herself with rage and anxiety. Once confronted with a child she has to feed, Mrs. Keen is ready to leap out of her skin under the lash of time. Nothing is fast enough for her; the human body does not have the capacity to take in food at a pace that satisfies her rage for speed. She wants to fly at the child, shove the food into his stomach all at once—pour it on his head. This feeding-time frenzy comes out regardless of whether she is feeding an infant or a grown boy, and she is prepared to reduce Paul (see next section) to the level of an infant—she will hurdle all obstacles if she can—in order not to be terrified when his pace is too slow for her.

In "primitive utopias"—which, by the way, are not utopian at all—there is one thing which, from our point of view, is truly utopian: the concept of time for one person is usually the same for others;* what is a right pace for one person is the right pace for others; mothers do not rush their babies' feeding; people do not rush one another or slow others down. There is a *mutuality of pace* that runs all the way through the society. Now, we have seen that the pace at which Mrs. Keen feeds her children is not their pace; but I have shown, in earlier research, that the forcing of the pace can be seen in a maternity ward in a good hospital too.† It is very likely that many mothers, forced into the temporal framework of this time-obsessed society, impose a compulsive feeding pace on their children. Mrs. Keen, then, is merely extreme.

* It is interesting that the one area in which tribal people regularly become alienated from one another in time is in prestige economics, where debtor and creditor often wish to work on different time schedules. Everywhere debt and credit tend to become enemies in time. If God is good, he must be against indebtedness.

† In "Child Rearing, Culture and the Natural World" by Jules Henry and Joan Boggs, *Psychiatry*, Vol. XV (1962), pp. 261–71 (*op. cit.*).

For many, the beginning of *alienation in time*, the beginning of furtive hatred of time as an alien "thing," occurs in earliest infancy, even in the maternity ward. It is the point where cultural time is first shoved down many an infant's throat, where nurses and even mothers become merciless in the interest of time, where mothers, captives of the benign hospital, first enslave their infants to time—where babies are annealed to it.

Let us now look at some material on the feeding of Paul, the ten-and-a-half-year-old.

Feeding Paul

(First day.) Mrs. Keen served Paul his lunch, then went into the living room and sat down with her feet up. I went into the kitchen and soon Mrs. Keen came in and started to yell at Paul to hurry up, that he didn't have much time to get back to school. "Hurry up and eat," she said. Since he didn't seem to be eating fast enough for her, she started to feed him, and apparently referring to me, he said, "Don't feed me in front of that—" and stopped. After he finished his lunch his mother said he could have an apple to eat on the way back. She kept telling him to go to the bathroom and wash his hands and go off to school.

(Second day.) Mrs. Keen said Paul was coming home for lunch and he soon did. She had a hunk of cheese and a piece of bread out for him and gave him some tomato soup. When Paul said he wanted ham instead of cheese she said, "Eat it anyway." Though he had just sat down, she told him to hurry up and drink his soup down, because it was getting late. While he was eating it I noticed he sounded as if the soup were catching in his throat. He took an apple and left for school.

Nothing in the notes describes Paul as a slow eater, but there is a great deal that proves his mother is a fast feeder. In this family, food, which should bring parents and children close together, creates a gulf between them. What still remains of the mother's coercive feeding pattern is power, her insistence on her own pace and her determination that food not be left on the plate.* Even though Paul is ten and a half years old, his mother will not relinquish power over his eating, and she will reduce him to an infant if he does not submit.

In the next example Paul uses food against his mother:

(Sixth day.) Paul said something about wanting a good lunch, and his mother gave him soup and a ham sandwich. He said, "What, no mustard?" She was busy at the sink but finally came and gave him the mustard.

He said he likes his grandmother's cooking or her pies—apple and cherry. He said he likes her chicken too and his mother asked, "Well, Mom makes good chicken, doesn't she?" He replied, "Yes, but Grandma makes the little pieces so good," and she said, "Oh." I asked which grandmother and he said his mother's mother. Mrs. Keen started to tell me that she was his favorite grandmother, and Paul sort of smiled.

* It is true that many Americans consider it immoral to leave food, yet I do not believe that is the issue in the Keen family. A very good example of the relationship between eating and power is to be seen in "Dinner on the Last Day" (p. 377), where Paul says he doesn't want any corn but his stepfather insists that some be put on his plate.

He didn't want to eat the rest of his sandwich but his mother said, "Eat it, eat it." She kept telling him to eat it and he said he didn't want it, whining as he spoke. At last she said, "Okay, you don't have to eat it if you don't want to," and took it away. She asked if he wanted an apple or orange and he said, "Oh, the same old thing all the time," and she said, "Well, I can't help it." He chose an apple way back in the refrigerator and she remarked, "You always have to choose the apple that's way in the back, don't you?" and his answer was, "Yes, it's the biggest." He said good-bye and left.

This is the first weekday she didn't go through this come-on-Paul-hurry-up-and-eat-your-lunch-because-you-have-to-get-back-to-school routine—perhaps because he had come back a few minutes earlier than usual.

Compared to other feedings, this one is very "normal" and Mrs. Keen scarcely exercises her power at all. Since tension appears to diminish as we go up the age scale from Carol to Paul, it may be that the greatest anxiety lies behind the feeding of the baby. Since Mrs. Keen seems to believe that Paul and Frankie are more or less capable of eating on their own, she does not act with them as if death itself were chasing her. Perhaps her wild feeding of Carol is an expression of her flight from death. But with her boys she now feels safer. Thus her peculiar reversal, noted earlier, of the primordial human pattern of punishing older children more than younger ones occurs here in the face of death, in order to preserve the baby.

In the next example we are back with time again and with the last hurrah—a piece of sandwich left on the plate, a crack in the door to freedom!

(Seventh day.) Paul came home for lunch and we stood on the steps talking. His mother came to the door and said, "Hurry up, Paul, and get in there and eat." Mrs. Keen and I had had ham and soup. She fixed Paul soup and a cheese sandwich. He ate a little soup and some of the sandwich. His mother came and sat down and asked him if some little boy or other had returned to school and Paul answered, "No, Mother, he moved away," and she said, "Well, he must have moved away, then."

While Paul ate, Mrs. Keen sat at the table twirling a knife. Paul took it and started to do the same, but she said, "Don't play, Paul, eat your lunch." Then she took off one of the rubber sandals she wears when she doesn't go barefoot (she goes barefoot quite a bit) and started to examine it closely. At this time Carol was screaming bloody murder. [Cause unknown.] Mrs. Keen looked at the hole through which the thong of the sandal attaches to the sole and started to pick the dirt out. I was reminded of her examining Carol's mouth and nose, which she does quite often. Mrs. Keen picked the dirt out of the hole in the sandal and threw it on the floor. She was very absorbed, and commented, "You just don't know how all this dirt gets in there."

Then she urged Paul to finish his lunch, but he said he didn't want the rest of the sandwich and she said, "Eat it," but he repeated that he didn't want it. Next she asked him if he wanted some cookies. He said, "Yes, four," and when she asked, "Why four?" he said, "Well, I'm going to eat them all; I'm not going to share them." She gave him three.

We cannot tell whether it is more important to these children to eat or not to eat. While eating does away with a merely biological craving, abstaining has a deeper meaning. Eating destroys hunger, but abstinence is freedom. Eating satisfies a biological need, but refraining gratifies a spiritual one. The conflict between eating and freedom is so great here that we do not know whether these children are ever really hungry. Frankie gives the impression of having no appetite at all. Mrs. Keen's underlying assumption that children do not want to eat has become a self-fulfilling prophecy, for in her anxiety she flings herself so upon her children that they end up acting as if they really did not want to eat.

Even as Mrs. Keen urges Paul to hurry, she does things that slow him down and might even make him lose his appetite: she gives him cheese, which he does not want and saves the ham for herself and Susan; as Paul tries to eat she twirls a knife and picks dirt out of her sandal. Thus, even as she urges her children to eat, Mrs. Keen tends to cancel their desire to.

AN AMERICAN DOCTRINE OF COMMENSALITY
(with apologies to Chu Hsi*)

A family should eat together in Proper Order, at one table, and remain together until all have eaten. The seating in Orderly and Constant Arrangement at the table expresses *li*, order, as it should be expressed in the family life. Food, and utensils too, should be arranged according to the Principle of *li*; forks should be on the left-hand side of the plate, and knife and spoon on the right, and dishes should be clean and of china.

Depending on nationality and social class, one or the other or both parents preside. Depending on social class and nationality, conversation may arise, but at table it should always be gentle and affirm the family. When the family is affirmed, personality is affirmed; when personality is affirmed, the family is affirmed; and when the family is affirmed, social class is solidified. In some nationalities and classes children may be permitted to talk, according to age, and in others, children—especially the young—are required to be silent. This follows the Traditional Laws of class and nationality. However, in well-ordered houses, there is always a Rule of Conversation, imposed by whoever presides.

A first Rule of the Table is that a meal should be like music, where musicians follow *li*. Food is pleasant and should therefore create pleasure in the family. However, it is natural that when food is plentiful, the family should be optimistic, and sad when food is scarce. Following *li*, eating and the passing of dishes should be harmonious, and when this is done the life of the family is as music.

As respect between husband and wife was the Law of Our Ancestors, so at table, respect between them should shine forth. When respect is mutual between husband and wife, love is mutual between parents and children and among the children.

To each child according to his need, from each child according to his capabilities, for in the Well-Ordered Home no one eats too much and each feeds or is fed according to his nature.

Table is not a place for a display of power, except that children, since they are admitted to table, should not behave in unseemly ways but, rather, play assigned roles in the harmonious interchange. In eating at table a child's maturity is maximized; children, no less than adults, should affirm the family by their behavior. Depending on social class, on tradition and

* Neo-Confucian philosopher (1130–1200).

national origin, in our multinational commonwealth, children shall be permitted to eat as much as they wish, or be obliged, in order to maintain the Ancient Morality of Parsimony, to consume what is on their plate, and they shall be required to eat each dish according to traditional Principles by the One Presiding, but only in order to conserve *li* and to affirm the Principles.

In families governed according to *li*, children do not eat to please their parents but to satisfy their own hunger. A parent punishing a child who does not eat disaffirms respect and love, undermines the family and violates *li*. It is an Ancient Principle that though a Monarch may use food to control his subjects, at table, in the family, food and power are kept apart. (A wise Monarch, however, does not use food to control his subjects, except in extremity, and with great care.) In general, it is an Ancient Principle that food and power are to be kept apart. Speaking to his pupils one day, the Ancient Sage said, "Food and power are as antagonistic as honey and vinegar, and painful to be swallowed together. Whoever is compelled to gulp another's power with his food suffers much pain, for he swallows that power along with a sense of his own powerlessness."

To each according to his own pace: some eat fast and some slowly. *Li* requires each musician to look to the consonance of the ensemble, and, so, at table, each in the rhythm proper to his nature, but all in unison also.

When these principles are kept, family unity is preserved at table, food is enjoyed and the family is reaffirmed.

It is not possible to break respect and retain *li;* it is not possible to break Arrangement and Order and preserve *li;* it is not possible to be boisterous or taciturn at table and preserve *li;* it is not possible to exercise power capriciously and preserve *li;* it is impossible to break pace, intruding on others and yet preserve *li*. The Ancients used to say that a family at table is a small model of the State; that the Laws of the Table are the Laws of the State writ small.

These maxims hold, one way or another, whether food is consumed at table or away from it.

On reading about mealtimes in "An Outing," "Dinner on the Last Day" and "The Keen Household Some Weeks Later" (pages 376, 377, 378), we experience an intense feeling of malaise. This arises from the fact that many of the principles of the table—principles which all of us feel intuitively, with no philosopher to codify them for us—are violated. There is no *li*, no regulation, and we are struck by the atomism of the family. I give below more material bearing on the problem.

Mrs. Keen was putting dinner on the table rather slowly and Mr. Keen was getting Frankie to wash his hands. When we at last sat down it was immediately apparent that Mrs. Keen had not put serving spoons in the food, had forgotten to put butter on the table and left the bread in its original wrapper. This disturbed her husband, for he asked her to please get a plate for the bread and he took the package off the table. He told me to take a piece of meat, and when I did he kept telling me to take more, because "there certainly is enough for everyone." Then he served Paul. Everyone else was serving himself, except Mrs. Keen. Her husband told her to pass me the salad. She buttered Paul's bread. She was the last one served.

Soon Mr. and Mrs. Keen began to talk about marriage and they both mentioned, in a jocular way, that they used to fight quite a bit. They seemed amused when Mr. Keen talked about the day he got the marriage license.

Perhaps one of the saddest things that happened today was just another joking interchange between husband and wife. It had something to do with getting away. Mr. Keen said something about taking off, and his wife said, "You know what would happen, don't you? You would end up with all the kids in the trunk of your car."

All during the meal Paul kept looking from one person to the other, and his eyes rested particularly long on his stepfather's face and on mine. He seemed very preoccupied.

During dinner Frankie seemed the less active of the boys. He sat next to his father while eating, but did not finish everything on his plate. Things were constantly being done for Paul—he seemed to be given no responsibility at all: his bread was buttered for him, his Kool-Aid was poured for him. Whenever he said anything his stepfather silenced him.

Mr. Keen was the first to leave the table, saying he was going into the living room to play with his daughter.

The notes do not indicate whether serving spoons and butter were ever forgotten again, whether Mrs. Keen ever again put bread on the dinner table in its wrapper, to whom the absence of serving spoons was "immediately apparent," whether anyone objected or whether anyone got up to get them. It may be that Mrs. Keen usually put bread on the table in its wrapper and that her husband objected just this time because there was a guest; and perhaps serving spoons were never used. These omissions interfere with a discussion of the Principle of Order; but more important is the fact that we do not know what principles of order are observed at working-class meals. Perhaps workingmen's wives often put bread on the table in its wrapper; perhaps they do not use serving spoons; and there is probably much variation among the "working class."

Mr. Keen obviously presides: at table he tends to take control, but his wife will intervene if she objects to what he does.

With its frightening suggestion of dead children ("in the trunk of your car"), the talk about breaking up ("disaffirming") the family may account for Paul's preoccupation and his apparent helplessness, and for Frankie's short appetite, this time. Divorce is a pretty constant theme in this house.

Nothing occurs at meals that intensifies enjoyment, but there is no observation of a meal at which something does not happen to diminish it. Family solidarity is negated rather than affirmed, and nobody stays longer at table than is necessary for him to eat what he has to.

The war between Mr. and Mrs. Keen stops where some agreement has been reached; where existence has been "neutralized," so to speak; where roles have been agreed upon. In general, food and feeding are one area. He leaves it up to her to feed the baby, and even though he may object if she is too severe with Carol, he will not intervene further. He controls the dinner table; there he has the right to issue orders and she accepts the traditional role of submissive housewife. Mr. Keen does the marketing, and since he is a far better cook than she, he cooks from time to time and she asks him what to do with leftovers. He often puts the finishing touches on sweeping up—perhaps because she is quite sloppy about it, or at least not meticulous enough for him. He leaves the children's bedtime to her, even though he objects to her sending them to bed so early. Thus, where life can be reduced to what the sociologists call "segregated roles"—even though it be the Keens' special variety of role segregation—things are relatively smooth.

The following record illustrates Mr. Keen's efficiency and his wife's sloppiness:

We were in the kitchen when Mr. Keen came home with two big shopping bags full of groceries. I remember there were apples and cabbage, and, I think, potatoes and carrots. After he put them away he wrapped the head of lettuce very carefully in wax paper and put it in the refrigerator. Then he unwrapped the stew meat.

He put out two pieces of wax paper and checked each piece of meat. He removed the little pieces of fat and put them on wax paper; then he sprinkled tenderizer on the meat, and some pepper. Then he began chopping an onion on a cutting board. He was very concentrated on his task—very absorbed. Mrs. Keen remained in the kitchen and occasionally distracted him by some comment. She took a dry mop and started swishing along the floor near the sink. Then she took a broom and swept rather haphazardly, stepping in the dirt.

All this time her husband was methodically preparing the stew. He put the onions in the pan and very carefully cut up another vegetable. Then he chopped the carrots, all the while watching what he was doing. He got out the potatoes and peeled them very carefully, picking out the eyes. He was almost too meticulous. It seemed to take him a very long time—from forty-five minutes to an hour—to get the stew ready for cooking; he did it step by step. To see him you would have thought he was some kind of chef. I asked him where he had learned to cook, and he said, "Oh, I just learned."

Mrs. Keen sat down by the refrigerator and he said, "Don't sit there. I'm going to go in that refrigerator," so she moved over by me. She was holding one of Carol's dresses. The baby had pulled the hem out and Mrs. Keen did not know how she had done it. "How could a baby do this?" As she began to sew the hem, she looked at the other side of it to see if the thread was coming through. She wasn't sewing very carefully.

One might say they have reached a détente on housekeeping.

Paul and Frankie may leave the table without excusing themselves when their eating has satisfied their father. The greatest power is exerted in getting the children to eat, but practically none in keeping the family together at table. Nobody gives a sign that he cares at all whether anybody remains, perhaps because they are only too glad when the meal is over. However, it makes good sense to let everybody go as soon as he feels like it. Why should they want to prolong the misery? At least the parents do not bind the older children to an unbearable situation: they do not compel them to stay where they are miserable, and they do not try to stay there themselves.

On the other hand, perhaps leaving the table as soon as one has finished eating is a common "working class" pattern.

Mrs. Keen and Her Children When There Is No Feeding

Carol: Negation and Pleasure

I have sifted the week's notes for all contacts between Mrs. Keen and Carol outside the feeding situation, and I have grouped them according to whether they seem good for the baby or dubious.

SEEM GOOD

#1

Mrs. Keen took the baby and kissed and hugged her, and the baby laughed and seemed quite happy with her.

#2

She decided that Carol needed some sun in order to grow big and strong, so she took her out of the playpen and sat with her on the porch. She talked about how the sun bothered her [Mrs. Keen] but she continued to sit there with the baby and at last took her back into the house.

#3

Carol was playing with her toys in the playpen in the living room. Sometimes she pulled herself into standing position on the sides and bounced up and down, delighting her mother. Mrs. Keen would laugh and coo at the baby, apparently delighted with every move she made. She alternated for about an hour between watching Carol and watching television.

#4

Mrs. Keen had Carol on her lap and Frankie wanted to kiss the baby. This is one of the few times I have seen him really close to Carol. Mrs. Keen was smiling all the time.

#5

Mrs. Keen got Carol into her pajamas and took her to kiss Mr. Keen good night. I was reminded that on the outing Mrs. Keen often told her husband to look at Carol, to look at what she was doing. She often calls his attention to the baby and then starts to smile—it's a sudden change of mood, and she just starts laughing.

SEEM DUBIOUS

#6

Mrs. Keen let the baby crawl around on the floor for a while. It was the first time [it was now almost noon] this morning that the baby had been free to crawl. Before that she had been either in the crib, the playpen or on her mother's lap. Every time the baby moved, her mother would say, "No, don't do that, you're going to hurt yourself," "You're going to fall off the step," or "You're going to knock the table over."

As Carol crawled on the floor she began to have a bowel movement and her mother looked over and said, "Oh, bet you're going to make a mess in your

pants—that's what I bet you're going to do." Mrs. Keen made a big fuss about this.
[Mrs. Keen went out on the porch to watch for Paul, who was expected home from school for lunch any minute.] She left me and the baby in the living room after telling the baby not to stand up by the coffee table because she might knock it over.

#7

Mrs. Keen told me that Carol loved her bath. I was able to test the water, and I noticed that it was really rather chilly for a baby's bath, even on a summer day like this one. When the baby was lowered into the water, she didn't look at all happy—as a matter of fact she looked very stiff. Her mother immediately took her hand and started splashing it around in the water. Carol splashed a little too, but not very much. Mrs. Keen had told me that Carol splashed and splashed.

Mrs. Keen washed the baby with her hands, saying that this was better than washing her with a cloth. She started to talk about a neighbor who used a special soap and said she didn't go along with that—she had been raised in a plain family and her husband too. . . .

After the bath she examined the baby's vagina rather roughly and then took a Q-Tip, dipped it in baby oil and cleaned out Carol's nostrils, saying she was supposed to do this. She also did it rather roughly. Then she cleaned her ears the same way and examined the baby's vagina again. She poured gobs of powder on Carol's chest and spread it over her in the same rough manner. The powder got on the babys' face. She handled the baby as if she were a hunk of meat or a sack of potatoes.

I had noticed, in the morning, that when Mrs. Keen dressed Carol, she pulled the baby's shoes on roughly and laced them very tightly.

#8

Mrs. Keen set the baby's hair, using pink curlers. She remarked that Carol doesn't like to have her hair set and that she fights before it is finished. She thought this was a riot, and laughed. Carol didn't seem to mind at first, but later on she clearly did. Mrs. Keen seemed to be rather rough in the way she set the baby's hair—she wound the curls so tight. She kept looking over at me and laughing. Then she took the baby and put her in the playpen in the living room. The baby fell over something and cried and cried. Her mother went over to her and started fixing one of her curls and the baby cried again. Mr. Keen said, "Alice stop it, you're hurting her," but she didn't seem to mind that she was hurting the baby.

#9

Mrs. Keen was sitting with Carol on the next-door neighbor's front porch, and I went over. One of the things the neighbor talked about involved Carol's hair. She said little girls shouldn't have their hair curled because they weren't ready to look for boy friends yet. Carol reached for the neighbor's cigarettes and the neighbor took away the pack and the ashtray, saying they weren't for her to play with. When Carol started to cry, the neighbor seemed alarmed. The baby was standing by the neighbor's chair, crying, but Mrs. Keen, unconcerned, was leaning on the porch railing. Looking from me to Mrs. Keen, the neighbor said, "Well, do something," and Mrs. Keen picked up Carol. She did not respond to the baby's crying until the neighbor spoke.

#10

Mrs. Keen put the baby on the bed and started to examine her nose and mouth. She examines her mouth quite often—apparently to see how many teeth she has. She said to the baby, "You've got a big booger [crust] in there [nose] and Mama has to get it out." The baby was protesting and crying. Mrs.

Keen got a Q-Tip and thrust it into the baby's nose. Carol was protesting and hollering but Mrs. Keen kept holding her arms and telling her not to move around. She poked in there three or four times but nothing came out. Finally she said, "Let me look and see if I got the booger." Then she said, "There," as if she had gotten it, but I didn't see anything on the Q-Tip.

#11

Dandling Carol on her knee, Mrs. Keen talked about how much the baby cost, and said to her, "I keep having things like you; you cost me a hundred and fifty dollars." She talked about people going to Fink's Department Store, where they could buy air conditioners. She wanted one, she said, but babies kept coming along, so they didn't have any money.

These notes show that Mrs. Keen can take delight in her baby and make the baby feel good. She is even willing to sit in the sun with her, although, for her own good, she should not. The field notes contain five entries in which mother and baby seem to enjoy each other—in which Mrs. Keen seems to be doing something that makes her and the baby feel good—and six entries (aside from the feeding) in which Mrs. Keen seems to restrict Carol unnecessarily, to deal roughly with her or even to cause her pain willfully and callously.*

In presenting the material on feeding Carol to a group in psychiatry, I was asked by a psychoanalyst whether I had thought of sadism in connection with Mrs. Keen. I replied that I found it impossible to decide, from those observations alone, whether Mrs. Keen was sadistic, and that it seemed to me that much of what she did to Carol may have derived from perceptual defects, combined with a tendency to fly into a rage and to react violently to slight frustrations. Yet, I added, there are some incidents, like the "sorry-bad" one, which make me suspect a sadistic impulse. What happened when she set Carol's hair now leads me to think that Mrs. Keen could take pleasure in her baby's pain. The matter is further complicated, however, by the fact that Mrs. Keen seems to want to hurt Carol also because it hurts her husband. Since she perceives that hurting the baby upsets Mr. Keen, this may override other perceptions, so that the baby's very discomfort becomes a motivation to continue it. Mrs. Keen allows her emotions to obstruct a clear perception of Carol's suffering and to prevent an appropriately maternal reaction. The baby's discomfort is a nuisance to Mrs. Keen when it makes Carol hard to manage, but to the degree that it offends her husband it is desirable.

Such socialization of perception conforms to a general law that perceptions involving human beings are affected by the relationship. It also conforms to a law according to which perceptions and actions are selected by the brain according to their emotional loading. These two together constitute what might be called the "black is white" law of perception: "I love him so that if he wants me to say black is white I will—and believe it"; "I hate him so that if he says it's black, I'll say it's white—and believe it!"

Continuing to hurt Carol may also express Mrs. Keen's determination not to let her husband put her down—not to let any man push her around. Thus the baby pays for the bad relationship between Mrs. Keen and her husband and for the bad relationship between male and female in our culture.

* Observer bias can never be ruled out of this or any other observation.

It is a unique accomplishment of *Homo sapiens* to have discovered the possibility and utility of one person's hurting another through inflicting pain on a third—as Mrs. Keen hurts her husband through hurting the baby. Another evolutionary achievement is the ability to take pleasure in the pain of others; and the name of the Marquis de Sade has been given it. As I pointed out in *Culture Against Man,* in studying the evolution of our species we have to take account of man's capacity to use every one of his evolutionary accomplishments against himself. We have to take account also of the emergence, in the course of evolution, of *viciousness,* another unique achievement of *Homo sapiens.* The point I stressed is that every emergent "accomplishment," with a potentially positive outcome, has also its potentially vicious backlash.

At any rate, when Mrs. Keen is dealing with her baby, it seems as if there were missing from *her* consciousness an essential element of the *human* consciousness that defines our culture, the idea that human beings in one's own family must be protected against pain. She knows that pain exists and that it can be used for control, but lacking the essential element, she has no compassion. Reflecting that her baby's pain does not move her and sometimes even gives her pleasure, we suddenly imagine the Roman Coliseum filled with agony so immense that after two thousand years we are still appalled by it, and it occurs to us that there can be whole populations in which pain has this character. Remembering Nero, Caligula, Domitian, and others, we understand that Mrs. Keen is merely extreme, and perhaps out of date. When we perceive that her uniqueness consists in the fact that the cruelty of which man in our culture has always been capable is, in her case, turned against her own baby, and that the cruelty without which no civilization ever became "great" has here entered the home, then we realize that the cruelty that makes supreme paratroopers, bomber pilots, napalm droppers, etc., is kept out of our own homes by chance alone.* Though some of the most competent brains in the world—chemists, physicists, biologists, etc.—are trained in the technology of cruelty and train others in it, there is no systematic training in compassion. It stands to reason, therefore, that what aggrandizes us will destroy us, and it will do it by surreptitiously entering our homes labeled "psychotic," "neurotic" or "disturbed." The number of American children mutilated and killed by their parents and the "incomprehensible" multiple murders by deranged men are an outcome of the historical mercilessness of our culture. It is true that we have the value of compassion also; and hospitals, I suppose, are one institutional expression of it. Organized religion, which likes to fancy itself the mother of compassion, long ago lost its right to that claim by its organized support of organized cruelty.

Now, it is clear from the observations under "Seem Good," that Mrs. Keen has love, or something like it, for Carol, that she wants to take pleasure in the baby and that she wants her husband (observation #5, page 419) to take pleasure in and love the baby too. Observation #2 (page 419) also shows that Mrs. Keen can do something unselfish to "make the baby

---

* If one asks oneself, "Why isn't my family as cruel as the Keens?" the answer is so difficult that one has to fall back on some vacuous answer like "It's just good luck." I refer the reader to the introductory essay on "The Miracle of Tenderness" (p. 367).

big and strong," by disregarding her own intolerance of the sun. But when she tries to do *for* the baby what is necessary to keep her alive, safe, clean or "attractive" (whether putting the baby's shoes on, feeding or bathing her, setting her hair), she over and over again does *against* her and mishandles her, so that solicitude is satanically mixed with destruction. The essence of the pathogenic process is the negation of solicitude in the very act of giving it. In the category "Seem Good" there is only one example (observation #2, above) in which Mrs. Keen is actually doing something to keep the baby either alive, safe, clean, healthy or "attractive," while in most of the observations in which she hurts the baby—in the "Seem Dubious" group and in the feeding series—she is doing something to keep the baby alive, safe, clean, healthy or "attractive." Fundamentally, then, *pathogenesis is a negation of basic life processes.*

Observation #6 (page 419) illustrates how Mrs. Keen is "overly restrictive" while trying to protect Carol. It suggests, also, that like many disturbed mothers, Mrs. Keen cannot get used to her baby's excrement. Thus the natural impulse to move around and the biological need to excrete are both challenged, restricted or given negative meaning. Yet even in the process of restricting Carol's baby activity, Mrs. Keen shows that she has the baby's safety at heart.

Frankie: Getting Away with Murder

Mrs. Keen punishes Frankie much less than Carol. She is forever saying no to Frankie, but most of the time he does what he wants to, and though she scolds him and threatens him with "the belt" and with telling his father, she never used the belt while the observer was there. She hit Frankie only once—with her hand and only after he hit her first—and there is no indication that Mrs. Keen ever carried out the threats to tell his father. The following documents the conclusion that Mrs. Keen is quite nice to Frankie and puts up with a great deal from him.

#1

(First day.) Frankie took a pair of scissors and pried a hinge cap off the refrigerator. He took it in to his mother and told her he couldn't get it back on, so she walked into the kitchen and said, "Oh, what did you do? Look what you've done now. Boy, you're going to get it when your dad gets home." [He did not.]

#2

(Second day.) Twice this morning Frankie came in and asked his mother for money to go to the store. She gave it to him the first time, and the second time he took it without permission and bought a balloon and some candy. She said he was really going to catch it when his father got home. [He did not.]

#3

Frankie came in to ask his mother for more money to go to the store, but she said no. Since she was busy with the baby and I was standing by the sink, she said, "Susan, don't let him take the money." I said I would hold the baby while she took care of Frankie, but that I couldn't interfere, so she went over and yelled at him not to take any money and that he was going to catch it anyway for having taken money. Frankie left. [He did not catch it.]

#4

(Sixth day.) Mrs. Keen suggested that Frankie make mud pies. He had gotten some candles out of the drawer and his mother suggested that he stick those in the mud pies. He wanted to take some water along but she said no. He wanted to take a spoon but she said no to that, too, but he took one, anyway. I asked her if it was all right for him to take the spoon and she replied, "Well, he's got it now." She explained her initial refusal by saying that his father didn't want the silverware outside any more. [Description here of observer's play with Frankie while he makes pies, using a paper plate.]

After we finished playing, he brought a plate of dirt into the house. I had asked him to leave it outside, but he said his mother wouldn't care if he brought it in. She had just washed the kitchen floor and he dumped the dirt on it. I said, "Oh, Frankie, look what you've done," and since Mrs. Keen was about to feed the baby, I said I would sweep it up. As I was sweeping, Frankie kicked his foot in front of my face. I said, "Don't kick me, Frankie," but he did. I asked him to please not kick me, because I didn't like it; I said I liked him but I didn't like his kicking. He said, "I can, too, kick you." Finally I asked him if he wanted to help me sweep up, so he took the dustpan and held it while I swept the dirt into it. Then he took the dustpan into the living room, saying, "Come in here— we can sweep the living room," but I said no, the broom wasn't used to sweep the living room. Then I discovered he had spilled some dirt in the doorway too.

I came into the house, after playing outside with Frankie, and then he came in, bringing some cherries. He said he had picked some more cherries from his tree, and he came over to me, saying, "See my cherries?" I said nothing, but his mother said he had been told he wasn't to pick those cherries—that they weren't ripe. He asked me if I wanted one, and I said no, they weren't ripe. Then he said he had eaten cherries off this tree before; I asked him what color they were and he said they were red. [Mrs. Keen left the room and Frankie started hitting the observer.] He finally did stop hitting me and then his mother came in and asked what we were talking about; Frankie said, "Cherries," but I said I was asking him why he hit me. She went down to the basement to do the laundry, and he followed her and brought up two badminton rackets although his mother told him, "Don't bring them up." Frankie asked me to play with him outside, but I said no, his mother had asked him not to bring the rackets upstairs, but he said, "Well, I can," and he went outside with them. [Observer went downstairs to be with Mrs. Keen while she was hanging up the clothes to dry, and then went into the bedroom to take a nap.]

Before I fell asleep I heard Frankie come in again and ask where I was, and his mother said I was asleep and that he should not bother me. He came into the room with the rackets and said, "Come outside and play," but I said, "No, Frankie, I'm resting now, I'll see you later." . . . He began hitting me with the rackets. At first he didn't hit hard. I was just lying there and then he hit me one on the back that was pretty hard. I jumped up suddenly and said, "Frankie, don't you do that," and he got a terrible look of fear on his face and started running toward the door, saying, "No!" I repeated that I was going to rest and would see him later. His mother told him to come out.

He went into the kitchen and apparently opened the refrigerator, for I heard his mother say, "Don't you get into the refrigerator." I fell asleep.

#5

Frankie and his little friend were playing with the ball I had bought for Carol, and although Mrs. Keen kept telling them not to play with it, she didn't take it away from them. At last it rolled out into the street and she said, "There, see what you've done. I bet I have to go down and get it." [The notes do not indicate whether she got it.] I guess it finally got to be too much for her, because she said she was going to get the belt.

Frankie took off his shoes and his mother said, "You're not going barefoot," but he said yes and began to walk around in his socks, so she said she was going to get the belt. Whimpering, and with a sad look on his face, Frankie asked me to put his shoes on, but when I started to, he said, "No, let me do it myself," so I let him. When he started to put a shoe on the wrong foot I pointed it out, but he said no, it was the right shoe. I kept quiet and he finally put it on the correct foot.

Taking the cap off the refrigerator violates the unwritten metaphysic of "durables" ("hard goods," placing them in the category of expensive-complicated taboo), which states that children are not to tamper with them and that they are to be dismantled only by skilled mechanics for repair purposes. Automobiles, toasters, TV sets, washing machines, driers, heaters, and so on, also belong in the "durables" category. The prices of durables fluctuate much less than those of nondurables, and durables have the special quality of being able to rise in price while demand for them is declining. One of the striking aspects of the rebellion of youth nowadays is that they can often repair durables which their fathers would not dare tinker with, and that often they own a "durable" themselves. Since American civilization is built on durables (including armaments, now affectionately called "hardware," which sort of brings them right into the kitchen and basement), there is a somewhat superstitious reverence for and delight in them that passes beyond their mere utility.

I find it striking that Mrs. Keen, a person presumed on the way to total disorganization, really cares about and understands this metaphysic and responds to its dynamic implications. With the intuition and élan, therefore, of a perfectly normal person, she understands, and is able to act on the fact, that damage to the hinge will impair the *efficiency* of the refrigerator, making it difficult to manage the food supply. She is able to relate one thing to another; in regard to the refrigerator she is "perfectly normal." In view of Frankie's violation, Mrs. Keen is remarkably restrained in her reaction. Frankie spit on the universe in this violation, and potentially there are grave consequences; yet his mother merely threatened—she did not punish him. A whacking would not have been too much to expect, and a strong scolding might have been very salutary. On the other hand, Mrs. Keen failed in that she did not explain to Frankie the enormity of his offense, but I think very few mothers would have, because the metaphysic lies below the level of awareness.*

Frankie seems to get quite a bit of money from his mother. I wish we knew enough about the working class to tell whether this is usual or not. Mrs. Keen appears rather indulgent in this regard, but Frankie is insatiable, so he steals. He steals—but what courage to let himself be found out! "Nor-

---

* It is for these unconscious systems that advertisers and other propagandists reach when they wish to use us; attempting to manipulate the very tissue of consciousness and sanity. They are like those malevolent scientists, seen in TV movies, who perform operations on brains in order to so modify the substratum of the mind that the victims will become their creatures. Advertising, etc., is not merely "messages" but a kind of plastic surgery, a kind of weaving-into the fabric of sanity, which *must* then function, in the interest of others, *competely outside our control*.

mal" children steal, usually very surreptitiously. The ease with which
Frankie is found out, however, suggests that when he stole before, he was
not punished severely. In some families stealing is such an enormous crime
that children may be beaten and denied freedom for a month, but Frankie
is merely scolded (is this a punishment?) and threatened with his father.
His mother is no policeman: she does not represent the ultimate threat to
Frankie; she does not impress him with the importance of being innocent,
nor even with the importance of being careful not to get caught.

In the ancient image, money, when honest, had the qualities of a chaste
woman, of clear water, of unpolluted space. Money is virginal, pure and
"cold" when owned or acquired honestly, but "dirty" and "hot" when stolen.
Stealing money is therefore another immense spitting on sacredness—perhaps not so bad in a child, but bad enough. Yet Frankie's violation of the
metaphysic of money does not bring retribution—merely a threat of it,
which is not carried out: Frankie knows his mother won't snitch. This principle is more sacred to his mother than the principles of hard goods and the
holiness of money. She apparently holds the protection of Frankie against
his father higher than the metaphysic of money. She has an *ontological
hierarchy*—a hierarchy of angelic Notions blowing gold and silver horns.
Like metaphysicians from Aristotle to Husserl, she holds some inherent,
intuitively accepted principles or concepts higher than others, and ranks
her feelings accordingly. At this point she is just like many "perfectly normal" mothers who hold protection against the father higher than money.

We continue with the spoon. Here nothing happened, except a faint stir
of disapproval. The metaphysic of silverware divides it into categories of
quality—"good," "second- and even third-line," kept in different places and
used for different occasions. We do not know the quality—or "line"—of
spoon Frankie took, but we do know that he committed a violation—but a
violation of a purely human mandate, for his father alone had objected.
Frankie's was not a mortal sin, like stealing money, for it is recognized that
the metaphysic of silverware, which holds that silverware is to be used only
in connection with food and the rooms in which it is manipulated, may be
modified in the case of children who need it for play. The culture stands
firm on that one! Thus, in our culture the laws of children may modify
universal laws of silverware. And furthermore, Mrs. Keen recognizes this
modification as a modification, so that she is willing to oppose Frankie's
father on the basis of it—perhaps she is even very willing, because it annoys h'm! Here again, the evidence points to sanity, to her capacity for
circumspection, to her strength, to her ability to tolerate the violation of the
law of silverware and to accept this childish violation of a merely idiosyncratic ordinance. Unlike stealing, violation of the law of silverware is not
violation of an immutable law of the universe, and hence merits punishment much less.

We cannot say as much as we might wish about Frankie's spilling the
dirt on the kitchen floor because we do not know how Mrs. Keen reacted.
But we can guess that since Frankie kicked the observer when she started
to sweep up the dirt, his "present" was intended for his mother, and that
Frankie was annoyed because the observer accepted it. At any rate, we
perceive that he is not very much afraid of his mother—that he is willing to
brave her anger in order to bother her or in order to do what he wants to do.

The large number of "violations" point to the fact that in spite of her threats and scolding, Frankie's mother is quite permissive with him. Since Frankie does not react as if he were being punished, we conclude that a decision by an observer about whether an act is punishment or not depends on the interpretation of the one punished as well as on the one who punishes. Punishment may turn out to be a reward in that the one who is punished knows he has succeeded in upsetting the person who punished him. The last hurrah is that of the man who enrages the king to the point where the king cuts off his head! Rats, pigeons—even chimpanzees—have not accomplished this evolutionary feat.

What is, perhaps, of most interest in the incident of the dirt spilled on the kitchen floor is Frankie's understanding of the relationship between dirt, mother and floor. He must have learned from his mother that she wants and believes in a clean kitchen floor. *The fact that he violates that floor is witness to his mother's sanity!* In the midst of her anguish, on the threshold of another nervous breakdown, far gone in pregnancy, anemic, and with the prodromal symptoms of her fatal illness perhaps even then undermining her constitution, this pathetic woman washes her kitchen floor. She grasps at this line to sanity and life.

Man does not eat what is unripe. Perhaps here and there particular fruits or vegetables are eaten so, but on the whole, *Homo sapiens* avoids and teaches his children to avoid the unripe. Thus, in objecting to Frankie's eating the cherries, Mrs. Keen joins the human race. She becomes a particle in the tide of humanity, which, through evolutionary time, has avoided unripe fruit, and in affirming her objection to unripeness, Mrs. Keen affirms her sanity too, for how else does man affirm his sanity except by affirming, in behavior, the perduring characteristics of the species? This *perception* of unripeness, plus the *predictable* negative response, shows us one more strength.

Sin against a purely human ordinance (as in the case of the spoon) confronts mother and child again in the case of the badminton rackets, and again Mrs. Keen refrains from enforcing the law—in this case, *her* law, for there is no metaphysic into which she can fit those rackets. She has, perhaps, a tendency to be more relaxed about purely human ordinances than about those which culture has validated as eternal—like the law of money —although she can sometimes become very, very angry and threatening about the former, as, for example, in the case of Carol's ball (see page 424). But there, I suppose, being pregnant and anemic, she got sick and tired of seeing the ball roll away. A metaphysical principle was also involved, however. Let us assume that by "street" is meant "middle of the street, where the autos run" and that she really did go and get the ball, bending over her big pregnant belly to pick it up. If *she* gets the ball, it is only to protect the children from being run over and to save the ball for the baby, in which case she is being a good mother in spite of her fatigue and discomfort. The metaphysical underpinning for this behavior is clear: *solicitude* embraces it. Perceiving certain functions of parenthood clearly, she is reasonable and even maternally self-sacrificing. Threatening with "the belt" is a commonplace of working-class child nurture and is found in many ethnic groups also. But even here we sense from the text that the threat fits the crime and that it was made only after a great exercise of *forbearance;* Mrs. Keen did not immediately threaten the belt but delayed until she had reached her *limit.* She is not always in a rush, not always driven by impulse to punitive behavior. Her psychological limit is felt by us to be *reasonable.*

In going after the ball, Mrs. Keen synthesizes her maternal role (solicitude), the character of the street (dangerous) and the status of her child (vulnerable and having a right to be protected by her). But her role has time, mood and reasonableness aspects too. She is affected by how long whatever is happening drags on (time); her mood changes accordingly along with her willingness to let things continue, and her intuition informs her correctly when her child has become unreasonable by continuing to do too long what she has asked him not to. Since the longer the ball-playing continues, the less she can stand it, her maternal role undergoes a change as her patience approaches its limit. This is *the inner calculus* of role performance. The limit of patience—or endurance, if one prefers—is related to Mrs. Keen's conception of her own *rights* and to an *obligation* she attributes to a child (as an aspect of *his* role) to desist—or, at least, to desist when his mother's patience is becoming exhausted.

The analysis of any act requires the study of the actual material environment (the street), the role and status of the persons involved (including rights and obligations), the moods, the reasonableness of the activity, the length of time it goes on, the limits and endurance of the person involved and the limits as *culturally defined.* ("No mother has to put up forever with a child's throwing the ball into the street—there's a limit, you know! Mrs. Burke has a lot more patience than I, and I suppose she's a lot stronger, too.")

No amount of analysis of psychosexual level, of reinforcement, of stages of intellectual development, and so on, would get us to this synthesis.

The fact that Mrs. Keen is more sensitive to Frankie's vulnerabilities than to Carol's requires further analysis. When Mrs. Keen herself is the threat, she does not perceive it, but when the threat is a force outside herself, she does. In this we are all very much like her. The point is an evolutionary one, for in the course of the evolution of mammals, provision for parental protection of the young against outside forces, and for the control of the destructiveness of parents, was directed by genetic factors. With the extinction of these genetic factors in man, parental protectiveness became more problematic, and the possibility of parental destructiveness—psychological and physical—became more likely. In the course of cultural evolution some societies must have drifted too far in the direction of underprotecting (called "indirect infanticide") or even of destroying ("direct infanticide") children.

Before examining the conflict over going barefoot, I would like to present two more observations to the reader, and then some quotes from *The Adventures of Tom Sawyer.*

(Second day.) While Mrs. Keen was feeding Carol, Frankie came in and asked his mother's permission to go barefoot. She told him he could, if he promised to take a bath later. He left. [The notes do not say whether he promised or whether he took the bath.]

Frankie came in crying, saying that a neighbor lady had sent him home because he was barefoot, and his mother told him just to tell her his mother had given him permission. Neighbors, she said, were always nosing into everything but their own business. She said to Frankie, "People are old goats, aren't they?"

From *The Adventures of Tom Sawyer**

Presently Tom checked his whistle. A stranger was before him. . . . This boy was well dressed, too well dressed on a weekday. This was simply astounding. . . . He had shoes on—and it was only Friday. (p. 15)

Tom . . . was called off to dress for Sunday School . . . He hoped that Mary would forget his shoes, but the hope was blighted; she coated them thoroughly with tallow, as was the custom, and brought them out. He lost his temper and said he was always being made to do everything he didn't want to do. But Mary said, persuasively:
"Please, Tom—that's a good boy."
So he got into his shoes, snarling. (pp. 30–1)

Huckleberry came and went, at his own free will . . . he was always the first boy that went barefoot in the spring and the last to resume leather in the fall; he never had to wash, nor put on clean clothes; he could swear wonderfully. In a word, everything that goes to make life precious, that boy had. So thought every harassed, hampered, respectable boy in St. Petersburg. (p. 46)

In the Keen household the American mystique of bare feet seems to bring Frankie and his mother together. "People are old goats, aren't they?" says Mrs. Keen in a rare, warm moment of transient reunion-in-hostility. Mother and son understand what it is to go barefoot—what it means. But there is more to this sanity than merely a traditional revolt against respectability: there is Mrs. Keen's perfectly rightful objection to her neighbor's sticking her nose into her affairs, and in referring to the neighbor as an "old goat," Mrs. Keen expresses the right to be free from the meddling of neighbors. Even her metaphor is linguistically correct and well within the limits of respectable derogation. Behind Mrs. Keen's objection to her neighbor's intervention lies Mrs. Keen's understanding of the primordial postulate: *no responsibilities, no rights*. If a person has no responsibility for my child, he has no right to discipline him, and a characteristic of tribal cultures in which children are disciplined by people other than the parents is that those others have specific personal responsibilities toward the child also.

But we have not finished elucidating Mrs. Keen's sanity. Consider the fact that she lets Frankie go barefoot on condition that he take a bath: what could be more maternal, what could be more mother-and-child-like? Behold, then, the principle of the parent-child bargain! Behold the price of maternal favor—that ineffable silk! Note also the fact that Frankie has learned to ask for permission to walk with his feet free of leather and that his mother knows how to extort a bath from him. Could anything be more normal? And she *wants* her child to bathe—it makes a difference to her;

* Quotes are from Mark Twain's *Adventures of Tom Sawyer* (Signet Classic; New York, New American Library, 1959).

she knows that cleanliness is next to godliness. The mother's sensitivity to *the mystique of bare feet,* her understanding of the relationship between obligations and rights, her awareness of the conventions of respectable derogation, her grasp of certain principles of parent-child bargaining and of the ontological import of bathing—are all lucidly implied in those few lines, and with them, her sanity.

And let us finally note that with delicate maternal sensibility, Mrs. Keen comforts her child's sorrow by calling the neighbor a name. She is trying to be a good mother.

By the sixth day the idyll of bare feet is destroyed (see observation #5, page 425), perhaps by the objections of the same neighbor lady, and Mrs. Keen is threatening Frankie with the belt for taking his shoes off. Mrs. Keen has merely switched to another normal phase of the foot-defined area of sanity, but now she has safety and respectability on her side; now she is squarely behind conformity just as a few days ago she was against it. This does not make things easy for Frankie, and he whimpers, because he does not understand that his mother has his own good at heart. It may be that she insists on his going shod just in order to preserve her name in the neighborhood as a good mother, but it is still in Frankie's interest to have it known that his mother does not "let her kids run around like gypsies." Mrs. Keen is trying to be a good mother.

Here are a few more examples.

#1

Mrs. Keen went out to get Frankie for his nap. When they came back, Frankie was protesting loudly, but she finally got him to go to bed. He came out of his room once to show me how to use a ball and bat, but his mother sent him off to bed again.

He slept for about an hour and when he awoke he was very anxious about something. His mother said he was cross, and she told him that if he had gone to bed earlier he wouldn't be so cross. He sat on her lap for a while. We were in the kitchen. He kept hitting his mother on the shoulders and saying, "Darn it." I didn't know what the reason was for all this.

#2

She got Frankie and made him come into the house. He didn't want to, but he finally went into his room. Mrs. Keen was lying down with Carol in her bedroom and I was in the living room reading the paper. Frankie got up once and went into his mother's bedroom and said something I couldn't quite hear. Then he came into the living room with a new shirt on; he wanted to see how it fit, but I said I thought he was supposed to be in bed. He said no, but his mother heard him and ordered him back to bed. He called out to her that he had to poo-poo, so he went to the bathroom. She kept telling him to get back to bed and he replied he was still in the bathroom.

Finally he did go and lie down. His door was open, and as I was leaving he asked where I was going. I told him I was going for a walk and to do some shopping.

#3

Frankie came in with his little friend Myrtle. She had a bag of peanuts but she wouldn't give any to him; his mother talked rather loudly about how she should give him some and if she wouldn't, she could go home. Myrtle left and Mrs. Keen proceeded to tell me that Frankie was always giving the little girl something and that she didn't want her kids to be selfish, but she didn't want them to be made fools of, either. This morning she told Frankie that if anyone hit him—girl or boy—he should hit right back, because she didn't like him getting hit; he had gotten a knock on the head and she didn't like that.

Mrs. Keen's effort to be a good mother takes place within well-recognized normalities of child care and protection. There is the maternal insistence on a nap, over the typical objections of a three-year-old, and the mother's effort to comfort the child when he wakes up anxious. Even her interpretation of his anxiety as crossness has the exquisiteness of a cultural cliché used right. The fact that Frankie goes and sits on his mother's lap demonstrates that he knows he will be accepted there, that he feels she is a good mother. The incident with the little girl who wouldn't share brings out Mrs. Keen's protectiveness and her awareness of the conventions of sharing. Like a good mother, Mrs. Keen wants to defend her child against exploitation; perhaps she is too eager, for too many defenses of this kind might lose Frankie friends. These three observations demonstrate again Mrs. Keen's awareness of her son's vulnerability and her eagerness to protect him—all within a culturally respectable configuration.

ANALYTICAL SUMMARY

A person observing Mrs. Keen only while she dealt with Carol would surely be convinced that she was mad, but on the other hand, if he saw her only while she was with Frankie, especially if the observer missed certain feedings, he would never suspect the madness that appears when she deals with Carol. She seems to pour out nearly all her potential for disturbed behavior on the baby, and this leads us to suspect that there is something about her relationship to Carol that makes her do it. I do not believe we have enough information to come to a conclusion. Mr. Keen gets upset when he sees her hurt Carol; on the other hand, he does not see her let Frankie get away with murder, but her permissiveness is experienced by him as a feeling that the kids are getting out of hand, and he frequently complains about it. When Carol is hurt and Frankie goes scot-free, the children are weapons against the father. It is impossible to say that Mrs. Keen is permissive with Frankie on purpose or that she is motivated by unconscious factors in this, but the result is the same: it makes him unruly. A consequence for Frankie is that it sometimes gets him into trouble with his father.

Analysis of the relationship between Mrs. Keen and Frankie has demonstrated how intricately sane Mrs. Keen is, for the *pattern of sanity* is complex, though psychiatry, as it must, has emphasized patterns of insanity. It is this pattern of sanity on which Mrs. Keen has a strong grip; it is this pattern of sanity which the logical analysis has attempted to lay bare. Beneath the outward skin of conventionality of all of us runs a fine network of metaphysical assumption, mystique and behavior; intuitions of limits, reasonableness, role, obligations and rights, etc. This network is the infrastructure of sanity; it has to be understood in diagnosis, prognosis and treatment.

Mrs. Keen and Paul

Paul was less than a year old when his mother and father separated, and it was not until Mrs. Keen remarried and Paul got a stepfather that there was a permanent adult male in his life. During those first years of his life, his mother boarded him out during the day and picked him up in the evening, on her way back from work, to take him home with her to her mother's house. Her father was dead. The record states that Mrs. Keen had reason to believe that the woman with whom she boarded Paul mistreated him. Paul is a pretty sad little boy. When he was tested several years ago Paul had an exceedingly low IQ, but the opinion of his teacher in special education was that he was not working at his potential, that he daydreamed and could not concentrate. He could not "get along" with the other children either. Urged to have Paul undergo a psychological examination, Mrs. Keen got the diagnosis: "Retarded, with behavior problems."

In view of Mrs. Keen's intervention, often violent and determined, in the functions of her children, and in view of Paul's history, the psychological diagnosis seems problematic—as, indeed, many such diagnoses are. As we shall presently see, Paul receives no demonstrations of affection from his mother; yet the other children receive little also. Paul does not get any money from his mother and he seems to have no toys—at least he was not seen playing with any toy other than the one the observer brought him. Yet, even as Mrs. Keen was "breaking down" for a third time, she thought principally of Paul. When the observer spoke to Mrs. Keen over the phone, just after Mrs. Keen returned from a checkup at the hospital, where the psychiatrist had expressed the opinion that she was so disturbed that she would probably have to be readmitted, Mrs. Keen did not mention the other children but said, crying quietly, "I wonder what is going to happen to Paul. Oh, I worry so much about Paul." Let us keep this in mind as we consider the following observations. The first three bear on the problem of her continuing to treat him like a three-year-old.

Mrs. Keen told Paul to wash his hands and dress and get ready for school. She followed him into the boys' room and remained there while he was dressing. Frankie and I played hide-and-go-seek, but I could see that Mrs. Keen was putting Paul's pants and shirt on him. Frankie and I went into the boys' room too, and as Mrs. Keen put Paul's shoes on, she said she certainly wished he would learn to tie his shoelaces, because it was very annoying for her to have to do it.

. . .

Mrs. Keen told Paul to get dressed, and she went into the boys' room with him . . . and helped him get dressed.

. . .

After breakfast Mrs. Keen went to the boys' room to be with Paul to see that he got dressed.

Students of psychopathology will not be impressed by these evidences of "retardation," for they are long familiar with *infantilization*. The following notes show the other side of the coin.

Paul told Frankie that I would sew the piece of plastic they were playing with and make it into a purse for Frankie, but *I said they could do it themselves.* So they got some string out of the drawer and got the scissors and Paul sewed the pieces together. As I watched Paul at work I got to thinking of yesterday morning, when he dressed himself. He had a pair of new tennis shoes, still without laces. He evidently laced them himself and came in to me and said, "Look!" I don't understand why his mother has to dress him in the morning, since he showed yesterday that he can do it himself.

. . .

When Paul was asked to dry the dishes he protested strongly, but finally complied.

Paul was again asked to dry the dishes, and he put up a bigger protest than before, yelling that he was not going to do them and his mother yelled back. Finally she told him to just do them and walked out of the kitchen. He was distracted several times, once by listening to the water going down the drain. He asked me if I wanted to hear it again. I asked him how many dishes he still had to dry, since I thought that it would bring his attention back to what he was supposed to do. He counted and said he had twenty-eight, and then finished the dishes. Meanwhile his mother kept yelling from the bedroom, "Please finish drying the dishes," and Paul looked at me and said, "I'm sure glad this world is in one piece."

As Mrs. Keen dresses Paul, they are close to each other, and he is like a baby to her. The two of them get something out of his "inability" to dress himself, though it is also a nuisance to the mother. Since the speed at which Paul dresses suits her no more than the speed at which he eats his noonday meal, her obsession with speed helps deprive her children of independence. At the present time, this kind of *radical* interference with the boy's independence seems to occur only when Mrs. Keen feels under some kind of pressure. When a parent is driven *on* by time, and her child has been driven *back* by time—because he has not been able to put up with his mother's pace-making and because he has suffered emotional deprivations—it is not surprising to find mother and child in the mutual, self-reinforcing time reversal called infantilization. When we consider the rewards Paul gets from this and what he would lose were he to mature, we can readily understand why he might appear to be "retarded," etc.: any move in the direction of appearing not to be a baby might be so frightening that Paul might even be willing to fail in school.

If we assume that during the years when she had no husband and was living with her mother, Paul was infantilized, partly perhaps because it was "easier" and more expeditious for the women to do everything *for* the child rather than let him do anything himself, partly because he, somehow, had to be "protected," we can account for Paul's "retardation" without introducing constitutional factors.*

I do not believe that Mrs. Keen's obsession with time was solely responsible for Paul's infantilization. Other aspects of the problem are discussed below.

Paul, it seems, can accomplish what he wants to do when it suits him and when he can do it at his own pace. On the other hand, doing what *he* wants to do is often inseparable from what his mother wants him to do. Drying dishes takes co-ordination and good sense, if for no other reason

* I have no data on unconscious factors motivating Mrs. Keen and/or her mother to infantilize Paul.

than that it is necessary not to break the dishes. In this particular case, there is no time pressure from his mother. And dish drying is not something —like dressing—which Mrs. Keen might be motivated to do for Paul. His mother sends Paul to the store too, and even though he sometimes forgets items, what child doesn't? Furthermore, his performance must be good enough, on the average, for her to continue sending him.

When Paul came home he went right to his room and got the Batman figure I had given him as a present. His mother asked, "Did you take that to school with you?" and he said, "No, Mom, I just went in and got it right out of my room." She said, "Go to the store and get some bread and milk," so off he went. But he came back without the milk, saying he had forgotten, and his mother yelled at him and sent him back for it.

Mrs. Keen's question about the Batman figure could be motherly interest. Yet, in the overall impression of their relationship, it might bring us to a more general problem—her constant intervention in Paul's life: he absolutely must be home from school by four o'clock, and if he is not, his mother questions him closely. He is not allowed to play with girls:

Paul came home from school, apparently a little late: it was around four-twenty. His mother had told me that he used to take a girl friend home until recently and that she had tried to stop it. Then he would be late but now he was getting home on time.
She began to ask him where he had been, and when he told her that he had run all the way home, she said he must have stopped somewhere. When she asked him where, he said he hadn't, but she insisted, "You don't need to lie to me, Paul—just where were you?" With the baby's crying and her being upset with Frankie [who had been pounding her legs asking for jello until she hit him], she started to scream at Paul. Finally we all went out on the porch to wait for Mr. Keen.

Mrs. Keen won't give Paul a chance to become mature or masculine by being with boys and girls his own age after school; he has to come home to be with his mother, the baby and his little brother. In this way he might be pushed in the direction of becoming "feminine" and babyish (in the American view). Consider the following:

Paul had taken Frankie's baseball mitt and Frankie was demanding it—it was his mitt, and he wanted it back. Their mother came to the door and told Paul to give it back, and Paul did; and as he went into the house he said he hated Frankie, that he was very selfish. He went to his room and began to cry.
.　.　.
Paul finished his breakfast and then got Carol out of the crib despite his mother's objections; she said the baby should stay there until her breakfast at nine o'clock. Mrs. Keen took the baby and hugged and kissed her, and they both laughed, and the baby seemed happy with her mother. Paul took the baby and brought her around to me and she sat on my lap for a while, until Mrs. Keen said, "Paul, put her back in bed," and he put her back. While the baby was on my lap Frankie was on his mother's lap, and although she kissed and fondled him, it was clear that she didn't enjoy him nearly as much as she did Carol.

I do not say that Paul's awareness of the baby—remember how he stood up to his stepfather, saying, "She's my sister and you don't have to pester her"? (page 378)—and his awareness of the observer as a woman "proves" that he is "feminine," but he certainly possesses a so-called feminine sensibility, not usually expected in a ten-and-a-half-year-old American boy. Running crying to his room, Paul shows his "femininity" and also his babyishness—not to mention his misery: at ten and a half years óf age Paul has no baseball mitt (supreme masculine symbol) but his three-year-old brother does, and his mother scolds Paul for trying to play with it instead of reprimanding Frankie for being selfish in not lending it.

Mrs. Keen usually takes Frankie's side in clashes between the boys.

Frankie started to open and close the door, apparently in an effort to hit Paul with it. When he succeeded, Paul hit him. Frankie went crying to his mother, and she told him to go out and hit Paul back because Paul had hit him first.

. . .

There was an argument when Paul took Carol's ball. Mrs. Keen told him to put it down because it wasn't his. Paul tried to take out the flying saucer but his mother told him to put it down because it was Frankie's.

Mrs. Keen goes by rules and does not go to the root of things; she takes matters as they appear on the surface: it is Frankie's mitt so Paul should give it back; Frankie was hit, Frankie complained and he is smaller, so Paul is in the wrong; but Frankie should "fight his own battles." It is Frankie's flying saucer and Paul has no right to it. That the boys should share does not seem to enter her head. She prevents or breaks up clashes rather than moderates them. In other words, she is like most untutored parents. In this way she burdens herself with irritation and deprives the children of each other. But by acting in a purely repressive capacity, she also interferes with maturation.

ANALYTICAL SUMMARY

Mrs. Keen is worried about Paul, yet she does not understand what she is doing to him. Paul has had a dreadful, stigmatizing diagnosis that will follow him through life, but nothing in the notes I am analyzing suggests that the observer had trouble communicating with him in a normal way. We may discount, on the grounds of his training in incapacity, Paul's "difficulties" in dressing and the fact that at table everything is done for him as if he could not do it himself. Since his mother makes him stay away from children his own age, because she insists that he come right home from school, he tends to be imprisoned in his social disabilities. Over the high walls of this infantile garden is the outer world of mature boys his age, but at home there is the constant pressure from his mother to be a Peter Pan.

Conclusions

As Mrs. Keen infantilizes her children she infantilizes herself—she says she feels like fifteen! Thus, she deprives herself of the maturing experience of dealing with maturing children. In *Culture Against Man** I called this

---

* *Op. cit.* See Chapter 9, the Ross family.

failure to take account of crucial differences "pathogenic even-handed-ness." —

All of us make our own world to some degree, and our inner disabilities help us distort it, always assisted by cultural factors that distort *us*. All of us construct a personal world which, in some ways, reacts against us in ways we have constrained it to. Mrs. Keen's troubles with her children are very much her own creation—as with all of us; only she is extreme. Because of what the culture has done to *her*, she develops her relationships so that they are undeveloped; depriving instead of enriching, infantilizing instead of maturing. Although it is the fatality of psychosis that the person who breaks down creates in others the very reactions that break him, we all have this potential both to break and to break others. And the emergence of this potential does not depend on us alone, for as social creatures we are always beyond ourselves, in other people: * though we can bring out the tenderness in others, too often we activate in them what may break us down. True, some monsters require precious little to activate them. But apart from these, other people who might under more usual circumstances be incapable of harm can be so provoked by a disturbed person that they have a pathogenic effect on him. When Mrs. Keen, at her wit's end, cries to her harmless baby, "What are you doing to me?" she is right—Carol *is* harming her mother, but without knowing it, and only because she has been driven, by the very need to survive, to do what upsets her mother. In the present group of observations, Mrs. Keen's cross-examination of Paul right in the middle of minor chaos is an excellent example of how she drives her children to drive her mad.

The following is a rather frightening example of Paul's reaction to his mother's troublesome surveillance:

[Observer and Paul were having a conversation.] Back in the kitchen Mrs. Keen asked, "What?" which she often does when she thinks I've said something and I haven't, or when I'm talking to the children and she can't quite hear what I'm saying. I answered, "Nothing," and she said, "I thought you were talking. I thought you said something." I explained, "I was talking to Paul." Paul gave me a sidelong glance and said out of the clear blue sky, "Isn't this a beautiful world?" His mother asked him, "What makes you think so?" and he said, "Well, it's pretty." His mother told him to hurry up and finish his soup—that he was going to be late. He had just sat down.

There is no such thing as a "paranoid disease" existing as a thing-in-itself, as an inevitable process of disintegration. Whatever potentialities a person has for paranoia are brought out in social interaction with people who respond blindly in the way he compels them to.

Mrs. Keen's distortion of time, space, temperature and objects is one of the most striking aspects of her pathology, but it seems as if time is the most important. It is especially in regard to time that she projects herself into her children—not only through insisting that her pace be theirs, but also through infantilizing them. As she insists on speed they slow down, and not alone in actual clock time—such as rate of food intake—but in

* The history of this idea in existentialist and pre-existentialist thought is important. We might, perhaps, start with Hegel's purely abstract analysis of the ought and the beyond in *The Science of Logic*, then go on to Heidegger's *Being and Time* and finish with "Concrete Relations with Others" in Sartre's *Being and Nothingness*.

social time, in rate of maturation. Therefore, in a contradictory way, her insistence on speed has the opposite result. She tries to project her feeling about time into her children but fails, and *thus* alienates them. Yet she binds Paul to her, for his failure in time contributes—though it is not the root of it—to his dependence on her. While time, space and the other fundamental components of the universe are mediated to us through social relations, so that we see the universe as social experience has trained us to, it is also true that the child comes to know and understand his parents through the manner in which they mediate time, space, etc., to him. The child develops his feelings for and understanding of his parents very much through how close they hold him, how fast they move and want him to move; how they handle him and the objects they give him, take away from him, let him go near, handle, etc.; through whether they let him be cold or get too hot, give him cold food or force it on him when it is too hot. The fundamental components of the universe may be impersonal for scientists and for metaphysicians, but in social life they are swollen with the sap of human existence.

Mr. Keen and the Children

Carol

Mr. Keen can be very harsh with Carol, but he is not as harsh as his wife and even protects the baby against her. He watches out for Carol: in the car he is worried that his wife may drop the baby if he stops suddenly; he is worried that as his wife plays with her, holding her over her head, she may drop her; and he is afraid she might fall off the table in the restaurant. His wife's handling of the baby makes him nervous; he distrusts her.

Mr. Keen seems to be fond of Carol: he plays with her occasionally, dandles her on his knee or picks her up when she keeps on crying. The observer notes: "He seems to like her very much and she likes to play with him," and the fact that Mrs. Keen takes Carol to him to be kissed good night and that she calls his attention to her "cuteness" suggests that he is responsive. Here is another observation:

Mr. Keen was playing with Carol on his knee and she was laughing. When she sort of tipped backward, he told her to be careful, or she would fall over.

When the observer paid a visit while Mrs. Keen was in the hospital, Mr. Keen seemed concerned about the baby. On the other hand, an interest in her as a toy and showpiece—in showing her off, regardless of her feelings —came through also:

[After breakfast.] Mr. Keen was telling me that Carol could walk, and took her out of the playpen to show me. She does walk—with legs apart, moving sideward and forward at the same time. She can go a way without having to lean against anything. When she did, her father told her to walk, and when she sat down on the floor he said, "No, no, get up and walk, get up and walk."

She came over to me and smiled, and he said, "Come here," and when she did, he put her back in the playpen, which she didn't appreciate at all. When he left the room for a moment to stop the boys' fighting, she sucked her thumb and played with her hair. When he came back he told her, "Take that thumb out of your mouth!" She obeyed, then lay back and put her hand in her crotch, and he said, "Take your hand out of there!" Then he added, "And you're not going to suck your thumb."

He took her out of the playpen a few moments later and put her in the rocking chair, saying, "Rock in the chair," but she didn't want to, and started to whimper and got out. At about ten-forty he put her to bed, saying she usually takes a nap at this time.

[Carol was on her little potty in the kitchen and Paul informed Mr. Keen that she had "made a pot"] and he came in and wiped her and put her in the playpen.

When I reflect on the activity of this man with his baby I feel inclined to remark that though the middle class sets high standards for itself, it rarely lives up to them. And I am also led to think, What does one expect of this man or of any man? That he should work himself ragged on hard materials in a hard world and still be tender to a babe? Where would a capacity for tenderness come from? I think Mr. Keen is much more predictable, more probable, than the middle-class paternal ideal.

Mr. Keen can take pleasure in a baby, and his baby can enjoy *him;* yet we must not inflate this enjoyment: in this world, in Carol's world particularly, a child has to be content with what he gets, and often he inflates the value of a little pleasure relative to much pain. A baby wants to be loved and wants to love, but he must often *extort* humanness from the world. This is the secret of sanity and survival in Carol's world—*in the world. The secret of sanity is to exaggerate the good of the world.*

Babies hope, too. The "sorry-bad" game was, from Carol's point of view perhaps, a game of blind hope—hope that when her mother said, "I'm sorry" and held her to her face, she meant it. So Carol, perhaps, hopes from her father: every time he is sweet to her it keeps her hope for affection alive; every time he relaxes and is nice to her she sucks it up; an ounce of affection becomes a bucket of hope.

One of the first tasks of a baby is to figure out how to get positive responses from the members of the family, not only because they will then like the baby but also because, having learned how to get positive responses, the baby will know how to get them from the rest of the world. Mrs. Keen's major problem is that she does not seem to know how to get a positive response. The same is true of Paul.

Mr. Keen, Frankie and Paul

I shall start with observations made on the very first day:

Finally we all ended up on the porch waiting for Mr. Keen's arrival. Everyone seemed calm now, just waiting for him. When he drove up, Frankie gave out a horrible wail: "Oh, it's Daddy!" He was obviously very frightened about something. It seems that he had been playing with a gun the day before, had broken a window and had been forbidden ever to take the gun out. Now there he was, standing on the porch with the gun, so he immediately went into the house to hide it, and then stood whimpering behind his mother. Mr. Keen came up, said hello to us and went into the house. He said something to his wife in a loud voice, which I didn't get, and she yelled back. When I went into the house, dinner was being put on the table rather slowly and Mr. Keen was getting Frankie to wash his hands.

In the backyard Frankie and Paul ran up the slide. Whenever Paul did it he had to say, "Dad, look," in order to attract his attention, but when Frankie ran up the slide his father's eyes followed him. Paul said, "Dad, you know, Frankie runs up the slide just like a squirrel," and Mr. Keen answered, "Yes, he does." Then Paul asked, "Dad, how does a squirrel run up the slide?" and Mr. Keen said, "Like Frankie." Meanwhile he was holding Carol on his lap and also dancing her around. He seemed delighted with this. Mrs. Keen was sitting at the picnic table, laughing occasionally at Carol's antics and paying little attention to those of Frankie and Paul. Finally she said she had to get up and give Carol her bottle and her husband said, "Oh, do you have to go now? It's really too early—she doesn't go to bed until eight," but his wife took the baby and went in.

Mr. Keen followed after a while, leaving me alone with the boys, and they kept up their play. Then Paul came over to me and asked, "Don't you think I'm great?" and I answered, "Oh yes, I do." Then he said, "Would you like to have me?" I asked, "What did you say?" and he said, "Would you like to have this?" showing me a package of candy cigarettes he had in his hand.

Before analyzing what seems to speak so eloquently "for itself," I feel I have to remind the reader what happened here, from the scientific point of view. Merely by being present for a few hours in the home, the observer was able to see with her own eyes, on the very first day, the essence of Mr. Keen's relationship to the boys. Although I have spoken to many professional groups, there has scarcely been a time when I have not been asked, "Doesn't the presence of the observer distort the picture?" Here we can see that the impulses of the children and the established relationships in the family do not suddenly change just because an observer is present.

Now to the analysis, for I do not believe that nature ever "speaks for itself" so well that it can be interpreted entirely without the intervention of a trained person.

Here we get the extremes of the relationship between Frankie and his father, ranging from pleasure to threat and terror. We also perceive the extremes of Mr. Keen's feelings toward the two boys—pleasure in Frankie, relative indifference to or cold rejection of Paul. Finally we observe that Paul's feeling is so intense that at that moment he says he wants to go away. This must, however, be a pain he feels constantly, that weighs him down, that must surely "impair his intellectual functioning." Thus Mr. Keen makes a big contribution to Paul's pathology by ignoring him—just as he does to his wife's; we could say that *if anybody in the family has a weakness, it is going to be made worse by Mr. Keen.* I leave open the question of whether there is some connection between Mr. Keen's attitude toward Paul and his attitude toward his wife.

When the whole family is outside in the backyard and the boys are playing on the slide, Paul's misery must be particularly sharp: while his stepfather's eyes are on Frankie and the baby, and his mother is enjoying the baby, nobody but the observer is watching Paul. He is not part of this fleeting moment of family pleasure. There was no sign, throughout the entire week, that Mr. Keen took any pleasure in Paul at all, or that Paul had found a way to get a positive response out of him. Neither his mother nor his stepfather are ever nice to him, and it seems to me that binding people to him by appearing incompetent is the only way Paul has found to line up the world on his side; yet incompetence will make it turn away too.

So Frankie is a much more "normal" child than Paul. Smiling, active, "likable," he is alternately treated nicely and indulged or restricted and hit by his mercurial, impulsive parents:

Frankie and his father decided to go down to the store to buy some beer.

Frankie and his father played catch in the backyard.

Frankie came over and asked his father some questions. An argument developed, and his father spanked him and sent him to his room.

I went into the kitchen and Frankie came in and asked whether the surprise I said I had bought was something for him and his father called out, "Does it always have to be something for you?" Frankie was crying. I told him I wanted to wait till his mother finished the dishes before giving the children their surprises, so we could all be together in the living room.

Frankie got up on his father's knee with a book and asked him to read it. His father tried to, but every time he started, Frankie would ask a question, like "What's this, Daddy? What's he doing?" and his father quickly became impatient. He said that he was going to read and that Frankie should be quiet, and that was it. So Frankie came over and asked me to read. His father said, "I told you I would read it," but Frankie said he was mad at his father, and his father repeated, "I told you I would read it." So finally Frankie went back to him. Mr. Keen seemed to enjoy very much having Frankie around.

This sequence illustrates the alternation and also illustrates the fact that Frankie actually has power sometimes to put his father on the defensive. He does it here by turning to the observer when his father becomes impatient, but if he could turn to his mother, it might give Mrs. Keen and Frankie more strength to cope with the father. Since, however, everyone in the house is alone and lonely, there is no force adequate to stand up to Mr. Keen's convinced strength, harshness and intelligence, so that whoever challenges him or provokes his anger faces him alone. It is true that once in a while Mrs. Keen or Paul becomes a transient ally of one of the children, but there is no permanent coalition to stand Mr. Keen off. Mrs. Keen, who could be the children's sanctuary, is too preoccupied, too disorganized and too harsh. No child can turn to any one for comfort; when he cries he grieves alone.

Every once in a while Mr. Keen acts like a father to Paul: once he sent him to his room because he wouldn't eat his spaghetti, and another time he compelled Paul to eat corn when he didn't want it. Here is a further example of this kind of I'm-doing-it-for-your-own-good negative parenthood:

Paul came in and said his dad wouldn't let him play. Apparently this had come up before: Mr. Keen won't let Paul play with little girls or with children younger than he is.* He is pretty strict about this. Mr. Keen said, "Honestly, Alice, these kids are getting really bad." Paul was crying very hard and said he was "going to kill Myrtle" (Frankie's playmate). His mother asked, "What are you going to do, shoot her dead?" and he replied, "No, I'm going to push her off a bridge." He was quite upset and cried for a long time. He went to his room because Mr. Keen came in and told him, "You're going to have to learn to mind. You're not going to get away with this just because somebody is here." Then he sent Paul to his room again. I'm not sure whether he hit him but he did threaten to spank him.

Later, when I went into the living room, I saw Mr. Keen sitting on the front step tossing a ball with some little boys out there.

For a child who receives so little, negative parenthood may be better than nothing. Note, however, that Paul got no comfort from his mother, merely a lively interest in the kind of murder he had in mind. Perhaps if he had sat beside her and explained in detail how he intended to go about it, his mother would have shown more interest in him, but one of Paul's problems is that he is too gentle, too "passive," too "feminine" in a household where activity and violence are valued. And for a ten-and-a-half-year-old boy to cry like this merely because he got bawled out—or even spanked—may seem "pretty girlish" or "kiddish" to these parents. There is just no way in which Paul can win; some day he may resign from the culture altogether.

The Brothers

Since there is little affection to be gotten from the parents and since Paul does not have much chance at what there is, there is little sibling rivalry between Frankie and Paul. We have seen that they occasionally quarrel over a toy, but actually, Paul has somewhat of an ideal parental attitude toward Frankie.

When Paul came home, the first thing he asked for after he said hello was Frankie. . . . He kept suggesting that I take Frankie for a walk—that Frankie would really like it.

And when their mother was in the hospital:

Frankie wanted me to ride him on my shoulders, so I did. . . . When I got tired I set him down on the bench, but he said, "No, I don't want to get off." Paul offered to give him a ride, and Frankie said, "Yes, let my brother do it." Paul put him on his back, but then they decided it would be better if Paul got down on his hands and knees with Frankie on his back. Paul started to buck and said that Frankie thinks he's a wild man—"Wild Man Paul."

· · ·

Their airplane went over the wire fence into the neighbor's yard. Frankie and Paul discussed who should pick it up and Paul decided he would let Frankie go. Frankie went and when he didn't return, we called to him, "Come on back and let's play with the airplane!" He brought back the plane, which was falling

---

* The reader will have noted that while Mr. Keen insists that Paul play only with children his own age, his wife interferes with this by insisting he come home from school as soon as it is out.

apart now, threw the tail fin over the fence and tried to jam the plane through the wire. His brother said, "No, don't do that; you'll break it." Finally Frankie got back.

Frankie picked up a steel bar, part of the swing set, and began throwing it at Paul. The first time, Paul said, "Oops, oops, almost got me," and laughed. When Frankie threw it again I asked him not to, but he wouldn't stop, so I took it from him and put it under some bushes.

Somewhere along in here Frankie hit me and Paul with his fists and he charged into my leg with his head. I told him not to—that it hurt. Then we flew the plane around some more, but Paul seemed more interested in it than Frankie.

Frankie wanted to be lifted up to the pole that holds the clothesline, so Paul did. Then Frankie asked Paul to boost him into a tree and he did. Frankie said he was going to get down by himself, and his brother said "Okay" and I stood below to see that he didn't fall. Frankie was holding on to a little branch and Paul said, "Now let go, Frankie, let go." I cautioned, "Maybe he ought not let go until he gets a hold," but he succeeded in getting down and went into the house. [While both boys were in the kitchen Mr. Keen suggested to them, "Why don't you show her (the observer) the game your Aunt Melba (his sister) gave you?" The game is Paul's but he wanted to watch TV, so Frankie brought it out and started to demonstrate it on the floor of the boys' room. Then] he got up, went into the kitchen, and said to his father that he was playing with the game too, and his father said, "Now, Frankie, that's Paul's game; you have your own game." Frankie came back to the room, stood over in the corner and started to cry. His brother asked Mr. Keen to let Frankie play with the game, and he said it was all right. Paul started to tell us how to work the game but went back to TV. Frankie came and sat down and Paul said, "Let's put the game away," but his brother didn't want to. I thought I would try to get them to play together but they wouldn't. A couple of times Paul tried to take a card from Frankie's hand but Frankie held on. [This broke up when their father called them to lunch.]

For all its squalls, the relationship between Frankie and Paul is good. The boys are not afraid of each other, they do not appear to try to hurt each other for the sake of hurting. Frankie, who is really a very violent little boy, who hits his mother and repeatedly attacks the observer, was rarely violent with Paul, and Paul was never seen to hit Frankie, although we know that Frankie once complained that he did. When we compare this relationship with that of Bobby and Jackie Jones (Part I) or even that of Irving and Benjamin Rosenberg (Part II), the way Paul and Frankie treat each other seems practically idyllic. We have already seen something of how they can play together peacefully; here is another example:

During breakfast Frankie got up and brought in his gun and Paul asked him if he was a big hunter. He asked me if I didn't think Frankie was a small hunter. Then they began to play a game. Frankie went into the living room; Paul followed and then came back, saying he had killed the monster. When I asked, "Who is the monster?" he answered, "Frankie." Paul hid in the living room, and Frankie came back, saying he had killed the monster—Paul. Then Paul said I should be Frankie's wife and when I asked why, he said, "Because wives are big and husbands are small." Paul began to pretend that he was a lion and Frankie a hunter, and they went into the living room again. After a while they came back, and Paul looked at me. "You're supposed to ask Frankie if he killed any lions!" When I asked him why, he answered, "Because Frankie is the husband." [Another game.] During this play Paul took the part of the father-king and Frankie took the part of the son.

The boys quickly become reconciled after a squabble. In the following example Frankie goes about it sensitively.

Some sort of fight started in the boys' room over what to watch on television; Mr. Keen went in and then Paul came out mad. Mr. Keen explained to me that Paul had been watching cartoons all morning long, so that Frankie hadn't had a chance to watch a program he likes.

Almost immediately after this fight, however, Frankie was preparing for a reconciliation:

Frankie soon came out of the room, went halfway down the hall and looked into the kitchen, where Paul was. Then he went back and brought out a paper plate with half of another plate tacked onto it, so it looked like a little carrier. Frankie said Paul had made it, and asked, "Isn't it nice?"

The boys want to keep their relationship going, and both try to patch up quarrels. Frankie identifies with his brother:

Paul said something like "Those men always think mean. I don't mean like Batman, because he's a fat gobbler." Frankie came in and repeated it and Mr. Keen said, "You don't have to say everything Paul says." They went into their room.

In dealing with the boys, Mr. Keen, like his wife, follows certain stereo-typed notions and doesn't go below the surface: he objects to Paul's monop-olizing the TV and does not take into consideration the fact that the set was a gift to Paul from his mother's mother, and that therefore, according to the rules of this house, he has exclusive right to it. Mr. Keen has some vague concept of individualism and objects to Frankie's imitation of Paul; he does not think this is proper for little kids, especially when they admire and are fond of each other. When the idea of property presents itself to Mr. Keen in one guise, he emphasizes sharing; when it presents itself to him in another, he insists on individual rights. His intervention stops at command and enforcement; he does not explain, he does not try to bring the kids together when his commands have forced them apart. He—like his wife—disjoins, and the children themselves have to fight their way back to each other. In this we are very much alike: entering arbitrarily, inconsistently and whimsically, as the children see it, into their lives with incomprehen-sible commands and then retreating, leaving sorrow and chaos to reconsti-tute themselves. It is like "the law": its function is to apprehend, to punish and to remove the offender—what happens in the aftermath is none of its affair.

SUMMARY OF THE RELATIONSHIP BETWEEN MR. KEEN AND THE CHILDREN

Mr. Keen is not "wild" about Carol, nor does he "dote" on her; we could not say that "almost from the moment he comes home Mr. Keen has the baby on his knee." When it suits him, he holds her; sometimes he seems to enjoy her. Often he is callous and sometimes he is harsh. Yet he watches out for her; he does not want her to be hurt. We could not say that he is indifferent to her, physically, but psychologically he is distant and sometimes even hurtful—in the case of the ruler, for example (pages 406–407).

Since Frankie is not confined to playpen and crib, he can approach his father and attempt to get more out of him of whatever it is that makes kids feel good. Mr. Keen definitely likes Frankie and goes through some typical routines of American fatherhood with him, like playing catch. He has bought him a mitt, symbol and augur of his masculinity, of his identity with his father. Giving Frankie a baseball mitt large enough for an adult hand, half wishing him and pushing him into adulthood, is the opposite of what Mrs. Keen does to Paul. Each parent rapes time in his own way. To buy a baseball glove for a three-year-old is perhaps somewhat premature, especially when the ten-and-a-half-year-old doesn't have one, but it is a bond between the maleness of the father and that of the son; their joint maleness is made to flow together through the artery of the Great National Game. In olden times a father gave his son a bow, or perhaps, like Aegeus, left a sword and sandals beneath a stone for the day when the son could lift it and use them.* Frankie's sword is the baseball mitt, with which he will someday catch the long fly or kill the hot grounder. Et cetera, and so on to the stadium and to the World Series on TV on a Sunday afternoon. All the rich promise of American maleness is projected in that mitt.

Mr. Keen sometimes lets Frankie say no to him—but often he spanks him until he screams, and he can be capricious and entrapping as well. At the same time there is enough there for Frankie to keep approaching his father for more. Does Frankie exaggerate the good in his world, does he see enough in his father to make him hope for more? He can get his father to read a book to him, and we have seen how he is able, by shrewd instinct, to put his father on the defensive and even tame him a little. But this is only because his father gives a damn: side by side with callousness, deception (entrapment) and impulsive harshness there is a fondness for Frankie which the child perceives and instinctively exploits. Frankie—and Carol—are indeed Mr. Keen's own children.

His attitude toward his stepson is different. Many iron gates shut Paul out: he can never be Mr. Keen's child, even legally, because Paul's real father will not release him for adoption. Paul is allegedly retarded, and that may be hard for Mr. Keen to take. And finally, many people feel ashamed to have a retarded child, and Mr. Keen may be no different. In order to free himself of shame he would have to go around telling everybody that Paul is not his child.

Life is miserable for Paul, and Mr. Keen's unconcealed coldness contributes to his depression and makes him want to go away with the observer. After many years he got a father who is not a father but a stone. What compels him to keep trying to squeeze water out of the stone? It may be Mr. Keen's very "negative paternity" that gives Paul hope: Mr. Keen does what seems to be for Paul's own good—all the way from commanding that he eat when he doesn't want to, to insisting that he play with kids his own size and punishing him when he does not. Since, in these respects, his "dad" acts as if he really cared, Paul may be led to believe that there may be a smile or even a word of praise for him somewhere. The logic is sound but wrong.

* See p. 321.

Perhaps most people would be pleased if Mr. Keen were "wild" about the baby and embodied the other traits in quotation marks at the beginning of the "Summary" (page 443). They would rejoice, because Mr. Keen would have made contact, through Carol, with the ontological springs of our cultural absolutes. Babies, or more precisely, ideas about babies, belong to the ineffabilities of cultural desire and hope, which is really where all metaphysics is basically lodged. Since Aristotle, "badness" has merely been a corruption of the good. But all metaphysical systems have been set down by élites, and some of the most famous have been the works of aristocrats. No prole has ever thought one out. The élite can write fine fancy notions about "being," but the lower classes have to live in a social hole and their unconscious formulations about it may contain nothing so fancy as the "absolute good." What, then, if they do not share the mountain-spring-pure conceptions of childhood that fine folk do? Are they sick? Pathogenic perhaps? How do we cope with this dilemma? How cope with this unwritten, but surely existent, metaphysic of the social hole? Well, perhaps in the first place by reserving judgment about Mr. Keen in general and turning our attention to how he handles the agonizing specific problems of *dolor* that confront him: the problem of his wife and the problem of Paul. He clearly cuts his wife to pieces by attacking her ego—he hits her when she is down; and Paul, who needs his shelter, sleeps in the cold backyard of his heart. So, relative or absolute élitist metaphysic, Mr. Keen makes misery worse.

Summary of the Keen Case

This is the only case in the book in which a parent has been reported to have had a nervous breakdown, and it is the only one in psychiatric annals in which a mother labeled psychotic was observed for a week in her home, carrying on her daily routine. Of course, the other cases in the book are unique, too, in the sense that no comparable material exists in the psychiatric literature. In the other cases my interest was focused on how parents drive children mad, but in the Keen case I am more interested in how one parent can drive the other mad and how children drive parents mad when parents drive them mad.

I have also used the Keen case for the following purposes:

1. To examine the metaphysical basis for judgments of sane and insane. Nowadays metaphysics is concerned with the structure of consciousness rather than with the structure of the universe and with ultimate causes. This structure of consciousness is the underpinning of *the mind called sane, and it provides the intuitive standards by which we judge the sanity of others.* Consciousness, say contemporary metaphysicians, is always consciousness of *something*, which means that there is no "pure" consciousness. From this the anthropologist draws the immediate inference that consciousness is culturally determined and that it is nothing more than the cultural configuration installed in the head, and ramifying through the tissues as the "psychosomatic reaction," i.e., appropriate to given events.

2. Another purpose of this chapter is to raise questions about the re-

lationship of perceptual defects to behavior labeled "disturbed." In this connection I tried to present an alternative to the death-wish–sadism–hate-her-children hypothesis, which, I believe, would be the more orthodox interpretation of Mrs. Keen's behavior with her children.

3. I also used this case to attack the idea, very current in psychiatric thinking, that the inherent temperaments of children somehow determine how their parents will treat them, for I have shown that Mrs. Keen feeds all her children in very much the same way, which is improbable in terms of the theory that children determine parents.

4. Study of the structure of *consciousness* was used to suggest the direction in which analysis of the structure of *sanity* might move. Since I have argued that consciousness is the cultural configuration installed in the head, study of the nature of sanity would necessarily require an exhaustive examination of its underlying metaphysics: the basic assumptions and conceptual differentiations that form the configuration. Such a phenomenological analysis would not be a series of categories but instead a network of irreducible ideas.

The analysis of the Keen case is not so theoretical that the reality of the Keen family is lost. On the contrary, their anguish and their satisfactions are always in the forefront, and sometimes, perhaps, the theoretical objective even becomes obscure. I think this is as it should be: humanity must always take precedence over theory.

Conclusions

In the essays on sham; anger and quarreling; time, space, motion, objects and people; availability; the metaphysics of infancy, and so on, I examined relationships between psychopathology and certain invariants of human existence. Now I shall discuss pathogenic factors, touched on in the studies but not analyzed in detail. Reviewing them here gives me the opportunity to stress them again and provides a framework for comparing the families.

Before summarizing I want to repeat that I do not believe that any single factor is alone responsible for psychopathology, except, perhaps, physical isolation from human contact: a baby alone in his room, where he sees no one except a mother who comes in only to feed and change him.

The reader will have seen that family interaction is complex, that many things are happening at once, and that even in families where people are sickest there is always some health, some alleviating condition. If it is a serious mistake to ascribe psychopathology to one cause only, it is also a serious mistake not to perceive the strengths in even the weakest.

The closest this study comes to placing the blame for psychopathology on any single factor is the Keen case. The Keen family is also the only family in this book in which a person was known to be actually on the way to having a nervous breakdown. There we saw that power, ruthlessly applied to the ego of a weak person, incapable of escape, was the principal cause. Cruelty—humiliation without possibility of stabilizing retaliation; destructiveness without emotional repair, so that the object loses all hope, so that the victim tears at himself and thus completes the destruction—this, I believe, is able to accomplish psychosis without any other intervening factor.

In our study Mrs. Keen is the only person subject to this; but even here we see that cruelty may not alone have been responsible for her breakdown. She was physically ill, and when Susan knew her she may have been suffering the prodromal symptoms of her fatal illness. Furthermore, she so drove her children that, in trying to escape, they "drove her crazy." Treating her children as she did, however, may itself have been a consequence of her husband's cruelty; as Susan put it, he acts as if he "could not bear the sight of her."

Considering the historic cruelty of our culture, the main question is not, "What makes people cruel?" but rather, "Considering our culture, how does it come about that many people are not cruel?" If, as Freud argued in "Thoughts for the Times on War and Death," cruelty is softened by love,* we still have the problem of accounting for love. In the light of our imme-

* "The influences of civilization cause an ever-increasing transmutation of egoistic trends into altruistic and social ones, and this by an admixture of erotic elements."

morial cruelty, love and naturally loving people* seem miracles. In the framework of the Freudian dialectic it appears that everyone needs love in order to save him from the consequences of his own cruelty.

Since man is a social animal, incapable of existing without the company of his own species, his inherent gregariousness provides the biologic under-pinning for love. Impulses to kill, to humiliate, to torture, must be con-trolled in order to maintain the social group; but the impulses can still be directed against those outside it. When destructiveness gets out of hand, so that it is directed against one's own, that is pathology.

If we do not adulterate our cruelty with love, we are compelled by society to suppress or repress it. But suppose, as in the case of an emperor with absolute power, one is under no compulsion to do so? What then? Then we get Neros, Caligulas, Galbas, and so on. Put absolute power in the hands of any man, give him power with no restraints, and he easily be-comes a monster visiting cruelty on the world, until his cruelty may turn even against his own society. Galba, himself a monster, was called to be emperor of Rome in order to save the people from Nero, whose merely conventional imperial cruelty had gotten out of hand, so that no one was safe. While Nero is not called mad by the principal historians of his time,† the test and proof of his insanity is the fact that in the expression of even imperial cruelty, which in the Rome of that period allowed immense lati-tude and self-indulgence, he went too far and began to threaten the very fabric of Roman society. By such a criterion Mr. Keen was at least as sick as his wife, though never so labeled.

I now summarize factors that seem to me to play an important role in the misery of the families discussed in this book.

Vulnerability and slipping away: Vulnerability is the dialectic necessity of cruelty, for without vulnerability, cruelty is impossible. Ego vulnerability is a primary fact of pathogenesis; the cruel man needs the vulnerable one as the sword needs flesh. In this book the most vulnerable people are Carol, Mrs. Keen and Albert Metz. But Albert's mother was very vulnerable too; only, since there was no person around cruel or strong enough to crush her, she gives the impression of strength. Her reaction to Albert suggests ex-treme vulnerability. His pathetic behavior or, as she saw it, misbehavior— his scattering and "showing off"—filled her with shame and rage. She is also vulnerable to Myra; for Myra, she feels, is all she really has/has not. Through Myra she suffers the vulnerability of uncertainty/certainty; which is to say she half imagines that Myra loves her but knows she does not; which is to say she hangs on tightly to what she does not have while telling herself she has it; she tries not to lose it because she knows it is slipping away. In this family, as in all the families, everyone is slipping away from everyone else. This, of course, is man in our culture. The only difference is that these families seem extreme—perhaps because they have been studied more closely than others.

Each one of us is vulnerable, it is just a matter of degree—and a matter of how cruel others are. This dialectic—vulnerable/cruel—follows us

* "Freud recognized that there are rare people, of whom Martha was one, who seem to be good and kind by nature in contrast with those, such as himself, who attain that level only after considerable inner struggle." Ernest Jones in Vol. I of his *Life and Work of Sigmund Freud* (New York, Basic Books, 1953), p. 124.

† Tacitus and Suetonius.

through life, so that we always look to our defenses. Cruelty is a function of others' vulnerability, and vulnerability is a function of others' cruelty. This is a two-dimensional life.

Compassion gives life a third dimension, gives it depth. In all these families—in all of history—compassion is a weak function, and that is why we have progressed. Progress, as it is understood in conventional history, depends upon the dominance of cruelty and the exploitation of vulnerability —but with a judicious application of compassion, to prevent the necessary cruelty from getting out of hand. In the families in this book we see a consequence of the misunderstanding of, the failure to learn about, the utility of compassion.

A person is viewed as an adversary and treated like one. "The child as enemy" is a fairly constant theme in these families: Tommy and Bobby Jones, Irving and Abraham Rosenberg, Albert Metz, Carol and Paul Keen are all, in some way, treated like enemies by their parents. Bobby is his mother's enemy, but not entirely. On the one hand she seems to define Bobby as enemy, but on the other, she tries to woo him; sometimes she shows her anger and contempt, sometimes she talks with the sugary voice of reconciliation. On both sides there is distrust, while both want peace— something that is clearer in Mrs. Jones than in Bobby. Irving Rosenberg and his mother are also somewhat in this state. Between Abraham and his parents there is an abyss of distrust and scorn. Albert Metz was treated as enemy by his mother as soon as he entered the house; and he ridiculed, burlesqued and distrusted her.

Jackie, Harriet, Benjamin, Myra, Norma and Frankie are not enemies in their families and they are in better shape than the other children.

"The enemy" is pushed to the periphery of the family, or even out of it, is felt to be inimical; and the family, or certain members of it, feel they have to *defend* themselves against him and have the *right* to punish, even to destroy him.

Perception of a person as enemy-inimical is the radical, lethal metamorphosis that is a necessary precondition for the formation of psychosis. Psychosis, one result of warfare in the family, is preceded by the same kind of transformation that occurs in warfare in international relations—or nonrelations. Before making war it is necessary to transform the adversary into some kind of legitimately destructible, inimical *thing.*

Turning the other person on. The phrase to "turn on" means to trigger underlying impulses of the body, consciousness or soul. The pathogenic person, however, turns on impulses of the "turnee" which destroy the latter; or which, when released against the turner, are likely to result in a clash in which the turnee is hurt. Mr. Rosenberg and Mr. Keen are good examples of turners, and Irving and Mrs. Keen are good examples of turnees. In both cases the turning on has the *appearance* of being innocent.

In order for a person to be turned on he has to be set up for it: the turner trains the turnee to be a kind of innocent who will always react to the provocation. This occurs through the long process of the relationship. The common, often nonlethal* forms of the turner-turnee configuration found in many families are: (1) A makes B feel guilty that he is not giving A what he needs. (2) A trains B to feel he has treated A unjustly. It is then

---

* Nobody is driven mad—just made miserable.

easy for A to turn B on by dropping a hint that he is not getting what he needs from the relationship or that he feels he is being treated unfairly. There is often good reason for an observer to think that the belief structure of the configuration is founded on reality. Irving turns his parents on by his attitude that they love Ben more than they love him and that they are always unjustly blaming him. Dr. Jones can readily turn his wife on by implying she is not solicitous of him—meaning she does not give him what he really needs; and Norma Wilson does the same with her mother. Since turning on occurs in the population as a whole, it is difficult to distinguish between pathogenic and nonpathogenic forms.

In order to escape the consequences of being turned on, a person must be able to restrain his reactions, but even better is to understand that he is being turned on. The long-standing configuration of a relationship, however, often makes this practically impossible without therapeutic help. For any family to be reasonably tranquil the members must love one another enough, or be restrained enough, or have enough insight, or be strong enough not to enjoy pathologically one another's vulnerabilities by turning one another on. It seems to me that Dr. Jones often resisted his wife's efforts to turn him on; on the other hand, Mrs. Keen could not resist her husband, nor he her.

Related to turning on is *the entrapment of innocence*, because if entrapment is well planned, it always turns innocence on. The outstanding examples in the book are the "sorry-bad" game Mrs. Keen imposed on Carol, and Mr. Keen's entrapment of Frankie when Frankie asked whom the puppet was for. It is probable that "pure" cases of this syndrome can be found only in relation to children.

Entrapment combined with turning on occurs also in the absence of innocence, however. When Dr. Jones throws the diaper into the toilet and thereby turns on his wife, she is not an innocent: she knows something about her husband; she does not respond like a child who blindly, because of his unscreened impulses, falls into a trap. A similar situation arose when Dr. Jones dried the dishes but did not put them away and made his wife angry.

The purpose of entrapment in human culture is to punish or destroy an enemy; it seems to be man's improvement on stalking. Predators, like lions, tigers, cats, and so on, which stalk their prey, have to learn the habits, including the vulnerabilities, of their prey. It would follow that in human beings, in families, the trapper has to know the vulnerabilities of his prey. This was exquisitely illustrated for us by Mr. Keen's entrapment of Frankie. It was clearly pathogenic entrapment.

Fighting when one ought to submit or, at least, be quiet. This is most prominent in the Keen family. Mrs. Keen fought her husband, but she simply did not have the strength for such a fight.

The tragic aspect of fighting in our culture is that, since fighting is necessary in order to become a self, too many people fight against overwhelming odds and become desperately ill. The masochistic, the yielding manipulative strategy is the best for weak people and belongs, therefore, primarily to women and children in the presence of power. The secret in fighting to gain self-validation is either to wear down the opposing force gradually or to wait until one is strong enough to confront it head-on. We see this problem in Ben and Irving Rosenberg. In Irving's case, while he achieved self-hood through fighting his parents, it weakened him too: on the one hand he became too dependent on his brother, and on the other he had a tendency to respiratory attacks when enraged. Ben had achieved an almost perfect masochistic adaptation, which he was slowly beginning to use to overcome his brother and parents.

Bobby Jones readily submitted to his father's authority but, feeling himself strong vis-à-vis his mother, he fought her. He fought his father, shrewdly, only when they were loving each other; there he could fight with all his strength without appearing to be serious. Jackie had sense enough not to fight anybody. In all families fighting is complexly patterned.

The deeply troubled person seems to create or reinforce the very conditions that contribute to his illness. This is clearest in the case of Mrs. Keen; she provokes rejection and perhaps hostility, even in her baby. Because she is driving her kids crazy, she thinks, "If you want to go crazy, just start having kids." With her kids she seems to have created, all by herself, a rejecting environment and to have had it within her power to make it different. With her husband it is a somewhat different story, because he appears to be a harsh man, poised for retaliation. She may be driving her kids crazy and they may be driving her crazy because, hurling herself feebly against her husband, he is driving her crazy.

We see a different aspect of the same factor in Paul Keen's infantilization. By compelling his mother, through his "ineptness," to be near him, he undermines his ability to get on in the culture.

The creation and/or reinforcement of what is bad for one can be circular because, having been taught to behave in a certain manner, a person continues, since in a way it is rewarding. It is what is known as the "neurotic paradox" or the "secondary gain."

Absence of mutual satisfaction: distortion in the means of satisfaction. In many families people cannot satisfy one another's emotional needs. This happens in all the families in this book, but the least satisfied family is the Keens. In all the others the picture is mixed. In the Jones family neither Ida nor Ed really understand what is missing in their relationship. The clearest statement of wants appears in Ed's life story, where he speaks of his willingness to be dependent on Ida and of the wonder of having a woman who was nice to him. What she wants never comes out.

In the Rosenberg family the boys obtain some satisfaction from each other, but it is distorted by pathological overtones and is muddied by hostility. The Metz household has reached a kind of stability through relationships that are full of hostile elements camouflaged as love but which give certain satisfactions that are subtle and ambiguous.

In the Wilson family, satisfaction emerges in the mother-daughter relationship only; but there, Mrs. Wilson's love is mixed with ambition; achievement rides like a monkey on love's back.

Inability of the troubled person to utilize what emotional resources the environment does have. Irving Rosenberg's mother had reached the point where she was willing to "be nice" to him if he gave her a chance, but he did not. Mrs. Keen rejected her husband when he was "lovey-dovey." Myra Metz was unable to get at her mother's underlying yearning for love, and Mr. Metz was marooned in his depression. Bobby Jones would not capitulate to his mother's desire to be loved by him. In all the families in this book we see the members walled off from one another's potentialities; they are frozen in attitudes of long standing, and can find no way to reach one another. This is the commonest condition in human families, "officially disturbed" or otherwise.

The compulsion to murder pleasure; accentuation of the negative component in existence. One is impressed by the absence of joy, of the capacity to enjoy one's self, in these families, but some are worse off than others. The Keen family seems to be the most obvious example. The Jones's seem the people best able to enjoy themselves as a family, but even there, good times were sometimes badly disturbed.

The killing of pleasure means that what should give joy is turned into misery, or that pleasure is not even permitted. There is also an inability to plan for pleasure. The fantastic holiday outing of the Keen family illustrates the point. In this family, fighting often starts as soon as pleasure is anticipated, as in the bickering over what Mrs. Keen should wear the evening of the anniversary celebration. Mealtimes are always grim in the Keen household too.

There is always some tension in living together—the negative component in existence—and always some satisfaction; but in pathology the former predominates. In the Keen family the tension overshadows everything, and the Rosenbergs suffer this almost as intensely.

Food and mealtimes actualize underlying tensions: people use food and mealtime against one another. In the Keen and Rosenberg households the situation seems worst. Mrs. Jones is afraid to feed anyone but the baby unless her husband is home, while Dr. Jones pays little attention to the hardships his delays impose on the family. The fantastic eating behavior of Bobby and Jackie offends their mother.

When Albert Metz came home his mother, a good cook, served supper on TV-dinner trays, reminiscent of institutional grub-trays, and he did not have a decent meal all day. His breakfast was a misery. She bought the cheapest hamburger for him. The fundamental separation of mother and daughter was revealed when Myra ate while her mother put away the groceries Myra had refused to carry, and when she snarled at her mother for bringing her ice cream with her cake the day she was "sick." In the Wilson family, cookies, fruit—goodies—are tangled up with problems of independence and accusation, highlighting the tension between mother and daughter.

This relationship between food on the one hand, and anxiety and hostility on the other, is the best indication that the psychosomatic system of the family has been invaded by pathology.

Negation of solicitude while giving it. This is most obvious in Mrs. Keen's caring for Carol and in Mrs. Portman's caring for Belle in *Culture Against Man.* Both women force-fed their infants, bathed them in cold water and were harsh in other ways during the bath. Mrs. Jones gave Harriet her medicine in milk that probably had a high bacteria count, and left butter and milk out in very warm weather. Probably Mrs. Rosenberg's unbelievable cooking can be brought under this heading, perhaps not so much because she was a bad cook as because, in spite of the fact that the boys obviously hated some of the things she gave them—the "soup," the dead canned peas—she never changed. The purchase of one bicycle for the two boys is an example of the same negation. I would also be inclined to include here Mrs. Wilson's transforming a ball game into a lesson in elementary arithmetic or spelling, obliging Norma to count the cookies we were eating and setting two tempting bowls of fruit in front of Norma but forbidding her to touch one. When the organism is faced with a negation within solicitude, the psychosomatic reaction must tear the personality in half.

One stress begets another; binding into duress. I pointed out that when Myra Metz refuses to carry in the bags of groceries, her mother, after a brief outburst, does not follow through with scoldings for other things: she does not bawl Myra out for sitting down to lunch while she is still putting food away and she does not compel her to take the detergent down to the cellar. On the other hand, Mrs. Keen holds Carol a prisoner in the highchair and will not permit her to reject food—she *binds her into duress,* forcing, yelling and hitting. In the conflict between Irving Rosenberg and his father there is no slacking off—it is blow for blow all the way; only in the living room, after Irving's respiratory attack, when Irving begins to play with the Venetian blind, does his father fail to follow up each of his son's provocations. When Albert Metz comes home, a similar situation develops: his mother gives him no rest, creating occasions for turning him on, reacting hostilely to almost every action of his. Binding into duress, giving no opportunity to escape, following each provocation by another are found here where people are sickest.

Pathogenic leveling. In this syndrome no account is taken of crucial differences: the sick are treated as if well, the young are treated as if they were older and vice versa, strangers are treated like old friends, and so on. Mrs. Keen sometimes treated infant Carol as if she were at least ten years old, and often treated the older children as if they were infants. In *Culture Against Man* I pointed out that Mrs. Ross, who tried to save money on food, fed her undernourished four-year-old only two meals a day on weekends, just as she did herself and her husband. Mr. Keen treated his disturbed wife as if he were trying to drive her back into psychosis when he should have been considerate, and Mrs. Metz did the same with Albert. Mrs. Metz, failing to take account of crucial differences, greeted all the men she knew as if they were long-standing friends or companions in flirtation.

No doubt different intrapsychic processes are involved in each case of pathogenic leveling, but they all distort cultural or biological patterns. In all cases there are probably involved either illusions about one's self and the other person, failures in learning, or, perhaps in extreme cases, even hallucinations.

The folie à deux. I do not mean the *folie à deux* in the classic sense of two people sharing the same delusional system. What I mean here is that, even in adults, psychosis is often a result of destructive interaction of at least two people. The Keen case is the paradigm.

People often say things like "He/she was badly disturbed before he/she ever married him/her"; but this is the uninformed talking. It is true that it often seems as if it would take superhuman restraint and understanding on the part of others to prevent some people from being punished into madness: "Poor James, Mary was *so* difficult. How did he stand it all those years?" Often, however, Mary's difficult temperament is in part a product of her husband's difficult temperament. One fine day Mary begins to have paranoid hallucinations. "Well, her brother/sister committed suicide, and . . ." Nobody knows the contributing role played by her remarkably restrained, cold, unbending spouse over the years. He was always patient, understanding, even kindly. Against this Mary threw herself—until she broke. What she wanted was warmth; what she got was patience, "tolerance" and a distant look.

There is no question but that parents play an important role in the psychopathology of children; we must extend the reasoning to married couples, for since psychopathology is a consequence of disturbed interpersonal relations, logic compels us to extend the idea to all interpersonal relations; even the relationship between patient and therapist can become pathogenic.

Reflections on Family Psychotherapy

No field in the human disciplines has developed intellectually as rapidly as psychiatry in the past fifteen to twenty years. This is due partly to psychiatrists' openness to insights from information theory, philosophy—particularly existentialism, phenomenology and logic*—and sociology. In bringing these insights together with earlier theory, psychiatry created a unique, quite stunning new synthesis. Something else, however, was involved besides openness; it was a fundamental alteration in the mode of approach to the patient—from seeing him alone, to seeing him together with his family; from seeing *him* as sick, to perceiving him as a member of a sick family. When psychiatrists started to observe and to treat families, theories that developed in the first half of this century seemed inadequate. With disturbed families in living interaction directly confronting them, psychiatrists, as they are frank to say, were at first emotionally and intellectually overwhelmed, but contact with the new universe led to immense improvement in perception and in theoretical sophistication; indeed, to the degree that an entirely new—and, at present, too awesome!—vocabulary emerged to label phenomena never observed and never thought about before.

Intensive Family Therapy, edited by Ivan Boszormenyi-Nagy and James L. Framo,† expresses beautifully this fundamental alteration. Yet, while from one point of view the development is encouraging, from another it is depressing, for it would seem, from the complexity of the problem, that only men and women of high intellectual endowment should engage in family therapy, or, indeed, try to treat schizophrenia or any mental/emotional disturbance at all.‡

* Not only these, however. The concept "transaction," which became a prestige word in the social sciences in the 1950s, is a twentieth-century restatement of the dialectic principle, and comes into psychiatry from the work of John Dewey and Arthur F. Bentley.

† Hoeber Medical Division, Harper and Row, 1965. This book is valuable not only because of the quality of the papers in it but also because the extensive bibliographies enable the reader to find his way to important source material.

‡ When I was studying a psychiatric hospital I became interested in a patient,

Another point at issue in the new literature on schizophrenia has to do with the great difficulty in separating cause from effect. While I am convinced that these disorders are caused by the total configuration of family interaction, supported and reinforced by the outer world's reaction to it, it is often—perhaps almost always—impossible to establish a baseline in the family which might enable one to say, "This is how and where it started." The creation of any pattern of social activity begins at birth and starts a circle, for the infant's reaction to what his parents do causes them to react to his reactions: existence has started—and since usually no researcher is present to take notes, the most important formative components of life are not recorded and can never be recovered. Life constantly conceals itself from observation. In psychopathology we can perceive, through direct observation, that somewhere along the line the circle became vicious, that the entire family got caught up in something that originated in the infancy of the person labeled "sick," and that it grew to monstrous proportions as each member of the family reacted, over the years, to the pathologic process. Thus, though perceptive researchers can now specify fairly well what *is* happening in the family therapy sessions—especially if they have video tapes of the sessions—it is logically impossible to say that it is causative.

As one reads the work of this new group of therapists, one cannot help feeling that they often conceptualize as specifically pathological what is really common to many families and perhaps emerges as a necessary consequence of living together—or as living together as Americans, "occidental," urban, etc., monogamous, "private," etc.—in families never considered or labeled "sick." I wonder where the family therapists would find *any* family lacking all the following "pathogenic" features:

- a mother's great emotional dependence on her daughter
- the need of mothers to feel superior
- self-protection through acquiescence
- "symbiotic" attachments among members of the family
- pressure ("excessive" pressure) to maintain the subculture of the family
- "emotional divorce," i.e., husband and wife lead outwardly tranquil and conforming lives but do not give each other what they need
- a parent cares largely for himself as reflected in his child
- children are rewarded when they behave as the family wishes and are punished for being independent
- parents keep much of what goes on and their own motivations secret from the children
- two members of the family form an alignment
  etc., etc., etc.*

I worry that we have here, perhaps, a sudden discovery of the contemporary *family* rather than the pathologic family, unless, of course, we urge that in our culture most families are pathogenic, in some sense—a position I take in this book.

Meanwhile, although many of the processes discussed by the family therapy group may not be specific to schizophrenogenesis, they are true discoveries and rank among the great discoveries of science. They give sys-

---

and asking her physician what the diagnosis was, I received the answer, "Piss-poor protoplasm." Soon after that the patient was sent to a state hospital.

* From *Intensive Family Therapy* (*op. cit.*).

tematic insight into family life never available before* and are necessary preliminary steps to discovering the etiology of emotional disorder. It is a credit to psychiatry that it has taken them.

* I stress the term "systematic." Obviously many novelists and playwrights have had the insights before. Freud, for all his genius, could never rise above Lady Murasaki!

Appendix

Rationale, Method and Difficulties in the Naturalistic Observation of Families of Disturbed Children

The following questions have been asked wherever I have spoken about my research: (1) What was your entree into the family? (2) Didn't your presence distort the family way of life? (3) What did you do? (4) How did you stand it? (5) What did you record?

1. Entree into the family was obtained by explaining to husband and wife that science was of the opinion that their child's illness was somehow related to family life, and that the best way to discover the relationship was by having a scientist study their family. It was further explained that, hopefully, my findings might contribute to the treatment of their child; and if not to their child, surely to future generations of children.

2. The problem of the distorting effects of the observer may be treated under several headings:

(a) *The family as a culture.* Every family is different, and this individuality maintains itself even in the presence of the determined efforts of a therapist to change it. Such resistance to change develops as a direct consequence of the social interaction of the members of the family with one another, and of their mutual adaptation and conflict. Interaction, adaptation and conflict, meanwhile, occur in relation to a set of values adapted by the family from the values of the culture. If, in one family, the values of struggle, male dominance, female subordination, permissiveness, and so on, have become frames of reference in terms of which all interaction takes place, these can arise only because they are present in the culture as a whole. If we put together the pattern of interaction and the value system, we have the family culture.

The interaction that takes place in a family can be described accurately; it can be shown that the interaction may be examined in terms of specific interactional constellations, and it is possible to count the number of possible interactional constellations in terms of the equation

$$I = 2^n - n - 1$$

This equation tells us that in a family of two parents and three children there is a total of twenty-six interactional constellations. Each is relatively stable in its structure. That is to say, mother and father have a relatively fixed type of interaction; mother and child-one have another; father and child-one another, and so on. These patterns change with great difficulty. All the features I have discussed contribute to a stable social environment —however pathological it may be—and we therefore accept with skepticism the hypothesis of ready modification in the presence of an observer. Since all biological systems tend to low entropy, and since an interactional constellation in a family is a biological system, the biosocially determined tendency is not easily disturbed.

(b) *The factors of custom and strain.* When an observer is in the home, playing the role of a benign relative who, while making no demands and getting involved in no family disputes, at the same time makes himself useful, the family becomes accustomed to him. This factor of custom cannot, however, be considered apart from the problem of strain. Though a family may wish to protect itself from the eyes of the observer, its members cannot remain on guard constantly and everywhere, for the strain is too great. The problem of strain, however, is related to the pressure of impulses and fixed patterns of behavior.

(c) *Impulses and fixed behavior patterns.* Since behavior deriving from unconscious impulses cannot readily be controlled, often the members of a family cannot hide crucial dimensions of their behavior and feeling, for the simple reason that they are unaware of them. In addition, we must take account of conscious impulses which, though conceivably socially unacceptable, are not hidden, because they are too violent to be controlled. There are, furthermore, many forms of overt behavior which, though deemed socially acceptable by the subjects, have critical dimensions that, if known to the subject, might make him think twice before behaving as he does in the presence of an observer. Thus, conscious and unconscious impulses and fixed action patterns of long standing in families reveal to an observer crucial dimensions of the family culture.

(d) *The position of the observer and the situation of the subject.* As scientists we are prone to imaginatively project our own learning and understanding into our subjects' minds. In my experience, persons skilled in dynamic psychology are particularly apt to do this, thinking that subjects understand the implications of their own behavior as well as a trained observer does. Since this is not so, it follows that much of the time the subjects do not even know what one should inhibit or conceal.

(e) *Participation of the subject in the research.* In the families studied so far, the mother and father were interested in participating in the research in the hope of helping emotionally disturbed children. Guilt because of their role in their own child's illness also played a role in helping them believe that what was discovered about their own family might help other children. Hence, we start in some cases with a reduced tendency to conceal.

(f) *The pressures toward habitual behavior exerted by children in the home.* The inner needs of children, especially young and disturbed ones, are so powerful that they tend to come out even when "company" is around, and when "company" is around, the strong impulses of the young may become an embarrassment even in so-called normal families. Since, however, I soon cease to be "company," the children's needs dominate them, and the expression of these needs pushes the parents into habitual modes of conduct even though they might choose to avoid them. An example is Irving Rosenberg's rage which forced his parents into a characteristic pattern of anxious, hostile response and culminated in his respiratory attack.

(g) *Inflexibility of personality structure.* Since, under ordinary circumstances, personality integration cannot readily change, this fact makes a massive contribution to the validity of naturalistic studies in the home.

For example, a rough-and-ready extroverted individualist cannot suddenly become a passive, clinging conformist; nor can an unintelligent, ineffectual man be miraculously transformed into the opposite because an observer is in his home. Yet these personality integrations, which are precisely the target of observation in naturalistic observation, prevent distortion of the normal situation, and hence inexorably make their contribution to family life at all times.

3. *What did I do?* When I had a room in the home, I got up when the family did, or maybe before, and retired when the parents did. If I was living outside I would get to the home around breakfast time and remain until the family went to bed. Since, during the week, the husband was away at work, I naturally spent my time with the wife and children. Most of the time I talked to the wife about whatever happened to come up: about her neighbors, about her concerns for her children, about food and how to cook it, about her husband and herself, and so on. When the mother was doing household chores or took care of the children, I watched. If she went shopping, took a child for a haircut, went to pick him up at school, etc., I went along. If the family went out of an evening, I went too. I went on picnics, to church, to bible study, to a meeting of the chamber of commerce, and so on. With the husband I could talk about business, the state of the nation, politics, jobs, etc. I was somewhat in the role of a visiting friend or relative. If the children wished to come up on my lap, take me out to play, show me what they had done, and such, they were welcome. I remained, on the whole, passive and compliant.

I intervened rarely in any activity, but I tended to follow one rule, which was to intervene when some accident seemed to have happened to a child, or when the parent asked me to hold a child.

4. *How did you stand it?* If one makes a commitment to a scientific enterprise, he thereby binds himself not to destroy the subject matter of his investigation. It would therefore have been preposterous to have hurled myself upon the parents every time I felt they were doing something pathogenic; and it would have been absurd also if I had become so overwhelmed by the pathogenic behavior I witnessed that I had to run screaming from the house. Having studied the Kaingáng Indians of Brazil and the Pilagá Indians of Argentina, and having spent months and years studying psychiatric institutions, I am long accustomed to the bizarre and the destructive. This being the case, I maintained calm. Living in the homes of these families, one constantly encounters situations that might be unsettling to an untrained observer. Experience and training, however, impose automatic restraints. I imagine it must be remotely akin to the experience of an officer watching his men die on the battlefield.

5. *What did I record?* I recorded everything I could remember. Whatever it was, whether a discussion with the mother on how to broil chicken, an observation of how the mother fed the baby, or what the father told me about his job, everything I could recall went indiscriminately into the record. The scientific study of human emotions has been hampered by decisions made long ago about what is important for the vicissitudes of the emotional life. It was obvious to me that if I were to start naturalistic observation with a preconception of what is important, I could not learn very much beyond my preconceptions. I therefore took the position that every-

thing was important, and as I dictated from memory I made no attempt to arrange the data in sequence or in categories, or to sift it. I felt it was scientifically unsound to "pre-think" the data, and I felt sure that when the record was finished I would be able to make sense of it. After all, I have behind me a great history of a science that made the confusing variety of the universe appear orderly. Why not profit by the tradition and its brilliant successes?

INDEX

D

M

N

About the Author

JULES HENRY was born in New York City in 1904. He died in St. Louis, Missouri, on September 23, 1969. He studied under Franz Boas and Ruth Benedict at Columbia University, where he received his doctorate in anthropology in 1936. Dr. Henry taught at Columbia University, the University of Chicago, and until his death at Washington University in St. Louis.

Jules Henry had completed and edited the manuscript of *Pathways to Madness* before his death—leaving only the final stages of copy reading unfinished. He spent much of his life urging social scientists to observe families—live with them as he did with the families in *Pathways to Madness* —in order to learn more about the development of so-called psychosis and mental illness. He believed that only through the contact of daily life could we begin to know the causes of mental illness—as well as the enduring human qualities that help us to resist breakdown.

He was a Research Associate at the Sonia Shankman Orthogenic School from 1953 through 1960. While working on this book, he was a Fellow at the Center for Advanced Study in the Behavioral Sciences at Stanford. He also served as consultant to the National Institute of Mental Health and the World Health Organization, among others, as well as a number of psychiatric hospitals. His articles have been widely published in professional and general journals. He is the author of "Doll Play of Pilagá Indian Children" (a monograph), *Jungle People* and *Culture Against Man.* Two volumes of essays have been published posthumously, *Jules Henry on Education* and *On Sham, Vulnerability and Other Forms of Self-Destruction.*

Dr. Henry married Zunia Lotte Gechtman; their daughter, Phyllis, is married to Peter Kingsmill.

VINTAGE BIOGRAPHY AND AUTOBIOGRAPHY

VINTAGE WOMEN'S STUDIES

VINTAGE HISTORY—AMERICAN